The Gospel Plan of Salvation

by

T.W. Brents

"Men and brethren, what shall we do?" – Acts 2:37
"Lord, what wilt thou have me to do?" – Acts 9:6
"Sirs, what must I do to be saved?" – Acts 16:30

© **Truth Publications, Inc. 2018.** All rights reserved. No part of this book may be reproduced in any form without written permission from the publisher. Printed in the United States of America.

ISBN 10: 1-58427-310-0

ISBN 13: 978-1-58427-310-3

Truth Publications, Inc.
CEI Bookstore
220 S. Marion St., Athens, AL 35611
855-492-6657
sales@truthpublications.com
www.truthbooks.com

PREFACE

A wise man has said, "Of making many books there is no end; and much study is a weariness of the flesh." Why, then, should we add another to the "many books" already before the public? It has now been all of *fifteen years* since we conceived the plan, and began the preparation of this work, only bestowing upon it, however, such fragments of time as we could spare from other labors. Sometimes we rested a month, sometimes a year, feeling by no means sure that we would ever finish the work, but intending to do so if permitted to live until our head become sufficiently gray. Some portions were occasionally given to the public as contributions to the Gospel Advocate and in tracts, in the hope that they might accomplish some good, if the entire work should never be published. A very general demand for the completion and publication of the book soon came from those who read the portions published; but we have deemed it prudent to "hasten leisurely" lest we might prematurely publish something of which we would be ashamed in maturer years. When we passed our *fiftieth* year we engaged the services of the publisher, and now, on our *fifty-first anniversary birthday,* we are writing a *preface,* and yet we are not quite sure that we are old enough to publish a book on a theme so transcendantly important as the "Gospel Plan of Salvation." Our highest ambition is to honor the name of our Master, and direct sinners to the way of life; hence we would not, for any earthly consideration, publish a sentence known to be untrue. We wish our book to live when we shall be sleeping the years away. Yes, and *live it will.* This is the frightful thought. LIVE IT WILL. A mistake from the pulpit may soon be forgotten—should we make a mistake in an article furnished a paper or periodical, it may be lost or worn out, and soon pass away; but a *book* will live on, when he who wrote it lives only in the work left behind him. How important it is, then, that every thought penned concerning THE GOSPEL PLAN OF SALVATION should be tried "as by fire" that not a single error should escape the refining crucible of Holy Writ, and make its way into the permanent literature of the age. Had this responsibility been rightly appreciated, surely many of the books now on the market would never have met the public eye.

But there is another side to the picture. While it is unquestionably true that much mischief has been done by the publication of error, it is equally true that much good has been done, and may yet be done, by publishing the truth. Ceasing to publish truth will never arrest the publication of error. It will continue to be published as long as man lives in a tenement of clay; hence the best that may be done is the publication of truth with which, in some degree, to counteract its influence. But for this the world would have been to-day overwhelmed in the stygian waters of infidelity and idolatry; hence we would not erase a single impression made by any truth ever given to man by any who has written before us. It is no part of our object to supersede any work that has appeared among us; rather would we be an humble co-worker with all lovers of truth in pointing sinners to the "Lamb of God who taketh away the sin of the world."

Every writer has a taste and a style as peculiarly his own as are his features or his temperament; hence no two are likely to select exactly the same field of labor, or adopt the same method of arranging the material used by each respectively. While others have written upon some, perhaps all, the subjects treated in this work, we are not aware of any *single book* filling the place which this is designed to occupy. While it is directly addressed to the *alien,* we hope it will aid the young *disciple* in obtaining a more extensive knowledge of the "form of doctrine" by which he was made free from sin: especially will *young preachers* find it a valuable compend of *argument* and *critical authority* in elucidation of many subjects which they will find it necessary to examine. They will here find an amount of authority which would cost them much labor and money were they compelled to get it from the original authors quoted by us. Many of the works are out of print, so that only second-hand copies can be had at all, and these only by importation at fabulous cost. We found it necessary to pay *ten, fifteen,* and even as high as *twenty-five* dollars for works from which to obtain the author's definition of a single word, which will be found in this work. Many of these authors define in Latin which could not be read by the common English scholar if he had them; here he will find only the English translation of the author's Latin, which all can read and easily understand.

We have made no effort at elegance of style, seeking rather to clearly and *forcibly* express as *much* truth as possible in the space occupied. We dare not hope that every thought is expressed in the best possible manner; but he who reads to be benefited will likely understand us, and for such readers only were our labors intended. If we have not spoken as the oracles of God speak, then prove all things, and hold fast that which is good. By the word of God we are ever willing that our teaching may be tried. It alone can build us up and give us an inheritance among them who are sanctified; hence to it we commend our readers in the fear of Him who will judge us all according to our works.

T. W. BRENTS.

RICHMOND, TENN., February 10, 1874.

CONTENTS

	PAGE
CHAPTER I.	
Predestination	7- 12
CHAPTER II.	
Election and Reprobation	13- 40
CHAPTER III.	
Calvinistic Proofs Examined	41- 73
CHAPTER IV.	
The Foreknowledge of God	74- 87
CHAPTER V.	
Hereditary Depravity	88-116
CHAPTER VI.	
The Establishment of the Church	117-133
CHAPTER VII.	
The Identity of the Church	134-150
CHAPTER VIII.	
The New Birth	151-166
CHAPTER IX.	
Faith	167-186
CHAPTER X.	
Repentance	187-197

CONTENTS

CHAPTER XI.
The Confession 198-209

CHAPTER XII.
Baptism, what is it? 210-313

CHAPTER XIII.
Who should be baptized 314-381

CHAPTER XIV.
The Design of Baptism 382-454

CHAPTER XV.
The Holy Spirit 455-527

THE
GOSPEL PLAN OF SALVATION

CHAPTER I.

PREDESTINATION.

Are you "aliens from the commonwealth of Israel, and strangers from the covenants of promise, having no hope, and without God in the world?" If so, we propose to assist you in arriving at a knowledge of your duty, in order that you may become citizens of God's government on the earth—children of God's family—members of Christ's body, the Church—that you may escape the punishment of the damned, and secure for yourselves the favor of God and the bliss of heaven. But while our primary object is to benefit the *alien*, it is hoped that a careful reading of our book will be interesting and profitable to the babes in Christ. They should not regard themselves as fully grown at birth, and therefore cease their investigations; but they should desire and feed upon the sincere milk of the Word, that they may grow to the stature of men and women fully grown in the kingdom and patience of Jesus Christ. Knowledge is one of the adjuncts of faith: "Besides this, giving all diligence, add to your faith virtue; and to virtue, *knowledge*." 2 Pet. i:5. "Wherefore I will not be negligent to put you always in remembrance of these things, though ye know them, and be established in the truth. Yea, I think it meet, as long as I am in this tabernacle, to stir you up by putting you in remembrance; knowing that shortly I must put off this my tabernacle." Vers. 12, 13.

But before we proceed to look for the conditions upon which aliens may secure the favor of our Heavenly Father, it may be well to inquire whether or not there is *any thing they can do* that will be conducive to this end. There are prominent doctrines taught by those for whose learning and piety we have the most profound respect, which, if true, render it wholly unnecessary, it seems to us, to spend time or labor in instructing the sinner with regard to his duty either to God or man.

That we may place these doctrines properly before the mind

of the reader, without any reasonable probability of misrepresenting them, we beg permission to make a few quotations from the fountain whence they flow.

"God, from all eternity, did, by the most wise and holy counsel of his own will, freely and unchangeably ordain whatsoever comes to pass." Presbyterian Confession of Faith, chap. iii, sec. 1. To the same import we have the answer to Question 12 (Larger Catechism), as follows: "God's decrees are the wise, free, and holy acts of the counsel of his will, whereby, from all eternity, he hath, for his own glory, unchangeably fore-ordained whatsoever comes to pass, especially concerning angels and men."

Now, if the doctrine here set forth is true, we think it impossible for man to err. Whatever he does, is in keeping with and brought about by God's fore-ordination or decree, and therefore can not be wrong. If he does any thing—it matters not what—whether good or bad—if God has ordained every thing, He has ordained that thing. If it comes to pass that a man *lies*, God has not only ordained that he should lie, but He has unchangeably ordained it. If it comes to pass that a man *steals*, God has unchangeably ordained that, too. If it comes to pass that a man *kills* his neighbor, God has unchangeably ordained that, also. It did come to pass that Cain killed his brother: why, then, did God put a curse upon him for it? It was not only in accordance with the most wise and holy counsel of His will, but He had freely and unchangeably ordained that Cain should do the very thing for which He cursed him!!! Can any sane man believe it? God has said: "Thou shalt not kill. Thou shalt not commit adultery. Thou shalt not steal. Thou shalt not bear false witness against thy neighbor." Ex. xx: 13-16. As God has thus plainly forbidden things which do come to pass, it can not be true that He has unchangeably ordained them. That God should unchangeably ordain that a certain thing should come to pass, and at the same time positively forbid it, is an inconsistency entirely incompatible with His divine character, especially when we add to it the thought that He threatens the guilty with endless punishment. Surely He, whose laws ever bear the impress of that infinite justice, goodness, love and mercy which characterize their Author, would not punish His dependent creature man in the rude flames of an angry hell forever for doing that which He had unchangeably ordained that he should do: "The Lord is good to all: and his tender mercies are over all his works." Ps. cxlv: 9. "The Lord is righteous in all his ways, and holy in all his works." Ver. 17. Therefore when the murderer stains his hands in the blood of his fellow, he can not take shelter under the doctrine of the creed by saying that God, in ordaining every thing that comes to pass, ordained that he should kill his neighbor, and thereby avoid the responsibility of the act and the punishment due his crime. It is true that the makers of the creed disclaim the consequences of the doctrine, saying, "Yet so as thereby neither is God the author of sin;" but they have failed to show us how His character may be vindicated from such a charge in harmony with such a doctrine; and we are unable to see how God is not the author of what He has unchangeably ordained should come to pass. If He has unchangeably ordained every thing that comes to pass, then how can man change God's unchangeable ordinance? and if he can not change it, surely no blame can attach to him for any thing he does. If God unchangeably ordained that a certain man, on a certain day, should do a certain thing, then there is no power left to man not to do the thing; for were he to avoid doing it, he would have changed God's unchangeable decree, and therefore had more power to change than God had to enforce. Is any one prepared to assume such a position as this? The reader will please note the extent of the doctrine in controversy. It is not that God has from all eternity ordained, but that he has unchangeably ordained; not *some things*, but *whatsoever* cometh to pass—every thing. Surely, the ordinances or decrees of God are broken every day. He has ordained that men shall not kill, yet they do kill. He has ordained that they shall not steal, yet they do steal. He has ordained that they shall not bear false witness, yet they swear falsely every day. God compels no man to keep His ordinances, but He will visit upon him merited punishment if he does not keep them. Paul tells us that "the powers that be are ordained of God. Whosoever therefore resisteth the power, resisteth the ordinance of God: and they that resist shall receive to themselves damnation." Rom. xiii : 1, 2. How can any one successfully resist that which God has unchangeably ordained? God said, "Yet forty days, and Nineveh shall be overthrown." Jonah iii : 4. Here was a positive decree or ordinance of God that did not come to pass, for "God saw their works, that they turned from their evil way; and God repented of the evil, that he had said that he would do unto them; and he did it not." Ver. 10. Was not this decree changeable? God said to Hezekiah, "Set thy house in order; for thou shalt die, and not live." 2 Kings xx:1. Here was another positive ordinance which was changeable, for Hezekiah turned his face to the wall and prayed, after which God said to him: "I have heard thy prayer, I have seen thy tears; behold, I will heal thee: on the third day thou shalt go up unto the house of the Lord, and I will add unto thy days fifteen years." Vers. 5, 6. Here was a decree concerning Hezekiah's death, which was changed, and his life prolonged fifteen years, and the change induced by his prayers and tears.

When David was at Keilah, he inquired of the Lord, saying: "Will Saul come down as thy servant hath heard? O Lord God of Israel, I beseech thee, tell thy servant. And the Lord said, He will come down. Then said David, Will the men of Keilah deliver me and my men into the hand of Saul? And the Lord said, They will deliver thee up. Then David and his men, which were about six hundred, arose and departed out of Keilah, and went whithersoever they could go. And it was told Saul that David was escaped from Keilah; and he forbare to go forth." 1 Samuel xxiii:11-13. When David left Keilah, Saul turned his pursuit in the direction of David's flight, and did not go to Keilah at all. Had God decreed, from all eternity, whatsoever comes to pass, it occurs to us that He would have answered David differently; perhaps something after the following style: "No, David, Saul will not come to Keilah, nor will the men of Keilah deliver you into his hands, for I have unchangeably ordained that you shall leave Keilah, and Saul will turn his pursuit in the direction to which you go." This was what did come to pass, and certainly God did not tell David what he had foreordained to be untrue. Had David remained at Keilah, Saul would have gone there; hence circumstances, and not immutable decrees, controlled this event, even as they do most others. Other examples might be given, but these are enough to show that God has issued decrees that never have come to pass, nor never will come to pass. Now, if it is true that God fore-ordained every thing that comes to pass, then it follows that He fore-ordained the reformation of the Ninevites, the prayers of Hezekiah, and the flight of David from Keilah; hence when He said, "Yet forty days, and Nineveh shall be overthrown," He had fore-ordained, before time began, that it should not be overthrown. When He told Hezekiah to set his house in order, for he should die and not live, He had fore-ordained that he should live fifteen years longer. And when He told David that Saul would come to Keilah, and that the men of Keilah would deliver him and his men to Saul, was it not telling him that events should happen which He had unchangeably ordained to be otherwise? How such a theory is to be harmonized with the word of the Lord, we know not.

By the mouth of his prophet, the Lord said (Jer. xviii:7-10): "At what instant I shall speak concerning a nation, and concerning a kingdom, to pluck up, and to pull down, and to destroy it; if that nation, against whom I have pronounced, turn from their evil, I will repent of the evil that I thought to do unto them. And at what instant I shall speak concerning a nation, and concerning a kingdom, to build and to plant it; if it do evil in my sight, that it obey not my voice, then I will repent of the good, wherewith I said I would benefit them." Here we see the same law obtains as to nations that we have seen applied to cities and individuals. If they, having done evil, turn from the evil, then the Lord proposes to turn from the evil which He purposes doing to them; on the contrary, if they persist in disobedience, they will suffer the consequences, even to extermination. Hence circumstances have ever varied God's dealings with men.

Again: "God saw that the wickedness of man was great in the earth, and that every imagination of the thoughts of his heart was only evil continually. And it repented the Lord that he had made man on the earth, and it grieved him at his heart." Gen. vi:5, 6. Now, if the Lord fore-ordained every thing that comes to pass, He fore-ordained every thing the antediluvians did: why, then, should He grieve over their wickedness, when every act was but the consummation of His own immutable and eternal decree? Really, it would seem like God grieving over His own folly.

The Lord said that the children of Judah had "built again the high places of Tophet, which is in the valley of the son of Hinnom, to burn their sons and their daughters in the fire; which I commanded them not, neither came it into my heart." Jer. vii:31. "They have built also the high places of Baal, to burn their sons with fire for burnt offerings unto Baal, which I commanded not, nor spake it, neither came it into my mind." Jer. xix:5. If God fore-ordained every thing, He fore-ordained these things, for they came to pass; yet He says He did not command them, nor speak them, *neither came they into His mind.* Will the advocates of the doctrine please to enlighten the world as to *how God fore-ordained things which never entered His mind?* But we will not press the argument further. If the doctrine be true, the whole theory of sin, accountability, rewards, and punishments, in harmony with justice and mercy, is to us utterly incomprehensible. Every act of man is but carrying out the immutable purposes of Jehovah; and when He gives a man a law, He does it expressly that he may violate it, so as to furnish a pretext for the punishment previously ordained for him. Take the sin of Adam as an example: God made him and placed him under law. It came to pass that he violated this law. He ate of the fruit whereof God commanded him not to eat. If God fore-ordained whatsoever comes to pass, then of course He fore-ordained that he should eat. Hence Adam was in a strait between the *law* and the *unchangeable ordination* or decree. It came to pass that he eat; therefore God ordained that he *should eat.* The law said he *should not eat.* One or the other must be broken. He must eat, and violate the law; or not eat, and change God's unchangeable decree. This was impossible: hence to eat and violate the law was a *necessity;* and yet God would punish him for it!! Surely, such a theory is at war with the Bible—with all reason and common sense—as well as a reproach upon the character of our Heavenly Father. But able and learned men have taught it, good and true men believe it; therefore we must treat it respectfully, yet examine it fairly, patiently, and thoroughly.

CHAPTER II.

ELECTION AND REPROBATION

We come now to examine the subject of *unconditional election* and *reprobation;* and that we may see the doctrine in its purity, we beg permission to quote again from the creed: "By the decree of God, for the manifestation of his glory, some men and angels are predestinated unto everlasting life, and others fore-ordained to everlasting death. These angels and men thus predestinated and fore-ordained are particularly and unchangeably designed, and their number is so certain and definite that it can not be either increased or diminished. Those of mankind that are predestinated unto life, God, before the foundation of the world was laid, according to His eternal and immutable purpose and the secret counsel and good pleasure of His will, hath chosen in Christ, unto everlasting glory, out of His mere free grace and love, without any foresight of faith or good works or perseverance in either of them, or any other thing in the creature, as conditions or causes moving him thereunto." Confession of Faith, chap. 3, secs. 3, 4, 5.

It is quite easy to see that the doctrine of *unconditional election* and *reprobation is true* if the doctrine of *unchangeable fore-ordination* obtains as to every thing that comes to pass, unless we find relief in the more ample folds of *Universalism*. If God has unchangeably fore-ordained whatsoever comes to pass, then of course He has fore-ordained just who shall be saved, and who, if any, shall be lost; and if He has unchangeably fixed the destiny of every man before time began without any conditions whatever, then *Calvinism* or *Universalism* must be true. But we think we have seen that God did *not* so ordain every thing, and hence this doctrine can not support either of the others. If either stands at all, it must be proved by other testimony. For the present, then, we propose to inquire whether or not God has unconditionally and unchangeably fixed the destiny of a definite number of two classes—the *elect* and the *reprobate*.

And first, we remark that the words elect, elected, election, reprobate, and reprobates, are Bible terms; hence there must be a Bible doctrine concerning them. Elect means to *choose;* hence the elect of God are God's *chosen*. God has elected persons, families, nations, and bodies or organizations in different ages of the world, for the benefit of his creatures, but the final salvation and happiness of the elected were by no means secured by their election. On the contrary, God's elect have to "work out their own salvation with fear and trembling." Phil. ii:12. Hence in very many instances they have sinned and fallen far from the favor of God, and often forfeited the positions to which they were elected. But to comprehend the whole subject we must inquire who were elected and for what purposes; then we may be able to see what effect, if any, their election had upon their final destiny.

"Behold my servant, whom I uphold; mine elect, in whom my soul delighteth; I have put my Spirit upon him; he shall bring forth judgment to the Gentiles; he shall not cry nor lift up, nor cause his voice to be heard in the street. A bruised reed shall he not break, and the smoking flax shall he not quench: he shall bring forth judgment unto truth." Isa. xlii:1-3. That the servant of God here called His *elect* was Jesus the Christ may be seen by reference to Matt. xii:17-21, where this prophecy is quoted by Jesus as fulfilled in himself. Surely, it will be admitted that Jesus was not elected to secure His own salvation, but to be the Saviour of men. "Wherefore also it is contained in Scripture, Behold I lay in Zion a chief corner-stone, elect, precious: and he that believeth on him shall not be confounded." 1 Pet. ii:6. Here Jesus is represented as the *elect* corner-stone of the church, on whom others believe to their salvation. But we are more concerned in examining the election of *men*, as individuals, collective bodies, and nations.

Abraham was elected of God to be the father of the faithful, in whose seed all families of the earth were to be blessed in Jesus Christ. Gal. iii:16. But as Abraham had more sons than one, it was necessary that an election take place in his family, for Ishmael and Isaac could not both be the father of the family from which Jesus the promised seed should come; hence God said, "In Isaac shall thy seed be called." Gen. xxi:12; Rom ix:7. Isaac had two sons, Esau and Jacob, both of whom could not be the father of the royal family; hence God said, "Thou, Israel, art my servant, Jacob whom I have chosen, the seed of Abraham my friend." Isa. xli:8. Jacob had twelve sons; Judah was elected.

And so election has been a necessity all the way from Abraham to Jesus the promised seed—not to benefit the elected exclusively, but to benefit the world through them.

When God determined to deliver the children of Israel from Egyptian bondage, He elected Moses for their leader and lawgiver: "Therefore he said that he would destroy them, had not Moses his *chosen* stood before him." Ps. cvi:23. But Aaron was elected as speaker for Moses; hence "He sent Moses his servant and Aaron whom he had *chosen*." Ps. cv:26. Notwithstanding Moses and Aaron were elected—chosen of God to conduct the Hebrews from Egypt to Canaan, a type of the final home of the righteous; and Moses was the Jewish lawgiver, in this respect a type of Christ our lawgiver; and Aaron was anointed high priest, in this respect a type of Christ our High Priest; and he was permitted to enter the most holy place, which was typical of heaven, where Jesus our High Priest hath for us entered—yet they both sinned, and incurred the displeasure of God, in consequence of which neither of them were permitted to enter the land of Canaan, the type of the Christian's home in heaven. "And the Lord spake unto Moses and Aaron, because ye believed me not, to sanctify me in the eyes of the children of Israel, therefore ye shall not bring this congregation into the land which I have given them." Num. xx:12. Concerning this decree, Moses said: "The Lord was angry with me for your sakes, and sware that I should not go over Jordan, and that I should not go in unto that good land, which the Lord thy God giveth thee for an inheritance: but I must die in this land, I must not go over Jordan: but ye shall go over, and possess that good land." Deut. iv:21, 22. After taking Moses to the top of Pisgah and showing him the beauties of the land, the Lord said to him: "This is the land which I sware unto Abraham, unto Isaac, and unto Jacob, saying, I will give it unto thy seed; I have caused thee to see it with thine eyes, but thou shalt not go over thither. So Moses, the servant of the Lord died there in the land of Moab, according to the word of the Lord." Deut. xxxiv:4, 5.

Aaron and his sons were not only elected, but consecrated and anointed priests of God, and officiated in that most sacred office for themselves and the people. In the eighth chapter of Leviticus may be found an account of the grand and sublime ceremony with which they were inducted into that holy office. Thus the male portion of a family were elected and inducted into the priesthood; and what became of them? The Lord said: "Aaron, shall be gathered unto his people, for he shall not enter into the land which I have given unto the children of Israel, because ye rebelled against my word at the water of Meribah. Take Aaron and Eleazar his son, and bring them up unto Mount Hor; and strip Aaron of his garments, and put them upon Eleazar his son, and Aaron shall be gathered unto his people, and shall die there. And Moses did as the Lord commanded: and they went up into Mount Hor in sight of all the congregation. And Moses stripped Aaron of his garments and put them upon Eleazar his son; and Aaron died there in the top of the mount." Num. xx:24 to 28. "Nadab and Abihu, the sons of Aaron, took either of them his censer, and put fire therein, and put incense thereon, and offered strange fire before the Lord, which he commanded them not. And there went out fire from the Lord and devoured them, and they died before the Lord." Lev. x:1, 2. Now, if the doctrine of eternal unconditional election and reprobation be true, to which class did Nadab and Abihu belong? The destiny of all being unalterably fixed before time began, it follows that these were of the eternally elect, or of the eternally reprobate. Did God *elect* them of the *non-elect*, or eternally reprobate, and anoint them priests to officiate in the tabernacle, having previously determined upon their destruction, and unchangeably fore-ordained the wickedness for which He intended to kill them? Or were they of the eternally elect, and their interest in heaven made sure before "the foundation of the world," and God killed them for wickedness which he had unchangeably fore-ordained they should do, that he might take them home to glory? Is it not more rational to conclude that God elected them, anointed and consecrated them priests, intending to be with and bless them as long as they were faithful to Him, and punish them when they forsook Him; and that their unhappy end was the result of their own voluntary rebellion against the law of the Lord?

God elected Saul to be the first king over Israel. He told Samuel how he might know him; and having presented him to the people, "Samuel said to all the people, See ye him whom the

Lord hath chosen, that there is none like him among all the people? And all the people shouted and said, God save the king." 1 Sam. x:24. He not only elected him, but he gave him the spirit of prophecy, and when "a company of the priests met him, the Spirit of God came upon him, and he prophesied among them." 1 Sam. x:10. Nor was this all, but he sacredly anointed him to reign over his people. "Then Samuel took a vial of oil, and poured it upon his head, and kissed him, and said, Is it not because the Lord hath anointed thee to be captain over his inheritance?" 1 Sam. x:1. The Lord was with and prospered him in battle, as long as he was faithful to Him, but when he disobeyed him, Samuel said: "Hath the Lord as great delight in burnt offerings and sacrifices, as in obeying the voice of the Lord? Behold, to obey is better than sacrifice, and to hearken than the fat of rams. For rebellion is as the sin of witchcraft, and stubbornness is as iniquity and idolatry. Because thou hast rejected the word of the Lord, he hath also rejected thee from being king." 1 Sam. xv:22, 23. Will the reader observe the fact that he was rejected, not because God had eternally reprobated him, or unchangeably fore-ordained his rejection, but because he *rejected the word of the Lord.* From all these examples we learn that when God elected any one to any position however important, it did not unconditionally secure for him an entrance into the climes of endless bliss, or even a continuance in the office to which he was elected; but on the contrary the general principle is quite apparent that He blessed and prospered him as long as he continued faithful to His will, and failed not to punish and reject him when he rebelled against Him.

Thus far we have seen individuals in the age of types and shadows elected to peculiar privileges, for the benefit of themselves and others; and we have seen many of the elect perish on account of their sins; and the time would fail us to record all the cases which illustrate these principles in the government of God; we come now to look for the election of *nations* and *bodies* to religious promotion on the same principles.

One of the first promises made to Abraham by the Lord was: "I will make of thee a great nation, and will bless thee, and make thy name great; and thou shalt be a blessing; and I will bless them that bless thee, and curse him that curseth thee: and in thee shall all families of the earth be blessed." Gen. xii:2, 3. In due time God gave Abraham a son, Isaac, to whose wife Rebecca the Lord said: "Two nations are in thy womb, and two manner of people shall be separated from thy bowels; and the one people shall be stronger than the other people; and the elder shall serve the younger." Gen. xxv:23. As we will have occasion to notice this passage again, it is sufficient here to remark that this was said to her concerning Jacob and Esau, as the representatives of two *nations* which were to descend from her through them, one of which was to be stronger than the other, and bear rule over it; and this was "that the purpose of God according to election might stand." Rom. ix:11. Thus we find that the descendants of Jacob were elected the national family of God; hence he said: "O Jacob, my servant; and Israel, whom I have chosen." Isa. xliv:1. "For Jacob my servant's sake and Israel mine elect." Isa. xlv:4. God changed the name of *Abram* to *Abraham*, because He made him the father of many nations. Gen. xvii:5. He also changed the name of Jacob to Israel, saying: "Thy name shall be called no more Jacob, but Israel: for as a prince hast thou power with God and with men, and hast prevailed." Gen. xxxii:28. Henceforth the descendants of Jacob were called the "children of Israel;" and very often only *Israel*, the adopted name of their illustrious progenitor—an example of which Paul gives, Rom. x:1: "Brethren, my heart's desire and prayer to God for Israel is, that they might be saved." These God clearly recognized as *His people.* When He appeared to Moses for the purpose of sending him to deliver them, He said: "I have surely seen the affliction of my people which are in Egypt." Ex. iii:7. And verse 10, he says: "Come now therefore, and I will send thee unto Pharaoh, that thou mayest bring forth my people the children of Israel out of Egypt." Moses said to them: "The Lord hath taken you, and brought you forth out of the iron furnace, even out of Egypt, to be unto him a people of inheritance, as ye are this day." Deut. iv:20. Again: "Because he loved thy fathers, therefore he chose their seed after them, and brought them out in his sight with his mighty power out of Egypt." Deut. iv:37. "The Lord had a delight in thy fathers to love them, and he chose their seed after them, even you above all people." Deut. x:15. "For thou art an holy people unto the

Lord thy God, and the Lord hath chosen thee to be a peculiar people unto himself, above all the nations that are upon the earth." Deut. xiv:2. "For thou art an holy people unto the Lord thy God: the Lord thy God had chosen thee to be a special people unto himself, above all people that are upon the face of the earth. The Lord did not set his love upon you, nor choose you, because ye were more in number than any people; for ye were the fewest of all people: but because the Lord loved you, and because he would keep the oath which he had sworn unto your fathers, hath the Lord brought you out with a mighty hand, and redeemed you out of the house of bondmen, from the hand of Pharaoh king of Egypt." Deut. vii:6-8. Though we are here to prove that those *children of Israel were the elect people of God* in that age of the world, yet in passing we may note the additional fact apparent in the last quotation, that He loved them, not because they were elected from all eternity as *individuals;* nor did He elect them because He loved them *personally* "before the foundation of the world was laid," but because He loved their fathers and had entered into a covenant with them; and He refers their election to a time when they had, not only an *individual* and *personal,* but a *national* existence, and were few in number compared with other nations, associating it with the time of their deliverance from Egyptian bondage. We need not refer the reader to other recognitions of the Israelites as the national family of God, but it is necessary to our purpose that we note one other fact, which is, that they constituted *the church* in that dispensation; hence says Stephen, concerning Moses: "This is he, that was in the church in the wilderness with the angel which spake to him in the mount Sina, and with our fathers: who received the lively oracles to give unto us." Acts vii:38. Paul mentions some of the eminent privileges of these people: "Who are Israelites; to whom pertaineth the adoption, and the glory, and the covenants, and the giving of the law, and the service of God, and the promises; whose are the fathers, and of whom as concerning the flesh Christ came." Rom. ix:4, 5. Next we would call the attention of the reader to the all-important fact that the same general principle characterized God's dealings with this *elect national family,* or *typical church,* that we have seen prominent in His dealings with *elect individuals*—

namely, that He blessed and prospered them when they were faithful to His laws, and that He punished them, and finally exterminated them as a nation, for their wickedness.

Soon after God delivered them from Egyptian bondage, He called Moses to Him and said: "Thus shalt thou say to the house of Jacob, and tell the children of Israel; ye have seen what I did unto the Egyptians, and how I bear you on eagles' wings, and brought you unto myself. Now therefore, if ye will obey my voice indeed, and keep my covenant, then ye shall be a peculiar treasure unto me above all people; for all the earth is mine; and ye shall be unto me a kingdom of priests, and an holy nation. These are the words which thou shalt speak unto the children of Israel. And Moses came and called for the elders of the people, and laid before their faces all these words which the Lord commanded him. And all the people answered together, and said, All that the Lord hath spoken we will do." Ex. xix:3-8. God prefaces this solemn covenant by calling the attention of the people to the wonderful exhibition of His power put forth in their salvation, and the destruction of their enemies; and promises that they should be a peculiar treasure to Him on condition that they *obey His voice*, which on their part they solemnly promise to do. But they very soon forgot their obligations to God; hence "with many of them God was not well pleased; for they were overthrown in the wilderness." 1 Cor. x:5. For their idolatrous worship of the calf made by Aaron, three thousand fell in one day. (Ex. xxxii:28.) For their fornication, twenty-four thousand died in the plague. (Num. xxv:9.) Twenty-three thousand of them died in one day. (1 Cor. x:8.) For their murmuring against God, many of them were destroyed by serpents. (Num. xxi: 6.) And for their crimes of various kinds, God abandoned them in their conflicts with the nations around them, until multiplied thousands were slain in battle, their cities were burned to ashes, and their homes made desolate, and strangers devoured their land in their presence. (Isa. i:7.) They were taken captive into Babylon and kept there for seventy years. Thus did God afflict and scourge them as a father scourgeth his rebellious son, but they would not reform; until finally He asks, "Why should ye be stricken any more? ye will revolt more and more." Isa. i:5. Nor did He afflict them without warning, for He said to them: "If ye shall at all turn from following me, ye or your children, and will not keep my commandments and my statutes which I have set before you, but go and serve other gods and worship them: then will I cut off Israel out of the land which I have given them; and this house which I have hallowed for my name, will I cast out of my sight, and Israel shall be a proverb and a byword among all people." 1 Kings ix:6, 7. Never was there a more faithful picture of human wretchedness than is here given of the present condition of this once elect and highly favored people of God. He has utterly destroyed them as a nation from the face of the earth. They are not only cut off from the country which God gave them to be a permanent inheritance, but they are scattered among the nations, until there is not a place on the globe where civilization has gone where straggling Jews may not be found; and the very name *Jew* is a name of reproach to him who wears it—a "proverb and a byword among all people." And what was the condition set forth in this most solemn warning to them? Was it, "If you are of the eternally reprobate?" Nay, verily, they were God's own elect. But will it do to assume that, because there was no hell threatened in the Jewish law, these were merely temporal punishments inflicted upon God's elect, and hence he has taken, or will take them to heaven? Were there any others worse than these? Before any one so assumes, let him remember that almost, perhaps quite, every known species of crime was practiced by these elect; and if these whoremongers, idolaters and tempters of God were fit for heaven, then it must be true indeed that *election,* and not *character,* qualifies for that place. Before any one so assumes, let him further remember that these Jews, the elect of God, rejected and murdered the Lord of glory; and he said, "If ye believe not that I am he, ye shall die in your sins." John viii:24. Notwithstanding the gospel was first preached to the Jews, and some of them believed on Christ as the promised Messiah, yet not one of the Jews can be found who, as a Jew, believes, to-day, that Jesus was or is the Christ, the Son of God. How then are they to be saved over his declaration that "If ye believe not that I am he, ye shall die in your sins?" Are they to die in their sins, and be saved in their unbelief? He says, "He that believeth not shall be damned." Mark xvi: 16.

Now, we would note the fact that the Jewish age was a typical age: the church in the wilderness was, in a sense, a type of the church of God; Moses, the Jewish lawgiver, was, in a sense, a type of Christ our lawgiver; Aaron, the Jewish high priest, was a type of Christ our High Priest; the Jewish priests were types of Christians in the gospel age who are priests now.—Hence says Peter, "Ye also, as lively stones, are built up a spiritual house, a holy priesthood, to offer up spiritual sacrifices, acceptable to God by Jesus Christ." 1 Pet. ii:5. And again, verse 9, he says, "But ye are a chosen generation, a royal priesthood, a holy nation, a peculiar people." Then if these elect types, from the least to the greatest, both as individuals and as a body, had to be faithful to God or forfeit their election, may we not in the same way forfeit our election? After telling us that "with many of them God was not well pleased, for they were overthrown in the wilderness," Paul says: "These things were our examples, to the intent we should not lust after evil things, as they also lusted. Neither be ye idolaters, as were some of them; as it is written, The people sat down to eat and drink, and rose up to play. Neither let us commit fornication, as some of them committed, and fell in one day three and twenty thousand. Neither let us tempt Christ, as some of them also tempted, and were destroyed of serpents. Neither murmur ye, as some of them also murmured, and were destroyed of the destroyer. Now all these things happened unto them for ensamples: and they are written for our admonition, upon whom the ends of the world are come. Wherefore let him that thinketh he standeth take heed lest he fall." 1 Cor. x:5-12. We know not how the apostle could have given more conclusive proof that the number of the elect composing the church of God at Corinth, was liable to be diminished by apostasy than is here given. He tells them of the overthrow of many of the Jews, and mentions, specifically, the sins for which thousands of them fell, and tells them that these things happened to them as examples, and are written for our admonition; "wherefore let him that thinketh he standeth take heed lest he fall." But why this admonition, if the numbers of the elect and reprobate are so certain and definite that they can neither be increased nor diminished? Were this true, Paul's most solemn warning to his brethren was a mere "rawhead and bloody bones," to alarm them when there was no danger, for none of them could fall! And the creed is consistent with itself, if not with the Bible at this point; for it says: "They whom God hath accepted in his Beloved, effectually called and sanctified by his Spirit, can neither totally nor finally fall away from the state of grace; but shall certainly persevere therein to the end and be saved. This perseverance of the saints depends not upon their own free will, but upon the immutability of the decree of election, flowing from the free and unchangeable love of God the Father; upon the efficacy of the merit and intercession of Jesus Christ; the abiding of the Spirit and the seed of God within them; and the nature of the covenant of grace; from all which ariseth also the certainty and infallibility thereof." Chap. xvii, secs. 1, 2.

The doctrine here set out is a necessary outgrowth of the doctrine of unconditional election and reprobation. If God has unchangeably fixed the destiny of every man before time began, then it follows that such destiny can not be changed by any act of the creature—nay, not even by the Creator; for that which is unchangeable can not be changed even by God himself. Therefore none of the eternally elect can fall if that doctrine obtains; and whenever it is clearly shown that a Christian may apostatize, and be lost, the whole theory of unconditional election and reprobation is exploded. We will therefore be somewhat careful to see how this is. And if there was not another sentence in the Bible touching the subject, Paul's most solemn warning to the Corinthians would be quite sufficient to settle the question forever. He tells them of the falls of the Jews as examples to his brethren, and that their deplorable end was recorded as a solemn admonition to others, lest they, feeling secure, might fall. What could be more conclusive? In the last verse of the preceding chapter, the apostle says, "I keep under my body, and bring it into subjection: lest that by any means, when I have preached to others, I myself should be a castaway." 1 Cor. ix:27. If Paul, the great apostle to the Gentiles, had to keep such constant watch-care over himself, lest, after all his labor, he should be lost, is it not possible that others may fall? It is not necessary to show that Paul was one of the elect, for this will surely be admitted: yet he was in danger of falling; and had he fallen, would not the number of the elect have been diminished thereby, and the number of the reprobate correspondingly increased?

Jesus said: "I am the vine, ye are the branches. He that abideth in me, and I in him, the same bringeth forth much fruit; for without me ye can do nothing. If a man abide not in me, he is cast forth as a branch, and is withered; and men gather them, and cast them into the fire, and they are burned." John xv:5, 6. Why charge them to abide in him, if they could not do otherwise than abide in him? and why liken them to withered and dried branches which men gather and cast into the fire to be burned, if by reason of the immutability of the decree of election they could not do otherwise than persevere to the end and be eternally saved?

Paul tells Timothy of "Hymeneus and Philetus; who concerning the truth have erred, saying that the resurrection is passed already; and overthrow the faith of some." 2 Tim. ii:18. Here were persons who had faith, and that faith was overthrown by false teaching. Surely, these persons were of the elect, for the creed tells us that "The grace of faith whereby the elect are enabled to believe to the saving of their souls, is the work of the Spirit of Christ in their hearts." Chap. xiv, sec. 1. Without stopping for the present to inquire how the *elect*, whose souls never could have been lost, can believe to the *saving* of their souls, we remark that faith is the work of the Spirit in the heart of the elect, according to the creed; hence Hymeneus and Philetus diminished the number of the elect just as many as there were persons whose faith they overthrew.

But we will hear what Paul has to say to the Hebrews, chap. xi:verses 4-6: "For it is impossible for those who were once enlightened, and have tasted of the heavenly gift, and were made partakers of the Holy Ghost, and have tasted the good word of God, and the powers of the world to come, if they shall fall away, to renew them again unto repentance; seeing they crucify to themselves the Son of God afresh, and put him to an open shame." Here it is most clearly taught that even those who had been blessed with those extraordinary spiritual manifestations peculiar to the age of the apostles, might fall away; else why the language, "if they do fall away," when they could not so fall? But again he says: "If we sin wilfully after that we have received the knowledge of the truth, there remaineth no more sacrifice for sins, but a certain fearful looking for of judgment and fiery indignation, which shall devour the adversaries. He that despised Moses' law died without mercy under two or three witnesses; of how much sorer punishment, suppose ye, shall he be thought worthy, who hath trodden under foot the Son of God, and have counted the blood of the covenant wherewith he was sanctified an unholy thing, and hath done despite unto the Spirit of grace?" Heb. x:26-29. Here was a sorer punishment than death awaiting, under certain conditions, persons who had been sanctified by the blood of the covenant. Surely, these sanctified persons were of the elect, even according to the creed, for it says: "Sanctification is a work of God's grace, whereby they, whom God hath, before the foundation of the world, chosen to be holy, are, in time, through the powerful operation of his Spirit, applying the death and resurrection of Christ unto them, renewed in their whole man after the image of God." Larger Catechism, answer to Question 75. Then Paul intended to teach that God's elect, after sanctification by the blood of the new covenant, might sin wilfully and be worthy of sorer punishment than those who died without mercy under the law of Moses. But we will hear Peter on the same subject. He says: "If after they have escaped the pollutions of the world through the knowledge of the Lord and Saviour Jesus Christ, they are again entangled therein and overcome, the latter end is worse with them than the beginning. For it had been better for them not to have known the way of righteousness, than, after they have known it, to turn from the holy commandment delivered unto them; but it is happened unto them according to the true proverb, The dog is turned to his own vomit again, and the sow that was washed to her wallowing in the mire." 2 Pet. ii:20-22. Here we find that persons who have escaped the pollutions of the world may again be entangled in and overcome by them; and we are clearly told that if they are so overcome, then the latter end with them is worse than the beginning. Better for them not to have obeyed the gospel at all than to turn back into wickedness. As the sow that was washed may go back to wallowing in the mire, so may he who was cleansed from sin become worse than before.

Paul testified to such of his Galatian brethren as were circumcised, that "Christ is become of no effect unto you, whosoever of you are justified by the law; ye are fallen from grace." Gal. v:4. Here, it seems to us, all controversy on the possibility of "falling from grace" should cease. We see no place for further argument on the subject; indeed, we know not how to make an argument on a passage like this. We have learned how to reason from premises to conclusions, but here there is no room for reason. When Paul most solemnly testifies that such as had turned back to the law and been circumcised had "fallen from grace," it must simply be accepted as true, or the truth of the statement denied. Surely, these were once in grace—in favor with God—in Christ—for it would be the merest twaddle to talk about persons falling from positions which they never occupied. This being true, it follows that every person who thus falls diminishes the number of the elect and increases the number of the reprobate; hence the whole theory of unconditional election and reprobation is untrue.

But it is not only true that Christians, God's elect, may fall as *individuals,* but it is also true that *congregations* composing the "church of God" at certain places may fall. In proof of this position we would refer the reader to the several messages to the Asiatic churches, only a few extracts from which we have here room to make. After approving many good traits of character in the church at Ephesus, God said to them: "Nevertheless I have somewhat against thee; because thou hast left thy first love. Remember therefore from whence thou art fallen, and repent, and do the first works; or else I will come unto thee quickly, and will remove thy candlestick out of his place, except thou repent." Rev. ii:4, 5. Here was a church which had many elegant traits of character, yet it had left its first love, so that it had to repent and do its first works or have its candlestick quickly removed. Certainly, this had reference to the removal of the church as a body.

To the church of the Laodiceans he said: "I know thy works, that thou art neither cold nor hot; I would that thou wert cold or hot. So then because thou art lukewarm, and neither cold nor hot, I will spew thee out of my mouth. Because thou sayest, I am rich, and increased with goods, and have need of nothing; and knowest not that thou art wretched, and miserable, and poor, and blind, and naked: I counsel thee to buy of me gold tried in the fire, that thou mayest be rich; and white raiment, that thou mayest be clothed, and that the shame of thy nakedness do not appear; and anoint thine eyes with eyesalve, that thou mayest see." Rev. iii:15-18. Here was a church which God said he would spew out of his mouth, and after many epithets of reproach upon it he gives it such counsel as would enable it to reinstate itself in his favor by reformation and obedience. God said, "If the wicked will turn from all his sins that he hath committed, and keep all my statutes, and do that which is lawful and right, he shall surely live, he shall not die. All his transgressions that he hath committed, they shall not be mentioned: in his righteousness that he hath done he shall live. Have I any pleasure at all that the wicked should die? saith the Lord God: and not that he should return from his ways and live? But when the righteous turneth away from his righteousness and committeth iniquity, and doeth according to all the abominations that the wicked man doeth, shall he live? All his righteousness that he hath done shall not be mentioned: in his trespass that he hath trespassed, and in his sin that he hath sinned, in them shall he die. Yet ye say, The way of the Lord is not equal. Hear now, O house of Israel; is not my way equal? are not your ways unequal? When a righteous man turneth away from his righteousness, and committeth iniquity, and dieth in them; for his iniquity that he hath done shall he die. Again, when the wicked man turneth away from his wickedness that he hath committed, and doeth that which is lawful and right, he shall save his soul alive. Because he considereth and turneth away from all his transgressions that he hath committed, he shall surely live, he shall not die." Ezek. xviii:21-28. This general principle characterizes all God's dealings with man in every age of the world.

We come now to consider the doctrine of eternal unconditional election and reprobation in its bearing on the subject of the *atonement*. If God, before the foundation of the world, unconditionally ordained just who and how many should be saved, and who and how many lost, then of course the atonement made by Christ could not reach those who were fore-ordained to dishonor and wrath, and therefore they could not have any interest in his death. Indeed it is difficult, according to the theory, to see the benefits of Christ's death at all; for the atonement could not make the salvation of the elect any more secure, nor could it possibly change the condition or chances of the reprobate. Here again the creed is consistent with itself, as far as the reprobate are concerned, for it does not assume that the benefits of the atonement can in any way reach them; not because of any fault in them, but because Christ did not die for them. It says: "Neither are any other redeemed by Christ, effectually called, justified, adopted, sanctified, and saved, but the elect only." Chap. 3, sec. 6. *Then, when it is shown that Christ died for all men, the doctrine of unconditional election and reprobation will have been again exploded.*

Paul says, "We see Jesus, who was made a little lower than the angels for the suffering of death, crowned with glory and honor, that he by the grace of God should taste death for every man." Heb. ii:9. What can this mean? It can mean nothing less than that Christ *died for every man.* Surely, it would require elastic rules of interpretation to supply the word *elect* here, so as to make it read that "Jesus tasted death for every *elect man.*" Before making this addition to the word of the Lord, let the reader consider well the following quotation: "For I testify unto every man that heareth the words of the prophecy of this book, If any man shall add unto these things, God shall add unto him the plagues that are written in this book." Rev. xxii:18.

"For God so loved the world, that he gave his only begotten Son, that whosoever believeth in him should not perish, but have everlasting life; for God sent not his Son into the world to condemn the world; but that the world through him might be saved." John iii:16, 17. Here we find that the love of God extended to the world, and the object of sending His Son into the world was the salvation of the world. But here again we are asked to supply the word *elect,* so as to restrict the love of God to the elect. But the same apostle, in another place, supplies a word better calculated to give his use of the word *world* as connected with the atonement. He says, "He is the propitiation for our sins: and not for ours only, but also for the sins of the *whole world.*" 1 John ii:2. Could language be more ample or comprehensive? and would any one ever have thought of restricting its meaning to the *whole elect world*, had not the salvation of a theory required it? We know that the word *world* is sometimes used in a limited sense—that is, when it is intended to apply to a part, and not all of the human race; but it applies in such cases to the *wicked*, as distinguished from the elect. A single example will abundantly show this. Jesus said to his disciples: "If the world hate you, ye know that it hated me before it hated you. If ye were of the world, the world would love his own; but because ye are not of the world, but I have chosen you out of the world, therefore the world hateth you." John xv:18, 19. In this quotation the word *world* occurs several times in a limited sense, but every time it refers to the *wicked* as distinguished from the elect. But the context itself utterly forbids any such restricted use of the term in John iii: 16, 17. Let us examine it a little. The passage not only teaches that God loved the world, but also that the object of sending His Son into the world was that the *world* might not perish, but have everlasting life. Then if the love of God, and the *world* to whom He sent His Son, be confined to the *elect world*, it follows that whosoever of this elect world believes on Him may not perish; but *others of the elect world may not believe on Him, and therefore perish*. This view is quite prominent in the verse immediately following: "He that believeth on him is not condemned: but he that believeth not is condemned already, because he hath not believed on the name of the only begotten Son of God." John iii:18. That is, *he, of this elect world that God loved, and to whom He sent His Son, that believeth not, is condemned already*. This doctrine the advocates of the theory will not allow. And it will do no better to confine the word *world* to the Jews, reading it thus: "God so loved the Jewish world that he sent his only begotten Son," etc.: for that would *exclude all others* but Jews from the benefits of the atonement, even the makers of the creed themselves. Nor will it do to apply the word *world* here to the Roman Empire, for this would exclude the other nations, and thus come in direct conflict with the commission sending the apostles to disciple *all nations*, and into *all the world* to preach to *every creature*. Then it must mean just what it says: "He is the propitiation for the sins of the whole world." "Because we thus judge, that if one died for all, then were all dead: and that he died for all, that they which live should not henceforth live unto themselves, but unto him which died for them, and rose again." 2 Cor. v:14, 15. Here the apostle clearly teaches that Christ died for all affected by the sin of Adam; hence the language: "If one died for all, then were all dead." Then as "death passed upon all men" (Rom. v:12), even so Christ *died for all men.* "Therefore, as by the offense of one, judgment came upon all men to condemnation; even so by the righteousness of one the free gift came upon all men unto justification of life." Rom. v:18. Without turning aside to offer an exegesis of this verse, it is sufficient for our present purpose to call attention to the very obvious fact that, as Adam's sin affects all men, even so the benefits of Christ's death are offered to all men. To the same effect spake Jesus when He said: "I, if I be lifted up from the earth, will draw all men unto me. This he said, signifying what death he should die." John xii:32, 33. Surely, He did not expect all men to be drawn unto Him by His death unless *all were interested in His death.* What attraction could His death have for a reprobate, when he knew He died not for him, or any but the elect?

Again: Paul says, "There is one God, and one mediator between God and men, the man Christ Jesus; who gave himself a ransom for all, to be testified in due time." 1 Tim. ii:5, 6. Here, as usual, Paul is in contact with the theory which says substantially that Christ gave himself a ransom for the *elect* only. It is evident, from this connection, that the *ransom* was co-extensive with the mediatorial office—yea, with the reign of God himself —"For there is one God, and one mediator between God and men, the man Christ Jesus; who gave himself a ransom for all." Wherefore he is able also to save them to the *uttermost* that come unto God by him, seeing he ever liveth to make intercession for those he is able to save; and he is able to save to the *uttermost;* yet he can save none, only those for whom he died; therefore he died for the *uttermost* that come to God by him. Surely, we can not be mistaken in this.

When the angel of the Lord announced the birth of Christ to the shepherds who watched their flocks in the plains of Judea, he said, "Fear not: for, behold, I bring you glad tidings of great joy, which shall be to all people." Luke ii:10. It occurs to us that the angel would have spoken more like the creed had he said, "Behold, I bring you glad tidings of great joy, which shall be to the *elect*." Surely, the announcement of a Saviour born could not have been glad tidings of great joy to those who were eternally reprobate, and therefore could not hope for an interest in His mission and death, or the atonement made by Him. Nor is it very easy to see how the news of His birth could have been glad tidings of great joy even to the elect, for He could not make *their* salvation any more secure than it was made by the immutable decree of election. Peter did not so understand the subject, for he said, "Wherefore the rather, brethren, give diligence to make your calling and election sure." Then it was not already sure. But why strive to make it sure? "For if ye do these things, ye shall never fall." 2 Pet. i:10. Then if they did *not* do these things they *would* fall, and make void their election; at least they would be liable to do so. Hence, as the announcement of His birth *was glad tid'ngs of great joy to all people,* it is certain that Christ *died for all people;* and therefore *all people may be saved* through the atonement made by Him. It is certain that all will not be saved; but it will not be because the provisions of the atonement did not embrace them, but because they would not accept salvation as offered to them.

It is conceded by all parties that Christ died for the elect or saved; hence we propose next to show that He *also died for such as have been or may be lost.* Paul says: "But if thy brother be grieved with thy meat, now walkest thou not charitably. Destroy not him with thy meat, for whom Christ died." Rom. xiv:15. "And through thy knowledge shall the weak brother perish, for whom Christ died." 1 Cor. viii:11. These passages teach as clearly as language can teach anything that there were members of the church of God, both at Rome and at Corinth, for whom Christ died, who were liable to perish—be destroyed; hence *Christ died as well for those who perish—are destroyed—* as for those who are saved. These passages show, too, that the disciples at Rome and Corinth were liable to fall away—perish —be destroyed; hence his admonition to those in charge of the weaker members to guard against such result. How can it be, then, that the destiny of every one was immutably fixed by the decree of election? But we will hear another apostle on the same subject. Peter says: "But there were false prophets among the people, even as there shall be false teachers among you, who privily shall bring in damnable heresies, even denying the Lord that bought them, and bring upon themselves swift destruction." 2 Peter ii:1. Here were false teachers that denied the Lord that bought them, and thereby brought upon themselves swift destruction. How did the Lord buy them? Paul admonished certain persons "to feed the church of God, which he purchased with his own blood." Acts xx:28. Then it was with the blood of Christ that He bought or purchased these false teachers who denied Him, and destroyed themselves. Before leaving this passage, we may note another fact which appears in it. These false teachers brought destruction upon *themselves;* and this they could not have done if they were eternally and unchangeably ordained to dishonor and wrath by God's decree. The decree destroyed them, and no act of theirs—if such decree was made concerning them.

We next propose to show that salvation is attainable by all men, because the gospel of salvation is to be preached to all men. Jesus charged the apostles to "teach all nations, baptizing them." Matt. xxviii:19. And again: "Go ye into all the world, and preach the gospel to every creature." Mark xvi:15. Why preach the gospel to *every creature* when the larger portion were not embraced in its provisions? It occurs to us that something like the following would have been more appropriate: "Go ye into all the world and preach the gospel to *the elect,* that they may know the ample provisions made for them before the foundation of the world; but to the reprobate say nothing, for as they can not by any possibility avert the awful doom that surely awaits them, it is better to let them remain ignorant of their fate as long as possible." If this be true, we can see no use of all the labor and expense of printing Bibles, building meeting-houses, and preaching the gospel to either saint or sinner. If we are of the definite number elected and fore-ordained to eternal life, there is no chance for us to be lost; and if not, we can not be saved. We have often heard this doctrine preached from the pulpit, when the sermon closed with an exhortation to sinners to come to the anxious-seat to seek salvation or pray for pardon of sin. What a mockery! Why tell a man that God has unalterably fixed his destiny before time began, and then exhort him to "flee from the wrath to come" and "lay hold on eternal life"—as though he could either change or confirm God's eternal and immutable decree!! Surely, his efforts could do no good, nor could his negligence do any harm, for "Those of mankind that are predestinated unto life, God, before the foundation of the world was laid, according to his eternal and immutable purpose, and the secret counsel and good pleasure of his will, has chosen in Christ unto everlasting glory, out of his mere free grace and love, without any foresight of faith or good works, or perseverance in either of them, or any other thing in the creature, as conditions or causes moving him thereunto." Conf., chap. iii, sec. 5. Thus we see that *faith, good works,* nor *any other thing*, can avail, for the whole matter was unalterably fixed before time began. Salvation, upon certain conditions, was the great object of preaching the gospel to every creature; and among these conditions *faith* occupies a conspicuous place: "Faith cometh by hearing, and hearing by the word of God." Rom. x:17. Hence the necessity of preaching the gospel—teaching the word of God to every creature, that he might have the privilege of believing and obeying it; therefore the promise: "He that believeth and is baptized shall be saved; but he that believeth not shall be damned." Mark xvi:16. The fact that Jesus required the gospel to be preached among all nations, to every creature, promising salvation to those who would believe and obey it, is evidence high as heaven that all may have salvation who will accept it upon the conditions specified. Surely, God would not mock His creatures by preaching the gospel, and offering salvation to them on certain conditions, when He had eternally and unchangeably ordained that they should not be saved, and put it out of their power to comply with the terms offered. Nor is this all: He follows the promise of conditional salvation with the awful threat that "He that believeth not shall be damned." We can not see why any one should be required to believe and trust in a Saviour who did nothing for them, and believe and obey a gospel the provisions of which did not embrace them. Men are required to believe upon and trust in Jesus, in order to salvation: "Many other signs truly did Jesus in the presence of his disciples, which are not written in this book: but these are written, that ye might believe that Jesus is the Christ, the Son of God." And why believe this? "That believing ye might have life through his name." John xx:30, 31. Jesus said, "He that believeth on the Son hath everlasting life: and he that believeth not the Son shall not see life; but the wrath of God abideth on him." John iii:36. Thus we see that man is denied eternal life, and subjected to the abiding wrath of God, not because of any eternal decree against him personally, but because of his unbelief; hence "He that believeth on him is not condemned: but he that believeth not is condemned already." And why is he condemned already? Is it because of God's eternal decree against him? No; but "because he hath not believed in the name of the only begotten Son of God." John iii:18.

Thus the justice of God is vindicated in the punishment of man. If he is not saved, it will not be because God eternally and unchangeably ordained his destruction; nor will it be because God willed not his salvation. Hear Him most solemnly deny such an imputation: "If the wicked will turn from all his sins that he hath committed, and keep all my statutes, and do that which is lawful and right, he shall surely live, he shall not die. All his transgressions that he hath committed, they shall not be mentioned unto him. In his righteousness that he hath done he shall live. Have I any pleasure at all that the wicked should die? saith the Lord God: and not that he should return from his ways and live." Ezek. xviii:21-23. "For I have no pleasure in the death of him that dieth, saith the Lord God; wherefore turn yourselves, and live ye." Ver. 32. And again: "As I live, saith the Lord God, I have no pleasure in the death of the wicked; but that the wicked turn from his way and live." Ezek. xxxiii:11. This is either true or it is untrue. If God, from all eternity, fixed the destiny of all men, and ordained a definite number to life and a definite number to dishonor and wrath, and that "according to the unsearchable counsel of His own will, whereby He extendeth or withholdeth mercy as He pleaseth" (Conf., chap. iii, sec. 7), then we see not how God has not pleasure in and wills not that which is according to the secret counsel and good pleasure of His own will. It requires greater skill than we possess to harmonize the Bible and the creed here. "The Lord is not slack concerning his promise, as some men count slackness; but is longsuffering to us-ward, not willing that any should perish, but that all should come to repentance." 2 Pet. iii:9. How can this be true, if God fixed the destiny of each one in accordance with the unsearchable counsel of His will before time began? He who can, may explain.

Paul says: "I exhort therefore, that, first of all, supplications, prayers, intercessions, and giving of thanks, be made for all men; for kings, and for all that are in authority; that we may lead a quiet and peaceable life in all godliness and honesty. For this is good and acceptable in the sight of God our Saviour; who will have all men to be saved, and to come unto the knowledge of the truth." 1 Tim. ii:1-4. Here we learn that all men are the objects of prayer. And why? Because God wills the salvation of all men. Then if all are not saved, it will be because "ye will not come to me that ye might have life." John v:40. Their own obdurate will is the great barrier to the salvation of men. When Jesus beheld the wickedness of the people of Jerusalem, and the consequent destruction that awaited them, he said: "O Jerusalem, Jerusalem, thou that killest the prophets, and stonest them which are sent unto thee, how often would I have gathered thy children together, even as a hen gathereth her chickens under her wings, and ye would not!" Matt. xxiii:37. Mark well the reason: *"Ye would not."* Yes, the Son of God would gladly have saved them from the danger which threatened them, even as He would now save all who would come to God by Him; yet they would not—neither will ye. "The Spirit and the bride say, Come. And let him that heareth say, Come. And let him that is athirst come. And whosoever will, let him take the water of life freely." Rev. xxii:17. Not whosoever was elected from all eternity, but *whosoever will,* let him take the water of life freely. Then whosoever perishes is lost because he will not partake of that which is freely offered to him. His unending wail may be, "God is just, though I am lost."

Jesus said, "The Son of man is come to seek and to save that which was lost." Luke xix:10. Was there ever a time when the elect were lost? If so, when? The creed tells us that they were predestinated unto life before the foundation of the world was laid; hence, if they were ever lost, it must have been before that: therefore they could not have been the objects of Christ's mission, for these were lost when He came. Again He says: "They that are whole have no need of the physician, but they that are sick: I came not to call the righteous, but sinners to repentance." Mark ii:17; Luke v:31, 32. Were the eternally elect the sinners which Jesus came to call to repentance? Surely, they were not sick enough to invoke the aid of Jesus, the great Physician, for they were eternally and immutably ordained to eternal life; hence they were not sick—at all events they could not have been sick unto death.

The Scriptures abound with testimony showing that men are not elect before conversion. A few passages of this class are all for which we have room in this work. In speaking of himself and his Ephesian brethren, Paul tells us that they were "by nature the children of wrath, even as others." Eph. ii:3. If they had been elected to salvation before time began, we see not how, at any time, they could have been *children of wrath,* even as others not of the elect. Again: "Ye are not in the flesh, but in the Spirit, if so be that the Spirit of God dwell in you. Now if any man have not the Spirit of Christ he is none of his." Rom. viii:9. All persons know that, prior to conversion, the Spirit of Christ was not in them, and hence, at that time, they were none of His; yet according to the theory, they were *always* His. "As many as are led by the Spirit of God, they are the sons of God." Rom. viii:14. Then of course the converse is true, that as many as are not led by the Spirit of God are not the sons of God. All unconverted persons are led by the spirit of the wicked one, and not by the Spirit of God; therefore no unconverted man is a son of God. It will be conceded that the elect are sons of God; hence *when not sons of God, none are elect.* "Know ye not your own selves, how that Jesus Christ is in you, except ye be reprobates." 2 Cor. xiii:5. Prior to conversion, Christ is in no one. Paul says, "I travail in birth again until Christ be formed in you." Gal. iv:19. As Christ *has to be formed* in men, it follows that He was not always in them; and when He is not in them, they are reprobates: therefore none are elect until converted. "If any man be in Christ, he is a new creature: old things are passed away; behold, all things are become new." 2 Cor. v:17. If all the elect were in Christ from before the foundation of the world, then conversion makes no man a *new* creature in Him; for if in Him at all, they were always in Him. Paul says, "Salute Andronicus and Junia, my kinsmen, and my fellow prisoners, who are of note among the apostles, who also were in Christ before me." Rom. xvi:7. If Paul and his kinsmen were in Christ from before the foundation of the world, then he made a most egregious blunder here. When was it, and how is it that they were in Christ before him? Once more: "They that are Christ's have crucified the flesh with the affections and lusts." Gal. v:24. Then those who have *not* crucified the flesh with the affections and lusts are not Christ's. There was a time in the history of every man when he had not crucified the flesh with the affections and lusts, and therefore a time when he was not Christ's. All the elect are Christ's; therefore there was a time in the life of every man when he was not of the elect: hence none are personally and unconditionally elected to eternal life from before the foundation of the world.

Speaking of his brethren in the Lord, Peter said: "Ye are a chosen generation, a royal priesthood, a holy nation, a peculiar people; that ye should show forth the praises of him who hath called you out of darkness into his marvelous light: which in time past were not a people, but are now the people of God; which had not obtained mercy, but now have obtained mercy." 1 Pet. ii:9, 10. Here, again, we know not how to make an argument. This passage is so manifestly opposed to the whole theory of eternal and unconditional election and reprobation that there is no room to reason about it. These were a chosen generation, a royal priesthood; a holy nation, a peculiar people; hence they were God's elect beyond controversy: yet in time past they *were not a people,* but then were the *people* of God. Do you say these were Gentiles? Suppose they were: what relief does this bring to the theory? It only shows the more clearly that once they were not God's people; yet when the apostle wrote, they *were* God's people—yes, verily, they were His peculiar people. Were they elected in Christ before the foundation of the world! Then we would gladly know what time in the past it was at which they were not the people of God. Once they had not obtained mercy. When was this? Elected to eternal life before the foundation of the world, out of God's mere free grace and love, and yet had not obtained mercy!!!

But if the doctrine already quoted from the Confession is

true—that before the foundation of the world was laid, according to an immutable and eternal purpose of His own, without any foresight of faith, good works, or any thing else in man, God unconditionally elected some men and angels to eternal life, and at the same time fore-ordained the residue to dishonor and eternal wrath—then we know not how to avoid the conclusion that He is a respecter of persons. Against this imputation upon the character of our Heavenly Father, at least two inspired pens have given testimony. Paul said, "There is no respect of persons with God." Rom ii:11. Again: "He that doeth wrong, shall receive for the wrong which he hath done: and there is no respect of persons." Col. iii:25. Once more: "And, ye masters, do the same things unto them, forbearing threatening: knowing that your Master also is in heaven; neither is there respect of persons with him." Eph. vi:9. It is probable that Peter once had similar thoughts upon this subject to those of Calvinists now. Certain it is that he thought the privileges and blessings of the gospel were confined to the Jews, and it required nothing less than a miracle to convince him of his error; but when convinced, he at once replied: "Of a truth I perceive that God is no respecter of persons." Acts x:34. From that time he gladly taught the gospel to those previously regarded unworthy of its privileges. Finally, let us examine the subject of a general judgment through Calvinistic glasses.

"The times of this ignorance God winked at; but now commandeth all men every-where to repent: because he hath appointed a day in the which he will judge the world in righteousness by that man whom he hath ordained." Acts xvii:30, 31.

But why appoint a day of judgment in which to judge the world, if the numbers of the elect and reprobate were made certain and definite beyond increase or diminution before time began? Surely, the line of separation was drawn deep and wide between them by the immutable decree which assigned each one his position long in advance of his being. But God will judge the world in *righteousness;* therefore His judgment will be in accordance with principles of justice: "For we must all appear before the judgment seat of Christ; that every one may receive the things done in his body, according to that he hath done, whether it be good or bad." 2 Cor. v:10. John says: "And I saw the dead, small and great, stand before God; and the books were opened: and another book was opened, which is the book of life: and the dead were judged out of those things which were written in the books, according to their works. And the sea gave up the dead which were in it; and death and hell delivered up the dead which were in them: and they were judged every man according to their works." Rev. xx:12, 13. Why judge a man according to his works, when every thing he did was specifically ordained and put out of his control before time began? Why not judge him, if at all, *according to the eternal decree which immutably fixed his destiny?* From such a standpoint as Calvinism the whole theory of a future judgment seems to us a most sublimely ridiculous farce.

That the decree of election, and not the things done in the body, is the rule or law by which Calvinism proposes to judge the world, is further shown by the fact that reprobate infants that die in infancy are consigned to eternal misery for no other reason than that they were not of the elect. On page 64, chap. x, sec. 3, the creed says: "Elect infants dying in infancy are regenerated and saved by Christ through the Spirit, who worketh when and where and how he pleaseth. So also are all other elect persons who are incapable of being outwardly called by the ministry of the Word." Yes, elect infants are saved by Christ; but what of the non-elect? "Others not elected, though they may be called by the ministry of the Word, and may have some common operations of the Spirit, yet they never truly come to Christ, and therefore can not be saved." The words "elect infants" clearly imply non-elect infants. Elect means to choose. There can be no choice where there is but one person or class of persons. The above quotation tells us that elect infants dying in infancy are saved; and of course the non-elect infants dying in infancy, or in living to adult age, can not be saved, as Christ never died for them, or any but the elect. Though you may consign your infant to the tomb while so young that it never could have had a wicked thought or done a wicked act, yet you have no assurance of its ever being raised in the image of Christ, for the reason that you can not tell whether it is or is not one of the elect. No, you can not tell whether its little tongue will be employed in praising God, or in fruitless cries and bitter wailings in the eternal pit of despair, for no fault of its own, or any one else, but simply because God unchangeably decreed it that horrible fate. Calvinism has no escape from this difficulty. The numbers of the elect and reprobate having been made certain and definite before time began, it follows that he who is reprobate—at all, was so at birth; hence those who die in that condition are hopelessly lost. There is no remedy that can reach such cases. Therefore, Calvinists who are not prepared for such results should abandon a theory which necessarily produces them.

CHAPTER III.

CALVINISTIC PROOFS EXAMINED.

As the Bereans "were more noble than those in Thessalonica, in that they received the word with all readiness of mind, and searched the Scriptures daily, whether those things were so" (Acts xvii:11), even so we should search the Scriptures and receive the truth revealed in God's word with that readiness of mind that has ever characterized His true and devoted followers. Let us, therefore, very carefully consider the Scriptures relied on to prove the doctrine in question.

Ananias said to Saul, "The God of our fathers hath chosen thee." Acts xxii:14. This shows that Paul was elected or chosen; but for what was he chosen? Perhaps we may learn what Ananias meant here by reference to what the Lord said to him when He sent him to Paul: "The Lord said unto him, Go thy way: for he is a chosen vessel unto me." Chosen for what? "To bear my name before the Gentiles, and kings, and the children of Israel." Acts ix:15. Before giving this instruction to Ananias, the Lord said to Paul: "I have appeared unto thee for this purpose, to make thee a minister and a witness both of these things which thou hast seen, and of those things in the which I will appear unto thee; delivering thee from the people, and from the Gentiles, unto whom now I send thee, to open their eyes, and to turn them from darkness to light, and from the power of Satan unto God, that they may receive forgiveness of sins, and an inheritance among them which are sanctified by faith that is in me." Acts xxvi: 16-18. Taking these Scriptures together, we see very clearly what the object of Paul's election was; and his own salvation is not even mentioned in any one of the explanations given. He was elected to be a minister and a witness for Jesus, and to bear the gospel to the Gentiles; hence says he, "I speak to you Gentiles, inasmuch as I am the apostle of the Gentiles, I magnify mine office." Rom. xi:13. Here, then, was the office to which he was elected; but even his election to the apostleship did not secure his final salvation, for he says, "I keep under my body, and bring into subjection: lest that by any means, when I have preached to others, I myself should be a castaway." 1 Cor. ix:27. That Paul was not elected in Christ to salvation before the foundation of the world, is clearly shown by the fact that Andronicus and Junia were in Christ before him. Rom. xvi:7.

"And when the Gentiles heard this, they were glad, and glorified the word of the Lord: and as many as were ordained to eternal life believed." Acts xiii:48. This is relied on to show that men are ordained to eternal life from before the foundation of the world, and that this ordination is an indispensable antecedent to faith. First we beg permission to suggest that the translation of this verse, in the common version, is manifestly defective; but even in it there is not a word said about how long they were ordained to eternal life before they believed. That the ordination was from before the foundation of the world is assumption; nothing more. If men are ordained to eternal life before they believe, then they are in a state of condemnation, their ordination to the contrary notwithstanding; for the Lord said: "He that believeth not is condemned already, because he hath not believed in the name of the only begotten Son of God." John iii:18. It is difficult to see how a man who is ordained to eternal life can, at the same time, be a condemned unbeliever. Not only are they in a state of condemnation, but this theory teaches that they do not believe, in order to their justification; for they were ordained to eternal life before they believed in the eternal life to which they were ordained. This is not only sustained by the common rendering of this verse, but it is made doubly obvious by the fact that the theory places the ordination before the beginning of time. On the contrary, there is not a truth in the Bible better established than that men are required to *believe, that they may have eternal life:* "For God so loved the world, that he gave his only begotten Son, that whosoever believeth in him should not perish, but have everlasting life," John iii:16. When Jesus said, "He that believeth and is baptized shall be saved" (Mark xvi:16), did He intend to teach that he that would believe and be baptized had always been saved? or when Paul said to the jailer, "Believe on the Lord Jesus Christ, and thou shalt be saved" (Acts xvi:31), did he mean to teach that he had always been saved, having been ordained to eternal life from before the foundation of the world? Absurd as this may appear, it must be true, or Calvinism must be false.

CALVINISTIC PROOFS EXAMINED

But there are other difficulties hanging about the common rendering of this verse. McGarvey, in his Commentary, has the following very pertinent remarks:

"If it be true that 'as *many as were fore-ordained* to eternal life believed,' then there were none of the fore-ordained left in that community who did not believe. Hence all those who did not then believe, whether adults or infants, were among the reprobate, who were predestinated to everlasting punishment. Now, it is certainly most singular that so complete a separation of the two parties should take place throughout a whole community at one time." Truly, this would have been a most singular circumstance—such a one, indeed, as no sane man can believe ever occurred; hence that the translation is defective is obvious, even to those who know nothing of the original; for a faithful translation of God's word is always not only true, but perfectly consistent with itself. We have several translations of this verse, most of which substantially agree with the following version: "And the Gentiles hearing this rejoiced, and glorified the word of the Lord; and as many as were disposed for eternal life believed." (Compilation from George Campbell, Macknight, and Doddridge, by A. Campbell.) This rendering is perfectly consistent with the facts and the general teaching of the Scriptures; and, better still, is faithful to the original, and at once removes all ambiguity from the passage.

"For whom he did foreknow, he also did predestinate to be conformed to the image of his Son, that he might be the firstborn among many brethren. Moreover, whom he did predestinate, them he also called: and whom he called, them he also justified: and whom he justified, them he also glorified." Rom. viii:29, 30. First it will be observed that all these verbs are in the past tense, and express actions perfected at the time the apostle wrote. Persons seem to understand the passage to mean that God foreknew and predestinated the elect before time began, perhaps from eternity, and calls and justifies them now in his good time, and will glorify them in heaven finally. This can not be, for those of whom the apostle spake were glorified at the time he wrote, and for the same reason it can not apply to any who have lived since that time. The creed says: "God did, from all eternity, decree to justify all the elect; and Christ did, in the fullness of time, die for their sins, and rise again for their justification; nevertheless they are not justified until the Holy Spirit doth in due time actually apply Christ unto them." Conf., chap. 11, sec. 4. Thus we see that Calvinists themselves have justification to take place in the life-time of the party justified. Hence, as those of whom Paul wrote were justified before that time, it can not apply to any who have lived since, even according to the creed, but must apply to persons who had lived before the time he wrote. Hence the passage can not come to the support of Calvinism at all. Here we could well afford to rest our examination of the passage, seeing it proves not the doctrine in question; but we will endeavor to find persons to whom the language of the apostle will correctly apply. It is not important to inquire *when* God knew the persons here mentioned—we grant that He knew them when He predestinated them to be conformed to the image of His Son; and this was done before they were called and justified: this is all that can be claimed—the question which concerns us more directly is, *Who were these* of whom Paul spake as having been foreknown, predestinated, called, justified, and glorified prior to the time he wrote? While we look for an answer to this question, it may be well for us to bear in mind that God predestinated them to be conformed to the image of His Son, that He might be the first-born among many brethren. The word *conform* means "to shape in accordance with; to make like; to reduce to a likeness or correspondence in character, form, manners, etc." (Webster.) Then, to be conformed to the image of His Son is to be made like Christ, or in His image or likeness. Thus far all is plain. Let us try again. Paul says: "The first man is of the earth, earthy; the second man is the Lord from heaven. As is the earthy, such are they also that are earthy: and as is the heavenly, such are they also that are heavenly. And as we have borne the image of the earthy, we shall also bear the image of the heavenly." 1 Cor. xv:47-49. Paul is here speaking of the resurrection of the body, and after directing the mind to the time of that event, he says: "As we have borne the image of the earthy, we *shall also bear the image* of the heavenly"—thus teaching clearly that the children of our heavenly Father wear the image of Adam through life, but will wear the image of Christ when raised from the dead and furnished with immortal bodies like His: "And it doth not yet appear what we shall be; but we know that when he shall appear we shall be like him; for we shall see him as he is." 1 John iii:2. Though the image of Christ, in a certain sense, may have been begun in us when we put Him on by a birth of water and Spirit, yet it will never be complete until we are glorified with Him; and He was not glorified until after His death, resurrection, and ascension. John says, "The Holy Ghost was not yet given, because Jesus was not yet glorified." John vii:29. This clearly implies that the Holy Ghost was given as soon as Jesus was glorified; and as the Holy Spirit was not given until the day of Pentecost, it follows that his glorification did not long precede that event. Therefore, those of whom Paul spake were not only predestinated, called, and justified, but had also been raised from the dead, conformed to the image of Christ, and glorified prior to the time he wrote. This not only shows that the passage does not embrace all the elect, but it also shows that it did not refer to the apostles, as some suppose, for they were not all dead at that time, and hence could not have been then glorified. Then, when and where had any persons been raised from the dead to die no more prior to this writing by Paul? It could not have referred to Lazarus, Jairus' daughter, and the widow's son which were raised by Christ, for he was not the first-born among them, nor were they raised to glorification, but simply restored to life to live and die again. Let us look further, then, for we have not yet found persons to whom the passage can apply. "And the graves were opened; and many bodies of the saints which slept arose and came out of the graves after his resurrection, and went into the holy city, and appeared unto many." Matt. xxvii:52, 53. These persons were raised from the dead to die no more, but to be glorified with their risen Lord. We have seen that those of whom Paul wrote were predestinated to be conformed to the image of His Son, which image, if we are correct, was perfected when they were glorified. Then, for what were they thus to be conformed to the image of His Son? "That he might be the first-born among many brethren." When was He the first-born among many brethren? Certainly, it was not when He was born in the flesh, for many were thus born before Him; nor was He the first-born of water, for many were baptized by John before

Him. Paul says He is "the firstborn from the dead." Col. i:18. Then He was the first-born from the dead of the many brethren who came from their graves after His resurrection; and hence these were they who were predestinated to be conformed to the image of His Son, that He might be the first-born from the dead among them. Of these it may be correctly said that they had been foreknown, predestinated, called, justified, and glorified, at the time Paul wrote; but we know of no others of whom this may be truly said. Are we asked who these were? we answer that, as no inspired writer has given their names in this connection, of course we do not know their names; but we do know that He was the first-born from the dead among those who came from their graves after His resurrection: hence our argument is complete with or without their names. We think it likely, however, that they were Abraham, Isaac, Jacob, and the patriarchs and prophets of former times. That these were *foreknown, called,* and *predestinated* to the work assigned them, may be seen in the language of God to one of them. Jeremiah said: "The word of the Lord came unto me, saying, Before I formed thee in the belly I knew thee; and before thou camest forth out of the womb I sanctified thee, and ordained thee a prophet unto the nations." Jer. i:4, 5. Those of whom Paul spake were foreknown—Jeremiah was foreknown; those were predestinated—Jeremiah was ordained; those were called—Jeremiah was called. "The Lord said unto me, Say not, I am a child: for thou shalt go to all that I shall send thee, and whatsoever I command thee thou shalt speak. Be not afraid of their faces: for I am with thee to deliver thee, saith the Lord. Then the Lord put forth his hand and touched my mouth. And the Lord said unto me, Behold, I have put my words in thy mouth. See, I have this day set thee over the nations, and over the kingdoms, to root out, and to pull down, and to destroy, and to throw down, to build and to plant." Ver. 7-10. Then he was not only foreknown, predestinated, and called, but sanctified, too, and qualified for the work assigned him; hence he needed only to be justified in his obedience (which doubtless he was), raised from the dead, and glorified with Christ, to fill to repletion the character of those of whom Paul spake. Does any one doubt that he was one of them? then let him show to whom the language in question will more fitly apply, and we will acknowledge the favor.

We come next to examine the ninth chapter of Paul's letter to the church at Rome, in which he discusses the abrogation of the Jewish polity, and the election of a new people upon the principle of faith in Christ and obedience to His laws. The Jews, as we have seen, had been the only acknowledged family or people of God for many ages past; but in the fullness of time God broke down the middle wall of partition between Jew and Gentile and offered salvation to every creature, among all nations, who would accept it on the terms proposed; hence when the parents of Jesus brought Him into the temple, good old Simeon took him up in his arms and said, "A light to lighten the Gentiles, and the glory of thy people Israel." Luke ii:32. Paul says this: "In other ages was not made known unto the sons of men, as it is now revealed unto his holy apostles and prophets by the Spirit: that the Gentiles should be fellow heirs and of the same body, and partakers of his promise in Christ by the gospel." Eph. iii:5, 6. This extension of gospel privileges to persons so long regarded unworthy, very naturally excited the pride and envy of those accustomed to the exclusive enjoyment of such distinguished honors and privileges; hence they declined to enjoy salvation for no other reason than that the Gentiles were made fellowheirs with them. They refused to recognize the fact that "there is no difference between the Jew and the Greek: for the same Lord over all is rich unto all that call upon him." Rom. x:12.

They failed to see that the salvation of the Gentiles did not lessen the chances of the Jews; hence Paul quotes the language of Moses as applicable to them: "I will provoke you to jealousy by them that are no people, and by a foolish nation I will anger you." Rom. x:19. The election contemplated in the gospel was offered to the Jews first, and some embraced it and were content to become the elect of God; not as Jews by natural birth, but as Christians by a birth of water and Spirit. These Paul calls "The election," in opposition to those who made themselves reprobate by refusing the "election of grace," and adhering to their former election as the descendants of Abraham; hence "the election hath obtained it, and the rest were blinded." Rom. xi:7. "Not as though the word of God had taken none effect. For they are not all Israel, which are of Israel." Rom. ix:6. The election of a new church composed of Jews and Gentiles was not contrary to the promises of God to Abraham, saying, "I will establish my covenant between me and thee, and thy seed after thee, in their generations, for an everlasting covenant; to be a God unto thee, and thy seed after thee." Gen. xvii:7. God gave them very clearly to understand that the perpetuity of their covenant relation to Him depended on their obedience; hence said He, "If ye will obey my voice indeed, and keep my covenant, then ye shall be a peculiar treasure unto me above all people." Ex. xix:5. Hence when they ceased to obey Him, His promises to them were at an end; hence Paul asks, "Hath God cast away his people? God forbid." Rom. xi:1. If they were lost at all, it was their own fault. But even so, "For they were not all Israel, which are of Israel." Many of the descendants of Jacob had already fallen. The greater part of the ten tribes that were carried into captivity never returned to be again united to the Israel of God.

Hence this passage not only shows the rejection of the unbelieving Jews to be no infraction of God's promises to Abraham, but it shows the doctrine of eternal unconditional election to be false, for we have seen that all the children of Israel were once the elect of God; but when Paul wrote, many who were of Israel were not Israel, because they had fallen on account of their own wickedness.

But the apostle vindicates the justice of God in rejecting the unbelieving Jews by showing that many of the children of Abraham were not embraced in the promise of God to him at first. Said he: "Neither, because they are the seed of Abraham, are they all children"—for then the descendants of Abraham by Hagar and Keturah would have been included—"but, in Isaac shall thy seed be called. That is, They which are the children of the flesh, these are not the children of God: but the children of the promise are counted for the seed. For this is the word of promise, At this time will I come, and Sarah shall have a son." Rom. ix:7-9. The children of Abraham by Hagar and Keturah were children of the flesh, but God saw fit to promise him a son by him wife Sarah, when she was past age, through whom all the families of the earth were to be blessed in Jesus Christ; hence, in due time, Isaac, the child of promise, was born, in whom Jesus, the promised seed of Abraham, was called. But the calling of Jesus through the line of Isaac did not consign the descendants of Abraham by Hagar and Keturah to endless punishment; nor were their chances for heaven diminished by this election of Isaac. Jacob had twelve sons, which became the heads of twelve tribes; but God saw fit to call Jesus the promised seed of Abraham, through the tribe of Judah, Jacob's fourth son by Leah. Now, will any one assume that calling the Messiah through the line of Judah consigned all the others to endless punishment? If not, why should the descendants of Abraham be regarded as eternally lost because they did not come through the family of Isaac? God never promised Abraham that He would unconditionally save or damn any one. He promised him a son by Sarah, and He gave him Isaac. He promised to multiply his seed until they should become numerous as the stars of heaven or the sand upon the sea-shore, and He did it. He promised to give his seed the land of Canaan for a possession, and He did this also; but they forfeited it by their rebellion against Him. He promised that through his seed *all the families* of the earth should be blessed in Jesus Christ; but when Jesus came, according to the promise, they wanted to appropriate the blessing to *themselves,* to the *exclusion of the Gentiles:* hence *they* were seeking to thwart the very promise of God to Abraham which they thought was made void by carrying it into effect.

"And not only this; but when Rebecca also had conceived by one, even by our father Isaac (for the children being not yet born, neither having done any good or evil, that the purpose of God according to election might stand, not of works, but of him that calleth;) it was said unto her, The elder shall serve the younger. As it is written, Jacob have I loved, but Esau have I hated." Rom. ix: 10-13.

That we may understand this passage, it may be well to call the reader's attention to the fact that there are two quotations in it which should not be blended. One quotation is from Genesis, and was spoken before Jacob and Esau were born; the other is from Malachi, and was spoken long after they were both dead.

Before the children were born, it was said to their mother, "the elder shall serve the younger;" but in the next verse is a quotation from Malachi, where it is written, "Jacob have I loved, but Esau have I hated." By blending these quotations, God is made to say that He loved Jacob and hated Esau before they were born; or had, either of them, done good or evil. This is doing great injustice to the record. Let us see what was said of them before they were born: "And Isaac entreated the Lord for his wife, because she was barren: and the Lord was entreated of him, and Rebekah his wife conceived; and the children struggled together within her, and she said, If it be so, why am I thus? And she went to inquire of the Lord. And the Lord said unto her, Two nations are in thy womb, and two manner of people shall be separated from thy bowels; and the one people shall be stronger than the other people; and the elder shall serve the younger." Gen. xxv:21-23. Here is what was said before Jacob and Esau were born, and we find not a word about hating Esau and loving Jacob in the whole narrative. But as Paul said it was so written, we may expect to find it somewhere; hence let us try again: "The burden of the word of the Lord to Israel by Malachi. I have loved you, saith the Lord. Yet ye say, Wherein hast thou loved us? Was not Esau Jacob's brother? saith the Lord: yet I loved Jacob, and I hated Esau, and laid his mountains and his heritage waste for the dragons of the wilderness." Mal. i:1-3. This was said about fourteen hundred years after Jacob and Esau were both dead; hence it can not prove that God loved or hated either of them before they were born. But both passages refer to Jacob and Esau as the representatives of the two nations which descended from them; hence the language of God to Rebekah: "Two nations are in thy womb, and two manner of people shall be separated from thy bowels; and the one people shall be stronger than the other people; and the elder shall serve the younger." Please note the fact that it is not said "the *one man* shall be stronger than the *other man,*" but "one *people* shall be stronger than the other *people.*" Nor was it said the *elder man* shall serve the *younger man;* on the contrary, the inference is clear that the people who should descend from the elder were to be subject to the descendants of the younger. This passage was never fulfilled in the person of these two brothers. Esau never did, as an individual, serve Jacob; on the contrary, Jacob feared Esau, and came much nearer serving him. When Jacob, at the suggestion of his mother, fraudulently obtained his father's blessing, which was intended for Esau, the anger of the latter was kindled against his brother: "And Esau hated Jacob because of the blessing wherewith his father blessed him: and Esau said in his heart, The days of mourning for my father are at hand; then will I slay my brother Jacob. And these words of Esau, her elder son, were told to Rebekah: and she sent and called Jacob, her younger son, and said unto him, Behold, thy brother Esau, as touching thee, doth comfort himself, purposing to kill thee. Now therefore, my son, obey my voice; and arise, flee thou to Laban my brother to Haran; and tarry with him a few days, until thy brother's fury turn away; until thy brother's anger turn away from thee, and he forget that which thou hast done to him." Gen. xxvii:41-45. Jacob fled to Padan-aram, and there remained twenty years in the service of Laban, at the end of which he returned with two wives, two concubines, eleven sons, and great wealth. "And Jacob sent messengers before him to Esau his brother, unto the land of Seir, the country of Edom. And he commanded them, saying, Thus shall ye speak unto my lord Esau; Thy servant Jacob saith thus, I have sojourned with Laban, and stayed there until now; and I have oxen, and asses, and flocks, and menservants and womenservants, and I have sent to tell my lord, that I may find grace in thy sight. And the messengers returned to Jacob, saying, We came to thy brother Esau, and also he cometh to meet thee, and four hundred men with him. Then Jacob was greatly afraid and distressed: and he divided the people that was with him, and the flocks, and herds, and the camels in two bands; and said, If Esau come to the one company, and smite it, then the other company which is left shall escape." Gen. xxxii:3-8. Here we find that, in place of Esau serving Jacob personally, Jacob feared Esau greatly—called him his lord, and *himself the servant*. In his distress, he prayed God thus: "Deliver me, I pray thee, from the hand of my brother, from the hand of Esau: for I fear him lest he come and smite me, and the mother with the children." Ver. II. He also sent messengers with presents to give Esau, that he might buy his favor if possible.

Then it is evident that neither Jacob nor Esau was mentioned under any personal consideration, but only as the representatives of the nations which should descend from them respectively; nor was there any thing in the love of God for one, or in His hatred of the other, which could affect the eternal destiny of either. It is quite certain that all of Jacob's posterity were not saved, and it is equally certain that all of Esau's posterity were not lost. Indeed, it can not be shown that even Esau himself was eternally lost. He was wicked when he sold his birthright, and is called a "profane person" for so doing. It is also certain, that he was wicked about the time of his father's death, for we have seen that he would have killed Jacob had he not fled to the land of Padan-aram; but that he remained wicked as long as he lived is by no means certain. True, Paul says that, "When he would have inherited the blessing, he was rejected: for he found no place of repentance, though he sought it carefully with tears." Heb. xii:17. It was in his father that he found no place of repentance, and not in himself. He could not induce his father to revoke the blessing conferred upon Jacob, although fraudulently obtained. When Esau met Jacob returning from Padan-aram, "Esau ran to meet him, and embraced him, and fell on his neck, and kissed him: and they wept." Gen. xxxiii:4. Here we find that all his anger toward his brother had disappeared; and they lived in friendship ever afterward, as far as we know. "By faith Isaac blessed Jacob and Esau concerning things to come." Heb. xi:20. If the reader will examine these blessings, he will find that there was not a word about eternal life or eternal death in either of them. They pertained to national and temporal affairs entirely. To Jacob, Isaac said, "See, the smell of my son is as the smell of a field which the Lord hath blessed: therefore God give thee of the dew of heaven, and the fatness of the earth, and plenty of corn and wine: let people serve thee, and nations bow down to thee: be lord over thy brethren, and let thy mother's sons bow down to thee: cursed be every one that curseth thee, and blessed be every one that blesseth thee.' Gen. xxvii:27-29. To Esau, Isaac said: "Behold, thy dwelling shall be the fatness of the earth, and of the dew of heaven from above; and by thy sword shalt thou live, and shalt serve thy brother: and it shall come to pass when thou shalt have the dominion, that thou shalt break his yoke from off thy neck." Gen. xxvii:39, 40. Now we find no allusion to the final salvation or condemnation of either, in these blessings; but it is easy to see that they are connected with the purpose of God as expressed to their mother: "The one people shall be stronger than the other people; and the elder shall serve the younger." See the same thought in Jacob's blessing. "Let people serve thee, and nations bow down to thee: be lord over thy brethren, and let thy mother's sons bow down to thee." In Esau's blessing we have still the same: "By thy sword shalt thou live, and shalt *serve* thy brother." Thus we see, in these blessings, the servitude spoken of before the birth of the children, which was never fulfilled in them, but was fulfilled in their posterity.

That the language, "Jacob have I loved, but Esau have I hated," was intended to apply to the two nations, Israel and Edom, represented by Jacob and Esau, is evident from the language of the context from which Paul made the quotation: "Was not Esau Jacob's brother? yet I loved Jacob, and hated Esau, and laid his mountains and his heritage waste for the dragons of the wilderness. Whereas Edom saith, We are impoverished, but we will return and build the desolate places." Mal. i:2-4. Here the prophet uses the term *Edom*, the name of the nation which descended from Esau, and the plural pronoun *we*, agreeing with it, to designate the same people hated and punished by the Lord. Hence when the Lord, by his prophet, said, long after both men were dead, "Jacob have I loved, but Esau have I hated," He was speaking of *Israel* and *Edom* as nations, but not of *Jacob* and *Esau* as individuals.

It may not be out of place here to remark that the term *hate*, is sometimes used in the sense of *loved less—to regard with less favor*; *e.g.*: "And when the Lord saw that Leah was hated, he opened her womb: but Rachel was barren. And Leah conceived, and bore a son; and she called his name Reuben: for she said, Surely the Lord hath looked upon my affliction; now therefore my husband will love me. And she conceived again, and bore a son; and said, Because the Lord hath heard that I was hated, He hath therefore given me this son also: and she called his name Simeon." Gen. xxix:31-33. Here it is said that Jacob hated Leah; but by an examination of the preceding verse, it will be seen that nothing more is meant by it than that *she was loved less* than Rachel. "He loved also Rachel more than Leah, and served with him yet seven other years." Ver. 30.

Another example may be found in the language of the Saviour: "If any man come to me, and hate not his father, and mother, and wife, and children, and brethren, and sisters, yea, and his own life also, he can not be my disciple." Luke xiv:26. This is a pretty hard sentence—that, to be a disciple of the Lord, a man must not only *hate* all his kindred, but he must also *hate his own life;* but when we have the same thought in different language, it is quite plain: "He that loveth father or mother more than me is not worthy of me: and he that loveth son or daughter more than me is not worthy of me." Matt. x:37. Then, when God said, "I loved Jacob, and I hated Esau," if we interpret the passage in the light of this definition, the thought is that He loved the children of Israel *more* than Edom, the descendants of Esau. "What shall we say then? Is there unrighteousness with God" in rejecting the unbelieving Jews? "God forbid for; for he saith to Moses, I will have mercy on whom I will have mercy, and I will have compassion on whom I will have compassion." Vers. 14, 15. There was no injustice on the part of God in rejecting the unbelieving and rebellious Jews. As a Sovereign, He had a right to dictate terms of mercy to those who would become subjects of His kingdom. These terms were first offered to and rejected by the Jews; hence the apostle appealed to the declarations of God to Moses, their own lawgiver, to show them that God had always shown mercy to whom He would, and upon just such terms as pleased Him. At a very early period in Jewish history God gave them to know the terms upon which they might remain the recipients of His *mercy*. Said He: "I the Lord thy God am a jealous God, visiting the iniquity of the fathers upon the children unto the third and fourth generation of them that hate me; and showing mercy unto thousands of them that love me and keep my commandments." Ex. xx:5, 6. Then God will visit iniquity upon those who hate Him, *because they hate Him;* and He will show mercy to those who love Him, *because they love Him.* "He that covereth his sins shall not prosper: but whoso confesseth and forsaketh them shall have mercy." Prov. xxviii:13. Hence we find that God's mercy is not dispensed according to eternal and immutable decrees, but he that will *confess and forsake his sins shall have mercy.* Peter tells us of a people "which had not obtained mercy, but now have obtained mercy." 1 Pet. ii:10. Then they did not obtain mercy in a decree made before time began. Jesus said, "Blessed are the merciful, for they shall obtain mercy." Matt. v:7. And James says, "He shall have judgment without mercy that hath showed no mercy." Jas. ii:13. Hence the Calvinist, who imagines himself one of the chosen few to whom God hath shown mercy from before the foundation of the world, and is unwilling that the mercies of God extend to all men, may thus bring upon himself judgment without mercy.

"So then it is not of him that willeth, nor of him that runneth, but of God that showeth mercy." Rom. ix:16. It is possible that this verse alludes to the blessing conferred by Isaac upon Jacob. Isaac *willed* that Esau, the first-born, should have the blessing; Esau *ran* for the venison with which to secure it; nevertheless Jacob obtained it. The blessing, as we have seen, was not a personal one, but pertained to Jacob's descendants, and had no reference to eternal salvation, but conferred temporal blessings only. Hence it can yield no support to the theory in question. It is true, as shown in another part of the argument, that Jacob was elected to be the seed of Isaac, through whom *Christ should come*—but *this was before Jacob and Esau were born*—that the purpose of God according to election might stand, not of works, but of Him that calleth. Neither the purchase of his brother's birthright, nor the blessing conferred by his father, had any thing to do with this election.

"For the Scripture saith unto Pharaoh, Even for this same purpose have I raised thee up, that I might shew my power in thee, and that my name might be declared throughout all the earth." Rom. ix:17. Now, are we to understand by this that Pharaoh was one of the eternally reprobate, and that God foreordained the wickedness of his nature and the hardness of his heart? Is this the thought? Let us go back to the Scriptures from which Paul quoted, and see how this is: "For this cause have I raised thee up, for to show in thee my power, and that my name may be declared throughout all the earth." Ex. ix:16. Now, is there one word in the context about eternal unconditional election and reprobation? or is there any thing about election at all? It is said that God raised up Pharaoh that He might show His power in him; but who did He not raise up for this purpose? The same might have been truly said of Moses, in whom His mighty power was exhibited in the destruction of the Egyptians and the salvation of the children of Israel, yet I suppose no one will insist that he was raised up eternally reprobate. God commanded Pharaoh to let his people go, but he persistently refused to obey God; hence God overruled his rebellion to His own glory. Even so God offered salvation to the Jews, upon condition that they would believe and obey the gospel. Like Pharaoh, they rebelled against Him; hence He exhibited his power in their destruction as a nation, that his name might be glorified in all the earth. But surely this can not prove that they were eternally reprobate, for they had been God's elect or chosen people up to that time. Not only so, but salvation upon the terms of the gospel was first offered to them; and surely God did not offer them a salvation which was never intended for them, and which He had unchangeably ordained that they should reject.

But we are told that God hardened Pharaoh's heart: "Therefore hath he mercy on whom he will have mercy, and whom he will he hardeneth." Rom. ix:18. Are we to understand by this that God created Pharaoh with a stubborn and rebellious heart, and promoted a spirit of wickedness in him by the plagues inflicted upon him? If so, all the threatenings of God were but temptation to evil; yet James says, "Let no man say when he is tempted, I am tempted of God, for God can not be tempted with evil, neither tempteth he any man; but every man is tempted when he is drawn away of his own lust, and enticed." Jas. i:13, 14. The mercies and blessings of God tend always to *harden* or *soften* the hearts of those who receive them. If rightly appreciated, they tend to awaken a sense of gratitude in the heart; but if abused, they tend to harden the heart. When the hand of affliction falls heavily upon us, we are either wilted into submission to God's will, or, as in time of war, we become hardened until some care no more for the life of a *man* than for the life of a beast. Thus it was with Pharaoh: when the hand of affliction was upon him, he would promise to let the people go; but as soon as the affliction was withdrawn, the spirit of rebellion revived: "When Pharaoh saw that there was respite, he hardened his heart and hearkened not unto them, as the Lord had said." Ex. viii:15. "And Pharaoh hardened his heart at this time also, neither would he let the people go." Ver. 32. "And when Pharaoh saw that the rain and the hail and the thunders were ceased, he sinned yet more, and hardened his heart, he and his servants." Ex. ix:34. Then it can only be said that God hardened Pharaoh's heart because He sent afflictions upon him which he abused to the *hardening of his own heart*. In the same way it may be said that the *gospel hardens* men now. It is preached to them as the power of God to salvation, if they will accept it; but, *rejecting* it, they become hardened, until they can resist the most stirring appeals to which mortals can be subjected in this life. Hence said the apostle: "To the one we are the savor of death unto death; and to the other the savor of life unto life. And who is sufficient for these things?" 2 Cor. ii:16. We think it possible for men to continue in rebellion against God until they pass entirely beyond the reach of all the agencies of the gospel by which God proposes to save them. Such were some of the Jews in Paul's day: "Because that when they knew God, they glorified him not as God, neither were thankful, but became vain in their imaginations, and their foolish heart was darkened. Professing themselves to be wise, they became fools; and changed the glory of the incorruptible God into an image made like to corruptible man, and to birds and to four-footed beasts, and creeping things. Wherefore God also gave them up to uncleanness, through the lust of their own hearts, to dishonor their own bodies between themselves; who changed the truth of God into a lie, and worshiped and served the creature more than the Creator, who is blessed forever. Amen. For this cause God gave them up unto vile affections." Rom. i:21-26.

Thus we see that God gave them up to uncleanness and vile affections, not because they were eternally reprobate, and He had predestinated them to be wicked, and created vile affections within them, but because of their own willful and persistent rebellion against Him. Paul speaks of him whose "coming is after the working of Satan, with all power and signs, and lying wonders, and with all deceivableness of unrighteousness in them that perish; because they received not the love of the truth, that they might be saved. And for this cause God shall send them strong delusion, that they should believe a lie: that they all might be damned who believed not the truth, but had pleasure in unrighteousness." 2 Thess. ii:9-12. God sends men strong delusions, not because they were eternally reprobate, and predestinated to wickedness and destruction, but because they receive not the love of the truth, that they might be saved. And though many are thus deluded and hardened in falsehood, infidelity, and crime, it is the result of their own wickedness, and not because of any eternal and immutable decree against them. They "walk in the vanity of their mind, having the understanding darkened, being alienated from the life of God, through the ignorance that is in them, because of the blindness of their heart: who, being past feeling, have given themselves over to lasciviousness, to work all uncleanness with greediness." Eph. iv:17-19. Here were persons whose hearts were harder than that of Pharaoh, for he could feel even to the last chastisement laid upon him; but these were past feeling, and completely given over —not by any eternal decree, but they had *given themselves over* to the service of Satan.

"Nay, but, O man, who art thou that repliest against God? Shall the thing formed say to him that formed it, Why hast thou made me thus? hath not the potter power over the clay, of the same lump to make one vessel unto honor, and another unto dishonor? What if God, willing to show his wrath, and to make his power known, endured with much longsuffering the vessels of wrath fitted to destruction: and that he might make known the riches of his glory on the vessels of mercy, which he had afore prepared unto glory, even us, whom he hath called, not of the Jews only, but also of the Gentiles." Rom. ix:20-23. Here the apostle has reference to the language of God to the prophet concerning the potter, and the clay that was marred in his hand while attempting to make a vessel of it. Let us go back and see what was originally taught by it, and then we may be better prepared to understand Paul's use of it: "The word which came to Jeremiah from the Lord, saying, Arise, and go down to the potter's house, and there I will cause thee to hear my words. Then I went down to the potter's house, and, behold, he wrought a work on the wheels; and the vessel that he made of clay was marred in the hand of the potter; so he made it again another vessel, as seemed good to the potter to make it. Then the word of the Lord came to me, saying, O house of Israel, can not I do with you as this potter? saith the Lord. Behold, as the clay is in the potter's hand, so are ye in my hand, O house of Israel. At what instant I shall speak concerning a nation, and concerning a kingdom, to pluck up and to pull down, and to destroy it; if that nation against whom I have pronounced, turn from their evil, I will repent of the evil that I thought to do unto them. And at what instant I will speak concerning a nation, and concerning a kingdom, to build up and to plant it, if it do evil in my sight, that it obey not my voice, then I will repent of the good wherewith I said I would benefit them." Jer. xviii:1-10.

Here we find that this parable was used concerning the nation or kingdom of Israel: "As the clay is in the potter's hand, so are ye in my hand, *O house of Israel.*" But are we taught that nations and kingdoms are eternally and unconditionally ordained to prosperity or destruction? Surely, no language could have been employed which would teach more clearly the opposite. Though God may have spoken against a nation or kingdom to destroy it, yet if it turn from its wickedness for which it was condemned, He will turn from the evil which He said He would bring upon it. And though He may have spoken in favor of a kingdom or a nation to build and to prosper it, yet if it do evil, then He will turn from the good wherewith He said He would benefit it. True, the figure shows that God had the power to bless and prosper a nation, or to pluck up and destroy it—and who doubts this?—but the figure also shows that He will exercise His power in the salvation or destruction of nations, as they obey or rebel against Him, and not according to eternal decrees. The house of Israel as a nation and kingdom failed to accomplish the object designed in its creation, and hence was marred in the hand of the Potter. He therefore gave it a less honorable form, but did not cast it away entirely. They were captured, carried into Babylon, and there remained as slaves and captives in a strange land for seventy years. This they might have averted by turning from their wickedness; for God said, as we have already quoted, that "if that nation against whom I have pronounced, turn from their evil, I will repent of the evil that I thought to do unto them." They did not turn away; hence the threatened punishment came upon them. But it did not amount to their destruction. It was corrective as well as punitive, and brought them to repentance in Babylon; hence the Potter took the vessel that had been seventy years in dishonor, and made it again a vessel unto honor by restoring the Jews to their nationality.

The reader would do well to bear in mind that a vessel in *dishonor* is not necessarily a *vessel of wrath fitted to destruction;* for it may yet turn from its wickedness and be made a vessel unto honor. But at the time the apostle wrote, the Jewish kingdom had not only been marred in the hand of the Potter, but it was fast approaching the condition of a vessel of wrath fitted to destruction. The prophet gave a most appalling picture of the punishment which threatened them and very soon came upon them: "Thus saith the Lord, Go and get a potter's earthen bottle, and take of the ancients of the people, and of the ancients of the priests, and go forth unto the valley of the son of Hinnom, which is by the entry of the east gate, and proclaim there the words that I shall tell thee." Jer. xix:1, 2. After recounting the wickedness of which they had been guilty, he pronounces their doom as follows: "Therefore, behold, the days come, saith the Lord, that this place shall no more be called Tophet, nor The valley of the son of Hinnom, but The valley of slaughter. And I will make void the counsel of Judah and Jerusalem in this place; and I will cause them to fall by the sword before their enemies, and by the hand of them that seek their lives: and their carcasses will I give to be meat for the fowls of the heaven, and for the beasts of the earth. And I will make this city desolate, and a hissing: every one that passeth thereby shall be astonished and hiss because of all the plagues thereof. And I will cause them to eat the flesh of their sons and the flesh of their daughters, and they shall eat every one the flesh of his friend in the siege and straitness, wherewith their enemies, and they that seek their lives, shall straiten them. Then shalt thou break the bottle in the sight of the men that go with thee, and shalt say unto them, Thus saith the Lord of hosts; Even so will I break this people and this city, as one breaketh a potter's vessel, that can not be made whole again: and they shall bury them in Tophet, till there be no place to bury." Jer. xix:6-11.

While God was bearing with these vessels of wrath fitted to destruction, Christ came, as the promised seed of Abraham, their father, in whom all the families of the earth were to be blessed; but the Jews were unwilling that all families of the earth should enjoy salvation with them: hence the apostle alludes to the potter and the clay to teach them that when their government was marred in his hand, it was his prerogative to make of it just such government as pleased him. As the stubbornness and rebellion of the Jews caused them to be carried into Babylon, so their remaining stubbornness and rebellion prevented them from uniting with the Gentiles in forming one grand spiritual family most honorable of all others; hence, at the destruction of Jerusalem by Titus and his army, their nationality was literally destroyed, as predicted by the Lord through Jeremiah, and enforced by breaking the potter's earthen bottle into fragments, which could never be united again. While the material was clay it could be given another form when marred in the hand of the potter, but after it became an "earthen bottle" and was broken, the wreck was complete: "Even so will I break this people and this city, as one breaketh a potter's vessel, that can not be made whole again."

But not withstanding this was said of the *people* and the *city*, it took *individuals*, collectively considered, to make up the *people*; hence said the apostle: "What if God, willing to show his wrath, and to make his power known, endured with much long-suffering the vessels of wrath fitted to destruction, and that he might make known the riches of his glory on the vessels of mercy, which he had afore prepared unto glory, even us, whom he hath called, not of the Jews only, but also of the Gentiles? As he saith also in Osee, I will call them my people, which were not my people; and her beloved, which was not beloved. And it shall come to pass, that in the place where it was said unto them, Ye are not my people; there shall they be called the children of the living God." Rom. ix:22-26.

Thus the apostle most clearly proves to the Jews, by quotation from their own prophets, that the Gentiles, who had not been God's people, were to become the children of the living

God. Hence the argument can not apply to *individuals* only as making up the *classes* of which the apostle spake. Surely, we can not be mistaken here. But suppose we are, and the apostle intended to make a personal application of the argument, what then? Will the parable of the potter and the clay, thus applied, prove the Calvinistic theory of unconditional election and reprobation? Let us see. If the clay marred in the hand of the potter, it was not because he designed it to be so, for he intended to make a good vessel of it. Even so God wills not the death of any, but that all come to repentance and live. Calvinists teach that the non-elect were vessels of wrath from before the beginning of time; were never designed for any thing else—nay, were *unchangeably ordained* to dishonor and wrath.

Again: The potter did not make a vessel that he might destroy it himself. If the clay so marred in his hand that it was not fit for the more honorable vessel at first designed, he worked it over and made of the same lump another vessel of less value; but it was nevertheless made for use or sale, not that he might himself destroy it. But, according to the theory in question, God, the great Potter, made the non-elect to be vessels of wrath, and fitted them for destruction, that He might exhibit His power in their destruction—this being the object of their creation.

Once more: When the lump of clay marred in the hand of the potter, so that it would not make a vessel unto honor, as first contemplated, he worked it over and made of the *same lump* another vessel as it pleased him. The theory will not allow the purposes of God to fail; on the contrary, they insist that his vessels always come out just as He designed them. If so, the clay never mars in His hand, and hence there is no fitness in the parable. Indeed, they seem to have two lumps—one elect, and the other reprobate; and if the clay came from the elect lump, it can not make a reprobate vessel, for not an atom of that elect material can be lost: on the contrary, if the clay came from the reprobate lump, no mechanical skill can work it over and make an elect vessel of it. The theory makes every man elect or reprobate from before time began, and he must so remain while eternity endures. Therefore the parable will not fit Calvinism anywhere.

After mentioning many vices to be avoided, Paul says: "In a

great house there are not only vessels of gold and of silver, but also of wood and of earth; and some to honor and some to dishonor. If a man, therefore, purge himself from these, he shall be a vessel unto honor sanctified and meet for the master's use, and prepared unto every good work." 2 Tim. ii:20, 21. He speaks of "the house of God" as the "church of the living God." 1 Tim. iii:15. Then in the church or house of God there are vessels comparable to gold and silver, wood and earth; some more and some less honorable, while others are a disgrace to the cause they profess to love. And Paul here clearly shows that this difference is made, not by an immutable decree of God, but by the parties themselves: "If a man therefore *purge himself* from these"—not if God purge him, but if he *purge himself*—"he shall be a vessel unto honor."

But let us pursue the apostle's argument. He says, "Even so then at this present time there is a remnant according to the election of grace." Rom. xi:5. As there had been seven thousand men, in the days of Elias, who had not bowed the knee to the image of Baal, even so there was still a remnant when Paul wrote who had accepted salvation upon the terms of the gospel of the grace of God, and these are they of whom he spake, saying, "Israel hath not obtained that which he seeketh for, but the election hath obtained it, and the rest were blinded." Ver. 7. This remnant of Israel who accepted salvation upon gospel terms are denominated the *election,* and the rest were blinded; that is, all Israel except this remnant elected to salvation. Now, are we to conclude that those who were blinded were *eternally reprobate?* Before any one so affirms, let him remember that Israel was once God's elect people, and he must be prepared to show how they became reprobate after having been *eternally, immutably,* and *unconditionally elect,* according to his theory. Leaving Calvinism to grope its way out of this difficulty as best it can, let us go on to see whether or not it is possible for these reprobates to become elect again.

In the 8th verse we learn that God gave these reprobates "the spirit of slumber, eyes that they should not see, and ears that they should not hear." In the 9th verse, Paul quotes David thus: "Let their table be made a snare and a trap, and a stumblingblock, and a recompense unto them; let their eyes be darkened, that they may not see, and bow down their back always." Please remember that this was all said of those who were not of the election of grace, but were reprobates. Now let us read on: "I say then, Have they [these reprobates] stumbled that they should fall? God forbid: but rather through their fall salvation is come unto the Gentiles, for to provoke them to jealousy. Now if the fall of them [Then they were not eternally reprobate, else they could not have fallen] be the riches of the world, and the diminishing of them [The creed says they can neither be increased nor diminished] the riches of the Gentiles; how much more their fullness? For I speak to you Gentiles, inasmuch as I am the apostle of the Gentiles, I magnify mine office: if by any means I may provoke to emulation them which are my flesh, and might save some of them [the reprobates]. For if the casting away of them be the reconciling of the world, what shall the receiving of them [reprobates] be, but life from the dead?" Ver. 11-15. Then comes the figure of the olive-tree, showing that the Jews, or natural branches, were broken off because of their unbelief, and the Gentiles were grafted in. But even they must be faithful; for said he: "If God spared not the natural branches, take heed lest he also spare not thee. Behold therefore the goodness and severity of God: on them which fell, severity; but toward thee, goodness, if thou continue in his goodness: otherwise thou also shalt be cut off. [Ah, how can they be cut off if the number of the elect can neither be increased nor diminished?] And they also, if they abide not still in unbelief shall be graffed in; for God is able to graff them in again." Ver. 21-23. Thus reprobate Israel may again be elect if they will: "For I would not, brethren, that ye should be ignorant of this mystery, lest ye should be wise in your own conceits, that blindness in part is happened to Israel [those not elect], until the fulness of the Gentiles be come in. And so all Israel shall be saved." Vers. 25, 26. Is it possible that these blinded reprobates may yet be saved? They may be saved, if Paul is good authority: "For as ye [Gentiles] in times past have not believed God, yet have now obtained mercy through their [Jews] unbelief; even so have these also not believed, that through your mercy they [reprobate Jews] also may obtain mercy. For God hath concluded them all in unbelief [What for? That he might damn them all? No, but] that he might have mercy upon all." Ver. 30-32. Where, then, is the eternal decree of unconditional election and reprobation? Well may the apostle exclaim, "O the depth of the riches both of the wisdom and knowledge of God! how unsearchable are his judgments, and his ways past finding out" only as He has revealed them.

We come next to examine the same subject as taught in Paul's letter to the Ephesians. Will the reader open the divine volume and very carefully read the letter from its beginning to the 6th verse of the fourth chapter, inclusive? We have not room to transcribe it all, but every word deserves to be indelibly written upon every human heart.

We will begin with that portion of it supposed to give support to the theory of unconditional election. The apostle says: "Blessed be the God and Father of our Lord Jesus Christ, who hath blessed us with all spiritual blessings in heavenly places in Christ: according as he hath chosen us in him before the foundation of the world, that we should be holy and without blame before him in love: having predestinated us unto the adoption of children by Jesus Christ to himself, according to the good pleasure of his will, to the praise of the glory of his grace, wherein he hath made us accepted in the beloved: in whom we have redemption through his blood, the forgiveness of sins, according to the riches of his grace; wherein he hath abounded toward us in all wisdom and prudence; having made known unto us the mystery of his will, according to his good pleasure, which he hath purposed in himself; that in the fullness of times he might gather together in one all things in Christ, both which are in heaven, and which are on earth; even in him: in whom also we have obtained an inheritance, being predestinated according to the purpose of him who worketh all things after the counsel of his own will: that we should be to the praise of his own glory, who first trusted in Christ. In whom ye also trusted, after that ye heard the word of truth, the gospel of your salvation." Eph. i:3-13.

Without stopping to inquire after the meaning of the word *world* in the 4th verse, let us proceed to analyze the passage and see whether or not there is any thing like unconditional election in it: "According as he hath chosen us in him before the foundation of the world." Here we learn that certain persons were chosen in Christ before a certain time, but there is not yet a word as to whether they were chosen *conditionally* or *unconditionally*. This must be learned somewhere else. For *what* were they chosen? "That we should be holy and without blame before him in love." This is the character to be worn by the persons chosen, and it clearly shows that the apostle was speaking of a *class*, and not of individuals as such. What more? "Having predestinated us unto the adoption of children by Jesus Christ to himself." And how is it predestinated that children shall be adopted into God's family by Jesus Christ? "According to the good pleasure of his will." Then what is the good pleasure of his will in this matter? That the gospel shall be preached "among all nations, to every creature." "He that believeth and is baptized shall be saved; but he that believeth not shall be damned." Mark xvi:16. Then it is the good pleasure of His will that every creature who will believe the gospel and be baptized shall be saved, and all who are thus saved are His children by Jesus Christ, through whom He gave the conditions of adoption. This is all plain; let us go on: "Having made known unto us the mystery of his will, according to his good pleasure, which he hath purposed in himself." And what is the mystery of His will thus made known? "That in the dispensation of the fullness of times he might gather together in one all things in Christ, both which are in heaven and on earth; even in him: in whom also we have obtained an inheritance, being predestinated according to the purpose of him who worketh all things after the counsel of his own will." Now, if these persons were *unconditionally* and *personally* predestinated to this inheritance, then it follows that Universalism and not Calvinism gets the benefit of the quotation, for we have seen that He purposed to gather together all things in Christ—not the elect few, but *all things*. To whom was this made known, and what is the meaning of it? "By revelation he made known unto me the mystery, as I wrote afore in few words"—back yonder in the first chapter—"whereby, when ye read, ye may understand my knowledge in the mystery of Christ, which in other ages was not made known to the sons of men, as it is now revealed unto his holy apostles and prophets by the Spirit." Eph. iii:3-5. To whom was this long-concealed mystery made known by the Spirit? His holy apostles and prophets.

Then they were the persons referred to by the pronouns *we* and *us*, from the 3d to the 12th verse (inclusive) of the first chapter, to whom this mystery was made known, as Paul wrote afore in few words in the 10th verse of that chapter. And what was this long-concealed mystery? "That the Gentiles should be fellow heirs, and of the same body, and partakers of his promise in Christ by the gospel." Eph. iii:6. Then these holy apostles and prophets were the persons chosen in Christ before the foundation of the world, that they as a class should be holy and without blame before Him in love; and though as a class they were of this character, yet as an individual, one of them betrayed the Lord for money. Does this prove the doctrine of unconditional election?

That we may see, if possible, more clearly that the pronouns *we* and *us* in this context do refer to a particular class of persons of which Paul was one, and that the calling of these did not embrace all the elect as taught by Calvinists, we will pursue the connection a little further. The apostle says, "That *we* should be to the praise of his glory, who *first* trusted in Christ." Here is the same pronoun *we*, including Paul and others, to whom he referred as the called and predestinated, "who *first* trusted in Christ. In whom ye *also* trusted, after that ye heard the word of truth, the gospel of your salvation." Vers. 12, 13. Now, if *we* who *first* trusted in Christ included all the elect, who were the *ye* who *also* trusted in him after they heard the gospel of their salvation? The apostles and prophets were of the Jews who first trusted in Christ, and the Ephesians were Gentiles, who also trusted in Him after they heard the gospel: "Wherefore remember, that ye being in time past Gentiles in the flesh, who are called Uncircumcision by that which is called the Circumcision in the flesh made by hands; that at that time ye were without Christ, being aliens from the commonwealth of Israel, and strangers from the covenants of promise, having no hope, and without God in the world; but now, in Christ Jesus, ye, who sometime were far off are made nigh by the blood of Christ. For he is our peace, who hath made both one, and hath broken down the middle wall of partition between us; having abolished in his flesh the enmity, even the law of commandments contained in ordinances; for to make in himself of twain one new man [or church], so making peace; and that he might reconcile both unto God in one body by the cross, having slain the enmity thereby; and came and preached peace to you which were afar off, and to them that were nigh; for through him we both have access by one Spirit unto the Father." Eph. ii:11-18. Therefore, "keep the unity of the Spirit in the bond of peace. There is one body [composed of Jews and Gentiles], and one Spirit, even as ye are called in one hope of your calling; one Lord [who died for both Jew and Gentile], one faith [common to Jew and Gentile], one baptism [enjoined upon all, for there is] one God and Father of all, who is above all, and through all, and in you all," if Christians, whether Jew or Gentile. Eph. iv:3-6.

The next passage to which we are referred as proving eternal unconditional election is found, 2 Thess. ii:13, 14: "But we are bound to give thanks to God for you, brethren beloved of the Lord, because God hath from the beginning chosen you to salvation, through sanctification of the Spirit and belief of the truth: whereunto he called you by our gospel, to the obtaining of the glory of our Lord Jesus Christ."

In examining this passage, it is important to inquire what beginning it was from which these persons were elected or chosen. Was it the beginning of eternity? Eternity had no beginning. Was it the beginning of time? Then the theory of eternal election is false, for time had a beginning, and is not eternal. As the election was through sanctification of the Spirit and belief of the truth, it is impossible that the election could have antedated the belief of the truth through which it was effected. John says: "I write no new commandment unto you, but an old commandment which ye had from the beginning. The old commandment is the word which ye have heard from the beginning." 1 John ii:7. And again: "Let that therefore abide in you, which ye have heard from the beginning." Ver. 24. Now, what beginning was this? Surely, not the beginning of time, the beginning of the world, or any other time or thing which began before their birth, for this they "heard from the *beginning*." Nor was it the beginning of the Christian dispensation, for it is most likely that none of them heard the gospel until long after that beginning. Then it was the beginning of their spiritual life—the time of their conversion. From that beginning they had heard the gospel—had the old commandment, and knew God; hence to this beginning the apostle undoubtedly refers; and we suppose Paul refers to the same beginning from which the Thessalonians were chosen to salvation through sanctification of the Spirit and belief of the truth. Were we to say that the sheriff was elected through the votes of the people, no one would understand that he was elected before he received the votes of the people. When Paul said persons were "saved through faith" (Eph. ii:8), he certainly did not mean to teach that they were saved through faith before they had faith. Then, when the same apostle said that the Thessalonians were chosen through sanctification of the Spirit and belief of the truth, he surely did not mean that they had been chosen from before time began, or at any time before they believed the truth and had their hearts purified by it.

But we are referred to 1 Pet. i:2, where the apostle addresses his brethren as "elect according to the foreknowledge of God the Father, through sanctification of the Spirit, unto obedience and sprinkling of the blood of Jesus Christ." This election is according to the divine foreknowledge, not contrary to it. The whole scheme of redemption was in the mind of God before it was revealed to man. Therefore, when the conditions of salvation were embodied in the gospel and proclaimed to the world, they were presented just as they had existed in His mind before; hence, when any one complies with the conditions of salvation, he is elected according to the foreknowledge of God, because elected according to a plan previously known to Him. When we say of the governor that he was elected according to the constitution of the State, we do not mean that the constitution elected him, but that he was elected by a majority of the votes of the people, according to the provisions of the constitution, and not against its provisions. So when any one obeys the gospel, he is elected according to the foreknowledge of God, because God foreknew the provisions of the gospel; but the foreknowledge of God did not elect him.

Finally, we come to examine the last passage in the Bible which we have ever known brought to the support of unconditional election and reprobation: "The beast which thou sawest was, and is not; and shall ascend out of the bottomless pit, and go into perdition; and they that dwell on the earth shall wonder, (whose names were not written in the book of life from the foundation of the world,) when they behold the beast that was, and is not, and yet is." Rev. xvii:8. It is the parenthetical portion of the quotation which is believed by some to give support to the doctrine in question. As there are persons here spoken of whose names were not written in the book of life from the foundation of the world, it is inferred that there are persons whose names were so written. This, we admit, is a legitimate inference, but inferences rarely ever stop within proper bounds. It is further inferred that when a person's name is written in the book of life, his interest in heaven is secure to him; hence there are those whose names were written in the book of life and made sure of heaven from the foundation of the world, without regard to any thing done by them, whether good or evil. This is not deducible from the language of the text, and is at war with the spirit of the whole Bible, which rewards or punishes man according to his works, and is most plainly contradicted in the same book from which the quotation is made. "He that overcometh, the same shall be clothed in white raiment; and I will not blot out his name out of the book of life, but I will confess his name before my Father, and before his angels." Rev. iii:5. Now, let us apply the same rules of inference here that were admitted applicable to the other passage. As it is said of certain persons that their names were *not* written in the book of life, it is inferred that the names of others *were* so written: then when the Lord said of a certain character, "I will *not* blot out his name out of the book of life," the inference is equally clear that the names of others *would be blotted out* of the book of life. From this conclusion there is no escape; hence the fact that the name of a person is written in the book of life is not conclusive proof that he will finally be saved in heaven. "For I testify unto every man that heareth the words of the prophecy of this book, if any man shall add unto these things, God shall add unto him the plagues that are written in this book: and if any man shall take away from the words of the book of this prophecy, God shall take away his part out of the book of life, and out of the holy city, and from the things which are written in this book." Rev. xxii:18, 19. Then, a man may have a part in the book of life, and yet so conduct himself that it may be taken away from him.

Nor was this a new thought first revealed to John in the isle of Patmos; for when Aaron made the golden calf, and the children of Israel were threatened with destruction for worshiping it, Moses prayed the Lord to forgive their sin, and said: "If not, blot me, I pray thee, out of thy book which thou hast written. And the Lord said unto Moses, Whosoever hath sinned against me, him will I blot out of my book." Ex. xxxii:32, 33. As sin or disobedience causes God to erase or blot out the names of persons from the book of life, and obedience causes their names to be retained or not blotted out (Rev. iii:5), is it not probable that obedience caused their names to be enrolled when first written in the book? "They that feared the Lord spake often one to another, and the Lord hearkened, and heard it, and a book of remembrance was written before him for them that feared the Lord, and that thought upon his name." Mal. iii:16. This book seems to have been written before the Lord for those who feared Him and thought upon His name. It will be observed that the names were written *from*, not *before*, the foundation of the world. Then, as persons have lived and feared the Lord, their names were inserted in God's book. We do not suppose that God had a *literal book* in which the names of His people were written before or after the foundation of the world; but in the mind of God they are recognized as His from the time they bear His name and become obedient to His will. If God had a literal book in which the literal name of every person was written before time began, it follows that all parents and others concerned in giving children their names must have been inspired in order that they might give the child the name designed for it, otherwise they might miss the name occasionally. One thing is certain, however, whether the book be literal or figurative, viz: that names, though written in the book of life, are still liable to be blotted out of it; and surely, while the names of any persons remain written in the book of life, they are elect. Jesus said to his disciples, "Rejoice, because your names are written in heaven." Luke x:20. Paul told his brethren that they had come "to the general assembly and church of the first-born, which are written in heaven." Heb. xii:23. To another he said: "I entreat thee also, true yokefellow, help those women which labored with me in the gospel, with Clement also, and with other of my fellow laborers, whose names are in the book of life." Phil. iv:3. After John described the heavenly Jerusalem, he said: "There shall in no wise enter into it any thing that defileth; neither whatsoever worketh abomination, or maketh a lie: but they which are written in the Lamb's book of life." Rev. xxi:27.

From all these quotations it is evident that, while the names of persons are written in the book of life, in heaven they are elect; but when their names have been so written and blotted out of the book of life, they become reprobates, and, unless reinstated, must be lost. Therefore the number of the elect can be diminished, and hence the doctrine of eternal unconditional election and reprobation can not be true.

Now, we believe we have examined every passage of Holy Writ supposed to favor the doctrine of *personal unconditional election* and reprobation, and we feel sure that many readers will rejoice with us in the conviction that no such monstrous absurdity is taught in God's holy word. We conscientiously believe it not only antagonistic to the teaching of the Bible, but contrary to the spirit and genius of the Christian religion, and at war with the love, mercy, and justice of God. He had the entire control of man's creation, and certainly would not have created him, having unalterably consigned the greater portion of his posterity to eternal misery, dishonor, and wrath, for no fault of their own, or any thing in their power to prevent. How God could be glorified by the eternal punishment of man, in order to carry out a decree made by Himself before the creation of man, is a matter utterly incomprehensible to us. The doctrine makes God an embodiment of cruelty, tyranny, and oppression too horrible to contemplate; and we see not how any one who believes it can acceptably obey God. "He that cometh to God must believe that he is, and that he is a rewarder of them that diligently seek him." Heb. xi:6. Do Calvinists believe that God will reward the reprobates, however diligently they may seek Him?

How can he who believes himself either one of the elect or one of the reprobate, and that therefore there is nothing he can do that will in any way affect his salvation, ask such a question as, "What must I do to be saved?" (Acts xvi:30) or in faith *obey any command as a condition of salvation?* We speak with all due respect when we say we think such a thing impossible until such persons can correct their faith on this subject. If we believed it, we would never make another effort to persuade any person to make his calling and election sure; because, if the doctrine is true, no effort which man can make in the way of obedience to God can in the least increase his chances for future bliss, or in any way change the final destiny of any one of Adam's race.

Let us turn our backs upon the theory, and our eyes to the word of the Lord, and with hearts lifted in gratitude to God, seek to realize the grand truth perceived by Peter at the house of Cornelius—"that God is no respecter of persons: but in every nation he that feareth him and worketh righteousness, is accepted with him." Acts x:34, 35.

CHAPTER IV.

THE FOREKNOWLEDGE OF GOD.

Finally, we come to examine the last strong fortress of *Calvinism*, which it holds in alliance with *Universalism* by the common consent of those who oppose them. It is based upon the assumption that *God, from all eternity, foreknew every thing that ever has or ever will come to pass;* therefore, He foreknew just who and how many would be saved, and who, if any, would be lost. And as the final destiny of every person must be exactly as foreseen by God, it follows that such foreknowledge amounted to an immutable decree. If God knew, ere time began, that Cain would kill his brother, then there was no possibility left to Cain to avoid the deed. Had there been such possibility, Cain might have availed himself of it, and failed to do that which God foreknew he would do, thereby falsifying the foreknowledge of God. If God foreknew that Cain, or any one else, would act wickedly and be lost, then there was no possibility left him to have acted righteously and to have been saved; for had he availed himself of such a possibility and been saved, it would have been in despite of God's foreknowledge to the contrary. Ergo, as God *foreknew* every thing, He must have decreed every thing; and as He foreknew the destiny of every man, it follows that He decreed the destiny which man had no power to avert.

We believe this is a fair exhibit of the Calvinistic side of the argument; but Universalism applies the same principle to *all* men that Calvinism applies to the elect. It assumes that God will not punish man for that which he had no power to avoid (and yet we see that he is so punished every day); and as all must pursue the course marked out for them in the foreknowledge of God, none will be punished for carrying out the immutable purposes of Jehovah. Forgetting that God has such attributes as *justice* and *vengeance*, it draws largely upon His *love*, *goodness*, and *mercy:* "God is *infinite love*, and must have desired the salvation of all men. As He foreknew the destiny of every man, and had power to *create only* such as seemed good to Him, He would, of course, create only such as He foresaw would be saved. Hence all men were created for salvation, and will finally be saved."

Thus we have presented the arguments respectively drawn by Calvinists and Universalists from what they are pleased to call the *unlimited foreknowledge of God;* and it is but the part of candor to admit that they are not without some degree of plausibility. There are, however, at least three sides to this argument, viz: the Calvinist's side, the Universalist's side, and the Lord's side, and of the three we prefer the last. Many have been the efforts to harmonize the *free-agency* of man and the *unlimited foreknowledge* of God, and though we have read every thing written on the subject that has fallen under our notice, we have never yet read a plausible theory concerning it. From our stand-point, therefore, the premises are doubtful, to say the least of them: may we not, then, with becoming reverence, inquire *whether or not God eternally foreknew every thing that ever has or ever will come to pass?*

In approaching the examination of the subject we wish to state most plainly that we pretend not to comprehend the mind and purposes of God, *only* as He has revealed them to us. We pretend not to have fathomed the depths of the wisdom and knowledge of the infinite Jehovah. With Paul, we are ready to exclaim: "O the depth of the riches both of the wisdom and knowledge of God! how unsearchable are his judgments, and his ways past finding out! for who hath known the mind of the Lord? or who hath been his counselor?" Rom. xi:33, 34. Oh, the insignificance of man in the presence of God! Indeed, it seems to us unsafe to build a theological system upon an incomprehensible foundation; hence those who base their theory upon the supposed attributes of God, to say the least of them, *are liable* to build upon the sand. Do they not thereby say that they have sounded the depths of the wisdom and knowledge of God, and have found them extending to a perfect knowledge of every thing that ever has or will come to pass? Do they not, in theory, say that they *have searched His judgments,* and have found that a definite number were *approved,* and the reprobates *condemned,* before time began, or that *all* were unconditionally *approved?* Do they not say that they have searched His ways and known His mind to perfection, and can therefore safely build a theological system, involving the destiny of the human race, upon their knowledge of the attributes of God? We may know God's will, and the extent of His knowledge where He has revealed them to us, but beyond this we dare not go. When God *speaks*, it is the province of man to *hear* and *believe*, whether he can or can not see to the end. When God commanded Abraham to *go*, he *went*, not knowing whither he went (Heb. xi:8); hence, when God says He purposed to do any thing, we must accept it as *true*, whether He did it or not; and when He says *He did not know* a thing, it is unsafe to say that *He did know it, His word to the contrary notwithstanding.* But has God spoken to man on the subject? Let us see: "And God saw that the wickedness of man was great in the earth, and that every imagination of the thoughts of his heart was only evil continually. And it repented the Lord that he had made man on the earth, and it grieved him at heart. And the Lord said, I will destroy man whom I have created from the face of the earth." Gen. vi:5-7. Now, if God knew before He created man just how wicked he would be, and what he would do, what can this mean? "God saw that the wickedness of man was great." Did He not always see? And why did God grieve over a result which was as plain to Him before He created man as when He saw the overt acts of wickedness performed? And if the wickedness of man was such as to cause God to destroy him, why would not this wickedness *foreseen* have prevented his creation at first? If seeing the wickedness of man caused God to repent making him, and to determine to destroy him, does not it follow that He did not know, prior to his creation, how wicked he would be? Surely, He would not have created man for the purpose of bringing grief to His own heart, and destruction to His creature. But why did God not know the wickedness of the antediluvians, from eternity? Certainly, it was not because He was not capable of knowing future events, for we know He did foretell many things long before they came to pass. The Psalmist says, "Great is our Lord, and of great power: his understanding is *infinite*." Ps. cxlvii:5. "Could there be any thing unknown to him whose understanding is infinite?" Let us see. God is as *infinite in power* as He is in *understanding*. No one, we suppose, will deny that He is *omnipotent* as well as *omniscient*, yet there are some things He *can not do;* e.g., God can not lie. Titus i:2; Heb. vi:18. God could not have made two hills without a low place between them. Then if there are *some things which God can not do, though omnipotent, may there not be some th:ngs wh:ch He* DID *not know, though omniscient?* But it may be said that God can not lie, because it is incompatible with His nature, and not because He has not power to lie. Very well; then He did not know, before making man, just how wicked he would be, simply because such foreknowledge would have been incompatible with the free-agency and responsibility of man. To be responsible, man must be free. If God knew before He gave Adam the law in the garden that he would violate it when given, then he was not free; for he could not have falsified God's foreknowledge if he would: hence to violate the law was a necessity. The great scheme of salvation conceived by Infinite Wisdom contemplated human responsibility based upon freedom of will, and God had power to avoid the foreknowledge of every thing incompatible with His attributes and the scheme of salvation devised by Him. He who says God *could not avoid knowing every thing,* limits the power of Him who is omnipotent. God can limit the exercise of His own attributes, but it is dangerous for man to assume such power. *We* dare not limit the knowledge of God; but if *He* saw fit to limit the exercise of His own knowledge, we fear to say He had not the *power* and the *right* to do so. *Infinite power* does not *require* God to do every thing, but it implies the *ability to do whatever is in harmony with His attributes and purposes.* He could instantly kill every man who violates His law, but, in great mercy, He has seen fit to limit the exercise of His power, and permits us to live: so, in the morning of the first day, God could have looked down the stream of time and have seen the secret intentions of every heart that would ever be subjected to His law, but, in infinite mercy, He saw fit to *avoid* a knowledge of every thing *incompatible with the freedom of the human will* and the system of government devised by Him for man. Does any one say *God had not power* to do this? then let him explain how it was that God grieved over the wickedness of man *when He saw* that it was great in the earth; yea, let him explain why it was that the wickedness of man caused God to repent that He had made him, if He as clearly saw it before He made him as afterward; and let him further explain why it was that the wickedness of man, which caused God to determine to destroy him from the earth after He had made him, if clearly foreseen by Him, did not prevent God from creating man at first.

God exercises His attributes through means, or without them, as may best serve His purposes. When He would exert His power in the creation of any thing, He *said, Let it be, and it was*. When He would bear witness to the divine character of His Son, a voice came from the eternal throne, saying, "This is my beloved Son, in whom I am well pleased." Matt. iii:17; xvii:5. When He would rebuke the madness of Balaam, He enabled the beast on which the ungrateful wretch rode, to speak in the language of man. Num. xxii:28. When He would rebuke Belshazzar for the unholy use to which he applied the sacred vessels of His house, He caused the fingers of a man's hand, *where there was no man*, to write the king's doom on the plastered walls of his own palace. Dan. v:5. When He gave His law to the Jews at Sinai, He inscribed it on tables of stone with His own finger; but when He established the new covenant, He wrote His laws upon the hearts of His people with the tongues and pens of men. Even so He could know or not know whatever He desired to know, with or without means. When He would test the complaints that had reached Him concerning the wickedness of the cities of the plains, He said: "Because the cry of Sodom and Gomorrah is great, and because their sin is very grievous, I will go down now, and see whether they have done altogether according to the cry of it which is come unto me; and if not, I will know." Gen. xviii:20, 21. Certainly, God *could* have known what was going on in these cities without going down there to see about it, but He *declined* to know until He employed His angels, in the likeness of men, as means for the purpose of obtaining the information. But this was not a case of *foreknowledge*, but simply a case where God made use of means to acquire a knowledge of what had already occurred. This is certainly true, but does it remove the difficulty? Did God know, before time began, all about the wickedness of these cities, and *forget* it, so as to make it necessary to send His angels to acquire a knowledge of that which He had previously known? Surely, no one is prepared to take a position like this. Do words mean any thing? If so, when God said, "I will go down now, and see whether they have done altogether according to the cry of it, which is come unto me; and if not, *I will know,*" what did He mean? Had He always known?

"But this language was used in an accommodated sense." Was it, indeed? Then let us seek for its meaning in this sense. To whom was it accommodated? Not to God, certainly, for He needed no accommodation. He could have made the communication in any set of words which contained it, either through a medium or without one. Then, if the language was accommodated at all, it must have been to Abraham, to whom it was spoken, and to us for whose benefit it was recorded; but if it conveyed *some other idea* than is usually conveyed by the same set of words, then we see not how it was accommodated to any one. The only way by which language can be accommodated to any one consists in its adaptation to the comprehension of the party addressed and the thought to be conveyed by it; *e.g.:* If a German would communicate any thing to me, he must speak to me in English, as I would not be likely to understand him were he to address me in the German language. Hence, by speaking English, he would accommodate his language to me. But this is not all: he must use such English words as would embody the *thought*, otherwise I might still fail to understand him. If he wanted to buy a horse of me, and he should say, "I want to sell you some goods to-day," I would fail to understand him, because the idea of buying a horse is not in the words, "I want to sell goods." Nor is this all: he would *deceive* me by using words calculated to convey one thought when he designed to convey another. Then when God substantially said to Abraham, "I will go down and see whether or not things are as reported to me; and if not, I will know"—if He meant that He had *always seen* and *always known* the things spoken of, we insist that the language used not only failed to be accommodated to the thought, but was calculated to make a false impression upon all before whom it might come. Let us try a few other passages of like construction by the same accommodated rules of interpretation. In the same chapter from which we have quoted the language in question, God twice said to Abraham, by the mouths of the same angelic messengers, "I will return unto thee, according to the time of life, and Sarah shall have a son." Vers. 10, 14. Did God mean that He *had already returned,* and that Sarah had already been blessed with the promised son? Again: The Lord said to Abraham, "I will make thee exceeding fruitful." Did He mean that Abraham had always been fruitful? "I will make nations of thee." Did He mean that nations had always been made of Abraham? "I will give unto thee, and to thy seed after thee, the land wherein thou art a stranger, all the land of Canaan, for an everlasting possession." Did He mean that He had, from eternity, given the land of Canaan to Abraham? Once more: When Jesus said, "On this rock I will build my church" (Matt. xvi:18), did He mean that His church had always been built? If not, how can we accommodate the language "I *will* know" to the thought "I have *always* known?"

When Abraham, in obedience to the command of God, had placed his beloved son upon the sacrificial altar, and had stretched forth his hand, and taken the knife to slay his son, "the angel of the Lord called unto him out of heaven, and said, Abraham, Abraham. And he said, Here am I. And he said, Lay not thy hand upon the lad, neither do thou any thing unto him; for *now I know* that thou fearest God, seeing thou hast not withheld thy son, thine only son, from me." Gen. xxii:11, 12. What can this mean? "*Now I know* that thou fearest God." Did He always know it? Nay, how did He then know it? "*Seeing* thou hast not withheld thy son, thine only son, from me." Does not this language imply that God saw in Abraham a degree of faithfulness unseen before? Paul says God tried Abraham here. Heb. xi:17. Why did God try him, if He knew perfectly well what Abraham would do before He tried him? But it is said that this trial of Abraham was to show *him* the strength of his own faith. Then God should have said, "Now *you* know you fear God, because *you* see you have not withheld your son, your only son, from me." It occurs to us that an *accommodation* of language to thought would require a change like this.

Respecting the idolatry of the Jews, God, by the mouth of His prophet, said: "They have built the high places of Tophet which is in the valley of the son of Hinnom, to burn their sons and their daughters in the fire; which I commanded them not, neither came it into my heart." Jer. vii:31. Here were things done by men which the Lord said came not into His heart. Did He know from eternity that which never came into His heart? But we are told that this only means that it never entered into God's heart *to command* the wickedness which they did. He plainly says He did not command it before using the words "neither came it into my heart." Surely, something additional was implied by these words; if not, why use them at all? Let us examine the construction of the quotation. What did they do? They burnt their children. What was *it* which God commanded them not? *That which they did.* What was *it* that came not into the mind of the Lord? *That which they did,* the burning of their children. In the sentence, "Neither came *it* into my heart," if the pronoun *it* does not refer to burning their sons and daughters in the fire, then we confess our inability to construe it at all. In another place the Lord said: "They have built also the high places of Baal, to burn their sons with fire, for burnt-offerings unto Baal, which I commanded not, nor spake it, neither came it into my mind." Jer. xix:5. Let us examine the *pronouns* in this quotation. "*Which* I commanded them not." To what does the relative *which* refer? To the act of burning their sons with fire. "Nor spake *it*." To what does the pronoun *it* refer? That which they did, and were commanded not. "Neither came *it* into my mind." Now, to what does this *it* refer? Certainly, to that which they *did*, which God commanded them not, nor spake it. Unless we take the liberty of adding to the word of the Lord, we see not how to construe the language otherwise.

But we are told that these passages are explained by another: "They built the high places of Baal, which are in the valley of the son of Hinnom, to cause their sons and their daughters to pass through the fire unto Molech; which I commanded them not, neither came it into my mind, that they should do this abomination, to cause Judah to sin." Jer. xxxii:35. And how does this passage explain the other two? Perhaps this is explained *by* the other two. If we understand the auxiliary *should* in the sense of *would,* then we have most perfect harmony in all of them. But it matters not which rendering is adopted here, for when the passages are all considered they abundantly show that it never entered into the mind of God that they either *would* or *should* do the things they did. Let it be remembered that Calvinism assumes that God eternally and immutably fore-ordained every thing that comes to pass. It did come to pass that the Jews did these things; therefore it follows that God fore-ordained that they should do them; and yet He says it never came into His mind that they should do them. In another part of the argument we invoked the aid of Calvinists to explain how God fore-ordained that which never came into His mind. All must see that this is impossible, and hence God did not fore-ordain these things. Calvanism further assumes that whatever was *foreknown* was fore-ordained: then, as these abominations were *not fore-ordained,* it follows that they were *not foreknown;* hence, even from this stand-point, they never entered the mind of the Lord. Universalism is also entangled in the meshes of this net, for it and Calvinism agree that all things *foreknown* were *fore-ordained,* and must come to pass accordingly. Let Universalists, therefore, join with Calvinists in showing how God fore-ordained that which never came into His mind; for whenever they admit that the foreknowledge of God does not amount to an immutable decree, and that things may turn out otherwise than as foreseen by God, then their argument drawn from the unlimited foreknowledge of God will have been exploded, and the strongest prop which ever gave support to Universalism will have been withdrawn.

When the children of Israel worshiped the golden calf made by Aaron at the foot of Sinai, the anger of the Lord was kindled against them, and He said to Moses, "Let me alone, that my wrath may wax hot against them, and that I may consume them: and I will make of thee a great nation." Ex. xxxii:10. Moses interceded for the people with arguments too powerful to be resisted. Said he, "Wherefore should the Egyptians speak and say, For mischief did he bring them out to slay them in the mountains, and to consume them from the face of the earth? Turn from thy fierce wrath, and repent of this evil against thy people. Remember Abraham, Isaac, and Israel, thy servants, to whom thou swearest by thine own self, and saidest unto them, I will multiply your seed as the stars of heaven, and all this land that I have spoken of will I give unto your seed, and they shall inherit it forever." Vers. 12, 13. Was there ever a more powerful speech, of the same length uttered by mortal lips? He reminds the Lord of His deliverance of this people, and what His enemies would say of His motives in doing so—of His devoted servants whose children these were, and His *oath* of promise to them. This speech prevailed, "And the Lord repented of the evil which he thought to do unto his people." Ver. 14. Was the Lord deceptive in His pretensions of anger to Moses against the people? Were His threats of destruction all hypocrisy? The earnest appeals of Moses show that he did not so understand them; yet they were mere sound if He knew, when making them, that He would not execute them. But He repented of the evil which He thought to do unto His people, and *did not do that which He thought He would do*. But if He eternally foreknew every thing that comes to pass, it follows that He foreknew He would not do this evil to His people; hence *He knew He would not do that which He thought He would do*. Can this be true? Is it possible to *think* we will do that which we *know* we will not do? Men sometimes say they think they will do that which they know, at the time, they will not do; but they do that which it is impossible for God to do when they so speak. Surely, we should be slow to cast such an imputation upon the God we adore. The inspired Word is the *measure of our faith;* hence, when it says God thought He would do a thing, we accept it as *true*, feeling sure that no valid objection can be brought against it. The Book of God, to be worthy of its Author, must be harmonious in all its teaching.

But the disciples of the Saviour once said to Him, "Now are we sure that thou knowest all things." John xvi:30. And Peter once said, "Lord, thou knowest all things; thou knowest that I love thee." John xxi:17. Will the reader bear in mind that it is one thing to *know all things,* and quite another to foreknow all things—one thing to know a *thing,* and quite another thing to know a thing *before it is a thing,* or when it has no existence. If we make these texts prove that Jesus had unlimited foreknowledge of every thing that has or will take place, we come in conflict with His own word, when he said, "Of that day and of that hour knoweth no man, no, not the angels which are in heaven, neither the Son, but the Father." Mark xiii:32. Now, here is one thing which it is certain he did *not* know; hence the fact that Jesus *knew* all things did not imply that He *foreknew* every thing. But John said, "God is greater than our heart, and knoweth all things." 1 John iii:20. Yes, and in just as strong terms he said to his brethren, "Ye have an unction from the Holy One, and ye know all things." 1 John ii:20. Then, if the fact that God knows all things proves that He *foreknew* all things, the same language proves that the disciples to whom John wrote also had unlimited foreknowledge! Does any one believe this? Then the language has no application to foreknowledge whatever. Further: There is no fact more clearly established than that the word *all* is often used in the Bible to indicate a *great amount* or a *great number,* when it must not be understood without limit; *e.g.:* It is said that *all* the people in a certain region were baptized by John, and yet many rejected the counsel of God against themselves by not being so baptized. And even the very words *all things* are used in a limited sense. Paul says charity "beareth all things, believeth all things, hopeth all things, endureth all things." 1 Cor. xiii:7. Are we to believe all things, whether true or false? Surely not. Then the sum of John's teaching was that his brethren, having an unction from the Holy One, know all things about which he was writing to them. Then we shall continue to believe that our Heavenly Father had power to limit the exercise of His knowledge to an extent compatible with the free-agency and accountability of man and the scheme of salvation devised for him, until we are shown a more excellent way. This being so, neither Calvinism nor Universalism can be sustained by their long cherished hobby, unlimited "foreknowledge;" but how they will be successfully met by those who admit it, is more than we can *foreknow.* We must *see* it done, *then* we will, perhaps, know how it has been done.

When we wrote the foregoing we were not aware of a single authority, save the Bible, from which we might derive the slightest encouragement; since we sent it to press, however, we have found an article from the pen of Dr. Adam Clarke, from which we make the following very significant extract; not because there is any thing additional in it, but that our readers may see that we are, at least, in good company:

"As God's omnipotence implies his *power to do all things,* so God's omniscience implies his *power to know all things;* but we must take heed that we meddle not with the infinite *free-agency* of this Eternal Being. Though God *can* do all things, he does not all things. Infinite judgment directs the operations of his power, so that though he *can*, yet he *does not* do all things, but only such things as are proper to be done. In what is called illimitable space, he *can* make millions of millions of systems, but he does not see proper to do this. He *can* destroy the solar system, but he does not do it: he can fashion and order, in endless variety, all the different beings which now exist, whether material, animal, or intellectual; but he does not do this, because He does not see it *proper* to be done. Therefore it does not follow that, because God *can do all things*, therefore he *must do all things*. God is omniscient, and *can know* all things, but does it follow from this that he *must know all things?* Is he not as free in the *volitions* of his wisdom as he is in the volitions of his *power?* The contingent as absolute, or the absolute as contingent? God has ordained some things as *absolutely certain:* these he knows as *absolutely certain*. He has ordained other things as *contingent*: these he knows as *contingent*. It would be absurd to say that he foreknows a thing as only *contingent* which he has made *absolutely certain*. And it would be as absurd to say that he foreknows a thing to be *absolutely certain* which, in his own eternal counsel, he has made contingent. By *"absolutely certain"* I mean a thing which *must* be in that order, time, place, and form, in which Divine wisdom has ordained it to be; and that it can be not *otherwise* than this infinite counsel has ordained. By *"contingent,"* I mean such things as the infinite wisdom of God has thought proper to poise on the possibility of *being* or *not being*, leaving it to the will of intelligent beings to turn the scale. Or *contingencies* are such possibilities, amid the succession of events, as the infinite wisdom of God has left to the will of intelligent beings to determine, whether any such event shall take place or not. To deny this would involve the most palpable contradictions, and the most monstrous absurdities. If there be no such things as *contingencies* in the world, then every thing is *fixed* and *determined* by an unalterable decree and purpose of God, and not only all *free-agency* is destroyed, but *all agency* of every kind, except that of the Creator himself, for on this ground God is the only operator, either in time or eternity: all created beings are only instruments, and do nothing but as impelled and acted upon by this almighty and sole Agent. Consequently, every act is his own, for if he have purposed them all as absolutely *certain,* having nothing *contingent* in them, then he has *ordained them to be so;* and if no contingency, then no free-agency, and God alone is the sole actor. Hence the blasphemous, though, from the premises, *fair conclusion,* that God is the author of all the evil and sin that are in the world, and hence follows that absurdity—that, as God can do nothing that is wrong, WHATEVER IS, IS RIGHT. Sin is no more sin, a vicious human action is no crime, if God have decreed it, and by his foreknowledge and will impelled the creature to act it. On this ground there can be no punishment for delinquencies, for if every thing be done as God has predetermined—and his determinations must necessarily be all right—then neither the instrument nor the *agent* has done wrong. Thus all vice and virtue, praise and blame, merit and demerit, guilt and innocence, are at once *confounded,* and all distinctions of this kind confounded with them. Now, allowing the doctrine of the contingency of human actions (and it must be allowed in order to shun the above absurdities and blasphemies), then we see every intelligent creature accountable for its own works, and for the use it makes of the power with which God has endued it; and, to grant all this consistently, we must also grant that God foresees nothing as *absolutely* and *inevitably certain* which he has made *contingent;* and because he has designed it to be *contingent,* therefore he can not know it as *absolutely* and *inevitably certain.* I conclude that God, although omniscient, is not obliged, in consequence of this, *to know all that he can know,* no more than he is obliged, because he is *omnipotent,* to *do all that he can do.*" Commentary on Acts ii:47.

Although Dr. Clarke offers not a single scriptural quotation or reference in proof of the positions taken, yet we regard his reasoning upon the attributes of God, and the bearing of foreknowledge upon the free-agency and accountability of man, as simply irresistible. We have long entertained these views, but have never preached them from the pulpit, nor until now given them to the press. We were forced to them while preparing for a debate with a Universalist, some twenty years ago, since which we have studied the subject, until a position then cautiously taken has become a *settled conviction*. We feel strengthened by finding ourself in company with a man of such power as Dr. Clarke.

CHAPTER V.

HEREDITARY DEPRAVITY.

Having previously disposed of unconditional election and reprobation as taught by the Presbyterian Confession, we come now to notice another doctrine taught by the same authority, as well as by most of the denominations, which obtains much more general acceptance than the Calvinistic view of election and reprobation, but which is equally fatal to the obedience of faith required in the gospel, to which we deem it proper to call attention before we set out to learn the duty of man in order to his adoption into the family of God. This is what is called by its advocates *"Hereditary Total Depravity."*

We will make a few quotations from the Presbyterian Confession of Faith, as the highest authority known to us that contains this doctrine, which will correctly set it before the reader. And we do not make these quotations for the purpose of following this doctrine into all its legitimate results in detail, but for the purpose of showing *its bearing* upon the subject of *obedience to God:*

"By this sin (eating the forbidden fruit) they (our first parents) fell from their original righteousness and communion with God, and so became dead in sin, and wholly defiled in all the faculties and parts of soul and body. They being the root of all mankind, the guilt of this sin was imputed and the same death in sin and corrupted nature conveyed to all their posterity descending from them by ordinary generation. From this original corruption, whereby we are utterly indisposed, disabled, and made opposite to all good, and wholly inclined to all evil, do proceed all actual transgressions."

Now, it seems to us that if this picture correctly represents the disposition of the human heart at birth, the devil can be no worse. His Satanic Majesty can not be more than utterly indisposed, disabled, and opposite to all good, and wholly inclined to all evil. Nor can we very well see how man can get any worse in the scale of moral turpitude. He can not get worse than wholly defiled in all the faculties of soul and body—and this is his condition at birth, if the doctrine be true—yet Paul tells Timothy that "evil men and seducers shall wax worse and worse." 2 Tim. iii:13. How can they get worse? Wholly defiled in all the faculties of soul and body! Opposite to all good, and wholly inclined to all evil, and still wax worse and worse! Does not the common observation of every man contradict this doctrine? The theory is, as we shall see directly, that this corrupt nature remains until the man is converted to Christianity, as some teach, while others insist that it remains through life even in those truly regenerated. Then we can not be wholly defiled, opposite to all good by nature, for we see many men who make no pretension to Christianity at all, quite as ready to visit the sick and administer to the wants of the poor as many who claim to have had their hearts cleansed by the Spirit of God. These persons are surely not opposed to all good while thus doing good; if they are, then their feelings and actions are strangely inconsistent.

But we are told that from this original corruption do proceed all actual transgressions. If this be true, how came Adam to sin? This corruption of nature is the cause of all actual transgression, and it was the consequence of Adams's sin, but not the cause of it, according to the theory, and hence he was not under its influence until after he sinned. As this inherited corruption of nature is the source of all actual transgression *now*, what caused his transgression *then*? His transgression must have been caused by some other influence than the corruption of nature supposed to be the consequence of his sin; and if so, why may not the same or similar causes influence others now? We are *now* subject to many temptations from which he was *then* free. He could not have been tempted to steal from his neighbor, for there was no one then living to be his neighbor, and no one owned any thing but himself. He could not have been tempted to kill, for there was no person to kill but his wife. He could not have had a temptation to adultery, for the only woman on earth was his wife. Notwithstanding he was free from many sources of temptation that beset our pathway, he failed in the first trial he had of which we have a record. Then, surely, other causes than corruption inherited from him on account of his sin may cause transgression now.

But we are told that "this their sin God was pleased, according to his wise and holy counsel, to permit, having purposed to order it to his own glory." Chap. vi, sec. 1. It does not seem to us that "permit" is exactly the word here. We have already been told that "God, from all eternity, did, by the most wise and holy counsel of his own will, freely and unchangeably ordain whatsoever comes to pass." It did come to pass that they ate of the fruit whereof God commanded them not to eat. Then does it not follow that God not only permitted them to eat, but unchangeably ordained that they should eat the fruit and violate the law He had given, having "purposed to order it to his own glory?"

But how God could be glorified by this violation of His law, especially if we contemplate its results in the light of this theory, we are not very well prepared to see. We have been accustomed to think that the best way to glorify God is to honor His authority by obedience to His commands. How could God be glorified by the direct violation of His positive command, when it made man wholly defiled in all the faculties of soul and body? Did He glory in man becoming opposite to all good and wholly inclined to all evil, that He might punish him in hell forever? Could there be any justice in placing man under a law which God had unchangeably ordained he should break? Was it not downright mockery for God to command him to obey when He had previously decreed that he should disobey?

But was God glorified by the corruption of His creature man? Let us see: "And God saw that the wickedness of man was great in the earth, and that every imagination of the thoughts of his heart was only evil continually. And it repented the Lord that he had made man on the earth, and it grieved him at his heart." Gen. vi:5, 6. Did God grieve on account of His own glorification? If God was glorified by Adam's sin, the consequence of which was the entire corruption of the nature of his offspring, from whence flow all actual transgressions, the wickedness of the antediluvians was as much the result of it as the wickedness of any other people; hence we can not see how He would grieve over the result of an act which He had previously determined to order to His own glory, and which He had unchangeably ordained should come to pass.

Again: Would God have given man a command that He had unchangeably fore-ordained to be broken, that He might subject him to "death, with all miseries, spiritual, temporal, and eternal," then tell us that He "so *loved* the world that he gave his only begotten Son, that whosoever believeth in him should not perish, but have everlasting life" (John iii:16), and at the same time restrict the benefits of His death to a few elect ones, and allow the devil to have the many, and thus be glorified by their destruction—it being no fault of theirs? But if all actual transgressions proceed from this supposed corruption of nature, it is difficult to account for the difference of inclination to sin which we see manifested by different persons. We are accustomed to expect the same cause, when surrounded by the same circumstances, to produce the same effect on all occasions; yet we see persons, even in the same family, surrounded by as nearly the same circumstances as human beings can be in this life, somewhat differently inclined to sin; and, as circumstances differ, these differences increase, until one is a moral, upright man, another a drunkard, another a thief, and another a murderer. Can any one tell, in keeping with this theory, why Cain killed his brother? They were both possessed of the same corrupt nature, and precisely to the same extent. Why, then, was one more vicious than the other? We can not increase or intensify the meaning of such words as *wholly, all, total*, etc. We can not say *more* wholly defiled, *more* all the faculties, *more* all evil, *more* all good. If all Adam's progeny are *wholly* defiled in *all* the faculties of soul and body, opposed to *all* good and *wholly* inclined to *all* evil, Cain could not have been more corrupt than Abel. And if this corrupt nature is the source of all actual transgressions, it was the cause of Cain's sin; and Abel being possessed of this corruption of nature to the same extent, would have been just as much inclined to kill Cain as Cain would have been to kill Abel. Men differ as widely in their inclinations to sin as it is possible for them to differ in any thing, and they could not thus differ if the same corrupt nature influenced all and was possessed by all to the same extent.

But worse still: From our stand-point the theory necessarily damns every infant that dies in infancy. If all infants come into the world with natures inherited from our first parents, wholly defiled in all the faculties of soul and body, then those who die in infancy must go to hell on account of this defilement, or go to heaven in this defilement, or they must have it removed in some way unknown to the Bible. The makers of the creed plainly saw this difficulty, and attempted to provide for it. Chap. x, sec. 3, they tell us that "*elect infants*, dying in infancy, are regenerated and saved by Christ through the Spirit, who worketh when and where and how he pleaseth." Thus they provide for elect infants dying in infancy, but they make no effort to save any but the elect, telling us plainly that Christ died for none others.

But the Calvinists are but a very small part of those who adopt this theory—how will the others escape? The Cumberland Presbyterian Confession of Faith substitutes the word *all* for *elect*, thus: "All infants dying in infancy are regenerated and saved by Christ, through the Spirit, who worketh when, and where, and how he pleaseth." Chap. x, sec. 3. And how did the authors know this? Where is the proof that Christ, by the Spirit, removes this depravity from those dying in infancy and allows it to remain in the living ones? The creed refers us to Luke xviii:15, 16: "And they brought unto him also infants, that he would touch them: but when his disciples saw it, they rebuked them. But Jesus called them unto him, and said, Suffer little children to come unto me, and forbid them not: for of such is the kingdom of God." We have two objections to this proof: "First, These were living and not dead or dying children: how can it, therefore, prove any thing about what the Spirit does for those dying in infancy? Second, *It proves just the opposite* of infantile depravity. If Jesus had said, "Suffer little children to come, and forbid them not, that the total depravity and corruption of their little defiled hearts may be removed by the Spirit, for of such as they *will then be* is the kingdom of God," then the text would have been appropriate. But as it is, it would fill the kingdom of God with subjects wholly defiled in all the faculties of soul and body, opposed to all good, and wholly inclined to all evil. "Suffer little children to come unto me, and forbid them not, for of such [not as they will be, but are now] is the kingdom of God"—that is, of such total depravity, and subjects wholly defiled in all the faculties of soul and body, is the kingdom of God!!!

Mr. Jeter, the great Baptist luminary of Virginia, says: "Infants dying in infancy, must, by some process known or unknown, be freed from depravity—morally renewed or regenerated, or they can never be saved—never participate in the joys of heaven." Jeter's Campbellism Reexamined, pages 51, 52. And on page 49 he says: "I shall now proceed to show that, in the case of dying infants and idiots, regeneration takes place by the agency of the Spirit, without the Word." Thus we see that one error assumed and adopted creates the necessity for perhaps many others. The false assumption that infants are wholly depraved has forced upon these authors and their ilk the doctrine of infant *regeneration* and *abstract spiritual influences.* Nor is this all: *the doctrine of infant baptism originated here.* Does any one demand proof? He shall have it. Dr. Wall, the most voluminous and authoritative writer that has ever wielded a pen in defense of infant baptism, says:

"And you will see in the following quotations that they often conclude the necessity of baptism for the forgiveness of sins, even of a child that is but a day old." Wall's History, vol. i, page 48. After making a quotation from Justin Martyr, who wrote about forty years after the apostles, and about A.D. 140, our author says: "I recite this only to show that in these times, so very near the apostles, they spoke of original sin affecting all mankind descended of Adam; and understood that, besides the actual sins of each particular person, there is in our nature itself, since the fall, something that needs redemption and forgiveness by the merits of Christ. And that is ordinarily applied to every particular person by baptism." *Ibid,* 64.

On pages 104, '05, Dr. Wall quotes Origen, one of the most learned of the Greek fathers, as follows:

"Besides all this, let it be considered, what is the reason that, whereas the baptism of the Church is given for forgiveness of sins, infants also are, by the usage of the Church, baptized; when, if there were nothing in infants that wanted forgiveness and mercy, the grace of baptism would be needless to them. . . . Infants are baptized for the forgiveness of sins. Of what sins? Or when have they sinned? Or how can any reason of the laver in their case hold good, but according to that sense that we mentioned even now: none is free from pollution, though his life be but of the length of one day upon the earth? And it is for that reason, because by the sacrament of baptism the pollution of our birth is taken away, that infants are baptized."

In the writings of Cyprian, bishop of Carthage, is a letter written by a council of sixty-six bishops to one Fidus, about the close of the second century. Dr. Wall gives that part of this letter which pertains to the subject in hand, and says of it: "These bishops held that to suffer the infant to die unbaptized was to endanger its salvation." Wall's History, vol. i, page 139.

In support of infant baptism, Mr. Wesley says: "If infants are guilty of original sin, then they are proper subjects of baptism, seeing, in the ordinary way, they can not be saved unless this be washed away by baptism. It has been already proved that this original stain cleaves to every child of man, and that hereby they are children of wrath, and liable to eternal damnation." This comes to us not only as written by Mr. Wesley, but it was "Published by order of the General Conference" in New York, in 1850. Doctrinal Tracts, page 251. Many other quotations might be given from various authors held in high esteem by the various parties of these days; but surely these are sufficient to show that infant baptism grew out of the false assumption that infants are totally depraved in all the faculties and parts of soul and body —children of wrath, and liable to eternal damnation for Adam's sin, unless baptized. We know that modern defenders of the practice are unwilling to admit this, but Dr. Wall, as a historian, gives authority for what he says; and historical facts, though ignored, can not be wiped out. They are events of the past, and must so remain, though erased from the pages of every book on earth. If, therefore, we have succeeded, or do succeed, in showing that the dogma of hereditary total depravity is untrue, *we will have shown not only that man has the power to believe and obey God*, but also that the doctrine of *abstract spiritual influences, infant regeneration*, and *infant baptism*, as dependencies upon it, are necessarily untrue. Then, seeing the importance of our subject, let us continue our examination of it. If Adam's posterity inherited the corrupt nature described after the fall, then why do not children of Christians inherit their parents' purified natures after their conversion? Surely, if God directly controlled the matter, He would have had as much pleasure in the transmission of purity of nature to the children of the faithful, as He would have had in entailing corruption of nature on the children of the disobedient. And if He had not specially controlled it, but left it to the laws of nature, we can see no reason why purity of heart would not have been as readily transmitted to the children of the Christians as defilement of nature would have been to the children of the wicked. But the creed tells us that "this corruption of nature, during this life, doth remain in those that are regenerated." Presbyterian Confession, chap. vi, sec. 5, page 41. Here, as usual, the creed and the Bible are in direct antagonism. When Peter addressed his fellow-apostles and elders, on one occasion, he said: "Men and brethren, ye know how that a good while ago God made choice among us, that the Gentiles by my mouth should hear the word of the gospel, and believe. And God, which knoweth the hearts, bare them witness, giving them the Holy Ghost, even as unto us; and put no difference between us and them purifying their hearts by faith." Acts xv:7-9. In writing to his brethren, he says, "Seeing you have purified your souls in obeying the truth." 1 Pet. i:22. Now, if this corruption remains in those who are truly converted, how is it possible for persons to be wholly defiled in all the faculties and parts of soul and body, utterly indisposed, disabled, opposite to all good, and wholly inclined to all evil, as described by the creed, and yet their hearts purified by faith, and their souls by obedience, as described by Peter. Surely, the converts to the creed are not the brethren of Peter; nor are they the blest of the Lord, for he says, "Blessed are the pure in heart: for they shall see God." Matt. v:8.

Jesus, in his explanation of the parable of the sower, (Luke viii:15), says, "But that on the good ground are they, which in *an honest and good heart,* having heard the word, keep it, and bring forth fruit with patience." If there was not another passage of scripture in the Bible bearing on the subject, this one would be quite sufficient to spoil the whole theory. Had Jesus been educated in the theological schools of our day, He would not have spoken of honest and good hearts receiving the Word, for He would have been therein taught that there *are none* such; but, on the contrary, all Adam's race are wholly defiled in all the faculties of soul and body, opposed to all good, and wholly inclined to all evil. It seems to us that all speculative theorizing about doubtful interpretations of Scripture, to sustain our favorite dogma, should bend before such direct, plain, and positive statements of the Saviour as the above quoted.

But we are told in the creed that our natures are not only made totally corrupt by Adam's sin, but that the GUILT of it was imputed to all his descendants. This we regard as a fatal mistake growing out of a failure to discriminate between *guilt* and *consequences*. It is certainly true that we suffer in *consequence* of Adam's sin, but that we are in any sense guilty of it, or morally accountable for it, is not exactly clear to us. To suffer the consequences of an act is one thing, but to be held guilty of it, by imputation or otherwise, is quite a different thing. A man, for illustration, may own an estate sufficient to abundantly supply the wants of his family for life, but, by gambling, he may have it all swept away in a single day; his wife and children may be reduced to poverty and want by his wickedness, and thus made to keenly feel the consequences of his act, but surely no one would regard *them guilty* in consequence of their misfortune. So we suffer death as a consequence of Adam's sin, as we will more clearly see directly; but this is not quite sufficient to show that we are guilty of or responsible for it. If we are guilty of or responsible for his *first* sin, why are we not accountable for *all other sins* commmitted by him? As he was childless when driven from the garden, and was an hundred and thirty years old when Seth, his third son, of which we have an account, was born, and was nine hundred and thirty years old when he died, it follows that he lived more than eight hundred years after eating the interdicted fruit. It is next to certain, therefore, that he did many things wrong during this long period. Is there any good reason why we are guilty of his *first* sin, and guilty of *no other* sin committed by him? And if we are responsible for and guilty of Adam's sin, are we not equally guilty of all the sins committed by our own father? He is much nearer us than Adam, and we can plainly see in ourselves some things inherited from him. If, then, we are guilty of the sins of Adam, we see no escape from the guilt of our father's sin. And as these are but two extremes in the long chain of parentage from us to Adam, we can see no reason why we may not be held guilty, according to the same rule, of all the sins of every parent between them. If so, well may we ask, "Lord, who then can be saved?" When we do the best we can, we have quite enough in our own record to answer for; and if we are thus charged with the sins of those who have lived before us, then the last lingering ray of hope for the salvation of man is forever extinguished. We are encouraged, however, by the fact that God has contradicted the whole theory, saying: "The soul that sinneth, it shall die. The son shall not bear the iniquity of the father, neither shall the father bear the iniquity of the son: the righteousness of the righteous shall be upon him, and the wickedness of the wicked shall be upon him." Ezek. xviii:20. It seems to us that the prophet intended to describe the false reasoners of our day, when he said: "The Gentiles shall come unto thee from the ends of the earth, and shall say, Surely our fathers have inherited lies, vanity, and things wherein there is no profit." Jer. xvi:19.

But is it possible, in the nature of things, *that sin can be transmitted from parent to child?* In order to arrive at a satisfactory solution of this question, it may be well to ascertain what sin is; and this we can do with great certainty, for we have a definition of it given by inspiration. John says "sin is the transgression of the law." 1 John iii:4. In the light of this definition, how is it possible that a transgression by one man may be transmitted to another, or from parent to child? God has said, "Thou shalt not kill." In violation of this law, a man thrusts a dagger to the heart of his neighbor. This is sin. Now this act, being the act of a father, can not possibly become the act of his child; nor can the child be made responsible for it. He may *approve* the act, and for this approval may receive merited punishment; but it was the wicked approval that brought guilt to him, and not the act of the father. Without such approval, he may suffer in consequence of his father's act—may be made an orphan by it—but surely the act itself can not become his act. Sin is nowhere in God's word defined to be a weakness, or hereditament, but a transgression or act of the guilty himself. "God is love," and can not punish man for that which he has no power to prevent.

But we have said that we die as a consequence of Adam's sin. This is true, and yet we are not guilty of it. *When Adam fell from the plastic hand of God, he was as mortal as he was after he ate of the interdicted fruits:* how, then, is death a consequence of that act? He was placed in a garden or orchard, in which grew, among others, two trees, respectively called *The tree of life*, and *The tree of the knowledge of good and evil*. For his government in this garden, God gave him a law, saying: "Of every tree of the garden that mayest freely eat: but of the tree of the knowledge of good and evil, thou shalt not eat of it: for in the day thou eatest thereof dying thou shalt die." Gen. ii:16, 17. We have adopted the marginal reading of the Polyglot Bible, because it is agreed, by scholars, to be an improvement upon the King's translation. It will be seen, by an examination of this law, that Adam had access to the tree of life before he ate of the interdicted fruit, and the properties of the fruit of this tree were such as to counteract the mortal tendencies of his nature, and keep him alive as long as he had access to it. But when he violated God's law, it was only necessary that he should be driven from the garden, so that he might no longer have access to this life-giving fruit, that, under the laws of mortality to which his nature subjected him, he might suffer the penalty of the law which said, "dying thou shalt die." Hence, God said: "Behold, the man has become as one of us, to know good and evil: and now, lest he put forth his hand, and take also of the tree of life, and eat, and live forever: therefore the Lord God sent him forth from the garden of Eden, to till the ground from whence he was taken. So he drove out the man: and he placed at the east of the garden of Eden cherubim, and a flaming sword which turned every way, to keep the way of the tree of life." Gen. iii:22-24. Thus we see how Adam died in consequence of his sin, and that he would not have died had he not sinned; hence says Paul, "By one man sin entered into the world, and death by sin." Rom. v:12. Not that he possessed physical immortalty before he sinned, for he did not, but he had a remedy for his mortality of which he was deprived after he sinned. We are sometimes asked whether or not the lower animals die as a consequence of Adam's sin? We answer they do not, but they die as a result of the common laws of mortality to which the whole animal creation are subject. They have been subject to these laws from the time they were created, not having had access to the fruit of the tree of life, as Adam did before he sinned. From this stand-point it is easy to see how Adam's posterity died as a consequence of his sin. His children inherit from him just such an organization as he had both *before* and *after* he sinned and as they are born out of the garden of Eden, and away from the tree of life, they can not have its fruit to counteract the mortal tendencies of their nature, and hence, like him, dying they die. Shall we hence conclude that Adams offspring are guilty of his sin? As well may we conclude that the African child that falls a victim to cannibalism sinned by being born in Africa. It was its misfortune to be born in a locality where men eat each other: so it is our misfortune to be born out of the garden of Eden, where, for a time we can not get fruit from the tree of life; but if we do our Father's commandments, there is coming a period when we will have a right to the tree of life, and may enter through the gates into the city. There is much speculation in the world with reference to the *kind of death* Adam and his posterity died as a consequence of his sin. Mr. Ewing, in his Lectures (page 63), tells us that, "By reason of our union with our federal head and representative, we sinned in him, and fell with him, and death is the consequence—death spiritual, temporal, and eternal." If the death which Adam and the human race died was not only spiritual and temporal, but *eternal,* then we see no remedy that can reach such a case. *Eternal must mean without end—of endless duration.* Then, if this death be eternal, there can be no more life and hence all our efforts to save those who are eternally dead can do no good, and the whole family of man is lost—hopelessly lost. If a single son of Adam be saved, it follows that he was not eternally lost; for—it matters not in what sense he be dead —if ever made alive, that is an end to his death, and, consequently, his death could not have been eternal.

But Mr. Ewing further tells us (page 62): "The whole soul of man is entirely depraved, corrupt, and alienated from God—a child of wrath, an heir of hell, going astray from the womb, conceived in sin, an enemy to God, having a heart deceitful above all things and desperately wicked; the understanding darkened, the affections earthly, and the whole man sensual and devilish." Truly, this is an appalling picture of our nature at birth, entailed upon us for no other reason than that we descended from Adam, with whom, by a single act of his, we fell into this deplorable condition six thousand years before we were born. And when we add to this thought the language of the Presbyterian Confession—that "this corruption of nature, during this life, doth remain in those that are regenerated"—we have a most ridiculous description of Christian character manufactured by this theory. Behold a Christian with a heart not only entirely depraved, sensual and devilish, but hating God, and an heir of hell!!! We do not suppose the authors of these books believed this monstrous absurdity themselves, or intended to teach it to others, but they were involved in it by the blinding influences of a false theory. Be this as it may, however, we can not admit that this is a correct picture of that "holiness without which no man shall see the Lord."

The mind of man is composed of numerous faculties, which may be divided into two grand divisions, called, respectively, *Animal* and *Intellectual*. By "animal faculties," we mean such as are possessed by man and beast; or we might simply say by *animals*, for man is only an intellectual animal. As examples of this class of faculties we may mention Alimentiveness, Combativeness, Detructiveness, Amativeness, Philoprogenitiveness, etc., etc. In man they are usually called *propensities*, but in lower animals they are called *instincts*. Paul calls them "the carnal mind," and tells us "it is not subject to the law of God, neither indeed can be." Rom. viii:7. It would do but little good to read the Ten Commandments to a horse, as he would not be subject to them —neither, indeed, could he be; and it would do about as little good to read them to the purely carnal mind of man (if it were possible to do so), composed of similar constituents, which knows no law but animal gratification. But God has given to man an *intellectuality* capable of appreciating law, and has given him a law adapted to his organization, by which his carnal propensities are to be exercised, and by which the whole man is to be governed. And while the whole man is governed by laws received from God, and applied by the intellectual man, all is harmony and order, and without sin; but when these laws are superseded by animal propensities, such as appetite, passion, and lust, then come confusion, violence, and crime. And *thus originated sin in the garden of Eden*. God gave Adam a law for the government of his appetite, and while he obeyed it he had life and peace; but when law was supplanted by appetite, sin came, and death by sin. From the description of man's nature found in the creeds, it would seem that the authors regard these animal propensities as filling the entire measure of the human mind. But the *duality* of mind is well established by experience, observation, metaphysics, reason, and the Bible. The carnal mind we have seen already: the *perceptive* and *reflective* faculties, of which there are many, and the *moral sentiments*, such as Benevolence, Veneration, Conscientiousness, Firmness, Hope, etc., make up the intellectual and moral nature of man, to which God's law is addressed, and Paul tells us, "they that are after the flesh do mind the things of the flesh; but they that are after the Spirit, the things of the Spirit. For to be carnally minded is death; but to be spiritually minded is life and peace." Rom. viii:5, 6. The antagonism of these two departments of man's nature is well shown in Paul's description of himself. "I find then," says he, "a law, that, when I would do good, evil is present with me. For I delight in the law of God after the inward man. But I see another law in my members, warring against the law of my mind, and bringing me into captivity to the law of sin which is in my members." Rom. vii:21-23. Had this dual nature been dispensed with in the creation of man, he must have been *all animal*, and therefore nothing more than a brute; or he must have been *all intellectual and moral*, without any counter-tendencies in his nature, and therefore would have been a mere machine, acting as compelled to act, under one set of principles, and hence there would have been neither merit nor demerit in any thing he did; nor could he have had the slightest freedom of will, and, therefore, could not have been in the slightest degree accountable to his Creator, Who, in that event, would have been operating him as a mechanic does his machine.

But if we can arrive at the meaning of the language, "dying thou shalt die," as connected with the law given to and violated by Adam, then we think we may arrive at a knowledge of the kind of death he died. This we certainly can do with great clearness, as we have an exegesis of the language by God Himself. After Adam violated the law, God adjudicated his case, and pronounced the sentence upon him. Both as the *Giver of the Law* and as God, He certainly knew what He meant by the language of the law, and He certainly pronounced the sentence in accordance therewith. What, then, was the sentence? "Dust thou art, and unto dust shalt thou return." Gen. iii:19. Surely, this must mean literal, physical death; nothing more, nothing less. Moses wrote the history of this affair about two thousand five hundred years after it occurred, when the word *die*, in all its forms, was of no doubtful import, but had a well-settled meaning in the current usage of that day. A few examples may not be out of place here. In the fifth chapter of Genesis we have the word employed by the same writer no less than eight times, as follows: "And all the days that Adam lived were nine hundred and thirty years: and *he died.*" Ver. 5. "And all the days of Seth were nine hundred and twelve years: and *he died.*" Ver. 8. "And all the days of Enos were nine hundred and five years: and *he died.*" Ver. 11. "And all the days of Cainan were nine hundred and ten years: and *he died.*" Ver. 14. "And all the days of Mahalaleel were eight hundred ninety and five years: and *he died.*" Ver. 17. "And all the days of Jared were nine hundred sixty and two years: and *he died.*" Ver. 20. "And all the days of Methuselah were nine hundred sixty and nine years: and *he died.*" Ver. 27. "And all the days of Lamech were seven hundred seventy and seven years: and *he died.*" Ver. 31. These cases clearly show what Moses understood by the word *die*, and as he is the same writer that recorded the law violated by Adam, he must have meant the same by *"die,"* in the law, that he meant in the other cases referred to. Again, the word *die* must certainly mean just the *opposite* of the word *live*. This word in its various forms occurs in the same chapter to indicate physical life. Had God afflicted Adam with greater punishment than the terms employed indicated to him, then would He not have deceived him? And He determined upon other and greater punishment for him, after he committed the act, than that threatened in the law violated, then we insist that it was *ex post facto* in its character, and therefore unjust. The circumstances under which Adam violated God's law would have rather invoked a *commutation* of punishment than an increase of it. He did not know good and evil until he acquired a knowledge of it by eating the fruit of the tree of the knowledge of good and evil. This is evident from the language of God after he ate of it: "Behold, the man is become as one of us, to know good and evil."

Gen. iii:22. He could only appreciate the law as a *positive* prohibition, but his *moral* obligation to obey God, as his Creator, he could not appreciate. He did not so much as know that he was naked, for God said: "Who told thee that thou wast naked? Hast thou eaten of the tree whereof I commanded thee that thou shouldest not eat?" *Ibid*, 11. Certainly, then, if ignorance be a mitigating circumstance, Adam was entitled to the full benefit of it.

From our stand-point such a thought as spiritual corruption by inheritance is utterly impossible. Paul says, "We have had fathers of our flesh which corrected us, and we gave them reverence: shall we not much rather be in subjection unto the Father of spirits, and live?" Heb. xii:9. Does not this passage plainly prove that the fathers of our flesh are not the fathers of our spirits? To our mind it shows that while our bodies are inherited from our parents, the Spirit is not so inherited, but comes directly from God. Hence the style: *"Fathers of our flesh," "The Father of spirits."* Our bodies we inherit from our parents, and, consequently, physical impurities may be transmitted from parent to child, but we suppose all will agree that the mind, the spiritual or inner man, is the seat of moral depravity. If, then, we do not get our spirits by inheritance, it is impossible that we should inherit spiritual depravity from Adam. May we further examine the Scriptures on this subject? "The burden of the word of the Lord for Israel, saith the Lord, which stretcheth forth the heavens, and layeth the foundation of the earth, and formeth the spirit of man within him." Zech. xii:1. If God *forms the spirit within man*, it seems improbable that he gets it by inheritance. Again: Solomon says, "Then shall the dust return to the earth as it was, and the spirit shall return to God who gave it." Eccl. xii:7. By this we learn not only that the spirit returns to God at death, but that God originally *gave* it. The words *"returns to God"* clearly imply that it had been there before. We can not say we returned to a place to which we had never been. In returning, it did not go in or with the body, as the body returned to the ground as dust. As, therefore, the spirit returns independent of the body, is it not likely that God gave it to man, not *by* or *through* the body, but *for* the body? The words "God who gave it" have somewhat the same ring, too; nevertheless, they alone would not be quite conclusive, for He gives us food, raiment, and many other things through *means* prepared to produce them. The question for us, then, is does he give the spirit *through* means or *without* means—does He give it directly or indirectly—does He give it as we have seen that He takes it—or does He give it by procreation, organization, or some other means? Let us see. When Jesus restored the ruler's dead daughter to life, Luke says "her spirit came again, and she arose straightway." Luke viii:55. The spirit of the damsel *came again.* From whence did it come? Solomon says the spirit returns to God, who gave it. Then it is clear that her spirit went to God when she died, and came directly from Him when she was made alive. The words "came again" imply that it had done the same thing before; and as we have no account of her being miraculously made alive before it follows that it was at the beginning of her existence that her spirit came directly from God the previous time.

But we are told that the spiritual man did not come directly from God, but is the creature of the organization. We have not room for a thorough examination of this objection here, but we must notice it briefly—not by way of respect for materialistic infidelity, of which it is the cornerstone, but in respect to our own argument, against which it may be presented. First, then, if the spirit came not from God, how are the scriptures above quoted and the reasonings therefrom to be met? And how can a *material* organization create an *immaterial* soul capable of existence separate from the organization after the latter has ceased to be? Or if the soul, created by materiality, is itself *material*, why is it not subject to chemical analysis? The material organization is not only subject to chemical analysis, but has been analyzed repeatedly. The ultimate elements of it have been found, and if the soul is also material, why has it not been subjected to the same process? Surely, the advocates of materialism have the ability to do it if it were possible—and the defense of their theory would invoke the disposition to do it—if they, then, have not done it, it is clear that, because of the soul's immateriality, they can not do it. That the soul is capable of existence after the separation of soul and body, is clear from what we have already quoted from Solomon—that the body returns to the ground and the spirit returns to God, who gave it; not only so, but it is also clear from numerous other passages. Paul says: "Therefore we are always confident, knowing that, whilst we are at home in the body, we are absent from the Lord. . . . We are confident, and willing rather to be absent from the body, and to be present with the Lord." 2 Cor. v:6, 8. John "saw under the altar the souls of them that were slain for the word of God." Rev. vi:9. We might further quote Luke xvi:24, 27, concerning the rich man and Lazarus, and many other scriptures on this subject; but enough has been quoted to satisfy those who read and believe the Bible, and others will not likely read what we write about it. The body may be likened to a machine controlled by the mind or spiritual man. No machinery has ever been known capable of generating its own motive power; hence the "Perpetual Motion" has not been invented. If the human organism creates the soul, its own motive power, then it is an exception to all known law on the subject. If, then, our argument holds good, and the spirit came, not by inheritance, but directly from God, it follows that when it is given, it is not only good, but very good, and the whole theory of hereditary depravity is most certainly false. The child comes into the world with its infantile mind composed of numerous faculties susceptible of being cultivated and developed by impressions made upon it through the senses, and when all its faculties are properly balanced, educated, and governed, they are calculated to make the man useful and happy, but if neglected may make him vicious and miserable—and his inclinations to virtue or vice depend much upon the circumstances and influences surrounding him; hence inclinations to sin are as different in different persons as the circumstances have been different by which they have been influenced from infancy to manhood. We most firmly believe that many men who were raised under improper influences and became desperately wicked—perhaps terminated their lives upon a scaffold—if they had been raised under wholesome influences, would have been useful members of society and finally saved in heaven, and *vice versa*. Thus we see the importance of observing Solomon's admonition: "Train up a child in the way he should go, and when he is old he will not depart from it;" with which Paul agrees, saying, "Bring up your children in the nurture and admonition of the Lord."

But there are differences of mental power manifested by different persons, growing out of a difference in the physical machinery *inherited from our parents*. This we not only admit, but firmly believe; but these do not affect our position in the least. An engine may run a vast amount of well-made and properly applied machinery, and thus exhibit great power, but were we to apply the *same engine* to heavy, cumbersome, unwieldy, unbalanced machinery, it could do but little, though the same man operated it. So a man who has inherited a fine organization, large and well balanced brain, of fine material, will exhibit much more mental power than one who had inherited an imperfect organization of coarse material. But inherited weakness, whether physical or mental, is not sin—no guilt can attach to it—and therefore the differences in mental power spoken of can not prove the doctrine of total depravity; on the contrary, if they prove any thing concerning it, they contradict it, for these differences can not be the result of total depravity, because all who are totally depraved are, in this respect, exactly alike. There is no comparative degree in *total* depravity.

But we must briefly notice some of the proofs relied on to sustain the doctrine. First, we are told that the infant gets angry as soon as born, and thus gives evidence of total depravity. If this be proof conclusive, then God is totally depraved, too, for He said to Moses, when the people worshiped the calf made by Aaron, "Let me alone, that my wrath may wax hot against them." Ex. xxxii:10. And again: "God is angry with the wicked every day." Ps. vii:11. Does the infant smile as well as cry? And does it not very soon divide its toys and food with its associate, thus exhibiting feelings of kindness as well as anger?

But we are referred to some scriptures which we must notice: "As it is written, There is none righteous, no, not one; there is none that understandeth; there is none that seeketh after God; they are all gone out of the way; they are together become unprofitable; there is none that doeth good, no, not one. Their throat is an open sepulchre; with their tongues they have used deceit; the poison of asps is under their lips; whose mouth is full of cursing and bitterness; their feet are swift to shed blood; destruction and misery are in their ways, and the way of peace have they not known. There is no fear of God before their eyes." Rom. iii:10-18. Now, we only need to carefully read this quotation in order to see that it can not apply to any inherited corruption of nature existing at birth, but to such as had *corrupted themselves* by wicked works. Infants are not expected to be righteous, for righteousness consists in doing right. Nor are they expected to understand—to seek God—to have gone out of the way, or in the way—to have done good or evil. Their tongues have not used deceit, nor are their mouths full of cursing and bitterness, for they can not talk at all. Their feet are not swift to shed blood, for they can not hurt any one. And it will be borne in mind that the passage is relied upon to prove an inherited corruption of nature that comes into the world with us by ordinary generation. Paul makes this quotation from David—Ps. xiv—where he tells how they became corrupt: "They have done abominable works." Hence their corruption came not by Adam's sin, but by their own wickedness.

Next we examine the language of David—Ps. li:5: "Behold I was shapen in iniquity, and in sin did my mother conceive me." Whatever may be the meaning of this passage, it *can not be the imputation of sin to the child.* "In sin did *my mother* conceive me;" that is, *she* acted wickedly when I was conceived. Were the wife to say, "In *drunkenness* my husband beat me," or the child that "in *anger* my father whipped me," surely no one would attribute drunkenness to the wife or anger to the child; neither can they impute the *sin of the mother* to the child. We come now to notice the language of the prophet with regard to "Judah and Jerusalem"—Isa. i:5, 6: "Why should ye be stricken any more? ye will revolt more and more: the whole head is sick, and the whole heart faint. From the sole of the foot even unto the head there is no soundness in it; but wounds and bruises and putrefying sores." This was not spoken with regard to any inherited defilement attaching to any one, but with regard to the Jews as a nation. As a nation they had become corrupt—not by inheritance, but by actual transgressions of their own. And God had scourged them, and afflicted them for their own wickedness (not Adam's sin), until, as a nation, they were comparable to a man full of wounds and bruises and putrefying sores, and still they would not reform; hence, by His prophet, He asks, "Why should ye be stricken any more? ye will revolt more and more?" —as much as to say: "I have sent fiery serpents to bite you, by which thousands have died; I have allowed you to go to war with the nations around you until multiplied thousands have been slain in battle; and in various ways I have chastened you as a father chasteneth his children; but all to no purpose. Why should I afflict you further? it will only make you worse and worse." "Your country is desolate; your cities are burned with fire; your land strangers devour it in your presence, and it is desolate as overthrown by strangers"—thus clearly speaking of national calamities that had befallen them as a nation. Not a word of allusion to Adam's sin or its consequences in the whole connection.

We are next referred to the language of David—Ps. lviii:1-8: "Do ye indeed speak righteousness, O congregation? do ye judge uprightly, O ye sons of men? Yea, in heart ye work wickedness; ye weigh the violence of your hands in the earth. The wicked are estranged from the womb: they go astray as soon as they are born, speaking lies. Their poison is like the poison of a serpent; they are like the deaf adder that stoppeth her ear: which will not hearken to the voice of charmers, charming never so wisely." Here, again, we need only read the passage carefully to see that it can not apply to infants at birth. In heart *these* work wickedness: children at birth do not work wickedness.

The wicked are estranged from the womb: the theory says all are wicked and estranged. They go astray as soon as they are born—speaking lies: the theory says they are *born* astray. These persons spake lies: infants can not speak at all. Shall we hear David's prayer for them? "Break their teeth, O God, in their mouth." Do infants have teeth in their mouth at birth? He continues: "Break out the great teeth of the young lions, O Lord. Let them melt away as waters which run continually: when he bendeth his bow to shoot his arrows, let them be as cut in pieces." Surely, this was a singular prayer coming from David for the punishment and destruction of infants!!! This was simply strong language used to describe the wickedness of the *congregation* and *judges* mentioned in the first verse.

We are next referred to the language of Paul to the Ephesians—Chap. ii:1-3: "And you hath be quickened who were dead in trespasses and sins." This does not fit the theory, for then it should read *"dead in a trespass or sin."* But how came their death? "Wherein in time past ye walked according to the course of this world, according to the prince of the power of the air, the spirit that now worketh in the children of disobedience: among whom also we all had our conversation in times past in the lusts of our flesh, fulfilling the desires of the flesh and of the mind; and were by nature the children of wrath even as others." This shows us clearly how their nature became corrupt, which was by wicked works, or, as Paul expresses it, fulfilling the desires of the flesh. Not a word about Adam's sin: they were dead in their own sins.

But we are referred to Rom. v:12: "Wherefore, as by one man sin entered into the world, and death by sin; and so death passed upon all men, for that all have sinned." This passage does have reference to Adam's sin and its consequences, but it falls very far short of proving that all men, or even Adam, became totally depraved. David sinned very grievously; yet his *heart was perfect with the Lord his God* (1 Ks. xv:3), insomuch that he was a man after God's own heart. (1 Sam. xiii:14; Acts xiii:22.) If his sin left his heart perfect with God, how did a single sin of Adam totally deprave him and all his posterity? If a man were to commit a crime worthy of death, and were to have the sentence of death passed upon him, still all this could not prove him totally depraved, opposed to all good, and wholly inclined to all evil; he may have some good emotions yet. Here we might safely dismiss the passage, having shown that it does not prove that for which it is introduced; but can we learn the meaning of it? The fact that almost every exponent of it has a theory of his own, derived from it, is quite enough to prove the import of it to be doubtful. *A doubtful interpretation of an obscure passage must not come in contact with a plain passage about the meaning of which there can be no mistake.* When the phrase "all have sinned" is interpreted to mean that the whole race of man sinned in Adam, it seems to us a plain contradiction of God's law, which says: "The soul that sinneth, it shall die. The son shall not bear the iniquity of the father, neither shall the father bear the iniquity of the son: the righteousness of the righteous shall be upon him, and the wickedness of the wicked shall be upon him." The theory says the children of Adam do bear his iniquity, and his wickedness is not only on him, but also on them. It is also antagonistic to John's definition of sin—that "sin is the transgression of the law;" and also with the fact seen already—that a transgression or act (for sin is an act) of one man can not be transmitted to or become the act of another. We regard the passage as clearly *metonymical*. The consequences of Adam's sin being suffered by all, the sin is said to have been committed by all; the consequences being put for the act. The apostle alludes to the sin of Adam, as a consequence of which all suffer death in accordance with the laws of their mortal nature inherited from Adam, they not having fruit from the tree of life with which to counteract mortality as Adam had before he sinned; and thus "death reigned from Adam to Moses, even over them that had not sinned after the similitude of Adam's transgression." Ver. 14.

It is somewhat strange to us that those who profess to disbelieve Universalism can believe that the death here spoken of is spiritual death. If spiritual death passed upon all men because they all sinned in Adam, then Universalism must be true; for the apostle goes on to say: "If through the offense of one many be dead, much more the grace of God, and the gift by grace, which is by one man, Jesus Christ, hath abounded unto many." The grace of God and the gift by grace has abounded to just as many through Christ, the last Adam, as are dead by the offense of the first Adam; "therefore, as by the offense of one, judgment came upon all men to condemnation, even so by the righteousness of one, the free gift came upon all men unto justification of life." Ver. 18. The same *all* who suffer by the offense of one, are made alive by the righteousness of another. This is not only the teaching of Paul here, but he communicates the same thought to his brethren at Corinth. The fifteenth chapter of his first letter to them is devoted to the resurrection of the dead, and in the 22d verse he has the following very significant language: "For as in Adam all die, even so in Christ shall all be made alive." As in Adam all *die*—not *died* back yonder in the garden, but die now in Adam. And who dies in Adam? All men, most certainly. Even so in Christ shall the same *all* be made alive: the infant and the aged, the wicked and the just, all die, and their "dust returns to the earth as it was;" but when the trump of God shall sound, they will be raised from the dead through Christ—"but every man in his own order: Christ the firstfruits; afterward they that are Christ's at his coming." Ver. 23.

But we are sometimes told that if man is not guilty of Adam's sin, then Christ's mission and death were useless. Surely, such persons have very narrow views of the subject. How shall we escape the punishment due us on account of *our own* sins? And how shall we be raised from the dead only through Christ? It is nowhere said in the word of the Lord that Christ died to save man from Adam's sin; but we have abundant testimony proving that He came to save man from *his own* sins. Joseph was told by the Lord to call the infant Saviour *Jesus,* because He should save His people from *their sins,* not Adam's sin. Peter commanded his hearers, when preaching from Solomon's porch: "Repent ye therefore, and be converted, that your sins may be blotted out." It was *their sins* which were to be blotted out, and not Adam's sin. God's promise, in the new covenant, to His people was: "And their sins and iniquities will I remember no more." The new covenant made no provision for Adam's sin; therefore, if God ever remembered it against His people under this covenant, He is remembering it yet. Paul said to the Colossians, "You being dead in *your sins* and the uncircumcision of *your flesh."* They were not dead in *Adam's sin,* nor in the uncircumcision of *his flesh.* Under the Jewish law, God made provisions for pardon of sins committed against it, and He mentions many sins for which offerings were to be made in a prescribed form; but He provided no remedy for Adam's sin, nor did He ever speak of it as chargeable to the Jews. Surely, if God has Adam's sin in remembrance against Adam's posterity, He would have mentioned it somewhere, or in some dispensation made provision for the pardon of it. Christ came, then, "who his own self bare our sins in his own body on the tree;" but He came not only that we might have pardon of our sins, but, as we have already seen, that we may have a resurrection of the dead; hence, the language of Paul: "If Christ be not raised, your faith is vain; ye are yet in *your sins.* Then they also which are fallen asleep in Christ are perished." Surely, these are objects sufficiently important to invoke the mission and sufferings of the Christ the Son of God—salvation from sin, a resurrection from the grave, and eternal life.

We come now to notice the practical bearing of the doctrine of total depravity, as an effect of Adam's sin, upon the reception of the gospel as the power of God unto salvation. The Prebyterian Confession of Faith tells us that "Man, by his fall into sin, hath wholly lost all ability of will to any spiritual good accompanying salvation . . . is not able, by his own strength, to convert himself or to prepare himself thereunto." Chap. ix, sec. 3. Now, if the alien has lost all ability of will to any spiritual good, it follows that he can not even will or desire his own salvation. What can he do, then? Just nothing at all! he is as passive as a block of marble in the hands of the sculptor. But "when God converts a sinner, and translates him into the state of grace, he freeth him from his natural bondage under sin, and by his grace alone enables him freely to will and to do that which is spiritually good." *Ibid*, sec. 4. Thus we see that this theory brings man into the world wholly defiled in all the faculties of soul and body, opposed to all good, and wholly inclined to all evil, not even able to will any spiritual good accompanying salvation, until God converts and translates him into the state of grace, so as to free him from his natural bondage, and enable him freely to will and to do that which is spiritually good. Then, if God never converts him and he is finally lost, who is to blame for it? Surely, not man, for he could not even will or desire his own salvation, or prepare himself thereunto. Why did Christ command that the Gospel be preached among all nations, and to every creature, promising salvation to those who would believe and obey it, when He must have known, if this theory be true, that they *could neither believe nor obey* it?—nay, they could not even so much as will or desire their salvation, or any thing good connected therewith, to say nothing of doing any thing to secure it. And why did He threaten them with damnation if they did not believe it, when, according to the theory, they have no more power to believe it than they have to make a world?

We insist that the doctrine is too monstrously absurd to be entertained by any one for a moment—antagonistic to the whole tenor of God's word and the spirit of the Christian religion—

alike dishonoring to God and destructive to man. And when we remember that the world has been taught this doctrine for centuries by the large majority of those who have spoken and written concerning it, we are made to wonder, not that infidelity is abroad in the land, but that there are not an hundred infidels where there is one. God never, at any time, commanded man to do that which he was unable to do; and the very fact that He commands man to believe and obey Him, is evidence, high as heaven, that he has the ability to do the things required of him. All things necessary for man's salvation and happiness which he is unable to do for himself, God has done or will do for him; but what he is able to do for himself, God requires of him, and will not do for him. These fundamental truths, however, we must leave the reader to amplify for himself: we can not pursue this branch of our subject further at present; though we have not exhausted it, we fear we may exhaust his patience ere we get before him some remaining thoughts deemed important to our investigation.

If God charged Adam's posterity with the guilt of his sin, we wish to know when it was or will be, forgiven. Was it forgiven when Jesus made the atonement? If so, the whole theory of man's present guilt of that sin is destroyed, for he can not be guilty of a sin already pardoned. Is it pardoned when man is pardoned for his own sins? No, for the creed tells us that it remains through life in those who are regenerated; and it also tells us that it is appointed unto all men once to die, for that all have sinned. Surely, he would not yet have to die for a sin that had been pardoned. Is it forgiven at death? Where is the proof of it? And what are the conditions, if any, upon which it is to be done? Or, if unconditionally pardoned, what are the means to accomplish it? Is it forgiven in the intermediate state between death and the judgment? If so, why can not all other sins be pardoned in that state? And if they can, why the necessity of having them pardoned in this life? Is it pardoned at the final judgment? If so, then we will be judged according to the deeds done in *Adam's body*, and not every one according to the deeds done in *his own body*. Is it not pardoned at all? Then, will the Christian be damned for the guilt of *Adam's sin after having been pardoned for his own sins?* If so, the sentence will not be, "Depart from me, ye workers of iniquity," but, "Depart from me, all ye that have washed your robes, and made them white in the blood of the Lamb." Though *your sins* have all been canceled from the book of God's remembrance, in accordance with the provisions of the new covenant, and though *your righteousness* is as robes of linen clean and white, there is one sin which, though not committed by you, is imputed to or charged against you, for which you must go with the devil, that deceived you *in Adam*, into the lake of fire and brimstone, where the beast and the false prophet are, where you shall be tormented day and night forever and ever. Or, if he does not go to hell on account of it, will he go to heaven with it still charged against him—with a nature totally depraved, wholly opposed to all good, and inclined to all evil? We most confidently deny that any one of Adam's posterity ever has been or will be sent to hell for Adam's sin. As we have stated more than once, all die as a consequence of it, and through Christ will be raised from the dead. Those who are intelligent, and therefore responsible, and who have heartily accepted and complied with the terms of pardon for *their own* sins, as offered them in the Gospel through Christ, will be raised to the enjoyment of life eternal. Here they will gain even more in Christ than they lost in Adam. As saith the poet:

> "In him the tribes of Adam boast
> More blessings than their father lost."

They exchange not only temporal for eternal life, but they exchange *mortal* for *immortal* bodies, and for the first time will they have put on immortality. Having done the commandments, they will have a right to the tree of life, and will enter through the gates into the city. In these immortal and spiritual bodies they will not again be subject to temptation and sin. The devil, who seduced Adam, will not be there; but they will have the society of God their Father, Jesus their elder brother, and, as saints of the Most High, they will join the angelic host in praising God and the Lamb forever and ever.

> "There pain and sickness never come,
> And grief no place obtains;
> Health triumphs in immortal bloom,
> And endless pleasure reigns!

> No cloud these blissful regions know,
>   For ever bright and fair!
> For sin, the source of every woe,
>   Can never enter there.
> There no alternate night is known,
>   Nor sun's faint sickly ray;
> But glory from the sacred throne
> Spreads everlasting day."

But what of the wicked? "As in Adam all die, even so in Christ shall all be made alive." The wicked die as a consequence of Adam's sin, without their volition or agency; so, without their volition or agency, they will be raised from death through the merits of the resurrection of Jesus the Christ; but not to life eternal: *"These* shall go away into *everlasting punishment:* but the *righteous* into life eternal." They will be judged, every man according to *his works,* not Adam's works. They will be judged, not for *his sin,* because they are not, never have been, nor can they ever be, guilty of it, but for *their own sins* of which they are guilty. And having refused the terms of pardon offered them in the gospel, by which they might have been pardoned, they will be condemned: "The fearful, and unbelieving, and the abominable, and murderers, and whoremongers, and sorcerers, and idolaters, and all liars, shall have their part in the lake which burned with fire and brimstone." And how long will this awful inheritance be theirs? "They shall be tormented day and night forever and ever." O! friendly sinner, is this to be thy final doom?

> "What could your Redeemer do
> More than he has done for you?
> To procure your peace with God,
> Could he more than shed his blood?
> After all this flow of love,
> All his drawings from above,
> Why will you your Lord deny?
> Why will you resolve to die?"

But there is yet another class. Infants, idiots, and other irresponsible persons, die as a consequence of Adam's trangression, and will be raised from the dead by the same power and through the same means employed in the resurrection of others. We have seen that sin is the violation of law; and as they have never been subject to any law requiring any obedience of them, it follows that they have violated no law, and are hence without sins of their own. And as Adam's sin was not committed by, and therefore never charged to them, there is no sin for which they need forgiveness, and, therefore, for which they may be condemned to endless punishment. Jesus said, "Of such is the kingdom of God," and required others to be converted and become as they are, in order to enter it; therefore if their purity of heart and innocence of character were such as to constitute the standard of purity for those who would enter the kingdom of God on earth, we think they will scarcely be refused admittance into heaven by the same adorable Son of God, who pronounced blessings on them here. In coming from the dead however, they will exchange their natural, mortal bodies for spiritual, immortal bodies, and will be thus prepared to enter

> "Where the saints of all ages in harmony meet,
> Their Saviour and brethren transported to greet;
> While the anthems of rapture unceasingly roll
> And the smile of the Lord is the feast of the soul."

CHAPTER VI.

THE ESTABLISHMENT OF THE CHURCH.

It will be admitted by all that God has an organized government on the earth. This government is variously called in the New Testament "the kingdom of God," "the kingdom of heaven," "the kingdom of God's dear Son," "church of God," "the body of Christ," etc. We do not mean to say that the phrases "kingdom of God" and "the kingdom of heaven" always mean the same thing—namely, the church in all its parts; on the contrary, they frequently occur, especially in the *parables* of the Saviour, when only a particular feature or constituent *part* of the kingdom is indicated. A few examples illustrative of this position may be examined with profit. Jesus said:

"It is easier for a camel to go through the eye of a needle than for a rich man to enter into the kingdom of God." Matt. xix:24.

"Many shall come from the east and west, and shall sit down with Abraham, Isaac, and Jacob, in the kingdom of heaven; but the children of the kingdom shall be cast out into outer darkness: there shall be weeping and gnashing of teeth." Matt. viii:11, 12.

These passages with others which we might give, have manifest reference to the kingdom of *ultimate glory*. On another occasion, Jesus said: "The kingdom of God cometh not with observation: neither shall they say, Lo here! or, Lo there! for, behold, the kingdom of God is among you." Luke xvii:20, 21. This, with other passages which we might give, had reference to Jesus as King, who had come not with pride, ostentation, and show, but was then among them.

In the parable of the *sower* and the *seed*, a record of which we have in Matt. xiii, the gospel, as the law of induction into and government for those in the kingdom, is the feature represented. The parable of the *tares* and the parable of the *fisher's net*, found in the same chapter, have reference to the *character* of those in the kingdom, some of whom were *good* and others *bad*.

The parable of the *mustard-seed* and the parable of the *leaven* hid in three measures of metal, refer to the *growth* or extension of the kingdom.

With one example from Paul, we close these illustrations. He says: "The kingdom of God is not meat and drink, but righteousness, and peace, and joy in the Holy Ghost." Rom. xiv:17. Here the words "kingdom of God" refer to the *characteristics* of those in the kingdom. Other examples might be given, but these are quite sufficient to show that, while the phrases "kingdom of God" and "kingdom of heaven" are sometimes synonymous with *church,* they must *not always* be so understood.

As respects law, the church is truly a *kingdom*—an *absolute monarchy.* All its laws emanate from the King, and its subjects have no part in making them. There is no *representative democracy* connected with it. No council, convention, or legislative assembly has power or authority to abolish, alter, or amend them. It is a *kingdom,* not a *republic.* As respects *organization,* it is called a *body,* of which Christ is the *head,* all its subjects are *members,* and *in* which dwells the Spirit, by which it is vitalized or kept alive, and without which it would become a dead body. As respects relationship to the world, it is fitly called the church—*"ecclesia,"* or *called out* of the world, and is, therefore, not of the world. It was *set up, established, organized, begun* on earth, in the city of Jerusalem, on the day of Pentecost, by the authority of the Lord Jesus Christ, under the immediate agency of the apostles, guided by the direct inspiration of the Holy Spirit. A brief examination of the teaching of the Scriptures on this subject is important to the development of "the gospel as the power of God unto salvation," and will repay the attentive reader.

That we may properly appreciate the importance of arriving at truth on this subject, it may not be amiss to state that there are several theories differing from each other with regard to the time when this kingdom was set up, each one of which has its own doctrines growing out of its own theory. And if we are correct in the proposition stated as to *time* and *place,* it follows that all theories setting up the kingdom, organizing the body, or beginning the proclamation of the gospel, and laying, first, the foundation of the church at any other time or place, are not only wrong, but all doctrines growing out of such theories are false. And if we succeed in uprooting the trunk, all the branches drawing support from the parent trunk fall with it. To be more specific:

One theory begins the church in an *eternal covenant,* as its advocates call it, which is supposed to have been entered into between God and His Son before the foundation of the world was laid. It is assumed that in this covenant the salvation of the *elect* was *unconditionally* secured, and the balance of the human race consigned to eternal misery. If God and His Son were the contracting parties to the covenant, and the final destiny of man, the consideration about which the covenant was made, is it not passingly strange that the devil should be the largest beneficiary? He was not represented in the covenant at all, unless God represented him, or acted as his proxy. We are told that few go in at the strait gate, while many go the broad road and enter in at the wide gate that leadeth to destruction. If this be the result of such a covenant, why was God so liberal to the devil and so illiberal to His Son? But we do not propose to discuss these theories here: we call the attention of the reader to them, at the threshold of our investigation, for the purpose of awakening attention to the importance of arriving at the truth in the premises. Passing from this theory, then, there is another which establishes the kingdom or church of God in the family of Abraham. The advocates of this theory insist that, as *infants* were included in the provisions of the covenant made by God with Abraham, they are in the church now, and hence comes the doctrine of *infant church membership.* They further assume that *baptism came in the room of circumcision,* and, as infants were then circumcised, they must now be baptized; and thus some of them think they have Divine authority for infant baptism—which will be considered in due time.

Others set up the kingdom in the days of John the Baptist; hence the name "Baptist Church," etc. Thus we see that the time when the kingdom of God was set up on the earth is a most important matter—one that, rightly understood, would tend much to heal the wounds in the body caused by the many unfortunate divisions among those professing to be the people of God.

It is said: "Behold, the days come, saith the Lord, when I will make a new covenant with the house of Israel and with the house of Judah: not according to the covenant that I made with their fathers in the day when I took them by the hand to lead them out of the land of Egypt; because they continued not in my covenant, and I regarded them not, saith the Lord." Heb. viii:8, 9. Then we need not look to the covenant made at the time of the deliverance of God's people from Egyptian bondage for the beginning of the covenant under which the church of our day was established. It was to be a new covenant, and not according to that one. It was to be "a more excellent ministry"—"a covenant which was established upon better promises." Ver. 6. And wherein was it a better covenant? The old was "a figure for the time then present, in which were offered both gifts and sacrifices, that could not make him that did the service perfect as pertaining to the conscience; which stood only in meats and drinks, and divers washings and carnal ordinances, imposed on them until the time of reformation." Chap. ix:9, 10. "But in those sacrifices there is a remembrance again made of sins every year; for it is not possible that the blood of bulls and of goats should take away sins." Chap. x:3, 4. But "in that he saith, A new covenant, he hath made the first old. Now that which decayeth and waxeth old is ready to vanish away." This old covenant was ready to vanish away and give place to the new one. And what were to be its provisions? "This is the covenant that I will make with the house of Israel after those days, saith the Lord; I will put my laws in their mind, and write them in their hearts; and I will be to them a God, and they shall be to me a people: and they shall not teach every man his neighbor, and every man his brother, saying, Know the Lord: for all shall know me, from the least to the greatest. For I will be merciful to their unrighteousness, and their sins and their iniquities will I remember no more." Heb. viii:10-12. Under the old covenant, sins were only pardoned a year at a time, and thus were remembered again; but, under the new and better covenant, God has promised to be merciful to their unrighteousness, and sins and iniquities once pardoned are to be *remembered no more.*

But we did not come here to follow out the superior advantages of one and the disadvantages of the other, but to learn—as we think we have—that we live, not under the *same* covenant that was made with the Jews, under which they offered sacrifices according to the law, but under a *new* covenant, *superior* in its provisions to the old. We have now arrived at the proper point to look for the *beginning* of this *new* and *better* order of things.

THE ESTABLISHMENT OF THE CHURCH

During the time the Jews were held captive by Nebuchadnezzar, king of Babylon, God made known to him, in a dream—which was interpreted by Daniel, one of the Jewish captives—certain great national changes that were to take place, in which were foretold the destruction of his own government and three others which were to consecutively arise after it; and finally the establishment of the kingdom of God, which was never to be destroyed, but was to fill the whole earth and stand forever. As these kingdoms were to succeed each other in regular chronological order, we have only to follow them up and see the rise and fall of each, noting carefully the *dates* as we proceed, in order to see *when* God established His kingdom.

For a full account of this remarkable revelation from God, the reader is referred to the whole of the second chapter of Daniel. We have only room to transcribe the dream, and the interpretation of it, contained in the 31st to the 45th verse, inclusive:

"Thou, O king, sawest, and behold, a great image whose brightness was excellent, stood before thee; and the form thereof was terrible. This image's head was of fine gold, his breast and his arms of silver, his belly and his thighs of brass, his legs of iron, his feet part of iron and part of clay. Thou sawest till that a stone was cut out without hands, which smote the image upon his feet, that were of iron and clay, and brake them in pieces. Then was the iron, the clay, the brass, the silver, and the gold broken to pieces together, and became like the chaff of the summer threshing floors, and the wind carried them away; that no place was found for them: and the stone that smote the image became a great mountain, and filled the whole earth. This is the dream, and we will tell the interpretation thereof before the king. Thou, O king, art a king of kings: for the God of heaven hath given thee a kingdom, power, and strength, and glory; and wheresover the children of men dwell, the beasts of the field and the fowls of the heaven hath he given into thine hand, and hath made thee ruler over them all. Thou art this head of gold. And after thee shall arise another kingdom inferior to thee, and another third kingdom of brass, which shall bear rule over all the earth. And the fourth kingdom shall be strong as iron; forasmuch as iron breaketh in pieces and subdueth all things: and as iron that breaketh all these, shall it break in pieces and bruise. And whereas thou sawest the feet and toes part of potter's clay and part of iron: the kingdom shall be divided; but there shall be in it of the strength of the iron, forasmuch as thou sawest the iron mixed with the miry clay: and as the toes of the feet were part of iron and part of clay, so the kingdom shall be partly strong and partly broken. And whereas thou sawest iron mixed with the miry clay, they shall mingle themselves with the seed of men: but they shall not cleave one to another, even as iron is not mixed with clay. And in the days of these kings shall the God of heaven set up a kingdom which shall never be destroyed: and the kingdom shall not be left to other people, but it shall break in pieces and consume all these kingdoms, and it shall stand forever. Forasmuch as thou sawest that the stone was cut out of the mountain without hands, and that it brake in pieces the iron, the brass, the clay, the silver and the gold; the great God hath made known to the king what shall come to pass hereafter: and the dream is certain and the interpretation thereof sure."

Now, it will be observed that the Lord here tells Nebuchadnezzar that he was the head of gold. This kingdom embraced the countries of Chaldea, Assyria, Syria, Arabia, and Palestine, and ended with the death of Belshazzar, B.C. 538 years, when it was overthrown by Cyrus, king of Persia, and Darius, king of Media. These two kings were kinsmen; and after they had thus broken up the Chaldean or Babylonian empire, the government assumed the name of the Medo-Persian kingdom, that was represented by the breast and arms of the image, and was the second government in numerical or chronological order. It began, as we have seen, 538 years B.C., and was overthrown by Alexander (son of Philip), king of Macedon, B.C. 331 years. But he died B.C. 323 years, having reigned only a little more than seven years. But as the Macedonian empire is represented by the belly and *thighs* of the image, we must look for a division in it. Hence, after the death of Alexander, his government became divided among his generals. Cassander had Macedon and Greece; Lysimachus had Thrace and those parts of Asia which lay on the Hellespont and Bosphorus; Ptolemy had Egypt, Lybia, Arabia, Palestine, and Syria; Seleucus had Babylon, Media, Persia, Susiana, Assyria, Bactria, Hyrcania, and all other provinces, even to the Ganges. Thus this empire founded on the ruins of the

Medo-Persian "had rule over all the earth." But as the thighs of brass in the image represent the divided state of the empire, the above four divisions are soon merged into two, viz: those of the Lagidae and Seleucidae, reigning in Egypt and Syria. A distinguished historian says: "Their kingdom was no more a different kingdom than the parts differ from the whole. It was the same government still continued. They who governed were still Macedonians."

When did these thighs end? In the year B.C. 30, Octavius Caesar overturned the Lagidae, and Egypt, one of the *thighs*, became a Roman province. Not many years after this (we have forgotten the date; our pencil notes here have become dim, and we have not the history by us just now to which to refer), Pompey overthrew the Seleucidae, dethroned Antiochus, and thus Syria, the other thigh, became a Roman province. Thus we find the Roman government succeeded the Macedonian, and is evidently the fourth kingdom represented by the feet and toes of the image that stood before Nebuchadnezzar, composed of iron and clay.

Without going into a minute application of the Scriptures to each of these governments, it is sufficient for our present purpose to show, as we think we have done, that these governments did, in their order, overthrow and succeed each other. Then, as they are numbered first, second, third, and fourth in the interpretation given by Daniel, it is certain that they, following in that numerical order, and each one consuming its predecessor, are the kingdoms indicated. And as they all merged into the Roman government thirty years before the coming of Christ, it follows that *some time after that period, and during the existence of the Roman government, we may look for the God of heaven to set up a kingdom.*

We can not go back behind the date of this dream to look for the kingdom, for it was to smite the image on its *feet*—that is, it was to be set up during the existence of and come in contact with the government represented by the *feet*. And Daniel tells Nebuchadnezzar that the whole affair was designed to make "known to the king what shall come to pass *hereafter*"—not before the foundation of the world, or in the days of Abraham, but *hereafter*.

As this prophecy brings us down to within thirty years of the coming of Christ to establish the government—in the time of which the kingdom of heaven was set up—we may expect the harbinger of the Saviour soon to commence preaching about it. Accordingly, Matthew says: "In those days came John the Baptist preaching in the wilderness of Judea, and saying, Repent ye, for the kingdom of heaven is at hand." Matt. iii: 1, 2. Here we find John announcing the near approach of the kingdom for the origin of which we have been looking. But we are sometimes told that John set up the kingdom himself. Let us hear the Saviour on this point. After John was cast into prison, and his labors were at an end, Jesus taught his disciples to pray as follows: "Our Father, who art in heaven, Hallowed be thy name. Thy *kingdom come*," etc. Matt. vi:10. Would Jesus have instructed his disciples to pray for the kingdom to come if it had already come? It is true, many repeat this petition *now* who believe that the kingdom has long since come; but surely such persons think little about what they are saying. Like the schoolboy, they find it in their lesson and must repeat it. We may pray for the kingdom to be advanced in the earth, but we can not pray for it to come after it has come, any more than we may pray for God to send down the Spirit, since it was sent from heaven to the earth on the day of Pentecost, and has been here ever since. Once more: When John heard of Jesus, he sent to Him to know if He were the Christ, or whether he should look for another. After Jesus had answered and sent the messengers away, He said to those around Him: "Verily I say unto you, Among them that are born of women, there hath not risen a greater than John the Baptist: notwithstanding, he that is least in the kingdom of heaven is greater than he." Matt. xi:11. Then, as he that was least in the kingdom of heaven was greater than John, it follows that He was not in it; and surely He did not set up the kingdom and fail to enter it himself. Nor were the disciples of Jesus, though they had left all and followed Him, in the kingdom, for He once rebuked them, saying: "Verily I say unto you, Except ye be converted and become as a little child, ye shall not enter into the kingdom of heaven." Matt. xviii:3. He did not say, "Except ye be converted, etc., you shall be *turned out* of the kingdom," but, "ye shall not *enter*" it—clearly showing that they were not then in it, which surely they would have been had it then existed. They were to seek the kingdom (Luke xii:31), for it was the Father's good pleasure to give it to them (ver. 32). Persons do not seek for that which they already have, but may seek for that which is to be given or has been promised to them. As the kingdom had been promised to them, and they were still to seek it, we conclude that it did not then exist.

But we are not done with the Saviour's teaching on this point yet. When He sent forth the twelve apostles, under their restricted commission, He told them what to preach; and it is worthy of remark that the language is, *verbatim*, the same as that used by John—"The kingdom of heaven is at hand." Matt. x:7. When He sent out the seventy, He gave them, in substance, the same message—"The kingdom of God is come nigh unto you." Luke x:9. Now, it is very apparent that the object of all this teaching was to let the people know that the kingdom was approaching, that they might be prepared for it when it came. But when He came into the coasts of Cesarea Philippi, and learned, by inquiry, what was said of Him, and Peter confessed Him as "the Christ, the Son of the living God," He said to Peter, "Upon this rock I *will build* my church." Matt. xvi:18. This language is too plain to admit of doubt. There would be no sense in saying, "I will build my house in a certain place" if it had been built long years before; and there would have been just as little sense in the language used by the Saviour if He had intended to teach that His church or kingdom had been built prior to that time. Thus we must press our investigations still further—its erection is still later than the time He used this language.

Six days before His transfiguration He said: "Verily I say unto you, That there be some of them that stand here, which shall not taste of death till they have seen the kingdom of God come with power." Mark ix:1. Here we not only find Him teaching that the coming of the kingdom was yet future, but that it would come in the life-time of those then living. But later—when Jesus instituted the Supper—He said: "For I say unto you, I will not drink of the fruit of the vine until the kingdom of God shall come." Luke xxii:18. Thus we see that near the end of the Saviour's sojourn on the earth He still taught the people *to look ahead* for the coming of the kingdom; and we next propose to show that those to whom He spake so understood His teaching: "And as they heard these things, He added and spake a parable, because He was nigh unto Jerusalem, and because they thought that the kingdom of God should immediately appear." Luke xix:11. Thus we see they understood it was yet future, but thought its approach nearer than it really was. Coming down, now, to the time of His death, "Joseph of Arimathea, an honorable counselor, which also waited for the kingdom of God, came and went in boldly unto Pilate, and craved the body of Jesus." Mark xv:43; Luke xxiii:51. Here was a man of capacity to understand the Saviour's teaching, who *waited for* the kingdom to come even after the Saviour was dead. Surely, he was not waiting for that which had already come.

Let us next examine a prediction made by the prophets: "And it shall come to pass in the last days, that the mountain of the Lord's house shall be established in the top of the mountains, and shall be exalted above the hills; and all nations shall flow unto it. And many people shall go and say, Come ye, and let us go up to the mountain of the Lord, to the house of the God of Jacob; and he will teach us of his ways, and we will walk in his path; for out of Zion shall go forth the law, and the word of the Lord from Jerusalem." Isa. ii:2, 3. This very interesting prophecy was uttered by Micah (chap. iv: 1, 2), in very nearly the same words: "But in the last days it shall come to pass, that the mountain of the house of the Lord shall be established in the top of the mountains, and it shall be exalted above the hills; and the people shall flow unto it. And many nations shall come and say, Come, and let us go up to the mountain of the Lord, and to the house of the God of Jacob; and he will teach us of his ways, and we will walk in his paths: for the law shall go forth of Zion, and the word of the Lord from Jerusalem." This prophecy gives us to know that the establishment of the mountain of the Lord's house was to take place in the last days; and we can see no other *last days* that could have been intended, only the last days of the Jewish dispensation—the last days of that covenant which Paul tells us had waxed old and was ready to vanish away.

But we get another important item of information from this prophecy; and for the sake of it, we have delayed the introduction of the whole, until the mind of the reader was prepared for it. *The word of the Lord was to go forth from Jerusalem.* Hence, when Jesus was instructing and preparing His apostles for the establishment of His kingdom, "He said unto them, Thus it is written, and thus it behooved Christ to suffer, and to rise from the dead the third day; and that repentance and remission of sins should be preached in his name among all nations, beginning at Jerusalem." Luke xxiv:46, 47. Jerusalem is the place from which the word of the Lord was to go forth, and it consisted in preaching repentance and remission of sins among all nations, and this was to begin there. Jerusalem *is the place,* beyond the possiblity of a doubt.

But to establish a kingdom, there must be *persons* duly qualified for the work; hence Jesus, at the beginning of His personal ministry, selected twelve men and took them under His immediate care, and for three years and a half instructed them in the work they were to perform—not only so, but He selected one of them to lead off as foreman, in the opening of His kingdom, and said to him: "Thou art Peter, and upon this rock I will build my church, and the gates of hell shall not prevail against it; and I will give thee the keys of the kingdom of heaven, and whatsoever thou shalt bind on earth shall be bound in heaven, and whatsoever thou shalt loose on earth, shall be loosed in heaven." To Peter, then, was given the exaltd privilege of first opening the kingdom, with power to bind and to loose on the earth, with the assurance that his act would be recognized in heaven. Notwithstanding Peter had been a constant attendant upon the teaching of the Saviour, this work was too important to be entrusted to unaided human frailty—man is imperfect and forgetful: an important item of instruction given by the Lord might be forgotten by Peter when the final destiny of the human race trembled in awful suspense upon his decision—hence says the Saviour: "But the Comforter, which is the Holy Ghost, whom the Father will send in my name, he shall teach you all things, and bring all things to your remembrance, whatsoever I have said unto you." John xiv:26. Thus he is secured against the frailties and imperfections of human recollection. But operations are to begin at Jerusalem; therefore he must go there and wait the time appointed of the Father; hence Jesus says to him, with the other apostles: "Behold, I send the promise of my Father upon you: but tarry ye in the city of Jerusalem, until ye be endued with power from on high." Luke xxiv:49. "Jerusalem is the place you are to begin, Peter; therefore go there, and wait for the coronation of Jesus Christ as King of the kingdom to be set up; then He will send you the promised aid from on high." Shall we go with him to the appointed place and wait the developments of the time when Jesus is crowned King of kings and Lord of lords? Without a king there can not be a kingdom. "He led them out as far as Bethany, and he lifted up his hands, and blessed them. And it came to pass, that while he blessed them, he was parted from them, and carried up into heaven." Luke xxiv:50, 51. Angelic hosts escort Him to the throne appointed of His Father. On nearing the portals of the skies, His attendants demand admittance, saying: "Lift up your heads, O ye gates; and be ye lifted up, ye everlasting doors; and the King of glory shall come in." Before the porters of heaven admit the parties demanding entrance, they ask, "Who is the King of glory?" The attendants answer, "The Lord strong and mighty, the Lord mighty in battle." And again the demand is repeated: "Lift up your heads, O ye gates; even lift them up, ye everlasting doors; and the King of glory shall come in." Then the question again comes from within, "Who is the King of glory?" and the same announcement is made: "The Lord of hosts, he is the King of glory." Ps. xxiv. He is admitted, crowned King—angels, principalities, and powers are made subject to Him. The Holy Spirit is dispatched with the joyful tidings from heaven to Jerusalem—"And they were all filled with the Holy Ghost, and began to speak with other tongues, as the Spirit gave them utterance." Acts ii:4. And what did they say? Here is Peter, the proper person, at Jerusalem, the proper place; and Jesus, as King, is on His throne—surely, all things are ready now. Among other things, Peter said: "Therefore being by the right hand of God exalted, and having received of the Father the promise of the Holy Ghost, he hath shed forth this, which ye now see and hear. For David is not ascended into the heavens: but he saith himself, The Lord said unto my Lord, Sit thou on my right hand, until I make thy foes thy footstool. Therefore let all the house of Israel know assuredly, that God hath made that same Jesus, whom ye have crucified, both Lord and Christ."

THE ESTABLISHMENT OF THE CHURCH

Acts ii:33-36. Here, for the first time, is the grand fact announced to the denizens of earth—that Jesus reigns in the kingdom of heaven. Persons ask admittance: Peter uses the keys of the kingdom; they enter and are added to *them*. Them! who? The disciples—the hundred and twenty. After this, the church being organized, the "Lord was adding daily those that were being saved."* If, prior to this time, the kingdom had been in existence, it would have been a *kingdom without a king*, for Jesus was not then crowned King—"the Holy Ghost was not yet given (John vii:39); because that Jesus was not yet glorified." Then, if the "body, which is the church" (Col. i:24), had existed prior to the glorification of Jesus, and the descent of the Holy Spirit, it would have been a *body without a spirit*, and therefore a *dead body*, as "the body without the spirit is dead." Jas. ii:26. Again: "He is the head of the body, the church." Col. i:18. When did he become the head of the body? "The eyes of your understanding being enlightened; that ye may know what is the hope of your calling, and what the riches of the glory of his inheritance in the saints, and what is the exceeding greatness of his power to us-ward who believe, according to the working of his mighty power, which he wrought in Christ, when he raised him from the dead, and set him at his own right hand in heavenly places, far above all principality, and power, and might, and dominion, and every name that is named, not only in this world, but also in that which is to come: and hath put all things under his feet, and gave him to be head over all things to the church." Eph. i:18-22. Then, as He was never given to be the head of the church until He was set at His Father's right hand, and obtained His exalted name, it follows that, if the church or body existed prior to that time, it was *a body without a head*. And for the very same reason, if the kingdom, church, or body was not then set up, Jesus was a king without a kingdom, and a head without a body, and the Spirit was upon the earth without a habitation or dwelling-place.

One more point, and we are done on this branch of the subject. When Peter was making his defense before his brethren, for going down to the house of Cornelius—in speaking of the

---

* Twofold New Testament, by T. S. Green—Acts ii: 47.

events that occurred there, he says: "And as I began to speak, the Holy Ghost fell on them, as on us at the beginning." Acts xi:15. Here we have the very word *beginning*, referring to the time when the Holy Ghost fell on the disciples on the day of Pentecost. The Holy Ghost fell on them on that day, and Peter refers to it as at the *beginning*. Beginning of what? Let him who thinks the kingdom or church began some time prior to the day of Pentecost, tell us what *beginning* is here referred to.

Prior to the day of Pentecost the church was always spoken of as a thing of the future; subsequently it was spoken of as having a real existence. John, Jesus, and the disciples preached that it was *at hand*. We have seen that Jesus taught His disciples to pray *for it to come*—said He *would build* it—that it *should come* in the life-time of those present. After that day, Luke says "great fear came upon all the *church*." Acts v:11. "There was a great persecution against the *church* which was at Jerusalem." Acts viii:1. "Tidings of these things came unto the ears of the *church* which was in Jerusalem." Acts xi:22. "A whole year they assembled themselves with the *church* and taught much people." Ver. 26. Paul addressed his letters to "the *church* of God at Corinth." 1 Cor. i:2; 2 Cor. i:1. And he said: "God is not the author of confusion, but of peace, as in all the *churches* of the saints. Let your women keep silence in the *churches*." 1 Cor. xiv:33, 34. He admonished them to "give none offense, neither to the Jews, nor to the Gentiles, nor to the *church* of God." 1 Cor. x:32. "If any man seem to be contentious, we have no such custom, neither the *churches* of God." 1 Cor. xi:16. "I persecuted the *church* of God." 1 Cor. xv:9; Gal. i:13. These passages, with others which we might present, show that after Pentecost the church was spoken of as a thing of *real existence*. Why this difference in the phraseology of the New Testament before and after that day? If the church existed before Pentecost, why was it not spoken of in the same way it was afterward? Before that day, Jesus charged Peter to feed His lambs—feed His sheep (John xxi:15, 16); after that time, Paul exhorted the elders "to *feed the church* of God." Acts xx:28. Before the day of Pentecost, Jesus said, "On this rock I *will build my church;*" after that day, Paul told the church at Corinth that it was "God's *building*" (1 Cor. iii:9)—"the *temple* of God." Ver. 16. Before

Pentecost, Jesus said to the disciples that, unless they were converted, they *should not enter into* the kingdom (Matt. xviii:3); but after that, Paul told the disciples that they had been translated *into* the kingdom. (Col. i:12). Why were the disciples spoken of as *having to enter* the kingdom before Pentecost, but as *in it* afterward? These distinctions might be greatly multiplied, but enough has been presented to show a difference in style inexplicable upon any other hypothesis than that the church began on the day of Pentecost, and was therefore spoken of as a thing future before that day, but as an existing organization afterward.

We are not unaware that there are scriptures which seem to indicate the existence of the kingdom at the time Jesus was personally on the earth; but we take it to be an inflexible rule of biblical interpretation that no obscure passage must be so construed as to come in contact with a principle, doctrine, or fact clearly taught elsewhere. The Bible must be harmonious in all its teaching, otherwise it can not be of God. Hence we need not seek a theory contradicting any thing so clearly taught as is the fact that the church of God began on the earth, in Jerusalem, on the first Pentecost after the crucifixion of Jesus. Such efforts are much more likely to make skeptics than Christians of the untaught.

Before the temple was built by Solomon, all the material was so prepared that when every piece was placed in its position the building was complete without the sound of a hammer in its construction. All parties agree that this was typical of the church of God. If so, we may expect to find material prepared for the Christian temple before its erection. John began the preparation of this material, Jesus completed it. John preached the baptism of repentance for the remission of sins (Mark i:4), and the sins of those who complied with the terms imposed were remitted, in accordance with the gospel preached by him. When he was cast into prison and his ministry ceased, that of Jesus began (Matt. iv:12-17); hence, in *this respect*, the ministry of Jesus was but a continuance of the preparatory ministry begun by John. While Jesus did many things which John could not do, their preaching, in this respect, was the same. Jesus established His claims to be King—gave laws for the establishment and government of His church—qualified men to organize it—entered heaven with His blood, where He made the atonement for the world—was crowned King, and sent the Holy Spirit with the news of His coronation—thus perfecting the preparations for the building of His temple. The builders, guided by the Holy Spirit, put the material in position and the spiritual temple stood forth. As the material which composed the temple of Solomon was prepared before it was placed together, so the material which first constituted the temple of God was made ready by John and Jesus for position in it. Hence it existed in its materials before the day of Pentecost; but, as an organic structure before that time, it had no existence.

We could give much testimony from learned men who differ from us on other matters, yet agree with us here. In Smith's Dictionary of the Bible, article Church, we find the following paragraph:

"From the gospels we learn little in the way of detail as to the kingdom which was to be established. It was in the great forty days which intervened between the resurrection and the ascension that our Lord explained specifically to his apostles the things pertaining to the kingdom of God (Acts i:3); that is, His future church. *Its origin:*—The removal of Christ from the earth had left His followers a shattered company, with no bond of external or internal cohesion, except the memory of the Master whom they had lost, and the recollection of his injunctions to unity and love, together with the occasional glimpses of His presence which were vouchsafed them. They continued together, meeting for prayer and supplication, and waiting for Christ's promise of the gift of the Holy Ghost. They numbered in all some 140 persons—namely, the eleven, the faithful women, the Lord's mother, his brethren, and 120 disciples. They had faith to believe that there was a work before them which they were about to be called to perform, and, that they might be ready to do it, they filled up the number of the twelve by the appointment of Matthias 'to be a true witness,' with the eleven, 'of the resurrection.' The day of Pentecost is the birthday of the Christian church. The Spirit, who was then sent by the Son from the Father, and rested on each of the disciples, combined them once more into a whole—combined them as they never had been before combined, by an internal and spiritual bond of cohesion. Before, they had been individual followers of Jesus; now they became his mystical body, animated by his Spirit."

CHAPTER VII.

THE IDENTITY OF THE CHURCH

We have found that the *Church of God* was organized in the city of Jerusalem, on the day of Pentecost; and it is worthy of note that all the forms of speech used to indicate it are in the singular number; thus: "kingdom of heaven," "kingdom of God;" "kingdom of his dear Son," "church of God," "household of faith," "house of God," "the pillar and ground of the truth," "the body," "temple of God," etc., etc. Where the word *churches* occurs in the plural number, it has reference to the congregations worshiping at particular places, and not to the kingdom, body, or church, which has been the object of our search. Paul tell his Ephesian brethren that "there is one body, and one Spirit, even as ye are called in one hope of your calling; one Lord, one faith, one baptism, one God and Father of all." Eph. iv:4-6. The connection in which we here have the phrase "one body" as clearly shows that there is *but* one body as does the phrase "one God" show that there is *but* one God. But, in Rom. xii:4, 5, we are told that, "as we have many members in one body, and all members have not the same office: so we, being many, are *one body* in Christ." And again: "But now are they many members, yet *but one body.*" 1 Cor. xii:20. Thus we see that language can not more clearly indicate any thing than that Christ has but one organized body on the earth. What constitutes this one body? What is this one body? With reference to Christ, Paul says "he is the head of the body, the church." Col. i:18. And again, verse 24, he says: "Who now rejoice in my sufferings for you, and fill up that which is behind of the afflictions of Christ in my flesh for his body's sake, which is the church." Here we are expressly told that the body is the church. Once more: "And hath put all things under his feet, and gave him to be the head over all things to the church, which is his body, the fulness of him that filleth all in all." Eph. i:22, 23. Here the order is reversed—the church is His body. Then the *church* and *body* are the same is His body. Then the *church* and *body* are the same, and are used interchangeably; but the *unity* of thought is quite apparent. "The body," "the church"—not *a church, some church,* or *any church*, but THE CHURCH. There being but one body, and that being the church, it follows that there is but *one church*. Then if, in kindness, we may be plain and candid, without being offensive, we would like to inquire how it comes to pass that there is a Catholic Church, an Episcopalian Church, several kinds of Presbyterian Churches, several kinds of Methodist Churches, several kinds of Baptist Churches, etc., etc., each claiming Divine authority for its existence, and yet all acknowledging the Bible to be true, and an *infallible rule of faith* and practice. Is there not something wrong here? We hear Paul addressing "the church of God at Corinth," but he never speaks to or instructs the Presbyterian Church, the Methodist Church, the Baptist Church; nor does he ever address any class of persons as a church at all, only those who compose the one body, or kingdom, of which Christ is the Head and King.

But we are told that these sectarian organizations are *branches* of the one church, or body, of which Paul speaks. This makes the matter no better, but rather worse. Paul nowhere addresses the *Presbyterian branch* of the church, the *Methodist branch* of the church, or the *Baptist branch* of the church. In order to sensibly speak of branches of the church, one of three figures must be before the mind, viz.: a tree with trunk and branches, a vine with its stem and branches, or a stream with its tributaries. A tree and its branches and a vine and its branches are so nearly alike in their illustrative character, that we may consider them together, while we see if either or both of them will symbolize the church. When did these branch organizations shoot forth? We do not know that we can correctly date the origin of all of them; nor is it necessary that we should go back to the beginning of the Roman Catholic and Greek Churches; for those who advocate the branch church doctrine do not admit these to be sister branches with them at all. According to history, the

Episcopal Church began about the year 1521.
Presbyterianism began about the year 1537.
Scotch Presbyterianism about the year 1558.
English Presbyterianism about the year 1572.
Baptistism began about the year 1611.
Quakerism began about the year 1655.

Methodism began about the year 1729.

Secederism began about the year 1733.

Cumberland Presbyterianism, according to Burder, began on Cumberland River about the year 1810.

The church of God began in Jerusalem about the year 33.

We believe these embrace the most prominent organizations of this country, and we see that we can not get a single one, except the church of God, further back than the sixteenth century. Was the church without branches for the first fifteen hundred years of its existence? and did she bring no fruit during that time? Neither tree nor vine can maintain its life and bring forth fruit without branches; yet if these organizations are the branches, then it follows that the church was a branchless, fruitless, lifeless thing until they came into being. Since then, in one-third of that time, it has put forth a host of branches, and branches of branches, and branches of branches of branches, until they have become so thick that we are inclined to think that the pruning-hook is necessary. Each of the branches differs in constitution, character, and fruit from all the others. Such a tree! such a tree!! What a monstrosity!!! A tree bearing apples, pears, peaches, apricots, quinces, plums, cherries, berries, nuts of all kinds, "hard-shell" and soft, melons, pumpkins, squashes, etc., etc., and yet all come from the same "incorruptible seed"—the word of God! Strange as such a sight would appear, it would take a tree with more different kinds of branches and fruits than we have mentioned to represent the church of God, if it has as many branch churches growing out of it as there are denominations claiming to be branches of it at present. But we may be told that this variety was produced by grafting. If so, the grafting was not done by Paul, nor in accordance with his formula; for he speaks of branches which were "cut out of the olive tree which is wild by nature, and were graffed *contrary to nature* into a good olive tree." Rom. xi:24. Naturally, branches bear fruit like that of the tree from which they were taken, but Paul's grafts bore fruit contrary to nature, like the natural branches of the tree into which his grafts were inserted, they were taken from the world, and were ingrafted into Christ, the true Vine— made members of his body, or church; and, whether they were Jews or Gentiles, Christianity, or pure and undefiled religion, was the fruit. Therefore, if these sectarian parties were graffed branches of the one church of God, they would all partake of its "root and fatness," and there would be no difference in them or their fruit. One could not bear sprinkling as baptism, another pouring, another immersion, another all three, and another none at all; another, vicarious atonement, total hereditary depravity, abstract spiritual operations, unconditional election and reprobation, and many other doctrines differing as widely as these do.

Once more: Men usually take branches for grafting from other trees than the one into which they are to be inserted. It is true, Paul tells us that these natural branches that were broken off because of unbelief, might be grafted in again if they abode not in unbelief; but when they were broken off they were as foreign as the unnatural branches. Then, as the one church of God is supposed to be made up of these branch churches, where is the trunk into which they were grafted? and where is the tree from which they were taken before grafting? Is this great church tree all branches? and from what church were these branch churches taken before grafting? These branches are *churches*, according to the theory, and not *individuals*. Then whence came they? They were not taken from the church of God, for there would be no use in taking a branch from a tree and grafting it back into the same tree. Then from what tree or vine were they taken? or, to speak without a figure, from what church did these branches come, before they became part and parcel of the church made up of them? It will not do to say they were taken from the world, for they came from there as individuals, not as organizations.

And if we look at it under the figure of a great stream and its branches or tributaries, the same difficulties are in the way. As these organizations are branches, where is the main stream into which they flow? and where are the fountains whence they come? They come not from Christ, the Fountain of living water; for all the branches making up a great stream come not from the same spring, for then they would be a unit from the first, and there could be no branches at all. Then, if they come not from the inexhaustible Fountain of the human imagination, we know not their source. Let us go to Christ, whence flows the pure, limpid stream of living water, of which he who drinks shall thirst no more, but have a well of water springing up in him unto eternal life.

But we do read of *branches,* and we will now try to find what a branch is. Jesus says, "I am the vine, ye are the branches." John xv:5. Here, Jesus speaks of his disciples as branches of Him, and in Him. "Abide in me," says He, verse 4. Paul speaks of himself and brethren as having been "baptized into Christ." Rom. vi:3. His baptism did not give him a literal entrance into Christ, but it gave him entrance into His body, or the body organized by His authority, by which a relationship was created like that of a vine and its branches, or a body and its members. The same writer tells us that "by one Spirit are we all baptized into one body." 1 Cor. xii:13. By the authority and according to the teaching of one Spirit we are all baptized in water into one body, or church, and become members of it; and when speaking to the Romans, with regard to the same relationship, he says, by baptism we enter into Christ; and thus *individuals,* as such, become branches of Him, the true Vine; but an organized body of persons or an organized church can not, as such, be termed a branch of the one body, or church, of God. If any one insists that it can, then we would gladly see the scriptural process by which such a relationship is created. We are profoundly ignorant of any such instructions, as well as any precedent or authority of any kind authorizing it; hence when asked, as we frequently are, to what branch of the church we belong, we answer, that we claim to be an humble branch ourself, but know nothing about belonging to branches.

Jesus, as King, has but one kingdom; as Head, has but one body; as Bridegroom, has but one bride, and is the Author of but one church, and His people should be one people, and no divisions among them. But we have heard persons—yes, indeed, preachers too—thank God for divisions, so as to furnish an organization suited to the taste of every one, that the people may be without excuse for disobedience to the gospel. "Thank God," say they, "that there are so many different denominations, each holding a different doctrine, that all can be suited. If *our* church don't suit you, in the multitude of others you can find one suited to your fancy; so you can not fail to be suited." Such persons, to say the least of it, have a different view of this subject from that entertained by the Saviour, for He considered *unity among* His people as of the utmost importance, and prayed for it in His most solemn prayer to His Father: "Neither pray I for these alone, but for them also which shall believe on me through their word; that they all may be one, as thou, Father, art in me, and I in thee, that they also may be one in us: that the world may believe that thou hast sent me." John xvii:20, 21. Thus we see that Jesus considered divisions among those claiming to be His people as a most fruitful source of infidelity; and He was not mistaken. We verily believe that divisions among those claiming to be the people of God have made more infidels than all the writings of Voltaire, Paine, Gibbon, Hume, Owen, and every other avowed infidel that has ever wielded a pen on the earth. A celebrated Indian chief, when asked by a missionary what he thought of the religion of the Bible, said: "Go home, and agree among yourselves, and then come to me, and I will consider the matter." Hence Paul, unlike those who love and create divisions, said: "I beseech you, brethren, by the name of our Lord Jesus Christ, that you speak the same thing, and that there be no divisions among you." 1 Cor. i:10.

But we have been asked why the Lord's people are not one, if such be the import of His prayer? It is said that his Father always heard Him when He prayed, and not only heard Him, but granted His petitions, or that for which He prayed: why, then, are His people divided? Is it not possible that the class of persons for whom he prayed *are all one?* He prayed for unity among those who should believe on Him *through the words of His apostles*. He did not pray for such as might believe on Him through the traditions of their fathers, or the teachings of men, as set forth in Disciplines, Confessions of Faith, Catechisms, etc., which might be taught them from childhood. These are the sources of much of the faith that is in the world, and persons whose faith comes in this way come not within the range of the prayer made by the Saviour.

It is sometimes said that these different organizations are only as many different roads leading to heaven, and when we get there, we will not be asked which road we came, or what kind of conveyance brought us there. We are willing to grant that no such questions will be asked those who get there. But will we get there? This is the important inquiry. We would be glad to see proof of the fact that there are *as many ways to heaven as there are denominations in the world,* before we accept the doctrine as safe. The greatest Teacher that has ever condescended to instruct man on this subject said: "Strait is the gate, and narrow is *the way,* which leadeth unto life, and few there be that find it." Matt. vii:14. Again He said, "I am the way." John xiv:6. The Pharisees, recognizing this fact, said: "Master, we know that thou art true, and teachest *the way* of God in truth." Matt. xxii:16; Mark xii:14; Luke xx:21. Even wicked spirits gave testimony to the same fact, for through a damsel one said, "These men are the servants of the most high God, which show unto us *the way* of salvation." Acts xvi:17. Peter says "*the way* of truth shall be evil spoken of." 2 Pet. ii:2. Verse 15, he says certain persons had "forsaken *the right way.*" And again, verse 21, he says "it had been better for them not to have known *the way* of righteousness." Apollos "was instructed in *the way* of the Lord," but when Aquilla and Priscilla found that he knew only the baptism of John, they "expounded unto him *the way* of God more perfectly." Acts xviii:25, 26. The Holy Spirit signified that *the way* into the holiest of all was "not made manifest while the first tabernacle was standing." Heb. ix:8. Thus we find Jesus, the Holy Spirit, evil spirits, opposing Pharisees, apostles, and other disciples, all speaking of *the way* to heaven, but none of them speak of the *ways,* or in any way imply that there are more ways than one from earth to heaven; hence we conclude that there is one way, and only one way. We read of "wicked ways," "pernicious ways," "the ways of death," etc., but *the way* to heaven is so straight and narrow that it is found by few. Indeed, there can be but one straight line between any two points; hence those who do not travel the *straight* and *narrow* way, must necessarily travel crooked ways, which are marked out by men, and not by the Lord. "It is not in man that walketh to direct his steps." Jer. x:23. Surely, then, we had better walk as God directs. Guided by Him, we are safe, but there is safety nowhere else.

But there is another thought connected with these organizations which demands our attention just here. Quite a number of them recognize each other as *orthodox,* yet they differ very widely in their teaching upon matters vital to the interest of Christianity. As an intended compliment to the society of his town, a distinguished clergyman once said: "There is great unanimity among the orthodox denominations of our town—that is, Methodists, Baptists, Presbyterians, and Cumberland Presbyterians." As the Christian Church was the only church, in the town alluded to by the gentleman, not mentioned in his list of orthodox denominations, of course it was regarded by him as heterodox—so much so, indeed, that it was important to specify the orthdox denominations, lest their "good name" be injured by an association with what he was pleased to call "Campbellism" under the general name of orthodoxy. We have no complaint to make as to the motives which prompted the statement, for we doubt not that it was made, as Saul persecuted Christians, in all good conscience, but we mentioned it because it gives us a pretty fair idea of the general use, or rather *abuse*, of this term; and we propose to examine briefly the claim of these denominations to it.

We have the word *orthodoxy* from *orthos*, right, true, and *doxa*, opinion, from *dokeo*, to think; hence its import, to think right—soundness of faith—a belief in the genuine doctrines taught in the Scriptures. Modern divines, however, define the term about thus: "Orthodoxy is *my* doxy, and heterodoxy is *your* doxy, to the full extent of your difference from me. Then, as orthodoxy means to think right—a belief in the genuine doctrine taught in the Scriptures—soundness of faith, etc., it will be expected that these so-called orthodox denominations will agree among themselves; for it can not be maintained that they are all sound in faith, and believe the genuine doctrine taught in the Scriptures, while they believe and teach doctrines contradictory to each other. Things which are equal to the same thing, are equal to each other; hence if each of these is equal to the genuine doctrine of the Bible, they will be found equal to or exactly like each other. Are they thus united, speaking the same thing? We will see.

The Presbyterians say, "God, from all eternity, did, by the most wise and holy counsel of his own will, freely and unchangeably ordain whatsoever comes to pass." Confession of Faith, chap. iii, sec. 1. The Methodist, Baptists, and Cumberlands say: Not so: it comes to pass that men kill, steal, and do many other things which God has positively forbidden; hence He could not have ordained that they should thus act, and then threaten the guilty with endless punishment for carrying out His own ordination. The Presbyterians say: "By the decree of God, for the manifestation of his glory, some men and angels are predestinated unto everlasting life and others fore-ordained to everlasting death. These angels and men thus predestinated and fore-ordained are particularly and unchangeably designed, and their number is so certain and definite that it can not be either increased or diminished." Conf. Faith, chap. iii, sec. 3, 4. The others say: Not so: every man may make his election or condemnation sure, as he chooses; hence they seek with commendable zeal, to increase the number of the elect, and thus diminish the number of the reprobates. Presbyterians say: "Elect infants, dying in infancy, are regenerated and saved by Christ through the Spirit, who worketh when, where, and how he pleaseth; so, also, are all other elect persons who are incapable of being outwardly called by the ministry of the Word. Others not elected, although they may be called by the ministry of the Word, and may have some common operations of the Spirit, yet they never truly come to Christ, and therefore *never can be saved.*" Conf. Faith, chap. x, secs. 3, 4. The others say: Not so: *all* infants, dying in infancy, are saved; and all other persons, who are incapable of being outwardly called by the ministry of the Word, are saved, if they die in that condition. The Presbyterians, Baptists, and Cumberlands say: "Once in grace, always in grace"—that is, after a man is truly converted, he can not fall away and be lost. The Methodists say: Not so: let him that thinketh he standeth take heed lest he fall; for though he be a child of God, an heir of heaven, still there is great danger that he may fall away and be lost forever. The Presbyterians, Methodists, and Cumberlands say that infants of believing parents are proper subjects of baptism, and are entitled to membership in the church. Baptists say: Not so: faith is a prerequisite to baptism, and as infants can not believe, they should not be baptized. They are not capable of appreciating law, and hence are not subjects of government, and therefore are not fit subjects for the Lord's kingdom. Presbyterians, Methodists, and Cumberlands say that baptism is rightly administered by sprinkling or pouring water on the head of the candidate. Baptists say: Not so: there is as much authority for putting water on the feet as on the head for baptism. The Presbyterians, Methodists, and Cumberlands say all Christians should eat at the Lord's table together when convenient. Baptists say: Not so: Presbyterians, Methodists, and Cumberlands are good Christians, and therefore fit to surround the throne of God in heaven, but they can not eat at a Baptist table. When they come to our house, they may preach, pray, sing, exhort, and labor for us, but they shall not eat with us. Presbyterians say, "Neither are any others redeemed by Christ, effectually called, justified, adopted, sanctified, and saved, but the elect only." Conf. Faith, chap. iii, sec. 6. The others say Christ tasted death for every man. And thus we might multiply differences almost *ad infinitum*. Now is it possible that these contradictory doctrines are all the "genuine doctrine taught in the Scriptures?" They are the doctrines of these so-called orthodox denominations. *Orthodoxy* means "to believe the genuine doctrine taught in the Scriptures." One of two things is, therefore, certain: the Scriptures teach these contradictory doctrines held by these denominations, or the word *orthodoxy* is a misnomer when applied to them, and they have no right to appropriate it to themselves.

But say they: "We all believe in one great God, the Author of the Bible, the efficacy of the blood of Jesus, the operation of the Spirit in conversion, the importance of a hearty faith in Christ as the Saviour of sinners, a thorough change of heart, and repentance for sins committed, and a turning from sin to holiness: and as we are agreed in these great leading features of the genuine doctrine of the Bible, we claim to be orthodox, though we may and do differ in these minor matters of which you have been speaking." But stop! Do we not believe in these great leading features of doctrine, and insist upon them as strongly as you do, and do you not still regard us as heterodox? What, then, is the matter? It must be something else that constitutes you orthodox and us heterodox. What is it? It is this: these denominations all unite in telling penitent sinners to come to the altar, anxious-seat, or mourner's bench, to pray and be prayed for in order to remission of sins, and we tell the same persons to repent and be baptized in the name of Jesus Christ for remission. This is the true secret of the whole matter. Here is the line between so-called orthodoxy and heterodoxy. Can they find authority for their instructions in the Bible? Not if the salvation of the world depended on it. Can we find authority for our teaching in the Bible? Most assuredly we can find it, both in precept and example. We have the precise words: "Repent and be baptized, every one of you, in the name of Jesus Christ, for the remission of sins." Acts ii:38. "Arise, and be baptized, and wash away thy sins." Acts xxii:16. "He that believeth and is baptized shall be saved." Mark xvi:16. Then, if to believe and teach the genuine doctrine taught in the Scriptures constitutes orthodoxy, we are orthodox according to the true import of that term. There is no escape from this position. From our very heart have we been grieved at efforts made to make Christianity look as much like sectarianism as possible, in order to court the popular cant of orthodoxy. While we continue to believe and practice the genuine doctrine taught in the Bible, we are orthodox; but when we forsake these truths, in order to get the world to call us orthodox, we give evidence that we love the praise of men more than the approbation of God. "Tis better to show that we have a valid claim to the title, by believing the truth, than seek to make our faith look like error to induce the world to call us orthodox.

But we often hear persons say, when called on to obey the gospel, that "there are so many denominations differing so widely from each other in their teaching of what is in the Bible, that we know not which is the right church. They all teach different doctrines, and hence may all be wrong, but can not all be right, for the Bible must be harmonious in all its parts, if it be a revelation from God. There is the most perfect harmony in all His laws governing the material universe; hence we are not prepared to receive contradictory theories as law from Him for the government of His creature man, for whom all other things were made. We see not why His laws for the government of the noblest of His work, made in His own image, should be less harmonious and perfect than laws given by Him in the great book of nature. We therefore conclude that some of these organizations, if not all, are spurious; and if the trumpet give an uncertain sound, who shall prepare himself to battle?" Truly, this is a difficulty, but we beg such persons to remember that there never was a spurious coin yet that was not an imitation of something pure; hence, as there are spurious churches, we may be sure that there is one of pure origin somewhere; and we propose to assist the reader in recognizing the one body, or church of God, of which all others are counterfeits; and many of them but poorly executed, at that. We think that if we subject the church to the same criteria by which we test the identity of persons and things, it will be found with such marks, features and other means of recognition as will enable us to identify it with great certainty.

Were you hunting for a man who was personally a stranger to you, whose name was Martin Luther, and you were to find a man whose name was John Wesley, you would know at once that he was not the man for whom you were hunting, unless he had changed his name. If you knew him to bear the character of an honest man, you would continue your search until you found a man wearing the name of the man you desired to see. Then, if you wish to find "the church of God" (1 Cor. i:2; 2 Cor. i:1), and you find a church calling herself the Roman Catholic Church, the Episcopalian Church, the Baptist Church, the Presbyterian Church, the Methodist Church, or any other unscriptural name, is it not enough to cause you to suspect that you have not found the true church, and continue your search a little further? There are doubtless many *good* persons in each of these sectarian organizations, but this proves not that any one of them, or all of them together, is the church of God. God had a people in Babylon, but He admonished them to come out of her, that they partake not of her sins, and receive not of her plagues (Rev. xviii:4).

But we are told that there is nothing in names. Then why not as well expect salvation through one name as another? Speaking of Christ's name, Peter says: "Neither is there salvation in any other: for there is none other name under heaven given among men, whereby we must be saved." Acts iv:12. But if there is nothing in names, we may as well expect salvation through the name of Beelzebub as through the name of the Lord. If there is nothing in these denominational names, why think so much of them as to prefer to wear them rather than the name that honors Christ our head? Do they not tend to keep up divisions and gender strife among good people? and if there is nothing in them, why not give them up? Let us not strive about words or names, to no profit; for if there is nothing in them, we may give them up and lose nothing; but by exchanging them for the name authorized of God we may gain much.

The church is said to be "the bride, the Lamb's wife" (Rev. xxi:9), and, as such, should wear the name of her Bridegroom. "The head of the woman is the man" (1 Cor. xi:3), and hence she honors her head by wearing his name; and she dishonors her head when she refuses to wear his name and assumes another. Suppose a citizen of your neighborhood were to marry a wife, and when she is called by his name, she objects to it, saying, "There are so many branches of my husband's family that, for the sake of distinction, I prefer to be called by some other name," and thereupon assumes another—perhaps the name of some other man of her acquaintance—what would you think of her? and how would you treat her if she were your wife? Would she not have dishonored you, as her husband? dishonored him whose name she wished to assume? and dishonored and disgraced herself? and would you not regard her as unworthy to be your wife or enjoy the privileges of your house? Would she not have placed a foul blot upon her character, that would render her unworthy the confidence and respect of the virtuous and good of every age and clime? and would you not feel a little like telling her to go and live with him whose name she preferred to wear? What say you? Then if the wife of a citizen would so far dishonor her husband, and degrade and debase herself by refusing to wear the name of her husband, will it be less dishonoring to Christ for His bride to refuse to wear and be called by His name? and will it be less a blight upon the character of His bride for her to assume and wear other names than His? Will He own that organization as His bride, before His Father in the great day of the marriage, that has, owns, and willingly wears some other name than His? Will He say: "My wife hath made herself ready, and to her was granted that she should be arrayed in fine linen, clean and white: for the fine linen is the righteousness of saints." Rev. xix:7, 8. Is the assumption of other names than that of the husband, the righteousness of saints that is comparable to fine linen, clean and white, with which the church is to be clad as a bride adorned for her husband when he comes to receive her?

By the way, what will our Baptist friends do for a name now? They adopted the official name of John the Baptist as their denominational name, preferring to honor the *servant* of the Bridegroom rather than the Bridegroom himself; but the Bible Union, to which, as a church, they are fully committed, wiped the word *Baptist* from the revised edition of the New Testament, giving us *"Immerser"* instead thereof; thus, "John the Immerser." (See revised New Testament, Matt. 3:1.) Will they keep pace with the translation and adopt the name *"Immerser Church?"* This would be rather wanting in euphony, to say the least of it; but the word *Baptist* is not in the revised Scriptures put forth by the Bible Union at all. They have very correctly and faithfully translated the original into *Immerser*, and every scholar, if honest, will approve the translation. Then, will they give up the name *Baptist?* The late John Waller, of Kentucky, saw this in prospect, while president of the Bible Union, and said: "If a faithful and pure version of God's holy word takes from me my denominational name, then I say *let it go!* LET IT GO!! LET IT GO!!!" Are his surviving brethren capable of rising with him above every earthly consideration to a reception of the name given in a pure version of God's word, to the exclusion of every thing else? To this question time will furnish an answer.

Another means of knowing persons and things is by *their age*. If you wish to find a man known to be forty years old, and you meet a lad of ten or twenty years old; or a man whose whitened locks, furrowed cheeks, and bowed frame betoken that the weight of many years is upon him: in either case you will know that this is not the man you wish to see; and this assurance will be made doubly sure if he wears not the proper name. The church of God, like every thing not eternal, has its age; and as the age of a man is reckoned from the time of his birth, so the age of the church is computed from the time of its organization. We have seen that this took place on the first Pentecost after the crucifixion of the Messiah; any organization, therefore, which began at any other time, either before or since, is not the church of God. Every theory teaching that the church began at any other time, before or since, is wrong—surely wrong. Were I, or an angel from heaven, to teach that the church of Jesus Christ began in eternity—in the days of Abraham—in the days of John the Baptist—it would be error, and unworthy of reception.

Again: The record says that Jesus was born in Bethlehem of Judea; and had any one appeared at the time He came, claiming to be the Messiah, who had been born anywhere else, he would have been known to be an impostor. Even so we have seen that the church of God was organized in Jerusalem; any organization, therefore, that began at any other place, is not the church of God. Should we find a church which began in eternity—in the garden of Eden—in Mesopotamia—at Sinai—in the Wilderness of Judea—at Augsburg—at Westminster—at Geneva—at Philadelphia—on Cumberland River—or at Bethany—we would know it could not be the church of God.

Again: The church of God was "built upon the foundation of the apostles and prophets, Jesus Christ himself being the chief corner-stone." Eph. ii:20. Should we find a church claiming to be built upon the experience of uninspired men, however wise and good they may have been, it can not be the church of God.

Again: The organic law of the United States is the constitution thereof. A government having any other organic law can not be the government of the United States of America. The organic law of the church of God is the New Covenant dedicated with the blood of Jesus; hence any church having any other organic law than this covenant can not be the church of God. The church that has the Mormon Bible as its organic law can not be the church of God. Why not? Because its organic law is the production of men, and not the covenant dedicated with the blood of Jesus. Then, can a church be the church of God, the organic law of which is the Westminster Confession of Faith, the Cumberland Presbyterian Confession of Faith, the Philadelphia Confession of Faith, the Methodist Discipline, or any other human production? Will the reader ponder well this question?

The church of God is entered by a birth of water and Spirit; any church which admits to membership in any other way can not be the church of God. Hence a church that receives infants to membership can not be the church of God, because born of water they may be, but born of water and of the Spirit they can not be.

All the subjects of the church of God know the Lord, from the least to the greatest of them: this being so, a church whose members are, in part, infants, can not be the church of God, because such can not know the Lord.

This line of thought might be pursued much further; but we have seen that the church of God was organized in Jerusalem, nowhere else—on the day of Pentecost, at no other time—wears a name honoring the Bridegroom, and no other—is built upon the foundation of apostles and prophets, Jesus Christ being the chief corner-stone, and other foundation can no man lay—has for its organic law the covenant dedicated with the blood of Jesus, nothing else, more or less—has only such members as have been born of water and of the Spirit, and know the Lord, from least to greatest. An organization, therefore, which bears all these marks of identity, may be the church of God; none other can be. If such an organization can not be found, then the church of God has no existence on the earth.

Suppose a man were to come into a community with the constitution and by-laws of the Good Templars, and by teaching its doctrines he were to make a number of proselytes to its principles, and were to initiate them according to its forms, and organize them, at a particular place, as a body built thereon, what would we call the organization? A society of Good Templars. Very well. Another man comes with the Mormon Bible, and by preaching its doctrines makes proselytes to Mormonism, and organizes them upon the Mormon Bible, according to its provisions: what shall we call this organization? A Mormon Church, most certainly. Very well. But suppose another man comes with the Presbyterian Confession of Faith and preaches its doctrines, makes proselytes, and organizes them according to its provisions, what shall we call this organization? A Presbyterian Church. Very well. It would not be a Mormon Church, certainly; and why not? Because it is not organized upon the Mormon Bible or indoctrinated with its teaching. Well, another man comes, and having the Methodist Discipline, he teaches its doctrines, makes proselytes and organizes them upon it as a basis of future action: what shall we call the organization? A Presbyterian Church? No. Why not? Because it has not been taught the doctrines of or organized upon the Presbyterian Confession of Faith. But it must be called a Methodist Church, because it has been taught the doctrines of that Discipline and organized upon it.

Then suppose another man comes with the Word of God, and by preaching its doctrines he makes proselytes and organizes them according to its provisions, to keep the ordinances therein inculcated, what shall we call this organization? Shall we call it a Presbyterian Church? No; the word of God, by which it has been created, says nothing about a church called by that name. Shall we call it a Methodist Church? The word of God says nothing about a Methodist Church. Shall we call it a Baptist Church? The word of God says not a word about a Baptist Church. Then, of what church does the word of God speak? It speaks of *the church of God*. Then, as the word of God is what was taught the proselytes, in accordance with which the organization was effected, and it speaks of the church of God, is not this organization likely to adopt a name found in its organic law? If so, we feel sure that we have given such marks as will enable us to find the church which has been the object of our search. Surely, it is worthy of all acceptation, and we will not seek another, but seek an entrance into *this* one.

CHAPTER VIII.

THE NEW BIRTH.

We have said that persons enter the church of God in one way, and in only one way. In this we are sustained by the positive statement of Jesus himself. In a conversation with Nicodemus on this subject, He said: "Except a man be born again, he can not see the kingdom of God." John iii:3. And in the 5th verse He said: "Except a man be born of water and of the Spirit, he can not enter into the kingdom of God." By the phrase "kingdom of God," here, He meant the church of God, or system of government established by God's authority on the earth. To this, we suppose, all agree. When we speak of entering the kingdom of God, then, we do not mean heaven, the holiest of all into which Jesus, our adorable High Priest, hath for us entered, but the kingdom established on the earth, on the day of Pentecost. Into this kingdom or church he that is not born again *can not enter*. This kingdom is a system of government, and those who enter it must be subjects of government, capable of understanding and obeying its laws. Infants, idiots, and irresponsible persons are not such; it was not, therefore, established for them, and their salvation is not suspended upon an entrance into it. Jesus says: "Of such is the kingdom of heaven"—that is, of such as they *are now*, without being born again.

Having seen that *a man* must be born again, in order to enter the kingdom, and that it is the office of the new birth to introduce the party born into the kingdom, it follows that a more important subject never engaged the attention of man; we will, therefore, examine it carefully, and somewhat in detail, in the hope that the class of persons for whose benefit we write may ponder well what may be said, and that some good may be done in the name of Jesus.

The first thing necessary to a birth is parentage. There must be a father and a mother, or there can be nothing born. Who, then, can be our spiritual parents? Paul salutes the brethren to whom he wrote, thus: "Grace, to you and peace, from God our Father, and the Lord Jesus Christ." Rom. i:7; 1 Cor. i:3; 2 Cor. i:2; 1 Thess. i:1; 2 Thess. i:2; 1 Tim. i:2; Philem. 3. In all these places, Paul, in the same words, recognizes God as our Father; and Jesus taught His disciples to address God, in prayer, as "*Our Father* who art in heaven." Matt. vi:9. John says: "Behold what manner of love the Father hath bestowed upon us, that we should *be called the sons of God.*" And again: "Beloved, now are *we the sons of God.*" 1 John iii:1, 2. Other scripture might be quoted, but these are sufficient to identify our Father with great clearness. Paul, in his allegory with reference to the two covenants, tells us that "Jerusalem which is above is free, which is the mother of us all." Gal. iv:26. This heavenly Jerusalem, answering in the allegory to the free woman, is our spiritual mother; hence, in the 31st verse, he says: "So, then, brethren, we are not children of the bondwoman, but of the free." But, before there can be a spiritual birth, the subject must have been begotten. Man is *begotten of his father* and *born* of his *mother*, both physically and spiritually. He is not born of his father, at all, either at the same time when born of the mother or at any other time. The father may have been in his grave long ere the child is born, and how he is born of his father when born of his mother, is not very clear to us. John says: "Whosoever believeth that Jesus is the Christ is begotten of God: and every one that loveth him that begat loveth him also that is begotten of him." 1 John v:1. Also, verse 18th, it is said: "We know that whosoever is begotten of God sinneth not; but he that is begotten of God keepeth himself." In keeping with the Bible Union and Anderson's translations, we have exchanged the word *born* for *begotten,* in each of the verses quoted, and we venture to state further that there is not a place in the New Testament where the words "born of God" occurs, that a faithful translation would not render "begotten of God." In no place will the Spirit's teaching, faithfully translated, represent us as born of God—*born of our Father.* Such a thought is absurd in the very nature of things; and no one who understands the new birth, or the natural birth, from which the figure was drawn, will entertain such a thought or use such language.

But to proceed. Peter speaks of his brethren as "being born [begotten] again, not of corruptible seed, but of incorruptible, by the word of God, which liveth and abideth forever." 1 Pet. i:23. Here we learn that the word of God is the spiritual seed with which persons are spiritually begotten. And in order that we may be begotten of this incorruptible seed, our Father has ordained that human agents shall preach it to the world. Hence, in this sense, Paul calls Timothy and Titus his sons in the common faith; and also to the Corinthians, he said: "In Christ Jesus I have begotten you through the gospel." 1 Cor. iv:15. Then, when Paul preached the word of God, gospel, or incorruptible seed, to the Corinthians, and they believed and received it, they were begotten of God, and Paul speaks of them as having been begotten of him through the gospel, because he was the person through whom God made known the gospel to them. Hence says James: "Of his own will begat he us with the word of truth." Jas. i:18. The gospel is the power of God unto salvation only to those who believe it; but "how shall they believe in him of whom they have not heard? and how shall they hear without a preacher?" Rom. x:14. So, then, "it pleased God by the foolishness of preaching to save them that believe." 1 Cor. i:21. Then, when a man believes the gospel, is he not born again? "Devils believe and tremble." Jas. ii:19. They also acknowledge Jesus the Son of God. Mark iii:11. Were they born again? "Among the chief rulers also many believed on him; but because of the Pharisees they did not confess him, lest they should be put out of the synagogue; for they loved the praise of men more than the praise of God." John xii:42, 43. There are *now* many such as these chief rulers were *then;* are they born again? If a man be born again when he first believes the gospel, when is he *begotten,* and where are the elements of birth—water and Spirit —of which Jesus said he should be born? John says Jesus "came unto his own, and his own received him not: but to as many as received him, to them gave he power to become the sons of God, even to them that believe on his name." John i:11, 12. Jesus came to His own prepared people, and many of them did not receive Him, or believe on Him; but to as many of them as did receive Him by believing on his name, He gave the power or privilege of becoming sons of God. Believing on His name, then, did not make them sons, but prepared them to become sons.

When a man believes the gospel, and with meekness receives it into a good and honest heart, he is then *begotten* of God, and is prepared *to be born.* The vital principle is then implanted in the heart; but he is no more born again at that time than he was physically born the moment he was conceived. As it is not the office of a birth to give life, but to bring the subject to the enjoyment of life previously possessed in a different state, so without being begotten by the Father through the gospel, and thus having the principle of life implanted in the heart, the subject born would be dead when born, if it were possible for him to be born at all. When he is spiritually begotten, he may avail himself of the means of God's appointment for a birth, and be born into the kingdom, or he may refuse them, as he may elect. In this particular there is no analogy between a physical and a spiritual birth. In the former we have no agency in being begotten or born, nor is either in the least under our control; in the latter both are to a considerable extent, under the control of the subject. He may (as many do) refuse to hear the gospel at all, or he may refuse to believe it after he has heard it. If he believes it not, his doom was pronounced by Jesus when He said, "He that believeth not shall be damned." He may also refuse to obey it after he has believed it; if so, he "believes in vain," and his faith is dead, not having been made perfect by obedience.

Faith causes us to love and fear God, and desire to do His will; it also causes us to hate sin because it is contrary to His will; hence Peter, in speaking of the conversion of the Gentiles, said that God "put no difference between us and them, purifying their hearts by faith." Acts xv:9. This, the effect of faith, is what is called a *change of heart,* and must *precede* the new birth. But a change of heart is one thing—the new birth a different thing. The conversion of Saul of Tarsus will make apparent the truth of this position. While he was "yet breathing out threatenings and slaughter against the disciples of the Lord, he went unto the high priest, and desired of him letters to Damascus, to the synagogues, that if he found any of this way, whether they were men or women, he might bring them bound unto Jerusalem. And as he journeyed, he came near Damascus: and suddenly there shined round about him a light from heaven, and he fell to the earth, and heard a voice saying unto him, Saul, Saul, why persecutest thou me? And he said, Who art thou, Lord? And the Lord said, I am Jesus whom thou persecutest."

Acts ix:1-5. It will be seen that Saul set out on his journey with his heart filled with bitterness against the disciples, and thought he was doing right to persecute and punish them. Jesus convinced him by a miracle that He was what He professed to be. Saul's faith was changed from believing that Jesus was an impostor to the belief of the truth that He was the Son of God. This change in his faith produced a corresponding change in his heart, and he abandoned his errand of persecution, and was willing to become a disciple himself. He was then begotten of God; but was he born again? If this was the birth, when and where were the elements of birth with which he then came in contact? Three days hence he was born of water and of the Spirit, in obedience to a divine command given him by Ananias: "Arise and be baptized, and wash away thy sins, calling upon the name of the Lord." Acts xxii:16. His heart was changed by the way, but he was born again three days afterward.

Faith produces repentance, and repentance changes the practices of the subject—causes him to cease doing evil and commence doing right—but he is not yet born again. His heart may be as submissive to God's will as it can ever get to be; yes, he may be a worshiper of God to the best of his knowledge, and still not be born again. The new birth does not consist in a reformation of life. An examination of the character of Cornelius will give proof of this: "There was a certain man in Caesarea called Cornelius, a centurion of the band called the Italian band, a devout man, and one that feared God with all his house, which gave much alms to the people, and prayed to God always. He saw in a vision evidently, about the ninth hour of the day, an angel of God coming in to him, and saying unto him, Cornelius. And when he looked on him he was afraid, and said, What is it, Lord? And he said unto him, Thy prayers and thine alms are come up for a memorial before God." Acts x:1-4. Here was a devoted, charitable, praying, and God-fearing man, quite as good as the best of our day, as far as reformation of life can make them good, and yet he was not born again. But says an objector, "He *was* born again, for he saw an angel that told him so." Not exactly: he did see and converse with an angel that told him his prayers and his alms were coming up for a memorial before God, and he told him more than this—"Send men to

Joppa, and call for Simon, whose surname is Peter; who shall tell thee words, whereby thou and thy house shall be saved." Acts xi:13, 14. Was he born again and still unsaved? The promise "shall be saved" clearly shows that he was unsaved; and not only so, but he was to hear words of Peter by which he was to be saved. Was he saved by the words before he heard them? If so, why did not the angel shape the language thus: "who shall tell thee words by which you *are* or *have been saved.*" If he was at that time born again, it follows that there is no salvation in being born again, for it is as clear as language can make any thing, that he was not then saved, in the gospel sense of that word. If he was born again when the angel appeared to him, he was born again without ever having heard the gospel, and therefore without gospel faith.

Peter, in alluding to this matter, said that "God made choice among us, that the Gentiles by my mouth should hear the word of the gospel, and believe." Acts xv:7. Then Cornelius had neither heard the gospel nor believed it until Peter preached it to him, and surely a cause must be desperate that could assume that he was born again prior to that time. Then as his conduct was as good before birth as after it, it follows that the birth did not consist in a reformation of life in this case.

A birth contemplates a change of state—a transition or passing from one state to another. A change of state, then, and the beginning of a new life, is the thought conveyed by the expression "born again," and we have the same thought presented by Paul, in his epistles, in other figures, varied to suit the circumstances under which he wrote. He expresses it by the figure of marriage, Rom. vii:4; by the figure of grafting, Rom. xi:24; by the figure of adoption, Rom. viii:15, Gal. iv:5; and by the figure of translation from one government to another, Col. i:13. If an individual be married to Christ, his state is changed—he is born again. If he be taken from the wild olive-tree and grafted into the tame olive-tree, or from the world and grafted into Christ, the true Vine, his state is changed—he is born again. If he be taken—as a child—from one family and adopted into another, the family of God, his state is changed—he is born again. If he renounce his allegiance to one government, the devil's, and be legally translated into another, the kingdom of God's dear Son, his state is changed—he is born again. We might amplify each of these figures of speech, and show the correctness of the position assumed; but our space will only allow us to use a single one of the illustrations given:

A gentleman visits and seeks the hand of a lady under unfavorable circumstances, and is rejected. There may be a single cause or many causes co-operating to produce his rejection. She may be unfavorably impressed with his character, or she may worship at the shrine of another, whose heart she hopes to win, or both causes may cooperate in producing his rejection. Circumstances change, however, and she finds her first suitor an unworthy man, and she becomes disgusted by him. Meanwhile, she learns more of the character of the man she rejected, and finds him chaste in his conversation, courteous, polite, and accomplished in manners—that a social, warm, and undissembling heart controls him—that he has a mind well stored with valuable information—that he has descended from a good family—and, above all, that he is possessed of inexhaustible wealth. A knowledge of these facts changes her heart, and she now admires and loves the man she once rejected. She receives him gladly, and is willing to become the sharer of his prosperity or adversity through life, but she is not yet his wife. Though her heart is changed, her state is not; she was in the single or unmarried state, at first, and is so yet. The parents may consent, the license be secured, the proper officer be present for the solemnization of the nuptials, the supper prepared and the wedding furnished with guests, and still she is not married; and were the process here arrested, she would not be entitled to the privileges of his house, to wear his name, or to inherit his estate. When she is married and her state legally changed, then, and not till then, is she entitled to all these privileges growing out of the new relation. Now for the application. The gospel is preached to the sinner—he is in love with the transient pleasures afforded in the service of the devil. The carpenter's Son, born in Bethlehem and cradled in a manger, has no charms for him. By-and-by he finds that the pleasures of sin are deceptive, and the devil, in whose service he delighted, has nothing with which to reward him but misery and woe. Meanwhile he learns more of Him who proposes to save all who will come to God by Him. He finds

Him so chaste in conversation, that guile is not found in His mouth; so amiable in disposition, that when He is reviled He reviles not again, and yet so powerful, that the furious winds and boisterous waves are calm at His bidding, the grave yields up the dead to live again, and devils tremble at His word; the waters are firm as a pavement beneath His majestic tread, God is His Father, and He the only Son and Heir to all things—He is chief among ten thousand and altogether lovely. With faith like this, he can not fail to feel grieved that he ever loved the devil or his service, because he is the enemy of Him whom he now loves supremely. Surely, his heart is now changed—is he born again? If so, there is no fitness in the figure, for he is not married yet. Though his *heart* is changed, his *state* is not; and if he stops at this point, he can no more claim the Christian name and character than can the unmarried woman claim the name and patrimony of him to whom she is espoused. But it is insisted that this change of heart is the new birth, and (strange enough, too) the same persons insist that *we* have no change of heart, and deny the importance of it, when, in reality, we have their change of heart and new birth, in our change of heart.

We insist that we must not only love our betrothed, but we must be married to the Bridegroom according to law, before we can claim the privileges of His bride. He will not permit us to live with Him in adultery if we were so disposed. A change of heart, then, is not a change of state; it must precede the new birth, but it is not the new birth.

The language "born again," was unique when used by Christ to Nicodemus. No inspired man had used such language before: is there any reason for its use then? The Jews believed that Jesus had come to re-establish the kingdom of David and literally sit on his throne on the eartr; hence when he entered Jerusalem, on one occasion, "They that went before, and they that followed, cried, saying, Hosanna; Blessed is he that cometh in the name of the Lord: Blessed be the kingdom of our father David, that cometh in the name of the Lord." Mark xi:9, 10. And even His apostles did not understand the nature of His kingdom until after they received the Holy Spirit on the day of Pentecost, and were by it guided into all truth. "When they therefore came together, they asked of him, saying, Lord, wilt thou at this time restore again the kingdom to Israel?" Acts i:6. It is not unreasonable that Nicodemus had the same mistaken views of the kingdom, and he knew well that he was born into that kingdom, and had a right to citizenship in it by virtue of Abrahamic parentage; and being "a ruler of the Jews," "a master of Israel," he may have expected to be entitled to an office in Christ's kingdom on that account. Jesus corrects this mistake by telling him that the kingdom of God was not to be entered in that way; but as a birth gave him entrance into that, he must be born again to enter this.

There is much speculation about the import of this language; but as Jesus attempted to explain the matter to Nicodemus, and then asked, "Art thou a master of Israel and knowest not these things?" we are encouraged to approach the examination of the subject in the belief that He intended to be understood, and, as "a teacher come from God," He was competent to make clear what He attempted to explain. Let us, then, take up the language in which the conversation is recorded, and see whether or not we may understand it: "There was a man of the Pharisees named Nicodemus, a ruler of the Jews." So reads the first verse, and from it we learn that, at one time in the world's history, there lived a man whose name was Nicodemus; that he belonged to the sect of the Jews' religion called the Pharisees; and that he was a distinguished personage or ruler among the Jews. 2d verse: "The same (Nicodemus) came to Jesus by night (not in daylight) and said unto him, Rabbi, we know that thou art a teacher come from God: for no man can do these miracles that thou doest, except God be with him." Here we learn that Nicodemus was convinced by the miracles which Jesus did that He was really a teacher come from God. This is all plain; let us try again. 3d verse: "Jesus answered and said unto him, Verily, verily I say unto thee, except a man be born again, he can not see the kingdom of God." Here we learn, *not how* a man may be born again, but the indispensable *necessity* of being born again in order to see or enjoy the privileges and blessings of the kingdom of God. 4th verse: "Nicodemus saith unto him, How can a man be born when he is old? can he enter the second time into his mother's womb, and be born?" Here we find that Nicodemus knew nothing of but one birth, and this was a birth of the flesh, and that he could not understand how a man, when old, could be born in this way; he therefore asks an explanation, "How can a man be born when he is old?" Jesus attempts to tell him *how* it can be; hence the 5th verse: "Jesus answered, Verily, verily I say unto thee, except a man be born of water, and of the Spirit, he can not enter into the kingdom of God." Here we learn that the elements of birth are *water* and *Spirit*, and that a man must be born of *both* to be born again—not *born of water* and *begotten* by the *Spirit*, as some translations would indicate, but he must be born of *both* to be born at all. How is he to be born of water and of the Spirit? One answers that he must get religion in the altar, grove, or elsewhere, and being then baptized with the Spirit, he is born of the Spirit, and after a time he is baptized in water and is then born of water. Well, this theory makes baptism in water *indispensable* to entering the kingdom. Will the reader think of this? It also makes two births where there should be but one. The language is *born again*, not again and again, or twice more—once at the altar and once at the creek. This is not all; the order is transposed. Jesus said born of water and of the Spirit; this theory says born of the Spirit and of water. It is out of joint at every angle. Another theory says that we are "born of water when we are born into the world, and born of the Spirit when we get religion." This will provoke a smile on the face of our readers; but it is taught by men of lofty pretensions, and must be noticed, whether worthy of respect or not, because it is regarded important by those who present it. It makes the answer of Jesus wholly inapplicable to the question asked by Nicodemus, who did not inquire how a *child* had been born *into the world*, but "How can a *man be born when he is old?* The answer was, not that you have once been born of water, and must be born again of the Spirit, but you must be born again. How? Of water AND of the Spirit.

Another theory makes that part of the Saviour's language which applies to the Spirit apply to the belief of the gospel at the time the subject is spiritually begotten. While this theory may not be, practically, as mischievous as those already noticed, it is quite as unphilosophic and foreign from the truth as any one of them. It breaks up the order of the Lord's arrangement and takes the term *Spirit*, which comes after water, and places it in theory as far before water as faith precedes baptism. If this be the thought, it occurs to us that the Lord was unfortunate in the selection of terms in which to express it. It would have been as easy to have said, a man must be *begotten* by the Spirit and *born* of water, as he have said what He did say. But we are told that the Greek word *genneethee,* here rendered *born,* is elsewhere rendered *begotten,* and hence may have that meaning here. We grant that it is often so rendered; but should it be so rendered *here?* If so, it must mean *begotten* as to *water* as well as Spirit, and hence the process is *all begetting,* and there is no birth about it. Is any one prepared for this? Will he render the passage, "begotten of *water* and of the Spirit?" But may not the word *genneethee* mean *begotten* as to Spirit and *born* as to water? It must be thus divided in meaning, to fit the theory; and hence our neighbors may be right in saying that *eis* [for], in Acts ii:38, means *in order to* as to repentance, but *because of* as to baptism. Such renderings are at war with all rules of exegesis on the subject. "THE SENSE OF A WORD CAN NOT BE DIVERSE OR MULTIFORM AT THE SAME TIME AND IN THE SAME PLACE." *Ernesti,* p. 9. Again: "IN NO LANGUAGE CAN A WORD HAVE MORE THAN ONE LITERAL MEANING IN THE SAME PLACE." *Ernesti,* p. 11. According to these rules, we may translate *genneethee* either *begotten* OR *born,* as the sense may require, but we can not translate it by both in one place; yet we might as well so render it in words *as in theory.* Let those who do so, agree with our neighbors that *baptidzontes* means *sprinkle, pour,* AND *immerse,* in Matt. xxviii:19. If we may thus bifurcate the meaning of *genneethee,* in John iii:5, and make it mean both *begotten* AND *born* at the same time and in the same place, then we may as well have an end to all rules of interpretation, and no longer complain of others for doing that which we do ourselves. Surely, Jesus understood the figure He employed; and if so, the theory is wrong. To be begotten of God is entirely a different thing from being born of water and of the Spirit. He who believes the gospel, and is truly begotten of God, is not half born, but has the full measure of a birth of water and of the Spirit between him and the kingdom of God, and must be born of BOTH to be born at all. Begetting must precede a birth, but it is no part of a birth.

But as one error often begets others, so this theory has led to the notion that "regeneration and the new birth are identical." *Generate* means *to beget;* *re*, as a prefix, means *again*. Hence *regenerate* must mean *to beget again*. *Born* means *brought forth*, and *born again* is synonymous with *reborn*, hence, if language means any thing, *to regenerate* or *beget again* is one thing, and *reborn* or *born again* is a different thing. Physically, a man is generated or begotten and subsequently born; spiritually, he is regenerated (*i.e.*, begotten again), and subsequently reborn (*i.e.*, born again). Regeneration is the *beginning*, that may *end* in salvation. We are saved by the washing of regeneration and renewing of the Holy Spirit. Titus iii:5. The washing that belongs to or follows regeneration is not regeneration. The regenerated man may be born again—no one else can be; but it is re-birth, not regeneration, that reaches salvation.

But our question is yet unanswered, and having been gone from it so long, we must repeat it, lest it may have been forgotten: *How is a man born of water and of the Spirit?* We answer that he is born of *water as a means appointed by the Spirit for a birth*. How is a man begotten of God? Not literally. How then? He is begotten with the word of truth, the gospel, as the means appointed for this purpose. Then why not a man *be born of the Spirit when born of water as the means appointed by the Spirit* for a birth? Baptism is the act by which we are placed in and delivered from the water, according to the teaching of the Spirit, and thus we are born of water and of the Spirit; hence we are "buried with him in baptism, wherein also we are risen with him." Col. ii:12. To be, if possible, more plain—*to be born* contemplates a delivery, a coming forth from one state into another. Then were we to immerse a man in water, without faith, repentance, or any thing else (as we are often accused of doing), when delivered from the water he would be born of water, but not of water and of the Spirit, because the process was not in accordance with the teaching of the Spirit; then it is equally clear that if born of water, as taught by the Spirit, he is born of water *and* of the Spirit. But we are told that the word *water*, in the sentence "water and of the Spirit," does not mean *water;* and one quibbler will say it means *grace*, another that it means *Spirit;* and a third will say that he does not know what it means, but it can not mean *water*, for then he must be baptized or into the kingdom of God he can not go—and his theory tells him baptism is a non-essential. So the word of the Lord is made to bend to suit the theory instead of giving shape to the theory. But we are told that the Greek particle *kai*, here rendered *and*, is sometimes rendered *"even"* and that this sentence should read thus: "Except a man be born of water, even of the Spirit," etc. It is true that the word is sometimes so rendered, but can it be rendered *"even,"* in this connection? *And* is the primary meaning of the word, and the rules of translation give preference to the primary meaning, unless the sense requires its removal. Does the sense require that *and* should give place to *even,* in the sentence before us? Theories may require such a change, but the sense does not either require or allow it. The word *water* has no qualifying term, and wherever we find water, whether in the Jordan or elsewhere, we have the proper element. But not so of the Spirit. It is made definite, *the Spirit*—not spirit, a spirit, some spirit, or any spirit, but *the Spirit*. "Born of water and of the Spirit"—immersed in and born of water, according to the teaching of the Spirit. How perfect the sense! But another tells us that the word *water* is exegetical of the word Spirit; hence to be born of water and of the Spirit, is to be born of the Spirit like an overflow of water. Whoever saw an exegesis given in advance of the word explained? We feel ashamed that it is necessary to notice such quibbles as these. Suppose a man living at the time the Saviour was on the earth, who had witnessed the many immersions performed in those days, had heard Jesus say, "Except a man be born of water and of the Spirit he can not enter into the kingdom of God," and he had no theory or prepossessions to give shape to his conclusions, but had to form them only by the language used, would he conclude that the word *water* meant *grace, Spirit,* or any thing else but *water?* Would he not more likely conclude, with Wesley, Clarke, and others, that it had reference to water baptism? Is there a man out of the lunatic asylum who can believe that any one of these quibbles would ever have been thought of had it not been necessary to devise some means to save some theory from being destroyed by the obvious meaning of the Saviour's language?

There were two questions asked by Nicodemus, in the 4th verse: The first, "How can a man be born when he is old?"

Jesus answered as we have seen in the 5th verse. The second question, "Can he enter the second time into his mother's womb and be born?" shows that he had entirely mistaken the kind of birth required. This mistake Jesus corrects, in the 6th verse, by saying: "That which is born of the flesh is flesh; and that which is born of the Spirit is spirit"—as much as to say to him: "You are thinking of a birth of the flesh, and a second birth of this character would be indeed impossible. But I am speaking of a moral transition of the spiritual or inner man. The man born again is the same physical man as he was before, but the temper and disposition of the inner man are not like they were before. 'That which is born of the Spirit is spirit. Marvel not that I said unto thee, Ye must be born again.' Seeing your difficulty grows out of a failure to recognize the existence of an invisible or 'inner man' (Eph. iii:16) dwelling in 'our earthly house of this tabernacle' (2 Cor. v:1), and which is the subject of the change produced by the new birth, I will use an illustration which will make plain the fact just stated, that 'that which is born of the Spirit is spirit,' hence the 8th verse, 'The wind bloweth where it listeth, and thou hearest the sound thereof, but canst not tell whence it cometh or whither it goeth; so is every one that is born of the Spirit.'" The mist and fog that men have thrown around this verse envelop it in darkness thick as that with which God cursed the land of Egypt. And we are of the opinion that most of it has grown out of a failure to keep before the mind the difficulty under which Nicodemus was laboring, for the removal of which Jesus introduced the illustration, and failing to get the point in the comparison at the right place. We once listened to a very eloquent man through a labored effort to *explain* the new birth, at the close of which he said that this verse was designed to teach us that the new birth is incomprehensible to all finite minds. Others can see that it teaches the doctrine of abstract and mysterious spiritual operations; others say that, as the wind blows down a large oak, and leaves others standing around it, so the Spirit is partial in its operations, converting one or two out of the many who were with him or them at the mourner's bench. Jesus did not say, "So is the Spirit," or "So is the operation of the Spirit"—no such comparison was made or intended. Others say that the language was addressed to Nicodemus, and is not applicable to us at all, because we can tell where the wind comes from and where it goes to. "He bringeth the wind out of his treasure." Ps. cxxxv:7. "Who hath gathered the wind in his fist." Prov. xxx:4. And what is gained by these quotations? Where is God's treasure from whence the wind comes? and where is His fist in which it is gathered? But suppose we can tell where the wind comes from and goes to, what light has been thrown on the new birth by the discovery? We confess ourself unable to see any at all. If we go back to the 4th verse and see the difficulty in the mind of Nicodemus to be a second birth of the flesh, then come to the correction given to this mistake in the 6th verse—"That which is born of the Spirit is spirit"—and then regard the 8th verse as an illustration used to teach the existence of an invisible principle or spiritual man, which is changed by the new birth, then, it seems to us, there need be no difficulty in understanding the matter. We have seen many translations of this verse, quite a number of which we have before us at this writing; and it is worthy of note that, whether the Greek *pneuma* be rendered *wind* or *spirit,* the illustrative qualities of the figure are still the same: they are both invisible—recognized by sound and not by sight. "So is every one that is born of the Spirit"—it being spirit that is so born.

While the kingdom was yet in prospect, Jesus taught the people by parables and figures; but after its establishment, figures gave place to facts, commands, and promises. Jesus commissioned his apostles to preach the gospel to every creature, promising salvation to those who would believe and obey it. He also promised them the Holy Spirit to guide them into all truth, and enable them to unerringly perform the work He had assigned them. When it came, they began to preach as it inspired them —persons were cut to the heart and made to cry out, "Men and brethren, what shall we do?" Peter did not tell them to be born again, because the time for figures had passed; he therefore said to them: "Repent, and be baptized every one of you in the name of Jesus Christ for the remission of sins." Acts ii:38. Thus he told them plainly, without a figure, to do that which would translate them into the kingdom of God's dear Son, and produce that change of state indicated by the figurative language of Jesus as used in the conversation with Nicodemus when He said: "Except a man be born of water and of the Spirit, he can not enter into the kingdom of God." When Peter thus addressed them, "they that gladly received his word were baptized; and the same day there were added unto them about three thousand souls." Now, are they born again? Surely, they are. When were they born again? Just when they did what Peter commanded them to do. Then, if they were born again when they were baptized in the name of Jesus Christ for the remission of sins, will you not be born again when you do as they did? and if it took this to introduce them into the kingdom of God *then*, will any thing less do you *now?*

CHAPTER IX.

FAITH.

We hope that the reader has carefully studied the lessons already given, and that he has not forgotten the marks on the guide-posts along the road to the Tree of Life. But as we started far back in the brush, bogs, muck, and mire of Calvinism, our journey thence to citizenship in the kingdom of God has been necessarily a long one, and made rapidly; it may not be amiss for us to go back and familiarize ourselves a little with the scenery along the road.

We have seen that the destiny of each individual was not unalterably fixed in heaven or hell before time began, and that God is no respecter of persons, but in every nation he that feareth Him and worketh righteousness is accepted with Him; and hence every one may make his calling and election sure—that you did not enter the world laden with *hereditary depravity*, by reason of which you are wholly opposed to all good, and irresistibly inclined to all evil, and unable to do any thing commanded you of God; but, on the contrary, you are quite competent to fear God and keep His commandments, and in doing so you will have discharged your whole duty. We have further seen that God has one kingdom, body, or church, on the earth, and only one; that it was set up on the day of Pentecost, in Jerusalem, by the authority of the Lord Jesus Christ, through the agency of the apostles, as guided by the Holy Spirit; and may be as surely known and identified, as men and things may be known by the features peculiar to them. And men must enter it by being born of water and of the Spirit; and thus, as individuals, they become branches of Christ, the true Vine, or members of his body, the church; but to speak of *organizations* as branches of the church of God, is nothing less than the confused dialect of Babylon. We have further seen that before we can be born again, we must have been begotten with the word of God, as the incorruptible seed necessary to the accomplishment of this end, and that this Word must be preached, heard, and believed, in order to the production of that change of heart, and reformation of life, which must necessarily precede the new birth.

As faith is the grand mainspring which propels the human machinery in all acceptable obedience to God, we propose to pause here while we open our Bibles and examine it in the light of inspiration. We think it likely that more has been said and written on the subject of *faith* than on any other subject connected with theology; and if every trace of every thing that uninspired men have spoken and written could be blotted out of human memory, we are not sure that the world would be greatly injured by the sacrifice. Indeed, it seems to us that the greatest labor on the part of those who would understand the subject, is to disentangle it from the speculations of men with regard to it. *What, then, is faith? whence cometh it? and what is its office in the plan of salvation?*

What is Faith?

Many persons speak of it as some indescribable gift infused into the heart by God, when they neither expected nor desired it; while others seem to think it a gift, only to be obtained after hours, perhaps days, weeks, months, or even years, spent at the mourner's bench, or elsewhere, in imploring God to bestow it upon them. Paul says: "Faith is the substance of things hoped for, the evidence of things not seen." Heb. xi:1. This verse is perhaps better rendered by Anderson, thus: "Faith is a sure confidence with respect to things hoped for, a firm persuasion with respect to things not seen." Christianity is a system of *faith,* and is not susceptible of demonstration like a problem in mathematics. We do not know that there is such a place as heaven, like we know that there is such a place as Nashville; because the latter we have seen, the former we have not seen. We have a sure confidence with respect to it—a firm persuasion that it exists, because we believe the testimony concerning it, "For we walk by faith, not by sight." 2 Cor. v:7. Faith, then, may be defined as *a firm, unshaken confidence, conviction,* or *belief in the truth of a proposition, based upon testimony* concerning it. The order is: *Fact,* Testimony, FAITH. First, a fact must exist, then it must be revealed with testimony sufficiently strong to establish its truth, then the confidence in, or firm belief of this testimony is faith. In support of this position, it may be well to make a quotation or two.

When Jesus saw the centurion's confidence that a word from the Master would heal his servant, He said to them following Him, "I have not found so great *faith*, no, not in Israel," and then said to the centurion, "As thou hast *believed*, so be it done unto thee. And his servant was healed in the self-same hour." Matt. viii:10, 13. Here Jesus used the words *faith* and *belief* interchangeably, showing clearly that the centurion's *belief* was his *faith*.

Again: Paul tells us that "without *faith* it is impossible to please God, for he that cometh to God must believe that he is." Heb. xi:6. Here the necessity of belief is given as a reason why persons can not please God without faith; and the fact that we can not please God without faith, is as good a reason why we must believe; therefore, with Paul, *faith* and *belief* were synonymous terms.

Once more: "Abraham believed God, and it was accounted to him for righteousness." Rom. iv:3. What was accounted to Abraham for righteousness? Belief; and that this *belief was faith* is seen in the 9th verse in which it is said, "Faith was reckoned to Abraham for righteousness." Surely, nothing could be more clear than that believing God constituted Abraham's faith. Why, then, was not *faith* used in the 3d verse in place of the word *believed?* Because the word *faith* is always used as a *noun,* and never as a *verb;* nor is there any power as a *noun,* and never as a *verb;* nor is there any power in the English language to convert it into a verb. We can not say, "Abraham *faithed* God," but we can say, "Abraham *believed* God, and his *faith* was accounted to him for righteousness." We can not say, "Faith on the Lord Jesus Christ, but we can say, "*Believe* on the Lord Jesus Christ and thou shalt be saved." We can not say, "He that *faitheth* not shall be damned," but we can say, "He that *believeth* not shall be damned." We can not say, "If thou *faithest* with all thy heart, thou mayest," but we can say, "If thou *believest* with all thy heart, thou mayest." Nor can we convert the word *faith* into a *participle,* and say, "That *faithing* ye might have life through his name," but we can say, "That *believing* ye might have life through his name." When the thought is expressed in the shape of a *command* to be obeyed, or as having been obeyed, or as a condition to be complied with as an act of the mind precedent to further obedience to the gospel, the style is: *believe, believeth, believest, believed, believing,* etc.; but when used as a *noun,* to indicate the conviction which *exists* in the mind, with one single exception (2 Thess. ii:13), the word *faith* is always used. These facts will be further developed as we proceed with the examination of our second question, viz.:

How Does Faith Come?

After asking, "How can they call upon him in whom they have not believed? and how shall they believe in him of whom they have not heard? and how shall they hear without a preacher?" (Rom. x:14) intending, doubtless, to make the impression that they could do neither, and clearly showing that after the facts of the gospel exist, the order is: *preaching,* HEARING, BELIEVING, Paul remarks, "So then *faith cometh by hearing,* and hearing by the word of God." Rom. x:17. Hence, after Jesus had taught the grand *facts* of the gospel to the apostles, His first charge to them was, "Preach the gospel to every creature." Mark xvi:16. And why? Certainly, that those interested might *hear,* BELIEVE, and OBEY it. In His most solemn prayer to His Father He said, "Neither pray I for these alone, but for them also who shall *believe on me through their word.*" John xvii:20. Observe, he prayed for them who should believe on him through the words of the apostles; and as He required them to preach the gospel, the people were expected to *believe in Him by hearing the gospel* which the apostles were required to preach. In keeping with this arrangement, Peter preached to the Pentecostians, and "when they *heard* this they were pricked in their heart." Acts ii:37. So *their faith came by hearing,* and they were of the class of believers for whom Jesus prayed. The faith of the Gentiles, too, came in the same way; for Peter said, "Brethren, ye know that a good while ago God made choice among us, that the Gentiles by my mouth should *hear the word of the gospel, and believe.*" Acts xv:7. Luke further tells us that "many of the Corinthians *hearing believed,* and were baptized." Acts xviii:8. "It came to pass in Iconium, that they [Paul and Barnabas] went together into the synagogue of the Jews, and *so spake,* that a great multitude both of the Jews and also of the Greeks *believed.*" Acts xiv:1. The Samaritans also "*believed* Philip *preaching* the things concerning the kingdom of God, and the name of Jesus Christ, and were baptized, both men and women." Acts viii:12. Many other examples might be given illustrative of the same fact; indeed, there is not a single example on record where faith came not in this way.

We once saw an educated *mute*, who was quite an intelligent member of the church of God. We wrote on a slip of paper and handed him the following question: "Sir: Paul says 'faith comes by hearing; as you can not hear, how came your faith?'" He was a good penman, and quickly wrote the following answer: "Though I can not hear, thank God I can read. I heard the gospel like I heard the question you asked me. John says: 'Many other signs truly did Jesus in the presence of his disciples which are not written in this book; but *these are written that ye might believe that Jesus is the Christ, the Son of God;* and that believing ye might have life through his name.' John xx:30, 31. I read, understood, believed, and obeyed *what was written*." We were pleased with his answer, for it evinced that he knew much more about the faith required by the gospel than many who have ears to hear but seem not to understand what faith is, or how it comes.

We have often heard persons praying most earnestly to God to give them faith, and the preachers exhorting them to believe, without presenting one word of testimony to produce faith, as though their loud vociferations could scare them into the exercise of faith, or awaken their God (who, like Baal, was either asleep or on a journey), that He might hear and answer their prayers for faith. Such persons always have the deepest sympathy of our heart; hence, in great kindness, we say to them, "Come, now, and let us reason together."

When they *ask for faith, they have not faith,* for surely they would not so earnestly beg for that which they already have. James says: "Let him ask in faith, nothing wavering, for he that wavereth is like a wave of the sea, driven by the wind and tossed; let not that man think that he shall receive any thing of the Lord." Jas. i:6, 7. Now, as he asks for faith, and would not knowingly ask for that which he has, it follows that he *has not* faith, and therefore can not ask *in* faith; therefore let him not think that he will receive any thing of the Lord, or that the Lord will *give* him the faith for which he asks. Again: "Whatsoever is not of faith is sin." Rom. xiv:23. Then, as they pray for faith, and therefore *have not faith*, their prayers can not be *of faith;* and as whatsoever is not of faith is sin, it follows that all such prayers are sin. Once more: "Without faith it is impossible to please God." Heb. xi:6. As prayers *for faith* are not made *in faith*, but without faith and as without faith it is impossible to please God, therefore such prayers are not pleasing to God. And as they are sinful, and therefore not pleasing to God, and nothing can be received in answer to them, it surely would be better not to make them.

But an objector says: "It is certainly legitimate to ask God, in prayer, for that which He has promised to give us; and the Bible says *faith is the gift of God;* therefore we may ask Him for it." Most assuredly we may pray to God for that which He has promised to give us; but do the Scriptures teach that He has promised to give faith to those who are without it? Before we proceed to examine the proofs relied on to support the theory, we beg permission to remark to our contemporaries that consistency looks quite as well in them as in us, and the demand to reconcile scriptures seemingly at war with positions taken should extend to them as well as to us. This is not always remembered. Every knotty quotation is reserved for us to explain, every seeming contradiction is zealously sought after and brought forward for us to harmonize, and every quibble that can be thought of is expected to be attended to by us, while the objector's theory may be flatly contradicted by the plainest teaching of inspiration, and no attempt is made by him to explain or harmonize any thing.

We are tired of this. We want to see an objector *be a man*, and dig up the briers, thistles, and thorns from his own garden before he points at the weeds and grass in ours. Come, then: what do you think of the quotations already made from Jas. i:6, 7, Rom. xiv:23, and Heb. xi:6, and our reasonings thereon? And when you shall have harmonized these with the right of such as have *no faith* to pray *for* faith (and many others which you can easily find), then try the following: "He that believeth not shall be damned." Mark xvi:16. Will God punish men in hell forever for not believing, when He has to give them faith? While you smooth these kinks out of the theory that faith is a direct gift from God to the sinner, we will see whether or not your proofs contradict us.

The first passage we will examine may be found in 1 Cor. xii:8-10, where Paul, in speaking of the miraculous gifts of the Spirit, says: "For to one is given by the Spirit the word of wisdom; to another the word of knowledge by the same Spirit; to another *faith* by the same Spirit; to another the gifts of healing by the same Spirit; to another the working of miracles; to another prophecy; to another discerning of Spirits; to another divers kinds of tongues; to another the interpretation of tongues." We have given the sentence with reference to faith with is context, and the connection most clearly shows that the faith which enumerated among the gifts of the Spirit is not the faith for which the alien is taught to pray. If he may pray for faith because it is here said to be the gift of the Spirit, then he may pray for the power to work miracles, prophesy, speak with tongues, and interpret tongues, for they are all in the same connection and by the same authority said to be gifts of the same Spirit. Surely, no one will say that *this* faith, or any of these gifts, is to be given to the unconverted alien, in answer to prayer, or in any other way. There was a faith of which Jesus said: "If ye have faith as a grain of mustard seed, ye shall say unto this mountain, Remove hence to yonder place; and it shall remove: and nothing shall be impossible unto you." Matt. xvii:20. And again: "If ye had faith as a grain of mustard seed, ye might say unto this sycamine tree, Be thou plucked up by the root, and be thou planted in the sea; and it should obey you." Luke xvii:6. We hear Paul also calling Titus his "son after the *common faith*." Tit. i:4. Paul had preached the gospel to Titus, and when he believed it he was begotten by the incorruptible seed, or word of God; and this belief of the gospel Paul calls the *common faith*, because this is the faith common to all God's people. But the word *common* implies *uncommon;* hence, as Paul spake of the *common* faith, he did it in contrast with the *uncommon* or miraculous faith given by the Spirit. Does any one think he has it now? Then let him remove the mountain or tree by his word, and thereby establish his claim.

The next and last passage to be examined is in the following words: "For by grace are ye saved through faith; and that not of yourselves: it is the gift of God." Eph. ii:8. Is faith the thing here said to be the gift of God? The demonstrative *that* never refers to the thing nearest us or last spoken of. For such purpose *this* is preferred. *That*, as a demonstrative, refers to the thing farther off or previously spoken of; hence, in this sentence, it must refer to something behind faith. We would paraphrase the sentence thus: "By grace are ye *saved* through faith; and that *salvation* is not of yourselves: it is the gift of God." This is the obvious import of the passage.

But we are told that faith is the gift of God because He has given us the testimony which produces it. To this we do not greatly object; but still there can be no propriety in praying for it, nor can their prayers avail any thing if they do pray. They have the testimony: why not believe it? Is God to give them *more* testimony? If they believe *all the testimony*, they have faith enough and need not pray for more. Faith is produced by testimony, and as far as testimony goes, faith may go; but where the testimony stops, faith must and will stop. The testimony concerning Jesus tells us that He was born of Mary in Bethlehem —was baptized by John in Jordan, and commenced His ministry in the hill country of Galilee—was crucified on Calvary, and was buried in Joseph's new tomb. Now, suppose the testimony had stopped at this point, how much faith would any person have had to-day in His *resurrection, ascension,* and *glorification?* Just none at all. As far as testimony goes, faith may go, but no further; all beyond is mere speculative opinion. Our faith may be strengthened or weakened by increasing or weakening the testimony. We have faith in the testimony of men, and we have faith in the testimony of God, but our faith in the testimony of God is as much stronger than our faith in the testimony of men as we regard God superior to man and His testimony more reliable than that of man. This difference—no more, no less. "If we receive the witness of men, the witness of God is greater." 1 John v:9. "For my thoughts are not your thoughts, neither are your ways my ways, saith the Lord; for as the heavens are higher than the earth, so are my ways higher than your ways, and my thoughts than your thoughts." Isa. lv:8, 9.

But we are told that the belief of testimony is merely *historic* faith. And what kind of faith is not historic faith? If by *historic* faith is meant a belief in the historic account of Jesus, heaven, hell, salvation, and condemnation given in the word of Truth, then we hesitate not to admit that we have that kind of faith, and know of no other. But you tell us you want *divine* faith. If by *divine* faith you mean that which is predicated upon divine testimony, then we have divine faith, and want no other. But you want *evangelical* faith. And what sort of faith is that? Is it to believe all that the evangelists have spoken and written? If so, we have evangelical faith. But you want *saving* faith. What is meant by saving faith? If it is, with all the powers of the soul, to believe in Jesus Christ as the Son of God and our Saviour, then we have saving faith. But you want the faith of *credence*. And what do you mean by this? Is it to give full *credit* to all the divine testimony? Then we have the faith of credence. But you want the faith of *reliance*. And what kind of faith is this? Is it to *rely*, with full confidence, on the testimony of inspiration? Then we have the faith of reliance. But you want a *trusting* faith. Do you mean by this a faith which enables you to *trust* in Jesus Christ and the efficacy of His blood for salvation? Then this is the kind of faith we have, and want no other. Then of what use are all these qualifying terms as applied to faith? They serve only to becloud the subject, and never can do any good. We have heard persons taught that they must believe that God *had pardoned* them, and whenever they would believe *this* they would realize that it was so. It is not strange that persons feel like they are pardoned when they believe that God *has pardoned* them; but if we must *believe that we are pardoned in order to be pardoned,* then we confess, frankly, that we neither have nor want that kind of faith. Are we to believe that there are as many different kinds of faith as there are qualifying terms here used? Paul said, "There is one Lord and *one faith.*" Eph. iv:5. When you believe all that God has said, through inspired men, to the world, and believe it *because* God has said it, you have all the faith which mortals can have or God requires of them. Pollok has well said:

> "Faith was bewildered much by men who meant
> To make it clear, so simple in itself;
> A thought so rudimental and so plain,
> That none by comment could it plainer make.
> All faith was one. In object, not in kind,
> The difference lay. The faith that saved a soul,
> And that which in the common truth believed,
> In essence were the same. Hear, then, what faith,
> True Christian faith, which brought salvation was—
> *Belief in all that God revealed to men;*
> Observe, in all that God revealed to men,
> In all He promised, threatened, commanded, said,
> Without exception, and without a doubt."

WHAT IS THE OFFICE OF FAITH?

Having seen what faith is and how it comes, we are now prepared to inquire what it does. And we may as well say at once that *it induces the performance of every act of acceptable obedience to God*—every one. We are lost in attempting to find any thing done in hearty obedience to God that is not, either directly or indirectly, the result of faith. Is your heart subdued to the will of God, and your affections and passions all mellowed by love, that God-like principle that enables you to love your enemies, and do good to and pray for them that persecute and evilly treat you? This is the work of faith. Are you heartily sorry for all your past sins and determined to forsake them and walk humbly and uprightly henceforth? These are the results of the subjugation of your heart to the will of God by faith. Have you confessed with the mouth the Lord Jesus before men, that He may confess you before His Father and the holy angels? Then you have but confessed with the mouth what the heart believed. Have you been buried with Christ in baptism and arisen to walk in newness of life? If so, Jesus, in the commission which authorized the performance of this act, associated it with faith, saying, "He that believeth and is baptized shall be saved;" and Philip made the eunuch's faith an indispensable prerequisite to his baptism, saying, "If thou believest with all thy heart thou mayest." And, as without faith it is impossible to please God, had he baptized him without faith, it would not have been pleasing to God; and hence were you to be baptized without faith, it would not be a service well pleasing to Him. Do you, as Christians, love mercy, deal justly, walk humbly and uprightly before God? If so, it is all the result of faith; for the Christian lives by faith, walks by faith, and dies in faith. But we are not yet ready to develop the life of the Christian; hence we must go back and assist the *alien* through that CHANGE IN THE AFFECTIONS OF THE HEART which we have seen to be the first result of faith.

Paul says: "Ye have obeyed *from the heart* that form of doctrine which was delivered you; being then made free from sin, ye became the servants of righteousness." Rom. vi:17, 18. By this we learn that the obedience which freed the Romans from sin was *from the heart;* and we may safely affirm that all acceptable obedience must come from a heart sincerely desirous to honor God's authority. All else is downright mockery. But no alien can obey from the heart without a changed heart; hence it may be well to inquire what a change of heart is, and how it is brought about. In order to acquire any thing like a satisfactory knowledge of the subject, it is important to know what the spiritual heart is, and then we may better understand how and when it is changed. As the physical heart is the center of the physical circulation, from whence passes the vital current, giving life and nutriment to all parts of the body, so the *mind* of man is the great center of all spiritual impressions and emotions, and is therefore called the heart—if you please, the *spiritual heart.* If in this we are not mistaken, then all reference of spiritual emotions and changes to the physical heart is out of place. Let us see how this is. "And God saw that the wickedness of man was great in the earth, and that every imagination of the thoughts of his heart was only evil continually." Gen. vi:5. It can not require an argument to show that thoughts originate in the *mind,* which is here denominated the heart. Solomon says: "The heart knoweth his own bitterness." Prov. xiv:10. "The heart of the righteous studieth to answer." Prov. xv:28. As study is the work of the mind, and as the mind is the store-house of all knowledge, we can not be at a loss to know that it was the mind which Solomon called the heart. "Jesus perceiving the thought of their heart." Luke ix:47. As thoughts proceed from the mind, it is evidently what Jesus here calls the heart. "The heart also of the rash shall understand knowledge." Isa. xxxii:4. Here it is quite clear that the prophet used the term *heart* with reference to the mind. With a single quotation from an apostle, we must close our proof on this subject: "With the heart man believeth unto righteousness." Rom. x:10. Until it can be shown that the physical heart can believe and appreciate testimony, it is unnecessary to make an argument to show that Paul here used the word *heart* as equivalent to the mind. Thus we see that God, Jesus, Solomon, Isaiah, and Paul used the term *heart* with reference to the *mind or intellect, with all its faculties, with which we think, understand, feel, and receive impressions*. We may cultivate and develop the faculties of the mind so as to enlarge our powers of thought and capabilities of acquiring and retaining knowledge, by making impressions on it through the senses; but this is not what is meant by the phrase "change of heart," as used by theologians with reference to conversion. And it may be well to remark that we use the phrase "change of heart" by way of accommodation to the parlance of our times, and not because we find such language in the Bible. It is not there. It is true that, in Dan. iv:16, it is said of Nebuchadnezzar: "Let his heart be changed from man's and let a beast's heart be given him;" but this had no reference to conversion to Christianity. Indeed, while we confine ourselves strictly to the literal signification of the terms we are by no means sure that such a thing as a *change of heart* is at all possible. We may change the affections and purposes of the heart or mind, but how we may change the heart or mind itself, is not very clear to us. The affections and purposes of the heart are no more the heart than the fruit of a tree is the tree. In the Scriptures, however, the term heart is sometimes used in this sense—*i.e.*, to indicate the affections and purposes of the mind; and as these may be changed, it is with reference to them that we use the phrase "change of heart." When we speak of a change of heart, then, we mean a *change of the affections and purposes of the heart*. Nothing more—nothing less.

Many persons are prating about a "change of heart," who are wholly destitute of any just conceptions of what it is, or how it is produced. One of them will tell you that "It is the work of grace in the heart," while another will tell you that "It is the new birth," "Getting religion," "Remission of sins," "Salvation from sin," "Justification," etc.; and they will tell you that "It was brought about by the *baptism* of the Holy Ghost;" or at least they will insist that "It was by the *operation* of the Holy Ghost." Hence the importance of knowing what a change of heart is, that we may know when we have it, if not how it was brought about. We have often seen persons, as truly penitent as they were capable of being, who were still praying for a change of heart, while their hearts were wilted into perfect submission to the will of God as far as they knew it. Did they not love God, and fear Him with all the powers of the mind? Yes. Then if their hearts were changed they must cease to love and fear God, and might love the devil and his service. Did they not believe in Jesus Christ as the Son of God and the Saviour of sinners? Yes; if not, they would not have gone to the mourner's bench, for it was to obtain salvation through Him that they went there. Change their hearts from this, and it is bound to land them in infidelity or unbelief, for this is the opposite of belief in Jesus. Is he not heartily sorry for sins? Then change his heart, and he is not sorry. Is he not willing and determined to forsake them? Then change his heart, and he is determined to practice them. Does he not love the company and society of the people of God? Then change his heart, and he loves the company and association of the vicious and wicked. But you ask why was he not pardoned if his heart was submissive to the will of God? Simply because he had not complied with the conditions upon which God had offered him pardon. And the failure, upon his part, was not because of any perversity of heart in him, but because his instructors had failed to teach him what those conditions are. For want of proper instructions, he must go home with his head bowed down as a bulrush, and continue to pray for a *change of heart* through long weeks, months, years, or perhaps through life, because he can not work himself up to a *sufficient degree of excitement* to believe his heart changed in some supernatural way. This is the literal meaning of it. And what is the result? If he is of Calvinistic persuasions, he may conclude that he is not one of the elect, and in an effort to drown his emotions he may go back into the practice of wickedness, and perhaps become tenfold worse than before; or he may plunge into the dark pool of infidelity, and conclude that there is no truth in any thing. We very recently had a conversation with a very intelligent infidel manufactured just in this way.

When a man's affections are won from sin to holiness, a love of Satan to God, and all the purposes of his heart are submissive to the will of God as far as he knows it, he has all the change of heart that God requires of him prior to obedience. And we propose, now, to examine a few passages of Scripture to see how this change is produced, to which we invite the very careful attention of those who would understand the subject: "And on this manner did Absalom to all Israel that came to the king for judgment: so Absalom stole the hearts of the men of Israel." 2 Sam. xv:6. How did Absalom steal the hearts of the people? Go back a few verses, and you will find that he placed himself by the gate, and when any one who had a controversy came to present his grievance to the king, he would say to him: "Thy matters are good and right, but there is no man deputed of the king to hear thee. Oh, that I were made judge in the land, that every man that hath any suit or cause might come unto me, and I would do him justice. And it was so, that when any man came nigh to him to do him obeisance, he put forth his hand and took him and kissed him." Thus it was that he stole their hearts; that is, he won their affections. Hence, the term *heart* is here used to indicate the affections of the mind, and not the heart itself; and thus we see what is meant by a change of heart. The affections of the people were won *from* the king and *to* Absalom; and it was done by making them believe that the king was indifferent to their interests, and that Absalom was their friend, and thus their faith changed their hearts.

What a vast cloud is removed from the subject by taking this view of it! From this stand-point we can see a beauty and fitness in the language of Peter to his brethren, when he said: "Men and brethren, ye know how that a good while ago God made choice among us, that the Gentiles by my mouth should hear the word of the Gospel, and believe. And God, which knoweth the hearts, bare them witness, giving them the Holy Ghost, even as he did unto us; and put no difference between us and them, purifying their hearts by faith." Acts xv:7-9. Thus we see that, though God gave the Gentiles the Holy Ghost, it was not to purify their hearts, for He did this work by faith. And as He put no difference between the Gentiles and Jews in this respect, it follows that He purified the hearts of the Jews by faith. Then let us go to Jerusalem on the day of Pentecost, when and where the hearts of three thousand were purified in one day, and see if we can find how it was done. And first we premise by saying that it was not done by the Holy Ghost, for Jesus said they [the world] could not receive it, and it was poured out upon the disciples before the multitude came together. When the apostles were filled with it, and under its influence began to speak forth in different languages, the wonderful works of God, the people assembled, with hearts full of bitterness, to hear what was being said. They believed Jesus an impostor, and that they did right in putting Him to death; and that the apostles were a drunken rabble. Thus we see that their wicked feelings were the result of improper faith, and to change their feelings it was necessary to correct their faith, which produced the feelings. And as faith is dependent upon testimony, it was necessary, in order to correct their faith, to present such testimony as would convince them that Jesus was not an impostor, as they had believed, but was what He professed to be—the Son of God. Hence Peter began to instruct them by telling them that the apostles were not drunk, as they supposed, and that God had raised up that same Jesus whom they had wickedly slain, and made Him both Lord and Christ; and that He had shed forth what they then saw and heard. And as with many other words he taught and exhorted them, it may be that he called their attention to the fact that Jesus was once happy in heaven, in company with God and angels, while they were without hope and without God in the world, destined to misery and woe; that to avert their punishment and secure their salvation, He left the realms of bliss and came to the world a stranger and pilgrim, without a place whereon to lay His head. That while He had come on a mission of love for them, and mercy to them, they had ungratefully persecuted and slain Him; that to increase and protract His sufferings, they had compelled Him to bear His own cross up the rugged steeps of Calvery, until from fatigue and exhaustion, He sunk beneath its weight; that to intensify the infamy with which they intended to load down His memory, they compelled Him to die between two thieves; that to mock His pretensions as King, they had put on Him a purple robe, and encircled His head with a crown of thorns, then buffeted Him, spat upon Him, and hailed Him in derision as King of the Jews; that they had suspended Him upon nails driven through His tender hands to the cross, and, when in the midst of His agony He asked them for drink, they gave Him vinegar mingled with gall. And while suffering all this for them, He loved them still—yes, He even loved the man that drove the nails through His hands, and prayed, "Father, forgive them; they know not what they do."

> "See, from His head, His hands, His feet,
> Sorrow and love flow mingled down;
> Did e'er such love and sorrow meet,
> Or thorns compose so rich a crown?
> Were the whole realm of nature mine,
> That were a present far too small;
> Love so amazing, so divine,
> Demands my soul, my life, my all."

When they heard these things they were pierced in their hearts. And is it surprising that they were? Ah! would it not have been surprising beyond measure had they not been deeply affected by the scenes that had been made to pass afresh before them on that occasion? They then knew how to appreciate the testimony that God had borne to the divine character of His Son, through the convulsions that took place in the laws of nature when He expired upon the cross. They had felt the earth tremble beneath their unhallowed feet, until the rocks about them had been shaken to atoms, and the vail of their sacred temple, that had stood for ages, had been rent in twain from top to bottom. The king of day, for the first time since God had placed him in the firmament, refused to give his light, and the world was enveloped in darkness, while all nature was clad in the habiliments of mourning because the Son of God was dead. Why all this? "God so loved the world that He gave His only-begotten Son, that whosoever believeth in Him should not perish, but have everlasting life."

> "He left His radiant throne on high,
> Left the bright realms of bliss,
> And came to earth to bleed and die—
> Was ever love like this?
> Oh! for this love let rocks and hills
> Their lasting silence break,
> And all harmonious human tongues
> Their Saviour's praises speak."

Reader, have you no place in your heart's deepest affections for a Saviour like this? But we are wandering from the point before us.

The testimony was believed with all the heart, and by it their enmity was subdued. They saw their lost and ruined condition, and hence felt their need of a Saviour. Their law had been: "He that sheddeth man's blood by man shall his blood be shed." Seeing no means of escape, in deep anguish of soul they cry out: "Men and brethren, what shall we do?" We can scarcely forbear quoting the answer, but it must bide its time. How simple the process! They had improper views of the Saviour when they killed Him; but the statements made by Peter, and the miraculous confirmation of them by the Holy Spirit, convinced them that they had been mistaken, and thus corrected their faith, and different faith produced different feelings and actions. Surely, this is clear enough.

We have said that the testimony was believed with *all the heart*. When the eunuch demanded baptism of Philip, he answered: "If thou believest with *all thy heart* thou mayest." Acts viii:37. There is a depth of meaning in this expression that we fear is not comprehended by all. The word *all* implies that there may be such a thing as *a part* of the whole; and when Philip said, "If thou *believest with all thy heart*," he certainly left us to infer that there is such a thing as believing *without* engaging all the powers of the heart. Hence there may be a sort of passive assent of the mind to the propositions of the Bible that falls very far short of that faith which works by love and purifies the heart. When a scribe once asked the Saviour for the first commandment, Jesus said: "Thou shalt love the Lord thy God with all thy heart, and with all thy soul, and with all thy mind, and with all thy strength." Mark xii:30. The same thought is here intensified by repeating it in different forms of speech, so as to forcibly impress us with the fact that God intends to engage the whole powers of the heart; and the faith which falls below this is worth nothing to any one. Hence says David: "I will praise thee, O Lord, with my *whole* heart." Ps. ix:1. Our faith must be sufficiently strong to subjugate the lusts, appetites, and passions—in a word, the whole man to the will of the Lord, and fill the heart with love. It must enable us to appreciate our dependence upon God, and feel the need of a Saviour, and put our trust in Him. It must enable us to rise above all the influences of earth, and disregard what friends, relatives, or the world may say of us, and feel, in the great deep of our hearts, to say, "Speak, Lord, thy servant will hear; command, and he will obey."

> "Through floods and flames, if Jesus lead,
> I'll follow where He goes;
> Hinder me not, shall be my cry,
> Though earth and hell oppose."

If heaven is worth any thing it is worth every thing; and he who stops to reason with himself about what it will cost him, or the sacrifices he will have to make to obey God, or the conveniences and inconveniences attending the requirements which God has made of him, is not in a fit frame of mind to obey God acceptably in anything, and need not attempt it until he can bring himself more fully into subjection to His will.

But we are told that God has to purify or change the heart before faith, so as to enable us to believe, and the language of the prophet is invoked to prove this position: "A new heart also will I give you, and a new spirit will I put within you: and I will take away the stony heart out of your flesh, and I will give you a heart of flesh." Ezek. xxxvi:26. And again: "I will give them one heart, and I will put a new spirit within you; and I will take the stony heart out of their flesh, and I will give them a heart of flesh: that they may walk in my statutes, and keep mine ordinances, and do them: and they shall be my people, and I will be their God." Ezek. xi:19, 20.

If these quotations prove that God, by His Spirit, purifies and renews the heart, and until He does this we can not believe and obey Him, and He never does it, will He send us to hell for an impurity of heart which He alone could remove? With this interpretation of these quotations before us, let us try another: "Cast away from you all your transgressions, whereby ye have transgressed, and *make you a new heart and a new spirit;* for why will ye die, O house of Israel? For I have no pleasure in the death of him that dieth, saith the Lord God; wherefore turn yourselves and live ye." Ezek. xviii:31, 32. Now what is to be done with these quotations? They are all from the same prophet, inspired by the same God. Does God contradict Himself? It certainly will be conceded that the phrase "stony heart" was used to indicate that hardness of heart which the Jews had produced in themselves by indulgence in crime, the consequences of which they had keenly felt in the numerous disasters which had befallen them. It will be conceded, also, that the phrase "heart of flesh" was intended to indicate that subdued state of mind in which God proposed to again receive them into His favor. As man is a creature subject to be influenced by motive, God, through the prophet, in the same chapter, recounts their afflictions and wickedness as follows: "When the house of Israel dwelt in their own land, they defiled it by their own way, and by their doings. . . . Wherefore, I poured my fury upon them for the blood that they had shed upon the land, and for their idols wherewith they had polluted it: and I scattered them among the heathen, and they were dispersed through the countries: according to their way and according to their doings I judged them." Ezek. xxxvi:17-19. Then, after presenting their sufferings and their wickedness, He proposes to take them from among the heathens, cleanse them from their idolatry, restore to them their country, and be to them a God. Were not these high incentives to reformation? And can we not see great similarity in the process by which their hearts were proposed to be changed, and the process by which the hearts of the Pentecostians were changed? In both cases the wickedness of the parties and its dire consequences were exhibited, and a plan of reconciliation proposed, embracing the grandest motives of which the mind can conceive, to induce acceptance. The arrangement of the terms in both cases was the work of God; the acceptance in one case was to be, and in the other case was, the work of man; and thus, in one sense, God changes the heart, while in the other, and more common signification of the terms, man does it himself. There are other passages we might notice, but they will be examined in another department of our work.

What faith does not do, or the doctrine of justification by faith *alone*, will receive attention when we come to consider objections to the design of baptism.

CHAPTER X.

REPENTANCE.

We have arrived at a proper stand-point from which to consider the subject of *repentance*, and to it we invite the reader's attention for the present. Its importance is admitted by all religious parties and teachers of our times. When John came to prepare a people for the reception of the Messiah, though he came to the Jews who had long been the recognized people of God, he found them steeped in wickedness; hence he said: "Repent ye, for the kingdom of heaven is at hand." Matt. iii:2. When John was cast into prison and his ministry ended, "Jesus began to preach, and to say, Repent: for the kingdom of heaven is at hand." Matt. iv:17. When Jesus sent the twelve apostles to the lost sheep of the house of Israel, "they went out and preached that men should repent." Mark. vi:12. Jesus said to those who came to Him, "Except ye repent ye shall all likewise perish." Luke xiii:3, 5. When He gave the final commission to His apostles He said that "repentance and remission of sins should be preached in his name among all nations, beginning at Jerusalem." Luke xxiv:47. When the apostles began to operate under this authority, they commanded believers to "repent and be baptized . . . in the name of Jesus Christ for the remission of sins." Acts ii:38. When the disciples were convinced that salvation was not confined to the Jews, they "glorified God, saying, Then hath God also to the Gentiles granted repentance unto life." Acts xi:18. Then, as repentance is so important a condition in the gospel plan of salvation, it is important that we know what it is, that we may know when we have obeyed the divine mandate.

We find that the word *repent* occurs in our common English Bible forty-two times; *repented* occurs thirty times; *repentance* twenty-six times; *repenteth* five times; and *repentest, repenting,* and *repentings* one time each—in all, one hundred and six times. *Repent* is used with reference to God sixteen times, and with reference to man twenty-six times. It is used to indicate sorrow eleven times, a change of mind or purpose fourteen times, and includes the idea of reformation of life eighteen times. *Repented* is used with reference to God thirteen times, and with reference to man seventeen times. It is used to indicate sorrow twelve times, a change of mind eight times, and includes a change of life or reformation ten times. *Repentance* is used with reference to God twice, and with reference to man twenty-four times. It is used to indicate sorrow twice, a change of purpose once, and extends to reformation of life twenty-three times. *Repenteth* is used with reference to God three times, and with reference to man twice. Twice it indicates sorrow, once a change of mind, and twice includes a change or reformation of life. *Repenting* and *repentest* are each used once with reference to God to indicate a change of purpose. *Repentings* is once used with reference to God to indicate sorrow. With reference to God the word is sometimes used in a *negative* sense; as, "God is not a man that he should repent" (Num. xxiii:19); "The Lord hath sworn and will not repent." Ps. cx:4; Heb. vii:21. Sometimes it is used with reference to God *affirmatively;* as, "It repented the Lord that he had made man on the earth;" "It repenteth me that I have made them." Gen. vi:6, 7. At other times it is used with reference to God *conditionally;* as, "If that nation against whom I have pronounced turn from their vile, I will repent of the evil I thought to do unto them. . . . If it do evil in my sight, that it obey not my voice, then I will repent of the good wherewith I said I would benefit them." Jer. xviii:8, 10. Again, it is sometimes used in petition or supplication to God; as, "Turn from thy fierce wrath, and repent of this evil against thy people." Ex. xxxii:12. In all the forms in which the word is used it refers to God thirty-seven times, and with reference to man sixty-nine times. It is used to indicate sorrow or regret twenty-eight times, a change of mind or will twenty-five times, and a *change of mind resulting in reformation of life fifty-three times.* We are not concerned or interested in the use of the term as applied to God; its application to man is that which more directly concerns us, and to it we will confine our examination.

When used in the New Testament as a command to the alien in order to the remission of sins, it always indicates such a change of mind as produces a change or reformation of life under circumstances warranting the conclusion that sorrow for the past would or had preceded it. When so used it is invariably a translation of the Greek word *metanoio;* and when used to indicate sorrow or regret it is always from *metamelomai*—a different word, though improperly rendered the same in English. Had these words been properly translated we think it likely that much of the confusion on the subject of repentance would have been prevented. *Regret* is certainly a much more fitting representative of *metamelomai* than repentance, and why it has not been so translated is more than we can tell.

A striking example of the difference in the meaning of the word *repent* when derived from these different Greek words will be found in 2 Cor. vii:8-10: "For though I made you sorry with a letter, I do not repent [*metamelomai*, regret], though I did repent [*metamelomen*, regret], forI perceive that the same epistle hath made you sorry, though it were but for a season. Now I rejoice, not that ye were made sorry, but that ye sorrowed to repentance [*metanoian*, reformation]: for ye were made sorry after a godly manner, that ye might receive damage by us in nothing; for godly sorrow worketh repentance [*metanoian*, reformation] to salvation not to be repented [*metameleton*, regretted]." Surely, nothing could be more apparent than the difference in the use which Paul makes of these two Greek words, though both rendered repent in the common version. Paul wrote the Corinthians a letter which made them sorry, and he regretted it, but he ceased to regret it when he saw that their sorrow worked in them repentance: *i.e.*, such a *change of mind* as culminated in their reformation.

The words *repentance*, in the commission, Luke xxiv:47, and *repent*, as used by Peter, Acts ii:38, and iii:19, are from the Greek *metanoio*, and not from *metamelomai*, and hence means *more* than sorrow for past sins. We say *more*, because that change of mind which we call repentance always implies that sorrow for the past has preceded it. When the Jews at Jerusalem, on the day of Pentecost, heard Peter's preaching, and by it were convinced that they had truly crucified and slain the Son of God; they were pierced in their hearts, and cried out, "Men and brethren, what shall we do?" Acts ii:37. Can we conclude that the hearts of those who asked this soul-stirring question were not filled with sorrow for the sins from which they desired salvation? Yet they were commanded to repent. But it may be said that the sorrow which they had was not godly sorrow, and this is the reason why it was not repentance. Their sorrow was the product of their faith, and their faith was produced by Peter's preaching, which was dictated by the Holy Spirit, sent that day from heaven, by Him who sat at God's right hand. Surely, if this was not godly sorrow, then there can be no such thing connected with conversion. But is godly sorrow repentance? Paul did not so think. He says: "Now I rejoice, not that ye were made sorry, but that ye sorrowed to repentance, for ye were made sorry after a godly manner, that ye might receive damage by us in nothing. For godly sorrow worketh repentance unto salvation not to be repented of; but the sorrow of the world worketh death." 2 Cor. vii:9, 10. Here we learn that godly sorrow precedes repentance, but certainly is not repentance. Godly sorrow is produced by respect for God and His violated law, and produces a change of mind which induces reformation or change of life; while the sorrow of the world may be produced by the fact that the party has been detected in crime—is subjected to the frowns of men or the punishment inflicted by human laws—perchance because his schemes have proven unprofitable and have resulted in loss to him. Such is the sorrow of the world, and makes no man better, but ends in death. The repentance contemplated in the commission, and required by Peter of those to whom he spake, began where they gladly received his words, with a fixed purpose to reform their lives in accordance therewith, and it was preceded by deep sorrow for the wrongs they had done.

But we have a definition of repentance incidentally given us in the Scriptures which will make the matter, if possible, more plain. Jesus on one occasion said: "The men of Nineveh shall rise in judgment with this generation, and shall condemn it, because they repented at the preaching of Jonas; and, behold, a greater than Jonas is here." Matt. xii:41. Jesus here says that the men of Nineveh repented at the preaching of Jonas; if, therefore, we can learn what the Ninevites did, we can thence learn what Jesus meant by repentance. "God saw their works, that they *turned from their evil way;* and God repented of the evil that he had said that he would do unto them, and he did it not." Jonah iii:10. Then, the change of mind which resulted in turning the Ninevites from their evil ways constituted their repentance.

The determination to reform must be such as will lead the party to a *reparation* of injuries done to others, as far as may be in his power to make restitution. In vain may any one tell me that he repents slandering me while he refused to correct his false statements concerning me, or that he repents stealing my horse while he continues to ride him without my consent. A circumstance recorded on page 256, Ch. Syst., which, whether real or imaginary, so aptly illustrates our view of this subject, that we feel constrained to transcribe it:

"Peccator wounded the reputation of his neighbor Hermis, and on another occasion defrauded him of ten pounds. Some of the neighborhood were apprised that he had done both. Peccator was converted under the preaching of Paulinus, and, on giving in a relation of his sorrow for his sins, spoke of the depth of his convictions and of his abhorrence of his transgressions. He was received into the congregation and sat down with the faithful to commemorate the great sin-offering. Hermis and his neighbors were witnesses of all this. They saw that Peccator was penitent and much reformed in his behavior, but they could not believe him sincere because he had made no restitution. They regarded him either as a hypocrite or self-deceived, because, having it in his power, he repaid not the ten pounds, nor once contradicted the slanders he had propagated. Peccator, however, felt little enjoyment in his profession, and soon fell back into his former habits. He became again penitent, and, on examining the grounds of his falling off, discovered that he had never cordially turned away from his sins. Overwhelmed in sorrow for the past, he resolved on giving himself up to the Lord, and, reflecting on his past life, set about the work of reformation in earnest. He called on Hermis, paid him his ten pounds, and the interest for every day he had kept it back, went to all the persons to whom he had slandered him, told them what injustice he had done him, and begged them, if they had told it to any other persons, to contradict it. Several other persons whom he had wronged in his dealings with them, he also visited, and fully redressed all these wrongs against his neighbors. He also confessed them to the Lord, and asked Him to forgive him. Peccator was then restored to the church, and, better still, he enjoyed a peace of mind and confidence in God which was a continual feast. His example, moreover, did more to enlarge the congregation at the cross-roads than did the preaching of Paulinus in a whole year. This was unequivocally *sincere* repentance."

Dr. Adam Clarke, in his commentary on Genesis, says: "No man should expect mercy at the hand of God, who, having wronged his neighbor, refuses, when he has it in his power, to make restitution. Were he to weep tears of blood, both the justice and mercy of God would shut out his prayers if he make not his neighbor amends for the injury he has done him."

This principle seems to have ever characterized God's dealings with men. In the Jewish law it is said: "When a man or a woman shall commit any sin that men commit, or do a trespass against the Lord, and that person be guilty, then they shall confess their sin which they have done; and he shall recompense his trespass with the principal thereof, and add unto it the fifth part thereof, and give it unto him against whom he hath trespassed. But if the man have no kinsman to recompense the trespass unto, let the trespass be recompensed unto the Lord, even to the priest." Num. v:6-8. Now, it will be seen that, during the existence of this law, a trespass against a man was regarded as a trespass against God, the Giver of the law forbidding the trespass; and it was not only necessary to recompense to the party aggrieved, but it was necessary to add a fifth part to it. And if he could not find the party to whom recompense was due, he should make it to his kindred if he had any; and if there were none, then it was required to be made to the Lord through the priest. There was no escape from making restitution. See also Lev. vi:1-7. Indeed, it is difficult to conceive it possible for the heart of a man to be wholly subjugated to the will of the Lord and he not feel a *desire* to restore any thing unjustly taken from any one. If his pretensions be real he will make restitution if in his power to do so. We do not mean that all this must be consummated before remission of sins and adoption into the family of God can take place; but we insist that the disposition or purpose of heart must be present before the party is in a fit frame of mind to further obey God in anything. And if the purpose thus formed is abandoned and not carried out, "it had been better for them not to have known the way of righteousness, than after they have known it to turn from the holy commandment delivered unto them." 2 Pet. ii:21. Zaccheus said: "If I have taken any thing from any man by false accusation, I restore him fourfold. And Jesus said, This day is salvation come to this house." Luke xix:8, 9. Thus we see that the principle of restitution met the approval of Jesus, even to the extent of fourfold.

Once more: Jesus once said to a distinguished lawyer: "Thou shalt love thy neighbor as thyself." Matt. xxii:39. If we do this, will we not do by our neighbor as we do by ourselves? As the golden precept which crowned the rich casket of jewels contained in the sermon on the mount, it is said: "Whatsoever ye would that men should do to you, do you even so to them." Matt. vii:12. Do we desire that others *withhold from us* that which they have wrongfully taken from us? Or do we not rather desire them to restore to us that which is our own? If so, then we are bound to make that restitution to others which, under like circumstances, we would have them make to us. True, this is a strait and narrow path, and few there be who walk therein; but it is nevertheless "the law and the prophets." He who would come to God must come with a clean breast; hence "let us draw near with a true heart in full assurance of faith, having our hearts sprinkled from an evil conscience, and our bodies washed with pure water." Heb. x:22.

We come now to look for the order or place of repentance in the scheme of salvation presented in the gospel. From the fact that repentance is mentioned before faith, in a few places in the New Testament, many have concluded that men must repent before they exercise faith. We will very briefly examine these scriptures, that we may see whether or not they prove the doctrine in question.

"Now after that John was put in prison, Jesus came into Galilee preaching the gospel of the kingdom of God, and saying, The time is fulfilled, and the kingdom of God is at hand: repent ye, and believe the gospel." Mark i:14, 15. These persons were not required to believe the same gospel that was to be preached to every creature alluded to in the commission given after the resurrection of Jesus, but they were simply to believe in the *good news* that the kingdom of God was at hand. This was the gospel which Jesus preached to them. They were Jews who had previous faith in God whose laws they had violated; hence for this they were required to repent and then believe in the coming reign of Messiah. In like manner Paul preached to the Ephesians "repentance toward God and faith in the Lord Jesus Christ." Acts xx:21. Their repentance was toward God, in whom they believed before the Messiahship of Jesus was proclaimed to them. Hence toward Him their repentance was directed. There is still another passage worthy of note in this connection: "John came to you in the way of righteousness, and ye believed him not; but the publicans and harlots believed him: and you, when you had seen it, repented not afterward, that ye might believe him." Matt. xxi:32. Here we not only have the word repentance before faith, but expressive of that which was necessary to faith; but it is from *metamelomai*, indicating *regret*, and not from the word indicative of that change of mind which is truly repentance. It was the pride of the self-righteous Pharisees that kept them from believing the proofs and accepting the ministry of John. When they saw the publicans and harlots acting more consistently in submitting to His teaching, as they believed in God by whom John was sent, they should have regretted that these outcasts outstripped them in obedience to the servant of the God in whom they believed; and had they been filled with such regret, it would have prepared them for faith in the glad tidings proclaimed by John.

Having seen that the strongest proofs relied on do not support the theory, it may be well to see whether the interpretation given to these scriptures by the advocates of the theory be not contradicted by other scriptures the import of which we can not mistake. Paul says: "Whatsoever is not of faith is sin." Rom. xiv:23. If repentance precedes faith, it can not be of faith, and is therefore sin. Again: "Without faith it is impossible to please him, for he that cometh to God must believe that he is, and that he is a rewarder of them that diligently seek him." Heb. xi:6. If repentance precedes faith, it is without faith, and hence can not be pleasing to God. Surely, then, there must be error in the theory. Finally: The advocates of this doctrine associate repentance with prayer, generally, at the mourner's bench. Now, if these prayers, connected with repentance, are *before faith*, they can not be *in faith*. James says: "Let him ask in faith, nothing wavering, for he that wavereth is like a wave of the sea, driven with the wind and tossed; let not that man think that he shall receive any thing of the Lord." Jas. i:6, 7. Will God hear and answer these prayers made in connection with repentance (so called) before faith? James says: "Let not that man think that he shall receive any thing of the Lord." If there be truth in Holy Writ, a prayer made before faith will not be answered.

Perhaps it may be well to examine the history of a few actual cases of repentance, and see whether it preceded or succeeded faith. We have seen that Jesus himself said that the Ninevites repented at the preaching of Jonah; let us see whether or not faith in Jonah's preaching preceded their repentance: "And Jonah began to enter into the city a day's journey, and he cried and said, Yet forty days and Nineveh shall be overthrown." Jonah iii:4. Here is the preaching; what was the first effect of it? "So the people believed God." *Here is their faith, the first thing.* What next? "They proclaimed a fast, and put on sackcloth, from the greatest of them even to the least of them. For word came unto the king of Nineveh, and he arose from his throne, and he laid his robe from him, and covered himself with sackcloth, and sat in ashes. And he caused it to be proclaimed and published through Nineveh, by the decree of the king and his nobles, saying, Let neither man nor beast, herd nor flock, taste any thing: let them not feed, nor drink water: but let man and beast be covered with sackcloth, and cry mightily unto God; yea, let them turn, every one, from his evil way, and from the violence that is in their hands. Who can tell if God will turn and repent, and turn away from his fierce anger, that we perish not? And God saw their works, that they turned from their evil ways." Jonah iii:5-10. Here is their repentance. Who can not see the order of events? First, Jonah preached the message which God gave him to say to them. Second, The people believed God. Third, They turned from their evil way. On the day of Pentecost the order was similar. Peter preached, the people heard, believed, were cut to the heart, asked what to do, were commanded to *repent* and be baptized. In the narrative already twice quoted from Paul, 2 Cor. vii:8-10, he wrote them a letter; they believed it—were made sorry by it—they sorrowed in a godly manner, and their godly sorrow worked repentance.

It will be admitted that repentance is produced in some way by some cause. If it precedes faith, faith can not be the cause of it, and we would be pleased to learn what does produce it. Do you admit that a belief with all the heart in God, Jesus, heaven, hell, apostles, prophets, and all things written and spoken by inspiration, precedes and causes repentance? then will you please give us a minute description of the faith that *follows repentance*—what it is, and how it comes. We acknowledge the want of light along here. We are not very well prepared to understand how we are to repent for transgressing the laws of a king in whom we have no faith. To us the doctrine seems not only contrary to the order of the Bible, but at war with every principle of reason and common sense.

But we may be told that repentance is the *direct gift of God*. The distinguished Watson says: "But if repentance be taken in the second sense, and this is certainly the light in which true repentance is exhibited in the Scriptures, then it is forgotten that such is the corrupt state of man that he is incapable of penitence of this kind. This follows from that view of human depravity which we have already established from the Scriptures, and which we need not repeat. In conformity with this view of the entire corruptness of man's nature, therefore repentance is said to be *the gift* of Christ, who, in consequence of being exalted to be a Prince and a Saviour, gives repentance as well as remission of sins—a gift quite superfluous if to repent truly were in the power of man and independent of Christ. To suppose man to be capable of a repentance which is the result of genuine principle is to assume human nature to be what it is not." *Watson's Institutes*, vol. ii, pp. 98, 99.

It seems to us that the dogma of *hereditary depravity* is the Pandora's box from which have sprung most, if not all, the errors which distract the religious world. This doctrine once received, and every thing else is tried by it. Hence man can not repent because the total depravity of his nature renders him incapable of it; and though God has commanded him to repent, and told him plainly that he shall perish if he does not repent, yet He must give him repentance before he can repent!! Suppose God never gives the man repentance, and per consequence the man never repents, what then? Will God damn him for His own neglect? Surely not. We know it is said: "Him hath God exalted with his right hand to be a Prince and a Saviour, for to give repentance to Israel, and forgiveness of sins." Acts v:31. Again: "Then hath God also to the Gentiles granted repentance unto life." Acts xi:18.

Are these passages sufficient to prove that man is incapable of repenting? God gives us bread, but we have to work and make it, nevertheless. So God gives us repentance by placing motives before us to induce it; hence Paul asks: "Despisest thou the riches of his goodness and forbearance and longsuffering; not knowing that the goodness of God leadeth thee to repentance?" Rom. ii:4. God has manifested His love for man in the gift of His Son, through whom salvation is offered on certain conditions, among which repentance holds a prominent place. He has revealed Himself to man in all the loveliness of His true character. The joys and bliss of heaven are set forth in a revelation adapted to his comprehension, and thus the goodness of God leads man to repentance; hence Paul says: "The servant of the Lord must not strive; but be gentle unto all men, apt to teach, patient; in meekness instructing those that oppose themselves; if God peradventure will give them repentance to the acknowledging of the truth; and that they may recover themselves out of the snare of the devil, who are taken captive by him at his will." 2 Tim. ii:24-26. Why should the servant of the Lord manifest such patience, and so meekly instruct the opposers, if God gives them repentance directly? Does not this case clearly show that God gives men repentance by a system of means calculated to produce it? He gives man faith by giving him testimony calculated to produce it, and will damn him if he does not believe it. He gives man bread by giving him the means with which to make it, but unless he uses the means he will starve for food. So God gives man repentance by causing repentance and remission of sins to be preached among all nations in the name of His Son, yet he who does not repent will surely perish. Then let no man wait for God to give him repentance directly, until he is willing to sit, with folded arms, and wait for God to give him *bread in the same way.*

CHAPTER XI.

THE CONFESSION.

It is very generally admitted that *some sort* of a confession of *something* should be made by everyone at *sometime* prior to admission into the church of God; but *what* this confession is, *how* and *when* it should be made, and its *office* in the plan of salvation, are questions which have greatly perplexed those who have spoken and written concerning them for the last three hundred years. In the earlier ages of the church persons were required to confess with the mouth their faith in Jesus Christ as the *Son of God* prior to baptism, and the only question worthy of our consideration at present is whether or not this practice was authorized by inspired precept or example. Paul says: "All scripture is given by inspiration of God, and is profitable for doctrine, for reproof, for correction, for instruction in righteousness, that the man of God may be perfect, thoroughly furnished unto all good works." 2 Tim. iii:16, 17. If the man of God is authorized to require the confession to be made by anyone, surely it is a good work; and if a good work, the Scriptures thoroughly furnish the man of God to it; *i.e.*, they thoroughly furnish the man of God with all needful instructions concerning it. If he is not therein thoroughly furnished to it, then It follows that it is not a good work, and should be abandoned. It may be well, then, for us to examine the Divine Volume, and see whether or not it furnishes authority for such a practice.

When the Ethiopian nobleman demanded baptism at the hands of Philip, the inspired teacher said: "If thou believest with all thy heart thou mayest. And he answered and said, I believe that Jesus Christ is the Son of God." Acts viii:37. That this was the proper confession is evident from the fact that it was satisfactory to the man of God, who thereupon proceeded at once to baptize him. And that it should be made *after faith* is evident from the fact that it would have been false had not the faith preceded it; and that it should be made before baptism is evident from the fact that it was demanded as a condition precedent to baptism. Here, then, we learn what is to be confessed: *i.e.*, that "I believe that Jesus Christ is the Son of God," and that the time to make it is *after faith* and *before baptism*. While this verse is regarded as genuine, the question of authority for this confession is not debatable at all. Here is a plain, unmistakable precedent which we dare not ignore. Our practice must conform to it, or the passage must be removed from the Divine Volume. But we are told that the passage is spurious—an interpolation which constitutes no part of the inspired text.

While our limits will not allow us to enter upon an extensive examination of the claims of this verse, nor have the means afforded us been such as to enable us to decide the matter, even to our own satisfaction, we are by no means satisfied that the proofs offered by those who would set it aside are conclusive. Indeed, we are not quite sure that there is, at this day, a *possibility* of knowing with certainty that it is spurious. This narrative (the Acts), like all the other books of the New Testament, was at first a separate manuscript, and was circulated by being copied by uninspired men. These copies were again copied, and copies of copies were copied, how far from the original we have no means of knowing. The first copy taken was in all probability imperfect, as it is very difficult to copy any thing without imperfections; and these imperfections must have increased, as the copies were more remote from the original, because each copy must contain the errors of the one from which it was taken, with the chance of incorporating others. As the only sure method of correcting these errors was to compare copies with the original, when it wore out, we see not how any further corrections could have been made. That the original manuscript, and all copies taken directly from it, have long since been *worn out* is next to certain.

How, then, are the claims of the verse in question to be settled? Were it wanting in all the manuscripts of the first thousand years, and only found in such us are of modern date, this would be a circumstance well calculated to cast suspicion upon it; but Dr. Hacket tells us that this interpolation was known to Irenæus as early as the year 170. Then it was bound to have been in copies taken at or before that period. It is fair to presume that the original and all the first copies were circulated among, and read, and handled by thousands of persons, and hence were most likely worn out before that time, so that we are not sure that even Irenæus had the privilege of comparing such copies as he saw with the original, so as to be assured that it was spurious. Hence, unless Dr. Hacket would furnish us with the testimony upon which Irenæus based his judgment, we can not accept it as conclusive.

Tregelles tells us that this verse was inserted by Erasmus, as being supposed to have been incorrectly omitted in his manuscripts; and from his edition this and similar passages have been perpetuated, just as if they were undoubtedly genuine. Are we to understand by this that the interpolation began with Erasmus? If so, how could Irenæus have known of it so early as A.D. 170, more than twelve hundred years before the time Erasmus lived? It occurs to us that those who would set aside this verse should harmonize their testimony, for when it is so plainly inconsistent we are inclined to reject it all.

The circumstance which casts the darkest shade upon the purity of the verse is the fact that the most profound critics, whose opportunities have been best for examining the subject, and whose peculiar labors called them directly into its examination, have decided against it. Tregelles tells us that "no part of this verse is recognized in critical texts." While the version of the New Testament put forth by the American Bible Union retains the verse, the translators have appended a foot-note, saying, "It is wanting in the best authorities." As it was their object to give the English reader a pure version of the mind of the Spirit, we see not why they retained the verse at all, if satisfied that it was spurious. Anderson has excluded the verse from his version of the New Testament, and many other men of great research have pronounced it an interpolation; but, as far as we have been able to examine the grounds of their decision, we regard them as inconclusive; and we think that attacks upon a verse that has had a place in the Bible, according to the testimony of its opposers, since the year 170, more than seventeen hundred years, should be very cautiously made, lest, unfortunately, we shake the confidence of the uninformed in the whole Bible.

Were this verse inconsistent with the sense of the context, we might give more credit to attacks upon its purity; on the contrary, as it is not only in harmony with the context, but indispensable to a completion of the sense, we insist that a presumption is created in its favor; and we wish to call attention to what we think is plain to the most ordinary reader, that there is evidently *a blank in the narrative without the 37th verse.* We quote from Anderson's version of the New Testament, in which the verse is omitted: "And as they went along the road they came to some water, and the eunuch said: See, here is water; what hinders me from being immersed? And he commanded the chariot to stand still, and they both went down into the water, both Philip and the eunuch, and he immersed him."

Now, please observe that when they came to water the eunuch asked a question, saying, "See, here is water, what hinders me from being immersed?" and to this important question his inspired instructor makes no answer whatever! none!! He knew that Jesus, in the very commission which authorized the act about to be performed, said: "He that believeth and is baptized shall be saved," and when asked what hindered baptism he made no answer at all, but acting upon the presumption that the eunuch believed, proceeded to baptize him, without asking whether he believed or not. And, stranger still, the eunuch commanded the chariot to stand still, and got out of it, without knowing whether Philip would baptize him or not. Are we to believe that Philip said nothing in answer to the question? and yet the eunuch commanded the chariot to be still—that both got out of it and went down into the water in silence. Can any sane man believe it? Is there not a perceivable blank which the sense requires to be filled with just such language as we find in the verse in question? We can not pursue the subject further, but dismiss it with the remark that the verse is fairly deducible from the connection, and it will require stronger proof than we have yet seen to shake our confidence in its purity. But whether it be real or spurious the confession can be justified by other scriptures, the authenticity of which will not be called in question by any believer in the inspiration of the Bible.

Upon the banks of Jordan, in the presence of the multitude that waited on the ministry of John, God bore witness to the divine character and mission of His Son, saying: "This is my beloved Son, in whom I am well pleased." Matt. iii:17.

Upon the truth of the grand proposition that *Jesus is the*

Christ, the Son of God, rests the salvation of the world, and in it are centered all the hopes which mortals can have that reach beyond the grave. It underlies the whole scheme of man's redemption. For if He be not the Son of God, He was an impostor, the Bible is a fable, and no man was, is, or ever will be under obligations to believe in or obey Him. On the contrary, if this is true, His pretensions were real, His claims are just, and every man who professes to believe it puts himself under obligations to accept the terms he imposes. Hence, Jesus said: "Whosoever therefore shall confess me before men, him will I confess also before my Father which is in heaven; but whosoever shall deny me before men, him will I also deny before my Father which is in heaven." Matt. x:33. Here He gives us plainly to know the importance of confessing Him before men. But *how* did they confess Him? When the parents of the blind man, whose eyes were opened by Jesus, were questioned, they feared the people, for "the Jews had agreed already that if any man did confess that he was the Christ, he should be put out of the synagogue." John ix:22. Then to confess Him was to *confess that He was the Christ,* and to deny Him was to deny that He was the Christ. Of course, some were making this confession, and others denying it, or the Jews would not have made such an agreement concerning those who did make it. These sayings among the people may have given rise to the question which Jesus asked His disciples, saying: "Whom do men say that I, the Son of man, am?" Matt. xvi:13. In answer to this question the disciples gave some of the opinions which the people expressed concerning Him, when He put the question directly to them, saying: "Whom say ye that I am? And Simon Peter answered, and said, Thou art the Christ, the Son of the living God. Matt. xvi:15, 16. Here the same grand truth is confessed by Peter; and Jesus assures him that on it His church is to be built: as much as to say, "All my claims upon the world rest upon this truth which you have now confessed, not because you have confessed it, but *because it is true.* You could not have known it, had not my Father, at my baptism, and at my transfiguration, and also through the mighty works I have done in His name, in your presence, revealed it to you. All who confess it put themselves under obligations thereby to accept the terms and obligations I impose, as much as if God, who sent me, did himself impose them; hence I will make this truth the foundation of my church." By making this confession the party puts himself under the strongest possible obligations to observe all the ordinances emanating from Jesus as *Head* of the church built upon the truth confessed. Hence says John: "Whosoever shall confess that Jesus is the Son of God, God dwelleth in him, and he in God." I John iv:15. And again: "Who is he that overcometh the world, but he that believeth that Jesus is the Son of God." 1 John v:5.

Having thus seen that this fact, which was attested by God and confessed by Peter, is the truth to be believed in order to overcome the world, and *confessed* in order that God may dwell in the party making it, it may be well to see *how* it is confessed. Paul says that "at the name of Jesus every knee shall bow of things in heaven, and things in earth, and things under the earth, and that every tongue should confess that Jesus Christ is Lord, to the glory of God the Father." Phil. ii:10, 11. Again: "As I live, saith the Lord, every knee shall bow to me, and every tongue shall confess to God." Rom. xiv:11. In these quotations two important facts are made apparent. First: The confession is to be made *with the tongue*. Second: God has determined that *it shall be made*, and, therefore, it can not be dispensed with or ignored by those who would honor His authority.

But from the pen of the same apostle we have another lesson on this subject. He says: "If thou shalt confess with thy mouth the Lord Jesus, and shalt believe in thy heart that God hath raised him from the dead, thou shalt be saved; for with the heart man believeth unto righteousness, and with the mouth confession is made unto salvation." Rom. x:9, 10. We here learn that the confession is not only to be *made with the mouth,* but it is a *condition of salvation,* and therefore precedes remission of sins. Mark well that Paul does not say "with a *nod of the head* confession is made unto salvation," nor does he say that by visiting the sick, or other acts of obedience through life, confession is made—but it is made WITH THE MOUTH *unto salvation;* and while Paul is thus specific we dare not accept it made in any other way, provided, the subject has the use of the tongue with which to make it.

Having learned that the confession with the mouth is a condition of and unto salvation, and therefore before it, and as Jesus says that "he that believeth and is baptized shall be saved" (Mark xvi:16), it follows that confession precedes baptism. As the baptized believer is saved, there is no period *between* his baptism and his salvation in which to make the confession; and hence, as it is made before salvation, it is certainly made before baptism. As it is with the heart man believeth that Jesus is the Christ, the Son of God, and *with the mouth* he confesses what the heart believes, it follows that the confession with the mouth is subsequent to faith or belief; hence, clearly *the confession is located after faith and before baptism.* As stated elsewhere, were a man to make the confession with the mouth before he believed with the heart, it would be a downright falsehood, for he would thereby say he believed what he did not believe.

Now, if the reader will review the ground over which we have traveled, he will find that God has determined that man shall confess with the mouth his faith in Jesus Christ as being the Son of God before he is baptized, and by so doing he puts himself under obligation to observe all the laws emanating from Him as Head of the church built upon the truth he thus confesses. Paul's account of Timothy's confession is in perfect harmony with this view of the whole subject. We quote from Anderson's version as follows: "Fight the good fight of faith; lay hold on eternal life to which you have been called, and for which you confessed the good confession before many witnesses." 1 Tim. vi:12. Jesus proposed to confess such as confessed Him *before men*—Timothy made the good confession *before many witnesses.* Paul tells the Romans that confession is made unto salvation; and when we supply the antecedent to which the relative "which" refers in his account of Timothy's confession, we find it reading thus: "For which, *eternal life,* you confessed the good confession." Then Timothy made the confession *unto salvation,* or for *eternal life,* "whereunto he was called" by the gospel when Paul preached it to him. Surely this is plain enough.

That the "good confession" made by Timothy consisted in confessing that Jesus was the Christ, the Son of God, is further shown by the fact that in the next verse Paul applies the very same words—*"the good confession"*—to the confession made by

Jesus before Pontius Pilate. And though in the account given by Matthew of what He said in answer to Pilate, the words *I am the Son of God* are not found, yet we are assured by the testimony of His enemies that this was embraced in His confession. In derision they said: "If thou be the Son of God, come down from the cross." And again: "He trusted in God, let him deliver him now, if he will have him: for he said, I am the Son of God." Matt. xxvii:40-43. If this, then, was what Paul called the good confession when made by the Saviour, it is also what he called the good confession when made by Timothy, before many witnesses, for eternal life, whereunto he was called by the gospel which was preached to him. Kind reader, have you made *this* confession with your mouth to your salvation? If not, you may have to make it to your eternal condemnation, for we have seen that the decree has gone forth that *every tongue shall confess that Jesus is Lord,* to the glory of God the Father.

But it is sometimes said that there was not time enough on the day of Pentecost, after Peter quit preaching, for three thousand to have made this confession before their batpism. Will the objector tell us how long it would have taken, on that occasion, for this same three thousand to have each told such an *"experience"* as HE requires previous to baptism? While it would have been possible for one speaker (and there were twelve present) to have propounded the question, "Do each one of you believe, with all the heart, that Jesus is the Christ, the Son of God?" and the response, "I DO" to have come simultaneously from three thousand tongues in as little time as it could have been asked of and answered by a single person, it could not have been possible for such experiences as are *now* told to have been told in that way. They may all differ in the details, and must therefore be told, listened to, and decided upon separately. Say, then, how long would it have taken to hear three thousand of them in that way? We have seen the inexorable law that every tongue shall confess that Jesus is Lord, and that with the mouth confession is made unto salvation; hence the presentation of *difficulties* can not *set aside the positive law* as long as there remains a *possibility* that the law was obeyed. The objector must show that obedience to the law *was impossible* before we are at liberty to presume that it was not obeyed, and even then the impossibility might constitute an *exception* to the law, but not an abrogation of it.

Were it profitable, we might entertain the reader with a feast of fat things sometimes narrated in those so-called experiences, but we forebear. We beg permission, however, to suggest a few plain questions for the reflection of our readers before leaving this branch of our subject:

If the belief of the fact that Jesus is the *Son of God* is the faith that overcomes the world, will believing that He is the *very and eternal God* do the same thing? If this is what must be confessed with the mouth unto salvation, after faith and before baptism, and it is not made, will we get the salvation unto which it should have been made? If Timothy made this good confession for eternal life, may we dispense with it, and still get the eternal life for which he made it? If God has determined that *every tongue shall confess* that Jesus is Lord, to the glory of God the Father, and we fail to make it unto our salvation, will we not *have to make it* in the final day to our eternal condemnation? If Jesus has promised to confess before His Father such as confess Him before men, will He still confess us if we fail to confess Him? If God dwells in those who confess that Jesus is the Son of God, will He also dwell in those who do not confess this fact? Does not the language imply that He *only* dwells in such as make this confession? If this is what has to be confessed, will it be safe to substitute a narrative of our dreams, feelings, and imaginations in the shape of an *experience* instead of the confession required by the law of the Lord? And if these dreams, feelings, and imaginations constitute all the confession made prior to baptism, *when do the parties confess that Jesus Christ is the Son of God,* or that Jesus is Lord to the glory of God the Father, to their own salvation, and for eternal life, and which secures the dwelling of God in those who make it?

But we have said that in the earlier ages of the church persons were baptized upon a simple confession of their faith in Jesus Christ. Neander says: "At the beginning, when it was important that the church should rapidly extend itself, those who confessed their belief in *Jesus* as the *Messiah* (among the Jews), or their belief in one God, and in *Jesus* as the *Messiah* (among the Gentiles), were immediately baptized, as appears from the

New Testament. Gradually it came to be thought necessary that those who wished to be received into the Christian Church should be subjected to a more careful preparatory instruction, and a stricter examination."—Neander's History of the Church, vol. i, p. 385.

Thus we have the testimony of this distinguished historian that in primitive times all that was required was that the candidate should confess his faith in the fact that Jesus was the Messiah. How long before this scriptural confession was abandoned he does not tell us, but it was gradual. Hence, as far as his authority goes, it shows what the New Testament confession was, and certainly the church had no right to change it.

Dr. Robinson says: "Among primitive Christians there was an uniform belief that Jesus was the Christ, and a perfect harmony of affection."—Benedict's History, vol. i, p. 99.

Again: "These churches were all composed of reputed believers, who had been baptized by immersion on the profession of their faith."—*Ibid*, p. 8.

Mosheim says: "Whoever acknowledged Christ as the Saviour of mankind, and made a solemn profession of his confidence in him, was immediately baptized and received into the church."—Maclain's Mosheim, First Century, p. 38. Part II, chap. 2, sec. 7.

Again, p. 42, chap. iii, sec. 5, he says: "In the earliest times of the church all who professed firmly to believe that *Jesus was the only Redeemer* of the world, and who, in consequence of this profession, promised to live in a manner conformable to the purity of his holy religion, were immediately received among the disciples of Christ."

These quotations might be extended almost indefinitely, but the foregoing are deemed sufficient to show that in primitive times the only confession demanded was a belief in the fact that *Jesus Christ was the Son of God*. As this was the confession authorized of the Lord, and required by the apostles and primitive Christians, who is authorized to demand any thing else now? Can we improve upon the work of the Lord? Surely, it is more safe to keep within the boundary prescribed in the New Testament. Has a church the right to determine whether or not a sinner may obey the Lord? Surely not; yet this is just what is assumed. A man wishes to be baptized in obedience to the Lord, but the church must hear his *experience,* and determine whether or not it is genuine before they will permit him to be baptized. And they decide upon the value of his experience, not by its approximation to the divine models given in the New Testament, but by comparing it with their own; and if his feelings have been like theirs, he is accepted, otherwise he is rejected. Paul says: "We dare not make ourselves of the number, or compare ourselves with some that commend themselves; but they, measuring themselves by themselves, and comparing themselves among themselves, are not wise." 2 Cor. x:12. Now, if these persons are not doing just the thing here pronounced unwise when comparing experiences, then we know not how they may do so. However much the man may desire to obey God, he can not be permitted to do so unless his experience is like that of each one who decides upon the merits of his. Who has the right to come between the sinner and his God and say he may or may not obey what God hath enjoined upon him? Surely, this is a most fearful responsibility. Nor is this the worst feature of the case; for however anxious a man may be to submit to baptism, and however anxious the administrator may be to wait upon him, he dare not do it until the church is convened to pass upon the merits of the experience. Was this the custom anciently? When the eunuch demanded baptism at the hands of Philip, the latter did not think of convening the church to hear and decide upon the experience of the candidate, but he said: "If thou believest with all thy heart thou mayest;" and when the eunuch said, "I believe that Jesus Christ is the Son of God," Philip proceeded at once to baptize him, without waiting to know what the church thought of it, or whether this was like theirs, yea or nay. It was what the Lord required, and this was enough for him.

Nor is the church any less liable to be imposed upon by these experiences than by a simple confession of faith in Christ. If the man be insincere, he can just as easily fabricate a narrative of falsehoods suited to his purpose as he could falsely confess his faith in Jesus Christ. Is man capable of improving upon the plan instituted by the Lord? If so, why could he not devise *a system of salvation* without invoking the wisdom of heaven at all? And if we may introduce such an addition to the confession, where will such interpolations stop? If the word of God is perfect, let us come to it, and be satisfied with it.

CHAPTER XII.

BAPTISM.

The subject of baptism has engaged the attention of many of the wisest heads, and employed the tongues and pens of many of the ablest speakers and writers that have blessed the world by their labors since the days of the Apostles. In the examination of a subject upon which there has been so much spoken and written, it will not be expected that we shall be able to present a single thought that has not been presented in some shape by some one who has preceded us. If there is a subject connected with man's salvation that has been *exhausted,* surely this one has. We have read every thing that has come in our way on the subject, and have profited especially by the writings of Campbell, Carson, Conant, Booth, Gale, Hinton, Bailey, and Stuart, whose works we have by us at this writing; but we will write just as though nothing had ever been written on the subject before, presenting every thing we may deem important to a thorough examination of the subject in our own way, without regard to the source from which we learned it, whether from the Bible or the writings of men tried by the Bible. If we speak not as the oracles of God speak, then prove all things and hold fast that which is good. First, then, we inquire:

What is Baptism?

When Jesus commanded his disciples to teach all nations, *baptizing* them, did He mean any thing? if so, what? It is scarcely necessary to say to the reader that the words *baptist, baptism, baptize, baptized,* and *baptizing* are all Greek words anglicized in termination to satisfy the demands of English euphony, and *transferred* (not translated) to our version of the sacred Scriptures; hence, if we would comprehend the subject, we must learn correctly the meaning of these words, not as defined by authors whose works are made to reflect the faith of the party to which they belong, but we must get at their import at the time the Saviour and the inspired speakers and writers employed them.

The word *baptisma,* rendered *baptism,* occurs in the New

Testament twenty-two times. The word *baptismos* occurs four times, three times rendered *washing* and once *baptism*. *Baptistees* occurs fourteen times connected with John, and is rendered *baptist*. *Baptidzo* occurs eighty times, seventy-eight times rendered *baptize, baptized*, etc., and one time each *wash* and *washing*. This family of words is derived from *bapto*, and each derivative partakes of the primary import of this word. It occurs five times in the New Testament, and *embapto* once. Matt. xxvi:23, Mark xiv:20, Luke xvi:24, John xviii:26 (twice) and Rev. xix:13. This word is never used to indicate baptism, and hence is not transferred but translated every time; hence you will find it *dip, dippeth, dipped*. Language has no law that is better established than that derivative words inherit the radical form and primary meaning of the words from which they are derived. This being so, and the primary meaning of *bapto* being *dip*, does it not follow that its derivative *baptidzo* must be rendered *dip, immerse*, or by some word equivalent thereto? If baptism may be performed by sprinkling or pouring, is it not strange that we never have *baptidzo*, the word used to indicate it, rendered *sprinkle* or *pour?* These words often occur in the sacred Scriptures, but never from the word *baptidzo*. Sprinkle is always from its own representative *raino*, and pour from *cheo*.

While the primary meaning of *bapto*, and, per consequence, of its derivative *baptidzo*, is to dip, immerse, overwhelm, the meaning of sprinkle is to *scatter in drops*, and pour to *turn out in a stream*. As well might we expect purely English parentage to produce a progeny of baboons and monkeys as for *baptidzo*, or any other word derived from *bapto*, to mean sprinklor of pour.

Worcester, in his unabridged Dictionary, first defines the Greek word *baptismos* "a dipping," and then proceeds to define the same word (less two letters) as an English word thus: "Act of baptizing, a Christian rite or sacrament, symbolical of initiation into the church and consecration to a pure life; performed by immersion, ablution, or sprinkling, and accompanied with a form of words." Now, how we to reconcile his definition of *baptismos*, "a dipping," with his definition of *baptism*, "performed by immersion, ablution, or sprinkling?" The former is the primitive meaning of the Greek when Jesus used it to indicate His will, the latter is the modern *abuse* of the term defined in accommodation to present usage. The Greek *baptidzo* he defines "to dip or merge," and then defines baptize "to administer baptism to; to immerse in water, or to sprinkle with water, in token of initiation into the Christian church; to christen." Here again we see that the word employed by the Lord means to *dip* or *merge*, while its modernized equivalent means to *immerse* or sprinkle.

Webster, in his unabridged Dictionary, defines "*baptisma baptismos*, from *baptidzein*, to baptize, from *baptein*, to dip in water." Then he defines baptism as from these: "The act of baptizing, the application of water to a person, as a sacrament or religious ceremony, by which he is initiated into the visible church of Christ. This is usually performed by sprinkling or immersion." When defining the Greek it means to dip, but in these days it is usually performed by sprinkling or immersion! Can dipping be done by sprinkling?

We introduce these authors, not for the purpose of objecting to them, for they were bound to define words as used when they wrote, but we introduce them, first, to show the marked difference between the Greek words employed by inspiration and the modern *abuse* of them; and, secondly, that we may have the benefit of their authority in showing that the Greek, from which we have the words in controversy, means *to dip* or *immerse*. Had there been any such meanings as sprinkle and pour in the Greek, surely they would have found them, and the definitions they give to the anglicized equivalents show that had they found them they would have given them. Ours is a living, growing, and, therefore, a changing language, and the import of adopted words is as liable to be changed by usage as native English words. Surely, it would have astonished the Greek writers of eighteen hundred years ago to have found a definition to *baptisma*, like those given to baptism by Webster and Worcester, saying, "it may be performed by immersion, ablution, or sprinkling." But let us examine the works of those whose peculiar business it is to define Greek words:

1. PICKERING defines *baptidzo* "to dip, immerse, submerge, plunge, sink, overwhelm; to steep, to soak, to wet, to wash one's self, or bathe."

2. GROVES: "*Baptidzo* (from *bapto*, to dip), to dip, immerse, immerge, plunge; to wash, cleanse, purify."

Mr. Groves and many others show that *baptidzo* comes from *bapto*, to dip; hence, however numerous the meanings of *bapto*, *baptidzo* inherits only the primary meaning *dip*, in accordance with the law already laid down.

3. ROBINSON: "*Baptidzo*—to immerse, to sink; for example, spoken of ships, galleys, etc. In the New Testament, to wash, to cleanse by washing; to wash one's self, to bathe, perform ablution," etc.

Mr. Robinson was a Presbyterian and gives the primary meaning of the word *baptidzo* to immerse, and then gives the meanings *wash, cleanse,* etc., from the New Testament, from such passages as do not speak of baptism, and where the word is translated, as Mark vii:4, Luke xi:38.

4. LIDDELL and SCOTT: "*Baptidzo*—to dip in or under water; of ships, to sink or disable them. Pass., to be drenched. 2. 2. Metahp., soaked in wine, over head and ears in debt; being drowned with questions or getting into deep water. To draw wine by dipping the cup in the bowl. 3. To baptize. Mid., to dip oneself; to get oneself baptized. [Latest edition].

"*Baptismos*—a dipping in water, ablution.

"*Baptistas*—one that dips, a baptizer, the Baptist, N.T."

In the first American edition of Liddell and Scott's lexicon *to pour upon* was in the definition of *baptidzo*, but this was expunged from subsequent editions.

In a discussion at Flat Creek, our opponent read these definitions from his edition of Liddell and Scott, remarking that this work had been tampered with by immersionists until it is difficult to tell when we have the real definitions of the authors—that it is likely an edition will be presented not having *pour upon* in its definition of baptidzo. When asked who was the editor of his edition, he said, "Drisler." Drisler is the editor of our edition, and, as far as we are informed, is the only American editor who has ever published Liddell and Scott. So it is certain that the same editor had control of the work when *pour upon* was *in* the definition, and when it *came out;* and could such a definition have been verified by examples it would doubtless have been retained. As it could not be sustained and had to come out, it is quite clear that sectarianism put it there and would have kept it there if any such meaning belonged to the word.

5. DONNEGAN: "*Baptidzo*—to immerse repeatedly into a liquid, to submerge; to soak thoroughly, to saturate, hence to drench with wine. Metaphorically, to confound totally; to dip in a vessel and draw. Passive, to be immersed."

Some lexicographers regard the termination *"zo"* as a *frequentative*, indicating a repetition of the act; hence they define *baptidzo* "to dip repeatedly." But Moses Stuart, a justly celebrated Presbyterian critic, in his work on baptism, has clearly shown this to be an error. Indeed, those who oppose us can not base an objection on this hypothesis, for then would they have to repeat their sprinkling as often as we our immersion.

6. SCHREVELLIUS, whose definitions are given in Latin, defines *baptidzo*, "*baptizo, mergo, abluo, lavo;*" which we translate, I baptize, I immerse, I cleanse, I wash.

The foregoing definitions we have taken directly from the original works of the authors quoted. The definitions following we collate from debates where they were presented in presence of opponents competent to have exposed any want of fidelity to the works from which they were taken. That they are correct we have no doubt.

7. SCAPULA: "*Baptidzo*—to dip, to immerse; also, to submerge or overwhelm, to wash, to cleanse."

8. STEPHANUS: "*Bapto* and *baptidzo*—to dip or immerse, as we dip things for the purpose of dyeing them, or immerge them in water."

9. ROBERTSON: "*Baptidzo*—to immerse, to wash."

10. PASOR: "*Bapto et baptidzo*—to dip, immerse, to dye, because it is done by immersing. It differs from *dunai,* which means to sink to the bottom and to be thoroughly submerged."

"Metaphorically, in Matthew, afflictions are compared to a flood of waters, in which they seem to be immersed who are overwhelmed with the miseries and misfortunes of life, yet only so overwhelmed as to emerge again."

11. PARKHURST: "*Baptidzo*—to immerse in or wash with water, in token of purification." "Figuratively, to be immersed or plunged into a flood or sea, as it were of grievous afflictions and suffering."

12. BRETSCHNEIDER: "*Baptidzo*—properly, often to dip, often to wash; to wash, to cleanse; in the middle voice, I wash or cleanse myself. An entire immersion belongs to the nature of baptism. This is the meaning of the word; for in *baptidzo* is contained the idea of a complete immersion under water; at least so is *baptisma* in the New Testament. In the New Testament *baptidzo* is not used unless concerning the sacred and solemn submersion, which the Jews used."

"*Baptisma*—immersion, submersion. In the New Testament it is used only concerning the sacred submersion, which the Fathers call baptism."

13. SUIDAS: "*Baptidzo*—to sink, to plunge, immerse, wet, wash, cleanse, purify."

14. GREENFIELD: "*Baptidzo* means to immerse, immerge, submerge, sink." In New Testament, "to wash, perform ablution, cleanse; to immerse, baptize, and perform the rite of baptism."

15. BASS: "*Baptidzo*—to dip, immerse, plunge in water; to bathe one's self; to be immersed in sufferings or afflictions."

16. DR. JOHN JONES: "*Baptidzo*—I plunge, I plunge in water, dip, baptize, bury, overwhelm."

17. WAHL: "*Baptidzo* (from *bapto*—to immerse; more frequently, to immerse in N. T.) To immerse (always in Josephus, Ant. IX, 10, 2, etc. Polyb. etc.). Properly and truly concerning sacred immersion."

18. HEDERICUS: "*Baptidzo*—I plunge, immerse, overwhelm in water, I cleanse, wash, I baptize, in a sacred sense. *Baptisma*—immersion, dipping, baptism. *Baptistees*—one who immerses, who washes; one who baptizes; a baptizer.

19. EWING: "*Baptidzo*—in its primary and radical sense, I cover with water or some other fluid, in whatever manner this is done, whether by immersion or affusion, wholly or partially, permanently, or for a moment; and in the passive voice, I am covered with water or some other fluid, in some manner or other. Hence, the word is used in several different senses, referring either mediately or immediately to the primary idea. It is used to denote, First: I plunge or sink completely under water. Second: I cover partially with water, I wet. Third: I overwhelm or cover with water by rushing, flowing, or pouring upon. And in the passive voice, I am overwhelmed or covered with water in that

mode. Fourth: I drench or impregnate with liquor by affusion. Fifth: I oppress or overwhelm, in a metaphorical sense, by bringing afflictions or distresses upon. Sixth: I wash, in general, without specifying the mode. Seventh: I wash for the special purpose of symbolical, ritual, or ceremonial purification. Eighth: I administer the ordinance of Christian baptism; I baptize.

20. Vossius: "*Baptidzo*—to baptize, signifies to plunge. It certainly, therefore, signifies more than *epi polazin,* which is to swim lightly on top, and less than *dunein,* which is to sink to the bottom so as to be destroyed."

21. Trommius: "*Baptidzo*—to baptize, to immerse, to dip."

22. Bagster: "*Baptidzo*—to dip, to immerse, to cleanse, or purify by washing, to administer the rite of baptism, to baptize.

"*Baptisma*—immersion, baptism, ordinance of baptism.

"*Baptismos*—an act of dipping or immersing."

23. Sophocles: "*Baptidzo*—to dip, to immerse; sink, to be drowned (as the effect of sinking), to sink. Trop., to afflict; soaked in liquor; to be drunk, intoxicated."

24. Leigh: "*Baptidzo*—the native and proper signification of *baptidzo,* is to dip in water, or to plunge under water."

25. Richardson: "*Baptidzo*—to dip or merge in water, to sink, to plunge or immerse."

26. Schottgenius: "*Baptidzo,* from *bapto*—properly, to plunge, to immerse, to cleanse, to wash."

27. Castel: "*Baptidzo*—to bathe, baptize, immerse."

28. Constantine: "*Baptismos*—baptism, the act of dyeing; that is, of plunging.

29. Minhert: "*Baptidzo*—to baptize; properly, indeed, it signifies to immerse, to plunge, to dip in water. But because it is common to plunge or dip a thing to wash it, hence it signifies also to wash, to wash away.

"*Baptisma*—immersion, dipping into, washing, washing away; properly, and according to its etymology, it denotes that washing that is done by immersion."

30. Thayer: "*Baptidzo*—1 Prop. to dip repeatedly, to immerge, submerge . . . 2. to cleanse by dipping or submerging, to wash, to make clean with water . . . to wash one's self, bathe. Met. overwhelm. *Baptisma*—N.T. *immersion, submersion.*

31. SUICER: "*Baptidzo*—properly denotes an immersion or dipping into."

32. ANTHON: Dr. Anthon, though not a lexicographer, as a scholar has no superior in America. He says: "The primary meaning of the word *(baptidzo)* is dip or immerse, and its secondary meanings, if it ever had any, all refer to the same leading idea. Sprinkling, pouring, etc., are entirely out of the question."

33. STOKIUS: Stokius defines in Latin, and is supposed to give some comfort to those who practice affusion and aspersion. The plan of his work is somewhat different from other lexicographers, as indicated in the title page, which we give, as follows: "Clavis of Christian Stokius, Professor in Public Academy at Jena; Opening the way to the sacred tongue of the New Testament; exhibiting, in convenient order, first, the *general* and then the *special* meanings of words; assisting especially the studies (or efforts) as well of tyros as of the cultivators of homiletics and exegesis; and then supplying the place of concordances with an index of words. Fourth edition, enlarged and improved."

By this it will be seen that he gives, first, the *general* and then the *specific* meanings. Hence he defines *baptidzo* "to wash, to baptize," and then proceeds to define the word specifically as follows: "Generally, and by force of the word, it obtains the notion of a dipping and an immersion. Second: Specifically and properly, it is to immerse or to dip into water. Figuratively, by metalepsis, it is to wash, to cleanse, because a thing is accustomed to be dipped or immersed in water that it may be washed or cleansed; although washing or cleansing can and is accustomed to be done by sprinkling water." [Thus we see how it is that *baptidzo* comes to mean *wash*, because things are accustomed to be dipped that they may be washed.]

"*Baptisma*—baptism: 1. Generally, and by force of its origin, it denotes immersion or dipping. 2. Specifically, properly it denotes the immersion or dipping of a thing into water that it may be cleansed or washed; hence, it is transferred to designating the first sacrament of the New Testament, which they call [the sacrament] of initiation—namely, baptism, in which those to be baptized were formerly immersed into water; though at this day the water is only sprinkled upon them, that they may be cleansed from the pollutions of sin, obtain the remission of it, and be received into the covenant of grace as heirs of eternal life. 3. By metaphor, it signifies the miraculous effusion of the Holy Spirit upon the apostles and other believers, not only on account of the abundance of the gifts of the Holy Spirit, just as formerly water was abundantly poured upon those baptized, or they were immersed deep into the water, but also on account of the efficacy and virtue of the Holy Spirit, which, like living water, refreshes in heart, cleanses from filth, and purifies."

Thus we have given a perfectly literal translation of the Latin of Stokius, made directly from his original work, that the reader may have the full benefit of it. He shows clearly that *baptidzo* primarily means to dip or immerse, and that it means *to wash* only because things are accustomed to be dipped that they may be washed. Nor is this all; he most clearly shows that the custom of the present day is a departure from the original practice. As to when, how, and by whom this departure from primitive practice was introduced we will see at the proper time. He also shows that persons were baptized, in early times, that they might be cleansed from the pollutions of sin and obtain the remission of it. Will the reader remember this when we come to examine the design of baptism?

34. SCHLEUSNER: "*Baptidzo*—properly, I immerse, and I dip (*intingo*), I sink into the water. From *bapto*, and corresponds to the Hebrew *tabal;* 2 Kings v:14, in the Alexandrian version; to *tabang*, in the writings of Symmachus, Psalmody 68:5, in anonymous Psalm 9:6. But it is never used in *this signification* in the New Testament, but is frequently thus used in Greek writers. * * * Now, because a thing is accustomed to be immersed, or dipped in water, that it may be washed, *hence* it marks (or denotes) I cleanse, I wash, I purge with water; thus it is used in Mark vii:4. * * * Jesus did not wash himself before dinner. Luke xi:38.

"Metaphorically, as in Latin, I wet, or I soak, I give and supply largely and copiously, I pour forth abundantly; *e.g.*, Matt. iii:11. 'He will baptize you *in* the Holy Spirit and fire.'

"It can be proved that *baptidzesthei*, in many places, signifies, not only to be washed, but also that one wash himself.

"*Baptisma*—baptism; a verbal noun from the passive participle of *bebaptisma*, of the verb *baptidzo*, (1) properly, immersion, dipping into water, a washing. Hence, it is transferred to the sacred rite which, par excellence, is called baptism, in which *formerly* those to be baptized were plunged into water that they might be bound to the true divine religion. Thus it is used concerning the baptism which John the Baptist administered by divine command (Matt. iii:7, Luke vii:29), which, par excellence, is called the baptism of repentance, because he bound men to a willing obedience to God and an emendation of their spirits. Here, truly, it should be observed that the expression 'the baptism of John' has sometimes a wider signification, and by synecdoche it signifies the whole function, institution, and doctrine of John the Baptist.* * * By metaphor, the heaviest afflictions and calamities were endured on account of religion, in which those who sustained them were as if they were submerged, which formerly were not improperly called a baptism in blood.

"*Baptismos*—a washing, cleansing, purification."

As Schleusner's Lexicon, like that of Stokius, is in possession of but very few, and is not published in America making it almost impossible to purchase it without an order to London, we have given a literal translation, made directly from the Latin of his work. And as his language is most cruelly perverted, and those who have not the lexicon are imposed upon by those who are willing to support a favorite dogma at the expense of truth, we have given all he has said which we regard at all calculated to throw any light on the subject. His definition of *baptidzo* is quoted thus: "Properly to immerse or dip, to plunge into water, from *bapto*** but in this sense it never occurs in the New Testament." See Louisville Debate, page 487. It was also thus used in debate with us at Flat Creek. By leaving out the words to which the author refers when he says "in this sense it never occurs in the New Testament," he is made to say that *baptidzo* never occurs in the sense of immerse, dip, or plunge into water, in the New Testament. By reference to his definition it will be seen that he says in the sense of *tabang* it is never used in the New Testament. *Tabang* means to sink, to be sunk, immersed, as in mire or a pit; and the examples referred to are cases where *baptidzo* is used in this sense, without any reference to *emersion* from that into which the *immersion* occurred. The author's definition of the noun *baptisma* (which was left out in the debates referred to), shows that because it *does mean* immerse, dipping, etc., it is *transferred* to the sacred rite which, par excellence, is called baptism, in which those formerly to be baptized were plunged into water. Thus Schleusner was made to say just the opposite to what he did say. Certainly the whole weight of his authority is in favor of immersion as baptism.

Thus we have the definition of *baptidzo* from thirty-four lexicons, most if not all of which were made by Pedobaptists, and with great unanimity they give *dip, immerse,* or some equivalent word as its *primary* meaning. Surely, if authority can settle the meaning of a word, the settled meaning of *baptidzo* is to dip or immerse.

But we have the testimony of other profound scholars who have *incidentally* defined the word *baptidzo* when writing on other subjects. At the risk of wearying our readers we will hear them also:

1. MICHAELIS: "To baptize, to immerse, to bathe."
2. SCHAAF: "To bathe one's self, to bathe, to dip, immerse in water, baptize."
3. GUIDO FABRICUS: "To baptize, dip, bathe."
4. BUXTORF: "To baptize, dip, bathe one's self."
5. SCHINDLER: "To baptize, dip, bathe, immerse in water."
6. PASCHAL AUSCHER: "To baptize, to wash by plunging in water."
7. MEKITAR VARTABED: The same as Auscher.
8. ENCYCLOPEDIA AMERICANA: "Baptism, that is, dipping, immersion, from the Greek word *baptidzo*."
9. EDINBURGH ENCYCLOPEDIA: "In the times of the apostles the act was very simple. The person was dipped in water."
10. KITTO's ENCYCLOPEDIA: "The whole person was immersed in water."
11. ALSTEDIUS: "*Baptidzein* signifies only to immerse, and not to wash, except by consequence."
12. WILSON: "Baptize, to dip in water, or plunge one into water."
13. DR. WILLIAM YOUNG: "To dip all over, to wash, to baptize."
14. BAILEY: "Baptism, in strictness of speech, is that kind of ablution or washing which consists in dipping, and, when ap-

plied to the Christian institution, it was used by the early Christians in no other way than that of dipping, as the learned Grotius and Casaubon observe."

15. BUTTERWORTH renders *baptidzo* "to dip, immerse, or plunge." Bliss' Let. p. 16.

16. JOHN ASH'S Dictionary, London, 1776, renders baptize "to dip, plunge, to overwhelm, to administer baptism."

17. BRANDE'S ENCYCLOPEDIA of Science, Literature, and Art, article Baptism: "*Bapto*—I dip. Baptism was originally administered by immersion. At present sprinkling is generally *substituted* for dipping—at least in northern climates."

18. BEZA: "Christ commanded us to be baptized, by which word it is certain immersion is signified. To be baptized in water signifies *no other* than to be immersed in water, which is the external ceremony of baptism."

19. ALTINGIUS: "Baptism is immersion when the whole body is immersed, but the term baptism is *never* used concerning aspersion."

20. BISHOP BASSUET: "To baptize signifies to plunge, as is granted by all the world."

21. HOSPINIANUS: "Christ commanded us to be baptized, by which word it is certain immersion is signified."

22. GURTLERUS: "To baptize, among the Greeks, is undoubtedly to immerse, to dip; and baptism is immersion, dipping. The thing commanded by our Lord is baptism, immersion in water."

23. BUDDEUS: "The words *baptizein* and *baptismos* are not to be interpreted of aspersion, but *always* of immersion."

24. VENEMA: "The word *baptizein*, to baptize, is nowhere used in the Scripture for sprinkling."

25. PROFESSOR FRITSCHI: "Baptism was performed, not by sprinkling, but by immersion; this is evident not only from the nature of the word, but from Rom. vi:4."

26. PROF. PORSON: "The Baptists have the advantage of us; baptism signifies a total immersion."

27. CATTENBURGH: "In baptism the whole body is ordered to be immersed."

28. KECKERMANUS: "We can not deny that the first institution of baptism consisted in immersion, and not sprinkling."

29. STOURDZA, a native Greek: "The verb *baptizo* has only one acceptation. It literally and perpetually signifies to plunge. Baptism and immersion, therefore, are identical; and to say *baptism by aspersion* is as if one should say *immersion by aspersion,* or utter any other contradiction of the same nature."

30. JEREMIAH, the Greek Patriarch: "The ancients were not accustomed to sprinkle the candidate, but to immerse him."

31. DANIEL ROGERS: "That the minister is to dip in water, the word denotes it. None of old were wont to be sprinkled."

32. BISHOP JEREMY TAYLOR: "The custom of the ancient churches was not sprinkling, but immersion—in pursuance of the sense of the word in the commandment and the example of our blessed Saviour."

33. DR. GEO. CAMPBELL: "The word *baptizein,* both in sacred authors and in classical, signifies to dip, to plunge, to immerse, and was rendered by Tertullian, the oldest of the Latin fathers, *tingere,* the term used for dyeing cloth, which was by immersion. It is always construed suitably to this meaning."

34. DRS. STORR AND FLATT'S THEOLOGY: "The disciples of our Lord could understand his command in no other manner than as enjoining immersion. Under these circumstances, it is certainly to be lamented that Luther was not able to accomplish his wish with regard to the introduction of immersion in baptism, as he had done in the restoration of the wine in the eucharist."

35. LONDON QUARTERLY REVIEW: "There can be no question that the original form of baptism—the very meaning of the word—was a complete immersion in the deep baptismal waters, and that, for at least four centuries, any other form was either unknown or else regarded as exceptional, almost a monstrous case."

36. CURCELLIUS: "Baptism was performed by plunging the whole body into water, and not by sprinkling a few drops, as is now the practice. Nor did the disciples that were sent out by Christ administer baptism afterwards *in any other way.*"

37. MARTIN LUTHER: "The term *baptism* is a Greek word; it may be rendered into Latin by *mersio*—when we immerse any thing in water, that it may be entirely covered with water. And though this custom be quite abolished among the generality (for neither do they entirely dip children, but only sprinkle them with a little water), nevertheless they ought to be wholly im-

mersed, and immediately to be drawn out again, for the etymology of the word seems to require it."

38. KNAPP's THEOLOGY: "*Baptisma*, from *baptizein*, which properly signifies to dip in, to wash by immersion."

39. DR. BLOOMFIELD, on Mark i:9: "The sense of '*was baptized in*' is '*was dipped or plunged into*.' He underwent the rite of baptism by being plunged into the water."

40. VETRINGA:' "The act of baptizing is the immersion of believers in water. This expresses the force of the word. Thus also it was performed by Christ and the apostles."

41. PROF. MOSES STUART: "*Bapto* and *baptizo* mean to dip, plunge, or immerse into any thing liquid. All lexicographers and critics of any note *are agreed in this*."

42. CALVIN: "The word *baptize* signifies to immerse, and the rite of immersion was practiced by the ancient church."

43. WITSIUS: "It can not be denied that the native signification of the words *baptein* and *baptizein* is to plunge, to dip."

44. ZANCHIUS: "The proper signification of baptize is to immerse, plunge under, overwhelm in water."

45. DR. CHALMERS: "The original meaning of the word baptism is immersion, and, though we regard it as a point of indifference whether the ordinance so named be performed in this way or by sprinkling, yet we doubt not that the prevalent style of administration in the apostles' days was by *an actual submerging* of the whole body under water."

46. SMITH's DICTIONARY OF THE BIBLE: "*Baptisma*, baptism (the word *baptismos* occurs only four times, viz: Mark vii:4, 8, Heb. vi:2, ix:10). The verb *baptidzein* (from *baptein*, to dip) is the rendering of the Hebrew by the LXX, in 2 Kings v:14. The Latin fathers render *baptidzein* by *tingere, mergere,* and *mergitare*. By the Greek fathers the word *baptidzein* is often used, frequently figuratively, for to immerse or overwhelm with sleep, sorrow, sin, etc. Hence *baptisma* properly and literally means *immersion*."

47. PICTET: "They immerse the whole body in water in order that the baptized might be counted a child of the covenant. Now, John (the Baptist) administered the rite among the Jews in the manner above described, and the same rite was used by Christ."

48. SALMASIUS: "Baptism is immersion, and was administered in former times according to the force and meaning of the word." R. Fuller, p. 20. "Baptism signifies immersion, *not aspersion*, nor did the ancients baptize any but by dipping." Witsius' Works, vol. III, pp. 390, 391.

49. AUGUSTI: "The word baptism, according to etymology and usage, signifies to immerse, submerge, etc., and the choice of the expression betrays an age in which the latter custom of sprinkling had not been introduced."

50. BRENNER: "The word corresponds in signification with the German *taufen*, to sink in the deep."

51. PAULLUS: "The word *baptize* signifies in Greek sometimes to immerse, sometimes to submerge."

52. SCHOLZ: "Baptism consists in the immersion of the whole body in water."

53. IKENIUS: "The Greek word *baptismos* denotes the immersion of a person or a thing into something."

54. CASAUBON: "To baptize is to immerse." Fuller, p. 72. "This was the rite of baptizing that persons were plunged into the water, which the very word *baptizein*, to baptize, sufficiently declares." Judson p. 11.

55. CHRISTOPHULUS, a Greek: "We follow the examples of the apostles, who immersed the candidate under the water."

56. RIDGELEY: "The original and natural signification of the word *baptize* imports to dip."

57. LIMBORCH: "Baptism consists in washing or rather immersing the whole body in water, as was customary in primitive times."

58. SIR JON FLOYER: "Immersion is no circumstance but the very act of baptism."

59. POOLE'S CONTINUATORS: "To be baptized is to be dipped in water; metaphorically, to be plunged in afflictions."

60. VALESIUS, in his edition of Eusebius' Eccl. Hist., speaking of the pouring of water all over Novatian while he was sick, says: "Moreover, since baptism properly signifies immersion, such perfusion (pouring over) could hardly be called baptism."

61. COLEMAN: "The term *baptism* is derived from the Greek word *bapto*, from which term is formed *baptizo*, with its derivatives *baptismos* and *baptisma*, baptism. The primary significa-

tion of the original is to dip, to plunge, immerse. The obvious import of the noun is immersion."

62. EDINBURGH REVIEWERS: "They tell me (says Carson) that it was unnecessary to bring forward any of the examples to prove that the word signifies to dip, that I might have commenced with this as a *fixed point universally admitted.*"

63. WETSTENIUS: "To baptize is to plunge, to dip. The body, or part of the body *being under water,* is said to be baptized."

64. MELANCTHON: "Baptism is an entire action; to wit: a dipping and a pronouncing the words I baptize," etc.

65. ISAAC BARROW: "The action is baptizing or immersing in water."

66. BURMANNUS: "*Baptismos* and *baptisma,* if you consider the etymology, properly signifies immersion."

67. RICHARD BENTLY: "*Baptismos*—baptism, dipping."

68. BECKMANUS: "Baptism, according to the force of its etymology, is immersion and washing or dipping."

69. BUCANUS: "Baptism, that is, immersion, and by consequence washing. *Baptistery,* a vat or large vessel of wood or stone in which we are immersed for the sake of washing,. *Baptist,* one that immerses or dips."

70. OTTO VON GERLACH: "The Greek word *(baptizo)* properly signifies dip. Baptism was performed in the first times of Christianity by *immersion* in water."

The foregoing quotations are mostly from Bailey's Manual, where he gives references to the works from which they are taken, many of which we have examined and know that they are correct. Added to the lexicographers quoted, they make one hundred and four scholars who say, one and all, that the word used by the Lord to indicate the act required by Him of those who would become obedient to Sis will, *primarily* and *literally* means to dip or immerse. He who will not be satisfied with this testimony would not likely be satisfied by the presentation of much more that might be adduced.

We propose next to examine the use of the term by those who lived before, during, and subsequent to the time when Christ and the apostles used it. Carson, Stuart, and Conant have given us perhaps every known occurrence of the word in the whole range of Greek literature. Dr. Conant, in his "BAPTIzein," has given two hundred and thirty-six examples of its use, of which he says: "The examples of the common meaning and use of the word in Sections I and II, are from every period of Greek literature in which the word occurs. They include all that have been given by lexicographers, and by those who have written professedly on this subject; and these, with the examples added from my own reading, exhaust the use of this word in Greek literature.

"The quotations have been copied, in every instance, by myself or under my own eye, from the page, chapter, or section referred to. Special pains have been taken to make these references as definite and clear as possible, that any passage may be easily found; the author's name being given, the name of the treatise and its divisions (if any are made), and the volume and page of the edition in most common use, or of the one accessible to me."

We have not room to give our readers the benefit of all the examples given by Dr. Conant, but we will give a sufficient number to indicate the import of the term at the time it was used by the authors of the New Testament. We give the number attached to each example in Dr. Conant's work, by which they may be found by any one who may choose to look for them. We do not follow the numerical order of the Doctor, because we wish to present such examples as will give the use of the word at a sufficient period *before* the days of the Saviour, and coming down through His time to a sufficiently *late period* to give its use at the time He employed it.

Example 62.

PINDAR, born 522 before Christ, *Pythic Odes*, II, 79, 80 (144-147). Comparing himself to a cork of a fisher's net, floating at the top, while the other parts of the fishing tackle are doing service in the depth below, he says:

"For, as when the rest of the tackle is toiling deep in the sea, I, as a cork above the net, am undipped (unbaptized) in the brine."

Example 1.

POLYBIUS, born 205 before Christ, History, book i, chap. 51, 6. In his account of the sea fight at Drepanum, between the Romans and Carthagenians, describing the advantages of the latter in their choice of a position, and in the superior structure and more skillful management of their vessels, he says:

"For, if any were hard pressed by the enemy, they retreated safely, on account of their fast sailing, into the open space; and then, with reversed course, now sailing round and now attacking in flank the more advanced of the pursuers, while turning and embarrassed on account of the weight of the ships and the unskillfulness of the crews, they made continued assaults and SUBMERGED (BAPTIZED) many of the vessels."

EXAMPLE 2.

The same work, book viii, ch. 8, 4. Describing the operations of the engines which Archimedes constructed for the defense of Syracuse when besieged by the Romans, and with which he lifted the prows of the besieging vessels out of the water, so that they stood erect on the stern, and then let them fall, he says:

"Which being done, some the vessels fell on their sides, and some were overturned, but most of them, when the prow was let fall from on high, being SUBMERGED (BAPTIZED), became filled with sea-water and with confusion."

EXAMPLE 6.

The same history, book xxxiv, ch. 3, 7. In his description of the manner of taking the sword-fish (with an iron-headed spear or harpoon), he says:

"And even if the spear fall into the sea, it is not lost, for it is compacted of both oak and pine, so that when the oaken part is IMMERSED (BAPTIZED) by the weight, the rest is buoyed up, and is easily recovered."

EXAMPLE 7.

The same work, book iii, ch. 72, 4. Speaking of the passage of the Roman army, under the consul Tiberius, through the river Tebia, which had been swollen by heavy rains, he says:

"They passed through with difficulty, the foot soldiers IMMERSED (BAPTIZED) as far as to the breast."

Example 50.

AESOPIC FABLES; fable of the mule, who, finding that he lightened his load of salt by lying down in the water, repeated the experiment when loaded with sponges and wool.

"One of the salt-bearing mules, rushing into a river, accidentally slipped down, and rising up lightened (the salt becoming dissolved), he perceived the cause and remembered it; so that always, when passing through the river, he purposely lowered down and IMMERSED (BAPTIZED) the pannier." Of uncertain date (related in Plut. Moral., *Skill of Water and Land Animals*, xvi).

Example 86.

AESOPIC FABLES; writer and date unknown; *fable of the Man and the Fox:* "A certain man, having a grudge against a fox for some mischief done by her, after getting her into his power contrived a long time how to punish her, and DIPPING (BAPTIZING) tow in oil, he bound it to her tail and set fire to it."

Example 71.

HOMERIC ALLEGORIES, ch. 9; (B. C., uncertain how long). The writer explains the grounds of the allegory (as he regards it) of Neptune freeing Mars from Vulcan thus: "Since the mass of iron drawn red hot from the furnace is PLUNGED (BAPTIZED) in water; and the fiery glow, by its own nature quenched with water, ceases."

Example 9.

STRABO, born about 60 years B. C., *Geography*, book xii, ch. 2, 4. Speaking of the underground channel through which the waters of the Pyramus (a river of Cilicia in Asia Minor) forced their way, he says:

"And to one who hurls down a dart from above into the channel, the force of the water makes so much resistance that it is hardly IMMERSED (BAPTIZED)."

Example 10.

The same work, book vi, ch. 2, 9: "And around Acragos Agrigentum in Sicily: are marsh lakes, having the taste indeed of sea-water, but a different nature; for even those who can not swim are not IMMERSED (BAPTIZED) floating like pieces of wood."

EXAMPLE 11.

The same work, book xiv, ch. 3, 9. Speaking of the march of Alexander's army along the narrow beach (flooded in stormy weather) between the mountain called Climax and the Pamphilian Sea, he says:

"Alexander happening to be there at the stormy season, and accustomed to trust for the most part to fortune, set forward before the swell subsided, and they marched the whole day in water, IMMERSED (BAPTIZED) as far as to the waist."

EXAMPLE 12.

The same work, book xiv, ch. 2, 42. Speaking of the *asphalt* in the lake Lirbanus, which floats on the surface on account of the greater specific gravity of the water, he says:

"Then floating at the top on account of the nature of the water, by virtue of which we said there is no need of being a swimmer, and he who enters in is not IMMERSED (BAPTIZED), but is lifted out."

EXAMPLE 61.

STRABO, born about the year 60 B.C., *Geography*, book xii, ch. 5, sec. 4. Speaking of the lake Tatta, in Phrygia (which he calls a natural salt pit), he says:

"The water solidifies so readily around every thing that is IMMERSED (BAPTIZED) into it, that they draw up salt crowns when they let down a circle of rushes."

EXAMPLE 13.

DIODORUS wrote his history about 60-30 B.C., *Historical Library*, book xvi, ch. 80. In his account of Timoleon's defeat of the Carthagenian army on the bank of the river Crimissus, in Sicily, many of the fugitives perishing in the stream, swollen by a violent storm, he says:

"The river, rushing down with the current, increased in violence, SUBMERGED (BAPTIZED) many, and destroyed them attempting to swim through with their armor."

Example 14.

The same work, book i, ch. 36. Describing the effects of the rapid rise of water during the annual inundation of the Nile, he says:

"Most of the wild land animals are surrounded by the stream and perish, being SUBMERGED (BAPTIZED) but some, escaping to the high grounds, are saved."

Example 16.

JOSEPHUS, born A.D. 37, *Jewish Antiquities*, book xv, ch. 3, 3. Describing the murder of the boy Aristobulus, who (by Herod's command) was drowned by his companions in a swimming-bath, says:

"Continually pressing down and IMMERSING (BAPTIZING) him while swimming, as if in sport, they did not desist till they had entirely suffocated him."

Example 17.

The same writer, *Jewish Wars*, book i, ch. 22, 2, relating to the same occurrence, says:

"And there, according to command, being IMMERSED (BAPTIZED) by the Gauls in a swimming-bath, he dies."

Example 18.

The same writer, *Jewish Wars*, book iii, ch. 8, 5:

"As I also account a pilot most cowardly, who, through dread of a storm, before the blast came, voluntarily SUBMERGED (BAPTIZED) the vessel."

Example 19.

The same writer, *Jewish Wars*, book iii, ch. 9, 3. Describing the condition of the vessels in the port of Joppa, during a storm, he says:

"And many [of the vessels] struggling against the opposing swell toward the open sea (for they feared the shore, being rocky, and the enemies upon it), the billows, rising high above, SUBMERGED (BAPTIZED)."

EXAMPLE 20.

The same writer, *Antiquities of the Jews,* book ix, ch. 10, 2. In his narrative of Jonah's flight, and of the events that followed, he says: "The ship being just about to be SUBMERGED (BAPTIZED)."

EXAMPLE 21.

The same writer, *Life of Himself,* sec. 3, says:
"For our vessel having been SUBMERGED (BAPTIZED) in the midst of the Adriatic, being about six hundred in number, we swam through the whole night."

EXAMPLE 24.

PLUTARCH, born A.D. 50, *Life of Theseus,* xxiv, quotes the following oracle of the Sybil, respecting the city of Athens:
"A bladder, thou mayest be IMMERSED (BAPTIZED), but it is not possible for thee to sink."

EXAMPLE 25.

The same writer, *Life of Alexander,* lxvii. Describing a season of revelry in the army of Alexander the Great, when returning from his eastern conquests, he says:
"Thou wouldest not have seen a buckler, or a helmet, or a pike, but the soldiers, along the whole way, DIPPING (BAPTIZING) with cups, and horns, and goblets, from great wine-jars and mixing-bowls, were drinking to one another."

EXAMPLE 64.

The same writer, on Superstition, iii. The superstitious man, consulting the jugglers on his frightful dreams, is told:
"Call the old Expiatrix, and PLUNGE (BAPTIZE) thyself into the sea, and spend a day in sitting on the ground."

EXAMPLE 65.

The same writer, *Gryllus,* vii. He says of Agamemnon:
"Then bravely PLUNGING (BAPTIZING) himself into the lake

Capais, that there he might extinguish his love and be freed from desire."

Example 28.

Lucien, born about 135 A.D., *Timon or the Man-hater*, 44. Among the resolves for the direction of his future life (to testify his hatred of mankind) is the following:

"And if the winter's torrent were bearing one away, and he with outstretched hands were imploring help, to thrust even him headlong, IMMERSING (BAPTIZING) so that he should not be able to come up again."

Example 29.

The same writer, *True History*, book ii, 4. In this satire on the love of the marvelous, he pleasantly describes men walking on the sea (having cork feet), and says:

"We wondered, therefore, when we saw them not IMMERSED (BAPTIZED), but standing above the waves and traveling on without fear."

Example 31.

Dion Cassius, born A.D. 155, *Roman History*, book xxxvii, ch. 58. In the description here given of the effects of a violent storm of wind, he says:

"So that very many trees were upturned by the roots, and many houses were thrown down; the ships which were in the Tiber, and lying at anchor by the city and at its mouth, were SUBMERGED (BAPTIZED), and the wooden bridge was destroyed."

Example 32.

The same work, book xli, ch. 42. Describing the defeat of Curio by Juba, king of Numidia (at the siege of Utica, in Africa), and the fate of the fugitives, many losing their lives in their eager haste to get aboard of their vessels, and others by overloading and sinking them, he says:

"And many of them who had fled perished; some thrown down by the jostling in getting on board the vessels, and others SUBMERGED (BAPTIZED) in the vessels themselves by their own weight."

Example 38.

PORPHYRY, born A.D. 233, *Concerning the Styx*. Describing the *Lake of Probation*, in India, and the use made of it by the Brahmins for testing the guilt or innocence of persons accused of crime, he says:

"The depth is as far as to the knees; . . . and when the accused comes to it, if he is guiltless he goes through without fear, having the water as far as to the knees; but if guilty, after proceeding a little way he is IMMERSED (BAPTIZED) unto the head."

Example 44.

GREGORY, A.D. 240, *Panegyric on Origen*, xiv. Describing him as an experienced and skillful guide through the mazes of philosophical speculations, he says:

"He himself would remain on high in safety, and, stretching out a hand to others, save them as if drawing up persons SUBMERGED (BAPTIZED)."

Example 54.

ACHILLES TATIUS, A.D. 450, *Story of Clitophon and Leucippe*, book iii, ch. 1. The vessel being thrown on her beam ends in a storm, the narrator says:

"We all, therefore, shifted our position to the more elevated parts of the ship, in order that we might lighten that part of the ship that was IMMERSED (BAPTIZED)."

Example 55.

The same writer *(ibidem)*.

"But suddenly the wind shifts to another quarter of the ship, and the vessel is almost IMMERGED (BAPTIZED)."

Example 82.

ACHILLES TATIUS, A.D. 450, *Story of Clitophon and Leucippe*, book ii, ch. 14: "And there is a fountain of gold there. They PLUNGE (BAPTIZED) into the water, therefore, a pole smeared with pitch, and open the barriers of the stream. And the pole is to the gold what the hook is to the fish, for it catches it; and the pitch is a bait for the prey."

Many other examples might be given, but these are deemed sufficient to show that *baptidzo*, at the time the Saviour and the writers of the New Testament used it, primarily meant to *dip* or *immerse*. It is admitted that classic Greek writers often employed the word in a *metaphorical* sense, but we are seeking for its *primary* and *literal* meaning, as used in the New Testament.

The examples given cover a period of nearly a thousand years, embracing the time when the Lord and the apostles lived. Josephus was born A.D. 37, and hence lived and wrote contemporaneously with the apostles. He was a native Jew and wrote in the Greek language, and certainly understood the word as used by his people. As a scholar he was inferior to no man of his day. He says: "Now, my father Matthias was not only eminent on account of his nobility, but had a higher commendation on account of his righteousness, and was in great reputation in Jerusalem, the greatest city we have. I was myself brought up with my brother, whose name was Matthias, for he was my own brother, by both father and mother; and I made mighty proficiency in the improvements of my learning, and appeared to have both a great memory and understanding. Moreover, when I was a child, and about fourteen years of age, I was commended by all for the love I had to learning; on which account the high-priests and principal men of the city then came frequently to me together, in order to know my opinion about the accurate understanding of points of the law," etc.

Again: *Ant.*, book xx, ch. xi, sec. 3, p. 139, he says: "I am so bold as to say, now I have so completely perfected the work I proposed to myself to do, that no other person whether he were a Jew or a foreigner, had he ever so great an inclination to it, could so accurately deliver these accounts to the Greeks as is done in these books. For those of my own nation freely acknowledge that I far exceed them in the learning belonging to the Jew. I have also taken a great deal of pains to obtain the learning of the Greeks, and understand the elements of the Greek language, although I have so long accustomed myself to speak our own tongue that I can not pronounce Greek with sufficient exactness," etc.

Although these extracts were written by Josephus himself,

yet the literary world awards him all the ability claimed in them, as the following paragraph will show:

"JOSEPHUS, FLAVIUS, a celebrated Jewish historian, was born at Jerusalem 37 A.D. He was of both royal and sacerdotal lineage, being descended, on the mother's side, from the line of Asmonean princes, while his father, Matthias, officiated as a priest in the first of the twenty-four courses. The careful education he received developed his brilliant faculties at an unusually early period, and his acquirements both in Hebrew and Greek literature—the two principal branches of his studies—soon drew public attention upon him." Chambers's Encyclopedia.

Josephus used the word *baptidzo*, in some of its forms, fourteen times, several examples of which we have given, and surely he knew the meaning his people attached to it; and had they used it in a sense different from him, it is likely it would have been mentioned by him somewhere. It is sometimes said that he used the word in the sense of drowning, but this is manifestly an error. The boy Aristobulus, of whom he speaks, was indeed drowned, but we know the fact, because it is so stated, and not because of any such meaning in the word *baptidzo*.

Many persons admit that the word *baptidzo* in classic Greek means to dip or immerse, but they insist that it has a different meaning in the New Testament. The reader will remember that the seventy authors already quoted defined the word in its scriptural application, and they say it means immerse when used to indicate baptism; and the examples given from the classics show that with the Greek classic writers it meant the same thing. Moses Stuart says: "That the Greek fathers and the Latin ones who were familiar with the Greek understood the usual import of the word *baptidzo* would hardly seem to be capable of a denial. That they might be confirmed in their view of the import of this word, by common usage among the Greek classic authors, we have seen in the first part of this dissertation."—Stuart on Baptism, p. 154. How could the fathers be confirmed in the fact that *baptidzo* meant *immerse* by classic usage, if their use of it differed from its use among the classics? Mr. Hughey, a distinguished Methodist debater, of great learning and research, in his debate with President Braden, p. 81, says: "I will show by examples from the classics that the classical usage agrees with the Hellenistic and patristic usage of the word." After giving some examples of its use, on page 82, he says: "These examples show, by the usage of the word, that classical usage agrees exactly with the scriptural usage and also the usage of the fathers." When summing up his argument, on page 157, he says: "I showed by a number of examples from the classics that classical usage agrees with Scripture and patristic usage." Thus we have his testimony, in three different places, that the classic usage of *baptidzo* differs not from scriptural and patristic usage. Such is his testimony, though different from some of his brethren.

Dr. H. A. W. Meyer, in his Manual on the Gospels of Mark and Luke, says: "The expression in Mark vii:4, is not to be understood of the *washing of hands* (as interpreted by Lightfoot and Wetstein), but of the immersing—which the word always means in the classics and in the New Testament." Bailey's Manual, p. 294. Thus, with Dr. Meyer, it means the same in both places.

Dr. George Campbell says: "The word *baptidzein*, both in sacred authors and classical, signifies to dip, to plunge, to immerse." Campbell on Baptism, p. 142. Dr. George Campbell, as a scholar and biblical critic, had no superior in his time, and he unites his testimony with the others given, and still others which might be given, in proving that *baptidzo* means to *dip* or *immerse* in both sacred and classic usage. It is true, as shown by Schluesner, that the Greek classic writers sometimes used the word to indicate *sinking* without regard to *emersion*, while in the Scriptures it is used in the sense of *dip*, as in 2 Kings v:14, which includes the idea of emersion. Hence says Paul: "Buried with him in baptism, wherein also ye are risen with him." Col. ii:12. But this is rather a difference in application than in primary import. Immersion is the leading idea in the classics as well as in the Scriptures. But were we to admit a difference in the primary import of the word, unless it be shown to mean *sprinkle* and *pour* in the New Testament, the admission could not serve sprinklers any purpose. This is the point which they must prove.

That dip, immerse, or some equivalent word, is necessary to express the *primary* meaning of *baptidzo*, is admitted by all; but it is insisted that wash, wet, stain, dye, etc., are figurative meanings; and, as washing, wetting, staining, and dyeing may be done by pouring or sprinkling, therefore baptism may be performed in either of these ways.

Wash, wet, stain, dye, etc., can not be real meanings, but are purely metonymical—that is, they are effects of the true or real meaning of the word.

No two meanings can be given to the same word which are antagonistic to each other. *Stains* are removed by *washing*, and, therefore, the same word can not literally mean both wash and stain. Washing may be the effect of immersing in clean water, while staining and dyeing may be done by immersing in impure or coloring fluids; hence these opposite meanings can not be otherwise than metonymical—that is, they are effects produced by the real meaning, dipping or immersing. All these figurative meanings, so-called, may be the effect of immersion, but they can not all be the effect of sprinkling or pouring, for washing and dyeing are not done in either of these ways. Sprinkling a few drops of water on a filthy garment would not be likely to wash it well, nor would pouring a little water on one end of a garment be very apt to wash or cleanse the balance of it. And if it were a coloring fluid it would not be a good process by which to dye a whole web to sprinkle or pour a little of the fluid on one end of it.

But does the word *baptidzo* ever mean to color or dye? We beg the attention of the reader to the following very appropriate remarks of Dr. Carson on this subject. He says:

"The word BAPTO, from which is formed BAPTIDZO, signifies, primarily, *to dip;* and, as a secondary meaning, obviously derived from the primary, it denotes to *dye.* Every occurrence of the word may be reduced to one or other of these acceptations." Carson on Baptism, p. 18.

On page 19 he says: "There is a very obvious difference in the use of the words, and a difference that materially affects the point at issue. This difference is, BAPTO IS NEVER USED TO DENOTE THE ORDINANCE OF BAPTISM, AND BAPTIDZO NEVER SIGNIFIES TO DYE. But the derivative is formed to modify the primary only, and in all the Greek language, I assert that an instance is not to be found in which it has the secondary meaning of the primitive word. If this assertion is not correct, it will be easy for learned men to produce an example in contradiction. That *bapto* is never applied to the ordinance of baptism any one can verify who is able to look into the passages of the Greek Testament where the ordinance is spoken of. Now, if this observation is just, it overturns all those speculations that explain the word, as applied to baptism, by an allusion to dyeing; for the primitive word that has this secondary meaning is not applied to the ordinance, and the derivative word, which is appointed to express it, has not the secondary signification of *dyeing*. *Bapto* has two meanings; *baptidzo* in the whole history of the Greek language has but one. It not only signifies to dip or immerse, but it never has any other meaning. Each of these words has its specific province, into which the other can not enter, while there is a common province in which either of them may serve. Either of them may signify to dip generally, but the primitive can not specifically express that ordinance to which the derivative has been appropriated, and the derivative can not signify *to dye*, which is a part of the province of the primitive. The difference is precise and important."

While we think it likely that Dr. Carson's language is rather strong in some respects, he shows most conclusively that *baptidzo* can not mean to *dye*. Indeed, we have no faith in the transmission of secondary or metonymical meanings from primitive to derivative words. They inherit the primary but not foreign meanings of the words from which they came. But as Dr. Carson was an immersionist it may be well to hear from those who practiced affusion and aspersion. Dr. Moses Stuart says:

"I have already intimated that *baptidzo* is distinguished from *bapto* in its meaning. I now add that it is not, like the latter word, used to designate the idea of *coloring* or *dyeing;* while in some other respects it seems, in classical use, to be nearly or quite synonymous with *bapto*. In the New Testament, however, there is one other marked distinction between the use of these verbs. *Baptidzo* and its derivatives are exclusively employed *when the rite of baptism is to be designated* in any form whatever, and in this case *bapto* seems to be purposely as well as habitually excluded."

Here we have a confirmation of Dr. Carson's statement by one whose authority will not be questioned by those who oppose us. If these authors are worthy of credit, *baptidzo* does not mean to dye. But suppose that in this they are mistaken, as immersion is admitted by all to be the *primary* meaning of the word representing baptism, we wish to know why *it* is to give place to figurative or metonymical meanings, such as wash, wet, stain, dye, etc.? All philological laws require preference to be given to the primary meaning of words, unless good reason be shown for its removal. We submit the following rules for the use and interpretation of words, arranged by Moses Stuart, of Andover, aided by Edward Robinson, author of Robinson's Greek Lexicon, Robinson's Gesenius' Hebrew Lexicon, etc.

1. "To every word in Scripture there is unquestionably assigned some idea or notion, otherwise words are useless, and have no more signification than the inarticulate sounds of animals." Ernesti, p. 7.

2. "The literal meaning of words is the sense that is so connected with them as to be spontaneously presented to the mind as soon as the sound of the word is heard, and that is first in order. The literal sense does not differ from the sense of the letter." Ibid.

3. "A particular meaning being attached to a word can no more be changed or denied than any historical event whatever. All men in their daily conversation and writings attach but one sense to a word, at the same time and in the same passage, unless they design to speak in enigmas. The sense of a word can not be diverse or multifarious at the same time and in the same passage or expression." Ibid., p. 9.

4. "There can be no certainty at all in respect to the interpretation of any passage, unless a kind of necessity compels us to affix a particular sense to a word, which sense must be one, and unless there are special reasons for a tropical meaning, it must be literal." Ibid, p. 10.

5. "The sense of words depends upon the *usus loquendi.*" Ibid., p. 13.

6. "Words are proper and tropical, literal and figurative. First: A proper or literal word is a definite name given to a cer-

tain thing. Originally, words were undoubtedly used in their proper and literal sense. Second: Tropes or metaphorical words are called by Aristotle strangers, foreigners. Ibid, p. 21.

7. "In no language can a word have more than one literal meaning in the same place." Ibid.

By these rules we see that a word can have but one meaning at the same time and in the same place, and that the primary meaning must be given to words unless there be special reasons for its removal. These rules come to us from the very fountain of authority in America, and have existence in the nature of all language. Having thus found that the primary meaning of *baptidzo* is to dip or immerse, dare we set it aside and adopt a metonymical, metaphorical, or figurative meaning, for no better reason than to save a favorite theory or to avoid going into the water whre the Lord commanded us to go?

In the Septuagint Greek of the Old Testament we have *baptidzo* as a translation of the Hebrew word *taval*, which modern theologians insist means sprinkle or pour. Although this word is never employed to indicate baptism, as *baptidzo* once a translation of it, it may be well for us to examine it briefly. In the Hebrew Bible it is used fourteen times, and is rendered by King James' translators *dip*, every time; hence, we have the unanimous testimony of the forty-seven distinguished scholars employed by him in the translation of the Hebrew Bible, that this is the meaning of the word. The following are the connections in which it occurs:

Genesis xxxvii:31: "And they took Joseph's coat and killed a kid of the goats, and *dipped* the coat in the blood."

Exodus xii:22: "And ye shall take a bunch of hyssop and *dip* it in the blood that is in the basin."

Leviticus iv:6: "And the priest shall *dip* his finger in the blood;" chap. ix:9: "And the sons of Aaron brought the blood unto him, and he *dipped* his finger in the blood;" chap. xiv:6: "And shall *dip* them and the living bird in the blood of the bird that was killed;" verse 16: "And the priest shall *dip* his finger in the oil;" verse 51: "And he shall take the cedar wood and the hyssop, and the scarlet and the living bird and *dip* them in the blood of the slain bird and in the running water."

Numbers xix:18: "And a clean person shall take hyssop and *dip* it in water."

Deut. xxxiii:24: "Let him *dip* his foot in oil."

Joshua iii:15: "The feet of the priests that bear the ark were *dipped* in the brim of the water."

Ruth ii:14: "And *dip* thy morsel in the vinegar."

1 Sam. xiv:27: "Wherefore he put forth the end of the rod that was in his hand and *dipped* it in an honeycomb."

2 Kings v:14: "And *dipped* himself seven times in Jordan," chap. viii:15: "He took a thick cloth and *dipped* it in water."

In Lev. ix:9, we have *dipped* and *poured* in the same verse; *dipped* is from *taval*, but poured is not. In Lev. xiv:16, we have *dip* and *sprinkle* in the same verse; *dip* is from *taval*, sprinkle is not. Why is this? If *taval* means to sprinkle and pour, why was it not used to express sprinkling and pouring even when it was employed in the same verse? We have four Hebrew lexicons by us as we write, which define the word as follows: "*Taval*—to dip, to dip in, to immerse, to dip or immerse one's self. Ex. 2 Kings. v:14: *He went down and dipped himself seven times in Jordan.*" ROBINSON'S GESENIUS' Heb. Lex., p. 364.

"*Taval*—1, to dip, immerse, plunge; 2, to tinge or dye with a certain color, which is usually performed by *dipping.*" PARKHURST, page 255.

"*Taval*—1. He dipped; 2. He was dipped." ROBERTSON'S Hebrew Dictionary by Joseph, page 111.

"*Taval*—dip, dip in, immerse, submerge." STOKIUS, Vet. Test., vol. i, p. 421.

"*Taval*—merge, immerse." M. STUART, Chr. Bap., p. 119.

SCHLEUSNER incidentally defines *taval* in his definition of *baptidzo* thus: "to immerse, dip, plunge into water; from *bapto*, and *corresponds to the Hebrew taval.*"

Besides these, we have in other works the following definitions of *taval*, viz.:

1. By DAVIDSON: "*Taval*—1, to dip, to immerse; 2, to stain."

2. BUXTORF: "*Taval*—to dip, to dip into, to submerge, to immerse."

3. DR. KLEEBURG, a celebrated Jewish rabbi, of Louisville, Ky., answered certain interrogatories propounded to him, thus: "1. What does *taval* mean? It means to immerse, to dip. 2.

242 THE GOSPEL PLAN OF SALVATION

Does it ever mean to sprinkle or pour? It never means to sprinkle or pour. 3. Did the Hebrews always immerse their proselytes? They did. The whole body was entirely submerged. 4. Were the Jewish ablutions immersions? Before eating and prayer, and after rising in the morning they washed; when they have become unclean they must immerse." Louisville Debate, p. 652.

Thus we see these authors concur in giving the import of *taval* to dip or immerse; hence, as far as it throws any light upon *baptidzo*, it certainly does not give any support to sprinkling or pouring.

We next present the reader with a table of versions of the New Testament, showing the several languages into which it has been translated, when the translations were made, and the word representing *baptidzo* in each of the languages, which we copy from Bailey's Manual, pages 121, 122, 123:

Version	Date.	Word.	Meaning.
SYRIAC:			
Peshito,	2d century,	amad,	immerse.
Philozenian,	6th century,	amad,	immerse.
ARABIC:			
Polyglot,	7th century (?)	amada,	immerse.
Propaganda,	1671,	amada,	immerse.
Sabat,	1816,	amada,	immerse.
PERSIC,	1341,	shustan and shuzidan,	wash.
ETHIOPIC,	4th century,	tamaka,	immerse.
Amharic,	1822,	tamaka,	immerse.
EGYPTIAN:			
Coptic,	3d century,	tomas	immerse.
Sahidic,	2d century,	baptizo,	plunge.
Basmuric,	3d century,		immerse.
ARMENIAN,	5th century,	mugurdel,	immerse.
SLAVONIC,	9th century,	krestiti,	cross.
Russian,	1519,		
Polish,	1585,		
Bohemian,	1593,	same root,	cross.
Lithuanian,	1660,		
Livonian,	1685,		
Dorpat Esthonian,	1727,		
Gothic,	4th century,	daupjan,	dip.
German,	1522,	taufen,	dip.
Danish,	1524,	dobe,	dip.

BAPTISM

Version	Date.	Word.	Meaning.
Swedish,	1534,	dopa,	dip.
Dutch, etc.,	1460,	doopen,	dip.
Icelandic,	1584,	skira,	cleanse.
ANGLO-SAXON,	8th century,	dyppan,	dip.
ANGLO-SAXON,	8th century,	fullian,	cleanse.
LATIN:			
Of the early Fathers,	2d century,	tingo,	immerse.
Ante-Hieronymian,	3d century,	baptizo,	immerse.
Vulgate,	4th century,	baptizo,	immerse.
French,	1535,	baptizer,	immerse.
Spanish,	1556,	baptizar,	immerse.
Italian,	1562,	baptizzan,	immerse.
English (Wickliffe),	1380,	wash, christen, baptize,	immerse.
Tindal,	1526,	baptize,	
Welsh,	1567,	bedyddio,	bathe.
Irish,	1602,	baisdim,	bathe.
Gaelic,	1650,	baisdean,	bathe.

Here are thirty-eight versions of the New Testament, made at periods extending from the latter part of the second century to 1822, none of which represent baptism by a word indicating to sprinkle or pour, nineteen of which represent it by a word meaning to immerse, six by a word meaning to dip, and one to plunge, while others use words meaning to bathe and cleanse, which manifestly refer to the same leading thought.

But it is insisted that the Syriac word *amad* means to pour or shed forth. In support of our table of versions we offer the following testimony as to the meaning of this word:

SCHAAF: "*Amad*—to bathe one's self, to bathe, dip, immerse into water, baptize." Syriac Lex., Lyons, 1708.

MICHAELIS: "*Amad*—to bathe, baptize, immerse." Syriac Lex., Gottingen, 1788.

GUIDO FABRICUS: "*Amad*—to baptize, dip, bathe." Syro-Chal. Lex. accompanying Antwerp Polyglot, Antwerp, 1592.

BUXTORF: "*Amad*—baptize, dip, bathe one's self." Chaldee and Syriac Lex., Basle, 1662.

BEZA: After remarking that *baptidzo* properly means to immerse and never to wash, except as a consequence of immersion, says: "Nor does this signification of '*amad*,' which the Syrians use for 'baptize,' differ at all from this." Appendix to Stewart on Baptism, p. 249.

ULEMAN: "*Amad*—to suffer one's self to be dipped, to suffer one's self to be baptized. *Amada*—dipping, baptism." Syriac Gram. with Sex. by Hutchinson, p. 359.

EPHRAIM CYRUS was a native Syrian, who lived in the fourth century; speaking of Christ, says: "How wonderful is it that thy footsteps were planted on the waters; that the great sea should subject itself to thy feet; and that yet, at a small river, that same head of thine should be subject to be bowed down and baptized in it." Gotch's Bible Questions, p. 130.

These definitions and examples of the meaning of *amad* are quite sufficient to sustain our table of versions as to this word. But it is further insisted that the German *taufen* signifies to sprinkle or pour. If this be so, our table needs correction at this point. Let us see how this is:

LUTHER says: "The Germans call baptism *tauff*, from depth, which they call *tieff* in their language, as if it were proper those should be deeply immersed who are baptized. And truly, if you consider what baptism signifies you shall see the same thing required." Luther's Works, vol. i, p. 72, Wittenberg, 1582.

HEINSIUS: "*Taufen* signifies, in a general sense, to plunge into water (as a bomb dipped in pitch and rosin); in a more limited sense, to immerse in water in a religious way." German Dict., 4 vols., Hanover, 1822.

SMILTHENNER: "*Taufen*, in old German, *taufian*, from *taufa*, which signifies *tiefe*, (*i.e.*, deep), consequently it means to immerse." Etymol. Dict., 1834.

KALTSCHMIDT: "*Taufen*—to immerse (eintauchen) to consecrate to Christianity, to name." Germ. Lex., Leipsic, 1834.

SCHWENCK: "*Taufen*—to immerse in water; specially, to purify with water for admission to the Christian church. *Taufen* is the same as *tauchen*." Etymol. Dict. 3d ed., 1838.

GEMTHE: "*Tauchen* and *taufen* were originally the same; the act expressed by taufen was performed by immersion (untertauchen). At present the word *taufen* retains its proper signification—overwhelm with water." Gemthe's Germ. Synonyms, 1838.

WIEGAND'S GERMAN SYNONYMS: "*Taufen*—originally equivalent to *untertauchen* (to dip under), signifies, in its religious use, *to immerse in water*."

KNAPP's THEOLOGY, vol. ii, p. 501, Andover edition, *taufen* is incidentally defined. This great German scholar says: "*Baptisma*, from *baptidzein*, which properly signifies to *immerse*, like the German *taufen*, to dip in, to wash by immersion."

WEBSTER and WORCESTER each give *taufen* as the German synonym of dip.

Surely these authorities are sufficient to establish immersion or dipping as the meaning of *taufen*, the German word representing baptism.

The Chaldee word *tseva* is also brought into the service of sprinklers in modern times. GESENIUS defines it thus: "To dip in, to immerse; hence to tinge, to dye." Heb. and Chal. Lex., p. 891. M. STUART says: "The Syriac has a word like the Chaldee *tseva* . . . which means to plunge, immerse." Christ. Bap., p. 155. Thus it will be seen that there is not much appearance of sprinkle or pour in it.

Having viewed the word *baptidzo* through the light of thirty-four lexicographers, seventy commentators and critics, numerous examples of its use among the classics, and its representatives in thirty-eight different versions, made at different times and in different countries, and every-where found that its primary import is *to dip* or *immerse,* and that the laws of interpretation require us to retain the primary meaning, unless good reason be found for its removal, we are now prepared to open the New Testament and see what the Lord required of those commanded to be baptized.

THE COMMISSION.

To the apostles Jesus said: "Go teach all nations, baptizing them into the name of the Father, and of the Son, and of the Holy Spirit." Matt. xxviii:19. Here, He who was possessed of all authority in heaven and upon earth commanded his apostles to do something, to which the obedient of all nations were bound to submit. We have found a rule of interpretation saying: "To every word in Scripture there is unquestionably assigned some idea or notion, otherwise words are useless, and have no more signification than the inarticulate sounds of animals." What particular idea, notion, or thought is attached to the word "baptizing" in the commission given by the Lord? Did

He employ the term in its ordinary, current signification, or did He attach to it some figurative or tropical meaning? If He used the word out of its current signification, and gave no notice thereof, we see not how He expected to be understood by those who heard Him. Unless a command is understood it can not be obeyed; hence, we see not how persons are to submit to baptism when they know not what is required of them. Therefore, as it was necessary that He should be understood in order to be obeyed, we conclude He used the term *baptizing* in its ordinary or current acceptation; and if so, He commanded the apostles to *immerse* the people, for we have shown this to be the current meaning of the word used by Him. Indeed, if the word means to sprinkle and to pour, it is difficult to see how the command can be obeyed at all; for the command requires the *people* to be baptized and not the water to be baptized upon the people. If sprinkling or pouring be the act required, then it is the water or element used that is baptized, and not the people; for it is certainly water that is sprinkled or poured. We are aware that Paul says: "When Moses had spoken every precept to all the people, according to the law, he took the blood of calves and of goats, with water, and scarlet wool, and hyssop, and sprinkled both the book and all the people." Heb. ix:19. But we regard this as no valid objection to the position we have taken, for Paul's language was evidently elliptical, as may be seen by reference to the historical account of what Moses did: "And he took the book of the covenant and read in the audience of the people, and they said, All that the Lord hath said will we do, and be obedient. And Moses took the blood and sprinkled it on the people, and said, Behold the blood of the covenant, which the Lord hath made with you concerning all these words." Ex. xxiv:7, 8. Hence, the ellipsis in Paul's language being supplied, it means that Moses sprinkled the blood upon the people. But we may be asked, is not the commission also elliptical? Suppose it is; this will not affect our argument at all, as may be seen by supplying the ellipsis: 1. Teach the people, sprinkling (water upon) them. 2. Teach the people, pouring (water upon) them. 3. Teach the people, immersing them (in water). Though the ellipsis be supplied, it changes not the act indicated. The government is not changed when the ellipsis is supplied as to immersion, the object of the action expressed by the participle is the *people;* hence they are immersed; but as to the act of sprinkling and pouring the government is entirely changed—the act expressed by the active participle sprinkling takes effect upon the water, and the word people is governed by a preposition. The same remark applies to pouring. The act expressed by it takes effect upon the water or element poured, and the word *people* is governed by a preposition. Then, when the word *baptizing* in the commission is made to mean pour it is the water that is baptized, because it is the thing poured, and when it is made to mean sprinkle it is the water that is baptized, because it is the thing sprinkled; but when it means immersing, the command can be obeyed by the people, for they may be immersed but can not be sprinkled or poured.

But there is another difficulty involved in the idea of substituting sprinkling or pouring for immersion. The verb *sprinkle* means to *scatter in drops,* and is always followed by the material to be sprinkled, either expressed or understood. We may sprinkle blood, water, sand, or ashes on a man, but we can not sprinkle a man on any thing. We sometimes speak of sprinkling a man with water when we mean to sprinkle water upon him, but the language is an outrage upon all grammatical accuracy. If we say, we sprinkle a man with water, the language must mean one of two things: first, that we sprinkle (that is, scatter in drops) both the man and the water together, as we eat butter with our bread; or, second, that the water is the instrument with which we sprinkle or scatter the man, as we sprinkle water with a broom. In the first construction, the nouns *man* and *water* are the objects of the action expressed by the verb sprinkle; and in the second construction, the noun *man* is alone the object and water the instrument—either of which involves a physical impossibility.

The verb *pour* means *to turn out in a stream,* and is followed by the thing poured, which must be something fluid or composed of small particles. It is as much impossible to *pour a man* as to *sprinkle him.*

But those who practice sprinkling, pouring, and immersion as baptism tell us that the only authority they have to baptize any body is found in this verse: Matt. xxviii:19. (See Louisville Debate, p. 15.) Then, when they sprinkle water upon any one as baptism they derive authority from this verse; when they pour water upon any one as baptism they derive authority from this verse; and when they immerse a man in water as baptism they get their authority from this same verse; hence, the word *baptizing* must mean sprinkle, pour, and immerse in this one place, in clear violation of the rule of interpretation, which says: "The sense of a word cannot be diverse or multifarious at the same time and in the same passage or expression;" and again: "In no language can a word have more than one literal meaning in the same place."

Sprinkling, pouring, and immersion are three separate, distinct, and specific acts, diverse from each other; hence they can not all be used as the meaning of "baptizing" in this place. But it may be said that sprinkle and pour are tropical meanings. This does not relieve the difficulty, for we have shown that immersing is the *literal* import; hence, you can not give a literal and tropical meaning to the same word in the same place. If you do, the word becomes "multifarious" in violation of the laws of interpretation.

Again: if sprinkling, pouring, and immersing are all required to make up the full import of the word indicating the command in this place, then no one has been baptized in obedience to the command until he has submitted to all three of these acts—that is, until he has had water sprinkled upon him, poured upon him, and has been immersed in it.

But if it be insisted that in this one place the word authorizes one man to be immersed, another to have water sprinkled upon him, and a third to have water poured upon him, and that each case is a baptism, it follows that as they are different acts performed by different persons, each being a baptism, they are not one but three baptisms, and Paul was mistaken when he said that there is "one baptism;" for the phrase "one baptism" as much implies that *there is but one baptism* as does the phrase *"one God"* imply that there is but one God. Hence, we conclude that when the Lord said "go teach all nations, baptizing them," He intended one specific act, and not three different acts. This one act is baptism—nothing else is.

The Baptism of Jesus.

We propose now to examine an example of baptism furnished in the baptism of Jesus by John, an account of which we have in Mark i:9, 10, as follows: "And it came to pass in those days, that Jesus came from Nazareth of Galilee, and was baptized of John in Jordan. And straightway coming up out of the water, he saw the heavens opened, and the Spirit like a dove descending upon him." Here we learn that Jesus was baptized by John in Jordan, after which He came up out of the water. For thus going into and coming out of the water there could have been neither reason nor propriety had sprinkling or pouring water upon Him been the baptism to which He submitted. It is true that in modern times we hear of persons going down into the water and having some of it poured or sprinkled upon them. This seems to be an artifice on the part of the administrator to satisfy the credulous subject, if possible, without at all doing the thing commanded. Surely, none will dare say the Lord ever commanded such a procedure.

But we are told that *apo*, the Greek word here rendered *out of*, primarily means *from*, and that nothing more was signified by it than that Jesus came up from the margin of the water. If *apo* be the correct word in the original text—about which we will see directly—is it not bound by the nature of the transaction, and by the meaning of the other words related to it in this connection, to mean *out of?* Mark tells us that John baptized Jesus *in* Jordan. Hence, if the baptism took place *in* Jordan, must not the subject (Christ) come from within Jordan, or the place where the baptism occurred?

But we are told that the Greek word *eis*, here rendered *in*, is sometimes rendered *at*, and may be so translated in this passage. Hence, John simply baptized Jesus *at* Jordan. But the whole force of this argument is based upon the *primary* meaning of *apo;* why, then, shall we not be allowed to demand the *primary* meaning of *eis?* We grant that primary meanings are to be preferred unless good reason be given for another. We dare not adopt or reject the meanings of words just as they may chance to favor or oppose our peculiar views. The primary meaning of *eis* is *into*, and were it so rendered, the connection would show that John baptized Jesus *into* Jordan.

As Jordan was a river, into the water of which Jesus was baptized, it is easy to see why He came "up out of the water;" and although *apo*, as contended, may primarily mean from, it is only from the place that *eis* put Him, and as this was *into the water*, the necessity of the case demands, as our rules of interpretation allow, a secondary meaning for *apo*, *out of*. Nor is there any thing in *apo* making it unreasonable that *from*, in the passage, means from within the water. A man might say, "I came from Nashville," when in truth he came from the Maxwell House in the very heart of the city.

Pickering, in his Greek Lexicon, gives us an example in which we see that *apo* means *out of;* as, From or out of Egypt. He further says: "It is also used instead of the prepositions *ek*, *epi*, *peri*, and *hupo;* as, Out of a hundred and twenty youths one only escaped;" thus showing us clearly that *apo* may and does often mean *out of*. But some of the very best authorities known have *ek* in place of *apo* in the original text, among whom we may mention Tregelles, Tischendorf, Alford, Greene, Bengel, Lackman, and Meyer.

When, in connection with all this, we consider the additional fact that the multitudes were being baptized by John in the river of Jordan, the conclusion that he was immersed by John in Jordan is irresistible. If John did not baptize *in* the river, he did not preach *in* the wilderness. Matt. iii:1. If Jesus was only baptized *at* the Jordan, then He was only led by the Spirit *at* the wilderness, for both are expressed by the same original word.

We have no confidence in the pictures exhibited by debaters in modern times, showing that John poured water on the head of the Saviour. But there is a thought or two connected with them to which we would solicit the attention of the reader. We have seen some ten or twelve of these, each representing the scene in a different manner from the others. No higher evidence than this is needed to prove them unfaithful in delineation, for, as He was baptized but once, it is not possible that a dozen modes were adopted.

Some of them represent Him as standing up to the waist in water, at least sufficiently deep to be immersed, while their criticisms upon *eis* and *apo* have Him baptized *at* or near the margin of the stream, and not in the water at all. Thus their own pictures contradict their criticisms. Truly, "the legs of the lame are unequal."

But it is said that "John baptized the people with water," and hence applied the water to the subject and not the subject to the water. And, by way of illustration, they give us examples like the following: "I shave *with* a razor," "I write *with* a pen," etc. As an offset to these examples we might give the following: "The tanner tans his leather *with* ooze," "The lady colors her web *with* dye," etc. Surely, it will not be insisted that the tanner makes his leather by sprinkling a little ooze upon it, or that the lady colors her web by sprinkling a few drops of her dye thereon. Hence, the examples given by the objector can prove nothing. The original word from which we have the word *with* in the connection, "I indeed baptize you *with* water" (Matt. iii:11; Mark i:8), is the Greek *en*, the primary meaning of which is *in*, and which must be the meaning used, as our rules say, unless there is some circumstance compelling some other. But so far from there being those compulsory circumstances, the other words and circumstances compel the retention of the primary meaning *in*. But we are told that *en* conveys the idea of instrumentality and must be rendered *with* if so, when John baptized the people *(en)* with the river Jordan, we suppose he had rather an unwieldy instrument, to say the least of it.

But we are told that the fearfully impetuous current of the Jordan would have rendered it impossible for John to have stood in it and baptized the people. As the testimony of Lieut. Lynch is invoked upon this subject, it will be well for us to hear what he says about it. On page 255 of his work titled the "DEAD SEA AND THE JORDAN," he says:

"At 9:30; P.M. we arrived at 'El Meshra,' the bathing place of the Christian pilgrims, after having been fifteen hours in the boats. This ford is consecrated by tradition as the place where the Israelites passed over with the ark of the covenant, and where our blessed Saviour was baptized by John. Feeling that it would be desecration to moor the boats at a place so sacred, we passed it, and with some difficulty found a landing below.

"My first act was to bathe in the consecrated stream, thanking God first for the precious favor of being permitted to visit such a spot; and, secondly, for his protecting care throughout our perilous passage. * * * Tradition, sustained by the geographical features of the country, makes this also the scene of the baptism of the Redeemer. The mind of man, trammeled by sin, can not soar in contemplation of so sublime an event. On that wondrous day, when the Deity, veiled in flesh, descended the bank, all nature, hushed in awe, looked on, and the impetuous river, in grateful homage, must have stayed its course, and gently laved the body of its Lord."

Thus it will be seen that Lieut. Lynch did not think it impossible for the body of the Lord to have been gently laved by the waters of the Jordan.

In describing a visit by a company of pilgrims to the Jordan, he says: "The party which had disturbed us was the advanced guard of the great body of the pilgrims. A 5, just at the dawn of day, the last made its appearance, coming over the crest of a high ridge, in one tumultuous and eager throng. In all the wild haste of a disorderly rout, Copts and Russians, Poles, Armenians, Greeks and Syrians, from all parts of Asia, from Europe, from Africa, and from far distant America, on they came; men, women, and children, of every age and hue, and in every variety of costume; talking, screaming, shouting, in almost every known language under the sun. Mounted as variously as those who had preceded them, many of the women and children were suspended in baskets or confined in cages; and, with their eyes strained toward the river, heedless of all intervening obstacles, they hurried eagerly forward, and dismounting in haste and disrobing with precipitation, rushed down the bank and threw themselves into the stream. They seemed to be absorbed by one impulsive feeling, and perfectly regardless of the observations of others. Each one plunged himself, or was dipped by another, three times below the surface, in honor of the Trinity; and then filled a bottle or some other utensil from the river. The bathing-dress of many of the pilgrims was a white gown with a black cross upon it. Most of them, as soon as they dressed, cut branches either of the *agnus castus* or willow, and, dipping them in the consecrated stream, bore them away as memorials of their visit.

"In an hour they began to disappear, and in less than three hours the trodden surface of the lately crowded bank reflected no human shadow. The pageant disappeared as rapidly as it had approached, and left to us once more the silence and the solitude of the wilderness. It was like a dream. An immense crown of human beings—said to be 8,000, but I thought not so many—had passed and repassed before our tents and left not a vestige behind them. Every one bathed, a few Franks excepted, the greater number in a quiet and reverential manner, but some, I am sorry to say, displayed an ill-timed levity." Pages 261, 262.

This needs no comment. We leave it with the single remark, that where so many in so short a time could bathe themselves without difficulty, surely John the Baptist could have no difficulty in baptizing those who came to him.

Rev. D. A. Randall visited the Jordan at the time of harvest, when it "overfloweth his banks all the time." In consequence of the falling rains and melting snows of the far distant mountains of Herman, it was near its greatest depth, yet he and his comrades enjoyed the pleasure of a bath in its waters. Handwriting of God, Part ii, p. 233.

The river Jordan, like all other streams, has its rapids and its eddies, in the latter of which there are doubtless numerous places in which it would be safe to immerse. It is a little remarkable to what extremes the opponents of immersion will go in their zeal to show the impossibility of performing this act in the Jordan. Heretofore, some have contended that immersion could not have been the act, because this river is so small that "a man might step across it, or arrest its current with his foot," but since the observations of Lynch, Randall, and others have been published, it suddenly becomes so impetuous and deep as to make it impossible for John to have immersed the people in it.

Before leaving this part of the subject we deduce another argument in favor of immersion from John's clothing: "John had his raiment of camel's hair and a leathern girdle about his loins," Matt. iii:4; Mark i:6. Why was he thus clad? I suppose it means something or it would not have been recorded. Some suppose that the coarse hair-cloth with which he was clad used as the best protection against the water. Certain it is that leathern girdles were then and now are used to strengthen the loins under physical exertion. We can see propriety in this girdle to sustain him while immersing the vast crowds baptized by him, but none whatever if he only sprinkled water upon them. Surely, his loins needed no support for such labor as this, since the most fashionably clad may now administer the rite without physical effort or damage to silks or satins.

As a further evidence that John practiced immersion we find he "was baptizing in Aenon, near to Salem, because there was much water there." John iii:23. Why should he have gone there to sprinkle or pour a few drops of water upon the people? This could not have required *much water.* We suppose a single gallon would be quite sufficient for a modern preacher for a whole day. But we are told that much water was necessary to supply the people and their animals with drink while attending his preaching. Then the passage should read, "John was holding a meeting at Aenon, near Salem, because there was much water there." Would not this have been much more appropriate? But, on the contrary, "he came into all the country about the Jordan preaching the baptism of repentance for the remission of sins." Luke iii:3. Thus we see that John preached every-where, but when he went to baptize he went where there was much water. It is reasonable to suppose that quite as many people attended his preaching in the country as witnessed his baptism at Aenon, yet much water is not mentioned as an accommodation for those who attended his preaching, but is given as a reason for his "baptizing at Aenon." For a beautiful description of the waters of Aenon and their adaptation to the purposes for which John selected them, see Barclay's "City of the Great King," pp. 559-562.

Convertible Terms.

We now pass to the examination of a law of translation found in the convertibility of terms, which may be stated substantially in the following words: "When the *correct* meaning of a word, in a given place, is substituted for the word, *it must make sense,* and harmonize with the other words in construction with the word for which the substitution is made." This rule lies at the foundation of all translation and must obtain, though in some instances, from force of habit, the euphony may seem somewhat impaired. Be it further observed that the demands of the rule are not that *every* meaning a word *may have* will make sense *every-where* it occurs, but the *correct meaning* of a word in a given place must make sense in that place. By this rule we will try the meaning of the word baptize in a few passages, and see whether or not it may mean sprinkle or pour—remembering, in the meantime, that sprinkle means *to scatter in drops*, and pour means *to turn out in a stream*. Let us now read the passages and submit these definitions to the rule stated: "Then went out to him Jerusalem and all Judea, and all the region round about Jordan, and were *sprinkled* (scattered in drops) of him in Jordan, confessing their sins. But when he saw many of the Pharisees and Sadducees come to his *sprinkling* (scattering in drops) he said unto them," etc. Matt. iii:5-7. Were the people scattered in drops by John in Jordan? "He that believeth and is *sprinkled* (scattered in drops) shall be saved." Mark xvi:16. "Repent and be *sprinkled* (scattered in drops) every one of you." Acts ii:38. "When they believed Philip preaching the things concerning the kingdom of God and the name of Jesus Christ, they were *sprinkled* (scattered in drops), both men and women." Acts viii:12. These scriptures need only to be read—no comment is necessary to show that *sprinkle* will not bear the test. Will *pour* do any better? We will try it. "Then went out to him Jerusalem and all Judea, and all the region round about Jordan, and were *poured* (turned out in a stream) of him in Jordan." "He that believeth and is *poured* (turned out in a stream) shall be saved." "Repent and be *poured* (turned out in a stream) every one of you." "When they believed Philip preaching the things concerning the kingdom of God and the name of Jesus Christ, they were *poured* (turned out in a stream), both men and women." Thus we see that the sense is as completely destroyed by substituting *pour* as by *sprinkle*.

Now, let us subject *immersion* to the same ordeal; if it will do no better, away with it. "Then went out to him Jerusalem and all Judea, and all the region round about Jordan, and were *immersed* of him in Jordan, confessing their sins." "But when he saw many of the Pharisees and Sadducees come to his *immersion*, he said unto them," etc. "He that believeth and is *immersed* shall be saved." "Repent and be *immersed* every one of you." "When they believed Philip preaching the things concerning the kingdom of God and the name of Jesus Christ, they were *immersed*, both men and women." Thus we might try every place in the New Testament where the word occurs, and the result would be the same. A man may be immersed in water, blood, oil, grief, suffering, debt, etc., but sprinkled or poured he can not be, and live.

As the Holy Spirit was shed forth on the day of Pentecost, when the apostles were baptized with it, it is sometimes insisted that this is the meaning of baptize. Then let us try it. "Go teach all nations, *shedding them forth* in the name," etc. Matt. xxviii:19. "And they went down into the water, both Philip and the eunuch, and he *shed him forth*." Acts viii:38. Will this do? Once more: At the house of Cornelius "the Holy Ghost fell on all them which heard the word." Acts x:44. It is therefore insisted that *fell on* is the meaning of the word baptize, and indicates the manner in which it should be performed. Then we will try this also. "Go teach all nations, *falling on them* in the name of the Father," etc. "And they went down into the water, both Philip and the eunuch, and he *fell on him*." We will not offer a word of comment to make these definitions more ridiculously absurd than they are in their own native deformity.

These illustrations clearly show that the lexicons and critics were right in giving *immerse* as the primary and literal meaning of *baptidzo*, as used in the New Testament. Hence the conclusion that John immersed Jesus and the multitudes who demanded baptism of him, in the waters of Jordan and Aenon, is irresistible. To the reader, then, we say, "go thou and do likewise."

The Birth of Water.

We deduce another argument in favor of immersion from the language of Jesus to Nicodemus, as follows:

"Except a man be born of water and of the Spirit, he can not enter into the kingdom of God." John iii:5.

The language "born again" is to be understood figuratively, of course; but the figure is based upon the real or natural birth, and as a figure must, in some sense, resemble the fact upon which it is based, so a birth of water must, in some sense, resemble a natural birth. Natural birth contemplates delivery, so when a man is born of water, he must be delivered from or come forth out of it. As he can not be delivered from or come forth out of that in which he has never been, it follows that a man must be placed in water before he can be delivered from or born of it. Hence, in order to be born of water, a man must be immersed in it that he may emerge from it. But what resemblance to a birth has sprinkling or pouring water upon any one? *Can a man be born of a substance less than himself?* Such a thing is impossible with every one save him who practices sprinkling or pouring water as baptism. How a grown man or woman may be born of a drop or a spoonful of water is a mystery which needs explanation.

For a full examination of the New Birth the reader is referred to the chapter on this subject, the object here being only to examine it so far as it bears upon the *action* of baptism. That the words "born of water" refer to baptism, see authorities quoted in argument based upon this verse in the chapter on the Design of Baptism.

Baptism a Burial.

"Therefore, we are buried with him by baptism." Rom. vi:4. "Buried with him in baptism, wherein also ye are risen with him." Col. ii:12.

That these passages refer to immersion is so manifestly plain that it seems almost an insult to common sense to attempt an argument to show it. There are three things which, though not all in the *word*, are implied in the *idea* of a burial. First, the thing buried; second, the thing buried in; and, third, the *act* of burying. A burial may differ as to the thing buried; it may be a seed, or it may be a man. It may differ as to the thing buried in; it may be in earth, it may be in water, but as to the *act* of burying there can be no difference; it must be a placing *in* and *covering up* in every burial, whether it be a seed or a man, in the earth or in water. Then, when a man has a few drops of water sprinkled on him, is he buried? Surely not. When he has a small stream poured upon him, is he buried? He is not. When he is immersed in water, is he buried? Most certainly he is.

We have shown that baptism means immersion; hence, when Paul said he and his brethren had been buried with Christ by baptism, is it not clear that he spake of that burial which was effected by immersion? Lives there a man beneath the sun, who has only had a few drops of water sprinkled on him, who can approach the mercy-seat of Christ, and, with his hand upon his heart, say "I have been buried with Christ by baptism?" We think not.

But we are told that Paul alluded to Holy Spirit baptism. Suppose he did, does this bring any support to those who oppose immersion? When they wish to make an argument in favor of pouring, they tell us that the Holy Spirit was poured upon the Pentecostians; and as that was Holy Spirit baptism, water baptism must be like it, and therefore must be pouring. Spirit baptism and water baptism must be administered in the same way. Well, then, if Paul spoke of Holy Spirit baptism, it was a burial, and if water baptism be like it, it must also be a burial. Hence this passage proves baptism to be immersion, whether he spoke of water or Spirit. If of water, the proof is direct; if of Spirit, it is by analogy, our opponents being judges.

But did Paul allude to Holy Spirit baptism? In submitting to it his brethren *obeyed* from the heart the form of doctrine delivered to them. See verse 17. Luke tells us that Jesus commanded his disciples "that they should not depart from Jerusalem, but wait for the promise of the Father, which, saith he, ye have heard of me." What promise? "For John truly baptized with water; but ye shall be baptized with the Holy Ghost not many days hence." Acts i:4, 5. Promises may be enjoyed, but can not be obeyed. We may obey commands, but can not obey promises. Then, as the baptism of the Spirit was a promise, and as submission to the baptism of which Paul spoke was obedience, it follows, clear as demonstration, that he spoke not of spiritual baptism.

Commentators and critics have, with great unanimity, in all ages, decided that Rom. vi:4, and Col. ii:12, refer to immersion in water. At the risk of being tedious we will collate a few extracts, which will serve to show the decision of the learned on this subject:

1. JUSTIN MARTYR, born A.D. 140: "We represent our Lord's suffering by baptism in a pool." Adkins, p. 127.

2. CLEMENT OF ALEXANDRIA, A.D. 200: "You were led to a bath as Christ was conveyed to the sepulchre, and were thrice immersed, to signify Christ's three days' burial." Adkins, p. 127.

3. ATHANASIUS, Bishop of Alexandria, A.D. 328: "To immerse a child three times in a pool or bath, and to emerse him; this shows the death and resurrection of Christ on the third day." Stuart, p. 148, Conant, Ex. 188.

4. GREGORY NYSSEN, A.D. 328: "Coming into water, the kindred element of earth, we *hide ourselves in it* as the Saviour did in the earth." Stuart, p. 147. "Let us, therefore, be buried with Christ in baptism, that we may also rise with him; let us go down with him, that we also may be exalted with him." Conant, Ex. 188.

5. AMBROSE, A.D. 340: "You were asked, 'Dost thou believe in GOD ALMIGHTY?' Thou saidst, 'I believe,' and thus thou wast immerged *(mersisti);* that is, thou wast buried." Stuart, p. 147.

6. CHRYSOSTOM, A.D. 347: "To be baptized and to submerge, then to emerge, as a symbol of descent to the grave and of ascent from it. And therefore Paul calls baptism a burial when he says: 'We are therefore buried with him by baptism into death.'" Westlake, ch. 3. Stuart, p. 147.

7. APOSTOLICAL CONSTITUTIONS, written in the fourth century: "Immersion denotes dying with him (Christ); emersion a resurrection with Christ." Stuart, p. 148.

8. CYRIL, Bishop of Jerusalem, A.D. 350: "Thou, going down into the water, and in a manner buried in the waters, as he in the rock, art raised again, walking in newness of life." Conant, Ex. 176. "Ye professed the saving profession and sunk down thrice into the water, and again came up, and thereby a symbol shadowing forth the burial of Christ." Conant, Ex. 178.

9. BASIL THE GREAT, Bishop of Caesarea in Cappadocia, A.D. 370: "By three immersions we represent the death of Christ—the bodies of those that are baptized are buried in water." Conant, Ex. 181.

10. FOURTH COUNCIL OF TOLEDO, Can. 5: "The immersion in water is, as it were, the descent into the grave, and the emersion from the water the resurrection." Adkins, p. 128.

11. PHOTIUS: "The three immersions and emersions of baptism signify death and the resurrection." Stuart, p. 148.

12. GELASIUS: "The three immersions and emersions of baptism signify death and the resurrection." Adkins, p. 129.

13. GREGORY: "The three immersions and emersions of baptism signify death and the resurrection." *Ut supra.*

14. PELAGIUS: "The three immersions and emersions of baptism signify death and the resurrection." *Ut supra.*

15. ARCHBISHOP CRANMER: "The dipping into water doth betoken that the old Adam, with all his sin and evil lusts, ought to be drowned and killed by daily contrition and repentance." Westlake, ch. 3.

16. SCUDDER: "Baptism doth lively represent the death, burial, and resurrection of Christ, together with your crucifying the affections and lusts: being dead and buried with him unto sin, and rising with him to newness of life and to hope of glory." Westlake, ch. 3.

17. PICTETUS: "That immersion into and emersion out of the water, as practiced by the ancients, signify the death of the old and the resurrection of the new." *Ut supra.*

18. NICHOLSON, Bishop of Gloucester, Expos. of Ch. Catechism: "The ancient manner of baptizing and putting the person baptized under the water and then taking him out again, did well set forth these two acts: the first his dying, the second his rising again. In our baptism, by a kind of analogy or resemblance, while our bodies are under the water we may be said to be buried with him." *Ut supra.*

19. DR. MANTON, Chaplain to the King of England: "The putting the baptized person into the water denoteth and proclaimeth the burial of Christ, and we, by submitting to it, are dead are buried; so that it signifieth Christ's death for sin and our death unto sin." *Ut supra.*

20. AUGUSTINE: "That thrice repeated submersion expresses a resemblance of the Lord's burial." *Ut supra.*

21. BENGELLIUS, Professor of Theology at Denkendorf, Germany, in 1713: "He that is baptized puts on Christ, the second Adam; he is baptized, I say, into a whole Christ, and therefore into his death; and it is like as if that very moment Christ suf-

fered, died, and was buried for such a man, and such a man suffered, died, and was buried with Christ." Westlake, ch. 3.

22. DR. GOODWIN, member of the Westminster assembly: "There is a further representation therein of Christ's death, burial, and resurrection, in the baptized's being first buried under water and then rising out of it. Therefore, it is said we are buried with him in baptism." *Ut supra.*

23. DODDRIDGE'S Family Expositor on Rom. vi:4: *"Buried with him in baptism.* It seems to me the part of candor to confess that here is an illusion to the manner of baptizing by immersion."

24. WHITBY'S Commentary on the New Testament—Note on Rom. vi:4: "It being so expressly declared here (Rom. vi:4, and Col. ii:12) that we are buried with Christ in baptism by being buried under water, and the argument to oblige us to a conformity to his death being taken hence, and *this immersion being religiously observed by all Christians for thirteen centuries,* and approved by our church, and the change of it into sprinkling, even without any allowance from the Author of this institution, or any license from any council of the church, being that which the Romanist still urges to justify his refusal of the cup to the laity, it were to be wished that this custom might be of general use, and aspersion only permitted, as of old, in cases of the clinic or present danger of death." Pengilly, p. 47.

25. WELLS' Illus. Bible on Rom. vi:4: "St. Paul here alludes to immersion or dipping the whole body under water in baptism." Pengilly, 46.

26. ADAM CLARKE, Com. on Rom. vi:4: "When he [the person to be baptized] came up out of the water, he seemed to have a resurrection to life. He was, therefore, supposed to throw off his old Gentile state, as he threw off his clothes, and to assume a new character, as the baptized generally put on new or fresh garments."

27. JOHN EDWARDS: "The immersion into the water was thought to signify the death of Christ, and their coming out his rising again, and did no less represent their own resurrection." Pengilly, p. 49.

29. EDINBURGH REVIEWERS: "We have rarely met, for example, a more weak and fanciful piece of reasoning than that by which

Mr. Ewing would persuade us that there is no allusion to the mode by immersion in the expression 'buried with him in baptism.' This point ought to be frankly admitted and indeed can not be denied with any show of reason." *Ib.*, p. 47.

30. BLOOMFIELD'S Greek Testament, note on Rom. vi:4: "By which the rite of immersion in the baptismal water and egress from it were used as a symbol of breaking off all connection with the present sinful life and giving one's self to a new and pure one. We have been thus buried in the waters of baptism. There is a plain allusion to the ancient custom of baptism by immersion, on which (says Bloomfield) see 31 SUICER's Eccl. in V. cited in confession.

32. BINGHAM'S Antiquities of the Chr. Ch.: "Immersion universally prevailed, since all the ancients thought that burying under water did more lively represent the death, burial, and resurrection of Christ." Bloomfield also cites to the same effect Bishops Sherlock and Warburton.

33. SAURIN'S SERMONS, vol. iii, p. 176: "Paul says we are buried with Christ by baptism into death; that is, the ceremony of wholly immersing us in water when we were baptized signified that we died to sin, and that of rising again from our immersion signified that we would no more return to those disorderly practices in which we lived before our conversion to Christianity." Benedict's History, p. 179.

34. ARCHBISHOP LEIGHTON: "'We are buried with him,' the dipping into the waters representing our dying with Christ, and the return thence our rising with him." Works, p. 277.

35. MATHIES' Biblical, Historical, and Dogmatical Exposition of Baptism, which obtained a prize in the University of Berlin, says: "Paul, as we have seen (Rom. vi:4), has in his mind only the rite of immersing and emerging; and in the apostolic church, in order that a communion with the death of Christ may be signified the whole body of the person to be baptized was immersed in the water or river, and then, in order that a connection with the resurrection of Christ might be indicated, the body again emerged or raised out of the water. That this rite has been changed is indeed a calamity, for it is placed before the eyes most aptly the symbolical meaning of baptism." Dr. I. Chase, on Bap., pp. 50, 51.

36. ROSENMULLER, Professor of Theology at Leipsic, says: "Immersion in the water of baptism and coming forth out of it was a symbol of a person's renouncing his former life, and, on the contrary, of beginning a new one. The learned have rightly reminded us, that, on account of this emblematical meaning of baptism, the rite of *immersion* ought to have been retained in the Christian church." I. Chase on Bap., p. 49.

37. JASPIS, in his Latin version of the Epistles, says: "Paul in this place (Rom. vi:4) alludes to the custom then usual of immersing the whole body, which immersion resembled the laying of a man in a sepulchre." *Ut supra,* p. 49.

38. TURRETIN: "For as in baptism, when performed in the *primitive manner,* by immersion and emersion, descending into the water and again going out of it, of which descent and ascent we have an example in the eunuch, in Acts viii:38, 39. Yea, and what is more, as by this rite, when persons are immersed in water they are overwhelmed, and as it were *buried,* and in a manner *buried* together with Christ; and again they emerge, seems to be raised out of a grave, and are said to be risen again with Christ." Frey on Baptism, p. 186.

39. THEOPHYLACT, a Greek commentator on Col. ii:12: "Baptism typifies by *immersion* the death, by *emersion* the resurrection of Christ." Adkins, p. 128.

40. LEO, bishop of Rome, Decret. 9: "Trine immersion represents the three days' burial of Christ." *Ut supra.*

41. THEOBUCK, on Rom. vi:4: "In order to understand the figurative use of baptism we must bear in mind *the well-known* fact that the candidate in the primitive church was immersed in water and raised out of it again." *Ut supra,* p. 130.

42. WINER, in his Manuscript Letters on Christian Antiquities, says: "In the apostolic age baptism was immersion, as its symbolical explanation shows." *Ut supra.*

43. PROF. LANG. on Infant Baptism, 1834: "As Christ died, so we die (to sin) with him in baptism. The body is as it were *buried* under water, is dead with Christ; the plunging under water represents death, and rising out of it the resurrection to a new life. A more striking symbol could not be chosen." *Ut supra.*

44. DR. JORTIN's Sermons. Of the baptized he says: "He that

descended into the water and stooped or laid down in it—this represents death and the grave. His ascending out of the water under which he had been hidden represents the resurrection of Christ for our justification, and the new life and second birth of the baptized person, who was thenceforward to live to God and to do good works." Frey on Bap., pp. 128, 129.

45. SUPERVILLE, Pastor of the French Protestant Church at Rotterdam, says: "You know that in ancient times baptism was administered by immersion, so that the person who was baptized, being entirely plunged into the water, appeared for a moment as one dead and buried; after which, emerging from the water, he seemed as one rising from the dead. Hence the language of the apostle in Rom. vi:4, Col. ii:12," *Ut supra.*

46. BURMANNUS, Synop. Theol.: "Immersion was used by the Jews, the apostles, and the primitive church, especially in warm countries. To this, various forms of speaking used by the apostles refer: Rom. vi:4, Col. ii:12, etc." Frey, p. 132.

46. PETER MARTYR: "As Christ by baptism hath drawn us into his death and burial, so he hath drawn us out into life. This doth the dipping into the waters and the issuing forth again signify when we are baptized." Westlake, ch. iii.

47. ALBERT BARNES: "It is altogether probable that the apostle in this place had allusion to the custom of baptizing by immersion." Note on Rom. vi:4.

48. ESTIUS: "Immersion, in a more expressive manner, represents the death, burial, and resurrection of our Lord and of us." Frey, p. 150.

49. BRAUNUS, in his Doctrina Federum: "By baptism we are plunged under water, and, as it were, buried; but we do not continue in a state of death, for we immediately rise again from thence, to signify that we, through the merits of Christ, and with Christ, mortify the old man, are buried with Christ, and with him arise to newness of life." Haynes' Bap. Cyclopedia, p. 78.

50. DR. BOYS' Works: "The dipping, in holy baptism, has three parts: the putting into the water, the continuance in the water, and the coming out of the water. The putting into the water doth ratify the mortification of sin by the power of Christ's death, as Paul in Rom. vi:4." *Ut supra,* p. 99.

51. RHEINHARD'S Ethics: "In sprinkling, the symbolical mean-

ing of the ordinance is wholly lost." Hinton's History, Bap., p. 52.

52. BISHOP BURNETT'S Expos. of the Thirty-nine Articles, pp. 374, 375: "They (the primitive ministers of the gospel) led them into the water, and with no other garments but what might cover nature. They first *laid them down in the water*, as a man is buried in a grave, and then they said the words 'I *baptize thee in the name of the Father, Son, and Holy Ghost.*' Then they raised them up again, and clean garments were put on them, from whence came the phrases of being baptized into Christ's death, of our being *buried with him by baptism into death, being baptized into Christ's death, of our being risen with Christ, and of our putting on Christ, putting off the old man and putting on the new man.*"

53. CARDINAL CAJETAN: "'We *are buried with him by baptism into death.*' By our burying he declares our death from the ceremony of baptism: because he who is baptized is put under the water, and by this bears a likeness of him that was buried, who is put under the earth. Now, because none are buried by dead men, from this very thing we are buried in baptism, we are assimilated to Christ when he was buried. Christ ascended out of the water, therefore he was baptized by John, not by sprinkling or pouring water upon him, but by immersion." Booth's Ped. Ex.

54. DR. CAVE'S Primitive Christianity: "As in immersion there are, in a manner, three several acts, the putting a person into the water, his abiding there for a little time, and rising again; so by these were represented Christ's death, burial, and resurrection, and in conformity thereunto our dying unto sin, the destruction of its power, and our resurrection to a new course of life. By the persons being put into water was lively represented the putting off the body of the sins of the flesh, and being washed from the filth and pollution of them," etc. Booth's Ped. Ex.

55. BISHOP DAVENANT, of Salisbury, Eng., 1641, Exposition of Col. ii:12: "In baptism, the burial of the body of sin, or of the old Adam, is represented when the person to be baptized is put down into the water, as a resurrection when he is brought out of it." Haynes' Bap. Cyclopedia, p. 186.

60. JOHN FELL, Bishop of Oxford, in his Paraphrase and Annotations on St. Paul's Epistles, Rom. vi:4: "The primitive fash-

tion of immersion under the water representing our death, and elevation out of it our resurrection, our regeneration." *Ut supra,* pp. 246, 247.

61. DR. QUENSTEDT (Lutheran): *"Immersion* is similar to a burial, *emersion,* to a resurrection." Wiberg, p. 83.

62. CH. STARK: "The apostle has reference to the then prevailing custom, according to which the candidate was entirely immersed in water, and after he had been left under a little while, was again taken up out of it. Baptism, consequently, does not only contain the image and power of the death of Christ, but of his burial; so that, as the Lord, by his burial, has done away with the curse that lay upon him, we also might be partakers of his burial when we were laid down under the water as in a grave and covered with it." Wiberg, p. 113.

63. LOCKE: "We did own some kind of a death by being buried under the water—even so we, being raised from our typical death and burial in baptism, should lead a new sort of life." Campbell and Rice, p. 235.

64. DR. G. C. KNAPP: "The image is here taken from baptized persons as they were *immerged* (buried) and as they *emerged* (rose again); so it was understood by Chrysostom." Theol., vol. ii, p. 525.

65. MACKNIGHT: "In baptism, the baptized person is buried under water, as one put to death with Christ on account of sin, in order that they may be strongly impressed with a sense of the malignity of sin and excited to hate it as the greatest of evils." On Epist., vol. i, p. 259.

"Christ submitted to be baptized, that is, to be buried under the water by John, and to be raised out of it again, as an emblem of his future death and resurrection. In like manner the baptism of believers is emblematical of his own death, burial, and resurrection." On Rom. vi:4.

66. JOHN WESLEY: "Buried with him—alluding to the ancient manner of baptizing by immersion." Notes on Rom. vi.:4; Col. ii:12.

67. GEORGE WHITFIELD: "It is certain that, in the words of our text, Rom. vi:4, there is an allusion to the manner of baptizing, which was immersion." Pengilly, p. 47.

68. DR. WALL: "St. Paul does twice, in an allusive way of

speaking, call baptism a burial." Defense of Hist. of Infant Bap., 131.

68. ARCHBISHOP TILLOTSON: "Anciently, those who were baptized were immersed and buried in the water, to represent their death to sin, and then did rise up out of the water, to signify their entrance upon the new life; and to these customs the apostle alludes in Rom. vi:4." Pengilly, p. 46.

69. ARCHBISHOP SEEKER: "Burying, as it were, the person in the water and raising him out again, without *question*, was anciently the more usual method, on account of which St. Paul speaks of baptism as representing the death, burial, and resurrection of Christ, and what is grounded on them—our being dead and buried to sin, and our rising again to walk in newness of life." Pengilly, p. 46.

70. SAMUEL CLARKE: "We are buried with Christ by baptism, etc. In the primitive times the manner of baptizing was by immersion, or dipping the whole body into water. And this manner of doing it was a very significant emblem of the dying and rising again referred to by St. Paul in the above mentioned similitude." *Ibid.*

71. BURKITT's Notes on the New Testament. On Rom. vi:4: "The apostle alludes, no doubt, to the ancient manner and way of baptizing persons in those hot countries, which was by immersion or putting them under the water for a time, and raising them up again out of the water, which rite had also a mystical signification, representing the burial of our old man, sin in us, and our resurrection to newness of life."

72. OLSHAUSEN's Commentary on Rom. vi:4: "In this passage we are by no means to refer the baptism merely to their own resolutions, or see in it merely a figure in which the one-half of the ancient baptismal rite—the *submersion merely* prefigures the death and burial of the old man—the second half the *emersion*, the resurrection of the new man."

73. CONYBEARE AND HOWSON's Life and Epist. of St. Paul: "Baptism was immersion, the convert being plunged beneath the surface of the water to represent his death to sin, and then raised from this momentary burial to represent his resurrection to a life of righteousness." Also on Rom. vi:4: "This passage *can*

not be understood unless it is borne in mind that the primitive baptism was by immersion."

74. Dr. Hammond on Rom. vi:4: "It is a thing that *every Christian* knows, that the immersion in baptism refers to the death of Christ; the putting of the person into the water denotes and proclaims the death and burial of Christ." Haynes' Last Reply to Cook and Towne, p. 107.

75. Bishop Hoadley: "If baptism had been then performed as it is now among us, we should never so much as heard of this form of expression, of dying and rising again in this rite." *Ibid.*

76. Dr. Storr and Flatt's Biblical Theol., Andover, 1826: "The disciples of our Lord could understand his command in *no other manner* than as enjoining immersion; and that they actually did understand it so is proved partly by those passages of Scripture which evidently allude to immersion: Acts viii:36, Rom. vi:4." *Ut supra.*

77. Martin Luther: "Baptism is a sign of both death and resurrection. Being moved by this reason, I would have those who are to be baptized to be altogether dipped into the water, as the word doth express and the mystery doth signify." *Ut supra*, pp. 109, 110.

78. Dr. R. Newton, on Rom. vi:4: "Baptism was usually performed by immersion or dipping the whole body under the water, to represent the death, burial, and resurrection of Christ together." Slack's Reasons for Becoming a Bap., p. 56.

79. Richard Baxter: "It is commonly confessed by us of the Anabaptists, as our commentators declare, that in the apostles' times the baptized were dipped over-head in the water, and that this signified their profession both of the believing the burial and resurrection of Christ, and of their own present renouncing of the world and flesh, or of dying to sin and living to Christ, or rising again to newness of life, or being buried and risen again with Christ, as the apostle expoundeth in the fore cited texts." Westlake, ch. v.

80. Bishop Smith: "Buried in baptism—all continue to render the fact as early ascertained far more reconcilable with Scripture than any contrary theory can be. If any one practice of the early churches is clearly ascertained, it is immersion." Bliss' Letters, p. 24.

81. WESTMINSTER ASSEMBLY OF DIVINES, Annotations on Rom. vi:4: "'Buried with him in baptism.' In this phrase the apostle seemeth to allude to the ancient manner of baptism, which was to dip the parties baptized, and as it were bury them under water." Judson, p. 24.

82. WILLIAM TYNDALE: "The plunging into the water signifieth that we die and are buried with Christ, as concerning the old life of sin, which is in Adam; and the pulling out again signifieth that we rise again with Christ in a new life." Westlake, p. 5.

83. DR. CHALMERS on Rom. vi:4: "In the act of descending under the water of baptism, to have resigned an old life, and in the act of ascending, to emerge into a second or new life—along the course of which it is our part to maintain a strenuous avoidance of sin."

84. GROTIUS: *"Buried with him by baptism.* Not only the word *baptism*, but the very *form* of it, intimates this. For an immersion of the whole body in water so that it is no longer beheld, bears an image of that burial which is given to the dead. So Col. ii:12. There was in baptism, as administered in former times, an image both of a burial and of a resurrection, which in respect of Christ was external, in regard to Christians internal." Rom. vi:4. Booth on Pedobaptism, abridged by Bryant, p. 52.

85. CHURCH OF ENGLAND: "As we be buried with Christ by our baptism into death, so let us daily die to sin, mortifying and killing the evil motions thereof. And as Christ was raised up from death by the glory of the Father, so let us rise to a new life and walk continually therein." Homily of the Resurrection, Booth. pp. 52, 53.

86. WOLFIUS: "Immersion into water, in former times, and a short continuance under the water, practiced by the ancient church, afford the representation of a burial in baptism." *Curae, ad* Rom. vi:4.

87. BISHOP PEARCE: "It seems to have been a metaphor taken from the custom of those days in baptizing, for the person baptized went down under the water and was (as it were) buried under it. Hence St. Paul says, in Rom. vi:4, and Col. ii:12, that they *were buried with Christ by baptism." Ibid*, p. 68.

88, 89. BISHOP SHERLOCK and BISHOP WARBURTON are cited

to the same effect in Bloomfield on Rom. vi:4: and still others might be given, but surely the reader is ready to say with us, these are enough. This list is mostly made up of those who practiced sprinkling and pouring, and surely were not influenced by any disposition to favor immersion, but when speaking as scholars and critics were compelled to testify to the truth, whether for or against their practice. The reader will please observe that some of them lived early in the second century; and we have taken some from every period in the history of the church from then until now, thus showing that, almost with one voice, the learned of all ages and countries testify that this passage refers to the ancient custom of baptizing by immersion. Surely, nothing but a cause reduced to desperation would demand of its advocates a departure from a meaning so plainly taught by all these authorities floating (as it were) upon the very surface of this passage.

Baptism a Washing.

"Let us draw near with a true heart in full assurance of faith, having our hearts sprinkled from an evil conscience and our bodies washed with pure water." Heb. x:22.

That the apostle here alludes to baptism is very generally admitted. He had been reasoning on the subject of the Jewish priesthood and the process of consecration connected with it, a partial account of which we have as follows: "Thus shalt Aaron come into the holy *place:* with a young bullock for a sin-offering, and a ram for a burnt-offering. He shall put on the holy linen coat, and he shall have the linen breeches upon his flesh, and shall be girded with a linen girdle, and with the linen mitre shall he be attired: these are holy garments; therefore shall he wash his flesh, and so put them on." Lev. xvi:3, 4.

Under the Christian dispensation every Christian is regarded as a priest. Speaking of his brethren, Peter said: "Ye also, as lively stones, are built up a spiritual house, an holy priesthood, to offer up spiritual sacrifices acceptable to God by Jesus Christ." 1 Pet. ii:5. Again, verse 9, he says: "Ye are a chosen generation, a royal priesthood." As Christians are priests, we can see a peculiar fitness in Paul's allusion to the washing of a Jewish priest in the ceremony of his consecration, illustrative of the washing of a Christian in the ceremony of his consecration. That it did not consist in the application of a small quantity of water to the face may be seen in the fact that the same general term *flesh is* used to indicate the extent of the washing, that is used to indicate the parts on which the priestly garments were worn. That the Jews understood the phrase *wash the flesh* in the sense of *bathing the whole body* may be seen in the washing of Naaman. "Elisha sent a messenger unto him, saying, Go *wash* in Jordan seven times, and thy flesh shall come again to thee, and thou shalt be clean * * * Then went he down, and dipped himself seven times in Jordan, *according to the saying of the man of God;* and his flesh came again like unto the flesh of a little child, and he was clean." 2 Kings v:10-14.

Here we see that Naaman was commanded to WASH himself seven times in Jordan; and, guided by those who are presumed to have understood what was meant, he DIPPED himself. That he correctly obeyed the command is evident from the fact that he dipped himself *according to the saying of the man of God,* and God recognized his act by *curing* him of his leprosy. This case throws a flood of light upon all the Jewish washings, and clearly shows what they did when they *washed* themselves, or any thing else, in accordance with their law. The word *dipped,* which expresses the act performed by Naaman, is from the Hebrew word *taval,* which the seventy Jews who translated the Hebrew Scriptures into Greek rendered *baptidzo,* the very word which the Lord subsequently employed to indicate baptism. Then, as King James' translators gave us *dip* as the English equivalent of *taval,* and the Jewish translators gave us *baptidzo* as its Greek representative, it follows that, in the judgment of the seventy scholars who made the Septuagint, and the forty-seven who made the common version, *baptidzo* in Greek and *dip* in English are synonymous. And since things which are equal to the same thing are equal to each other, it follows that *baptidzo* in Greek and *dip* in English, being equal to *taval* in Hebrew, are equal to each other, hence *dip* is demonstrably the proper translation of *baptidzo.*

In confirmation of our position on Heb. x:22, we quote Bloomfield as follows: "This is not an admonition to corporeal purity, but the expression turns wholly on a comparison with the legal rite of washing for purification; and there is an allusion to *baptism,* as also in the foregoing expression we have a parallel with a Jewish rite. The Jews (to use the words of Prof. Stuart) were sprinkled with blood in order that they might be purified, so as to have access to God—Christians are internally sprinkled; *i.e.,* purified by the blood of Jesus. The Jews were washed with water in order to be ceremonially purified, so as to come before God—Christians have been washed by the purifying water of baptism." The reader will observe that in this quotation we have not only the authority of Dr. Bloomfield, but also that of Prof. Stuart, approvingly quoted by him.

But Paul speaks of the *body* as washed in pure water. We are a little curious to know how it is that a drop of water applied to the head can be regarded as a washing of the body. The Greek word *lelumenoi* here used indicates a washing of the whole body, while *nipsosthai* is used to indicate a partial washing, as the hands or feet. (See Macknight on this verse.) It occurs to us that had the Lord intended a topical application of water in baptism He would have designated the part to which it should be applied. Surely, this was not a matter unworthy of note, for in matters perhaps less significant the parts involved are specifically named. When God instituted circumcision in the family of Abraham. He specifically named the part to be excised. When a man was slain by unknown hands among the Jews, the elders of the city next to him were to "wash their *hands* over the heifer that is beheaded in the valley." Deut. xxi:6. When Jesus washed the disciples' *feet,* the parts washed are specifically mentioned. John xiii:5. When Aaron and his sons were going to enter the tabernacle, they had to wash their *hands* and their *feet.* Ex. xl:31. In the consecration of a Jewish priest, there were applications to be made to the *head,* the *tip* of the *right ear,* the *thumb* of the *right hand,* and the *great toe* of the *right foot,* and each part is specifically designated. Then, if it were important to thus designate specifically and plainly each part to which an application was to be made in the examples given, it was not less important that the part to be wet in the act of baptism should have been designated with at least equal precision. Why should not Paul have mentioned this *part,* in place of the *body,* which he said was washed in pure water? We respectfully suggest that there is quite as much Scriptural authority for baptizing the hand or foot as there is for baptizing the head, and we may justly demand by what law of Christ or by what example of the apostles is any one authorized to apply water to the face or the head rather than to the hands, the feet, or any other part of the body?

Baptism of the Eunuch.

"And as they went on their way, they came unto a certain water; and the eunuch said, See, here is water; what doth hinder me to be baptized? And Philip said, If thou believest with all thy heart, thou mayest. And he answered, and said, I believe that Jesus Christ is the Son of God. And he commanded the chariot to stand still; and they went down both into the water, both Philip and the eunuch; and he baptized him. And when they were come up out of the water, the Spirit of the Lord caught away Philip, that the eunuch saw him no more; and he went on his way rejoicing." Acts viii:36-39.

We call the reader's attention to the progressive steps in the foregoing narrative and to the force of the several prepositions used. First, while on their journey, they came *unto* a certain water. This brings them *to* or at the water. Secondly, they went *down into* the water where the baptism took place. Thirdly, they come *up out* of the water. All this is perfectly rational if immersion was the act performed, but worse than useless if sprinkling or pouring was what was done. If the phrase *come unto a certain water* brought them *to* or at it, it follows that, if the phrase *they went down into the water* moved them at all, it must have carried them beyond its margin, hence a preposition indicating motion, *into,* was used to indicate the thought. We have *into* from the Greek word *eis,* which primarily means motion toward or *into,* and is, therefore, correctly rendered in the passage before us. *Out of* is from *ek,* the primary meaning of which is, *not from,* but *out of,* just as here rendered; and when construed with water, as it is here, it must mean literally *out of the water;* hence *eis* must have taken them just as far *into* the water as *ek* brought them out of it. If this language does not show that they really and literally went down into and came up out of the water, then we submit that it is beyond the power of language to express or embody the thought. No more appropriate language could have been used.

We have already seen that the rules of translation require the primary meanings of words to be retained unless good reasons be shown for their removal. Therefore, if we substitute the secondary meanings of *eis* and *ek* in the passage under consideration for *into* and *out of*, their primary meanings, there must be a better reason shown for it than the salvation of a favorite theory or the support of an unscriptural practice.

But as it is said that *eis* in this passage should be rendered *at* or *near to*, it may be well to examine a few passages where the word occurs. "It is better for thee to enter *(eis)* into life halt or maimed, rather than having two hands or two feet to be cast *(eis)* into everlasting fire." "And if thine eye offend thee, pluck it out, and cast it from thee: it is better for thee to enter *(eis)* into life with one eye, rather than having two eyes to be cast *(eis)* into hellfire." Matt. xviii: 8, 9. Here are four examples of *eis* in this quotation, which might be as correctly rendered *at* as in Acts viii:38: thus, enter *at* life—cast *at* everlasting fire, etc. Again: "Depart from me, ye cursed *(eis)* into everlasting fire, prepared for the devil and his angels." Matt. xxv:41. It would rejoice the hearts of many if *eis* in this place could be rendered *at* or *near* by. Verse 46: "And these shall go away *(eis)* into everlasting punishment: but the righteous *(eis)* into life eternal." Matt. xxv:46. While the translation of *eis* by *at* in the verse might bring joy to the wicked, it would destroy the hopes and happiness of the righteous. Numerous examples might be given, but these are deemed sufficient to show the absurdity of translating *eis* otherwise than by *into*, its primary meaning, in passages similar to the one under consideration.

But Prof. Stuart says "that if the phrase *'they both went down into the water'* is meant to designate the action of plunging or being immersed into the water, as a part of the rite of baptism, then was Philip baptized as well as the eunuch; for the sacred writer says that BOTH went into the water. Here, then, must have been a rebaptizing of Philip, and, what is at least singular, he must have baptized *himself* as well as the eunuch." Stuart on Bap., p. 97.

Here is a false issue made over a most ridiculous quibble by a truly great man; and we may well ask whether truth ever demands of its advocates a resort to such support? We insist that the very fact of such transcendent ability as Prof. Stuart possessed being reduced to such straits is evidence that he had a hard cause to defend. He knew well that the act of baptism was not expressed by the phrase "they both went down into the water," but was expressed by the phrase "he baptized him." All that is claimed for the language they *both went down into the water*, where the baptizing was done, and afterward *came up out of the water* is that it expresses acts wholly incompatible with the notion that baptism was sprinkling or pouring, but perfectly harmonious with the idea that Philip *immersed* the eunuch. Why was it necessary that Philip and the eunuch should have gone down into the water, or to have even got out of the chariot at all? When he commanded the chariot to stand still, why did he not order the driver to bring a pitcher, bowl, or cup of water with which to baptize the nobleman? Surely, any one traveling in such style, and so far as was this nobleman, might well be presumed to have such vessels. Nor will it do to presume them unworthy of mention had they been employed in connection with the sacred rite, for when Jesus washed the disciples' feet the basin that contained the water, and the towel wherewith he was girded were both thought worthy of their notice and are therefore recorded. Was the use of such implements of any more importance connected with the washing of feet, than a bowl, pitcher, or cup would have been in connection with baptism, had any such thing been employed? Is it not a little remarkable that we have no account of Peter, James, John, or Philip's taking a little water from any such vessel for the purpose of baptizing any one, since for the want of any such facility they were compelled sometimes to leave the house at midnight in order to perform this rite? Not only so, but we find them going where there was much water—baptizing in a river—going down into and coming up out of the water, none of which is more worthy of note than would have been a bowl or pitcher had it been employed.

But it is insisted that, as the eunuch was reading the 53d chapter of Isaiah when Philip approached him, it is likely he had previously read the 52d chapter, the 15th verse of which says,

"So shall he sprinkle many nations," and as Philip preached Jesus as the party referred to, when he came to the water the eunuch concluded that there was a suitable place for him to be sprinkled, as one of a nation referred to. We have the word sprinkle in Isaiah lii:15, from the Hebrew word *nazah*, which Gesenius thus defines: "To leap, to spring, to exult, to leap for joy; when applied to liquids, to spirt, to spatter, to be sprinkled." The reader will please note the fact that the word *nazah* only means to be sprinkled in the passive form, and only then when it refers to liquids; and as in Isaiah it refers to *nations* and not liquids, this meaning will not apply. Hence, we must adopt one of the first meanings, and these are all expressive of joy or rejoicing.

A distinguished scholar renders this verse: "So shall many nations exult on account of him." Bail. Man'l, p. 271. Perhaps the thought would be correctly expressed thus: "Many nations shall rejoice at his coming." Dr. BARNES, the celebrated Presbyterian commentator, says: "It may be remarked that whichever of the above senses is assigned, it furnishes *no argument* for the practice of sprinkling in baptism. It refers to the fact of his purifying or cleansing the nations, and not to the ordinance of Christian baptism; nor should it be used as an argument in reference to the mode in which that should be administered." Com. on Isa. lii:15.

BAPTISM OF THE JAILER.

"And when they had laid many stripes upon them, they cast them into prison, charging the jailor to keep them safely. Who, having received such a charge, thrust them into the inner prison, and made their feet fast in the stocks. And at midnight Paul and Silas prayed, and sang praises unto God: and the prisoners heard them. And suddenly there was a great earthquake, so that the foundations of the prison were shaken; and immediately all the doors were opened, and every one's bands were loosed. And the keeper of the prison awaking out of his sleep, and seeing the prison doors open, he drew out his sword, and would have killed himself, supposing that the prisoners had been fled. But Paul cried with a loud voice, saying, Do thyself no harm; for we are all here. Then he called for a light, and sprang in, and came trembling, and fell down before Paul and Silas; and brought them out, and said, Sirs, what must I do to be saved? And they said, Believe on the Lord Jesus Christ, and thou shalt be saved, and thy house. And they spake unto him the word of the Lord, and to all that were in his house. And he took them the same hour of the night, and washed their stripes; and was baptized, he and all his, straightway. And when he had brought them into his house, he set meat before them, and rejoiced, believing in God with all his house." Acts xvi:23-34.

It is insisted by those who oppose immersion that the jailer was baptized in the house at or after midnight, and hence was baptized by sprinkling or pouring. We frankly admit that, should we find, on examination, he was baptized in the house, it would raise a presumption in favor of their hypothesis, but, still, it would not be conclusive, for persons are often now and might then have been immersed in the house. On the other hand, should we find that he left the house, at the time indicated, in order to be baptized, it must raise a strong presumption in favor of immersion.

Let us, then, very carefully examine as to how this was. "Who, having received such a charge, thrust them into the inner prison, and made their feet fast in the stocks." Here we find that Paul and Silas were lodged in the inner prison. Let us watch them closely, and see how and when they leave and whither they go.

"Then he [the jailer] called for a light, and sprang in, and came trembling and fell down before Paul and Silas, and brought them out." Out where? "And they spake unto him the word of the Lord, and to all that were in his house." Here we learn that the jailer had brought them from the inner prison into his house where the preaching was done.

"And he took them the same hour of the night, and washed their stripes; and was baptized, he and all his, straightway." Remember that the preaching took place in the house, then the jailer took them to a place where there was water enough to wash their stripes and to baptize him and all his. Was this in the house? Surely not. For in the next verse we are informed that "when he had brought them into his house, he set meat before them." How could it be said that they were brought into the house after baptism if they had not left the house to be baptized? Seeing, then, that they were not baptized in the house, but left it in the night to be baptized, we claim the benefit of a strong presumption in favor of immersion—for surely no one would now think of leaving the house, at such an hour of the night, to sprinkle or pour a few drops of water on any one in lieu of baptism.

But we are told that, in the morning Paul and Silas refused to leave the prison, and it is unlikely they would have left it the night before as it would have been dissembling in them to do so. We beg the objector to remember that it was one thing to leave the prison in company with their keeper in the discharge of sacred duty and return in ample time to be ready to meet the charges which had been preferred against them, and quite another thing to leave the prison and the city privately, without a trial or an honorable acquittal, thus furnishing their enemies with a pretext for saying they had fled from justice. They had given abundant evidence of the fact that they did not wish to escape, by not leaving the prison when the doors were opened and their bands loosed; and as he had saved the jailer from a violent death at his own hands, it is reasonable to suppose that his confidence in them was such as allowed no fears of efforts on their part to escape.

All things considered, we are driven to the only probable solution of the matter—which is, that they left the house and went to where there was water in which to be immersed and *were immersed*.

In commenting on a phrase in the writings of Justin Martyr [They are led out by us to a place where there is water], Prof. Stuart says: "I am persuaded that this passage, as a whole, most naturally refers to immersion; for why, on any other ground, should the convert who is to be initiated *go out to the place where there is water?* There could be no need of this if mere sprinkling, or partial affusion only, was customary in the time of Justin." Stuart on Baptism, p. 144.

Now, if the fact that going to a place where there was water to baptize, in the days of Justin, was evidence of immersion, why is not the same fact evidence that the jailer was immersed, especially when we remember that he went at or after midnight? If Prof. Stuart's conclusion was a reasonable deduction from the language of Justin (and we think it certainly was), why does he not come to a like conclusion as to the baptism of the jailer? Yea, why should we not come to a like conclusion in a case surrounded by similar circumstances? That he did leave the house to be baptized is as certain as the language of Holy Writ can make any thing, yet Prof. Stuart gives the baptism of the jailer as one of three cases where immersion was not the act performed. As to whether or not he is consistent the reader will judge for himself.

The Baptism of Paul.

"Arise and be baptized, and wash away thy sins, calling on the name of the Lord." Acts xxii:16.

It would have been wholly unneccessary that Paul should *arise* to have water sprinkled or poured on him, but indispensable to his being immersed, as he could not go to a place suited to immersion without arising, while water could just as easily have been sprinkled or poured upon him lying, sitting, or in any other position, as standing, without the necessity of arising. Hence, the fact that he was told to arise raises a presumption that he was immersed; and this presumption is made a certainty by his own declaration that he was *"buried with Christ by baptism."* Rom. vi:4.

Baptism of the Israelites.

"Moreover, brethren, I would not have you ignorant how that all our fathers were under the cloud, and all passed through the sea; and were all baptized unto Moses in the cloud and in the sea." 1 Cor. x:1, 2.

That the baptism of the Israelites unto Moses in the cloud and in the sea, was in some sense typical of our baptism into Christ, is very generally admitted. As we will have occasion to introduce proof of this when we come to look for the design of baptism, we will not introduce it here.

In what sense are we to understand baptism in this passage? In a literal or figurative sense? If in a literal sense, the baptism consisted in specific action, as we have seen that the word primarily and literally indicates specific action.

Was there specific action in this baptism? If so, what was it?

The Israelites were not dipped in the cloud and in the sea, nor were they sprinkled or poured in the cloud and in the sea. Hence, the specific act of dipping, sprinkling, or pouring was in this baptism. Therefore, we conclude the baptism was figurative, not literal. As figures are based upon facts, and must resemble them, we may expect this figurative baptism in some sense to resemble the literal one. The word *baptidzo* is sometimes used metonymically; that is, the result reached by the specific action indicated by the term is put for the act itself. In such cases the result must be such as to resemble that produced by the specific act. The specific act indicated by *baptidzo* being dipping or immersion, the result must always be such as to resemble that produced by dipping or immersion—namely, overwhelming or burial. These things premised, we are now prepared to read an account of this baptism recorded in Exodus xiv:15-31, the sixteenth verse of which says to Moses: "Lift thou up thy rod and stretch out thine hand over the sea, and divide it: and the children of Israel shall go on dry ground through the midst of the sea." Again, verses 19-22: "And the angel of God which went before the camp of Israel, removed and went behind them; and the pillar of the cloud went from before their face, and stood behind them: And it came between the camp of the Egyptians and the camp of Israel; and it was a cloud and darkness to *them,* but it gave light by night to *these:* so that the one came not near the other all the night. And Moses stretched out his hand over the sea; and the Lord caused the sea to go back by a strong east wind all that night, and made the sea dry land, and the waters were divided. And the children of Israel went into the midst of the sea upon the dry ground, and the waters were a wall unto them on their right hand and on their left." Thus we see what Paul meant when he said they were *under* the cloud and passed *through* the sea. And as he understood baptism to be a burial (Rom. vi:4; Col. ii:12), it is not strange that he should call the passage of the Israelites through the sea and under the cloud a baptism, for truly they were buried, the sea being a wall on their right hand and on their left, and the cloud over and behind them.

But we are told that the Israelites were baptized by spray blown from the sea in their passage. When we remember that the hosts of Israel numbered six hundred thousand men, besides women and children, and that they all passed through the sea in a single night, taking every thing possessed by them, it will be seen that an opening several miles in width must have been required for their passage; and as a wind could blow spray but in one direction, and as it would fall much thicker and heavier on the side next its source, it must have deluged those on one side in order to have reached those of the other side at all, and yet we are told that all passed on dry ground. But, worse still, the sacred historian tells us that "the waters were gathered together, the floods stood upright as an heap, and the depths were *congealed* in the heart of the sea." Ex. xv:8. Now, it occurs to us that such a wind as would have blown *congealed water,* in spray, upon the Israelites would have blown them to the promised land before the time, or lifted them over the sea without passing through it at all.

But is said that the Psalmist comes to the aid of the objector, saying: "The clouds poured out water." Psalm lxxvii:17. But it will be observed that *clouds,* in the plural, poured out water, while it was *a cloud,* in the singular, which covered the Israelites, and was a cloud of fire and not of water. But the Psalmist is again quoted: "The earth shook, the heavens also dropped at the presence of God: even Sinai itself was moved with the presence of God, the God of Israel. Thou, O God, didst send a plentiful rain, whereby thou didst confirm thine inheritance." Psalm lxviii:8, 9. Truly, this quotation speaks of rain, but it was that which fell on the Israelites when at the base of Sinai, and not when passing through the sea.

If we would have David's description of their delivery and how they obtained water to drink, we have it briefly stated in the following words: "He divided the sea, and caused them to pass through: and he made the waters to stand as an heap: in the day-time also, he led them with a cloud, and all the night with a light of fire: he clave the rocks in the wilderness, and gave them drink as out of the great depths; he brought streams also out of the rock, and caused waters to run down like rivers." Ps. lxxviii: 13-16. Thus we see that David confirms rather than conflicts with the statement of Paul and Moses.

MOSES STUART says: "They went through the sea on *dry*

ground. Yet they were baptized in the cloud and in the sea. The reason and ground of such an expression must be, so far as I can discern, *a surrounding* of the Israelites on different sides by the cloud and by the sea, although neither the cloud nor the sea touched them. It is, therefore, a kind of figurative mode of expression, derived from the idea that *baptizing* is surrounding with a fluid. But whether this be by immersion, affusion, suffusion, or washing, would not seem to be decided. The suggestion has sometimes been made that the Israelites were *sprinkled* by the cloud and by the sea, and this was the baptism which Paul meant to designate. But the cloud on this occasion was not a cloud of rain; nor do we find any intimation that the waters of the Red Sea sprinkled the children of Israel at this time. So much is true, viz: that they were not *immersed.* Yet, as the language must evidently be figurative in some good degree, and not literal, I do not see how, on the whole, we can make less of it than to suppose that it has a tacit reference to the idea of *surrounding* in some way or other." Stuart on Baptism, p. 113.

This is a candid admission from one writing confessedly in the interest of sprinkling and pouring. Indeed, it is just the truth. No one ever supposed that the Israelites were immersed or dipped, but they were surrounded by the cloud and sea, suggestive of Paul's idea that *baptism is a burial.*

Baptism of Suffering.

"But Jesus answered and said, Ye know not what ye ask. Are ye able to drink of the cup that I shall drink of, and to be baptized with the baptism that I am baptized with? They say unto him, We are able. And he saith unto them, Ye shall drink indeed of my cup, and be baptized with the baptism that I am baptized with." Matt. xx:22, 23.

"But Jesus said unto them, Ye know not what ye ask; can ye drink of the cup that I drink of? and be baptized with the baptism that I am baptized with? And they said unto him, We can. And Jesus said unto them, Ye shall indeed drink of the cup that I drink of, and with the baptism that I am baptized with shall ye be baptized." Mark x:38, 39.

"But I have a baptism to be baptized with: and how am I straitened till it be accomplished!" Luke xii:50.

Upon these passages eminent critics have written as follows:

WITSIUS: "*Immersion* into water is to be considered as exhibiting the dreadful abyss of divine justice, in which Christ for our sins was for a time, as it were, absorbed; as in David, his type, he complains (Ps. lxix:2), 'I am come into deep waters where the floods overflow me.'" Bailey's Manual, p. 232.

DODDRIDGE's FAMILY EXPOSITOR: "Are ye able to drink the bitter cup of which I am about to drink so deep, and be baptized with the baptism, and *plunged* into that sea of sufferings with which I am shortly to be baptized, and, as it were, *overwhelmed* for a time? I have indeed a most dreadful baptism to be baptized with; and I know that I shall shortly be bathed, as it were, in blood, and *plunged* in the most *overwhelming* distress."

HERVEY: "He was baptized with the baptism of his sufferings, *bathed* in blood, and *plunged* in death." Bailey's Manual, p. 235.

SIR H. TRELAWNEY: "Here, I must acknowledge, our Baptist brethren have the advantage; for our Redeemer's sufferings must not be compared to a few drops of water sprinkled on the face, for he was *plunged* into distress and environed with sorrows." Ibid.

BLOOMFIELD's GREEK TEST: "This metaphor of *immersion* in water, as expressive of being overwhelmed by affliction, is *frequent*, both in the Scriptures and in classical writers." Vol. i, p. 97.

WESLEY's NOTES, p. 123: "Our Lord was *filled* with sufferings within, and *covered* with them without."

PROF. STUART: "I have a baptism to be baptized with—that is, I am about to be *overwhelmed* with sufferings, and I am greatly distressed with the prospect of them."

"Can ye indeed take upon you to undergo, patiently and submissively, sufferings like mine—sufferings of an overwhelming and dreadful nature?" Stuart on Baptism, p. 72.

The awful sufferings of Jesus may well be called a baptism, for truly he was overwhelmed in them. Will the reader follow Him to the garden of Gethsemane, and see Him, as it were, sweating great drops of blood, and say that such agony was in anticipation of a little sprinkle of suffering? Shall we enter the judgment hall of Pilate and see him clothed with a mock robe and crown of thorns, and still say this was a *little sprinkle of insult and injury?* Shall we stand upon the summit of Calvary and see the rusty nails sent hissing through His quivering flesh as He is made fast to the cross, and say this is yet only a sprinkle of suffering? Shall we stand by the cross on which he is suspended for three long hours, suffering all the horrors of a malefactor's death, derided by enemies, forsaken by friends, and for a time even forsaken by His God, and still say this is all a mere sprinkle of sufferings? Is not such a thought monstrously impious? Yet it is involved in the idea that sprinkling or pouring is baptism. We will not dignify it by a further examination in connection with the sufferings of our blessed Lord.

ARGUMENTS FOR SPRINKLING AND POURING CONSIDERED.

"I indeed baptize you with water unto repentance: but he that cometh after me is mightier than I, whose shoes I am not worthy to bear: he shall baptize you with the Holy Ghost and with fire." Matt. iii:11. This was a prophetic declaration made by John the Baptist; and before we proceed to look for its fulfillment it may be well for us to remark that the preposition *with*, which occurs three times in this passage, is from the Greek preposition *en*, the primary meaning of which is *in*, and should be so rendered here, unless good reasons, which we are not able to see, be shown for its removal. Thus translated, the passage reads: "I indeed baptize you *in* water ° ° ° he shall baptize you *in* the Holy Ghost and *in* fire." On the day of Pentecost this remarkable prediction was fulfilled as to the baptism in the Holy Spirit, an account of which we have as follows: "And when the day of Pentecost was fully come, they were all with one accord in one place. And suddenly there came a sound from heaven as of a rushing mighty wind, and it filled all the house where they were sitting. And there appeared unto them cloven tongues like as of fire, and it sat upon each of them. And they were all filled with the Holy Ghost, and began to speak with other tongues, as the Spirit gave them utterance." Acts ii:1-4. As we have elsewhere remarked, there was here an absolute impact of the human spirit and the Holy Spirit. They being filled with the

Spirit, it follows that their spirits were overwhelmed or immersed in the Holy Spirit.

But was this a baptism of the Holy Ghost? On a subsequent occasion Peter said: "As I began to speak [at the house of Cornelius] the Holy Ghost fell on them as on us at the beginning. Then remembered I the word of the Lord, how that he said, John indeed baptized with [in] water; but ye shall be baptized with [in] the Holy Ghost." Acts xi:15, 16. This shows that the baptism in the Holy Spirit was fulfilled on the day of Pentecost, and at the house of Cornelius.

But we are told that, as the Spirit was poured out on the day of Pentecost, that the *pouring* was the baptism. If this is true, it was the *Spirit that was poured*, and consequently it was the *Spirit that was baptized* and not the people.

That this is a figurative use of the term *baptidzo* is very generally admitted by the learned. In Dr. ROBINSON's Greek Lexicon of the New Testament, p. 126, he says: "Metaphorically, and in direct allusion to the sacred rite, baptize *en pneumati hagio kai puri*—to baptize in the Holy Ghost and in fire, to overwhelm, richly furnish with all spiritual gifts, or overwhelm with fire unquenchable. Matt. iii:11, etc."

CYRIL, Bishop of Jerusalem, A. D. 350, says: "As he who is plunged in the water and baptized in encompassed by the water on every side, so they that are baptized by the Holy Spirit are also wholly covered over." Bailey's Manual, p. 222. Substantially the same, Stuart on Bap., p. 148.

PROF. STUART on Baptism, p. 74, says: "The basis of this usage is very plainly to be found in the designation by *baptidzo* of the idea of *overwhelming*—i.e., of surrounding on all sides with a fluid."

GURTLERUS: "*Baptism in the Holy Spirit* is immersion into the pure waters of the Holy Spirit, or a rich and abundant communication of his gifts. For he on whom the Holy Spirit is poured out is, as it were, immersed unto him." Campbell and Rice Debate, p. 222.

BISHOP REYNOLDS: "The Spirit, under the gospel, is compared to water, and that not a little measure, to *sprinkle* or *bedew*, but to BAPTIZE the faithful in (Matt. iii:11; Acts i:5), and that not in a font or vessel, which grows less and less, but in a spring or living water." *Ut supra.*

IKENIUS: "The Greek word *baptismos* denotes the immersion of a thing or person into something. Here, also (Matt. iii:11, compared with Luke iii:16), the *baptism of fire*, or that which is performed *in fire*, must signify, according to the same simplicity of the letter, an *immission* or immersion into fire—and this the rather, because here, to *baptize in the Spirit and in fire* are not only connected but also opposed to being baptized *in water.*" *Ibid.*

LE CLERC: "*He shall baptize you in the Holy Spirit.* As I plunge you in water, he shall plunge you, so to speak, *in* the Holy Spirit." *Ibid.*

CASAUBON: "To baptize is to immerse—and in this sense the apostles are truly said to be baptized; for the house in which this was done was filled with the Holy Ghost, so that the apostles seemed to be plunged into it as into a fish-pool." *Ut supra.*

GROTIUS: "To be baptized here is not be slightly sprinkled, but to have the Holy Spirit abundantly poured upon them." *Ibid.*

MR. LEIGH: "Baptized—that is, drown you all over, dip you into the ocean of his grace; opposite to the sprinkling which was in the law." *Ut supra.*

ARCH'P TILLOTSON: "It (the sound from heaven, Acts 2) filled all the house. This is that which our Saviour calls baptizing with the Holy Ghost. So that they who sat in the house were, as it were, immersed in the Holy Ghost, as they who were buried with water were overwhelmed and covered all over with water, which is the proper notion of baptism." *Ibid.*

BISHOP HOPKINS: "Those that are baptized with the Spirit are, as it were, plunged into that heavenly flame whose searching energy devours all their dross, tin, and base alloy." *Ut supra.*

MR. H. DODWELL: "The words of our Saviour were made good, Ye shall be baptized (plunged or covered) with the Holy Spirit, as John baptized with water without it." *Ibid.*

THEOPHYLACT, commenting on the baptism of the Holy Spirit, says: "That is, he shall inundate you abundantly with the gifts of the Spirit." Bailey's Manual, p. 223.

These authors all concur in the fact that the word *baptidzo*, when applied to the Holy Spirit, indicates an *overwhelming* in

Spirit, drawn from the result reached by the primary meaning of the word, hence the *overwhelming* was the baptism, and not the outpouring. And if the spiritual or inner man was baptized in the Holy Spirit, as they were all filled with the Holy Spirit, we may well see why this was called a baptism or overwhelming of the human spirit in the Holy Spirit.

BAPTISM OF THE ALTAR.

"And he put the wood in order, and cut the bullock in pieces, and laid *him* on the wood, and said, Fill four barrels with water, and pour it on the burnt-sacrifice, and on the wood. And he said, Do it a second time. And they did it the second time. And he said, Do it the third time. And they did it the third time. And the water ran round about the altar; and he filled the trench also with water." 1 Kings xviii:33-35.

Origen, one of the most learned of the Greek fathers, was born A.D. 185, and probably wrote about the middle of the third century. He incidentally alludes to the baptism of the altar, wood, etc., by Elijah; and as the water was poured on the altar, the opponents of immersion insist that the *pouring* was what Origen called the baptism. If so, we again insist that he made an improper use of the term *baptidzo*, his great learning to the contrary notwithstanding; for, as the water was poured and not the altar or wood, it follows that the water was baptized upon the altar and the latter not baptized at all. Certainly, it was the complete saturation or overwhelming of the altar to which he alluded as a baptism, for he was, as before stated, one of the most learned of the Greeks, and as such knew well that *baptidzo* never meant to pour. What he understood baptism to be may be learned from his own words, as follows: "They are rightly baptized who are washed unto salvation. He that is baptized unto salvation receives the water and the Holy Spirit; such baptism as is accompanied with crucifying the flesh and rising again to newness of life is the approved baptism." Orchard's Hist., vol. i, p. 35.

But if the *pouring* constituted the baptism to which Origen referred, there must have been as many baptisms as there were pourings, hence he could not have spoken of *a baptism*, for there were twelve barrels of water used, and each one would have constituted a pouring, therefore there must have been twelve baptisms.

But we are told that there were no barrels in those days, and that Elijah only used twelve leathern bottles of water, a quantity wholly insufficient to have saturated or overwhelmed the altar. Such persons should take heed lest they deprive the prophet of the benefit of the trial between himself and the prophets of Baal, for the very object he had in applying the water was to so completely inundate the altar as to forbid the supposition or possibility of fire being concealed beneath it.

We come next to an examination of the bathing of Judith in or at the fountain in the valley of Bethulia. This case, recorded in the apochryphal books of the Bible, is no part of the inspired volume, and therefore has no just claim to our consideration, but as the advocates of sprinkling always introduce it, as drowning men catch at straws, we will therefore examine it.

"Then Holofernes commanded his guard that they should not stay her: thus she abode in the camp three days, and went out in the night into the valley of Bethulia, and washed herself in a fountain of water by the camp." Judith xii:7. Some copies have *at the fountain* in place of *in* the fountain. Hence it is insisted that she sprinkled a little water upon herself as a mere ceremonial cleansing, but we have quoted the above from Bagster's large family edition, which is one of the most authentic copies known.

Dr. Conant says: "One of the oldest Greek manuscripts (No. 58), and the two oldest versions (the Syriac and Latin), read immersed (baptized) herself in the fountain of water (omitting in the camp). According to the common Greek text, this was done at the fountain to which she went, because she had there the means of immersing herself. Any other use of water for purification could have been made in her tent." Baptizien, p. 85.

Surely, this is a rational conclusion. Why should she, like the Philippian jailer, have left her tent after midnight and gone out into the valley to sprinkle a few drops of water upon her person? The fact that she did go at such an hour proves that she went in obedience to the Jewish law that required her to bathe her whole person.

We have another case in the apocryphal writings suggested

in the following words: "He that washeth himself after the touching of a dead body, if he touch it again, what availeth his washing?" Eccles. xxxiv:25.

We need not say to the Bible reader that any one who had touched a dead body was regarded as unclean, and that the law required him to wash his clothes and bathe himself in water that he might be clean at even. See Numbers xix:19. Let it not be said that this bathing was a mere sprinkling, for they were required both to sprinkle and bathe, and both are specifically named in the same verse. Hence, all that is meant by baptizing from a dead body is that they baptized from the ceremonial uncleanness contracted by contact with a dead body. A similar form of expression is found in Heb. x:22, where we are said to be sprinkled from an evil conscience and the body washed in pure water.

We next come to examine the baptism of cups, pots, brazen vessels, and tables, recorded Mark vii:4, as follows: "And *when they come* from the market, except they wash, they eat not. And many other things there be which they have received to hold, *as* the washing of cups, and pots, brazen vessels, and of tables."

Although these washings had nothing to do with the baptism commanded by the Lord, yet, as the word wash is the translation of *baptidzo*, they are relied upon as expressive of its meaning. By reference to the Jewish law it will be seen that the washings here referred to were more than mere sprinkling. In Lev. vi:28, it is said: "The brazen pot shall be scoured and rinsed *in* water" —not a little water simply sprinkled upon it, but *scoured and rinsed in water*. As a brazen pot was one of the articles mentioned in Mark, it is fair to conclude that the other articles were cleansed as it was.

But again, the law says: "Upon whatsoever any of them, when they are dead, doth fall, it shall be unclean; whether it be any vessel of wood, or raiment, or skin, or sack, whatsoever vessel it be wherein any work is done, it must be put *into water;* and it shall be unclean until the even, *so it shall be cleansed."* Lev. xi:32. This puts the whole matter beyond the reach of cavil; they were to be put into water, and any thing short of this would have been an insult to the Giver of the law. Hence, the word *baptidzo* in Mark vii:4, should be rendered dip or immerse, according to its primary import; and Macknight, in his Harmony of the Gospels, so renders it.

THOMAS SHELDON GREEN, of London, in an improved version of the Greek Text, has this verse and a translation of it, by himself, as follows: "And coming from the market-place, they do not eat unless they dip themselves, and there are many other matters which they have received to hold, dipping of cups, and jars, and brazen vessels, and couches," etc.

On this verse BEZA remarks: "Christ commanded us to be baptized; by which word it is certain immersion is signified; *baptizesthai* in this place is more than *niptein,* because *that* seems to respect the whole body, this only the hands."

"DR. H. A. W. MEYER, in his Manual on the Gospels of Mark and Luke, says: 'The expression in Mark vii:4, is not to be understood of the *washing of* the hands (as interpreted by Lightfoot and Wetstein, but of the *immersing* which the word always means in the classics and the New Testament; that is here, according to the context, the taking of a bath. So Luke xi:38. Having come from the market, where among a crowd of men, they might have come in contact with unclean persons, they eat not without having first bathed themselves. The representation proceeds after the manner of a climax: before eating they *always* observe the washing of hands, but (employ) the *bath* when they come *from the market* and wish to take food.'" Louisville Debate, p. 563.

"VATABULUS, professor of Hebrew in Paris, says of Mark vii:4: 'They washed themselves all over.' GROTIUS, the great German writer, says: 'They cleansed themselves more carefully from defilement contracted at the market, to wit: not only by washing hands, but by immersing their bodies.'" Braden and Hughey Debate, p. 45.

The Sinaitic and Vatican manuscripts give us beds or couches in place of tables in the common version. Hence, it is insisted that baptism must have been a sprinkling, as beds could not have been immersed—basing their argument, of course, upon the assumption that beds then were such as are now used. They forget, however, that Jesus commanded persons to take up their beds and walk. See Matt. ix: 6; Mark ii:9-11; John vi:11, 12.

"Calmet says: 'The word bed is in many cases calculated to mislead the reader and perplex him. The beds in the East are very different from those used in this part of the world. They are often nothing more than a cloth or quilt folded double.'" Braden and Hughey Debate, p. 46.

Though not always so, it is evident that the beds of those times were often composed of a light fabric which could be conveniently spread down or taken up, folded and carried along at pleasure.

Maimonides, a Jewish rabbi, learned in the ceremonial law and traditions of the elders, says: "Wherever, in the law, washing of the flesh or clothes is mentioned, it means nothing else than dipping the whole body in a laver; for if a man dips himself all over except the tips of his little finger, he is still in his uncleanness. In a laver which held forty sacks (one hundred gallons) of water, every defiled man dips himself, except a proflunious man, and in it they dip all unclean vessels. A bed that is wholly defiled, if he dip it part by part, is pure. If he dip the bed in a pool, although its feet are plunged in the thick clay of the bottom, it is clean." *Ibid*, p. 45.

Maimonides was one of the greatest lights in the Jewish church, and lived about the twelfth century, when the baptismal controversy was not so rife as now, and surely had no motive to misrepresent the fact.

But we are told that some versions have sprinkle in place of wash, in Mark vii: 4. This is true, but we deny that it is a translation of *baptidzo*, here or elsewhere.

Schleusner says that some manuscripts have *rantizonti* in place of *baptizonti*, in Mark vii:4; hence any translator having such a manuscript before him must necessarily have sprinkle in his version. Although we thus account for the appearance of sprinkle in some versions, we have no idea that *rantizonti* is the correct word for the text, because we have seen that the washings referred to were immersions.

One other text, we believe, exhausts the proof of those who practice sprinkling for baptism, and, like the one just considered, it has no allusion to baptism whatever. It is found in Luke xi:38, as follows:

"And when the Pharisee saw it, he marveled that he had not first washed before dinner," etc.

GREEN, of London, translates this verse thus: "And as he spake, a Pharisee asked him to dine with him, and he went in and lay down. But the Pharisee wondered that he had not dipped before dinner." Twofold New Testament, p. 131.

We have already seen that this rendering is in harmony with the Jewish law. When any one went out where he was liable to come in contact with such things as would render him unclean, he must bathe his flesh in water as though he were really unclean. Hence, this can not be taken as evidence sufficient to justify the conclusion that the washing referred to was not an immersion.

We have abundantly shown that *baptidzo* means to immerse or dip; hence, wherever it occurs we are bound to presume that the act indicated was dipping or immersing as long as there remains a *possibility* that this was the act performed. A mere *possibility* that *it may have been done otherwise* is not sufficient to overturn the settled meaning of the word.

HISTORY OF BAPTISM.

We have now passed over and examined every scripture relied upon to prove sprinkling or pouring as baptism, and have not found a single passage where the word *baptidzo* occurs in the New Testament, where it may not justly be translated dip or immerse. And it is not a little remarkable that more importance is attached to the word in places where it has no reference to baptism, as commanded by the Lord, than in those places where He used it to express the act He required of His followers, or in places where any inspired apostle employed it with reference to the act enjoined by Him. Mark vii:4, and Luke xi:38, are regarded by them as of more importance than even the commission itself; and yet these passages have no reference to Christian baptism. No scholar has ever been found willing to hazard his reputation by pointing out a single place in the New Testament where the word *baptidzo* refers to the rite in question, and saying that it means sprinkle or pour and should be so rendered in that place, or who has ever been able to point to a single clear example of sprinkling or pouring for baptism.

We now pass to the history of baptism, and we will begin with the writings of those who lived contemporaneously with the apostles, and see if we can learn how the primitive Christians obeyed the command of the Lord in baptism.

HERMAS lived in the days of the apostles and wrote before John wrote his gospel. See Wall's History of Infant Baptism, vol. i, pp. 52-56. He says: "For before any one receives the name of the Son of God he is liable to death, but when he receives that seal he is delivered from death and is assigned to life. Now, that seal is water, into which persons go down liable to death, but come out of it assigned to life." *Ut supra*, p. 51. Here, we see, they went *down into* and *came up out of* the water.

BARNABAS was the companion of Paul. He says: "For these words imply, Blessed are they who, placing their trust in the Cross, have gone down into the water ° ° ° ° This meaneth that we, indeed, descend into the water full of sins and defilement, but come up, bearing fruit in our heart, having the fear of God and trust in Jesus in our spirit." Apostolic Fathers, p. 121.

JUSTIN MARTYR was a Christian, and put to death for his faith in Jesus Christ. He was born A.D. 114, and wrote about A.D. 150. He says: "Then we bring them to some place where there is water, and they are regenerated by the same way of regeneration by which we were regenerated: for they are washed with water in the name of God, the Father and Lord of all things, and of our Saviour Jesus Christ, and of the Holy Spirit. For Christ says: *Unless ye be regenerated, ye can not enter into the kingdom of heaven.*" Wall's Hist. Inf. Bap., p. 68.

Why should they have been taken to a place where there was water, to be "regenerated" (or, more properly, born again)? There is nothing in sprinkling or pouring resembling a birth or which could have created a necessity for going to a place where there was water in order to be born again.

MOSHEIM, in speaking of the first century, says: "The sacrament of *baptism* was administered in this century without the public assemblies, in places appointed and prepared for that purpose, and was performed by an immersion of the whole body in the baptismal font." Maclaine's Mosheim's Church Hist., Vol. 1, p. 49.

Of the second century he says: "The persons that were to be baptized, after they had repeated the Creed, confessed and renounced their sins, and particularly the devil and his pompous allurements, were immersed under water, and received into Christ's kingdom by a solemn invocation of Father, Son, and Holy Ghost, according to the express command of our blessed Lord." *Ibid.*, p. 69. This not only shows that the parties were immersed under water, but that it was done *according to the express command of our blessed Lord.*"

Of the fourth century the same author says: "Baptismal fonts were now erected in the porch of each church, for the more commodious administration of that initiating sacrament." *Ibid.*, p. 121. We are not here told expressly how baptism was administered in the fourth century, but surely it would have been unnecessary to erect fonts in connection with churches in order to practice sprinkling or pouring.

Mosheim is one of the most reliable ecclesiastical historians we have, and practiced sprinkling and pouring himself. It is not to be presumed, therefore, that he would misrepresent the facts of history in favor of immersion.

NEANDER, another church historian, says: "In respect to the form of baptism, it was in conformity with the original institution and the original import of the symbol, performed by immersion, as a sign of entire baptism into the Holy Spirit, of being entirely penetrated by the same. It was only the sick, where the exigency required it, that any exception was made, and in this case baptism was administered by sprinkling. Many superstitious persons, clinging to the outward form, imagined that such baptism by sprinkling was not fully valid, and hence they distinguished those who had been so baptized by denominating them the *clinici.*" Neander's Church History, by Torry, vol. i, p. 310. Neander is a voluminous and reliable author, and as the church of which he was a member practiced sprinkling, it is reasonable to suppose that he did also, and most likely gave unwilling testimony to the facts of history against his own practice.

DR. WALL, the Pedobaptist historian, says: "Their general and ordinary way was to baptize by immersion, or dipping the person, whether it were an infant or grown man or woman, into the water. This is so plain and clear by an infinite number of passages, that, as one can not but pity the weak endeavors of such pedobaptists as would maintain the negative of it, so also we ought to disown and show a dislike of the profane scoffs which some people give to the English anti-pedobaptists merely for their use of dipping. It is one thing to maintain that that circumstance is not absolutely necessary to the essence of baptism, and another to go about to represent it as ridiculous and foolish, or as shameful and indecent, when it was, in all probability, the way by which our blessed Saviour, and for certain was the most usual and ordinary way by which the ancient Christians did receive their baptism. I shall not stay to produce the particular proofs of this. Many of the quotations which I brought for other purposes, and shall bring, do evince it. It is a great want of prudence as well as of honesty to refuse to grant to an adversary what is certainly true and may be proved so. It creates a jealousy of all the rest that one says.

"Before the Christian religion was so far encouraged as to have churches built for its service, they baptized in any river, pond, etc. So Tertullian says: 'It is all one whether one be washed in the sea or in a pond, in a fountain or in a river, in standing or in running water; nor is there any difference between those that John baptized in Jordan and those that Peter baptized in the river Tiber.' But when they came to have churches, one part of the church, or place nigh the church, called the *baptistery*, was employed to this use, and had a cistern, font, or pond large enough for several at once to go into the water; divided into two parts by a partition, one for the men and the other for the women, for the ordinary baptisms." Wall's Hist. Inf. Bap., vol. ii, pp. 384, 385.

As Wall here refers to examples previously given as evidence of the correctness of his conclusions, it may not be amiss to give the reader the benefit of a few of them recorded in the first volume of his work.

On the language of Justin Martyr, which we have already quoted, he marks as follows: "I bring it because it is the most ancient account of the way of baptizing, next the Scripture, and shows the plain and simple manner of administering it. The Christians of these times had lived, many of them at least in the apostles' days." Vol. i, p. 69.

CLEMENT, of Alexandria, says: "If any one be by trade a fisherman, he will do well to think of an apostle and the children taken out of the water." Again, the same author says: "If there be engraved in a seal ring the picture of a fisherman [or rather, as Clement's own words are, *if a fisherman will have an engraving on his seal*], let him think of St. Peter, whom Christ made a fisher of men; and of the children, which, when baptized, are drawn out of a laver of water as out of a fish-pool." *Ibid.*, p. 86. These quotations from Clement show that after the introduction of infant baptism, even they were immersed, being drawn out of a laver of water as out of a fish-pool.

There was rather a novel question mooted before the Council of Neocaesarea, in the year 314 A.D., with regard to which Dr. Wall remarks as follows: "So much is plain, that some about that time and place had put this question: Whether a woman with child, that had a mind to become a Christian and be baptized, might conveniently receive baptism during her going with child, or must stay till she was delivered? And it is agreed likewise that the reason of the doubt was, because when she was immersed into the water, the child in her womb did seem to some to be baptized with her, and consequently they were apt to argue that that child must not be baptized, or would not need to be baptized, afterward for itself. This any one will conclude from the words of the council, which are these." (Here follow the words of the council.) *Ibid*, vol. i, p. 151. It strikes us that such a question would never have arisen with reference to the offspring of a mother who had had only a few drops of water sprinkled upon her head. Other examples might be cited, but these are sufficient to justify Wall in the conclusion to which he came.

PROF. STUART says: "Tertullian, who died in A.D. 220, is the most ample witness of all the early writers. In his works is an essay in defense of Christian baptism, which had been assailed by some of the heretics of his time. Passing by the multitude of expressions which speak of the importance of being cleansed by water, being born in the water, etc., I quote only such as are directly to the point." He then proceeds to quote Tertullian as follows: "*In aquam de missus,* let down into the water—*i.e.*, immersed—and *inter pauca verba tinctus*—*i.e.*, dipped between the utterance of a few words. * * * There is, then, no difference whether any one is washed in a pool, river, fountain, lake, or channel, *alveus* (canal), nor is there any difference of consequence between those whom John immersed (*tinxit*) in the Jordan or Peter in the Tiber. * * * Not that we obtain the Holy Spirit *in aquis* [*i.e.*, in the baptismal water], but being cleansed in the water we are prepared for the Holy Spirit. * * * Afterwards, going out from the ablution or bath, we are anointed. * * * Thence we are thrice immersed (*ter mergitamur*), answering, *i.e.*, fulfilling somewhat more than the Lord has decreed in the gospel." On these quotations from Tertullian Prof. Stuart remarks: "I do not see how any doubt can well remain, that in Tertullian's time the practice of the African church, to say the least, as to the mode of baptism, must have been that of *trine immersion.*" Stuart on Bap., pp. 144-46.

"But enough. 'It is,' says Augusti, 'a thing made out,' viz., the ancient practice of immersion. So, indeed, all the writers who had thoroughly investigated this subject conclude. I know of no one usage of ancient times which seems to be more clearly made out. I can not see how it is possible for any candid man who examines the subject to deny this." *Ibid*, p. 149. On page 152, Prof. Stuart quotes Augusti further: "Thirteen hundred years was baptism generally and ordinarily performed by the immersion of a man under water, and only in extraordinary cases was sprinkling or affusion permitted. These latter methods of baptism were called in question and even prohibited."

After quoting Chrysostom, Ambrose, Cyril, and Brenner to show that in their times persons were baptized in a nude state, Prof. Stuart says: "Still, say what we may concerning it in a moral point of view, the argument to be deduced from it in repect to immersion is not at all diminished. Nay, it is strengthened. For if such a violation of decency was submitted to in order that baptism might be performed as the church thought it should be, it argues that baptizing by immersion was considered as a rite not to be dispensed with." *Ibid*, p. 151.

After quite an array of testimony concerning the ancient practice, Prof. Stuart gives his conclusions in the following words: "We have collected facts enough to authorize us now to come to the following general conclusion, respecting the practice of the Christian church in general, with regard to the mode of baptism, viz: that from the earliest ages of which we have any account, subsequent to the apostolic age, and downward for several centuries, the churches did generally practice baptism by immersion, perhaps *by immersion of the whole person;* and that the only exceptions to this mode which were usually allowed were in cases of urgent *sickness* or other cases of immediate and imminent danger, where immersion could not be practiced. It may also be mentioned here, that *aspersion* and *affusion*, which had in particular cases been now and then practiced in primitive times, were *gradually* introduced. These became at length, as we shall see hereafter, quite common, and in the western church almost universal, sometime before the Reformation.

In what manner, then, did the churches of Christ, from a very early period, to say the least, understand the word *baptidzo* in the New Testament? Plainly, they construed it as meaning *immersion.* They sometimes even went so far as to forbid any other method of administering the ordinance, cases of necessity and mercy only excepted. If, then, we are left in doubt after a philological investigation of *baptidzo,* how much it necessarily implies; if the circumstances which are related as accompanying this rite, so far as the New Testament has given them, leave us still in doubt; if we can not trace with any certainty the Jewish proselyte baptism to a period as early as the baptism of John and Jesus, so as to draw any inferences with probability from this, still we are left in no doubt as to the more generally received usage of the Christian church down to a period several centuries after the apostolic age. That the Greek fathers, and the Latin ones who were familiar with the Greek, understood the usual import of the word *baptidzo,* would hardly seem to be capable of a denial. That they might be confirmed in their view of the import of this word by common usage among the Greek classic authors, we have seen in the first part of this dissertation. For myself, then, I cheerfully admit that *baptidzo* in the New Testament, when applied to the rite of baptism, does in all probability involve the idea that this rite was usually performed by immersion, but not always." *Ibid,* p. 153, 154.

Is it not strange that such a termination should follow such testimony and admissions? After telling us that *bapto* and *bap-*

tidzo mean to dip, plunge, or immerge into any thing liquid, and that all lexicographers of any note are agreed in this—that the churches of Christ, from a very early period, to say the least, understood the word *baptidzo* to mean *immersion in the New Testament*—that it could not be denied that those who so used it understood its import—that aspersion and affusion were gradually introduced—that he cheerfully admitted that *baptidzo* in the New Testament, when applied to the rite of baptism, in all probability involved the idea of immersion, he then closes with "not always." And he repeats, with emphasis, "I say *usually* and not *always*." And what are the examples to which he refers as exceptions? The reader shall have the benefit of them. He says: "To say more than this, the tenor of some of the narrations, particularly in Acts x:47, 48; xvi:32; 33, and ii:41, seem to me to forbid. I can not read these examples without the distinct conviction that *immersion* was not practiced on these occasions." p. 154.

Now, we confess ourself wholly unable to see any thing in these examples calculated to overturn the settled meaning of the word used to indicate the act required, and the construction placed upon it in the New Testament by the primitive Christians acknowledged competent to understand it, and the practice of the church from an early period in harmony with these authorities. May we briefly examine the exceptional cases to which he refers us? Acts x:47, 48, reads as follows: "Can any man forbid water, that these should not be baptized, which have received the Holy Ghost as well as we? And he commanded them to be baptized in the name of the Lord." On this passage Prof. Stuart says: "Observe that the idea in this case seems almost of necessity to be: Can any one forbid that *water should be brought in*, and these persons baptized? He does not say: 'Can any one forbid the bath, or the river—*i.e.*, the use of these, by which these persons should be baptized; but the intimation seems to be that they were to be baptized on the spot, and that water was to be brought in for that purpose." Stuart on Bap., p. 110.

Now, is it not strange that persons can see what is not said on one side and be blind as to what is not said on the other? He says: "He does not say: Can any one forbid the bath or the river?" No; nor does he say: Can any man forbid that water should be brought in, and yet he can easily infer it. Candor compels him to admit "that another meaning is not necessarily excluded which would accord with the practice of immersion." In view of the admissions of Prof. Stuart, as long as there remains a possibility that the command was obeyed as commanded, we have no right to infer that something else was done not indicated by the command.

The second example to which he refers, in Acts xvi:34, we have already examined, and we have seen that, according to rules of interpretation given by Prof. Stuart himself, we are bound to presume that the jailer was immersed. We refer the reader to the argument there presented without repeating it here. His third example claims a brief notice at our hands. The passage reads: "They that gladly received his word were baptized; and the same day there were added unto them about three thousand souls." Acts ii:41. On this passage Prof. Stuart asks: "Where and how were they baptized? Was it in the brooks or streams near Jerusalem? I can not find this to be probable. The feast of Pentecost, being fifty days after the Passover (Lev. xxv:15), must fall in the latter part of the month of May, and after the Jewish harvest. In Palestine this is usually a time of drought, or at least of great scarcity of rain." *Ibid.*, p. 108. How easy it is to imagine a thing just as we would have it to be! Prof. Stuart was anxious to find some testimony favoring baptism by *aspersion* or *affusion,* and hence he imagines that the Jewish harvest was at a time of great scarcity of water in Jerusalem, and therefore those baptized could not have been immersed. Joshua says: "Jordan overfloweth all his banks all the time of harvest." Josh. iii:15. Jordan was one of the chief rivers of that country, and is only eighteen miles from the city of Jerusalem by the ordinary road of travel. At a time when Jordan was overflowing his banks we can not easily imagine a great drought in Palestine. Josephus informs us that no less than two million seven hundred thousand two hundred persons assembled in Jerusalem to eat the feast of the annual passover. (Wars of the Jews, book vi, ch. 9.) Now, it occurs to us that a city which had water facilities for the accommodation of such a number of persons could furnish water enough to baptize them *all* in if necessary. "There were in Jerusalem the following pools: Bethesda, twenty-two rods long and eight rods wide; Solomon's pool, fifteen rods long and six rods wide; the pool of Siloam, fifty-three feet long and eighteen feet wide, with a smaller pool; Old pool, twenty rods long and thirteen rods wide; pool of Hezekiah, fifteen rods long and nine rods wide; lower pool of Gihon, thirty-six rods long and sixteen rods wide, *now,* in the days of the apostles it covered over four acres." Braden and Hughey Debate, p. 129. Here were acres upon acres of water, besides numerous other sources of water of which we have no names, and yet not water enough in which to immerse three thousand!! But Prof. Stuart admits that they might have been immersed even in baths or washing places. He says: "I do not say that this was impossible, for every one acquainted with the Jewish rites must know that they made much use of ablutions, and therefore they would provide many conveniences for them." Stuart on Bap., p. 109.

But we are told that the water was controlled by the enemies of the disciples, and hence they would have objected to their using it for such purpose. But Luke says they had "favor with all the people." Acts ii:47. Why should a people with whom God had given them favor forbid the use of the public watering-places for the immersion of those converted by their preaching?

After making an argument based upon the supposition that there was not time enough for the apostles to have baptized so many, Prof. Stuart says: "However, I concede that there are some points here which are left undetermined, and which may serve to aid those who differ from me in replying to these remarks. It is true that we do not know that baptism was performed by the apostles only nor that all the three thousand were baptized before the going down of the sun. The work may have extended into the evening, and so, many being engaged in it, and more time being given, there was a possibility that the work in question should be performed although immersion was practiced." Stuart on Bap., pp. 109, 110. Here he so completely meets his own argument that we feel disposed to dismiss it just where he left it—only asking the candid reader whether or not these three examples to which Prof. Stuart refers us are sufficient to overturn the evidence furnished by himself in favor of immersion? How are we to know what the Lord requires of us in any matter only as we learn it from the words employed by Him to express His will? We have seen a rule for the use of words given by Prof. Stuart himself, which says: "To every word in Scripture there is unquestionably assigned some idea or notion, otherwise words are useless and have no more signification than the inarticulate sounds of animals." Ernesti, p. 7. This being so, when the Lord used the word *baptidzo* there was unquestionably assigned to it some idea or notion—what was it? Prof. Stuart says: "*Bapto* and *baptidzo* mean to *dip, plunge,* or *immerge* into any thing liquid. All lexicographers and critics of any note are agreed in this." Stuart on Baptism, p. 51.

He gives us numerous examples from the classics, showing that this statement is true as far as they are authority. Then he quotes largely from the primitive fathers, showing that they so understood the word *baptidzo* in the New Testament, and admits that they did understand its import. Finally, he shows by undoubted historical testimony that the church practiced immersion only as baptism, from its organization on, for many centuries; then seeks to overturn it all by referring us to *three* cases in the New Testament which seem to teach otherwise; and yet, when he comes to examine them, his candor compels him to admit that they are not conclusive, and that even these may have been immersed. It is but just to Prof. Stuart to say that there is no higher authority in all the ranks of orthodoxy than he; yet with all his learning he was compelled to bring to the support of sprinkling and pouring mere *possibilities,* which he seeks to make *probabilities* by ridiculous quibbles unworthy of notice but for the fact that they emanate from a man whose fame, though starting at Andover, is not confined to America.

History of Sprinkling.

Having seen that primitive Christians practiced immersion only as baptism, we come now to inquire for the origin of sprinkling and pouring. The first case known to us is that of Novatian, in the year 251 A.D., an allusion to which we have, given by Wall, as follows:

"Novatian was by one party of the clergy and people of Rome chosen bishop of that church, in a schismatical way, and in opposition to Cornelius, who had been chosen by the major part and was already ordained. Cornelius does, in a letter to

Fabius, bishop of Antioch, vindicate his right, and shows that Novatian came not canonically to his orders of priesthood; much less was he capable of being chosen bishop; for that all the clergy and a great many of the laity were against his being ordained presbyter, because it was not lawful (they said) for any one that had been baptized in his bed in time of sickness, as he had been, to be admitted to any office of the clergy." Wall, Inf. Bap., vol. ii, pp. 385, 386.

Mosheim, in his Historical Commentaries, p. 62, vol. i, gives us the history of the baptism of Novatian. He says: "He was seized with a threatening disease and was baptized in his bed, when apparently about to die." He recovered from his sickness and was subsequently made a presbyter in the church by Bishop Fabian, contrary to the whole body of priests and of a large part of the church. The author says: "It was altogether irregular and contrary to ecclesiastical rules, to admit a man to the priestly office who had been baptized in bed—that is, who had been merely sprinkled, and had not been wholly immersed in water, in the ancient method. For by many, and especially the Roman Christians, the baptism of *clinici* (so they called those who, lest they should die out of the church, were baptized on a sick bed) was accounted less perfect, and indeed less valid, and not sufficient for the attainment of salvation." Louisville Debate, pp. 439, 440.

The reader will please observe that the objection made to the ordination of Novatian was that he had been *merely sprinkled* (in the language of the author), and not wholly immersed in water, *in the ancient method,* thus showing clearly that immersion was the ancient method. From this time sprinkling and pouring as baptism seem to have been practiced, but only upon persons dangerously ill. Much discussion of its validity ensued, until about eighty years afterward the question was laid before the Neocaesarean Council, the twelfth canon of which is: "He that is baptized when he is sick ought not to be made a priest (for his coming to the faith is not voluntary, but from necessity), unless his diligence and faith do afterward prove commendable, or the scarcity of men fit for the office requires it." Wall's Hist., vol. ii, pp. 386, 387.

On the validity of this baptism Bishop Cyprian remarks:

"The breast of the believer is washed, the soul of the man is cleansed by the merits of faith. In the sacraments of salvation, where necessity compels and God gives his permission, the divine thing, though outwardly abridged, bestows all that implies on the faithful." Neander's Church History, vol. i, p. 310.

Observe here, that while Cyprian held that clinic baptism secured the blessings implied in the rite, he acknowledges it to be an outward *abridgment of the divine thing*. Who has a right to abridge divine things?

"The first general law for sprinkling was obtained in the following manner: Pope Stephen II, being driven from Rome by Adolphus, king of the Lombards, in 753, fled to Pepin, who a short time before had usurped the crown of France. Whilst he remained there, the monks of Cressy, in Brittany, consulted him whether, in case of necessity, baptism poured on the head of the infant would be lawful. Stephen replied that it would. But though the truth of this fact be allowed—which, however, some Catholics deny—yet pouring or sprinkling was admitted only in *cases of necessity*. It was not till the year 1311 that the legislature, in a council held in Ravenna, declared immersion or sprinkling to be indifferent. In Scotland, however, sprinkling was never practiced in ordinary cases, till after the Reformation (about the middle of the sixteenth century). From Scotland it made its way into England, in the reign of Elizabeth, but was not authorized in the Established Church." Edinburgh Encyclopedia, article Baptism.

It has been insisted that sprinkling or pouring was first practiced in cold countries, but Dr. Wall says: "By history it appears that the cold climate held the custom of dipping as long as any; for England, which is one of the coldest, was one of the latest that admitted this *alteration of the ordinary way*. Vasquez having said that it was the old custom both in the East and the West to baptize both grown persons and infants that were in health by immersion, and that it plainly appears by the words of St. Gregory that the custom continued so to be in his time. * * * I will here endeavor to trace the times when it begun to be left off in the several countries in the West, meaning still, in the case of infants that were in health, and in the public baptism; for in the case of sickly or weak infants, there was always, in all countries, an allowance of affusion or sprinkling, to be given in haste, and in the house, or any other place.

"France seems to have been the first country in the world where baptism by affusion was used ordinarily to persons in health, and in the public way of administering it." * * *

"It came more and more into request in that country till, in Bonaventure's time, it was become, as appears by his words last quoted, as very ordinary practice; and though he says some other churches did then so use it, yet he names none but France.

"The synod of Angiers, 1275, speaks of dipping or pouring as indifferently used, and blames some ignorant priests for that they dip or pour the water but once, and instructs them that the general custom of the church is to dip thrice or pour on water three times. * * * From France it spread (but not till a good while after) into Italy, Germany, Spain, etc., and, last of all, into England. * * * In England there seem to have been some priests so early as the year 816 that attempted to bring in the use of baptism by affusion in the public administration, for Spellman recites a canon of a council in that year: 'Let the priests know that when they administer holy baptism they must not pour the water on the head of the infants, but they must always be dipped in the font.'" Wall's Hist., vol. ii, pp. 392-396.

On page 397, Dr. Wall quotes Wickliffe thus: "And the church has ordained that in case of necessity any person that is *fidel* [or that is himself baptized] may give baptism, etc. Nor is it material whether they be dipped," etc.

By this quotation from Wickliffe it will be seen that the *church ordained* the departure from the ancient custom by making it immaterial whether the subject was dipped, etc.

On page 398, Dr. Wall says: "From the time of King Edward, Mr. Walker (who has taken the most pains in tracing this matter) derives the beginning of the alteration of the general custom. He says that 'dipping was at this time the more usual, but sprinkling was sometimes used, which, within the time of half a century [meaning from 1550 to 1600], prevailed to be the more general (as it is now almost the only) way of baptizing.'"

We call the reader's special attention to *the beginning of the alteration of the general custom*. We might quote numerous other extracts from Dr. Wall, showing that the primitive practice was dipping or immersion, and that the church through her councils, popes, and bishops has assumed the right to change it, but the amount of testimony we wish to present from other sources forbids further quotations from him.

Dr. Kendrick, Archbishop of the Catholic Church in Baltimore, says: "When religion had consummated her triumphs over paganism in the various countries of Europe, the custom of Christians baptizing children being universal, ages passed away almost without an instance of the baptism of adults. Hence the necessity of receding from the mode of immersion became still more frequent, since the tender infant oftentimes could not be immersed without peril to its life. The cases thus multiplying, the more solemn method fell gradually into disuse, until it was in most places entirely superseded.

"Another cause contributed to favor affusion: A class of females formerly existed in the church, under the name of deaconesses, who, among other exercises of piety, instructed and prepared for baptism the catechumens of their sex, and performed some of the ceremonies preparatory to its administration. This class of females having ceased, from a variety of causes, it became expedient to abstain from the immersion of females." Kendrick on Baptism, pp. 172, 173.

And on page 174 he says:

"The change of discipline which has taken place in regard to baptism should not surprise us; for, although the church is but the dispenser of the sacraments which her divine spouse instituted, she rightfully exercises a discretionary power as to the manner of their administration. She can not change their substance."

Again, on same page: "The church wisely sanctioned that which, although less solemn, is equally effectual. The power of binding and loosing which she received from Christ warrants this exercise of governing wisdom, that, the difference of times and places being considered, condensation may be used with regard to the mode of administering the sacraments without danger to their integrity."

Dr. Johnson said: "As to giving the bread to the laity, they may think that, in what is merely ritual, deviations from the primitive mode may be admitted on the ground of convenience;

and I think they are as well warranted to make this alteration as we are to substitute SPRINKLING in the room of ANCIENT BAPTISM." Campbell, Debate with Rice, p. 173.

MR. BONNER says: "Baptism by immersion was undoubtedly the apostolic practice, and was never dispensed with by the church, except in cases of sickness, or when a sufficient quantity of water could not be had. In both these cases baptism by aspersion or sprinkling was allowed, but in no other." Booth on Baptism, p. 176.

CHAMIERUS: "Immersion of the whole body was used from the beginning, which expresses the force of the word BAPTIZO: whence John baptized in the river. It was afterward changed into sprinkling, though it is uncertain when or by whom it commenced." *Ibid,* p. 192.

BISHOP STILLINGFLEET'S Rites and Customs of the English Church: "Rites and customs apostolical are altered; therefore men do not think that apostolical practice doth bind, for if it did, there could be no alteration of things agreeable thereunto. Now, let any one consider but these few particulars, and judge how far the pleaders for a divine right of apostolical practice do look upon themselves as bound now to observe them." *Ut supra.*

DEYLINGIUS: "It is manifest, that while the apostles lived the ordinance of baptism was administered, not out of a vessel or a baptistery, which are the marks of later times, but out of rivers and pools, and that not by sprinkling but by immersion.° ° ° So long as the apostles lived, as many believe, immersion only was used, to which afterward, perhaps, they added a kind of pouring." *Ibid,* p. 194.

HEIDEGGERUS: "Plunging or immersion was most commonly used by John the Baptist and by the apostles. ° ° ° It is of no importance whether baptism be performed by immersion into water, *as of old,* in the warm Eastern countries, and even at this day, or by sprinkling, which *was afterward* introduced in colder climates." *Ut supra.*

EDWARD LEIGH: "The ceremony used in baptism is either dipping or sprinkling; dipping is the more ancient. At first they went down into the rivers; afterward they were dipped in fonts.° ° ° Zanchius and Mr. Perkins prefer (in persons of age, and in hot countries, where it may be safe) the ceremony of immersion under water, as holding more analogy to that of Paul (Rom. vi:4)." *Ut supra.*

HORNBEKIUS: "In the Eastern churches baptism was more anciently administered by immersing the whole body in water. Afterward, first in the Western churches, on account of the coldness of the countries, bathing being less in use than in the East, and the tender age of those that were baptized, dipping or sprinkling was admitted." Booth, Abridged, pp. 100, 101.

GROTIUS: "The custom of pouring or sprinkling seems to have prevailed in favor of those that were dangerously ill, and were desirous of giving up themselves to Christ—whom others call *clinics.* See the Epistle of Cyprian to Magnus." *Ibid.,* p. 101.

E. SPANHEMIUS: "In these northern and colder countries, out of regard to the tender age of infants, we use aspersion in the place of immersion, which, of old, was usually practiced, either in open rivers or in private baptisteries and vessels filled with water." *Ut supra.*

BISHOP BURNET: "The danger of dipping, in cold climates, may be a very good reason for changing the form of baptism to sprinkling." *Ut supra.*

DR. TOWERSON: "The first mention we find of aspersion in the baptism of the elder sort was in the case of the *clinici,* or men who received baptism upon their sick beds; and that baptism is represented by St. Cyprian as legitimate, upon the account of necessity that compelled it, and the presumption there was of God's gracious acceptation thereof because of it. By which means the lawfulness of any other baptism than by immersion will be found to be in the *necessity* there may sometimes be of another manner of administering it." *Ibid.,* pp. 101, 102.

SIR JOHN FLOYER: "The Church of Rome hath drawn short compendiums of both sacraments. In the eucharist they use only the wafer, and instead of immersion they introduced aspersion." *Ibid,* p. 102.

SCHLEUSNER, in defining *baptisma,* says: "Properly, immersion, dipping into water, a washing; hence, it is transferred to the sacred rite which, par excellence, is called baptism, in which *formerly* those to be baptized were plunged into water." New Testament Lexicon.

BAPTISM 309

STOKIUS, in defining *baptisma*, says: "Specifically, properly it denotes the immersion or dipping of a thing into water that it may be cleansed or washed; hence it is transferred to designating the first sacrament of the New Testament, which they call the sacrament of initiation—namely, baptism, in which those to be baptized were *formerly* immersed into water, though at this day the water is only sprinkled upon them." New Testament Lexicon. *Formerly* they were immersed, *now* they have water only sprinkled on them. How came the change?

DR. R. WITHAM: "The word baptism signifies a washing, particularly when it is done by immersion, or by dipping, or plunging a thing under water, which was formerly the ordinary way of administering the sacrament of baptism. But the church, which can not change the least article of the Christian faith, is not so tied up in matters of discipline and ceremonies. Not only the Catholic Church, but also the pretended reformed churches, *have altered this primitive custom in giving the sacrament of baptism, and now allow of baptism by pouring or sprinkling water on the person baptized.*" Booth, Abridged, pp. 102, 103.

MOSES STUART: "It will be seen from all this, that Christians began somewhat early to deflect from the ancient practice of immersion." Stuart on Chr. Bap., p. 175.

In debate with J. S. Sweeney, Dr. J. B. Logan, an eminent Cumberland Presbyterian debater, said: "The church claimed the right to *change the mode* but not the ordinance itself, and in that I agree with the church and can cheerfully admit it." Sweeney and Logan Debate, p. 72.

We have already quoted from Prof. Stewart "that aspersion and affusion, which had now and then been practiced in particular cases in primitive times, were gradually introduced." The fact that they were gradually introduced shows that they came not from the Lord. He says that these *became* at length quite common in the Western church, but "the mode of baptism by immersion the Oriental church has always continued to preserve, even down to the present time." Stuart on Bap., p. 151.

DEYLINGIUS says: "The Greeks retain the rite of immersion to this day, as JEREMIAH, the Patriarch of Constantinople, declares." Booth on Baptism, Abridged, p. 93.

BUDDEUS: "That the Greeks defend immersion is manifest, and has been frequently observed by learned men, which LUDOLPHUS informs us is the practice of the Ethiopians." *Ut supra.*

VENEMA: "In pronouncing the baptismal form of words, the Greeks used the third person saying, 'Let the servant of Christ be baptized in the name of the Father, and of the Son, and of the Holy Spirit,' and immerse the whole man in water." *Ut supra.*

Other authorities might be given, but these are deemed sufficient to show that, while the Western or Roman Catholic Church gradually introduced the practice of aspersion and affusion until they became common by the time of the Reformation, the Oriental or Greek Church has continued faithful to the commands of the Lord and still practices only immersion as baptism. As the Greeks are presumed to better understand the Greek language than others unaccustomed to speak it, the fact that they have always understood *baptidzo* to mean immersion, and have practiced accordingly, is an item of no small importance in arriving at a knowledge of what the Lord required as baptism. If any people may be presumed to know the import of the word used by the Lord it is certainly those by whom the Greek language has been always spoken. If they have not understood their native tongue, *who has* understood it?

PROF. STUART quotes *Calvin,* thus: "It is of no consequence at all whether the person baptized is totally immersed, or whether he is merely sprinkled by an affusion of water. This should be a matter of choice to the churches in different regions, although the word *baptize signifies to immerse,* and the rite of immersion was practiced by the ancient church;" and then says: "To this opinion I do most fully and heartily subscribe." Stuart on Bap., pp. 156, 157.

Thus we see that, after conceding immersion to be the meaning of the word used by the Lord to indicate His will, and that immersion was the practice of the ancient church, these two great lights in the ranks of orthodoxy think it a matter of indifference, and should be left to the choice of the church; hence, the church may decide whether the people shall obey the Lord or not. Kind reader, which will you obey? "If the Lord be God, serve him; if Baal, serve him."

But what are the reasons given by Prof. Stuart for the conclusion to which he comes? "1. The rite in question is merely external." Suppose it is, is that any reason why it should not be obeyed? Jewish circumcision was "outward in the flesh" (Rom. ii:28), yet God said: "The uncircumcised man-child whose flesh of his foreskin is not circumcised, that soul shall be cut off from his people; he hath broken my covenant." Gen. xvii:14. Does any one believe that God would have excused a Jew from circumcision or have justified him in changing the act to something else upon the ground that the rite was *merely external?* To obey is better than sacrifice, and to hearken than the fat of rams.

Prof. Stuart argues the right of the church to change the act of baptism at great length with all the plausibility of an ingenious sophist, but we have room only for a few short extracts, which we give as follow: "Must I show that we are not at liberty, without being justly exposed to the accusation of gross departure from Christianity, to depart from the *modes* and *forms* of the apostolic church in any respect? I have shown that all the churches on earth do depart from these, in their celebration of the Lord's Supper, and yet without any apprehension of being guilty of an impropriety, much less of being justly chargeable with the spirit of disobedience and revolt. * * * But what is the case in respect to baptism? Will nothing but the letter do here? So you may think and reason, but are you not entirely inconsistent with yourself? * * * Mere *externals* must be things of particular time and place. Dress does not make the man. One dress may be more convenient or more decorous than another, but neither the one nor the other is an essential part of the person. So the common feeling of men has decided about most of the external matters pertaining to religion the world over. They have always been modified by time and place, by manners and customs, and they always will be. * * * Accordingly, long before the light of the Reformation began to dawn upon the churches, the Roman Catholics themselves were gradually adopting the method of baptism by sprinkling or affusion, notwithstanding their superstitious and excessive devotedness to the usages of the ancient church. * * * All this serves to illustrate how there sprang up, in the bosom of a church superstitiously devoted to ancient rites and forms, a conviction that the mode of baptism was one of the *adiaphora* of religion—*i.e.*, something unessential to the rite itself, and which might be modified by time and place, without any encroachment upon the command itself to baptize. Gradually did this conviction increase until the whole Roman Catholic Church, that of Milan only excepted, admit it. By far the greater part of the Protestant world have also acceded to the same views. Even the English Episcopal Church and the Lutheran Church, both zealous in times past for what they supposed to be apostolic and really ancient usage, have had no difficulty in adopting modes of baptism quite different from that of immersion." Stuart on Baptism, pp. 169-172.

Thus we see that Prof. Stuart thinks that the church may change the forms and usages of worship just as a man may change his dress to suit time and place. He shows us, with an air of seeming pleasure, that the Roman Catholic Church had *gradually left her devotedness to the usages of the ancient church and adopted sprinkling and pouring,* and that the *Protestant churches had followed her example.* Daniel prophesied of a power that should "speak great swelling words against the Most High, and think to change times and laws; and they shall be given into his hand until a time and times and the dividing of time; but the judgment shall sit, and they shall take his dominion to consume and to destroy it unto the end." Dan. vii:25, 26. Does not the power assigned by Prof. Stuart to the church resemble that claimed by the government spoken of by Daniel? Though he seemed to triumph for a time, judgment came upon him in the end.

Let us learn a lesson here, and seek not to change laws and times which God has arranged in accordance with His own will. "Let no man deceive you by any means; for that day shall not come, except there come a falling away first, and that man of sin be revealed, the son of perdition; who opposeth and exalteth himself above all that is called God, or that is worshiped; so that he as God sitteth in the temple of God, showing himself that he is God." 2 Thess. ii:3, 4.

The Pope of Rome has gone on from one act of usurpation to another, changed the act of baptism in accordance with his views of propriety, and has, finally, had himself proclaimed infallible, thus sitting in the temple of God and seeking to show himself that he is God. But Daniel said a day of judgment would come that would break the power of the usurper, and we feel encouraged to hope that the day of his power is fast drawing to a close. Will Protestant parties continue to cling to the changes which he has made for them in the divine law? "Why call ye me Lord, Lord, and do not the things which I say?" Luke vi:46. "If ye love me, keep my commandments." John xiv:15.

CHAPTER XIII.

WHO SHOULD BE BAPTIZED?

When Jesus commanded the apostles to "Teach all nations, baptizing them into the name of the Father, and of the Son, and of the Holy Spirit," Matt. xxviii:19, there was an implied obligation upon those to whom they were sent, to submit to be baptized by them. Upon whom did this obligation rest? These may and should be baptized; none others may, unless other authority be shown for it. That penitent, believing adults should be baptized is admitted by all parties; we need not, therefore, stop to offer proof of what no one denies. But it is insisted that he who has submitted to the divine injunction himself, should also have his infant children baptized, and thus brought into the church with him. This we respectfully deny; hence the onus of proof rests upon him who so affirms. Our first duty, therefore, is to examine the proofs presented by him, and if these be found satisfactory and conclusive, our duty is clear without further investigation; for we may be assured that the Bible, faithfully translated and construed, will nowhere contradict that which is clearly taught in it.

We know of but three ways by which the practice of infant baptism could be taught in the Divine Volume, First: By the express command of the Lord, or some one speaking by inspiration. Second: By example; *i.e.*, where the Lord or some inspired man, baptized infants, or where it was done in his presence, by his consent or approval. Third: By a passage of Scripture from which the baptism of infants is a *necessary inference*. A merely *possible* inference is not sufficient, for while a thing is only *possibly true,* it is still *possible* for it to be *false.* We believe it is very generally admitted that there is no express command for, or example of, infant baptism recorded in the Bible, hence inferential proof is all we may expect from those who advocate the practice. It may be well to see how this is, for a concession so important, from those who advocate the practice in question, will greatly diminish the area of our investigation. We will hear what they say on the subject.

1. Dr. Moses Stuart says: "On the subject of *infant baptism* I have said nothing. The present occasion did not call for it;

and I have no wish or intention to enter into the controversy respecting it. I have only to say, that I believe in both the propriety and expediency of the rite thus administered, and therefore accede to it *ex animo*. Commands, or plain and certain examples, in the New Testament relative to it, I do not find. Nor, with my views of it do I need them." Stuart on Baptism, pp. 189, 190.

2. BISHOP BURNET: "There is no express precept or rule given in the New Testament for the baptism of infants." Expos. of 39 Articles, in Booth Abridged, p. 116.

3. DR. WALL: "Among all the persons that are recorded as baptized by the apostles, there is no express mention of any infant. There is no express mention of any children baptized by them." Hist. Inf. Bap. in Booth Abridged, p. 116.

4. LUTHER: "It can not be proved by the sacred Scriptures that infant baptism was instituted by Christ, or began by the first Christians after the apostles." *Ut supra.*

5. BAXTER: "I know of no one word in Scripture, that giveth us the least intimation that every man was baptized without the profession of a saving faith, or that giveth the least encouragement to baptize any upon *another's faith.*" *Ut supra.*

6. WILLS: "Christ did many things that were not recorded, and so did the apostles; whereof this was one, for aught we know, the baptizing of infants. Calvin, in his fourth book of Institutes, Chap. xvi, confesseth, that it is nowhere expressly mentioned by the Evangelists, that any one child was by the apostles baptized. To the same purpose are Stophilus, Melancthon, Turinglius quoted." Inf. Bap. Asserted in Booth Abridged, p. 117.

7. PALMER: "There is nothing in the words of the institution, nor in any after accounts of the administration of this rite, respecting the baptism of infants; there is not a single precept for, nor example of, this practice, through the whole New Testament." *Ut supra.*

8. LIMBORCH: "There is no express command for it in Scripture, nay, all those passages wherein baptism is commanded do immediately relate to adult persons, since they are ordered to be instructed, and faith is prerequisite as a necessary qualification, which are peculiar to adults alone. There is no instance that can

be produced, from whence it may indisputably be inferred that any child was baptized by the apostles. The necessity of Pedobaptism was never asserted by any council before that of Carthage, held in the year four hundred and eighteen." *Ut supra.*

9. ERASMUS: "Paul does not seem (in Rom. v:14), to treat about infants. It was not yet the custom for infants to be baptized." Annotations on Rom. in Booth Abridged, p. 118.

10. T. BOSTON: "It is plain that he [Peter, in Acts ii:38] requires their repentance antecedently to baptism, as necessary to qualify them for the right and due reception thereof. And there is no example of baptism recorded in the Scriptures, when any were baptized, but such as appeared to have a saving interest in Christ." *Ut supra.*

11. BISHOP SANDERSON: "The baptism of infants, and the sprinkling of water in baptism, instead of immersing the whole body, must be exterminated from the church—according to their principle; *i.e.*, that nothing can be lawfully performed, much less required, in the affairs of religion, which is not either commanded by God in the Scripture, or at least recommended by a laudable example." *Ut supra.*

12. CELLARIUS: "Infant baptism is neither commanded in the sacred Scripture, nor is confirmed by apostolic examples." *Ut supra.*

13. DR. KNAPP: "There is, therefore, no express command for infant baptism found in the New Testament, as Morris (p. 215, s. 12) justly concedes. Infant baptism has been often defended on a very unsatisfactory *a priori* grounds, *e.g.*, necessity of it has been contended for, in order that children may obtain by it the faith which is necessary to salvation, etc. It is sufficient to show; (1) That infant baptism was not forbidden by Christ, and is not opposed to his will, and the principles of his religion, but entirely suited to both; (2) That it was *probably* practiced even in the apostolic church; (3) That it is not without advantages." Lectures on Christian Theology, p. 494.

14. We may close this testimony by the declarations of *Henry Ward Beecher*, who is quoted in the *Louisville Debate*, page 173, as saying: *"That he had no authority from the Bible

---

* This was published in *The Christian Union* by Mr. Beecher.

for the baptism of infants, and that he wanted none; that he had better authority for it than if even the *Bible* commanded it; that he had tried it, and knew from actual experience that it was a good thing; he had the same divine authority for it that he had for making an ox-yoke—it worked well—and, therefore, it was from God."

The foregoing list might be extended much further; but these quotations are deemed sufficient to warrant us in regarding it as a fact, conceded that there is no divine *command,* nor apostolic *precedent* for the baptism of infants. It is insisted that the writers of the New Testament were all Pedobaptists; if so, is not such profound reticence on the subject a little remarkable, to say the least of it? They record the baptism of vast numbers of *believers,* just as though infant baptism had then never been heard of; and Luke tells us that when the Samaritans "Believed Philip preaching the things concerning the kingdom of God, and the name of Jesus Christ, they were baptized, both men and women." Acts viii:12. Is it not strange that he should be so specific as to mention the baptism of *men* and *women,* and say nothing about the multitudes of dear little children that were baptized? Their baptism could not have been a matter of less importance than that of the men and women, if indeed they were baptized at all. Would any of our Pedobaptist friends imitate Luke's example were they now writing the narrative? Would they not likely say "They were baptized, men, women, and *children?*" They are specifically mentioned in matters not less worthy of note. When the covenant of circumcision was instituted in the family of Abraham the Lord said: "He that is eight days old shall be circumcised among you, every male child in your generations, he that is born in thy house, or bought with money of any stranger, which is not of thy seed." Gen. xvii:12. Here is a rite applicable to infants, and we find that even the age of the child to be circumcised is specifically given. Numerous examples can be found recorded where this rite was performed according to the law. "Abraham circumcised his son Isaac, being eight days old, as God had commanded him." Gen. xxi:4. "And when eight days were accomplished for the circumcising of the child, his name was called Jesus, which was so named of the angel before he was conceived in the womb."

Luke ii:21. Is it not a little strange, if baptism was made obligatory on children, that we can not as easily find examples of it as of circumcision! When Pharaoh issued his decree for the destruction of the Hebrew children, he said: "When ye do the office of a midwife to the Hebrew women, and see them upon the stools, if it be a son, then ye shall kill him." Ex. i:16. When Herod determined upon the destruction of the infant Saviour, he "Sent forth, and slew all the children that were in Bethlehem, and in all the coasts thereof, from two years old and under." Matt. ii:16. When Jesus miraculously fed the multitudes, the children are not forgotten in the narrative. "They that had eaten were about five thousand men, beside women and *children*." Matt. xiv:21. Nor are they omitted in the record of the second occurrence. "They that did eat were four thousand men, beside women and *children*." Matt. xv:38. When infants were brought to the master that they might receive His heavenly benediction, He said: "Suffer little children, and forbid them not, to come unto me; for of such is the kingdom of heaven." Matt. xix:14. This account is preserved in the records of Mark and Luke also. When Paul and company bade a final adieu to the disciples at the city of Tyre, the historian informs us that "they all brought us on our way, with wives and *children*, till we were out of the city: and we kneeled down on the shore, and prayed." Acts xxi:5.

Thus we see that infants were deemed worthy of mention in all matters with which they were in any way connected; even in cases where they did nothing but to satisfy the demands of hunger, or were brought out of a city in company with those who were parting with a friend; where no doctrine is involved, no duty enforced, no dispute settled; yet we are asked to believe that they were baptized in obedience to the command of the Lord Jesus, by inspired men, and no record of the fact; when such a record would have prevented bitter contention and strife; much labor in preaching and writing; and would have secured the performance of a duty now bound to be neglected by many millions of devoted followers of the Master for want of the knowledge which such a record would have furnished.

Luke says: "Forasmuch as many have taken in hand to set forth in order a declaration of those things which are most surely believed among us, even as they delivered them unto us, which from the beginning were eyewitnesses and ministers of the word; it seemed good to me also, having had perfect understanding of all things from the very first, to write unto thee in order, most excellent Theophilus, that thou mightest know the certainty of those things, wherein thou hast been instructed." Luke i:1-4. Again he says: "The former treatise have I made, O Theophilus, of all that Jesus began both to do and to teach." Acts i:1. The sum of these quotations is that Luke had a perfect understanding of all things which Jesus did and taught; and that he wrote in order that Theophilus might know the certainty of the whole matter as believed among the disciples. Certainly, then, we may justly conclude that no important matter was omitted which had not been perfectly taught by some one else. Hence, as he says not a word about infant baptism we may feel tolerably sure that it was not taught or practiced by Jesus, nor believed among the disciples with whom he associated. When he tells us that "Saul made havoc of the church, entering into every house, and haling *men and women*, committed them to prison" (Acts viii:3), we may justly conclude that infants escaped the fierceness of his wrath, otherwise they would have been mentioned as well as *men and women*. We are strengthened in this conclusion by the fact already seen that it was his custom to mention them where they were connected with the matter recorded. Then as he speaks of the baptism of multitudes of *believers*, at different times and places, and under different circumstances, even mentioning *men* and *women*, and yet says nothing of the baptism of a single infant, we conclude that none were baptized, or he would have mentioned the fact somewhere; especially when he must have known that what he was writing would not only furnish an interesting history of past events, but *would constitute a rule of action for the government of God's people as long as time should endure.*

Paul told Timothy that "all scripture is given by inspiration of God, and is profitable for doctrine, for reproof, for correction, for instruction in righteousness: that the man of God may be perfect, thoroughly furnished unto all good works." 2 Tim. iii:16, 17. The Scriptures can not be profitable for the *doctrine* of infant baptism, for its advocates admit that they say nothing about it. If infant baptism be a duty, the Scriptures furnish no *reproof* for those who neglect it. If it be a crime to oppose infant baptism, the Scriptures furnish no *correction* for the error. If infant baptism be right, the Scriptures furnish no *instruction* to those whose duty it is to perform it. If the Scriptures are profitable for *doctrine, reproof, correction,* and *instruction* in righteousness, that the man of God may be *perfect,* as they say nothing about infant baptism, it follows that the man of God may attain to *perfection* without it. If the Scriptures not only *furnish,* but *thoroughly* furnish the man of God not only to *some,* but to *all* good works, as they are confessedly silent on the subject of infant baptism, it follows that it is not a good work, otherwise the man of God would be thoroughly furnished with instruction concerning the baptism of infants.

While considering the conceded fact that the Scriptures say nothing about the baptism of infants, we will hear another apostle on this subject. Peter says: "Grace and peace be multiplied unto you through the knowledge of God, and of Jesus our Lord, according as his divine power hath given unto us all things that pertain, unto life and godliness, through the knowledge of him who hath called us to glory and virtue." 2 Pet. i:2, 3. Here is a clear intimation that God has given us all things, through the knowledge of His Son revealed in the gospel, which pertain to life and godliness. And as He has given us nothing on the subject of infant baptism, we conclude that it neither pertains to *life* nor *godliness*. We are commanded to do all: "Whatsoever we do, in word or deed, do all in the name of the Lord Jesus, giving thanks to God and the Father by him." Col. iii:17. We understand this passage to teach that we are to do all things done at all by the *authority* of the Lord Jesus. How, then, can a man, standing in the presence of God, with his hand lifted toward heaven, say, "In the name or by the authority of the Lord Jesus, I baptize this child," when he acknowledges that the Word of the Lord furnishes neither *command* nor *example* for what he is doing? Could Prof. Stuart baptize a child in the name or by the authority of the Lord Jesus after saying: "Commands, or plain and certain examples, in the New Testament relative to it, I do not find?" Surely, he could not adopt the maxim of the justly celebrated *Chillingworth,* that "THE BIBLE ONLY IS THE RELIGION

OF PROTESTANTS." If this maxim is worthy of all acceptation, well may we ask, in the language of *Ambrose*, "Who shall speak where Scripture is silent?" Dare we baptize an infant in the name of the Lord Jesus if He has not appointed it? When Peter commanded the Pentecostians to be baptized, he did it in the "name of Jesus Christ." Acts ii:38. He also commanded the Gentiles at the house of Cornelius, "to be baptized in the name of the Lord." Acts x:48. And surely, such examples are worthy of our imitation; if so, there is an implied prohibition of administering this sacred rite in any other name or by any other authority. Surely, then, if Dr. Beecher was right when he said, in substance, that he had no higher authority for baptizing an infant than for making an ox-yoke, it had better be left undone. God will not condemn us in the great day of judgment for a failure to do that which He has nowhere commanded; but there may be danger in performing a thing in the sacred name of His Son for which we can not find authority in the Book by which we are to be judged.

The Lord said that the way of holiness should be so plain that "the wayfaring men, though fools, shall not err therein." Isa. xxxv:8. Hence, when Jesus sent chosen men to proclaim the gospel of peace and the approach of the kingdom of heaven, their mission was not confined to the wealthy who had been reared in opulence and learned in all the literature of the age in which they lived, but "the poor had the gospel preached to them." Matt. xi:5. Yet we are asked to believe that these uneducated poor were to learn the duty of baptizing their children from oral instructions which not once mentioned it, and in a country where they never once saw an example of it. And after the New Testament was written, the primitive Christians are expected to take a copy of it and learn the duty of baptizing their children from a record which furnishes not a command for it or an example of it. Nay, these unlettered fishermen, mechanics, and plowmen are expected to arrive at a knowledge of their duty from a careful examination of the covenants which God made with Abraham, and by identifying them with the New Covenant dedicated with the blood of Jesus. Those who lived later might also study the *Talmud*, and familiarize themselves with the writings of Maimonides and other Jewish rabbis and doctors of the law, from whom to learn that the children of proseltyes were baptized along with their parents, and infer therefrom that the Lord condescended to borrow the baptism of infants from those who believed Him an impostor and worthy of death. Nor must they stop here, but they must study the writings of Moses until familiar with the antiquated rite of circumcision; and, notwithstanding the many marks of dissimilarity, infer that baptism came in its room, and as *male* children were circumcised under the law, therefore *males* and *females* must be baptized under the gospel of the Son of God. Such are some of the sources from which the unlettered poor are expected to learn the duty of baptizing their children; and we next propose to examine them and see whether or not they furnish just grounds for even inferring infant baptism, though it were possible for all to understand them.

And, first, it is assumed that God has had but one church on the earth, and that it has existed at least since the days of Abraham; that the church *now* is the same church that then was; and that infants were members of the church then, and having never been put out, are members of it now; that all members of the church should be baptized—*ergo,* infants, being members, should be baptized.

We believe this is a fair statement of the argument, but before we enter upon an examination of its merits we would respectfully call attention to a want of consistency in the pleadings of those who advocate it. The argument is based upon the assumption that *infants are members of the church,* and *as such* should be baptized; yet they tell us that they should be baptized in order to bring them into the church. In the ministration of baptism to infants the Methodist Discipline instructs the administrator to say: "Dearly beloved, forasmuch as all men are conceived and born in sin, and that our Saviour Christ saith, Except a man be born of water and of the Spirit, he can not enter into the kingdom of God, I beseech you to call upon God the Father, through our Lord Jesus Christ, that of his bounteous mercy he will grant to this child that which by nature he can not have; that he may be baptized with water and the Holy Ghost, and received into Christ's holy church, and be made a lively member of the same."

Please observe that the minister instructs the congregation to pray that the child to be baptized may be received into the church and made a lively member of it. Then he leads them in the following prayer: "Almighty and everlasting God, who of thy great mercy didst save Noah and his family in the ark from perishing by water; and also didst safely lead the children of Israel, thy people, through the Red Sea, figuring thereby thy holy baptism: we beseech thee, for thine infinite mercies, that thou wilt look upon *this child:* wash *him,* and sanctify *him* with the Holy Ghost; that *he,* being delivered from thy wrath, may be received into the ark of Christ's church." Methodist Discipline, pp. 159, 160. What can this mean? Clearly, it means nothing less than that the child is baptized to introduce it into the church, and yet the very foundation of the argument stated is that it must be baptized because IN the church already.

Mr. Henry, in his Treatise on Baptism, p. 40, says: "The gospel contains not only a doctrine but a covenant; and by *baptism* we are brought into that covenant." And again: "Baptism is an ordinance of Christ, *whereby* the person baptized is solemnly admitted a member of the visible church." *Ibid,* p. 66. Then page 79, he says: "Baptism is a seal of the covenant of grace, and therefore belongs to those who ARE IN that covenant (at least by profession), and to NONE OTHER. The infants of believing parents ARE IN covenant with God, and therefore have a right to the initiating seal of that covenant." Again, page 66, he says: "Baptism is an ordinance of the visible church, and pertains, therefore, to those who are visible members of the church. Their covenant right and their church membership entitle them to baptism. Baptism doth not give the title, but recognizes it."

Other quotations might be given, but these are deemed sufficient to show the want of consistency on the subject referred to. The argument is as changeable as the colors of a chameleon. At one time parents are admonished to dedicate their children to God in baptism, and bring them into covenant and church relation with them; and we are severely reprimanded for denying the dear children the privilege of entering the church with their parents by baptism; and anon the order is reversed, and the little babes *are in the church*—in covenant relation with God with their parents, and for this very reason should be baptized. Thus it is that infants must be baptized because not in the church to bring them in; and they must be baptized because they are in it, and entitled to its ordinances as members of it.

But if all children of believing parents are born members of the church, and on that account are entitled to baptism, then we would be pleased to know what church they enter by baptism, and what means their so-called reception into the church when they are grown and make a profession of religion? First: We are told that infants of believing parents are born members of the church, and should be baptized because they are in it. Second: "Baptism is for the solemn admission of the party baptized into the church." What church? Third: They grow up to mature years, attend a protracted meeting, make a profession of religion; the doors are opened for the reception of members, and they join the church. What church? Is there one church into which they enter at birth, another into which they enter by baptism, and still another into which they enter by formal reception after "getting religion?" In a previous chapter, we have seen that there is one church, and only one. Are we to understand that the infant was born a member of it and subsequently re-entered the church of which it was born a member? If so, did it forfeit its previous membership in some way so as to make other admissions necessary? If it did, we would be pleased to know how, and when, or at what age the forfeiture was effected, and whether or not the church formally declared non-fellowship with it.

Again: If there be blessings conferred upon infants by baptism, why are they restricted to the children of believing parents? Are the children of unbelievers to be made responsible for the sins of their parents so as to deprive them of gospel privileges which belong to and are enjoyed by others of their age? Where is the authority for such discrimination? If one infant may be baptized, surely all others may. Indeed, we have observed quite a disposition to a change of position here in modern times. Formerly, debaters were willing to affirm that *the children of believing parents* were proper subjects of baptism; now they can not be induced to make such a discrimination, but will affirm only the general proposition that *infants* are proper subjects. We are rather pleased at this. If infant baptism be a blessing, let all have the benefit of it. But does not such shifting of ground show that there is nothing taught in the gospel in favor it? It occurs to us that if the practice were clearly taught it would be understood, and there would be no need of changing theories concerning it.

Once more: If infants enter the church either by birth or baptism, why are they not fit subjects for and admitted to the Lord's table? Surely, if they are members of the church, they should be entitled to all the privileges of full membership. Then, why not give them the bread and wine, as emblems of the body and blood of the Lord, which belong to all who are members of the body of which He is the head? Do you tell me that they can not partake of these emblems discerning the Lord's body? Then, for this very reason they are not competent for membership in the church where such a duty is enjoined upon them. We know of no reason why they should not be admitted to the Lord's table, which would not apply to their membership in the church with at least equal force. Does the gospel contain any special reason why they should be excused, as members of the church, from participation in the Lord's Supper? If not, are they not entitled to it? Nay, are they not bound to eat if members at all? No member of the church can be debarred from the emblematic body and blood of the Lord unless he has made himself unworthy by the commission of crime, such as infants are incapable of committing. Then, we insist that those who regard infants as members of the church should give them the bread and wine to which all members are entitled, or show the law excusing them.

Finally, as infants come into the church, according to the theory, without faith or repentance, it is not easy for us to see how such graces may be demanded of them in mature years. If they may enter the church without faith or repentance, surely they could remain members without them; why should they be treated as aliens or rebels for a want of faith or repentance in adult age, when they entered the church and lived in it for years without either? Indeed, no such qualifications were at all necessary to membership in the Jewish church; and if the church *now* is but a continuance of the same church which existed *then*, why should they be required now? No faith, change of heart, repentance, purity of life, or holiness was essential to membership in the Jewish churches. Every species of crime was perpetrated by those who lived and died in that church. If the same church exists now, and infants are in it because such were in it then, why may not adults be in it without faith, repentance, or any thing spiritual, seeing such were in it then. Persons were born members of the church then and continued in it until death, however wicked they may have lived; why not now? But suppose they are not born members of the church, but enter it by baptism, the same results must follow. Many thousands of those who are baptized in infancy become wicked, and remain through life as wicked as men ever get to be, even never making any pretense of Christianity in any way; hence, if they entered the church when baptized, they live and die in it, for we never hear of any such being excluded from the church because they become wicked; and therefore the church is as full of depravity and wickedness as is the dominion of Satan. There is no visible line of separation between the world and the church. Those in the church are just as wicked as those out of it, for we have never been able to see any difference in the ungodly who were baptized in infancy and those who were not. Nor is this the worst; if infants must be baptized because infants were in the Jewish church, then the wickedest man living may be baptized for a similar reason. We suppose there is not a worse man alive than lived in the Jewish church, and if infants may be baptized because infants were in that church, we see not why all other classes similar to those in that church may not be baptized. Will the advocates of the theory accept the results of their logic, and baptize every wicked man, because such were in the Jewish church? If not, the argument based upon infant membership must be abandoned.

In a previous chapter we attempted to show that the church now in existence was organized in Jerusalem on the day of Pentecost; we need not, therefore, further examine this subject here, but we may call attention to some facts, not presented there, showing that it can not be the same organization which existed in the days of Abraham, or in the days of Moses. The Church of Christ differs from the so-called Jewish church in the fact that it was based upon another covenant. There were two classes of promises made by God to Abraham. One pertained to the flesh and temporal interests, and the other to matters spiritual. God said, "I am the Almighty God: walk before me, and be thou perfect. And I will make my covenant between me and thee, and will multiply thee exceedingly. And Abram fell on his face: and God talked with him, saying, As for me, behold, my covenant is with thee, and thou shalt be a father of many nations. Neither shall thy name any more be called Abram, but thy name shall be Abraham; for a father of many nations have I made thee. And I will make thee exceeding fruitful, and I will make nations of thee, and kings shall come out of thee. And I will establish my covenant between me and thee and thy seed after thee in their generations, for an everlasting covenant, to be a God unto thee and to thy seed after thee. And I will give unto thee, and to thy seed after thee, the land wherein thou art a stranger, all the land of Canaan, for an everlasting possession; and I will be their God. And God said unto Abraham, Thou shalt keep my covenant therefore, thou, and thy seed after thee in their generations. This is my covenant, which ye shall keep, between me and you and thy seed after thee: Every man child among you shall be circumcised. And ye shall circumcise the flesh of your foreskin; and it shall be a token of the covenant between me and you." Gen. xvii:1-11.

In this covenant God promises Abraham a numerous fleshly offspring and the land of Canaan, as a permanent inheritance, and instituted circumcision as a token of the covenant thus made. This covenant was renewed with Isaac, Jacob, and Moses, and upon it the Jewish church or commonwealth was organized. That the covenant of circumcision was incorporated into the law of Moses may be seen by the language of the Savior, saying, "If a man on the Sabbath day receive circumcision, that the law of Moses should not be broken." John vii:23. That the covenant made with Abraham, and renewed with Isaac and Jacob, was renewed with Moses, is shown by the language of Moses himself. He says, "Keep therefore the words of this covenant, and do them, that ye may prosper in all that ye do. Ye stand this day all of you before the Lord your God; your captains of your tribes, your elders, and your officers, with all the men of Israel. Your little ones, your wives, and thy stranger that is in thy camp, from the hewer of thy wood unto the drawer of thy water: That thou shouldest enter into covenant with the Lord thy God, and into his oath, which the Lord thy God maketh with thee this day: That he may establish thee to-day for a people unto himself, and that he may be unto thee a God, as he hath said unto thee, and as he hath sworn unto thy fathers, to Abraham, to Isaac, and to Jacob." Deut. xxix:9-13. Thus we clearly identify the covenant concerning Abraham's fleshly descendants, the land of Canaan, and the right of circumcision with the covenant made with Moses; and Paul says Jesus "Blotted out the handwriting of ordinances that was against us, which was contrary to us, and took it out of the way, nailing it to his cross." Col. 11:14.

But there was another class of promises spiritual in their nature. When Abraham offered his son, as commanded of God, "And the Angel of the Lord called unto Abraham out of heaven the second time, and said, By myself have I sworn, saith the Lord, for because thou hast done this thing, and hast not withheld thy son, thine only son, that in blessing I will bless thee, and in multiplying I will multiply thy seed as the stars of the heaven, and as the sand which is upon the sea shore; and thy seed shall possess the gate of his enemies; and in thy seed shall all the nations of the earth be blessed; because thou hast obeyed my voice." Gen. xxii:15-18. Now let it be carefully observed that this promise was based upon the express ground of Abraham's obedience in offering Isaac. "Because thou hast done *this thing*," "Because thou hast obeyed my voice." And Paul quotes the language of this promise as fulfilled in Jesus Christ. He says: "Now to Abraham and his seed were the promises made. He saith not, And to seeds, as of many; but as of one, And to thy seed, which is Christ." Gal. iii:16. That these different sets of promises constituted at least a plurality of covenants, may be seen in the language of Paul concerning the Gentiles before the coming of Christ. He says: "At that time ye were without Christ, being aliens from the commonwealth of Israel, and strangers from the covenants of promise." Eph. ii:12. Here is a clear intimation that the promises made to Abraham constituted more than one covenant. Upon the promise made at the offering of Isaac was based the new and better covenant, established upon better promises (Heb. viii:6), which was predicted by the Lord through his prophet, as follows:

"Behold, the days come, saith the Lord, that I will make a new covenant with the house of Israel, and with the house of Judah: not according to the covenant that I made with their fathers, in the day that I took them by the hand to bring them out of the land of Egypt; which my covenant they brake, although I was a husband unto them, saith the Lord: but this shall be the covenant that I will make with the house of Israel after those days, saith the Lord: I will put my law in their inward parts, and write it in their hearts; and will be their God, and they shall be my people. And they shall teach no more every man his neighbor, and every man his brother, saying, Know the Lord: for they shall all know me, from the least of them unto the greatest of them, saith the Lord: for I will forgive their iniquity, and I will remember their sin no more." Jer. xxxi:31-34. That this new covenant was that of which Christ became the mediator is evident from the fact that Paul quotes the language as an argument to show that the old covenant had given place to the new. He says, "But now hath he obtained a more excellent ministry, by how much also he is the mediator of a better covenant, which was established upon better promises. For if that first covenant had been faultless, then should no place have been sought for the second. For finding fault with them, he saith, Behold, the days come, saith the Lord, when I will make a new covenant with the house of Israel, and with the house of Judah: not according to the covenant that I made with their fathers, in the day when I took them by the hand to lead them out of the land of Egypt; because they continued not in my covenant, and I regarded them not, saith the Lord. For this is the covenant that I will make with the house of Israel after those days, saith the Lord: I will put my laws into their mind, and write them in their hearts; and I will be to them a God, and they shall be to me a people: and they shall not teach every man his neighbor, and every man his brother, saying, Know the Lord: for all shall know me, from the least to the greatest. For I will be merciful to their unrighteousness, and their sins and their iniquities will I remember no more. In that he saith, A new covenant, he hath made the first old. Now that which decayeth and waxeth old is ready to vanish away." Heb. viii:6-13.

We would respectfully call the reader's attention to several important thoughts presented in the foregoing quotation. The Lord said He would make a new covenant, hence it was not an old one, made prior to the time He used the language quoted. Paul gives us several reasons why this new covenant was necessary, and he mentions several important points in which it differs from the old covenant. First: Those to whom the first covenant was given broke it—continued not in it, and hence God ceased to regard them. Second: The first was a faculty covenant, hence it became necessary to have a better covenant, established upon better promises, the provisions of which were not according to the old one. Third: The laws of the old covenant were engraven on stone; those of the new were to be written in the hearts of the people. Fourth: The subjects of the old covenant became such by natural birth, or were purchased with money, and hence could not know the Lord until taught by such as had reached mature years; the subjects of the new covenant have to be born again to enter the kingdom based upon it, and hence have to be all taught to know the Lord before they believe in Him, and become subjects of His government; this being so, there are no infants among them, because they can not know the Lord, or have his laws written in their hearts. Fifth: Under the old covenant those who violated its laws died without mercy under two or three witnesses (Heb. x:28); under the new covenant God is merciful to the unrighteousness of its subjects. Sixth: Under the old covenant, sins were pardoned only a year at a time. "For in those sacrifices there is a remembrance again made of sins every year. For it is not possible that the blood of bulls and of goats should take away sins." Heb. x:3, 4. Under the new covenant, one of its chief excellencies is that sins once pardoned *are remembered no more.*

As this position is fiercely assailed by some, and doubted by others, it may be well for us to give it more than a passing notice. If the sins pardoned under the old covenant were forever pardoned, why was it necessary that this should be mentioned as one of the superior provisions of the new covenant? Wherein is it a better covenant in this respect than the old? Was Paul mistaken when he said: "It is not possible that the blood of bulls and of goats should take away sin?" Surely the blood of these sacrifices did take them away if they were forever pardoned by them. Paul says: "How much more shall the blood of Christ, who through the eternal Spirit offered himself without spot to God, purge your conscience from dead works to serve the living God? And for this cause he is the mediator of the new testament, that by means of death, for the redemption of the transgressions that were under the first testament, they which are called might receive the promise of eternal inheritance." Heb. ix:14, 15. Why was it necessary that Jesus should die for the redemption of the transgressions which were under the first testament if they were forever pardoned by the offerings made according to its provisions? If we at all comprehend the language of Paul, he meant to teach that Jesus died for the redemption of the transgressions committed under the first testament, that those who were called by it might receive the eternal inheritance promised them. All the offerings made under the law looked to, and were perfected by, the death of Jesus Christ. "He taketh away the first, that he may establish the second. By the which will we are sanctified through the offering of the body of Jesus Christ once for all. And every priest standeth daily ministering and offering oftentimes the same sacrifices, which *can never take away sins;* but this man, after he had offered one sacrifice for sins forever, sat down on the right hand of God; from henceforth expecting till his enemies be made his footstool. For by one offering he hath perfected forever them that are sanctified. Whereof the Holy Ghost also is a witness to us: for after that he had said before, This is the covenant that I will make with them after those days, saith the Lord: I will put my laws into their hearts, and in their minds will I write them; and their sins and iniquities will I remember no more. Now where remission of these is, there is no more offering for sin." Heb. x:9-18. Thus we see that the apostle argues this question at great length, to show this as one of the great points of superiority in the new covenant over the old; and it seems to us that it could not have been made more plain. Then, as it is a *new* and *better* covenant, established upon better promises, why should any one want to get back under the old and faulty covenant, which has been taken out of the way to make room for a better one?

But we are told that it was the law given by Moses when the Jews were delivered from Egyptian bondage which was the old covenant which was taken out of the way, and not the covenant made with Abraham. We have seen that the covenant made with Abraham was renewed with Isaac, Jacob, and Moses (see Deut. xxix:9-13); and we have seen that even circumcision belonged to the law of Moses. (See John vii:23.) Surely this was given to Abraham (Gen. xvii:9-14); and we suppose no one, unless a Jew, will contend that it has not been taken out of the way; hence it is unsafe to affirm that a convenant has not been taken out of the way because it was given to Abraham. But it does not matter what covenant it was that was taken out of the way; the one of which Christ is mediator is the one which concerns us, and it is the new covenant; and the prophecy concerning it was made long *after*, not *before* the time when the Lord delivered the Jews from Egyptian bondage. Long after that time the Lord said, Behold the days come, (not have passed), when *I will make a new covenant* (not have made a covenant long years ago); hence it could not have been a covenant made with Abraham, or with any one else prior to the time God made this declaration by Jeremiah; and it was to be made with the house of *Israel* and with the house of *Judah*—houses which had no existence in the days of Abraham, nor until long years afterward. How, then, could it refer to a covenant made with him?

But the Jewish church was only half as large as the Christian church. While *that* was confined to the Jews, *this* is for every creature among all nations who will accept its blessings on the terms proposed. Here, too, is another striking evidence that the new and better covenant, of which Christ is the mediator, was based upon the promise of God to Abraham at the offering of Isaac. "In thy seed shall all the nations of the earth be blessed; because thou hast obeyed my voice." Gen. xxii:18. As long as the Jewish church existed, the Gentiles were refused the privileges of it. Paul says: "Wherefore remember, that ye being in time past Gentiles in the flesh, who are called Uncircumcision by that which is called the Circumcision in the flesh made by hands; that at that time ye were without Christ, being aliens from the commonwealth of Israel, and strangers from the covenants of promise, having no hope, and without God in the world: but now, in Christ Jesus, ye who sometime were far off are made nigh by the blood of Christ. For he is our peace, who hath made both one, and hath broken down the middle wall of partition between us; having abolished in his flesh the enmity, even the law of commandments contained in ordinances; for to make in himself of twain one new man, so making peace; and that he might reconcile both unto God in one body by the cross, having slain the enmity thereby." Eph. ii:11-16. Here we find that the law, which stood as a middle wall between Jews and Gentiles for ages, and had kept the latter from any participation in the worship of God *with* the former, was taken out of the way, by the death of Christ, and one new man or church was made of both Jews and Gentiles, who participated in its privileges upon terms of perfect equality. It is agreed by all parties that the phrase *new man* here simply means a *new church*. Under the the old dispensation the Gentiles were without Christ, aliens from the Jewish commonwealth, and strangers from the covenants of promise; but, under the new covenant, they enter into, and are members of the one church composed of all nations, to whom the gospel is preached, and for whom Jesus died. Observe it is not an enlarged church, an improved church, or a renewed church, but a NEW church, hence we see not how it can be the same old church which existed in the days of Abraham and Moses. Jesus says: "No man puttteth a piece of new cloth unto an old garment; for that which is put in to fill it up taketh away from the garment, and the rent is made worse. Neither do men put new wine into old bottles: else the bottles break, and the wine runneth out, and the bottles perish: but they put new wine into new bottles, and both are preserved." Matt. ix:16, 17; Mark ii:22; Luke v:36-38. Now it occurs to us that those who seek to retain the old Jewish church are doing just the thing which the Lord here condemned. They seek to enlarge it so as to include the Gentiles, leaving off its ceremonies, carnal ordinances, and festivals: and fill up the rents with infant baptism and other human traditions, and thus patch up the old garment with a little Christianity and a good supply of the commandments of men, and make a worse system than Judaism itself.

If the church of Christ or kingdom of God is the same church which existed in the days of Abraham and Moses, why did those who had been brought up in the Jewish church have *still to enter the church* established by the authority of the Lord? When Nicodemus recognized the divine character and mission of Jesus, he expected, doubtless, that, as a descendant of Abraham, he would be recognized as a ruler in the kingdom or church of God; but all his claims based upon Jewish birth were met with the solemn announcement that, "Except a man be born of water and of the Spirit, he can not enter into the kingdom of God." John iii:5. It is not strange that such a declaration should have astonished him, for he had the same notion of the continuance of the Jewish church which Pedobaptists seem to have now. As they view it could he not reply, "I have been in the church all my life, and am now a ruler of the Jews—a master of Israel, and you speak to ME of having yet to enter the church or kingdom into which I was born!" Still he is met with the cool reply: "Marvel not that I said unto thee, ye must be born again." Verse 7. Was not this equivalent to saying: "I know you were born into the *Jewish church,* but My kingdom or church is a very different organization. No spiritual qualifications were necessary to membership in that church, but a birth of flesh only, or even purchase with money was sufficient. My church is designed to make men holy; hence, purity of heart and submission to My will are the means of entrance; and, therefore, I tell you that, though a member of the Jewish church, of however great distinction, you must be born of water and of the Spirit, or into My kingdom or church you can not enter." Could language more clearly teach that the Jewish church was not the church which Jesus came to establish?

On another occasion Jesus said: "Among those that are born of women there is not a greater prophet than John the Baptist: but he that is least in the kingdom of God is greater than he." Luke vii:28. Though John was born of Jewish parentage, and filled with the Holy Spirit from birth (Luke i:15), a prophet, sent of God (John i:6), than whom there was not a greater, yet he that was least in the kingdom was greater than he. He lived and died out of the kingdom or church for which he prepared materials, because he died before it was established; but had the Jewish church been the one for which he prepared material, there would have been none greater than he in it, for there was none greater born of women, and he was born in it. When the Pharisees and Sadducees came to John, demanding baptism of him, he said: "Think not to say within yourselves, We have Abraham to our father: for I say unto you, that God is able of these stones to raise up children unto Abraham." Matt. iii:9. Does not this language imply that these Pharisees and Sadducees had set up peculiar claims on account of Abrahamic descent? And truly their claims would have been just, had the theory under consideration been true. If the Jewish and Christian churches were the same, and persons are to be baptized because in the church, surely they were in the Jewish church; were born members of it, and would have been entitled to baptism as such. Was it not, therefore, cruel in John to thus rebuke them; even cruel as we when we refuse to baptize infants because in the church? On one occasion Jesus said to the disciples: "Except ye be converted, and become as little children, ye shall not enter into the kingdom of heaven." Matt. xviii:3. Though the disciples of the Lord were selected from those prepared by John whose ministry was confined to the "lost sheep of the house of Israel," yet at the time Jesus used the language quoted they were not in the kingdom or church which Jesus came to establish, for the very good reason that it did not then exist. But with what propriety could Jesus have used such language had the Jewish church, in which they had lived all their lives, been the kingdom referred to? "Except ye become converted ye shall not enter a kingdom or church in which you have been all your lives." My blessed Lord never talked such nonsense. Other examples might be given, but these are deemed sufficient to show that those who were born and raised in the Jewish church, had nevertheless to enter the church of God or die out of it; and this fact is conclusive proof that they can not be identical. Similar in some respects they were, but identical they can not be.

But they are both called the *church*. Yes, but this proves not their identity, for different things are often called by the same name. How many different organizations are there now claiming to be the *church?* Joshua was called Jesus, so was Christ; yet they were not the same person. Joshua was called a Priest, so was Aaron, yet they were not the same person. Baalam was called a prophet, so were Elisha, Isaiah, John, Jesus, and many others, but still they were not identical; so Stephen speaks of the church in the wilderness, and Paul speaks of the church of God at Corinth, yet this proves not that they spake of the same organization. The Greek word *ekklesia*, from which we have the word *church*, means *called out;* hence, as God called the Jews out of bondage and separated them from the Egyptians, they were called the church in the wilderness; but they were not the church in our sense of this word. While there were some good people among them, yet, in the main, they were wicked, ungrateful, and idolatrous, lacking all the elements of character which should characterize the spiritual church of God. The word *assembly,* in Acts xix:34, is from the same word, *ekklesia*, rendered church, and is used to designate a rabble that would have taken Paul's life. Hence, the mere occurrence of the word can not identify the same church. The word *ekklesia* is variously rendered church, congregation, assembly, etc.; and we can only learn whether it is applied to a lawless mob, a political assembly, or a religious organization, from the context. Why, then, should the application of this word to the Jewish nation prove it to the church of God? Surely it can not.

But we are referred to the olive-tree, which is claimed to have been a figure of the Jewish church, into which the Gentiles were engrafted; hence it is but the same church under both dispensations. As this is an important argument, let us somewhat carefully examine it. Paul says: "For if the first-fruit be holy, the lump is also holy, . . . And if some of the branches be broken off, and thou, being a wild olive-tree, wert graffed in among them, and with them partakest of the root and fatness of the olive-tree; boast not against the branches. But if thou boast, thou bearest not the root, but the root thee. Thou will say then, The branches were broken off, that I might be graffed in. Well; because of unbelief they were broken off; and thou standest by faith. Be not highminded, but fear; for if God spared not the natural branches, take heed lest he spare not thee. Behold therefore the goodness and severity of God; on them which fell, severity; but toward thee, goodness, if thou continue in his goodness: otherwise thou also shalt be cut off. And they also, if they abide not still in unbelief, shall be graffed in: for God is able to graff them in again. For if thou wert cut out of the olive-tree which is wild by nature, and wert graffed contrary to nature into a good olive-tree; how much more shall these, which be the natural branches, be graffed into their own olive-tree?" Rom. xi:16-24.

In the first place, we remark that this passage says not a word about when the good olive-tree began, whether in the days of Abraham or on the day of Pentecost. In the next place, the natural and unnatural branches were supported by the *root*, and alike had to be graffed in. In the next place, those broken off were broken off for unbelief and those who stood, stood by faith. Infants can not exercise faith, nor is it probable that they are rejected for unbelief; hence, it can not apply to them in any sense. And if this good olive-tree represents the church, it is certain that it can not represent the Jewish church, because its branches stood by faith and were rejected for unbelief. Infants were in the Jewish church, hence the olive-tree could not represent it. The root, which gave support to all the members or branches, represents Christ. Isaiah says: "And in that day there shall be a root of Jesse, which shall stand for an ensign of the people; to it shall the Gentiles seek." Isa. xi:10. Paul quotes this language in this same letter to the Romans as fulfilled in Christ. He says: "Esais saith, There shall be a root of Jesse, and he that shall rise to reign over the Gentiles; in him shall the Gentiles trust." Rom. xv:12. The same thought is presented in the figure of the vine and its branches. Jesus says: "I am the true vine, and my Father is the husbandman. Every branch in me that beareth not fruit he taketh away: and every branch that beareth fruit, he purgeth it, that it may bring forth more fruit. Now ye are clean through the word which I have spoken unto you. Abide in me, and I in you. As the branch can not bear fruit of itself, except it abide in the vine; no more can ye, except ye abide in me. I am the vine, ye are the branches." John xv:1-5. Jesus, as the promised seed of Abraham in whom all nations were to be blessed, was the root of the good olive-tree or church established on the day of Pentecost among the Jews or natural descendants of Abraham, who very soon went back into Judaism and rejected the Messiah, and were thus broken off for their unbelief, and the Gentiles were brought in, and to-day stand by faith; but the Jews are not yet graffed in again, because they abide still in unbelief. But as all the members stand by faith, or fall by unbelief, infants are entirely out of the question. It can not embrace them. But we are referred to the language of James: "After this I will build again the tabernacle of David, which is fallen down; and I will build again the ruins thereof, and I will set it up." Acts xv:16. It is assumed that the tabernacle of David here means the Jewish church. But what may we not prove by assumption? Isaiah says: "And in mercy shall the throne be established: and he shall sit upon it in truth in the tabernacle of David, judging, and seeking judgment, and hasting righteousness." Isa. xvi:5. The throne of David was long unoccupied by any descendant of his, and it was predicted that that throne should be re-established in his family. Hence says Peter: "Therefore being a prophet, and knowing that God had sworn with an oath to him, that of the fruit of his loins, according to the flesh, he would raise up Christ to sit on his throne." Acts ii:30. Thus the tabernacle of David was simply the family of David, from which Christ was raised up to sit upon his throne—Christ was the fruit of his loins, according to the flesh. It had no allusion to such a thing as the church of David. Did David have a church? Mr. Robinson, a celebrated Pedobaptist Lexicographer, in defining the Greek word from which we have the word tabernacle in the above quotation, says: "Metaphorically, for the family, or royal line of David, fallen into weakness and decay." Louisville Debate, p. 78.

It occurs to us that if the Jewish church and the Christian church are the same, the Jews' religion and the Christian religion are the same. Paul was zealous in the Jews' religion while persecuting Christians. He says: "My manner of life from my youth, which was at the first among mine own nation at Jerusalem, knew all the Jews; which knew me from the beginning, if they would testify, that after the straitest sect of our religion I lived a Pharisee." Acts xxvi:4, 5. And again: "For ye have heard of my conversation in time past in the Jews' religion, how that beyond measure I persecuted the church of God, and wasted it: and profited in the Jews' religion above many my equals in mine own nation, being more exceedingly zealous of the traditions of my fathers." Gal. i:13, 14. Once more: "I persecuted the church of God." 1 Cor. xv:9. From these quotations it is evident that the Jewish and Christian religions differed very widely. While Paul was a rigid adherent to the Jewish religion, he was a most fanatical persecutor of the Christian religion. Nor will it change the argument to admit that he was mistaken in his views of Christianity, for had he been imbued with the spirit of the Christian religion he could not have given encouragement to the murder of Stephen, and the persecution of Christians, even granting them to have been wicked as he regarded them. The spirit which characterized him as a Jew, is not the spirit of Christianity at all. And while at this point, we would refer the reader to the sermon on the mount, where he may find a most wonderful and striking contrast in the principles of the Jewish and Christian religions. While one was a system of retaliation, sensuality, and revenge, the other is a system of love, mercy, good for evil, and self-denial. Can fruits so very different be the product of the same religion in the same church? Can the same fountain send forth bitter water and sweet? Surely no two organizations could be more different; and yet infant baptism derives its chief support from their supposed identity.

But we propose to show that there was no such thing as infant membership in the church in the days of the apostles. Paul says: "Those members of the body which seem to be more feeble are necessary." 1 Cor. xii:22. Are infants the more feeble members? If so, for what are they necessary? "That the members should have the same care one for another." Verse 25. What care has an infant for any one as a member of the church of God? "And whether one member suffer, all the members suffer with it; or one member be honored, all the members rejoice with it." Verse 26. *All the members* sympathize with each other in time of distress; and rejoice in times of honor with the honored ones. They rejoice with them that rejoice, and weep with them that weep. Infants can not do this, and as all did do it, there could have been no infants among them. We are aware that the word *all* must sometimes be understood in a limited sense, but we are not sure that it may be so understood here. The language seems to *individualize* the whole body. When *one member* suffers *all the members* suffer with it. When *one member* rejoices *all* rejoice.

When Ananias and Sapphira were put to death, it is said that "Great fear came upon all the church." Acts v:11. Were the little infants alarmed lest some great calamity should come upon the church? If not, none were in the church at that time, for such was the feeling of the church—*all the church*.

When the difficulty arose concerning circumcision, and Paul and Barnabas placed the matter before the church at Jerusalem, it pleased "the apostles and elders, with the WHOLE CHURCH, to send chosen men of their own company to Antioch with Paul and Barnabas." Acts xv:22. We know that the church may do things without every member engaging in the work, but in such cases it could not be said that it pleased the WHOLE church. When it is said that the WHOLE church did a thing, we are inclined to think that every member, great and small, engaged in it. Infants could not take part in such a settlement as the one referred to, and as the *whole church* did take part in, and sanction what was done, it follows that there were no infants in the church.

Paul gives us an instructive lesson on this subject: He says: "From whom the whole body fitly joined together and compacted by that which every joint supplieth, according to the effectual working in the measure of every part, maketh increase of the body unto the edifying of itself in love." Eph. iv:16. Here we learn that the great business of the church is to edify itself and convert sinners, that it may increase the number of the saved in the body. And in order to do this, *every joint* must supply some assistance, that the *whole body* be engaged in the work. The apostle declares that there must be an *effectual working* in the measure of *every part*. We not only have the *whole body* here engaged, but *every part* is *effectually working*. Can infants effectually work for the salvation of men and the edification of the church? If not, they have no place in it.

Peter says: "Ye also, as lively stones, are built up a spiritual house, a holy priesthood, to offer up spiritual sacrifices, acceptable to God by Jesus Christ." 1 Pet. ii:5. The church is not made of dead, inactive material, but of active, lively members who can work in God's building. They are spiritual priests, whose business it is to offer spiritual sacrifices—not mere lumps of flesh, without any spirituality connected with them. Can infants be thus actively engaged as lively stones in this great spiritual temple? If not, they have no place in it. There is no function belonging to the body which they can perform, unless it be to *weep* with them that weep. They do not know the Lord, and hence can not make spiritual sacrifices to Him, and therefore, have no place in the church of God on the earth.

We come now to examine the argument based upon the assumption that baptism came in the room of circumcision, and as infants were circumcised in the Jewish church they must now be baptized. Though in former days this was regarded as the chief argument supporting the practice, it has become about obsolete. Watson, in his "Institutes," makes it his strongest argument, and so did Rice, Hughey, and other debators; yet Mr. Ditzler says they were all wrong—that baptism did not come in the room of circumcision, and that the argument drawn from that source must be abandoned. He, though the recognized champion in Pedobaptist ranks, makes no argument based upon that hypothesis in support of his practice. Is not this significant? When a practice is to be supported for a time from one stand-point, and when driven from it, positions are shifted, and the same practice supported from other considerations, equally doubtful, we are inclined to regard it as of doubtful authority, and hard to defend, to say the least of it.

But why shall we consume time in the examination of an obsolete argument? Because it still has a place in the standard works and text-books of the various parties who practice infant baptism, and some may still be inclined to regard it as important, for long cherished arguments are usually abandoned reluctantly. But as this argument has its root in the doctrine of the identity of the Jewish and Christian churches, it necessarily falls with that theory. We will, however, present some additional arguments, designed to show that baptism did not come in the room of circumcision.

1. Circumcision was confined to the Jews, and those purchased with money by them; baptism is for all nations.

2. Circumcision was to be performed on native Jews at eight days old; baptism is for any age capable of believing the gospel.

3. Circumcision was confined to males only; baptism is for men and women. If baptism came in the room of circumcision, why baptize females?

4. Circumcision applied to those bought with money; baptism has no such application. No Christian man thinks of baptizing a servant, simply because of purchase; but why not, if baptism came in the room of circumcision?

5. No faith was required as a qualification for circumcision; but believers only are baptized. When the eunuch demanded baptism of Philip, the answer was: "If thou believest with all thy heart, thou mayest," clearly implying that if he did not believe he should not be baptized.

6. Circumcision was not an initiatory ordinance, but was for such as were already members of the Jewish family; and if not circumcised he was to be cut off from his people. Gen. xvii:14. Baptism, properly administered, admits or introduces the subject into the kingdom of God (John iii:5); therefore, baptism did not come in the room of circumcision.

7. Circumcision showed a man to be a Jew; baptism shows a man to be neither a Jew nor a Gentile, but a Christian only.

8. Baptism is administered in the name of the Father, Son, and Holy Spirit. Circumcision was not thus administered.

9. Baptism is administered to show the burial and resurrection of Christ. Circumcision was not administered for this purpose, because these events had not transpired when it was instituted, nor for many hundred years afterward.

10. Circumcision placed a man under obligations to do the whole law; baptism frees us from bondage, and puts no one under the law of Moses; hence it came not in the room of circumcision.

11. Baptism is administered for the remission of sins (Acts ii:38); circumcision had no such object.

12. Baptism is for the answer of a good conscience (1 Peter iii:21); circumcision had nothing to do with the conscience, but pertained wholly to the flesh.

13. Those baptized went on their way *rejoicing* (Acts viii:39;

xvi:34); we imagine that those who were circumcised were usually taken away crying. Therefore they were not much alike.

14. Circumcision was obedience to the law of Moses (John vii:23); baptism is obedience to the gospel of Jesus Christ.

15. No one can be a scriptural subject of baptism who is not first taught the gospel; but many were circumcised before they were old enough to be taught any thing.

16. The gift of the Holy Spirit was promised to those baptized on the day of Pentecost (Acts ii:38); this gift was never promised to any for being circumcised, or, as following it.

This list of distinctions might be extended much further, but these are enough to show, to every reflecting mind, that there is not a shadow of resemblance in baptism to circumcision, and that one came not in the room of the other. But there arose a difficulty in the church in the days of the apostles concerning circumcision, which it seems to us would have been a good time to have settled this whole question. "Certain men which came down from Judea taught the brethren, and said, Except ye be circumcised after the manner of Moses, ye can not be saved. When therefore Paul and Barnabas had no small dissension and disputation with them, they determined that Paul and Barnabas, and certain other of them, should go up to Jerusalem unto the apostles and elders about this question. And when they were come to Jerusalem, they were received of the church, and of the apostles and elders, and they declared all things that God had done with them. But there rose up certain of the sect of the Pharisees which believed, saying, That it was needful to circumcise them, and to command them to keep the law of Moses. And the apostles and elders came together for to consider of this matter." Acts xv:1-6. Had the apostles only thought of the fact that circumcision had given place to baptism, which had taken its place, they would have answered something after the following style: "Brethren, there need be no difficulty about circumcision, for baptism has come in its place, and hence you need only now be baptized, and have your children baptized, in place of having them circumcised, as under the law." Would not such an answer have been most natural under the circumstances? Did they so answer? Peter said: "Why tempt ye God, to put a yoke upon the neck of the disciples, which neither our fathers nor we were able to bear?" Verse 10. But he said not a word about baptism in room of circumcision. After due deliberation these inspired teachers wrote an answer as follows: "The apostle, and elders, and brethren, send greeting unto the brethren which are of the Gentiles in Antioch, and Syria, and Cilicia: Forasmuch as we have heard, that certain which went out from us have troubled you with words, subverting your souls, saying, Ye must be circumcised, and keep the law; to whom we gave no such commandment; it seemed good to us, being assembled with one accord, to send chosen men unto you with our beloved Barnabas and Paul. * * * For it seemed good to the Holy Ghost, and to us, to lay upon you no greater burden than these necessary things: that ye abstain from meats offered to idols, and from blood, and from things strangled, and from fornication; from which if ye keep yourselves, ye shall do well. Fare ye well." Verses 23-29. Now, be it observed that this letter was written by the apostles and elders, from the church at Jerusalem, who had duly considered the question of circumcision, and it *was approved by the Holy Spirit;* and yet it contains not a word about baptism coming in the room of circumcision; and circumcision was the very thing about which the difficulty arose! Would a Pedobaptist council now write thus? Would they not more probably write something after the following style: "Brethren, you need not now be circumcised, for baptism has taken its place. If you, therefore, have your children baptized and abstain from circumcision, you shall do well?" Paul labors this question at great length in his letter to the Galatians, who were inclined to go back to the law. He says: "Stand fast therefore in the liberty wherewith Christ hath made us free, and be not entangled again with the yoke of bondage. Behold, I Paul say unto you, that if ye be circumcised, Christ shall profit you nothing; for I testify again to every man that is circumcised, that he is a debtor to do the whole law. Christ is become of no effect unto you. Whosoever of you are justified by the law, ye are fallen from grace. For we through the Spirit wait for the hope of righteousness by faith; for in Jesus Christ neither circumcision availeth any thing, nor uncircumcision, but faith which worketh by love." Gal. v:1-6. Is it not strange that, while Paul was making this argument to keep his brethren from being circumcised, he never once thought of the fact that baptism came in the room of circumcision? Had he informed them of this fact it would have settled the question forever. But he could think of every other argument except this, the most important of all. He told them it was a yoke of bondage, from which to keep themselves free; that if circumcised they would have to keep the whole law; that they would lose all their hopes of salvation through Christ; that they would fall from grace; that in Christ circumcision could not avail them any thing; all this, but never once said, "Brethren, you need not be circumcised, for baptism has taken its place." Why did he not think of it? Will the reader think of it?

But we insist that baptism did not come in the room of circumcision from another consideration: both were in force, under the same covenant, among the same people, at the same time. We have seen that circumcision was instituted in the family of Abraham for the Jewish nation, and that the covenant to which it belonged was not taken out of the way until the death of Christ; hence it was in force up to the time of His death. John's ministry was confined to the Jews, and ended before Christ began to preach. See Matt. iv:12-17. Then, John's ministry began and ended during the existence of the covenant of circumcision; and his baptism and Jewish circumcision were both binding among the same people at the same time—with this difference only: infants were circumcised at eight days old; those only were baptized who had sinned and were willing to confess and forsake their sins. As circumcision and John's baptism were both in force at the same time, under the same covenant among the same people, how could one be in the place of the other?

Again: If baptism came in the room of circumcision, why was it necessary for Jews who had been circumcised to still be baptized? We have stated that John's ministry was confined to the Jews who had been circumcised, and yet he baptized vast numbers of them. The Pharisees were the straitest sect of the Jews, and were so zealous for the law of circumcision that they even wanted to bind it upon Gentiles after conversion to Christianity, and yet the "Pharisees and lawyers rejected the counsel of God against themselves, being not baptized of him." Luke vii:30. It may be that they made their objection to John's baptism because they had been circumcised; we suppose not; but whether they did or did not, one thing is certain; namely, it was the counsel of God that they should be baptized notwithstanding their circumcision. On the day of Pentecost the gospel was preached to Jews, who were commanded to repent and be baptized in the name of Jesus Christ, and three thousand of them were baptized, though, as Jews, they had all been circumcised. And Paul was a Pharisee, brought up at the feet of Gamaliel, and taught according to the perfect manner of the law touching which he was blameless; yet, under special instructions from the Lord, Ananias commanded him to "be baptized and wash away his sins." Acts xxii:16. Might he not have expostulated with the man of God thus: "Sir, I am a Jew, and have been circumcised; and as baptism came in the room of circumcision, however, important it may be to a Gentile, it can not be obligatory on me, as I have complied with the rite in the room of which it came, and for which it is a substitute? Why should I submit to the substitute, having received the original?" Surely, such a plea would have been in harmony with the theory. But, as no such plea was made by any Jew, but every one of them converted to the faith of the gospel had to be baptized notwithstanding his circumcision, we conclude that circumcision passed away with the old covenant, of which it was a part, and that baptism has no connection with it whatever. Indeed, as circumcision belonged to the old covenant which has passed away, baptism can not be in the place of circumcision, for it has no place. The covenant in which it had a place being gone, it would be quite as sensible to speak of a man having a place in a house which had been burned to ashes. A place in the house he may have had when it *was* a house, but when it ceased to exist he could no longer have a place in it. So, when the covenant to which circumcision belonged passed away its place passed away, and it is idle to talk of any thing coming in and filling its place. *It has no place* only in Jewish history.

But it is said that circumcision was a seal of the Jewish covenant, and that baptism is the seal of the new covenant, hence one is in the place of the other—*i.e.*, baptism sustains the same relationship to the new covenant which circumcision sustained to the old. Well, let us examine this theory. And, first, the reader will note the fact that this argument—or, rather, theory—abandons the whole doctrine of church identity based upon an identity of the covenants. Waving this, however, we will examine the theory upon its merits. God said: "And ye shall circumcise the flesh of your foreskin; and it shall be a token of the covenant betwixt me and you." Gen. xvii:11. Here we find circumcision called a *token*, but not a seal of the covenant. Paul says Abraham "received the sign of circumcision, a seal of the righteousness of the faith which he had yet being uncircumcised; that he might be the father of all them that believe, though they be not circumcised." Rom. iv:11. Here circumcision was a seal of the righteousness of Abraham's faith, not a seal of the covenant. And circumcision was to Abraham what it was to no other Jew. It was a seal of the righteousness of the faith which he had *before* he was circumcised. How much faith could a Jewish infant have before it was eight days old? Of course, none at all; and hence, circumcision could not seal the righteousness of the faith of those who had no faith.

But is baptism the seal of the new covenant? If so, where is the scripture which proves or teaches it? As to the covenant itself, it came nearer being sealed by the blood of Jesus Christ than by baptism; and the subjects are sealed by the Holy Spirit. Paul says: "In whom ye also trusted after that ye heard the word of truth, the gospel of your salvation; in whom also, after that ye believed, ye were sealed with the Holy Spirit of promise." Eph. i:13. And again: "Grieve not the Holy Spirit of God, whereby ye are sealed unto the day of redemption." Eph. iv:30. Thus we see that persons converted to God under the new covenant are sealed with the Holy Spirit, and not by baptism; nor is it even once called the seal, or a seal in all the book of God. Hence, if any thing sustains the same relation to the new covenant which circumcision did to the old, as taught by Pedobaptists, it is the Holy Spirit. Thus, were we to grant that circumcision was the seal of the Jewish covenant—or, rather, were it true— it would only be another evidence that baptism did not come in its place, for baptism is not a seal, nor is it anywhere called one. It comes much nearer performing, under the new covenant, the office which the natural birth did to a Jew under the old. Natural birth introduced a Jew into the Jewish commonwealth, or so-called church, and a birth of water and Spirit introduces men and women into the kingdom or church of God. Hence, there *is* some analogy between the natural birth of a Jew and the new birth which makes a man a child of God or a Christian, but none whatever between baptism and Jewish circumcision.

But suppose we admit, for a moment, that circumcision was the seal of the Jewish covenant, and that it is still in force, the seal being changed to baptism, then it follows that every Jew who is baptized is twice sealed in the same covenant—once with the sign of circumcision and once in baptism. Hence, if circumcision and baptism may be, and were administered to the same subject under the same covenant, why will not Pedobaptists rebaptize those who become dissatisfied with a baptism received in infancy? If the same persons may be twice sealed in the same covenent—once by circumcision, and again by baptism after it became a substitute for the former, then we see not why others may not be twice sealed by baptism upon the same principle. If they may receive the original and then the substitute, why not twice receive the substitute? Those who can, may explain; we can not.

We close our examination of the covenants with Paul's allegory. He says: "Tell me, ye that desire to be under the law, do ye not hear the law? For it is written, that Abraham had two sons, the one by a bond-maid and the other by a free woman. But he that was of the bond-woman was born after the flesh; but he of the free woman was by promise; which things are an allegory; for these are the two covenants; for this Agar is mount Sinai in Arabia, and answereth to Jerusalem which now is and is in bondage with her children, but Jerusalem which is above is free, which is the mother of us all. For it is written, Rejoice, thou barren that bearest not; break forth and cry, thou that travaileth not: for the desolate hath many more children than she which hath a husband. Now we, brethren, as Isaac was, are the children of promise. But as then he that was born after the flesh persecuted him that was born after the Spirit, even as it is now. Nevertheless what saith the scripture? Cast out the bond-woman and her son: for the son of the bond-woman shall not be heir with the son of the free woman. So, then, brethren, we are not children of the bond-woman, but of the free." Gal. iv:21-31.

In this allegory, Abraham's bond-woman Hagar represents the covenant made at Sinai, and his lawful wife Sarah represents the new covenant, of which Jesus Christ is the mediator. Each of these women had a son by Abraham. Hagar's son was born after the flesh, Sarah's son Isaac was given her by promise when she was past age. The question arose whether the child of the bond-woman should inherit Abraham's estate equal with the son of the free. God decided that he should not be heir with the son of the free woman, and ordered the bond-woman and her son to be cast out. Paul uses this circumstance to illustrate the two covenants. As the Sinaitic covenant required no spiritual qualifications for membership but a birth of flesh only, it was fitly represented by the woman whose son was born according to the flesh, and was rejected. But as the new covenant required spiritual qualifications for membership, and conferred spiritual blessings upon the subjects of it through Christ, it was fitly represented by the lawful wife, whose son Isaac was the child of promise and the seed of Abraham, from whom Christ the mediator of the new covenant should come. And Paul says we, as Isaac was, are the children of promise; not children of the bond-woman, but of the free. As the free woman represented the new covenant and we are children of the free woman, it follows that we are children of the new covenant represented by the free woman, whose children we are. And as God commanded to cast out the bond-woman and her son, which represented the old covenant and its membership, it follows that no one can inherit the spiritual privileges of the new covenant as a subject of the one which has waxed old and been cast out with its membership.

Nor will it do to assume that this bond-woman simply represented the covenant made at Sinai, but did not include the covenant made with Abraham, for we have already seen that the covenant made with Abraham was renewed with Isaac, Jacob, and Moses (See Deut. xxix:19); and even the covenant of circumcision originally given to Abraham was incorported in and became part of the law of Moses. Jesus says: "If a man on the sabbath day receive circumcision, that the law of Moses should not be broken; are ye angry at me, because I have made a man every whit whole on the sabbath day?" John vii:23. Then, as circumcision, which Pedobaptists tell us was the seal of the Abrahamic covenant, became part of the law of Moses or covenant made at Sinai, surely the covenant did also, for the seal would not have been transferred without the covenant to which it belonged. Then, as these were merged into the covenant made at Sinai, which was represented by the bond-woman and her son who were cast out, it follows that that covenant and the Jewish church based upon it, with its membership, are gone, forever gone. "So, then, brethren, we are not children of the bond-woman, but of the free," thank God.

We come now to examine the argument based upon *Jewish proselyte baptism*. It is assumed that the Jews, from the days of Jacob until now, have baptized female proselytes, and both baptized and circumcised male proselytes; and when they baptized parents they also baptized their children. The theory appears to be somewhat inconsistent, to say the least of it. Both circumcision and baptism practiced at the same time, among the same people, upon the same subjects, under the same covenant, and yet one came in the room of the other! Really, if both were in existence from the days of Jacob until the coming of the Messiah, it would seem that if He did any thing with them He rather consolidated them than substituted one for the other. Among the Jews, it seems that each is in its own place, for if both were practiced under the old covenant, each had a place; and as both are practiced now, we suppose they have not changed places yet. But as Pedobaptists admit that circumcision has passed away, but contend that baptism has taken its place, we feel a little curious to know what place it filled under the old covenant when circumcision was in its own place. If baptism is the *seal* under the new covenant, what office did it fill in the old covenant when circumcision was the seal? Leaving those who advocate the theories to harmonize them at their leisure, we propose to examine the testimony concerning the baptism of Jewish proselytes, and see whether or not it was practiced from the days of Jacob, or even before the days of John the Baptist. And we will first hear what eminent Pedobaptists, who have given the subject a careful and thorough examination, say about:

1. "Part of John's office consisted in baptizing—an external

rite, then in a particular manner appointed of God, and *not used before.*" Venema, in Booth Abridged, p. 161.

2. When speaking of John the Baptist and his ministry, Gerhardus asks: "Who would have embraced that *new and hitherto unusual ceremony, baptism,* without sufficient previous information." Gerhardus, in Booth Abridged, p. 161.

3. *"Why, then, baptizest thou?"* Hence, it appears the Jews were not ignorant that there should be some alteration in the rites of religion under the Messiah, which they might easily learn from Jer. xxxi. John most pertinently answers, professing that he was not the author, but only the administrator, of this *new rite.*" Beza, in Booth Abridged, p. 161.

4. "The baptism of proselytes, in our opinion, seems to have been received by the Jews after the time of John the Baptist, being very much influenced by his authority, and greatly admiring him. Certainly, it can not be proved by any substantial testimony, that it was in use among the Jews before the time of John." Deylingius, in Booth, p. 162.

5. "In fine, we are destitute of any early testimony to the practice of proselyte baptism antecedently to the Christian era. The original institution of admitting Jews to the covenant, and strangers to the same, prescribed no other rite than that of circumcision. No account of any other is found in the Old Testament; none in the Apocrypha, New Testament, Targums of Onkelos, Jonathan, Joseph the Blind, or in the work of any other Targumist, excepting Pseudo-Jonathan, whose work belongs to the seventh or eighth centuries. No evidence is found in Philo, Josephus, or any of the earlier Christian writers. How could an allusion to such a rite have escaped them all if it were as common and as much required by usage as circumcision?" Stuart on Baptism, p. 140.

Again he says: "Be this as it may, or be the origin of proselyte baptism as it may, I can not see that there is any adequate evidence for believing that it existed contemporarily with the baptism of John and of Jesus. But what has all this to do with the question, What was the ancient mode of baptism? Much; for it is on all hands conceded that, so far as the testimony of the Rabbis can decide such a point, the baptism of proselytes among the Jews was by immersion. * * * It is, therefore, a matter of no little interest, so far as our question is concerned, to inquire whether Christian baptism had its origin from the proselyte baptism of the Jews. This we have done, and have come to this result, viz.: that there is no certainty that such was the case, but that the probability, on the ground of evidence, is strong against it." *Ibid,* p. 142.

6. "But independently of its supposed scriptural sanction, an attempt has been made to prove this usage in the apostolic age, upon the alleged fact that the Jews then baptized proselytes from heathenism. Now, this alleged fact of the baptism of proselytes is very uncertain, and, even if admitted, would by no means establish the apostolic usage of infant baptism. The baptism of proselytes is first mentioned in the Mishna, a collection of Jewish traditions, completed in the third century [A.D. 219]; and the usage there mentioned (baptism of adults and infants) might have been derived, directly or indirectly, from Christians." Dr. Blunt, in Louisville Debate, p. 105.

With regard to the silence of Josephus on the subject, Dr. Blunt very justly remarks: "But whether this supposed Jewish usage existed at all (among Jews or Christians) in the apostolic age is uncertain. It is not mentioned by Josephus, even when we might fairly expect that it would have been recorded—as when he relates that the Idumeans were received among the Jewish people by circumcision, without mentioning baptism. Were the usage undoubted, it would only have been an unauthorized addition to the scriptural command, since it was by circumcision only that proselytes were to be added to the Jewish Church. Ex. xii:48." *Ut supra.*

On this subject Prof. Stuart says: "Nay, there is one passage in Josephus which seems to afford strong ground of suspicion that the rite in question was unknown at a period not long antecedent to the time of the apostles. This author is relating the history of John Hyrcanus, high priest and king of the Jews, a zealous Pharisee, and one who, according to Josephus, was favored with divine revelations. He says that Hyrcanus took certain cities from the Idumeans; 'And he commanded, after subduing all the Idumeans, that they should remain in their country if they would circumcise themselves and conform to the Jewish customs. Then they, through love of their country, underwent circumcision, and submitted to other modes of living which were Jewish; and from that time they became Jews.' Ant. xiii:9, 1." Stuart on Baptism, p. 129.

Now, is it not a little strange that Josephus should mention the circumcision of persons who became Jews, and say not one word about their baptism, when, if the Jews both circumcised and baptized their proselytes, they must have baptized these very persons which he speaks of being circumcised?

But we are not done with the testimony of Dr. Blunt yet. He says: "It is, however, very unlikely that the Jews would adopt the usage of baptism from the Christians; and the Mishna being founded on previous collections reaching to the apostolic age, there is just a probability that at the time of our Lord and His apostles the Jewish custom prevailed of baptizing proselytes and their children. Even admitting this, yet before this custom can be alleged in proof or confirmation of apostolic usage, it must be proved that the Jewish custom was adopted by our Lord and His apostles; but of this neither the Scriptures nor the early fathers offered any proof whatever. Besides, it should be considered that the baptism of proselytes widely differs in theory from the Christian doctrine of baptism. The convert to Judaism was baptized, and all his family then born; but if he had children born afterward, they were not baptized, the previous baptism of their parents being deemed sufficient." Blunt, in Louisville Debate, p. 105.

Thus testify Pedobaptists themselves on the whole question of Jewish proselyte baptism; and so far from tracing it back to the days of Jacob, it goes back to sometime in the third century, when even the church, to say nothing of Judiasm, was full of heresy and corruption. From that time it has been practiced as claimed by Pedobaptists, but all behind that is doubt and speculation.

But Dr. Robinson says: "Purifications of proselytes indeed there were, but there never was any such ceremony as baptism in practice before the time of John. If such a rite had existed, the regular priests, and not John, would have administered it, and there would have been no need of a new and extraordinary appointment from heaven to give being to an old established custom; nor would it have been decent for John, or any other man, to treat native Jews—especially Jesus, who had no paganism to put away—as pagan proselytes were treated. This uninteresting subject hath produced voluminous disputes, which may be fairly cut short by demanding at the outset substantial proof of the fact that the Jews *baptized* proselytes *before* the time of John—which can never be done." Robinson, in Louisville Debate, p. 104.

Again, the same author says: "The modest Dr. Benson was pleased to add that he wished to see all these difficulties cleared up, and that he could not answer all that Dr. Wall and Mr. Emlyn had said in support of proselyte baptism; but, with all possible deference to this most excellent critic, it may be truly said he hath, by stating his difficulties, fully answered both these writers; for what they call proselyte baptism was *not* baptism, and if there was *no* institution of such a washing as they call baptism in the Old Testament, and no mention of such a thing in the Apocrypha, or in Josephus, or in Philo, what, at this age of the world, signify the conjectures of a Lightfoot, and a Wall, or even an Emlyn?"

On the subject of Jewish washings, which some have been inclined to call baptism, he says: "A fact it is, beyond all contradiction, that this same proselyte washing, which learned men have thought fit to call baptism, is no baptism at all, but, as Dr. Benson truly says, a very different thing, and that in which infants could have no share. It was a person's washing himself, and not the dipping of one person by another." Robinson, in Louisville Debate, p. 104.

We could well afford to rest the argument with the authors quoted, but at the risk of being tedious we will offer a few thoughts for the consideration of the reader not suggested in the foregoing quotations.

These authors concede that the Bible furnishes not a trace of authority for the baptism of proselytes by the Jews, nor any account of a single example of it. Surely, then, divine authority can not be claimed for it; hence, it can furnish no authority for the baptism of infants, though we were to grant that it had been practiced from the days of Adam. If the practice began with man, without divine sanction, how can it furnish authority for any thing? Are we to conclude that the Lord borrowed the idea of baptism from the unauthorized practice of men when He sent John to baptize the people? When Jesus asked the people whether the baptism of John was from heaven or of men, they might have promptly answered that it was of men if it had come from the unauthorized practice of men. And it dare not be assumed that God authorized the practice. Let him that so assumes produce the passage of Holy Writ that proves it. God instituted circumcision, and we can find an account of it, and a record of cases under the law; why can we not do the same as to the baptism of Jewish proselytes? When a stranger would keep the passover among the Jews, God gave the law for it. "When a stranger shall sojourn with thee, and will keep the passover to the Lord, let all his males be circumcised, and then let him come near and keep it; and he shall be as one that is born in the land; for no uncircumcised person shall eat thereof. One law shall be to him that is home-born, and unto the stranger that sojourneth among you." Ex. xii:48, 49. Is it not strange that the Lord did not say: "Let all his males be circumcised, and his *males and females be baptized*, and then let him come near and keep it?" Surely, it would have been a good time to make the suggestion. But it is not contended that native Jews were to be baptized, but only proselytes; and here the Lord says one law shall be to him that is home-born, and unto the stranger; hence, as the home-born were only circumcised, it follows that nothing more was required of strangers, at least to prepare for eating the passover, and we suppose when any one could eat the passover he was in full fellowship. We regard this as settling the question as far as authority is concerned.

But if further proof be desirable, it may be found in the official title of John THE Baptist. If others had been baptizing since the days of Jacob, why call John *the* Baptist? A baptist he might have been, but THE Baptist he could not have been, for the Jewish priests would have been baptists as well as John. Indeed, it would not have required a special appointment from God to authorize John to do that which any Jewish priest could do, and had been doing, for ages.

Is it not a little strange that the Lord should give a commission to the apostles to baptize the nations, and yet leave those who are to submit to it to eliminate their duty from Jewish talmuds and targums in place of from His law? On this subject we wish to give the reader the benefit of a paragraph from the illustrious Booth. He says: "If, therefore, we obtain the useful intelligence about it, so as to help us in settling who are the subjects of our Sovereign's appointment, it must be by having recourse to the Jewish synagogue. Now, is it not far more probable that Christ intended his own commission for the observance of baptism as the *only law* of administration, and the practice of His apostles as the *only example* for His people to follow, than that He should leave either its mode or subjects to be learned from the traditions of an apostate people, or the records of their admired but impious talmuds? Can it be imagined that our Lord should appoint baptism for all his disciples; that He should give them a body of doctrine and a code of law in the New Testament; and, after all, tacitly refer them to the writings of His enemies; those writings which are the register of their own pride, and madness, and shame; writings, too, of which perhaps a great majority of Christians never heard, nor had in their power to read, in order to learn *whom He intended to be baptized?*" Booth Abridged, p. 166.

All the premises considered, it is quite apparent that there was no such thing as the baptism of Jewish proselytes until long after the introduction of Christianity, from which the practice was borrowed by the Jews. If any one thinks he can find an example of Jewish proselyte baptism earlier than two hundred years after John began to baptize, let him name the case, tell who he was, where it was done, and by whom. All this we can do as to John's baptism and Christian baptism from their introduction; why may it not be done with reference to the baptism of Jewish proselytes, if indeed they were baptized at all? As neither command nor example can be produced antedating Christianity, we conclude there was no such practice, and dismiss the subject with the question, upon which the reader may reflect at his leisure, whether it is more likely that the Lord borrowed the idea of baptism from an unauthorized Jewish custom, or whether the Jews borrowed the practice from John and primitive Christians?

We congratulate the reader upon his escape from Jewish covenants, talmuds, targums, and antiquated rites and ceremonies, and take much pleasure in introducing him to the New Testament, where we may at least find the *word* baptism, baptize, baptist, or some word *akin* to the subject under examination. Baptism is confessedly a New Testament ordinance, and why we should go to Jewish commands, talmuds, targums, any where and every where save the New Testament, to examine a question of purely New Testament origin, is, to say the least, a little strange. As we are in the negative of the question, we must go where others lead; but if the practice of *infant baptism* were clearly taught in the New Testament, it is likely we should be spared the trouble of looking for it elsewhere.

As John was the first to baptize the people, it may be well to see whether or not he baptized any infants. The record says: "Then went out to him Jerusalem, and all Judea, and all the region round about Jordan, and were baptized of him in Jordan, confessing their sins." Matt. iii:5, 6. "John did baptize in the wilderness, and preach the baptism of repentance for the remission of sins. And there went out unto him all the land of Judea, and they of Jerusalem, and were all baptized of him in the river of Jordan, confessing their sins." Mark i:4, 5. "And he came into all the country about Jordan, preaching the baptism of repentance for the remission of sins." Luke iii:3.

These quotations are deemed sufficient to give us a pretty clear view of John's baptism, so far as the present inquiry is concerned. They show us, with great clearness, that John's baptism was *for the remission of sins;* infants have no sins to be remitted, hence it was not for them. Nor could it have been the guilt of original sin, for the removal of which John baptized the people —*i.e.*, the dear babes, for then it must have been, not for the remission of *sins*, but for the remission of *a sin*—Adam's sin. And the scriptures quoted show that the people were all baptized by John in Jordan, confessing THEIR sins, not Adam's sin; hence, it was for the remission of the sins of the people that they were baptized. Again: These persons were not only baptized for the remission of sins, but they *confessed* their sins. This infants could not do, hence there were no infants baptized by John. Paul says: "John verily baptized with the baptism of repentance, saying unto the people that they should believe on him which should come after him; that is, on Christ Jesus." Acts xix:4.

Thus we see that faith in a coming Saviour was enjoined by John upon those he baptized. Infants could not have appreciated such preaching or exercised such faith, therefore they were not subjects of John's ministry. Finally: John preached the baptism of repentance; that is, it was a baptism which belonged to and grew out of repentance; infants can not repent, therefore the baptism of repentance was not for them. Collating these items, then, we find that John preached—the people heard, believed, repented, confessed their sins, and were baptized by John for the remission of them. Infants were not competent to do these things, hence they were not the subjects of John's preaching or baptism.

We come now to an examination of the commission given by the Lord, a record of which we have by Matthew in the following words: "All power is given unto me in heaven and in earth; go ye, therefore, and teach all nations, baptizing them in the name of the Father, and of the Son, and of the Holy Ghost; teaching them to observe all things whatsoever I have commanded you." Matt. xxviii:18-20.

This is truly an important text and well deserves our most serious consideration. John's mission was confined to the Jews, and so was that of the *twelve* and the *seventy* prior to the death of Jesus; now He claims all authority in heaven and on earth, and for the first time authorizes the baptism of the Gentiles. His language, then, must be regarded as *the organic law* of this *divine institution,* and not as a merely incidental allusion to the subject. It not only furnishes authority for baptizing *all nations,* but gives the only formula contained in Holy Writ in which the sacred rite is to be administered. The word teach occurs twice in the passage, and is from different Greek words, a circumstance which has given rise to much speculation on the subject to very little profit. It is insisted that *mathetusate,* rendered teaching, means to *make disciples;* and suppose it does. What is a disciple? A student, or learner; and could there be such a thing as a student without teaching? Where there is a student there must be something to study. Hence, the obvious import of the passage is, *teach* first the elementary principles of the gospel, so that the people may believe in Jesus as the Son of God and Saviour of man; then baptize them into the sacred names of

Father, Son, and Holy Spirit; then further teach them how to live the Christian life.

Mr. Baxter says: *"Go disciple me all nations, baptizing them.* As for those who say they are discipled by baptizing, and not before baptizing, they speak not the sense of that text, or that which is true or rational, if they mean it absolutely as so spoken; else why should one be baptized more than another? This is not a mere occasional or historical mention of baptism, but it is the very commission of Christ to His apostles for preaching and baptizing, and purposely expresseth their several works in their several places and order. Their first task is, by teaching to make disciples, which are by Mark called believers. The second work is, to baptize them, whereto is annexed the promise of their salvation. The third work is to teach them all other things which are afterward to be learned in the school of Christ. To condemn this order is to renounce all rules of order, for where can we expect to find it if not here?" Booth Abridged, p. 202.

Brugonsis says: "Christ commanded first to teach the nations that are strangers to God and the truth; afterward, when they have submitted to the truth, to teach them those precepts and rules of life which are worthy of God and the truth. *The order here observed,* says Jerome, *is excellent. He commands the apostles first to teach all nations; then to dip them with the sacrament of faith; and then to show them how they should behave themselves after their faith and baptism.* Before baptism, they are to be taught the truth of the gospel, especially matters of faith; after baptism, they are to be instructed in the Christian morals, and what concerns their practice." Booth Abridged, pp. 203, 204.

These statements made by Pedobaptists we will regard as so obviously correct that further comment is unnecessary; we will regard this as the settled meaning of the text and make our deductions accordingly.

It is claimed that, as infants compose a part of *all nations,* they are included in the command to "teach and baptize all nations." Will those who make the argument stand by the same rule throughout? The veriest *infidel* that lives is a part of *all nations*—should he be baptized for that reason? Idiots belong to all nations—should they therefore be baptized? If infants should be baptized because they are a part of all nations, then there is not an atheist or an infidel which may not be baptized for the same reason. The phrase *all nations* often occurs in the Scriptures, where only a class is embraced in it. The word *ethne*, rendered nations, occurs about eighty times in the New Testament, where the context clearly shows that infants are not included. There are no less than eight such passages in Matthew's gospel. We will give a few New Testament examples. "Ye shall be hated of all nations." Matt. xxiv:9. "This gospel of the kingdom shall be preached in all the world for a witness unto all nations." Ver. 14. "My house shall be called of all nations the house of prayer." Mark xi:17. "Made known to all nations for the obedience of faith." Rom. xvi:26. "Babylon is fallen, is fallen, that great city, because she made all nations drink of the wine of her fornication." Rev. xiv:8. "All nations shall come and worship before thee." Rev. xv:4. "By thy sorceries were all nations deceived." Rev. xviii:23. Similar examples may be found in the Old Testament. "I will gather all nations against Jerusalem to battle." Zech. xiv:2. Surely, we are not to understand by this that all the *infants, idiots,* and old women of all nations were to enter the army of Titus to fight against Jerusalem. These quotations need only be carefully read to see that in every instance infants were excluded, though the phrase *all nations* was used; then why should the same words necessarily include them in the commission? We think they are just as clearly excluded by the context as they are in either of the texts quoted above. "Go teach all nations, baptizing them." Infants nor idiots are subjects of gospel address, and can not be taught the gospel; hence, if the Lord required the apostles to teach such the gospel, He simply required of them an impossibility.

But worse still: If infants are included in the commission, then it follows that they must all be lost. Mark records the commission thus: "Go ye into all the world, and preach the gospel to every creature; he that believeth and is baptized shall be saved; but he that believeth not shall be damned." Mark xvi:16. Infants can not believe the gospel; hence, if the commission includes them, they must all be damned. The language of Mark is even more comprehensive than that of Matthew. He says teach all nations; Mark says go into *all the world* and preach the gospel to *every creature*. Surely, then, if the phrase *all nations* includes infants, then *every creature in all the world* would none the less include them; and if so, they can not believe; and as those who believe not must be damned, we see no chance for the salvation of one of them according to the Pedobaptist argument based on the commission.

Again: The language of the commission makes faith a necessary antecedent to baptism. Teach the nations, baptizing them —he that believeth and is baptized. Here the inference is clear that unbelievers are not to be baptized; nay, a *want of faith* is sufficient to bar any one from the sacred rite; infants can not believe, and therefore can not be scripturally baptized under this commission. More of this directly.

But we are now ready to make a little advance in the argument. Having seen that the commission does not authorize infant baptism, we respectfully suggest that it very clearly forbids the practice. When God gave specific directions for doing any thing, it was a clear violation of law to do it otherwise. When God commanded Noah to build an ark of *gopher* wood (Gen. vi:14), it clearly implied a prohibition to make it of *cedar* wood; and had he made it of cedar, it would have been as clear a violation of God's law as though he had not made it at all. When God commanded Moses to make a *serpent* of *brass*, and put it upon a pole in the midst of the camps of Israel (Num. xxi:9), it implied a prohibition to hang up a *brazen pot* in the camp. When God commanded a Jew to kill a *red* heifer, he dare not kill a *black* one, because it would have been a clear violation of the law. When God commanded a Jew to offer a ewe lamb of the first year, he dare not offer a male or an old sheep. When God commanded the apostles to teach the nations, baptizing them in the name of the Father, Son, and Holy Spirit, He clearly implied that they were not to baptize into other names; and were any one to baptize into the names of Abraham, Isaac, and Jacob, he would be regarded as an impious violator of God's holy law. Then, when the Lord told the apostles to teach all nations, baptizing them, the taught, the language as clearly implied that they were to baptize *none others*, as did the command to build the ark of gopher wood imply that he was not to make it of cedar wood. Hence, it is just as clear a violation of the commission to baptize an *untaught infant* as though the Lord had expressly forbidden it.

That we are correct in our interpretation of the commission, may be further seen by an examination of the various baptisms recorded in the Acts. That the Lord made faith an indispensable antecedent to baptism is confirmed by the fact that no case can be shown where any were baptized without it. Believers, and *believers* ONLY were baptized by divine authority. With this thought specially before us, let us examine every case on record, and see whether or not we can find an exception. And as we proceed we may note any evidence, of any kind, of the baptism of any infant by divine authority, if any such there be.

1. The first baptism which occurred under the commission just examined was the Pentecostian converts. Peter preached the gospel to the people; thousands heard, understood, and *believed* it; were cut to their hearts, and anxiously inquired what to do. Peter told them to repent and be baptized. He would not have addressed infants thus, for they could not repent; nor will it do to assume that some were infants, for the command says *every one of you*. As many as gladly received his word were baptized; no more, not another one. This is clearly the import of the language, *as many* as gladly received his word. Infants can not so receive the word, hence none were baptized. That *faith* preceded their baptism is evident from the fact that they were pricked in their hearts. This was a result of their faith in what Peter had preached. Infants would have heard Peter any length of time with perfect indifference, because they could not have understood him.

2. The second case of baptism recorded was at Samaria, where Philip preached the gospel to the people, and "when they believed Philip preaching the things concerning the kingdom of God and the name of Jesus Christ, they were baptized, both men and women." Acts viii:12. When they believed Philip they were baptized, not until then. Hence, Philip understood faith to be antecedent to baptism, and none but men and women were baptized.

3. "Then Simon himself believed also, and when he was baptized he continued with Philip, and wondered, beholding the

WHO SHOULD BE BAPTIZED? 363

miracles and signs which were done." Ver. 13. In Simon's case, the same order is observed—preaching, hearing, faith, *then baptism,* but not until then. Is not this in harmony with the commission? Preach the gospel; he that believeth and is baptized shall be saved. Preaching, hearing, faith, then baptism is the order ordained of the Lord, and as this order can not apply to infants, it follows that baptism was not intended for them.

4. But we have another example of baptism in this chapter. We find that Philip preached the gospel to a distinguished Ethiopian nobleman, who understood and believed it, and demanded baptism, saying: "See, here is water; what doth hinder me to be baptized? And Philip said, If thou believest with all thy heart thou mayest. And he answered and said, I believe that Jesus Christ is the Son of God." Acts viii:36, 37. This case most clearly shows that no one was allowed to be baptized who did not believe with the heart in Jesus Christ as the Son of God. When this man demanded baptism, he was told that if he believed he might be baptized, clearly implying that if he did not believe he was not a fit subject for baptism. Who, then, has a right to improve upon the work of Philip and baptize such as do not believe in Jesus Christ at all? Are there two baptisms, one requiring faith to prepare the subject for it, and another which may be administered without faith? Paul says there is one Lord, one faith, and *one baptism.*

5. The next case recorded is that of Saul of Tarsus, afterward called Paul, an account of which we have in the ninth and twenty-second chapters of the Acts, which we need not stop to examine, as no question important to our search can arise concerning it.

6. A case of much more interest and importance to our inquiry, is the introduction of the gospel to the Gentiles at the house of Cornelius, recorded in the tenth chapter of the Acts. Not to be tedious in unimportant details, it is sufficient to state that Peter visited the house of Cornelius in Cesarea, and preached the gospel to him and his friends who were there assembled. While he spake, the Holy Spirit fell on them who heard the word, and they of the circumcision heard them speak with tongues and magnify God. They were all old enough to talk, to say the least of it. And he commanded them to be baptized in the

name of the Lord. Then prayed they him to tarry certain days. Who solicited Peter to tarry certain days? They who had been baptized; nor is there any evidence that any one was baptized who did not join in this solicitation.

7. The next case recorded is the baptism of Lydia and her household, a record of which we have in Acts xvi:15. The subject of household baptisms has been one out of which more capital has been made by the advocates of infant baptism than perhaps any thing else. It is assumed that infants are in every family, and hence were baptized when and where there was a household baptized. To prove that infants were baptized with Lydia's household, it must be proved. 1. That Lydia was a married woman, or at least had children; 2. That some of these children were infants; 3. That these infant children were with her, though she lived in Thyatira and was then in the city of Philippi, three hundred miles from her home. We grant that it is *possible* that Lydia was a married woman; but what are the probabilities of the case? As she was three hundred miles from home, on a mercantile mission, is it not likely that if she had a husband he would have made the trip for her? or had she gone without him, is it not likely that he would have taken care of the children at home without burthening her with them? But is it likely that a husband composed a part of her household? Surely not. As the husband is, in the New Testament, regarded as the head of the family, the household would have been ascribed to him rather than to her. Nor is it at all likely that the husband would not have been named in the narrative by the historian had he been present, for the same writer did mention both on other occasions where they were present. See Acts v:1; xviii:2. And there is a fair intimation by Lydia herself that she did not have a husband; at least, if she had, that he was not with her. She says: "If ye have judged me to be faithful to the Lord, come into my house and abide there." Ver. 15. As a modest Christian woman, it is not likely that she would have claimed the house in presence of her husband; nor is it likely that she would have invited guests into *her* house on the sole ground of HER fidelity to the Lord, and say nothing of her husband had he been present. It was a delicate matter for her to invite men into her house to remain with her in the absence of a husband, and, knowing that good

men would feel a delicacy in doing so, she put the invitation upon the express ground of her fidelity to the Lord. Virtually, this was saying: "Though I am a long ways from home, where you can know nothing of my character, and my family is made up of such as are in my employment, yet if you have judged me to be faithful to the Lord, come into my house and abide there." The argument prevailed, and she constrained us, says the apostle; and that her family was composed of adults may be seen in the fact that after Paul and Silas had been released from prison they "entered into the house of Lydia; and when they had seen the brethren, they comforted them and departed." Acts xvi:40. Then, her family was composed of such as were capable of being comforted by the apostles, and there is not the slightest evidence that she even had a child there or at home. But suppose we grant that she had infants, and that they were with her, it would be no evidence that they were baptized, because they were not subjects of gospel address, and hence were not baptized in flagrant violation of the law of the Lord requiring faith before baptism. We have seen that the commission required the gospel to be preached to every creature in all the world, and yet it did not apply to infants, else they must all be damned. The import of it is, preach the gospel to every creature of the classes embraced in the gospel. So, when Lydia and her household were baptized, the clear inference is that, if there were infants or idiots in her house, they were not subjects of baptism and made no part of the household baptized. Nothing is more plainly apparent in the Scriptures than that the word *household,* and even the phrase *all the house,* are used in a limited sense—*i.e.,* where *a class* of persons, and not every one in the house, was included. It is said "the man Elkanah, and all his house, went up to offer unto the Lord the yearly sacrifice and his vow." Here it is expressly stated that Elkanah and *all his house* went to offer sacrifice to the Lord. This is strong language—all his house; but did every one go? "But Hannah went not up, for she said unto her husband, I will not go up until the child be weaned, and then I will bring him, that he may appear before the Lord, and there abide forever. And Elkanah her husband said unto her, Do what seemeth thee good; tarry until thou have weaned him." 1 Sam. i:21-23.

From this quotation it is clear that Elkanah's wife and child did not go to offer the yearly sacrifice, though it is said all his house went up. Then, were it granted that Lydia's household had infants in it, and it were said, not only that her household was baptized, but that all of it was baptized, still it would only imply that all for whom baptism was intended were baptized. Thus we see the utter impossibility of proving infant baptism from household baptisms, even were every thing granted that is claimed; but we have seen no evidence of an infant in Lydia's household to be baptized.

8. But we have an account of another family baptism in this chapter. The jailer "was baptized, he and all his, straightway." It is claimed that this jailer had infants in his family, and, as he and all his were baptized, his infants were baptized also. Is this position warranted by the proof? The record says: "They spake unto him the word of the Lord, and to all that were in his house." Ver. 32. The gospel was preached to all that were in his house. Why preach the gospel to senseless babes? But he and *all his* were baptized. Yes; "And when he had brought them into his house, he set meat before them, and rejoiced, believing in God with all his house." Ver. 34. Then the same, all his house, that were baptized were capable of *rejoicing* and *believing in God*. We think such should be baptized; but we submit to the unprejudiced judgment of the reader whether infants are capable of doing what is here said to have been done by the jailer and those baptized with him. Can they believe in God? Can they rejoice in the privileges of the gospel? If not, then no infants were among the baptized of this family.

9. "And many of the Corinthians hearing, believed and were baptized." Acts xviii:8. Here the order is in perfect harmony with the commission. The gospel was preached, the Corinthians hearing believed it, and their faith prepared them for baptism, to which they submitted. Of course, there were no infants baptized among them.

10. The twelve disciples found at Ephesus by Paul had been baptized with the baptism of John after the organization of the church on the day of Pentecost; hence, their faith was defective. John preached that they should believe on a Saviour to come after him, hence they were believing in a Saviour to come who

had already come. Their baptism was defective for these reasons: 1. It was not administered in the name or by the *authority* of the Lord Jesus Christ; 2. It was not *into* the name of the Father, Son, and Holy Spirit, as the baptism then in force required to be administered; 3. John's baptism had been superseded by another; hence, when Apollos only knew John's baptism, it was necessary that he be taught the way of the Lord more perfectly—*i.e.*, that John's baptism had passed away and was not *then* in force, and hence worthless to those who received it. When these disciples heard these things, "they were baptized in the name of the Lord Jesus." Acts xix:5. We will not insult the reader by offering an argument to show that there were no infants among these, and that faith preceded their baptism.

We believe we have now examined every case of baptism recorded in the Acts. There are a few incidental allusions to other cases in the epistles which throw no additional light on the subject. Now, will the reader bring himself as near the judgment of the great day as it is possible for mortals to come in this life, and ask himself the question, "Is there a case of infant baptism recorded in all the Book of God? Have we been able to find one?" We have found where *believers* were baptized by thousands. We have found where *men* and *women* were baptized in great numbers, and in families, but nowhere is there a record of the baptism of a single infant. Suppose a modern preacher had written the Acts of the Apostles, and things had been then as now, we imagine the narrative would have run about thus: "As many as gladly received his word were baptized, with their children, and the same day there were added three thousand *adults* and as many *infants*." "They were baptized *men*, WOMEN, and CHILDREN." "And he commanded *men*, WOMEN, and CHILDREN to be baptized in the name of the Lord." "And when she and the infants of her household were baptized." "And he took them the same hour of the night and washed their stripes and was baptized, he and all his infant children, straightway." Recently, I read a scrap from a preacher's journal of several years ago, running thus: "Baptized 20 adults and 21 children." "Sept. 3. Sunday, I preached, and then baptized 21 adults and 3 infants." "On the first Sunday in this month I baptized 34 adults and their children—48 in all." This shows us what the record kept—or, rather, made—by Luke would have been had infants been baptized them as they are now. On the contrary, we have found the same order every-where. As faith comes by hearing, the gospel was first preached that the people might hear, understand, and believe it. Jesus said: "He that believeth and is baptized shall be saved;" hence, when they believed, if they desired salvation, they were baptized, both men and women; but we may safely affirm that no one without faith in Jesus Christ was ever baptized by divine authority. Paul says: "Without faith it is impossible to please him." Heb. xi:6. Therefore, when any one is baptized who has no faith, such baptism can not be pleasing to God. "That which is not of faith is sin." Rom. xiv:23. Infants can not exercise faith hence their baptism can not be of faith, and is, therefore, sin. Hence, we conclude that an infant has never yet been baptized by divine authority anywhere.

Paul says Jesus gave Himself for the church, "that he might sanctify and cleanse it with the washing of water by the word, that he might present it to himself a glorious church, not having spot, or wrinkle, or any such thing; but that it should be holy and without blemish." Eph. vi:26, 27. When would the church attain to this state of perfection if the practice of infant baptism was universal, and baptism introduced infants into the church? (And if its advocates could succeed in their efforts it would be universal, and *should* be universal if right; if wrong, it should not be at all.) All distinction between the church and the world would be obliterated; nay, there would, in this sense, be *no world*. All would be in the church, good and bad. Drunkards, liars, murders, infidels, atheists, and all other classes would be *in the church,* having entered it by baptism in infancy; for none thus introduced are ever excluded for crime unless they make a profession of religion in maturer years. Such a church as there would then be!!! Was this the *glorious* church for which Jesus gave His life, that it might be *without spot, wrinkle, blemish,* or any such thing? Is *this* the *bride* which He is coming to receive, expecting her to be clad in robes of *righteousness* comparable to *fine linen, clean* and *white?* Rev. xix:8.

This theory perfected would make void the commission of Jesus Christ. If infant baptism universally prevailed, there would be no such thing as *believer's baptism.* When Jesus says: "He that believeth and is baptized shall be saved," infant baptism comes along and takes every subject from Him, leaving not one to grow *old enough to believe* the gospel and be baptized. Nor is this all; Peter's sermon on the day of Pentecost would not apply to such a state of things. Were all baptized in infancy, no one in mature years could be commanded to "repent and be baptized in the name of Jesus Christ for the remission of sins." Such a command could not apply to infants; and as there would be no *unbaptized men* and *women,* there would be none to whom such preaching could apply. Is it not clear, therefore, that the gospel plan of salvation given by Jesus Christ and carried into operation by His inspired apostles did not contemplate the baptism of infants?

Baptism, says Peter, is "the answer of a good conscience toward God." 1 Pet. iii:21. It was not to be a mere fleshly washing, but was intended to reach the conscience; but how can it reach the conscience of an infant? It may satisfy the consciences of some misguided parents; but the conscience of the infant subject has nothing to do with it; nor can it be in the least exercised thereby. One of the most pernicious tendencies of the practice is that it prevents many thousands of conscientious persons from intelligently obeying the Lord for themselves. They are informed by their parents or others that they were baptized in infancy, and they must be content with this statement. If they are more correctly taught in after life, and desire to be baptized in the name of Jesus Christ for the remission of sins, they must abandon the church of their infancy or they can not obtain the services of an administrator. Hence, nothing short of an abandonment of their entire system of theology can secure their emancipation from the bondage of a practice unauthorized by inspired precept or example, even as admitted by many wise and good men who practice it.

We come now to notice the argument which those who defend infant baptism base upon the *history* of the practice; and we promise our readers the utmost brevity in its examination, for we have already dignified the subject of this chapter with an undue portion of our space. Indeed, we confess our inability to see the importance which those who make the argument attach to it. Suppose it were true, and could be so proved by well authenticated history, that infant baptism was practiced even in the days of the apostles, unless it could be shown that it met their approval, it would not authorize the practice. In Paul's time he tells us that "the mystery of iniquity doth already work." 2 Thess. ii:7. He also says: "I know this, that after my departing shall grievous wolves enter in among you, not sparing the flock. Also of your own selves shall men arise, speaking perverse things, to draw away disciples after them." Acts xx:29, 30. If, therefore, innovations began to spring up even in the days of the apostles, and persons then among the disciples, who had been blessed with the personal instruction of the apostles, would, so soon after Paul's death, teach perverse doctrine which would draw disciples after them, is it surprising that infant baptism should be introduced in two hundred years? That it did not have the sanction of inspiration in any way, we have already shown by the admissions of as truly great and good men as belong to the Pedobaptist ranks; what, then, is gained by proving, what no one denies, that it has been practiced from the days of Origen until now? are we to practice every thing which came into the church in those days? If so, we must go to anointing with oil—casting devils out of persons before they are baptized —breathing on them in imitation of the Saviour—consecrating the baptismal water—applying salt and spittle to the tongue— giving honey and milk—anointing the eyes with clay—covering the head, and numerous other things which came into the church about the time infant baptism was introduced. They were practiced from about the close of the second century, on for several hundred years, why not practice them now? Do you say they were without divine authority? We grant it; but many of the wisest and best men who have practiced infant baptism *admit the same of it;* why not discard them all together; or practice them all, and be at least consistent?

We believe Irenæus is the first witness whose testimony is introduced in support of the practice. He wrote about the year 190, and is quoted by Neander, vol. i, p. 311. As Neander was a Pedobaptist historian, we will give what he says on the subject in connection with the quotation from Irenæus. He says: "Baptism was administered at first only to adults, as men were accustomed to receive baptism and faith as strictly connected. We have all reason for not deriving infant baptism from apostolic institution, and the recognition of it which followed somewhat later, as an apostolical tradition, serves to confirm this hypothesis. Irenæus is the first church teacher in whom we find any allusion to infant baptism, and in his mode of expressing himself on the subject, he leads us at the same time to recognize its connection with the essence of the Christian consciousness; he testifies of the profound Christian idea out of which infant baptism arose, and which procured for it at length universal recognition. Irenæus is wishing to show that Christ did not interrupt the progressive development of that human nature which was to be sanctified by Him, but sanctified it in accordance with its natural course of development and in all its several stages. 'He came to redeem all by Himself; all who through Him are regenerated to God; infants, little children, boys, young men and old. Hence, He passed through every age, and for the infants He became an infant, sanctifying the infants; among the little children He became a little child, sanctifying those who belong to this age, and at the same time presenting to them an example of piety, of well-doing, and of obedience; among the young men He became a young man, that He might set them an example and sanctify them to the Lord.'"

The reader will observe that Neander says that Irenæus is the first church teacher in whom we find any allusion to infant baptism, and hence the practice can not be traced further back than 190 A.D., even granting that Irenæus means baptism by "regenerated to God." Neander further testifies that baptism was administered at first only to adults, as men were accustomed to conceive baptism and faith as strictly connected. And why should they not be connected when Jesus so connected them, saying: "He that believeth and is baptized shall be saved;" and Philip made faith an indispensable condition upon which he would baptize the eunuch—"If thou believest with all thy heart thou mayest?" But Neander further says: "We have all reason for not deriving infant baptism from apostolic institution." These are surely strong admissions coming from one whose practice shows they were not suggested by partisan feelings.

Again he says: "But immediately after Irenæus, in the last

years of the second century, Tertullian appears as a zealous opponent of infant baptism; a proof that the practice had not as yet come to be regarded as an apostolical institution; for otherwise, he would hardly have ventured to express himself so strongly against it." Neander, vol. i, p. 312. On the same page Neander quotes Tertullian as follows: "Let them come, while they are growing up; let them come while they are learning, while they are being taught to what it is they are coming; let them become Christians when they are susceptible of the knowledge of Christ. What haste to procure the forgiveness of sin for the age of innocence! We show more prudence in the management of our worldly concerns, than we do in intrusting the divine treasure to those who can not be intrusted with earthly property. Let them first learn to feel their need of salvation, so it may appear that we have given to those that wanted."

Dr. Wall has a slightly different translation of this paragraph, as follows: "Therefore, let them come when they are grown up; let them come when they understand; when they are instructed whither it is that they come; let them be made Christians when they can know Christ. What need their guiltless age make such haste to the forgiveness of sins? Men will proceed more warily in worldly things; and he that should not have earthly goods committed to him, yet shall have heavenly. Let them know how to desire this salvation, that you may appear to have given to one that asketh." Wall's Hist. Infant Bap., vol. i, p. 94.

Neander comments upon this paragraph from Tertullian as follows: "It seems, in fact, according to the principles laid down by him, that he could not conceive of any *efficacy whatever* residing in baptism, without the conscious participation and individual faith of the person baptized; nor could he see any danger accruing to the age of innocence from delaying it; although this view of the matter was not logically consistent with *his own* view.

"But when, now, on the one hand, the doctrine of the corruption and guilt cleaving to human nature in consequence of the first transgression, was reduced to a more precise and systematic form, and, on the other, from the want of duly distinguishing between what is outward and what is inward baptism (the baptism by water and the baptism by the Spirit), the error became more firmly established that without external baptism no one could be delivered from that inherent guilt, could be saved from the everlasting punishment that threatened him, or raised to eternal life; and when the notion of a magical influence or charm connected with the sacraments continually gained ground, the theory was finally evolved of the *unconditional necessity of infant baptism.*" Neander, vol. i, p. 313.

Thus we see when and how the theory of infant baptism was finally evolved. Infantile depravity, or the guilt of original sin, was the foundation of it. The fathers drank down the notion that infants inherited the guilt of Adam's sin, and unless this was washed away in baptism they were lost if they died in infancy; hence, says Neander, was finally evolved the unconditional necessity of infant baptism. They must be damned for Adam's sin unless baptized. Modern Pedobaptists are unwilling to admit this, and seek to derive it from the identity of the Jewish and Christian churches, as we have seen, and yet, strange enough, they base an argument on the history of infant baptism which must develop the true foundation of the practice and destroy every argument made in its support. But is Neander correct in this statement? As he was a Pedobaptist himself, he could have had no motive to misrepresent the facts; nevertheless, it may not be amiss to see whether or not he had authority for what he said.

Dr. Wall was one of the most voluminous writers that has ever wielded a pen in defense of infant baptism. He makes a quotation from Justin Martyr, on which he comments as follows: "I recite this only to show that in these times, so very near the apostles, they spoke of original sin affecting all mankind descended of Adam, and understood that, besides the actual sins of each particular person, there is in our nature itself, since the fall, something that needs redemption and forgiveness by the merits of Christ. And that is ordinarily applied to every particular person by baptism." Wall, vol. i, p. 64.

When the fathers became well settled in the doctrine of infantile depravity, they very naturally desired a remedy for it, and, knowing that baptism was for the remission of sins, they conceived the idea of baptizing infants for the removal of the guilt of Adam's sin in them. By the close of the second century it made its appearance, and we have found Tertullian opposing it. In Origen's day it was more general, and we find him favoring it. He was born about 185 A.D.

Allowing him to have been fifty or sixty years old when he wrote, his writings would date near the middle of the third century. We have not much confidence in the authenticity of what is said to have been written by him, yet we will give some of it to the reader, and he can estimate it for himself.

Dr. Wall says: "The Greek (which was the original) of all Origen's works being lost, except a very few, there remain only the Latin translations of them. And when these translations were collected together, a great many spurious ones were added and mixed with them and went under Origen's name." Wall's History, vol. i, p. 106.

Though Dr. Wall goes on to say that "critics quickly smelt them out and admitted none for his but such as appeared to have been done into Latin either by St. Hierome or Rufinus," yet he says: "Rufinus altered or left out any thing which he thought not orthodox, * * whereas now, in these translations of Rufinus, the reader is uncertain (as Erasmus angrily says) whether he read Origen or Rufinus." Pp. 106-108.

The following paragraph is a translation of Rufinus' Latin of Origen's Greek by Wall: "Besides all this, let it be considered what is the reason that, whereas the baptism of the church is given for the forgiveness of sins, infants also are by the usage of the church baptized, when, if there were nothing in infants that wanted forgiveness and mercy, the grace of baptism would be needless to them." Wall, vol. i, p. 104.

The following paragraph was translated from Origen's Greek into Latin by St. Hierome, and thence into English by Wall, who exonerates Hierome from any want of fidelity to the original of Origen: "Having occasion given in this place, I will mention a thing that causes frequent inquiries among the brethren. Infants are baptized for the forgiveness of sins. Of what sins? Or when have they sinned? Or how can any reason of the laver in their case hold good, but according to that sense that we mentioned even now: none is free from pollution, though his life be but of the length of one day upon the earth? And it is for that reason, because by the sacrament of baptism the pollution of our birth is taken away, that infants are baptized." Wall, vol. i, pp. 104, 105. This comes to us from Origen through Hierome and Wall, and must, therefore, be received as genuine. In it Origen answers the inquiries of his brethren by plainly stating that *it is because the pollution of our birth is taken away by baptism that infants are baptized.*

But there is another passage translated from Origen's Greek by Rufinus, to which we must give some attention: "For this also it was that the church had from the apostles a tradition [or order] to give baptism even to infants. For they, to whom the divine mysteries were committed, knew that there is in all persons the natural pollution of sin which must be done away by water and the Spirit." Wall, vol. i, p. 106.

As this passage comes to us through Rufinus, an admitted interpolator of Origen's works, we can have no confidence in its purity; and even Dr. Wall has given us some evidence of overmuch zeal in his cause, by placing in brackets the phrase *"or order,"* as though *order* was the synonym of *tradition*, and thus seeking to make his author say that the church had an *order* to give baptism to infants. Does *tradition* amount to an *order?* Let us see. "Tradition is a very convenient word to excuse and retain those things that were brought into religion without the authority of Scripture, by the ignorance of the times and the tyranny of men." Turettenus, in Booth Abridged, p. 273.

"To convince the world how early tradition might either vary or misrepresent matters, let the tradition not only in, but before St. Irenæus' time, concerning the observation of Easter be considered, which goes up as high as St. *Polycarp's* time. If, then, tradition failed so near its fountain, we may easily judge what account we ought to make of it at so great a distance." Bishop Burnet, in *Ibid*.

"Irenæus, one of the first fathers, with this passage [John viii:57] supports the tradition, which he saith he had from some that had conversed with St. John, that our Saviour lived to be fifty years old, which he contends for. See what little credit is to be given to tradition." Mr. Henry, in *Ibid*, pp. 3, 4.

"As to the Scripture, instead of making that the only rule of faith, they [the Papists] have joined traditions with it; that is to say, the most uncertain thing in the world, the most subject to impostures, and the most mixed with human inventions and weaknesses, tradition is so far from being able to serve for a rule, that it ought itself to be corrected according to that maxim of Jesus Christ, *In the beginning it was not so.* There is, therefore, nothing more improper to be the rule of faith than that pretended tradition which is not established upon any certain foundation, which serves for a pretense to heretics, which is embraced *pro* and *con,* which changes according as times and places do, and by the favor of which they may defend the greatest absurdities by merely saying that they are the traditions which the apostles transmitted from their own mouths to their successors." Mr. Claude, in *Ibid,* pp. 274, 275.

Thus, we see that, when contending against Papal usurpation, Pedobaptists regard *tradition* as "the most uncertain thing in the world"—serves as a pretext for heretics, by the favor of which they may prove the greatest absurdities, even that *Jesus lived to be fifty years old;* but when defending infant baptism, and nothing better can be had, tradition does very well, and may be called an *order* from the apostles to give baptism to infants! With reference to Origen's remark, Neander says: "Origen, in whose system infant baptism could readily find its place, though not in the same connection as in the system of the North African church, declares it to be an apostolical tradition; an expression, by the way, which can not be regarded as of much weight in this age when the inclination was so strong to trace every institution which was considered of special importance to the apostles; and when so many walls of separation, hindering the freedom of prospect, had already been set up between this and the apostolic age." Neander, vol. i, p. 314.

These quotations are deemed sufficient to show what estimate is to be placed upon Wall's substitution of the word *order* for *tradition* in the quotation from Origen. He verifies the adage that "drowning men will catch at straws." As he has nothing better with which to support his practice, we leave him in the enjoyment of his *tradition,* but insist that he hold it as a *tradition,* not as an *order.*

Having seen that the history of infant baptism can not be traced further back than about the close of the second century, we feel no disposition to pursue it into later periods, being content to know that *it did not originate in the days of the apostles, or have their sanction;* this we have seen as surely as there is truth in the testimony of those who practice it. The reader will please remember that we have *found its origin*—not in the identity of the Jewish and the Christian churches—not in Jewish circumcision—not in Jewish proselyte baptism—not in the teaching of John the Baptist, Christ, or the apostles—but in the absurd dogma of *infantile depravity,* or the *inherited guilt of Adam's sin.* So testifies Tertullian, so testifies Origen, and all the primitive fathers who give testimony on the subject. My distinguished friend Mr. Ditzler says: "They all believed that infants were depraved, as their writings show. * * They believed that baptism was regeneration in the sense of washing away original sin; that infants were depraved by original sin, and could not be saved without this washing away of that sin; and, therefore, they baptized infants that they might be saved. Now, the apostolic fathers speak in this manner, and refer to the baptism of infants." Louisville Debate, p. 163. This is a frank admission of what is unquestionably true, limiting the words *apostolic fathers* to such as wrote after the introduction of the practice.

But we have later testimony than the so-called apostolic fathers on this subject. In a work, titled DOCTRINAL TRACTS, page 251, we find the following paragraph in a treatise on baptism:

"As to the grounds of it: if infants are guilty of original sin, then they are proper subjects of baptism; seeing, in the ordinary way, they can not be saved unless this be washed away in baptism. It has been already proved that this original stain cleaves to every child of man; and that hereby they are children of wrath and liable to eternal damnation." This work was published by Lane & Scott, New York, 1850, BY ORDER OF THE GENERAL CONFERENCE of the Methodist Church. Hence, the above paragraph comes to us indorsed by the Methodist Church through her General Conference only *twenty-three* years ago. And it clearly shows that infant baptism, in the judgment of that organization, was based upon the doctrine of original sin, or inherited guilt, by reason of which infants are children of wrath and liable to eternal damnation; and in the ordinary way can not be saved unless this original sin be washed away by baptism.

This tract was published, for about thirty years, by the General Conference as the production of Mr. Wesley's pen, but Mr. Jackson, the biographer of Mr. Wesley, denies that he wrote it. So far as the weight of its authority goes, it matters little whether Mr. Wesley wrote it or not; it was written by some one of no ordinary power, as the tract itself shows; and the fact that it was published by order of the General Conference gives it more authority than it could derive from Mr. Wesley or any other one man. But we do not regard Mr. Jackson's denial as quite sufficient to show that it was not written by Mr. Wesley. Of all writers known to us, as a class, biographers are least reliable. It is a well known fact that they ignore and often cover up the faults and exaggerate the virtues of their heroes; and when we add to this the fact that Mr. Jackson's partisan feelings would incline him to mould Mr. Wesley's teaching in accordance with his own views and the interest of his church, we are inclined to accept his denial, under the circumstances, with some degree of caution. What are the circumstances connected with the publication of this tract? In the advertisement following the title page it is shown that a number of tracts had been published with the Discipline for a time, but in 1812 the General Conference ordered them left out of the Discipline and published in a separate volume. Following this announcement, it is said: "Several new tracts are included in this volume, and Mr. Wesley's Short Treatise on Baptism is substituted in the place of the extract from Mr. Edwards on that subject." Here it is stated that the former tract by Mr. Edwards was taken out and this one by Wesley was put in. Did those who made this statement tell the truth, or were they mistaken in what they said?

On page 249, we find a footnote, as follows: "That Mr. Wesley, as a clergyman of the Church of England, was originally a *high-churchman*, in the fullest sense, is well known. When he wrote this treatise, in the year 1756, he seems still to have used some expressions in relation to the doctrine of baptismal regeneration, which we at this day should not prefer. Some such, in the judgment of the reader, may perhaps be found under this second head. The last sentence, however, contains a guarded corrective. It explains also the sense in which we believe Mr. Wesley intended much of what goes before to be understood."

As no name is attached to this note, we know not who wrote

it, but we suppose it was by the publishing committee. Be this as it may, it seems to have been written by some one acquainted with the facts, for it even gives the date when Mr. Wesley wrote the tract. This note, be it remembered, is attached to the tract itself. The whole Methodist Conference, publishers, publishing committee, and every body else connected with this tract, save Mr. Jackson, were mistaken for thirty years or Mr. Wesley wrote it. No child ever resembled its father more than does the style of this tract resemble the general style of Mr. Wesley's writings. But if those who practice infant baptism intend to repudiate the doctrine that infants are in danger of being lost unless baptized, we trust they will cease abusing us for opposing their baptism. If those who are unbaptized are in no more danger than those baptized, why abuse us for seeking to prevent that which can do no good? Surely, they do not wish to unjustly prejudice the minds of the people against us by making much ado about nothing. If infants need not baptism, why baptize them? We think they are good enough without baptism. Jesus said: "Of such is the kingdom of heaven." Not of such as they will be when they are baptized, but of such as they are without baptism.

But we are referred to the baptism of the Israelites in the cloud and sea as a clear case of the baptism of infants. Paul says: "All our fathers were under the cloud, and all passed through the sea; and were all baptized unto Moses in the cloud and in the sea." 1 Cor. x:1, 2. It is certain that infants were under the cloud and passed through the sea, hence it is insisted that they were in the typical baptism referred to by Paul, and should now be baptized to fill the antitype. Does the fact that they were under the cloud and in the sea prove that they were contemplated by Paul in the baptism referred to? If so, then the *flocks* and *herds* of the Hebrews were included also, for it is just as certain that they were under the cloud and in the sea as it is that the infants were there. Shall we baptize our flocks therefore, to fill the antitype? Why not? They were taken along without their volition just as were the infants; hence, if these were baptized, why not those? Paul says that those baptized "did all eat the same spiritual meat; and did all drink the same spiritual drink; for they drank of that spiritual Rock that followed them; and that Rock was Christ." Verses 3, 4. Thus we see that those contemplated by Paul were capable of receiving spiritual instruction concerning Christ, which Paul calls spiritual meat and drink. Hence, says he, "By faith they passed through the Red Sea as by dry land; which the Egyptians essaying to do were drowned." Heb. xi:29. Is it not clear that Paul did not contemplate infants; but alluded to such as could receive spiritual instruction, and pass through by faith? Infant baptism was never heard of in Paul's day; hence, when he spake of baptized persons, either in type or antitype, he contemplated only such as were legitimate subjects of the rite.

Suppose we try the *commission* by the same principle of interpretation applied to the baptism of the Israelites. Jesus said: "Go ye into all the world, and preach the gospel to every creature." Now, it is just as certain that infants are *creatures in the world,* as it is that they were under the cloud and passed through the sea—were they contemplated in the commission? If so, what next? "He that believeth and is baptized shall be saved; but he that believeth not shall be damned." Infants can not believe, therefore they must all be damned! Is any one prepared to accept the conclusion? Surely not; yet it is fairly deducible from the commission by the same rules applied to the baptism of the Israelites to prove infant baptism. Infants are not subjects of gospel address, and were not contemplated in the commission, nor are they *subjects of baptism;* hence they were not contemplated by Paul.

Baptism is not a mere unmeaning ceremony, but a solemn act of obedience to God. Gentle reader, have you intelligently submitted to His will in the act required of you? Jesus commanded the apostles to teach the nations, baptizing them, the taught—clearly implying that they should baptize none but the taught. We have seen that they, acting under this commission, preached the gospel to the people, and when they believed it they were baptized, both *men* and *women. Intelligent, believing, penitent men and women who desire salvation should be baptized into the sublime names of Father, Son, and Holy Spirit.* None others should be so baptized, for it would do them no good; and should it unfortunately keep them from obeying God in mature years, it would do them much harm. In vain may we attempt the worship of God by obeying the commandments of men. Be baptized yourself; you can not obey God for your children; but you can bring them up in the nurture and admonition of the Lord, and when they are old enough to understand the Lord's will, you will have the consolation of seeing them obey it for themselves.

CHAPTER XIV.

THE DESIGN OF BAPTISM.

The GOSPEL PLAN OF SALVATION is the grandest *system* of harmony and order ever devised by God for man. There is a place for every thing, and every thing should be in its place. We have found a place for *faith*, what it is, how it comes, and what it does; a place for *repentance*, what it is, how it is produced, and what it does; a place for the *good confession*, what it is, how it is made, when it should be made, who should make it, and what it is made for; a place for *baptism*, what it is, and who should submit to it; and now it remains for us to see what it is for, or to learn, if we can, the design of it—what office, if any, it fills in the great system of salvation to which it belongs.

It is not to be presumed that the Lord required *men* and *women* to be baptized into the awfully sublime names of the Father, and of the Son, and of the Holy Spirit, without some important design or end to be accomplished by it; and when we take from baptism this design, it becomes an unmeaning pageant, which may be attended to or neglected as the caprice of the clergy or the people may determine. If a sick man waits until he get well before he takes the medicine designed to cure him, it is scarcely necessary that he should then trouble himself to take it at all. So if a man must wait until he be saved from his sins, made a child of God and an heir of heaven, before he obeys the Lord, we see not why he should still be baptized for the remission of sins already pardoned. Hence, when we take from baptism its *design*, it matters little who is baptized, how it is done, or whether it is done at all.

That we may have something tangible and definite before us, we affirm that BAPTISM IS FOR, OR IN ORDER TO, THE REMISSION OF SINS. This is its design, as taught by Christ and those who wrote the New Testament. Before offering the proof of this affirmation, it may be well to get its import clearly before the mind of the reader. We fully realize the importance of the proposition, and feel, therefore, that we should well understand the import of the terms employed in its construction.

"Sin is the transgression of the law." 1 John iii:4. Not a law, some law, or any law, but *the* law. There are laws which, we suppose, it would be no sin to violate; but *sin is the transgression of divine law,* and whenever any other law comes in conflict with this law, it is no crime, but may be a virtue to violate it. That we be more plain, the wife is required to obey her husband, but were the husband to command her to steal, we suppose she had better obey God, who says "thou shalt not steal," than the husband who says "you shall steal." "All unrighteousness is sin." 1 John v:19.

There can be no enforcement of law without a penalty for its violation, and this penalty must be suffered by the guilty or it must be forgiven by the offended. By remission of sins, then, we mean *a release from the punishment due the violation of God's law.* The same thought is expressed in different forms; as: "Remission of sins," Matt. xxvi:28; Acts ii:38. "Forgiveness of sins," Acts v:31; xiii:38; xxvi:18. "Salvation from sins," Matt. i:21. "Cleansing from sin," 1 John i:7. "Blotting out of sin," Ps. li:1; Isa. xliii:25; Jer. xviii:23. "Washing away sins," Acts xxii:16. "Ceasing to remember sins," Jer. xxxi:34; Heb. viii:12, x:17. All these, and others which we might give are but different ways of expressing the same thought. A sin once committed can never be undone by any power, human or divine. The punishment may be commuted, suspended, or forgiven—undone it can not be, but must remain in the history of past events as long as eternity endures. How important, then, it is that we look well to the record we are making; and how wonderfully kind, too, has been our Heavenly Father in providing a plan of salvation by which we may escape the punishment justly due those who violate His law!

But while baptism is appointed of the Lord for the remission of sins, the pardon granted is retrospective, only for the sins of the past; hence says Paul: "Being justified freely by his grace through the redemption that is in Christ Jesus, whom God hath set forth to be a propitiation through faith in his blood, to declare his righteousness for the remission of sins that are past." Rom. iii:24, 25. But does any one suppose that baptism is for the remission of *all* the sins of the party baptized, *future* as well as *past?* If not, what means John Calvin by the following language: "Nor must it be supposed that baptism is administered only for the time past, so that for sins into which we fall after baptism it would be necessary to seek other new remedies of expiation, in I know not what other sacraments, as if the virtue of baptism were become obsolete. In consequence of this error, it happened in former ages that some persons would not be baptized except at the close of their life, and almost in the moment of their death, so that they might obtain pardon for their whole life—a preposterous caution, which is frequently censured in the writings of the ancient bishops. But we ought to conclude that at whatever time we are baptized we are washed and purified for the whole life. Whenever we have fallen, therefore, we must recur to the remembrance of baptism, and arm our minds with the consideration of it, that we may be always certified and assured of the remission of our sins." Calvin in Campbell on Baptism, pp. 262, 263.

This is an error into which Mr. Calvin and others fell by failing to recognize the fact that God has ordained a law of pardon or naturalization for the alien, by which he must become a citizen of His kingdom, and another law of pardon for him after he becomes a subject of His government—one law of pardon for the stranger and another for His children. We do not know whether there are any who now believe the doctrine of the foregoing paragraph from Mr. Calvin's pen or not, but we do know that many, like him, have failed to make any distinction in the law which applies to the *alien* and that which applies to the *erring Christian;* and, hence, the common objection to the doctrine of baptism for the remission of sins: "If baptism is for the remission of sins, why do you not baptize a man every time he sins?" We are not surprised when such an objection comes from those who never read the Bible, but when it comes from *good* men who *study* the Bible, we know not how to account for it. Our charity, however, inclines us to make great allowance for the blinding influences of a false theory, and to conclude that the objection is honestly made and must be met accordingly; we, therefore, proceed to show that God has given a law of pardon applicable to His erring children differing from the law of pardon given to the unconverted sinner.

Philip went down to the city of Samaria and preached Christ to the people, and "when they believed Philip preaching the things concerning the kingdom of God and the name of Jesus Christ, they were baptized, both men and women. Then Simon himself believed also; and when he was baptized he continued with Philip, and wondered, beholding the miracles and signs which were done." Acts viii:12, 13. Here is one law to which the Samaritans submitted, in doing which they became children of God. Jesus said: "He that believeth and is baptized shall be saved." Mark xvi:16. The Samaritans, Simon among them, did believe and were baptized, and hence were pardoned as surely as there is any truth in the record. Simon did just what the others did, and was saved if *they* were saved. But "when Simon saw that through laying on of the apostles' hands the Holy Ghost was given, he offered them money, saying, Give me also this power, that on whomsoever I lay hands he may receive the Holy Ghost." Ver. 18, 19. Here was a wicked thought which entered into the heart of Simon, but did the inspired teachers rebaptize him? No; but why not? This is a case exactly applicable to the objection under examination. He, with the other Samaritans, had believed and been baptized, and was, therefore, saved; yet he sinned. What shall he do now? Peter said: "Repent, therefore, of this thy wickedness, and pray God, if perhaps the thought of thine heart may be forgiven thee." Ver. 22. Here is the law which applies to those who sin after having been baptized in the name of Jesus Christ for the remission of their past sins. They must *repent* of the sin or sins committed, and *pray* to God for pardon, and, as His children, He will hear and pardon them. Being a child of God, "if any man sin, we have an advocate with the Father, Jesus Christ the righteous." 1 John ii:1. And, again: "If we confess our sins, he is faithful and just to forgive us our sins, and to cleanse us from all unrighteousness." 1 John i:9. Here are privileges which the children of God have, which aliens, while children of the wicked one, have not. It is their gracious privilege to *pray* to their Father, with the assurance that He will grant them such favors as they ask in accordance with His will.

But Mr. Ditzler says Simon "did not believe on Christ, but they simply believed Philip preaching the things concerning the kingdom of God * * * and were baptized. Acts viii:12. Ver. 13: Then Simon himself believed (*i.e.*, Philip preaching), and was baptized." Louisville Debate, p. 222. He says Simon did not believe on Christ, yet the scriptures he quotes show that he believed just what the others did; and no one doubts their faith. But he omits some words in the quotation, which, of course, he deems unimportant to the sense, yet we think them calculated to show just the opposite of what he said. They are the words "and the name of Jesus Christ" in the sentence, "They believed Philip preaching the things concerning the kingdom of God and the name of Jesus Christ."

Then Philip preached the things concerning the kingdom of God and *the name of Jesus Christ,* which they and Simon believed, yet he did not believe on Christ at all! Philip must have acted strangely inconsistent; for, in the same chapter (ver. 37), we find that he would not baptize the eunuch until he confessed his faith in Jesus Christ as the Son of God, and yet he baptized Simon and the Samaritans who did not believe on Christ! How is this? But he continues: "Now, because Simon was baptized, sorcerer as he was, though at once said to be in the gall of bitterness and the bond of iniquity." How does he know that as soon as Simon was baptized this was *at once* said to him? The record says: "When the apostles which were at Jerusalem heard that Samaria had received the word of God, they sent unto them Peter and John: who, when they were come down," etc. Ver. 14, 15.

This shows that after Simon's baptism a report of the success of Philip's preaching had to go from Samaria to Jerusalem (a distance of thirty-six miles); the apostles have a meeting, and Peter and John go from Jerusalem to Samaria before Peter could have said to him what Mr. Ditzler says was said *at once.* We suppose the news went from Samaria to Jerusalem by the ordinary intercourse between those cities; as we have no account of special messengers being sent to carry it, then it is impossible to tell how long a time elapsed from Simon's baptism to his rebuke by Peter. But when we take into consideration the means of travel in that country at that time, we know it was several days at least.

Mr. Ditzler continues: "Peter's very words, 'I *perceive* thou art in the gall of bitterness,' imply he discovered he never had been right." Do Peter's words show that Simon never had been right? Peter does not tell Simon to repent of all his sins, or even of sins, but of a specific sin—repent of THIS thy wickedness. Nor does he tell him to pray to God for the pardon of all his past sins, but for a specific sin—pray God if perhaps the *thought of thine heart may be forgiven thee*—*this thought of purchasing the gift of God with money.* We insist that this language clearly shows that *one sin,* and *only one,* stood charged against Simon, and that *all his former* sins had been pardoned prior to that time.

Nor is this all; Simon did not manifest a *wicked,* but a *penitent,* disposition after Peter rebuked him. Said he: "Pray ye to the Lord for me, that none of these things come upon me." Acts viii:24. And if Peter obeyed the instructions which were given to other disciples, to "pray one for another" (Jas. v:16), he did pray for Simon, and none of these things came upon him.

We have quoted Mr. Ditzler as expressing the generally received theory on Simon's case, because his language is a matter of record, and can be found by those who will take the trouble to find and read the page to which we have referred them. Simon's case as clearly shows *two laws of pardon*—one for the *alien* and another for the *erring Christian*—as it is possible to show any thing by proof; we shall, therefore, treat this as settled, and proceed to examine the testimony upon which we rely to prove that *baptism is for the remission of sins.*

Though John's baptism is not now binding upon any one, and has not been since the establishment of the kingdom for which it prepared material, yet a brief examination of it is deemed important to a proper understanding of the baptism to which the taught of all nations are now required to submit. Indeed, *that* differed from *this* rather in its *adjuncts* than in the baptism itself. John required those baptized by him to believe in a *Saviour to come.* John required those who came to his baptism to *confess their sins*—now those who would be baptized must *confess their faith in the Son of God.* Now, persons are baptized into the name of the Father, and of the Son, and of the Holy Spirit. What formula John used is not known, but it is certain he did not baptize into these sublime names. John's baptism prepared material for position in a kingdom *to be established,* or a temple or church *to be built;* now, persons are baptized into a kingdom *already established,* a temple which *has been built,* a church al-

ready in existence. While there are these differences in the *adjuncts,* John's baptism was *immersion* in water—*adults* only were subjects of it, and it was *for the remission of the sins* of those who submitted to it.

When John was named by the direction of the angel, his father Zacharias was filled with the Holy Spirit, and prophesied, saying: "Thou, child, shalt be called the prophet of the Highest: for thou shalt go before the face of the Lord to prepare his ways; to give knowledge of salvation unto his people by the remission of their sins." Luke i:76, 77. In fulfillment of the prophecy, and others made by the prophets, it is said "John did baptize in the wilderness, and peach the baptism of repentance for the remission of sins." Mark i:4. "And he came into all the country about Jordan, preaching the baptism of repentance for the remission of sins." Luke iii:3. If these scriptures do not prove, beyond the possibility of even respectable quibble, that John's baptism was for the remission of sins, then we know not how language might be shaped capable of proving that fact.

To keep within the range of English criticism, the preposition *of* in these quotations implies possession—*i.e.,* that baptism belongs to or grows out of repentance; hence, those baptized by John were truly penitent, and desired to obey God in baptism that they might have knowledge of salvation by the remission of their sins. But we are told that John's baptism did not follow repentance, but preceded and obligated to it. Then we are to understand that John baptized the *impenitent* upon a promise of future repentance. Suppose an applicant for baptism had said: "John, I have not repented, but if you will baptize me I will repent at a more convenient season," would John have baptized such an applicant? But let us suppose this theory true for a moment, and see what it will do for the theory of those who advocate it. They tell us that there never has been but one law of pardon from the days of Adam until now, and that repentance precedes faith in the order of their occurrence. Then, as the same law of pardon existed in John's day that exists now, and baptism preceded repentance, and repentance preceded faith, it follows that baptism is first in order, then repentance, and faith comes last; and, hence, we must baptize persons without faith or repentance. Paul says: "Without faith it is impossible to please

God," therefore such baptism could not be pleasing to God; and as that which is not of faith is sin, such baptism is sin. The advocates of this theory have often tantalized us for baptizing persons without sufficient preparation, but we would like to know how much preparation for baptism belongs to this theory. As it precedes repentance, and repentance precedes faith, what precedes and prepares for baptism? Just nothing at all.

But again: suppose their theory be true that repentance did follow, not precede, John's baptism, does it follow that his baptism was not for the remission of sins because it was not *last* in the order of conditions complied with?

We are told that Jacob served seven years for Rachel (Gen. xxix:20); was not the first year's service as much *for* Rachel as that of the seventh year? and could he ever have reached the seventh year without passing through all the preceding years? When Naaman dipped himself seven times in Jordan, that he might be cured of his leprosy, though the cure followed the seventh dipping, all the preceding were as much for his cure as was the seventh. We might give numerous illustrations of this principle, but these are enough to show that were we to concede that John's baptism preceded repentance, the concession would not prove that it was not for remission of sins.

When the Bible says that John preached the baptism of repentance for remission of sins, the language affirms nothing of repentance, but that the baptism which belongs to repentance is for remission of sins. But why argue the question further? It is plain enough.

But there are those who admit that John's baptism was for the remission of sins, and yet they tell us that those who submitted to it could not enter the kingdom on or after the day of Pentecost without being rebaptized. Now, if John's baptism was for the remission of sins, and those who submitted to it were pardoned—their sins remitted—for what must they be baptized on or after the day of Pentecost? *Must they again be baptized for the remission of the same sins remitted in John's baptism?* When the blood of Jesus was shed their pardon was complete. As the material prepared for the temple of Solomon was ready, as soon as brought together, for position in the building, so those baptized by John, and during the personal ministry of Jesus by the apostles, were ready to be placed in the great spirirtual temple erected on the day of Pentecost—all that was necessary was that they should be placed together, and the building was complete without the sound of axe or hammer. But more of this anon.

We base our second argument upon the language of Christ to Nicodemus: "Except a man be born of water and of the Spirit, he can not enter into the kingdom of God." John iii:5. Having devoted a chapter each to the *establishment of the kingdom* and the *philosophy of the new birth*, we need not stop here to enlarge upon either; but it is sufficient to remark that in the kingdom is a state of safety—out of it we know of no salvation for any one who belongs to the class of persons for whom it was established. Paul says: "Then cometh the end, when he shall have delivered up the kingdom to God, even the Father." 1 Cor. xv:24.

How shall those for whom the kingdom was established be delivered with the kingdom unless they be in it? He who enters the kingdom is saved, pardoned, justified; but if there is salvation for intelligent men and women *out of it*, why did Christ give His life to establish it? Surely it could do no good to establish a kingdom out of which persons could be saved as well as in it; and had such been the fact, when Jesus said "Except a man be born of water and of the Spirit he can not enter the kingdom," Nicodemus could have replied: "It matters not whether a man enters it or not, as he can be saved as well out of it as in it."

As it is an incontrovertible truth, then, that men who would be saved from their sins must enter the kingdom, and as they can not enter it without being born of water and of the Spirit, it follows that a birth of water and of the Spirit is indispensable to salvation from sins.

The only remaining question, then, is: *Did the Lord allude to baptism when He used the language "born of water?"* If not, to what did He allude? What other connection with water can there be to which He may have referred? The religious world, *with one voice*, from the days of Christ until quite recently, has ascribed this language to water baptism.

Speaking of the primitive fathers, Dr. Wall, the great Pedobaptist historian, says: "They understood that rule of our Saviour, '*Except one be regenerated* (or born again) of *water and of the Spirit, he can not enter into the kingdom of God,*' of water baptism, and concluded from it that without such baptism, no person could come to heaven—and so did all the writers of these four hundred years, not one man excepted." Wall's History of Infant Bap., vol. i, pp. 69, 70.

Thus we have Dr. Wall's testimony that every writer of the first four hundred years, without a single exception, understood the Saviour to refer to water baptism, and that no man could be saved without it.

Again: on page 147, of the same volume, Dr. Wall says: "There is not any one Christian writer of any antiquity in any language, but what understands it of baptism; and if it be not so understood, it is difficult to give an account how a person is born of water any more than born of wood." This is strong language, but no writer has ventured to dispute it. If it were not true, and any writer understood it otherwise, his writings would have been produced in refutation of the statement.

But what is the testimony of modern writers on this subject? Mr. Wesley says: "Except a man be born of water and of the Spirit—except he experience that great inward change by the Spirit and be baptized (wherever baptism can be had) as the outward sign and means of it." Wesley's Notes on John iii:5.

"By baptism, we who were 'by nature children of wrath,' are made the children of God; and this regeneration which our church in so many places ascribes to baptism is more than barely being admitted into the church, though commonly connected therewith; being 'grafted into the body of Christ's church, we are made the children of God by adoption and grace.' This is grounded on the plain words of our Lord, 'Except a man be born again of water and of the Spirit, he can not enter into the kingdom of God.' John iii:5. By water, then, as a means, the water of baptism, we are regenerated or born again; whence it is also called by the apostle 'the washing of regeneration.'" Doctrinal Tracts, published by order of the Methodist General Conference, pp. 248, 249.

BLOOMFIELD: "The purpose of the next verse (6) seems to be to set forth the indispensable *necessity* of this regeneration by water and the Spirit, in order to the attainment of everlasting salvation; for that as the natural or animal life depends on flesh and blood, so does the *spiritual* life depend on the baptism by water and by the Spirit." Greek Testament and Notes.

WHITBY: "*If a man be not born of water:* That our Lord speaks here of baptismal regeneration, the whole Christian church from the beginning hath always taught, and that with very good reason." Notes on John iii:5.

BARNES: "*Born of water:* By water here is evidently signified baptism; thus the word is used, Eph. v:26; Titus iii:5." Notes on John iii:5.

TIMOTHY DWIGHT, president of Yale College: "To be born again is precisely the same thing as to be born of water and of the Spirit; and to be born of water *is to be baptized;* and he who understands the nature and authority of this institution, and refuses to be baptized, will never enter the visible or invisible kingdom of God."

GEORGE WHITFIELD: "*Born of water and of the Spirit:* Does not this verse urge the *absolute necessity* of baptism? Yes, when it may be had." Works, vol. iv, p. 355.

While we do not indorse every thing quoted from these authors, they show that the learned of all ages understand *baptism* by the language *born of water*. Did space permit we might extend the list of quotations *ad infinitum*. The Methodist Discipline quotes John iii:1-8, in the baptismal ceremony. The Westminster and Cumberland Presbyterian Confessions refer to John iii:5, as a proof text under the head of baptism, showing that they understand the passage to refer to water baptism, otherwise they would not thus refer to it. The Episcopalian Church so understands it, as the following questions and answers from the Catechism will clearly show:

"*Question.* What is the inward and spiritual grace (of baptism)?

"*Answer.* A death unto sin and a new birth unto righteousness, for being by nature born in sin, and the children of wrath, we are hereby made the children of grace.

"Q. But are there not some conditions required on the part of man in order to his being saved by the death of Christ?

"A. We must become members of that spiritual society or body of which Christ is the head.

"Q. Why must we become members of this body?

"A. Because we can not partake of the Spirit of Christ unless we are members of the body of Christ. 'There is one body and one Spirit.' Eph. iv:4.

"Q. What is the body of Christ commonly called?

"A. It is called the church. Eph. i:23.

"Q. How are we made members of the church or mystical body of Christ?

"A. By baptism. 'We are all baptized into one body.' 1 Cor. xii:13.

"Q. For what end did our Lord institute the rite of baptism?

"A. To be the way and means of admitting man again into the favor of God. 'Except a man be born of water and of the Spirit, he can not enter into the kingdom of God.' John iii:5.

"Q. What favors or privileges does God grant to persons baptized in this new covenant?

"A. The forgiveness of all his own sins, if he hath committed any, and the sin of Adam so far as concerned him; a title to the Holy Spirit, as being the life of the body whereof he is now made a member, and the promise of a resurrection of his body, and a glorious immortality in heaven.

"Q. Can forgiveness of sin be obtained by those to whom the gospel is preached, out of the church?

"A. No; for it is obtained only through Jesus Christ.

"Q. Does baptism cleanse us from all the actual sins we have committed before it?

"A. Yes; as well as from original sin. 'Arise, and be baptized, and wash away thy sins.' Acts xxii:16.

"Q. Who instituted the sacrament of baptism and the Lord's Supper?

"A. Our Lord Jesus Christ, for the purpose of applying the merits of his death to us.

"Q. Is it, then, a great advantage to receive these sacraments worthily?

"A. It is the greatest blessing of this life, because they are the means of conveying grace into our souls, without which we can do no good thing."

This catechism teaches that baptism brings us into the church, out of which those to whom the gospel is preached can not be saved; it brings us into the body of Christ, out of which we can not partake of the Spirit of Christ, without which we are none of His; it is the means of obtaining the remission of all our sins, and Adam's sin as far as it pertains to us; it gives a title to the Holy Spirit, a promise of a resurrection of the body, and a glorious immortality in heaven. Is not this enough? Who ever attached more importance to baptism than this?

But our chief object in quoting it was to show that it refers the language of Jesus (born of water) to baptism. How comes it to pass NOW that men will abandon their own creeds and the plainest teaching of Holy Writ, as understood by the learned of all ages, and deny that the passage has any reference to baptism at all. When the Lord said: "Suffer little children to come unto me," and said not a word about water, or baptism, they can see plenty of water to baptize an infant; yet where the Lord uses the language "born of water and of the Spirit," they can not find a drop of water in the passage. Whether or not they are consistent the reader will judge for himself.

But we are told that if the kingdom was not established until the day of Pentecost, this language can not apply to it, for it was used before that time. It is true that the kingdom was not set up until the day of Pentecost; and it is also true that this language was used by Christ before that time, but the same is true of every thing He said while on the earth; hence it may all be wiped out by the same rule. The New Testament is the *last will* of the Saviour; was there ever a will the provisions of which were not arranged before the death of the testator? Jesus Christ arranged the provisions of His will before His death, and one very important provision was the manner of entering His kingdom when it should be established. The clause containing this provision was given to Nicodemus in a figure, and went into effect when His apostles were installed executors of the will on the day of Pentecost.

But the tenth verse—"Art thou a master of Israel, and knowest not these things?"—is supposed to show that the lesson contained in the conversation was one which Nicodemus was presumed to know as a teacher of the Jewish law; and as baptism for remission of sins was not taught in that law, he could not know it, and therefore it was not embraced in the conversation between Christ and him. As a teacher of Israel, it was presumed that Nicodemus was capable of understanding plain instruction such as Christ had given him, but after Christ had explained the whole matter to him, he still did not understand it; hence the question, "Art thou a master of Israel, and knowest not these things?" and Jesus proceeds to tell him the reason: "We speak that we do know, and testify that we have seen; and ye receive not our witness. If I have told you of earthly things, and ye believe not, how shall ye believe if I tell you of heavenly things?" Vs. 11, 12. Thus we see he did not know what Jesus had taught him because he did not receive the testimony presented. The Jewish age abounded with *types* and *prophecies* pointing to Christ and His kingdom, with which Nicodemus should have been familiar, yet he did not understand them when explained to him. Hence the objection amounts to nothing, and the argument stands forth in all its strength: When Jesus spake of a birth of water and Spirit, He referred to baptism, without which no man can enter the kingdom of God, and out of which there is no salvation for those to whom the kingdom comes.

Our third argument is based upon the commission as recorded by Mark: "And he said unto them, Go ye into all the world, and preach the gospel to every creature. He that believeth and is baptized shall be saved; but he that believeth not shall be damned." Mark xvi:16. To suit the theory of some who regard baptism a nonessential, and teach that man is justified by faith alone, the commission should read, "He that believeth and is saved may be baptized if convenient." Their theory confronts the Lord when He says, "He that believeth and is baptized shall be saved," and says, "Not so, Lord; he that believes is saved, whether baptized or not."

When a blessing is promised on certain conditions, it can not be enjoyed until the last condition is completed with. E.g.: When Naaman was commanded to wash himself *seven* times in Jordan, that he might be healed of his leprosy, he was not healed until he dipped himself the seventh time. When the Jews were required to go around the city seven days, and on the seventh day seven times, that they might possess the city, the walls were not thrown down until they came to the end of the conditions prescribed; so, when the Lord promises salvation to him who *believes* AND is baptized, no one need expect the promised salvation until he has complied with the last prescribed condition. If he believes, yet has not been baptized, the blessing promised can not be expected.

But we are told that the salvation here promised was salvation in heaven, or future salvation. This attaches much more importance to baptism than belongs to it. We can not be saved in heaven unless first saved from sin; and as baptism secures salvation in heaven, it must save us from sin, and every thing beyond that. This is too strong meat for us. As Peter was one of those to whom this commission was given, and had the Spirit to guide him into all truth, perhaps he might tell us what baptism saves us from. On the day of Pentecost, operating under this commission, he commanded persons to repent, and be baptized in the name of Jesus Christ for the remission of sins; hence he understood "remission of sins," or salvation from the punishment due sin, to be the salvation of the commission. And when he wrote to his brethren he said, "Baptism doth also NOW save us" (1 Pet. iii:21); hence it is not a future but a present salvation which is received by baptism—not salvation in heaven, for it *now* saves us.

But infidelity has furnished our neighbors an easier way of escape from the commission by Mark. Finding all other quibbles ineffectual, they now tell us it is an interpolation—a Roman Catholic forgery—"the whole of the chapter, from the ninth verse to the twentieth, inclusive, is spurious." This is a very convenient way of disposing of an argument which can not be met otherwise. If a passage is in harmony with our theory it is canonical, otherwise it is a forgery. We wish to enter our protest against the immolation of our Bible in this way. Interpolations in it there may be, but they must be incontrovertibly shown such before we can respect the attack of one against whose theory they chance to come. Such men can not blow a chapter out of our Bible with a breath.

We propose to submit some testimony which may not be in the possession of every one, with regard to the authenticity of this connection of Scripture. Prof. Stowe has made the authenticity of the books of the Bible a specialty, and we suppose has given the subject more attention than any man in America—perhaps than any man now living. He wrote a notice of Tischendorf's New Testament, which was was published in the "Christian Union," from which we extract the following:

"The New Testament in English, edited by Tischendorf and published by Tauchnitz, is a work of great merit, in a scholarly point of view; but to those not fully acquainted with the subject, altogether deceptive, though not intentionally so. Such are apt to think that the three oldest manuscripts must be the best authority for the original text, and that what can not be found in them could not have been a part of the New Testament as it came from the hands of the apostles. This is a great and mischievous mistake. The three oldest manuscripts used by Tischendorf date from the first quarter of the fourth to the middle of the fifth century; that is, some two hundred and twenty-five years, at least, after the New Testament had been written, read in the churches, and scattered all over the Christian world—liable to all the accidents incident to frequent transcription.

"Now we have *translations* of the New Testament in various languages—Syrian, Egyptian, Ethiopic, and others—beginning with the latter part of the second century. From the first century to the fifth there are not less than ten of these translations, and they certainly are a much better authority than manuscripts which had no existence till early in the fourth century. When these translations contain passages which are not contained in later manuscripts, the translations are much more likely to give the text as it stood in their time than the manuscripts. The loss of a leaf (for these manuscripts are all in *book* form, and not in rolls), the beginning in wrong places by the transcriber after a rest from writing, and various other circumstances, may easily account for an unintentional *omission* in the manuscripts, but an *interpolation* must be intentional. On these accounts, and others that might be mentioned, it is easy to see that, at least in regard to interpolations, a good translation of the *second or third century* is a far more reliable authority for the original of the text than the manuscript of the fourth or fifth century. The ten translations above alluded to are, therefore, on these points, far more trustworthy than the three manuscripts used by Tischendorf in his new edition of the New Testament.

"Again, we have numerous Christian writers—from the first

century to the fifth—who constantly quote the New Testament as it stood in their time; and the quotations of the first three centuries are an earlier authority for the original text than any of the Tischendorf manuscripts. There are some seventy-five of these writers, and their quotations are so numerous that if every manuscript of the New Testament were lost, the substance of it could be reproduced from their writings. Moreover, the manuscripts are all anonymous. We know not who wrote them; but the quotations are given with responsible names. We know the authors of the books in which they occur. It is true that these translations, and the writings of the early Christian fathers, are generally more or less incomplete, and the text somewhat varied, but the same is true of the New Testament manuscripts. In the very best manuscript (the Sinaitic), Tischendorf indicates four different *classes* or *kinds* of variation. On this point all the authorities, whether translations or manuscripts, need careful editing—they all stand on precisely the same ground.

"Now apply these principles to a single case by way of illustration. The last chapter of Mark's gospel, from the eighth verse onward, is omitted in the Sinaitic and Vatican manuscripts, but is contained in the Alexandrian. It is in all the Syrian, Egyptian, and other translations of the second and third centuries, and it is quoted as the last part of Mark's gospel by Irenæus, the most learned Christian writer of the second century, and the student of Polycarp, who had studied with the apostle John. Irenæus tells us that he had the books of the Christian Scriptures in his possession at the very time when he was on terms of familiarity with Polycarp, daily listening to his accounts of what he had himself heard from John and others, who had seen the Lord. * * * This chapter of Mark is also found in more than five hundred Greek manuscripts, and also in the Latin and Gothic. Now, which is the more probable that all these *most ancient* witnesses had been deceived by an interpolation, or that, by some accident, the last leaf of Mark's gospel had been dropped out from the manuscript from which the Sinaitic and Vatican were copied? From this statement of fact it is obvious that any one who should, in making a revised text of the New Testament, strike out all that is not contained in the three oldest manuscripts used by Tischendorf, must be guilty of a very faulty text.

It is a remarkable fact, not to be lightly estimated, that a whole column of space is left blank in the Vatican manuscript as if the copyist had intended, but for some reason had omitted, to fill it with the text."

In a subsequent paper Prof. Stowe enters into specifications as follows: "We are perfectly safe and within bounds in concluding that, at least, the historical books of the New Testament were in circulation in the Syrian churches in the Peshito translation as early as the latter part of the first century. If so, then the Syrian Christians, the near neighbors and contemporaries, and relations by language and race, of the apostles themselves, read this passage, the last verses of Mark's gospel, without question, as a genuine portion of the gospel of Mark, nearly three centuries before the oldest manuscript used by Tischendorf was written. Now take this in connection with the fact that no one knows either the origin or the history of the Tischendorf manuscripts, while both the origin and history of the Syrian translation are known and well attested as to substance, and also the fact that an accidental omission, especially of the last leaf, is much more easily accounted for than an interlined interpolation, which, at that early period, and in those circumstances, would have been well nigh impossible, and any one can see that the authority of the Syrian translation must be, in this instance, altogether superior to that of the Greek manuscript. To this add the authority on the same point of all the translations of the second and third centuries, and of more than five hundred Greek manuscripts, and the case is made out.

"*Second authority*, Irenæus. He was born in Smyrna, near the beginning of the second century; was the student of Polycarp, the celebrated bishop and martyr of that city, the disciple of John the apostle, and, not unlikely, the very *angel* of that church to whom John directed the epistle in Rev. ii:8-17, dictated by the Lord Jesus. He had resided at Rome and early went as a missionary to France, where he suffered martyrdom in the year 202. In writing to his friend Iconius, who was an elder in the church at Rome, he says: 'I saw thee when I was yet a boy in the lower class with Polycarp. I remember the events of those times much better than those of more recent occurrence. I can tell the very place where the blessed Polycarp was accus-

tomed to sit and discourse of his familiar intercourse with John, as he was accustomed to tell, as also his familiarity with those who had seen the Lord; how, also, he used to relate their discourses concerning his miracles, his doctrine; all these were told by Polycarp, *in consistency with the Holy Scriptures,* as he had received them from the eye-witnesses. These things I attentively heard, noting them down in my mind; and these same facts I am always in the habit of recalling faithfully to mind.'
* * * Is not Irenæus better authority on such a point as that which we are now considering than any anonymous manuscript written nearly two centuries after his time? Yet Irenæus, in his great work on *Heresies,* iii, 10:6, writes thus: 'Mark says in the end of his gospel (Mark xvi:19), And, indeed, the Lord Jesus, after he had spoken to them, was received up into heaven, and sat on the right hand of God.'

"*The third authority,* Hippolytus. Hippolytus was a student of Irenæus, the pastor of a church in the neighborhood of Rome, one of the most pious preachers and able writers of his time, and his works are still highly esteemed and widely read. In 1551, a statue of him, with biographical inscriptions, was disinterred near Rome, and in 1661 and 1832, important long-lost writings of his were discovered, all of which excited great interest and enthusiasm. In his work on spiritual gifts there is this passage: 'Jesus says to all, at the same time, concerning the gifts which shall be given by Him through the Holy Spirit. And these signs shall follow them that believe,' etc., etc., quoting the whole of Mark xvi:17, 18. We need pursue the subject no further, nor quote the later fathers, Augustine, Jerome, and others. So far as the weight of authority is concerned, is not the genuineness of the passage in question established beyond reasonable doubt? Tischendorf has no superior in regard to New Testament Greek *manuscript* authority; but as to authority of *translations,. church writers,* etc., which are more ancient than any of our existing New Testament Greek manuscripts, Lachmann is his superior, and Lachmann retains this passage as genuine. As to the internal evidence, without these verses how abrupt and awkward the closing words of the gospel: 'For they were afraid.' From the analogy of all the other gospels we could certainly expect something beyond this, and common sense would teach the same."

We offer no apology for these long extracts from Prof. Stowe, they throw a flood of light upon the whole subject, and we can well afford the space given if we may thereby *preserve the integrity of the Bible*. We could abundantly prove the doctrine of baptism for the remission of sins without this passage, but with it there can be no plausible opposition. In the Introduction to the Tischendorf New Testament we find the following admission: "The ordinary conclusion of the gospel of St. Mark, namely, xvi:9-20, is found in more than five hundred Greek manuscripts, in the whole of the Syriac and Coptic, and most of the Latin manuscripts, and even in the Gothic version. But by Eusebius and Jerome (the former of whom died in the year 340), it is stated expressly that in nearly all the trustworthy copies of their time the gospel ended with the eighth verse; and, with this, of all existing known Greek manuscripts, only the Vatican and the Sinaitic now agree."

We might quote numerous other authorities, but the foregoing are all for which we have room, and are deemed quite sufficient to establish the purity of the text beyond doubt. It is a positive utterance of Him who had all authority in heaven and upon the earth, that "he that believeth and is baptized shall be saved." Heaven and earth may pass away, but the words of Jesus can not fail. Reader, are you a believer? If so, have you been baptized? If not, can you feel that the promise, "he that believeth and is baptized shall be saved," offers any consolation to you while in your present condition? If not, "why tarriest thou? arise and be baptized, and wash away thy sins, calling on the name of the Lord."

We base our next argument upon the operations of the apostles under this commission. They were instructed to tarry at Jerusalem until endued with power from on high. They were all with one accord in one place when the Spirit came from heaven and took possession of their tongues, and spake forth the wonderful and mighty works of God to Jews, devout men, of every nation under heaven. The gospel was preached, they heard and believed it, and were cut to the heart by it, and cried out "Men and brethren, what shall we do?" To this important inquiry Peter replied: "Repent, and be baptized every one of you, in the name of Jesus Christ for the remission of sins." Acts ii:38. This answer was dictated by the Holy Spirit, and must therefore be accepted as applicable to the question asked. If there was ever a time when a plain, unambiguous answer was demanded, this was the time. His answer not only concerned the thousands then present, but as to him was committed the keys of the kingdom, and he was, for the first time, proclaiming the terms of admission, his answer must constitute a law of entrance for those who would become subjects of the kingdom until it shall have been delivered up to God even the Father. A plain answer was demanded, and we insist that such was the character of the answer given. There are two adjunctive phrases in the answer which we may first understand, and then remove for a moment in order to get the meaning of the trunk without them. Repent, and be baptized [every one of you, in the name of Jesus Christ] for the remission of sins. Every one of you. This shows that all are addressed, and this is the measure of its import. In the name of Jesus Christ. This shows by what *authority* he gave to the command. When Peter healed the lame man who lay at the gate of the temple, he said: "In the name of Jesus Christ of Nazareth rise up and walk." Acts iii:6. When the people were astonished at what was done, Peter explained: "Ye men of Israel, why marvel at this? or why look ye so earnestly on us, as though by our own power or holiness we had made this man to walk?" Ver. 12. This shows that the phrase "in the name of Jesus Christ" simply conveys the idea of authority or power. This settled, then we leave out the adjunctive phrases that the members of the trunk may stand closer together, and we read it thus: Repent, and be baptized for the remission of sins. This leaves no room to doubt the object or design of the obedience required. Repent, and be baptized. What for? For the remission of sins.

The preposition *for* connects *repent and be baptized* on the one hand with *remission* on the other; *of* connecting *sins* with *remission* and governing it in the objective case. Hence, the relation expressed by the word *for* is between *repent and be baptized* on one side, and *remission of sins* on the other. The word *for* can not be divided and made mean *one thing* as to *repent*, and *another thing* as to *be baptized*. We have already shown, by rules of language quoted more than once, that the same word can not have more than one meaning at the same time, and in the same place; hence, whatever may be the meaning of the preposition *for* as to repentance is its meaning as to baptism. They are connected by the copulative conjunction *and*, and must not be separated, but must sustain, in this sentence, the same relation to remission. This point being settled, we turn to Peter for an explanation of the relation existing between repentance and remission, feeling sure that baptism sustains the same relation. We read: "Repent ye, therefore, and be converted, that your sins may be blotted out." Acts iii:19. Do what? Repent and be converted. What for? That your sins may be blotted out. Then, as men are to *repent* that their sins may be blotted out, and baptism sustains the same relation to remission of sins, it follows that *men must be baptized that their sins may be blotted out*. From this decision there is no appeal; it is strong as Holy Writ and the laws of language can make a proposition.

Before leaving this argument we may say that were it shown that men must be baptized *because their sins are pardoned*, it would follow that they must *repent for the same thing, i.e., because their sins are pardoned*. As before stated, the preposition *for* can not mean *in order to* and *because of* at the same time and place. More than this, *for* is from the Greek preposition *eis*, which looks forward, not backward. Liddell and Scott define it, "*direction toward*," "*motion to*," "*on*," or "*into*." It is not used in the sense of *because of* a single time in the Bible. In Matt. xxvi:28, we have a similarly constructed sentence both in the Greek and in the English scriptures: "For this is my blood of the New Testament, which is shed for many for the remission of sins." The words "for the remission of sins," are not only the same as in Acts ii:38, but they are from the same Greek words, *eis aphesin amartioon*. No one believes that Christ shed His blood because the sins of the people were remitted, but in order that they might be remitted. Then if the same set of words means the same thing, Peter commanded the Pentecostians to repent and be baptized in order that their sins might be remitted, or as in the French Bible, *"in order to* OBTAIN *the remission of sins."*

But an objector says that "when Jesus cured a man of his leprosy, 'he charged him to tell no man: but go, and show thyself to the priest, and offer for thy cleansing according as Moses commanded, for a testimony unto them' (Luke v:14; Mark i:44)—thus showing that *for* means 'because of.' He was to make the offering because of his cleansing." In the first place, we reply that the word *for*, in the phrase "for thy cleansing," is not from *eis*, the word used in Acts ii:38. In the next place, by consulting the law of Moses for the cure of leprosy, it will be seen that there was first a cure, and then a ceremonial cleansing from leprosy; and it was *in order to this cleansing* that the *cured man* was required by the Lord to make the offering. Hence, even in this place, the preposition *for*, though not a translation of *eis* at all, means "in order to," and not "because of." And if it did mean "because of," as it comes not from *eis* the objection amounts to nothing.

But since Mr. Ditzler has come upon the arena, the argument based upon "because of," as a meaning of *eis*, has been very generally abandoned in this country. He says: "*Eis* is *always prospective*, and *never retrospective*. * * * The Baptists are all wrong on *eis*—making it retrospective—'in consequence of.'" Louisville Debate, p. 307. This position is well taken, but it takes away all chance of even a respectable quibble on Acts ii:38, against baptism for remission of sins. He says: "Neither repentance nor baptism is for remission, but conditions precedent to doing that which is for remission." P. 295. If this were true it could give no relief to his theory. How can he get to remission until he passes through the conditions precedent to it? But he continues: "The repentance would as much be for remission as baptism, since they are coupled with χαι—*and*—'repent and be baptized.' But it is never for remission of sins. Whatever *is for* remission, of necessity brings remission of sins. Faith does this—repentance *never*. The repentance here as usual precedes faith." *Ut supra*. Repentance is not for remission of sins, yet Peter commanded persons to repent and be converted, that their sins might be blotted out!! (Acts iii:19.) Wonder what difference there is in *remission of sins* and *blotting out of sins!* But he says repentance precedes faith; and as repentance precedes baptism, and both are conditions precedent to faith, which brings remission, it follows that they are without faith, and not pleasing to God; for "without faith it is impossible to please him." Heb. xi:6. And as that which is not of faith is sin, such repentance and baptism as precede faith are sin. But this reverses the order of the commission—"he that believeth and is baptized," not he that is baptized and then believes. It also reverses the order of Philip's operations. When the Samaritans believed Philip's preaching, they were baptized; and when the eunuch demanded baptism, Philip replied: "If thou believest with all thy heart thou mayest." No inspired man ever taught that repentance and baptism were conditions precedent to faith, or that any one should be baptized who did not believe.

The conversion of the Pentecostians may be regarded as an inspired commentary on the commission under which the apostles acted. The commission required teaching or preaching—Peter preached to Jews, devout men, who were present on the occasion. The commission required faith or belief—these were cut to the heart when they heard and believed what Peter preached. The commission, as recorded by Luke, associated repentance with remission of sins; so did Peter. The commission required believers of all nations to be baptized; so did Peter. The commission followed baptism by a promise of salvation—Peter made remission of sins the object of repentance and baptism. Thus we see how the apostles understood the commission.

But an objector says: "Anderson's Translation of Acts ii:47, says: 'The Lord added the saved daily to the church.' And as men are added to the church by baptism, it follows that they were saved before they were added by baptism." Anderson believed that the word εχχλεσια, here rendered *church*, simply meant a *local church* or *congregation*, and that after they were saved by obedience to the gospel they were daily added to the congregation, or placed together. Mr. Campbell's compilation of Campbell, Macknight, and Doddridge, renders this verse, "And the Lord daily added the saved to the congregation." Whether Anderson correctly translated the verse or not, no honest man will take advantage of his translation to pervert his teaching. T. S. Green, of London, renders the passage thus: "And the Lord was adding daily those that were being saved." Twofold New Testament. Thus he leaves out the word *church*, for which there is nothing in the original, and is faithful to the participial form and present tense of the Greek. This rendering comes to us from, and is supported by, very high authority, and is in harmony with the general teaching of the Bible on the subject. It should, therefore, be very carefully considered before it is rejected.

It is a fact beyond controversy that those who complied with the terms imposed on the day of Pentecost were pardoned at some time of that day. At what time were they pardoned? Were they pardoned when they came together that morning? No, for they believed that Jesus Christ was an impostor, and they had crucified Him as such. Were they pardoned when Peter began to preach? Surely not, for he accused them with the murder of the Son of God, and they believed him drunk with wine. Were they forgiven when, convinced of their great wrong, they cried out, "Men and brethren, what shall we do?" Such is not the style of those who are forgiven. Surely they did not cry out in the anguish of their souls, "Men and brethren, what shall we do because God has graciously forgiven us all our sins?" They were charged with the murder of Jesus Christ, and they wanted to know how to escape the punishment due them as sinners. Did Peter answer the question they put to him? We suppose he did. He commanded them to repent, and be baptized in the name of Jesus Christ for the remission of sins. As many as "gladly received his word were baptized." Now, are they pardoned? No one doubts it. When were they pardoned? When they complied with the conditions specified in the command; not before. Sinner, would *you* be saved? then do as they did. The command came fresh from heaven, and can not be wrong.

We base another argument upon the language of Ananias to Saul: "And now why tarriest thou? Arise, and be baptized, and wash away thy sins, calling on the name of the Lord." Acts xxii:16. Saul's conversion, though in some respects extraordinary, has within it all the elements contained in the commission and in the conversions of Pentecost. He was a violent persecutor of the people of God, and believed Jesus an impostor, and His followers worthy of punishment. Jesus presented Himself to him and made known the fact that He was truly the Son of God. Believing it, he cried out, "Lord, what wilt thou have me to do?" Here would have been a good time to have verified the theory of justification by faith alone. Saul had the faith, and, if justification was by it alone, he would have gladly known the fact.

As the Lord did not so inform him, we infer that no such theory was in operation at that time. Having delegated the proclamation of the gospel to men, the Lord did not usurp the authority delegated to others by telling Saul himself, but tells him where he might go and find one competent to furnish the desired information—"Arise, and go into the city and it shall be told thee what thou must do." Not what you *may* do or *can* do, if convenient, but what you *must* do. The Lord sent Ananias to answer the inquiry, which he did, saying, "Arise, and be baptized, and wash away thy sins, calling on the name of the Lord." He did not tell Saul to believe, for he had been a believer from the time the Lord appeared to him in the way, three days before; nor was he told to repent, because he had been truly penitent the same length of time; but the instructions began just where Saul's obedience had stopped, and at the point necessary to perfect it. We stop not to inquire what washed Paul's sins away—whether blood, water, or any thing else—sufficient it is for us to know that they were not washed away until he was baptized. Granting, as we do, that the blood of Christ cleanseth from all sin, Paul could not literally come in contact with it, but must approach it through some means appointed for that purpose. Commenting upon the phrase "be baptized and wash away thy sins," Mr. Wesley says: "Baptism administered to real penitents is both a means and seal of pardon. Nor did God, ordinarily, in the primitive church, bestow this on any, unless through this means." Wesley's Notes.

Burkitt says: "*Arise, and be baptized, and wash away thy sins.* Here note that sacraments are not empty, insignificant signs; but God, by His grace and blessing, renders His own ordinances effectual for these great ends for which his wisdom has appointed them: *Be baptized and wash away thy sins.* As water cleanseth the body, so the blood of Christ, signified by water, washes away the guilt of the soul. Where true faith is, together with the profession of it by baptism, there is salvation promised. Mark xvi:16. He that believeth and is baptized shall be saved." Burkitt's Notes.

But Mr. Campbell says: "Paul's sins were *really pardoned* when he believed, yet he had no solemn *pledge* of the fact, no *formal* acquittal, no *formal* purgation of his sins, until he washes them away in the water of baptism." Debate with MacCalla, p. 135.

Yes, Mr. Campbell said this in his debate with MacCalla in October of 1823, while he was a Baptist and believed and taught as Baptists do; but when he became a man he put away childish things.

But we are told that Paul was commanded to arise and be baptized and wash away his sins BY calling on the name of the Lord. We respectfully suggest that the language will not bear this rendering. The word επιχαλεσαμενος, is, i. Aorist, corresponding to the indefinite past tense of English, and, hence, must indicate a calling which had previously been made. Arise, and be baptized, and wash away your sins, *having called* on the name of the Lord.

We would transpose and paraphrase the passage thus: "Having called upon the name of the Lord for information, or to know what to do, He has sent me to tell you; and now why tarry? Arise, and be baptized, and wash away your sins." The *indefinite past tense* can not express a calling yet to be made.

"But Paul said to the jailer, 'Believe on the Lord Jesus Christ and thou shalt be saved, and thy house,' and it is not likely he would have given to the jailer a system of pardon differing from his own." What are we to do with such a passage as this? Shall we tear it from its context, and build a theory of justification by faith alone because it says nothing about repentance or baptism? If so, may we not take the language of Ananias to Saul, and construct a theory of justification by baptism alone because he was told to arise and be baptized, and not a word was said about faith or repentance? And may not a third party take Peter's language, "Repent, and be converted that your sins may be blotted out," and construct a theory of justification upon repentance alone, because faith nor baptism is mentioned? So a fourth party may quote Peter on Pentecost, saying, Repent, and be baptized, and build a theory on these *two* to the exclusion of faith because it is not mentioned, and thus we may have as many theories of justification as there are cases of conversion recorded.

We must allow the apostles to adapt their teaching to the condition of the taught. When Paul addressed the jailer in infidelity—one who believed Jesus an imposter and had Paul and

Silas in prison for performing a miracle in His name—it was necessary to begin at the beginning; hence, they told him to *believe* as the first thing necessary, and then they spake unto him the word of the Lord; that is, they further developed the plan of salvation to him. When Peter addressed believers on the day of Pentecost, he did not tell them to do that which they had already done, but added what was lacking, "Repent, and be baptized." But when Ananias addressed a believing penitent in the person of Saul, he did not tell him to believe and repent, for both of these he had done; but he told him to do the only thing which, at that stage of his conversion, he lacked "Arise, and be baptized."

But we propose now to show that Paul did impose the same conditions upon the jailer that Peter did upon the Pentecostians, and that Peter and Paul did not preach different gospels. Paul said to the jailer: "Believe on the Lord Jesus Christ and thou shalt be saved, and thy house, and they spake unto him the word of the Lord, and to all that were in his house." Acts xvi:31, 32. The reader will please note the fact that the *word of the Lord* was spoken to the jailer; and if we would know what was required of him we must learn what was embraced in the word of the Lord. The prophet said: "And many people shall go and say, Come ye and let us go up to the mountain of the Lord, to the house of the God of Jacob, and he will teach us of his ways, and we will walk in his paths; for out of Zion shall go forth the law and the word of the Lord from Jerusalem." Isa. ii:3. Thus we see that the word of the Lord spoken to the jailer was to go forth from Jerusalem; hence, if we can find what went forth as the word of the Lord from Jerusalem we may know what was preached to the jailer. The Lord said: "That repentance and remission of sins should be preached in his name among all nations, beginning at Jerusalem." Luke xxiv:47. The prophet tells us that the word of the Lord should go forth from Jerusalem, and the Lord explains this by saying it was written that repentance and remission of sins should be preached in His name among all nations, beginning there. Then how did the word of the Lord go forth from Jerusalem? and how was repentance and remission of sins preached in the name of Jesus, beginning there? Peter said: "Repent, and be baptized, every one of you, in the name of Jesus Christ for the remission of sins." This was what went forth as the word of the Lord from Jerusalem; and, as this constituted the word of the Lord at Jerusalem, it took the same thing to constitute it at the Philippjan jail; and as this was the way repentance and remission of sins began to be preached in the name of Jesus at Jerusalem, and was to be preached among all nations, and as the jailer and all his were a part of all nations, it is certainly what was preached as the word of the Lord to them. Not only so, but we find the same result produced by the preaching at both places. At Jerusalem "they that gladly received his word were baptized: and the same day there were added unto them about three thousand souls." Acts ii:41. At the jail "he took them the same hour of the night and washed their stripes, and was baptized, he and all his straightway." Acts xvi:33. Thus we see that the same gospel was preached at both places, and the parties understood and obeyed it in the same way. If baptism was not included in the word of the Lord spoken to the jailer, and especially if it be a mere non-essential, why did he so promptly attend to it the same hour of the night?

Before leaving Paul's case we must attend to another objection which comes in our way occasionally: "If baptism be for the remission of sins, then remission is made to depend upon third parties, and the subject is dependent upon an administrator." Had the Lord been disposed to have dispensed with the services of third parties, why did he not pardon Saul without sending him off to wait three days for Ananias, the third party? Why did He not pardon the devout Cornelius without sending to Joppa for Simon Peter, the third party? Why did He not pardon the Ethiopian nobleman without the services of Philip, the third party? God did specially interpose in each of these cases, and yet He dispensed not with the services of the third party. When an unclean person was to be purified under the law, "a clean person shall take hyssop, and dip it in the water, and sprinkle it upon the tent, and upon all the vessels, and upon the persons that were there, and upon him that touched a bone, or one slain, or one dead, or a grave; and the clean person shall sprinkle upon the unclean on the third day and on the seventh day." Num. xix:18, 19. Thus we see that God's law has ever required the services of third parties, or the services of one class in behalf of another. But if this objection be worth any thing, is the theory of justification by faith alone free from it? Paul tells us that faith comes by hearing, and hearing by the word of God, and asks: "How shall they believe in him of whom they have not heard? and how shall they hear without a preacher?" Rom. x:14. Then, as he can not get faith without a third party, the preacher, the difficulty rests with all its weight upon the objector. When he gets done preaching to him, if he has faith enough, it will not detain him much longer to baptize him and make a clean job of it at once.

"But in a desert he might believe in preaching previously heard." Yes; but the preacher was still present when the preaching was done by the third party, and when the sinner heard the gospel, then was the time he should have obeyed it; and if he declined to do it, it was his misfortune, and God will hold him responsible for opportunities thus slighted, just as he will another man who has the same opportunities and dies in place of falling in a desert.

In both cases it is the misfortune of the parties that they did not obey the gospel when they had the opportunity of doing so. The man who slighted ten thousand opportunities of obeying the gospel, until he gets into a condition that offers no opportunity, need scarcely expect to be held guiltless for slighting the overtures of the past. Now is the day of salvation. Now is your time—to-morrow to you may never come.

We come next to examine the epistles, in which are various allusions to our subject. In Paul's letter to the church at Rome we have the following very significant paragraph: "But ye have obeyed from the heart that form of doctrine which was delivered you. Being then made free from sin, ye became the servants of righteousness." Rom. vi:17, 18. Here we learn that the Romans obeyed a form, system, or mould of doctrine, in doing which they were made free from sin.

Having made the subject of a change of heart a theme of special examination in another part of our work, we need not stop to consider it here. It is sufficient at present to state that all acceptable obedience comes from the heart. God is not mocked, but seeks such to worship Him as worship Him in spirit and in truth. He that worships God to be seen of men, to gain popular applause, professional patronage, the hand of a lady, the approval of a companion, is but mocking Him with that which is an abomination in His sight. The Romans obeyed from the heart the form of doctrine delivered them. They did not obey the doctrine, but they obeyed the form of it. In order to recognize the form or likeness of any thing, we must be acquainted with that of which it is a form; *e.g.*, to recognize the form or likeness of a man, we must first be acquainted with the man of whom it is a likeness. Then, to recognize the form of doctrine obeyed by the Romans, we must know the doctrine itself. Paul says: "Moreover, brethren, I declare unto you the gospel which I preached unto you, which also ye have received, and wherein ye stand; by which also ye are saved, if ye keep in memory what I preached unto you, unless ye have believed in vain. For I delivered unto you first of all that which I also received, how that Christ died for our sins according to the Scriptures; and that he was buried, and that he rose again the third day according to the Scriptures." 1 Cor. xv:1-4.

Paul says he *delivered* to the Corinthians that which he received, and he says the Romans obeyed the form of doctrine *delivered* them. He further says that he preached the gospel to the Corinthians, and we suppose he preached the same gospel at Rome which he preached at Corinth, for he invokes the curses of heaven upon himself, or an angel, should either preach another gospel. Gal. i:8.

Then, what was the gospel preached by Paul? In its facts it was: "that Christ died for our sins according to the Scriptures; that he was buried, and that he rose again the third day according to the Scriptures." These three facts are the gospel which Paul preached, the form of which the Romans obeyed, in doing of which they were made free from sin. We are now prepared to look for the form.

Paul says: "If we be dead with Christ, we believe that we shall also live with him; knowing that Christ being raised from the dead dieth no more; death hath no more dominion over him. For in that he died, he died unto sin once; but in that he liveth, he liveth unto God. Likewise reckon ye also yourselves to be dead indeed unto sin, but alive unto God." Rom. vi:8-

11. Then the sinner dies unto sin—Christ died unto sin once. Going back to the third verse, we read: "Know ye not, that so many of us as were baptized into Jesus Christ were baptized into his death? Therefore we are buried with him by baptism into death; that like as Christ was raised up from the dead by the glory of the Father, even so we also should walk in newness of life; for if we have been planted together in the likeness of his death, we shall be also in the likeness of his resurrection." Christ died *for* sin—the sinner must die *to* sin. Christ was buried—the sinner must be buried with him by baptism; Christ was raised up from the dead—the sinner must be raised up from his baptism into death to walk in newness of life. Thus they are planted in the likeness of His death, and, raised to newness of life, should live in expectation of a final resurrection like His.

There is another thought connected with baptism into Christ's death. We are not baptized into Christ's death literally, but we are baptized into the benefits of His death; this being so, we can reach the benefits of His death only through baptism as the means of reaching it. A burial with Christ by baptism is the subject introduced in the beginning of the chapter, and Paul labors it and its results until he comes to the language quoted: "You have obeyed [in baptism] the form of doctrine delivered you [what was the effect of this obedience]?; being then made made free from sin, ye became the servants of righteousness,"

But we would next call attention to the fact that out of Christ there is no salvation. All the blessings of the gospel are to be realized in Him, none out of Him: "If any man be in Christ, he is a new creature: old things have passed away; behold, all things have become new." 2 Cor. v:17. "God was in Christ, reconciling the world unto himself, not imputing their *trespasses* unto them." Ver. 19. "In whom we have redemption through his blood, even the forgiveness of sins." Col. i:14; Gal. i:7. "Ye are complete in him who is the head of all principality and power." Col. ii:10. "For in him dwelleth all the fullness of the godhead bodily." Ver. 9. "It pleased the Father that in him should all fullness dwell." Col. i:19. "Who hath blessed us with all spiritual blessings in heavenly places in Christ." Eph. i:3. All things are gathered in Christ. Ver. 10. We trust in him. Ver. 12. Our redemption is in Christ. Rom. iii:24. While living, the Christian has hope in Christ. 1 Cor. xv:19. When dead, the Christian sleeps in Christ. 1 Thess. iv:16. Will be made alive from the dead in Christ. 1 Cor. xv:22.

Seeing, then, that all the blessings of the gospel are *in* Christ, and that if we enjoy them we must get into Christ, the question next in order is, How do we get into Christ? Paul says: "Know ye not, that so many of us as were baptized into Jesus Christ were baptized into his death." Rom. vi:3. And, again: "For as many of you as were baptized into Christ have put on Christ." Gal. iii:27. Of course, we are not speaking of baptism to a faithless impenitent, for we have labored the *antecedents* sufficiently to be understood on these subjects. By the above passages we find baptism to be the act by which a proper subject puts on Christ, where all spiritual blessings are.

Luther says: "This is not done by changing of a garment, or by any laws of works, but by a new birth, and by the renewing of the inward man, which is done in baptism, as Paul saith: 'All ye that are baptized have put on Christ.' Also: 'According to his mercy he saved us by the washing of regeneration, and renewing of the Holy Ghost.' Tit. iii:5. For, besides that, they who are baptized are regenerated and renewed by the Holy Ghost to a heavenly righteousness and to eternal life, there ariseth in them new and holy affections, as the fear of God, true faith, and assured hopes, etc. There beginneth in them also a new will; and this is to put on Christ truly and according to the gospel. Therefore, the righteousness of the law, or our own works, is not given unto us in baptism, but Christ himself is our garment. Now, Christ is no law, no lawgiver, no works, but a divine and an inestimable gift, whom God hath given unto us, that he might be our Justifier, our Saviour, and our Redeemer. Wherefore, to be appareled with Christ according to the gospel, is not to be appareled with the law or with works, but with an incomparable gift—that is, with remission of sins, righteousness, peace, consolation, joy of spirit, salvation, life, and Christ himself." Luther on Galatians in Campbell on Baptism, p. 261.

"For 'as many as are baptized into Christ,' in his name have' thereby 'put on Christ' (Gal. iii:27)—that is, are mystically united to Christ, and made one with him. For 'by one Spirit are we all baptized into one body' (1 Cor. xii:13)—namely, the church, 'the body of Christ' (Eph. iv:12). From which spiritual, vital union with Him proceeds the influence of His grace on those that are baptized; as from our union with the church, a share in all its privileges, and in all the promises Christ has made to it." Doctrinal Tracts, p. 248.

But we have another argument upon Paul's *seven units*, of which baptism is one. He says: "There is one body and one spirit, even as ye are called in one hope of your calling, one Lord, one faith, one baptism, one God and Father of all, who is above all, and through all, and in you all." Eph. iv:4-6. Having shown in the preceding chapters of this epistle that in the death of Jesus Christ God had broken down the middle wall which had long separated Jews from Gentiles, that He might make of twain one new church, reconciling both Jews and Gentiles in one body by the cross (ii:11-20), the apostle's argument culminated in the grand fact that there is now ONE BODY, or church, composed of both Jews and Gentiles—ONE SPIRIT sealing both Jews and Gentiles—ONE HOPE animating both Jews and Gentiles—ONE LORD, who died for all, both Jews and Gentiles—ONE FAITH common to Jews and Gentiles—ONE BAPTISM enjoined upon all, whether Jews or Gentiles—ONE GOD and Father of all, if Christians, whether Jews or Gentiles. Now, are all the items of this compendium of doctrine for the remission of sins?

1. We are to be reconciled to God in one body, and Jesus gave Himself for it. Eph. ii:16.

2. We must all drink into one Spirit (1 Cor. xii:13), and unless we have the Spirit of Christ we are none of his. Rom. viii:9.

3. We are saved by hope. Rom. viii:24.

4. Christ the one Lord died for man, and there is no salvation in any other name. Acts iv:12.

5. Without faith it is impossible to please God. Heb. xi:6.

6. Baptism doth also now save us. 1 Pet. iii:21.

7. It is God that justifieth. Rom. viii:33.

Now, are all these grand pillars in the spiritual temple essential save one which is unimportant? "But this is spiritual baptism." Then let us turn quaker, and repudiate water baptism, so that Paul may be consistent in saying "there is one baptism." The language *"there is one baptism"* just as clearly implies that there is *but one baptism*, as does the phrase *there is one God* imply that there is *but one God*. But the *one Spirit* is specifically mentioned in its own place; then why afterward mention one baptism, and refer it back to Spirit which fills its own place? Alexander Hall once made a remark on the use of prepositions as follows: "We now present five prepositions: *in, by, with, for,* and *into*. Upon these five prepositions we predicate five propositions, viz: that we are baptized *in* something, *by* something, *with* something, *for* something, and *into* something; and that all these refer to water baptism. They are, 1st, *in* the name of the Lord Jesus (Acts x:48; xix:5); 2d, by the Spirit of God (1 Cor. xii:13) —*i.e.*, according to its authority or directions; 3d, *with* water (Matt. iii:11, should be in); 4th, *for* the remission of sins (Acts ii:38; 5th, *into* Christ (Gal. iii:27); *into* one body (1 Cor. xii:13).

"Here, then, we have these five relations clearly expressed by these five prepositions; and thus we are baptized *in* the name of Christ, *by* the Spirit of God, *with* [in] water, *for* the remission of sins, and *into* the one body, which are all one and the same baptism—the same ordinance which brought three thousand penitent believers into the kingdom of God on the day of Pentecost." Gospel Proclamation, vol. ii, p. 342.

In this summary Paul groups the great fundamental pillars of the Christian religion; and that the one baptism is in water, has been the opinion of the learned until the baptismal controversy became rife in modern times. Dr. Clark's note on this passage is as follows: "*One baptism*—administered in the name of the Holy Trinity; indicative of the influences, privileges, and effects of the Christian religion." Wesley's note is composed of three words: "One outward baptism." In his *sermon upon the church*, however, he is more ample. He says: "There is one baptism, which is the outward sign our one Lord has been pleased to appoint of all that inward and spiritual grace which he is continually bestowing upon his church. Some, indeed, have been inclined to interpret this in a figurative sense, as if it referred to the baptism of the Holy Spirit which the apostles received on the day of Pentecost, and which, in a lower degree, is given to all believers. But it is a stated rule, in interpreting Scripture, never to depart from the plain, literal sense unless it implies an absurdity; and, besides, if we thus understood it, it would be a needless repetition, as being included in 'there is one Spirit.'"

Mr. Rice, in his debate with Mr. Campbell (p. 264), says: "This one baptism is an ordinance administered with WATER, in the name of the Father, and of the Son, and of the Holy Spirit, by an ordained minister of the gospel." Thus we see the very highest authority understands Paul to refer to water baptism when he says "there is one baptism;" indeed, we suppose no one ever thought of any thing else until this passage was brought into the recent controversy on the design of baptism.

But this is not all upon this subject. The apostle says: "Husbands, love your wives, even as Christ also loved the church, and gave himself for it, that he might sanctify and cleanse it with the washing of water by the word." Eph. v:25, 26. Christ gave Himself for the church, that He might sanctify and cleanse it *how?* With the washing of water by the Word. Not a washing *with* the Word—the washing of water by the Word; that is, in obedience to it, or in accordance with it—just as we are baptized by one Spirit into one body; that is, in obedience to it, and in harmony with its teaching. That the washing of water by the Word, here, is baptism, Watson, Wesley, Clark, Macknight, Stuart, and all other commentators, teach, as far as we have been able to examine. Then, if baptism be the means by which the church is sanctified and cleansed, how shall it be cleansed without the means? Surely, it can not be. If baptism be not the washing of water alluded to, what other washing of water is there connected with spiritual cleansing to which Paul may have referred? "But it is the church that is cleansed, not the people before they enter it." Yes, and Christ gave Himself for the church before it was a church; so the church is cleansed by cleansing the material of which it is made. Does any one suppose men and women are to enter the church uncleansed, or unpardoned, and then be cleansed by the washing of water? The objector might be willing to apply this theory to infants, but it would not do for men; and it would involve the necessity of rebaptizing even those baptized in infancy. But the creeds will not allow the theory, for they all teach that the washing with water brings them into the church. On page 247, Doctrinal Tracts, we find a comment on the verse under consideration, as follows: "And the virtue of this free gift, the merits of Christ's life and death are applied to us in baptism. 'He gave himself for the church, that he might sanctify and cleanse it with the washing of water by the word' (Eph. v:25, 26); namely, in baptism, the ordinary instrument of our justification. Agreeably to this, our church prays, in the baptismal office, that the person to be baptized may be 'washed and sanctified by the Holy Ghost, and, being delivered from God's wrath, receive remission of sins, and enjoy the everlasting benediction of His heavenly washing.'"

Again, the apostle says: "Ye are complete in him, which is the head of all principality and power; in whom also ye are circumcised with the circumcision made without hands, in putting off the body of the sins of the flesh by the circumcision of Christ; buried with him in baptism, wherein also ye are risen with him through the faith of the operation of God, who hath raised him from the dead. And you, being dead in your sins and the uncircumcision of your flesh, hath he quickened together with him, having forgiven you all trespasses." Col. ii:10-13. Here we learn that the Colossians put off the body of the sins of the flesh by the circumcision of Christ, in being buried with him in baptism; and thus they were forgiven all trespasses. On this passage Mr. Watson remarks: "Here baptism is also made the initiatory rite of the new dispensation, that by which the Colossians were joined to Christ, in whom they are said to be complete." Institutes, vol. ii, p. 621. If baptism be the act which joins us to Christ, then we ask whether or not we can be saved until we are joined to Christ? If not, we can not be saved until baptized, that we may be joined to Christ.

But the apostle says: "Not by works of righteousness which we have done, but according to his mercy he saved us; by the washing of regeneration and renewing of the Holy Ghost." Tit. iii:5. He saved us how? By the washing of regeneration and renewing of the Holy Ghost. What is this washing of regeneration? It can not be the renewing of the Holy Ghost, for that is specifically mentioned. The Spirit and the water are not the same, for "there are three that bear witness in earth, the Spirit, and the water, and the blood." 1 John v:8. Then, if this washing of regeneration is not baptism, what is it? Wesley and Whitby call this "the laver of regeneration." Clark says: "Undoubtedly the apostle here means baptism." Watson, Macknight, Alford, Bloomfield, Stuart, Smith, and Wall, say it means baptism. Well, what if it does mean baptism? Only this: Paul says *we are saved by it*. He saved us by the washing of regeneration and renewing of the Holy Ghost. Wall says: "The washing of regeneration (Tit. iii:5) is the washing of baptism." Vol. i, p. 70.

"But baptism is a work." Yes; so is faith. "Jesus answered and said unto them, This is the work of God, that ye believe on him whom he hath sent." John vi:29. Hence, if baptism may be set aside because it is a work, then faith goes the same road. "But faith is the work of God." Yes, and so is baptism, in the same sense, the work of God. They are both acts of man, but the works of God by authority, because God has ordained them. Paul says: "We are his workmanship, created in Christ Jesus unto good works, which God hath before ordained that we should walk in them." Eph. ii:10. The works which God has ordained are not the procuring cause of our salvation, but according to His mercy He saved us through just such means as He saw fit to appoint; and Paul says they were the washing of regeneration and renewing of the Holy Spirit.

We come now to examine the types and shadows of former dispensations, and their antitypes and substances in the Christian dispensation. We might begin with Adam, and show that from him until the coming of Christ there were numerous single types of Him. Moses, as lawgiver, mediator, etc., was a type of Christ. Aaron, as high-priest, was a type of Christ. But there were great systems of types adumbrating the deliverance of men from the guilt and pollution of sin under the gospel. Some of these we will briefly examine.

God proposed to save Noah and his family from the sin-cursed world with which he was identified prior to the deluge. With a view to this end, He revealed to Noah the plan by which his deliverance was to be effected. Noah believed it, and Paul says: "By faith Noah, being warned of God of things not seen as yet, moved with fear, prepared an ark to the saving of his house; by the which he condemned the world and became heir of the righteousness which is by faith." Heb. xi:7. Faith was the great principle which moved Noah. Faith alone, however, did not save him, but, moved with fear, he prepared an ark to the saving of himself and family. Peter says: "Once the longsuffering of God waited in the days of Noah, while the ark was preparing, wherein few, that is, eight souls, were saved by water. The like figure whereunto even baptism doth also now save us (not the putting away of the filth of the flesh, but the answer of a good conscience toward God), by the resurrection of Jesus Christ." 1 Pet. iii:20, 21. The words *like figure*, in the above quotation, are from the Greek *antitupon*, which should be rendered *antitype;* thus: the *antitype whereof baptism doth also now save us.* Here Peter says in plain terms that baptism saves us, and that it is the antitype of Noah's salvation in the ark by water. Now, if baptism does not save us from sin, from what does it save us? It does not save us from temporal punishment, such as persecution, insult, hunger, sickness, death, for the baptized man is as subject to these as the unbaptized. Nor can Peter allude to final salvation, for he says baptism NOW saves us. Then, if baptism does not save from sin, we repeat the question, with emphasis, *from what does it save us?* It does not save us from the filth of the flesh, for it is not a mere fleshly washing, but has to do with the conscience. "But it is the answer of a good conscience, and hence the conscience must be good before baptism." Waiving any objection to this rendering for the present, we inquire what is meant by a *good conscience?* Certainly a good conscience does not always imply that he who has it is a pardoned man. Paul had a good conscience when he was killing Christians; after his conversion he says: "I have lived in all good conscience before God until this day." Acts xxii:1. Yet, he had to be pardoned, and says: "But I obtained mercy, because I did it ignorantly in unbelief." 1 Tim. i:13. Then all that can be claimed for a good conscience is, that its possessor is an honest man; and we are quite willing to grant that such he must be, in order to acceptably obey God in baptism or any thing else. But the rendering might be improved, perhaps, by rendering it *seeking* of a good conscience; and we know not how a man might seek a good conscience more effectually than by being baptized in the name of Jesus Christ for the remission of his sins. If he were as correctly taught as the eunuch he would likely have a good conscience when done.

"Well but Noah was a good man *before* he was saved in the ark by water; hence we must be Christians before we are bap-

THE DESIGN OF BAPTISM 421

tized." If this proves any thing against baptism for remission, it proves just as much against faith; for Noah was as good a man before he had faith in the plan of his delivery as he was after the deluge, or when he was in the ark. Hence that which proves too much proves nothing at all. Watson says: "It is thus that we see how St. Peter preserves the correspondence between the act of Noah in preparing the ark as an act of faith by which he was justified, and the act of submitting to Christian baptism, which is also obviously an act of faith, in order to the remission of sins or the obtaining a good conscience before God." Institutes, vol. ii, pp. 624, 625.

Wesley says: "*The antitype whereof*—the thing typified by the ark, even baptism, *now saveth us.* That is, through the water of baptism we are saved from the sin which overwhelms the world as a flood; not indeed the bare outward sign, but the inward grace—a divine consciousness that both our persons and our actions are accepted through Him who died and rose again for us." Wesley's Notes.

Clark says: "Noah believed in God, walked uprightly before Him, and found grace in His sight; he obeyed Him in building the ark, and God made it the means of his salvation from the waters of the deluge. *Baptism* implies a consecration and dedication of the soul and body to God the Father, Son, and Holy Spirit. He who is faithful to his baptismal covenant, taking God through Christ, by the eternal Spirit, for his portion, is saved here from his sins, and, through the resurrection of Christ from the dead, has the well-grounded hope of eternal glory." Commentary on 1 Pet. iii:21.

"Baptism doth now save us if we live answerable thereto—if we repent, believe, and obey the gospel; supposing this, as it admits us into the church here, so into glory hereafter." Doctrinal Tracts, p. 249.

But we are told the word *rupos*, rendered *filth* in this verse (1 Pet. iii:21), means *sin;* and hence the parenthetical clause negatives the idea of baptism saving from sin; thus, "not the putting away sin." Let us see about this.

LIDDELL AND SCOTT: "*Rupos*—dirt, filth, dirtiness."

PICKERING: "*Rupos*—dirt, foulness, scurf; metaphorically, avariciousness; also, sealing-wax."

DONNIGAN: "*Rupos*—filth; metaphorically, sordid avarice," etc.

Rupos may sometimes, metaphorically, mean *sin*, but we are bound by the laws of exegesis to give its obvious meaning unless it involves an absurdity. No one will say that it does this here; hence it must simply mean *filth*, especially as it is qualified by the word *flesh—filth of the flesh*. Baptism is not for the removal of this, but has to do with the conscience.

Peter remembered the commission given by the Lord—"He that believeth and is baptized shall be saved"—and commanded the Pentecostians to repent, and be baptized for the remission of sins; hence he understood baptism to be for remission of sins, and hence, with great propriety, could say, "Baptism doth also now save us." Save us how? From our sins.

After the deluge the world was again peopled by the descendants of Noah, and they again became wicked; but He had entered into covenant not to a second time destroy the world by water; hence, finding Abram righteous before Him, he determined to separate him from the wicked people and of him make to Himself a great nation. In due time Isaac was born to Abraham, and then Jacob was born to Issac, and to Jacob was born twelve sons, who became heads of the twelve tribes of Israel. After a time, by their wickedness, they became slaves in Egypt, where, notwithstanding their sore oppression, they rapidly increased, until Pharaoh, fearing for the safety of his throne, issued an order that all male children born of Hebrew mothers should be put to death. Pending this order, Moses was born, and hid by his mother until she could conceal him no longer; she placed him in an ark on the river, where his sister lingered to see the result. Pharaoh's daughter found the child and adopted him as her own, and thus he was saved from death by the decree of her father. "By faith Moses, when he was come to years, refused to be called the son of Pharaoh's daughter; choosing rather to suffer affliction with the people of God than to enjoy the pleasures of sin for a season; esteeming the reproaches of Christ greater riches than the treasures in Egypt; for he had respect unto the recompense of the reward. By faith he forsook Egypt, not fearing the wrath of the king; for he endured as seeing him who is invisible. Through faith he kept the passover, and the sprinkling of blood, lest he that destroyed the first-born should touch them. By faith they passed through the Red Sea as by dry land, which the Egyptians essaying to do were drowned." Heb. xi:24-29.

In due time God appeared to Moses and revealed to him His purpose to deliver the Hebrews through him; "And Moses answered and said, But, behold, they will not believe me, nor hearken unto my voice: for they will say, The Lord hath not appeared unto thee. And the Lord said unto him, What is that in thine hand? And he said, A rod. And he said, Cast it on the ground. And he cast it on the ground, and it became a serpent; and Moses fled from before it. And the Lord said unto Moses, Put forth thy hand, and take it by the tail. And he put forth his hand and caught it, and it became a rod in his hand: that they may believe that the Lord God of their fathers, the God of Abraham, the God of Isaac, and the God of Jacob, hath appeared unto thee." Ex. iv:1-5. By this sign, and two others which we have not space to mention, God enabled Moses to bear witness to his brethren that he was sent of God, that they might *believe*. Moses went to them and delivered the message, confirming it by signs which God had enabled him to perform in their presence. They believed the message given them by Moses, and, with full confidence in Moses, they turned their backs upon their former taskmasters and set forward on their journey toward Canaan. After a time they came to the Red Sea, and, finding themselves closely pursued by their late masters, they murmured at Moses for bringing them out of Egypt to die in the wilderness. But Moses replied: "Fear ye not, stand still, and see the salvation of the Lord, which he will show to you to-day; for the Egyptians whom ye have seen to-day, ye shall see them again no more forever." Ex. xiv:13. Moses stretched his arm and raised his rod over the sea—the waters were divided, and stood as walls on either side; the people moved forward, the cloud overshadowed them, and they landed safely on the opposite shore. The Egyptians pursued them and were drowned in the sea: seeing which the children of Israel sang a song of deliverance and rejoiced, believing in God and His servant Moses. But though their enemies were gone, they were still far from Canaan; and for forty years they were in a state of probation, until, of the male adults who crossed the Red Sea, only Caleb and Joshua remained alive. Under the lead of these faithful men, Joshua being chief, they crossed the river Jordan and entered the land of Canaan—the inheritance promised to their fathers.

Touching the leading features of this narrative, Paul says: "Moreover, brethren, I would not that ye should be ignorant, how that all our fathers were under the cloud, and all passed through the sea; and were all baptized unto Moses in the cloud and in the sea; and did all eat the same spiritual meat; and did all drink the same spiritual drink; for they drank of that spiritual Rock that followed them: and that Rock was Christ. But with many of them God was not well pleased; for they were overthrown in the wilderness. Now these things were our examples." 1 Cor. x:1-6.

Let us now gather the chief features of this system of types, and see their application to the antitype:

1. The children of Israel became slaves in Egypt by their own wickedness—men become servants of sin by indulgence in crime.

2. God heard the groanings of His people in Egypt and provided for their deliverance—God so loved the world that He gave His Son to die for them.

3. Moses was the deliverer of the children of Israel—Jesus is our deliverer.

4. Pharaoh feared for the safety of his throne and ordered all male children born of Hebrew mothers to be put to death—when Jesus was born, Herod feared for the safety of his throne and sent and slew all the male children from two years old and under.

5. God preserved Moses from death by Pharaoh's decree—God sent Joseph with the infant Jesus into Egypt, there to remain until Herod was dead, and thus saved him from death by Herod's decree.

6. Moses was enabled to perform miracles in confirmation of his mission, that the people might believe that God had sent him—"Many other signs truly did Jesus in the presence of his disciples which are not written in this book; but these are written that ye might believe that Jesus is the Christ, the Son of God,

and that believing ye might have life through his name." John xx:30, 31.

7. Moses, through Aaron, made known to the Israelites the plan of their delivery, and they believed it, for Paul says they did every thing by *faith*—Jesus required His apostles to preach the gospel to every creature in all the world, that every one might believe it; for faith comes by hearing, and without faith it is impossible to please God.

8. The Israelites were required to quit serving the Egyptians and turn away from them—Jesus required the people everywhere to repent, turn away from the service of sin.

9. The Israelites were baptized unto Moses in the cloud and in the sea—Peter commanded the people to be baptized, in the name of the Jesus Christ, for the remission of sins.

10. The Egyptian task-masters of the Israelites were left just where the people were baptized unto Moses, and they saw them no more—those baptized in the name of Jesus Christ for the remission of sins, leave their sins just where they are baptized.

11. The Israelites rejoiced in their deliverance on the shore after their baptism—as soon as the eunuch was baptized he went on his way rejoicing.

12. The Israelites were not secure in Canaan as soon as baptized, but had to be faithful to God or die short of the promised land—those baptized in the name of Jesus Christ for the remission of sins, though freed from past sins, are not in heaven, but must live a life of devotion to God or be lost at last.

13. The Israelites who remained faithful to God through their period of probation were conducted across the Jordan and into the land of Canaan, the inheritance promised to their fathers—those Christians who remain faithful to God through life will be conducted across the Jordan of death into heaven, the everlasting Canaan which God has prepared for them that love Him.

Thus we have presented, as briefly as possible, the more important features of this great system of types, omitting, for want of room, many things which would have been of interest to the reader; but the great point to which we would especially direct his attention at present is the time when the Israelites were freed from their enemies, and the corresponding time when we are freed from sin. We are told that men must be saved from their sins before they are baptized—*i.e.*, that they are pardoned as soon as they believe on Jesus Christ. If so, then there is no fitness in this type. The Jews believed in the plan of their delivery when it was presented, otherwise they would not have set out under the lead of Moses; but they were not saved from their enemies at that time. Moses specifically locates the time of their salvation. "Stand still and see the salvation of the Lord, which he will show to you to-day" (Ex. xiv:13)—not *did* show you back in the place where you believed. And what was the salvation shown them that day? "The Egyptians whom ye have seen to-day, ye shall see them again no more forever." *Ut supra.* Where did they leave these enemies? In the sea where they were baptized. "Thus the Lord saved Israel that day out of the hand of the Egyptians." Ver. 30. Language could not more definitely locate the time of their salvation upon the day of their baptism than it here does. Then, if there be any fitness in type and antitype, we must be saved from our sins when we are baptized, not before. When a type spells the word *God*, the antitype can not spell *devil;* so when the type says *saved in baptism,* the antitype can not say *saved by faith alone before baptism.*

No one denies that the salvation of the Israelites from bondage was a type of our salvation from sin, and that their baptism in the cloud and sea was a type of our baptism; but some seek to evade the force of the argument by saying that God recognized the Israelites as *His people* when He appeared to Moses in the burning bush; and as this was *before their baptism,* we must be God's people before we are baptized. But if this objection amounts to any thing against *baptism* for remission of sins, it amounts to just as much against *faith,* for the Lord had not *then* revealed the plan of their delivery, but had then appeared to Moses for the purpose of revealing it to him. The Israelites knew nothing about it. So they were God's people before they had faith, as well as before they were baptized. Indeed, they were God's national people before the birth of Moses; hence, if we must be God's people at the same time they were, it follows that we must have been God's people before Jesus, the antitype of Moses, was born. This would be Calvinism sublimated. The objector forgets that the *type was in the salvation of the Israel ites from Egyptian bondage,* hence we can not go *behind the type* for impressions in the antitype.

In debate upon this subject once, our opponent replied that there was no remission of sins in the deliverance of the Israelites, and as there was no remission in the type there could be none in the antitype; yet he freely quoted, "As Moses lifted up the serpent in the wilderness, even so must the Son of man be lifted up; that whosoever believeth in him should not perish, but have eternal life." John iii:14, 15. Now, was there any remission of sins in the brazen serpent placed on the pole by Moses? Surely not; yet it could represent his system of justification by faith alone, as he thought. The idea that a figure can represent nothing not in the figure itself would simply destroy all figures. The serpent on the pole could not be a type of Christ unless Christ became a serpent; a lamb could not be a type of Christ until Christ is shown to have been a sheep. We dislike to dignify such an objection with a reply, but when great men make such objections, others may think there is something in them.

It was our original purpose to have followed these types through the Tabernacle of the wilderness and the consecration of a Jewish priest as types of the more perfect Tabernacle and the consecration of a Christian priest, but want of space compels us to forego the pleasure of doing so.

We must notice some of the more prominent objections urged by those who oppose our teaching. First, we are told that "there are two kingdoms, one *visible* and the other *invisible*—that the *visible* kingdom is the visible church, and is for the visible man. Baptism is purely a visible act of the visible man, who is pardoned when baptized, and thus introduced into the visible kingdom. This is *formal* pardon, indicative of *real* pardon which was secured by *faith*—a purely mental act, an act of the invisible man by which it was introduced into the invisible kingdom when he believed. And whether the visible man is ever justified and introduced by baptism into the visible kingdom, yea, or nay, is of but little importance as to the ultimate happiness and final salvation of the spiritual man."

This is substantially the theory of the two kingdoms, and we will examine it briefly. If it be true, it is evident that there are two churches or two kingdoms governed by the same King at the same time. And as the church is the body, and Jesus "is the head of the body, the church" (Col. i:18), it follows that He is the head of two bodies at the same time, or one of the bodies has no head, or if each has a head one of them has a human head. John saw a beast having *seven heads to one body* (Rev. xiii:1); but here we have a different beast—*two bodies to one head*. When Paul said "there is *one body*" (Eph. iv:4), and again, "now are there many members yet *but one body*" (1 Cor. xii:20), he was not aware of the existence of one of the bodies contemplated in this theory.

Once more: The church is said to be the "*bride*, the *Lamb's* wife." According to this theory, the Lamb has *two wives at the same time*, and one of them invisible; hence, He would be unfit for a *bishop* in the church, to say nothing of its head, for Paul tells us that a bishop must be "the husband of one wife." 1 Tim. iii:2. These visible and invisible brides must both belong to one husband, or one of them has either no husband or an illegitimate one. "There is one body and one spirit" (Eph. iv:4) in this body; and as one spirit can not animate two bodies at the same time, it follows that one of them is without a spirit (unless it be a human spirit); and as James tells us that "the body without the spirit is dead" (Jas. ii:26), it follows that one of these is a dead body.

It will be remembered that at the time, the subject believes, the invisible man is introduced into the invisible kingdom of the Lord, and baptism is the only way of introducing the visible man into the Lord's visible kingdom. Then, if a man believed twenty years ago, and by that act had the inner man introduced into the invisible kingdom at that time, and he has not been baptized until to-day, where was the visible man from that time until this? It was not in the visible kingdom, for it could only enter this kingdom by baptism; and as he was unbaptized, of course he was not in it. He was not in the *invisible kingdom*, for that was prepared for the *invisible man*, and is in heaven and he upon the earth. Then, we repeat the question, where is the visible man from the time faith is exercised until he is baptized? As we have seen that he is in neither of the theoretical kingdoms of the Lord, he must be in the dominion of Satan, and if so, then there must be a singular partnership between the Lord and his satanic majesty in the same person, the former having the invisible and the latter the visible man from the time he *believes* until he is *baptized*. Well might Paul ask: "What concord hath Christ with Belial?" 2 Cor. vi:15.

Once more: It will be remembered that the locality of the visible kingdom is on the earth, and that of the invisible kingdom is in heaven; and it will be admitted that the visible man is the dwelling-place of the invisible through life, and their separation takes place only at death. How, therefore, can the invisible man be translated to heaven, the place of the invisible kingdom, by faith or otherwise, and the body remain upon the earth during life, and no separation take place? When Paul said he was "willing to be absent from the body and be present with the Lord" (2 Cor. v:8), he had not learned the theory by which he could be with the body and the Lord at the same time. In this theory we have the very anomalous idea of a king having two kingdoms in different localities, the same subjects being in both at the same time.

But we come now to examine the foundation of the theory. Is faith purely mental, or does it require the cooperative exercise of mind and body? Paul says: "Faith comes by hearing." Rom. x:17. How do persons hear? Jesus quoted the prophet thus: "For this people's heart is waxed gross, and their ears are dull of hearing, and their eyes they have closed, lest at any time they should see with their eyes, hear with their ears," etc. Matt. xiii:15.

Then, if faith comes by hearing, and hearing is done with the ear, and the ear is a part of the physical or visible man, it is certain that the faith of which Paul spake is not purely mental. But the objector quotes Paul again: "With the heart (mind) man believeth unto righeousness." Rom. x:10. True, indeed; but how does he obtain possession of what he believes? Surely, through his senses. At the time faith is exercised, or is present, there has been an exercise of *mind* and *body,* and hence the theory is false that would justify the invisible man at that time, because nothing but mind had entered into the service.

Once more: The brain is as much the organ of the mind as is the eye the organ of sight, or the ear the organ of hearing, and we are as much compelled to use the brain in thought as we are the eye to see or the ear to hear. Then, if we are compelled to *think* in the act of *believing,* and the brain, a part of the physical and visible man, is used in thought, it follows that to have faith there must be an exercise of mind and body.

But is baptism purely a physical act? If so, why will not the advocates of the theory baptize a maniac in the absence of mind? If a man's reason is dethroned, no one will say he may be baptized. But why not? If there is nothing mental connected with its validity, surely he would be as fit a subject then as at any other time. In the administration of infant sprinkling they are more consistent, for here, indeed, there is nothing mental to accompany it. But even here they reverse the *order* of the theory. In the case of adults the *invisible man* is first saved *by faith,* then the *visible by baptism;* but here the *visible man* (infant) is introduced into the *visible kingdom,* and the *invisible* or *spiritual man* is left in the *devil's kingdom* for years, perhaps for life.

If we wish to baptize a man, we must first operate on his mind or invisible man until we convince his judgment that it is his duty to submit to it. When we have done this, the mind transmits the will to act, through the nerves to the muscles; they contract, in obedience to the will, upon the bones, and thus by a co-operation of *mind and body* the man steps forward. But whenever the mind ceases to co-operate the process is at once arrested. Hence, baptism can not be performed as an acceptable service to God without the action of *mind and body.* There is no foundation for the objection, and it therefore amounts to nothing.

But another very common objection is that when Jesus healed the woman of her plague, He said: "Daughter, thy faith hath made thee whole: go in peace, and be whole of thy plague." Mark v:34. And it is insisted that *this miraculous healing from disease must constitute the basis of a theory of conversion.* We insist that no one has a right to select one miracle and make it the basis of a theory, to the exclusion of other miracles of like character. If one man may make such selection, others may. One may select the healing of the centurion's servant. Jesus said to him: "Go thy way: and as thou hast believed so be it done unto thee. And his servant was healed in the self-same hour." Matt. viii:13. A servant may build a theory of conversion for him on this case and seek to be saved on the faith of the master.

But some are not servants and would prefer to be saved upon the faith of their parents, hence they select a different miracle. "Then Jesus answered and said unto her, O woman, great is thy faith; be it unto thee even as thou wilt. And her daughter was made whole from that very hour." Matt. xv:28. Again: "As soon as Jesus heard the word that was spoken, he saith unto the ruler of the synagogue, Be not afraid, only believe." Mark v:36. And on his faith Jesus restored his dead daughter to life, though twelve years of age. Then, if any one has parents he may get them to have faith for him, and upon their faith his sins may be pardoned.

But another may not be a servant, nor yet have parents, but may have brothers or sisters, hence he selects the following: When Jesus was standing over the grave of Lazarus, He said to Martha: "Said I not unto thee, that if thou wouldest believe, thou shouldest see the glory of God?" John xi:40. Then, if a man wishes to be saved, he may get his sister to have faith, and that will do for him.

But another has no relatives, and hence must select another example. "They brought a man sick of the palsy, lying on the bed; and Jesus seeing their faith said unto the sick of the palsy, Son, be of good cheer, thy sins be forgiven thee." Matt. ix:2. Taking this case as a foundation, a man may get his neighbors to have faith for him.

But as many have more faith in the preachers than any one else, they select another example suited to their taste. "Peter, fastening his eyes upon him, with John, said, Look on us. And he gave heed unto them, expecting to receive something of them. Then Peter said, Silver and gold have I none; but such as I have give I thee: In the name of Jesus Christ of Nazareth rise up and walk. And he took him by the right hand, and lifted him up." Acts iii:4-7. Then, with this case as a foundation, a man may get the preacher to have faith, and that will do for him.

But there are infidels who have no faith in any one. They may be saved too. "When Jesus was come into Peter's house, he saw his wife's mother laid, and sick of a fever. And he touched her hand, and the fever left her." Matt. viii:14. All the faith in this case was in Jesus. So of the blind man restored to sight. John ix:6, 7. These examples would justify the theory of justification upon the faith of Christ without any faith in the saved at all.

But there are those who seem to have more communion with evil spirits than with the Lord. They, too, may find examples suited to their taste. "Unclean spirits, when they saw him, fell down before him, and cried, saying, Thou art the Son of God." Mark iii:11. See also v:7. Luke iv:41. These examples would secure salvation upon the faith of evil spirits.

But we return now to the case whence we set out; and by an examination it will be seen that her faith did not make her whole until she d'd the thing contemplated in her faith. "When she had heard of Jesus, came in the press behind and touched his garment. For she said, If I may touch but his clothes, I shall be whole. And straightway the fountain of her blood was dried up; and she felt in her body that she was healed of that plague." Mark v:27-29. Then, this example would not do for justification by faith alone, for she did the thing contemplated in her faith before she was healed.

But what have all these miracles to do with remission of sins? If one man may select one of them on which to build a theory of conversion, others may do the same thing, and we may thus have as many different theories of conversion as there are miracles recorded. John said: "Many other signs truly did Jesus in the presence of his disciples, which are not written in this book; but these are written, that ye might believe that Jesus is the Christ, the Son of God; and that believing ye might have life through his name." John xx:30, 31.

Then these miracles were not written upon which to construct theories of conversion, but they were written that the people might believe in the divine character and mission of Jesus Christ. They could not have been done by unaided human power; hence, says Nicodemus: "We know that thou art a teacher come from God, for no man can do the miracles that thou doest except God be with him." John iii:2. This is the object of these miracles, and hence they have nothing to do with justification by faith alone.

"But the thief was saved without being baptized." To this

assumption we file three objections: 1. No man can prove that the thief was saved at all. 2. No man can prove that he was unbaptized. 3. This was before the kingdom was established, and before the law of remission began to be preached under the new covenant.

It is true that the thief "said unto Jesus, Lord, remember me when thou comest into thy kingdom. And Jesus said unto him, Verily I say unto thee, To-day shalt thou be with me in paradise." Luke xxiii:42, 43. It is doubtful whether the thief made this request in derision or in good faith, for the thieves had both derided Him (see Matt. xxvii:44; Mark xv:32). And, in the next place, if the thief understood the nature of Christ's kingdom, he had higher conceptions of it than did even the apostles, for they thought it a merely temporal kingdom. In the next place, Jesus only promised the thief that they would meet in *paradise*. Jesus was in the heart of the earth (Matt. xii:40), and when He arose from the grave He said He had not yet ascended to His Father. John xx:17. Then we think it would be difficult to prove that this amounted to a promise of salvation.

Was the thief baptized? We can not prove positively that he was, nor can any one prove that he was not. John was baptizing in that country, and there "went out to him Jerusalem, and all Judea, and all the region round about Jordan, and were baptized of him in Jordan, confessing their sins." Matt. iii:5, 6. That this language implies the baptism of large masses of the people no one will deny; then "Jesus made and baptized more disciples than John." John iv:1. Then, taking what John baptized and what Jesus, through his disciples, baptized in that country—and we suppose there were but few left unbaptized—hence the probabilities are strongly in favor of the presumption that the thief was baptized.

But whether he was or was not baptized affects not the doctrine of baptism for the remission of sins. While a man lives he may give his property to whom he will, but when he dies, leaving a will, there can be no more special bequests, but his property must be distributed according to the provisions of the will. So while Christ was upon the earth, He could say to a man, "Thy sins be forgiven thee," and it was so; but when He died, leaving a will, He would not afterward pardon, even Saul, contrary to the provisions of the will, but sent him where he might find a man to tell him how he might obtain pardon according to the provisions of the will. Granting, then, what can not be proved, that the thief *was saved without baptism,* while Christ was alive, it is no evidence that men may be so saved after the law went into force, which required them to be baptized in the name of Jesus Christ for the remission of sins.

But Paul says: "Therefore being justified by faith we have peace with God through our Lord Jesus Christ." Rom. v:1. By supplying the word *only* or *alone* after the word *faith,* this passage has been made to negative the doctrine of baptism for remission of sins by setting up the doctrine of justification by faith alone. If this be the correct interpretation of the passage, then the word *alone* may be supplied in the *reading;* thus: "Being justified by faith *alone* we have peace with God." Then how are we to reconcile this statement with others made by Paul himself? If we are justified by *faith alone,* we are justified by faith to the *exclusion* of every thing else; yet, in the same chapter from which the above quotation is made, he says: "Much more, then, being justified by his blood, we shall be saved from wrath through him." Ver. 9. Does Paul thus flatly contradict himself in the same chapter? Again he says: "Being justified freely by his grace through the redemption that is in Christ Jesus." Rom. iii:24. Once more: "Ye are justified in the name of the Lord Jesus, and by the Spirit of our God." 1 Cor. vi:11. Now, how can we be justified by ALL these things and justified by any one of them alone? We may be justified by grace, but not by grace alone; by Christ, but not by Christ alone; by blood, but not by blood alone; by the Spirit, but not by the Spirit alone; in the name of the Lord Jesus, but not by His name alone; by faith, but not by faith alone; by works, but not by works alone. We live by *breathing,* but not by breathing alone; we live by *eating* but not by eating alone; we live by *sleeping,* but not by sleeping alone; we live by *exercise,* but not by exercise alone. A place for every thing, and every thing in its place, is God's order every-where.

But if we may supply the word *alone* after the word *faith,* in Rom. v:1, why may we not do the same thing elsewhere? If the phrase "by faith" means *by faith alone,* then we may supply the word *alone* and make sense wherever this form of expression occurs. Shall we try a few passages, to see whether or not the phrase "by faith" means *by faith alone?* "By faith *alone* Abel offered unto God a more excellent sacrifice than Cain." Heb. xi:4. "By faith *alone* Noah, being warned of God of things not seen as yet, moved with fear, prepared an ark to the saving of his house." Ver. 7. "By faith *alone* Abraham, when he was called to go out into a place which he should after receive for an inheritance, obeyed; and he went out, not knowing whither he went." Ver. 8. That is, he sat perfectly still, went nowhere, nor did any thing only by faith! "By faith *alone* Abraham, when he was tried, offered up Isaac." Ver. 17. That is, by faith *alone* he went three days' journey to a mountain shown him by the Lord; by faith *alone* he built an altar; by faith *alone* he bound his son upon the altar; and by faith *alone* he raised his knife and would have slain him had not the Lord interposed!! And thus we might go through the whole list of examples given in this chapter, but these are sufficient to show the absurdity of supplying the word *alone* or *only* after faith. These ancient worthies *did* what they were commanded to do, in order to accomplish the object contemplated in their faith. They practically carried out their faith, and perfected it by obedience to the law of the Lord. James says: "By works was faith made perfect." Jas. ii:22. Surely, an imperfect faith can do no good—and if not, it can only be perfected in obedience. "Even so faith, if it hath not works, is dead, being alone." Ver. 17. And again: "As the body without the spirit is dead, so faith without works is dead also." Ver. 26. Can dead faith justify any one?

But by supplying the word *alone*, or only in the passage quoted, thus making Paul say, "Therefore, being justified by faith only, we have peace with God," we not only make him contradict himself, but we make him contradict James, when he says: "Ye see, then, how that by works a man is justified, and not by faith only." Jas. ii:24. Now, James does not say that a man is justified by works alone, to the exclusion of faith, for the phrase "not by faith only" shows that *faith is included.*

But we are told that Paul speaks of justification in the sense of pardon, and James speaks of justification in the sense of approval—that Paul draws his argument from Abraham's faith, by which he was *justified* or *pardoned of his sins*, when the covenant of circumcision was instituted, an account of which we have in the seventeenth chapter of Genesis—and James draws his argument from Abraham's justification as a righteous man when he offered his son, an account of which we have in the twenty-second chapter. Now, *we respectfully deny that Abraham was an unpardoned sinner up to the time of which Paul speaks*. The first account we have of him is as follows: "Now, the Lord had said unto Abram, Get thee out of thy country, and from thy kindred, and from thy father's house, unto a land that I will shew thee; and I will make of thee a great nation, and I will bless thee, and make thy name great; and thou shalt be a blessing; and I will bless them that bless thee, and curse him that curseth thee; and in thee shall all families of the earth be blessed." Gen. xii:1-3. Now, this precedes the time to which Paul refers by twenty-five years; and can any sane man believe that God fell in love with Abraham so as to induce his removal from among the wicked that he might be the father of God's peculiar people; and that God promised to bless them who blessed him, and curse them who cursed him, when he was a condemned, unpardoned sinner himself, and so remained for twenty-five years afterward? Abraham was as good a man the first account we ever have of him as he ever got to be, and both Paul and James allude to his justification in the sense of approval; but they did it to show the kind of faith which has *always* been required to meet the favor of God—a faith which *trusted in the promise* of God, and *perfected itself by obedience* to His will. *God never accepted any other faith than this from saint or sinner*. This is the doctrine taught by Paul *and* James, and there is neither discrepancy in their teachings nor difference in the justification to which they allude. The principle will apply to the alien or to the Christian, as an imperfect or dead faith will profit neither.

In the New Testament the word faith is used in at least three different significations. 1. As the synonym of belief; 2. To indicate a spiritual gift by which miracles were wrought; and 3. To indicate a *system* of justification by the gospel in contrast with the law of Moses. The first two of these we have examined sufficiently in the chapter on faith; the *system of faith* demands some further notice just here. We have seen that James says we are justified by works, yet Paul says: "Not of works, lest any man should boast." Eph. ii:9. How shall we reconcile these two statements? Paul says: "Knowing that a man is not justified by the works of the law, but by the faith of Jesus Christ, even we have believed on Jesus Christ, that we might be justified by the faith of Christ, and not by the works of the law; for by the works of the law shall no flesh be justified." Gal. ii:16. Then, when Paul said "not of works, lest any man should boast," he referred, first, to the origin of the plan of salvation, that it was by *grace* or *unmerited favor*, and, secondly, that it was not by the works of the law of Moses. By the faith of Jesus Christ, which Paul here contrasts with the law, is meant the system of faith or gospel plan of salvation given by Jesus Christ. By the phrase *works of the law* is meant the works of the law of Moses which had been taken out of the way by the death of Christ, by which if a man could be saved now he might have whereof to glory, for he would be saved upon a plan of his own, and not upon God's plan; hence, Paul asks: "Where is boasting then? It is excluded. By what law? of works? Nay; but by the law of faith. Therefore, we conclude that a man is justified by faith without the deeds of the law." Rom. iii:27, 28. What is the law of faith? Certainly, it is the gospel, and by it boasting is excluded because it is God's plan, which was given in mercy, from a principle of love, grace, or unmerited favor; and "was made known to all nations for the obedience of faith." Rom. xvi:26. Paul calls this same *law of faith* "the law of the Spirit of life in Christ Jesus," which he says "hath made me free from the law of sin and death." Rom. viii:2. To be made free from sin by a law we must comply with the requirements of the law; hence says Paul: "You have obeyed from the heart that form of doctrine which was delivered you, being then made free from sin." Rom. vi:17, 18.

But we are told that "Abraham believed God, and it was counted unto him for righteousness." Rom. iv:3. But when was faith counted to him for righteousness? James says: "Was not Abraham, our father, justified by works, when he had offered Isaac his son upon the altar? Seest thou how faith wrought with his works, and by works was faith made perfect? And the scripture was fulfilled which saith, Abraham believed God, and it was imputed unto him for righteousness; and he was called the friend of God. Ye see, then, how that by works a man if justified, and not by faith only." Jas. ii:21-24. Then, it was when Abraham obeyed God, and perfected his faith by obedience that his faith was counted to him for righteousness. Hence, if we would be justified by faith, as Abraham was, we must "walk in the steps of that faith of our father Abraham." Rom. iv:12. "By faith Abraham, when he was called to go out into a place which he should after receive for an inheritance, obeyed; and he went out, not knowing whither he went." Heb. xi:8. Abraham walked by faith, not by sight, and if we would walk in the steps of his faith, we must trust in God and go where He commands us to go, whether we can or can not see to the end.

But the advocates of justification by faith alone invoke the aid of John as well as Paul in support of their theory. He says: "Whosoever believeth that Jesus is the Christ is born of God; and every one that loveth him that begat loveth him also that is begotten of him." 1 John v:1. That the translation of this verse is defective any one can see by the context. The words *born, begat, begotten* are from the same original word, and the word born here should have been begotten, as the context clearly shows. "Whosoever believeth that Jesus is the Christ is *begotten* of God; and every one that loveth him that *begat* loveth him that is begotten of him." This harmonizes the passage with itself, and with the general teaching of the Scriptures on the subject of the new birth to the chapter on which the reader is referred. When a man believes the gospel he is begotten of God, and is prepared to be born. As an effect of his faith he must *love* God; hence "He that loveth is born [begotten] of God." 1 John iv:7. Nor is this all. "Every one that doeth righteousness is *born* [begotten] of God." 1 John ii:29. Whosoever, then, believes that Jesus is the Christ, is begotten of God—loves God, and does righteousness; for "Whosoever doeth not righteousness is not of God." 1 John iii:10.

That the word *born* in 1 John v:1, should be begotten is a point upon which critics are very generally agreed.

Dr. Clarke says: "He that believes that Jesus is the Messiah, and confides in him for the remission of sins, is *begotten of God.*" Commentary, John v:1.

T. S. GREEN, of London, translates the verse thus "Every one that believes that Jesus is the Christ has been begotten of God; and every one that loves the begetter loves him that has been begotten of him." Twofold New Testament.

When the translation is corrected, the difficulty is gone. He who makes a proper distinction between being *begotten of God* and the *new birth* knows that when a man believes the gospel he is begotten; but if *begotten of God* and *born again* mean the same thing, we see no use in correcting the translation.

John further says: "He came unto his own, and his own received him not; but as many as received him, to them gave he power to become the sons of God, even to them that believe on his name; which were born, not of blood, nor of the will of the flesh, nor of the will of man, but of God." John i:11-13. Jesus came to his own—John came to prepare a people for the Lord, and when they were made ready Jesus came to them, but as a people they did not receive Him. Some did, however, and believed on His name, and to them He gave the power or privilege of becoming sons of God. John baptized the people, saying "That they should believe on him which should come after him —that is, on Christ Jesus." Acts xix:4. Having been previously baptized by John, and made ready for the Lord, when they believed on Him He gave them permission to enter the family of God when it should be organized on the day of Pentecost. The style of expression shows that their faith did not make them sons of God, but simply prepared them to become such in future. It was a prospective privilege with them; but no persons are situated *now* as they were *then.* They were baptized before Jesus came, and when He came they believed on Him before His Father's family was organized, or the kingdom of God had come; hence they had permission given them to become His children when the fullness of time should arrive.

It is sometimes said the material prepared by John had to repent and be baptized, as others, on or after the day of Pentecost, in order to enter the spiritual family of God; but if this was true, the privilege of becoming sons of God was without meaning to them. All others had the privilege of becoming sons of God in this way, and therefore His own prepared people who believed on Him were not at all in advance of those who crucified Him; for *they* could repent, and be baptized in His name for the remission of sins, and enter the kingdom on the day of Pentecost. What did the Lord mean by giving His own prepared people who believed on Him the power or privilege of becoming the sons of God? Surely, this privilege amounted to something.

We come now to notice a class of proof texts more relied on to prove the doctrine of justification by faith alone than any others, perhaps, in the Bible. They are in the third chapter of John, and we begin to read with the fourteenth verse: "And so Moses lifted up the serpent in the wilderness, even so must the Son of man be lifted up; that whosoever believeth in him should not perish, but have eternal life. For God so loved the world, that he gave his only-begotten Son, that whosoever believeth in him should not perish, but have everlasting life." Vs. 14-16. Now be it observed that Jesus is here speaking to Nicodemus, to whom he had just said: "Except a man be born of water and of the Spirit he can not enter into the kingdom of God." Ver. 5. Does any one believe that Jesus intended to contradict this statement by what he said in the fourteenth to sixteenth verses? That is, "I know, Nicodemus, that I did say that a man must be born of water and of the Spirit, or into the kingdom of God he should not go; but I was wrong in that, for he that believeth on Me has everlasting life, whether born of water or not." Jesus had fully explained the new birth to Nicodemus, and he did not believe the testimony—"you receive not our witness;" hence Jesus appeals to an incident in Jewish history with which, as a teacher of Israel, Nicodemus was bound to be familiar, to confirm the fact that He was the promised Messiah, through Whom alone the world could hope for eternal life. The Israelites were bitten by poisonous serpents, and were dying without remedy, but God instructed Moses to make a serpent of brass, and place it upon a pole in the midst of the camp, and he that would look upon it should live. Now, Nicodemus, you are acquainted with this fact; then, "as Moses lifted up the serpent in the wilderness, even so must the Son of man be lifted up." And how was the serpent lifted up? Were the bitten Israelites cured by faith alone? They might have believed that the brazen serpent was on the pole, and they might have believed in the power of God to heal them, yet had they regarded the *look* as non-essential, and acted accordingly, they would have died without remedy. *They had to do the thing commanded or die;* even so may the sinner believe that Jesus was lifted upon the cross and died for sinners, yet if he refuses to look to God in His appointed way, he will die in his sins and be lost at last. Then, it was *believe, look, and live;* now, he that *believeth* and is *baptized* shall be *saved.* Baptism is the act of faith *now; look* was the act of faith then.

But Jesus makes another declaration to Nicodemus which, to understand, we must remember the circumstances under which it was said: "He that believeth on him is not condemned; but he that believeth not is condemned already, because he hath not believed in the name of the only-begotten Son of God." Ver. 18. We have seen that John's baptism obligated those who received it to believe on Jesus when He should come; hence those who believed on Him were not condemned, but had permission to become sons of God; but those who did not believe on Him had forfeited their obligations, and hence were in a state of condemnation for their unbelief. This could not have been applicable to those who had not heard the preliminary preaching of John, Jesus, or His disciples, for they surely would not have been ALREADY condemned for not believing in a Christ of Whom they had not heard. As these unbelievers were already condemned, it follows that they were such as had been under obligations to believe.

One more verse in this chapter demands a passing notice: "He that believeth on the Son hath everlasting life; and he that believeth not the Son shall not see life; but the wrath of God abideth on him." Ver. 36. We have no doubt that this declaration was made with reference to the same class of persons—namely, those who had been baptized. Paul says: "Moreover, brethren, I declare unto you the gospel which I preached unto you, which also ye have received, and wherein ye stand; by which also ye are saved, if ye keep in memory what I preached unto you, unless ye have believed in vain." 1 Cor xv:1, 2. How could a man *believe in vain* if he were in possession of *eternal life* the moment he believed? Every part of God's Word must be so interpreted as to harmonize with every other part; and nothing is more clearly taught in Holy Writ than that *man never has eternal life* otherwise than in *prospect* while he dwells in the flesh. "Eternal" means *without beginning or end—of endless duration;* hence, if any one has eternal life in actual possession, he can not believe in vain—he can not fall away and be lost; for, whenever he falls, that is an end to his spiritual life, which, therefore, could not have been *eternal.* That it is possible for a child of God to fall away and be lost, we have seen on pages 28-32, to which the reader is respectfully referred.

In further confirmation of the fact that the Christian has eternal life *only in prospect,* Jesus says: "There is no man that hath left house, or brethren, or sisters, or father, or mother, or wife, or children or lands for my sake and the gospel's, but he shall receive an hundred-fold now in this time, houses, and brethren, and sisters, and mothers, and children, and lands, with persecutions; and in the world to come eternal life." Mark x:29, 30. Luke gives an abridgement of this promise, thus: "Manifold more in this present time; and in the world to come life everlasting." Luke xviii:30. Here the Lord expressly tells us *when* His followers shall have eternal life—*in the world to come.* According to the theory of some, His disciples might have replied: "Lord, you said, 'He that believeth on the Son of God hath everlasting life;' we believe on you, and, therefore, have eternal life now: why do you say we shall have it in the world to come?" Paul says: "Now being made free from sin, and become servants of God, ye have your fruit unto holiness, and the end everlasting life." Rom. vi:22. Paul's brethren at Rome were then pardoned—free from sin—servants of God—and of course were *believers* in Jesus, yet they were *to have eternal life at the end.* Again: Paul speaks of the righteous judgment, when God "will render to every man according to his deeds; to them who by patient continuance in well-doing seek for glory, and honor, and immortality, eternal life." Rom. ii:6, 7. Those who persevere in well-doing *to the end will get eternal life* in the judgment of the great day, when the wicked "shall go away into everlasting punishment; but the righteous into life eternal." Matt. xxv:46. The eternal life of the righteous is co-etaneous with the punishment of the wicked. Paul admonished Timothy to fight the good fight of faith, that he might "lay hold on eternal life." 1 Tim. vi:12.

Surely, this man of God did not have to fight in order to lay hold on that which he already had. And to Titus Paul said: "Being justified by his grace, we should be made heirs according to the hope of eternal life." Tit. iii:7. He who is justified by grace *hopes for eternal life;* yet he can not hope for that which he already has; "but if we hope for that we see not, then do we with patience wait for it." Rom. viii:25. Then they who had been baptized by John, and believed on Jesus as the Son of God when He came, had everlasting life; but *how* did they have it? In *prospect*—by right or grant—were heirs of eternal life, and by patient continuance in well-doing, would lay hold on it in the world to come. And no man has it otherwise now, however confidingly he believes in Jesus Christ, or honestly he may have obeyed the gospel.

"Among the chief rulers also many believed on him, but because of the Pharisess they did not confess him, lest they should be put out of the synagogue, for they loved the praise of men more than the praise of God." John xii:42, 43. Here were persons who believed on Jesus, yet surely no one will say they had eternal life when they loved the praise of men more than the praise of God. They would not confess Jesus before men; and he says: "Whosoever, therefore, shall confess me before men, him will I confess also before my Father which is in heaven; but whosoever shall deny me before men, him will I also deny before my Father which is in heaven." Matt. x:32, 33; Luke xii:8. And again: "Whosoever, therefore, shall be ashamed of me and of my words, in this adulterous generation, of him also shall the Son of man be ashamed, when he cometh in the glory of his Father with the holy angels." Mark viii:38; Luke ix:26. If this does not cut off those rulers who believed on Jesus, no language could do it; and yet they did the very thing which, it is claimed, secures eternal life. Their faith was dead, and surely *dead faith* can not secure *eternal life*.

But we have another case. "As he spake these words, many believed on him." Here are believers—have they eternal life? We will see. "Then said Jesus to those Jews which believed on him, If ye continue in my word, then are ye my disciples indeed." John viii:30, 31. Jesus continues His address to "those Jews which believed on him" until at the fortieth verse He says: "But now ye seek to kill me, a man that hath told you the truth, which I have heard of God." To these same believers He says: "Ye are of your father the devil, and the lusts of your father ye will do." Ver. 44. Here were persons who believed on the Son of God, yet they sought to kill Him, and He tells them that they are children of the devil. Surely, then, he who believes on the Son of God, and does not perfect his faith by obeidence to His will, can not have eternal life, either in *possession* or in *prospect*, unless, indeed, he may be the son of God and a child of the devil at the same time.

If it be true that man is justified by faith *alone,* is it not a little remarkable that no case of conversion can be found on record where a man rejoiced in the pardon of his sins before, or without baptism after the new covenant went into operation on the day of Pentecost? Thousands were converted under the teaching of inspired men, and the cases are recorded for "our learning," yet not a case of justification, or pardon by faith alone—not one. "Yes, Cornelius was baptized with the Holy Ghost and spake with tongues before he was baptized in the name of the Lord; and, as the world can not receive the Spirit, he was, of course, pardoned by faith alone before baptism." This is the most plausible case, and we have put the objection in the strongest possible terms, that we may examine it in all its strength.

That the Holy Spirit or Comforter can not be received as an indwelling guest by a man of the world is a fact conceded; but the ability to speak with tongues was not always conclusive proof of the conversion of the party speaking by the Spirit, or that the Spirit had taken up its abode in him. Very wicked men have spoken by inspiration of God. Balaam prophesied against Balak by the immediate direction of God.* The Spirit of God came upon Saul, and he prophesied.† The old lying prophet of Bethel was enabled by the Spirit to foretell the sad fate of the man of God, whom by falsehood he had seduced from the word of the Lord.‡ Caiaphas, though one of the chief priests who conspired against the Lord, prophesied of the death of Christ for the Jewish nation.§ These men, though wicked as need be, proph-

---

* Num. xxiii, xxiv. Two chapters entire † 1 Sam. x:10.
‡ 1 Kings xiii:11-32.   § John xi:47-53.

esied truly by the Spirit of God; hence, the fact that Cornelius was enabled to prophesy can not prove that his sins were pardoned at that time. Cornelius was told to send to Joppa for Simon Peter, "who shall tell thee words whereby thou and all thy house shall be saved." And Peter says: "As I began to speak the Holy Ghost fell on them as on us at the beginning." Acts vi:14, 15. Now, if Cornelius had to hear words by which to be saved, he could not have been saved by the words until he heard them. And as the Holy Spirit fell on them as Peter *began to speak*, it follows that they had not heard the words when the Holy Spirit fell on them, and hence they were not saved at that time. From this decision there can be no appeal. Alluding to this event, "Peter rose up, and said unto them, Men and brethren, ye know how that a good while ago, God made choice among us, that the Gentiles by my mouth should hear the word of the gospel and believe." Acts xv:7. Then, if they were pardoned when the Holy Ghost fell on them at the beginning of Peter's discourse, they were pardoned before they heard and believed the gospel, and therefore they were pardoned without faith as well as without baptism.

Paul says: "Though I speak with the tongues of men and of angels, and have not charity, I am become as sounding brass or a tinkling cymbal." 1 Cor. xiii:1. Hence, were a man baptized with the Holy Spirit, and enabled to speak in all the languages of earth, yet without charity or love he would be nothing; and "this is the love of God that we keep his commandments." 1 John v:3. And what was His commandment to Cornelius? "He commanded them to be baptized in the name of the Lord." Acts x:48. What were they baptized in the name of the Lord for? To the Pentecostians Peter said: "Repent, and be baptized, every one of you, in the name of Jesus Christ for the remission of sins." Acts ii:38. Then Peter understood baptism in the name of the Lord to be for the remission of sins, and this is what he commanded Cornelius to do; and he says God "put no difference between us and them;" and again: "We believe that through the grace of the Lord Jesus Christ we shall be saved even as they." Acts xv:9-11. Then, unless God did make a difference between the salvation of the Jews and the Gentiles, which Peter says He did not, Cornelius was baptized in the name of the Lord for the remission of sins. For the design of his baptism with the Holy Spirit, see the chapter on that subject.

CONYBEARE and HOWSON say: "The case of Cornelius, in which the gifts of the Holy Spirit were bestowed *before* baptism, was an exception to the ordinary rule." Life and Epistles of Paul, p. 384. That they are right in this statement, is clear from the fact that the Pentecostian converts were not baptized with the Holy Spirit at all, and were only promised *the gift* of the Holy Spirit at all, and were only promised *the gift* of the Holy Spirit as a *sequence* to baptism in the name of Jesus Christ for the remission of sins, and from the additional fact that the Samaritans believed and were baptized, and yet the Holy Spirit fell upon none of them until Peter and John went there.*

But Peter said: "To him give all the prophets witness, that through his name whosoever believeth in him shall receive remission of sins." Acts x:43. Yes, believers get remission of sins through His name, and that is the reason Peter commanded Cornelius and the Pentecostians to be *baptized in His name*, that they might receive remission of sins as the prophets had testified; and we know of no other way by which believers may receive remission of sins in His name than by accepting remission as He proposed it, saying: "He that believeth and is baptized shall be saved." Mark xvi:16.

But we have an overwhelming objection to the doctrine of baptism for the remission of sins in the fact that Paul says: "Christ sent me not to baptize, but to preach the gospel." 1 Cor. i:17. This is an *elliptical* form of expression, like which we have many in the Bible; *e.g.*, "He that believeth on me, believeth not on me, but on him that sent me." John xii:44. Here the Saviour is made to contradict Himself in a single sentence, by saying he that believed on Him did not believe on Him; but when we supply the ellipsis all is plain. "He that believeth on me, believeth not [only] on me, but [also] on him that sent me." We suppose all will agree that the words *only* and *also* should be supplied in this quotation. Let us try another. "But when they deliver you up, take no thought how or what ye shall speak; for it shall be given you in that same hour what ye shall speak; for it

---

* See Acts viii: 13-16.

is not ye that speak, but the Spirit of your Father which speaketh in you." Matt. x:19, 20. Here, again, unless the ellipsis be supplied, Christ contradicts Himself by first saying it should be given them what *they should speak,* and then telling them that they should not speak at all. When the ellipsis is supplied the passage reads thus: "It is not [only] you that speak, but [also] the Spirit of my Father that speaketh in you." Do all agree to this? Then, why may we not understand Paul in the same way? "Christ sent me not [only] to baptize, but [also] to preach the gospel." If this ellipsis be not allowed, then we have Paul doing that for which he had no authority; for he says he did baptize even some of these Corinthians; and he says himself he baptized Crispus, and Gaius, and the household of Stephanus.

Now, can any one suppose that Paul raised his hand before God and said: "In the name of Jesus Christ I baptize you," when Christ gave him no authority to baptize at all? Surely not. Then Paul was sent not only to baptize, but also to preach the gospel.

"But Paul thanked God that he had baptized but few of them; and if baptism had been for the remission of sins he would have gladly baptized many of them." Paul did not thank God that but few had been baptized, but that but few of them had been baptized by him, and he gives a reason for this: "Lest any should say that I had baptized in mine own name." Ver. 15. He does not say that he had baptized but few persons at all, but only that he had baptized but few of the Corinthians, among whom this unfortunate division had sprung up. He may have baptized thousands elsewhere.

But had baptism been an unmeaning formality, it occurs to us that Paul would not have feared a disparagement of its value by a false report concerning the name in which it was administered. But some of them had claimed to be of Paul, some of Apollos, some of Cephas, and some of Christ; hence he asks: "Were you baptized in the name of Paul?" thus showing that they could not be of Paul unless they had been baptized in his name, nor could they *be of Christ unless baptized in His name.* The apostle asks: "Was Paul crucified for you?" thus showing that they were Christ's because He had died for them, and they had been baptized in His name, that they might enjoy the benefits of His death. Reader, will you be baptized in the name of Him who has been crucified for you, that you may be His and enjoy the benefits of His death?

"But what efficacy is there in water to wash away sins?" Just none at all. "Then why should we be baptized in water for the remission of sins?" Because God has required it: is not this reason enough? The blood of Christ cleanseth us from all sin; but as we can not come in contact with it literally, we must approach it through the means which God has appointed for that purpose. As God saw fit to appoint baptism for this purpose, it is our duty to submit, but not our province to object. Had He seen proper to appoint prayer at the mourner's-bench, or any thing else, for this purpose, then this, and not baptism, would have been the act of obedience for us. When God commands, the man of faith obeys without a *why* or an *if*, and the promised blessing is sure to follow. Naaman reasoned very much like the people do now.* He was afflicted with a loathsome leprosy which bid defiance to all the remedies at his command, when he was induced by a captive girl, who waited on his wife, to go to Samaria, that Elisha the prophet might cure him. He prepared himself with presents, and a letter from the king of Syria to the king of Israel, that he might be properly introduced on his arrival. When he presented his letter to the king, it gave offense to him, rather than secured his favor; but when Elisha heard of it, he ordered Naaman to be brought unto him, that he might know there was a prophet in Israel. When he stood before the house of Elisha, he did not even go out to see him, but "sent a messenger unto him, saying, Go and wash in Jordan seven times, and thy flesh shall come again to thee, and thou shalt be clean." But Naaman was angry, and went away, saying, "Are not Abana and Pharpar, rivers of Damascus, better than all the waters of Israel? may I not wash in them and be clean? So he turned and went away in a rage." But a servant, more prudent than himself, entreated him to go and do what the prophet had directed: "Then went he down and dipped himself seven times in Jordan, according to the saying of the man of God; and his flesh came again like unto the flesh of a little child." Just so people reason

---

* 2 Kings, chap. v, entire.

now. "What virtue is there in water? Why not go to the altar or to the grove and be pardoned?" But Naaman thought there was no virtue in the waters of the Jordan; and truly there was none; yet God healed him when he did the thing commanded. So there is no abstract virtue connected with the water in which we are baptized; but the Lord said, "He that believeth and is baptized shall be saved;" and as Naaman was cured when he obeyed, so will the sinner be saved who obeys the commandment of the Lord. God commanded Moses to make a serpent of brass and put it on a pole in the midst of the camps of Israel, promising that the bitten Israelite who looked thereon should live;* and it came to pass according to His word. Was there any virtue in the brass? None. Any in the peculiar form into which it was cast? None. Any in the pole on which it was reared? None. Any in looking at it on the pole? None. Yet God healed the bitten man when he did just what was required of him. Jesus made ointment of spittle and clay and anointed the eyes of one who had been born blind, and told him to go and wash in the pool of Siloam, which he did, and came seeing.† Was there any efficacy in the spittle? None. Any in the clay? None. Any in the waters of the pool in which he washed? None. Yet the Lord gave him sight when he availed himself of the means appointed for that purpose. These illustrations might be extended indefinitely; but surely the thought is sufficienty clear that we are baptized because God has required it of us, and in respect to His authority; and we expect remission of sins, not because of any virtue in water, or merit in any act of our own, but because the Lord has promised to bestow it upon us when we comply with His will.

But why should we have to thus explain a doctrine as though it were *new* which has been taught not only by the writers of the New Testament, but also by primitive Christians even from the days of the apostles. At the risk of being tedious, we must present a few extracts from the writings of the "fathers" in proof of this fact.

HERMAS says: "For before any one receives the name of the Son of God he is liable to death; but when he receives that seal,

---

* Num. xxi:8-12. † John ix:1-7.

he is delivered from death and is assigned to life. Now, that seal is water, into which persons go down liable to death, but come out of it assigned to life. For which reason to these also was the seal preached; and they made use of it that they might enter into the kingdom of God." Wall's History, vol. i, p. 51. (Paul salutes Hermas, Rom. xvi:14.) Wall says: "This book was written before St. John wrote his gospel." *Ibid*, p. 52. On page 54 he says: "The scope of the place is to represent the necessity of water-baptism to salvation or to entrance into the kingdom of God, in the opinion of the then Christians—*i.e.*, the Christians of the apostles' times." Thus we see, according to Dr. Wall, that Hermas lived in the days of the apostles, and wrote before John wrote his gospel; and he says *persons go down into the water liable to death, and come out of it assigned to life.*

BARNABAS says: "This meaneth that we indeed descend into the water full of sins and defilement, but come up bearing fruit in our heart, having the fear of God, and trust in Jesus in our spirit." Apostolic Fathers, p. 154. Barnabas is said to have been the companion of Paul. Orchard's History, vol. i, p. 12.

JUSTIN MARTYR wrote about ninety years after Matthew wrote his gospel. He says "that we should not continue children of that necessity and ignorance, but of will, or choice, and knowledge, and should obtain forgiveness of the sins in which we have lived, by water, [or in the water] there is invoked, over him that has a mind to be regenerated, the name of God the Father," etc. Wall's History, vol. i, p. 69.

Orchard quotes Justin as follows: "This food we call the eucharist, of which none are allowed to be partakers but such only as are true believers, and have been baptized in the laver of regeneration for the remission of sins." Orchard's History, vol. i, p. 24.

Wall comments on a quotation from Justin thus: "I recite this to show that in these times, so very near the apostles', they spoke of original sin affecting all mankind descended of Adam; and understood that, besides the actual sins of each particular person, there is in our nature itself, since the fall, something that needs redemption and forgiveness by the merits of Christ. And that is ordinarily applied to every particular person by baptism." Wall's History, vol. i, p. 64.

THE DESIGN OF BAPTISM 451

ORIGEN wrote about the year 185 A.D. He says: "They are rightly baptized who are *washed unto salvation*. He that is *baptized unto salvation* receives the water and the Holy Spirit; such baptism as is accompanied with crucifying the flesh, and rising again to newness of life, is the approved baptism." Orchard's History, vol. i, p. 35.

CYRIL, Bishop of Jerusalem, in the year 385 A.D., said: "If any one receive not baptism he can not be saved." *Ibid.*, p. 43.

ST. AMBROSE: "There is no regeneration without water." Wall's History, vol. i, p. 78.

TERTULLIAN. Wall comments upon Tertullian thus: "This author, in the places here first cited, treating of the necessity of baptism, speaks of that necessity as absolute, and of those who die unbaptized as lost men; and is enraged at those who maintain that faith without it is sufficient to salvation." Wall's History, vol. i, p. 96.

GREGORY NAZIANZEN. Wall comments on Gregory after the following style: "When he deters the baptized person from falling back into sinful courses, tells him 'there is not another regeneration afterward to be had, though it be sought with ever so much crying and tears,' and yet grants, in the next words, that there is repentance after baptism, but shows a difference between that and the free forgiveness given in baptism." *Ibid*, pp. 77, 78.

CYPRIAN: "If any one be not baptized and regenerated he can not come to the kingdom of God." *Ibid*, p. 146.

GREGORY, Bishop of Nysa, A.D. 388, says: "In baptism there are three things which conduct us to immortal life—*Prayer, Water* and *Faith*." Orchard's History, vol. i, p. 44.

AMBROSE, Bishop of Milan, A.D. 390, says: "The body was plunged into this water to wash away sin." *Ibid*.

In commenting upon the doctrine of Novatian, who figured in the middle of the third century, Neander says: "The church, he could say, has no right to grant absolution to a person who, by any mortal sin, has trifled away the pardon obtained for him by Christ, and appropriated to him by baptism." Neander, vol. i, p. 244.

Concerning baptism in the third century, Mosheim says:

"The remission of sin was thought to be its immediate and happy fruit." Maclain, Mosheim, vol. i, p. 91.

We might pursue this line of testimony on through the *Donatists,* the Albigenses, the Waldenses, and other parties of more recent date, showing that they all were of one mind on this subject, but we have not room to do so. Even the abuses of baptism point to the well-recognized doctrine of baptism for the remission of sins. In the previous chapter we saw that infant baptism grew out of the absurd dogma of original sin, and the well-known fact that baptism was for the remission of sins. "The Council of MELA, in Numedia in Africa, enjoin Christians to baptize their infants for forgiveness of sin, and curse all who deny the doctrine." Orchard's History, vol. i, p. 47. For abundant proof of this fact the reader is referred to the previous chapter. We have not the space, nor is it necessary, to elaborate it here— though a volume might be filled with proof of the fact.

But if baptism for remission of sins was taught by the writers of the New Testament, and by the primitive Christians for centuries after inspiration ceased, how comes it to pass that it is so zealously opposed by good men of modern times? From some cause a radical change has been effected in the theology of religious parties on this subject very recently. We have before us some two or three editions of the Methodist Discipline which differ from each other widely upon this subject. One of them was published by John Early for the Methodist Episcopal Church South in Louisville, in 1846, from which we quote a prayer used at the baptism of persons of riper years, as follows:

"Almighty and immortal God, the aid of all that need, the helper of all that flee to Thee for succor, the life of them that believe, and the resurrection of the dead; we call upon Thee for *these persons,* that *they,* coming to Thy holy baptism, may receive remission of *their sins* by spiritual regeneration. Receive *them,* O Lord, as thou hast promised by thy well-beloved Son, saying, Ask, and ye shall receive; seek, and ye shall find; knock, and it shall be opened unto you; so give now unto us that ask: let us that seek, find; open the gate unto us that knock; that *these persons* may enjoy the everlasting benediction of Thy heavenly washing, and may come to the eternal kingdom which Thou hast promised by Christ our Lord. **Amen.**"

Now we pick up another edition which was published by J. B. McFerrin, of Nashville, in 1858; and find that after the words "these persons" all the following words are omitted: "that *they, coming to Thy holy baptism, may receive remission of their sins by spiritual regeneration.*" Why were these words stricken out? If they were expressive of truth in 1846, were they not equally orthodox in 1858? If baptism was for the remission of sins when the first edition was published, is there any good reason why it should not be so yet?

But there is a change in the next prayer equally significant. In 1846 the minister was instructed to pray for the candidates thus: "Give Thy Holy Spirit to *these persons,* that they may be born again, and be made heirs of everlasting salvation through our Lord Jesus Christ." But in 1858 he prays, 'Give Thy Holy Spirit to *these persons,* that they, being born again, may be made heirs of everlasting salvation," etc. *Then* he prayed that "they may be born again" in baptism; *now* he must recognize them as already born again before baptism. And still he must pray that they be made heirs of eternal life—as though they could be *born again without being heirs of eternal life.* But why cease to pray that they should be *born again in baptism?* If it was true then that men must be born of water and of Spirit, it is certainly true yet. We do not object to the abandonment of error when it is discovered, but these changes show that these parties found *themselves teaching the doctrine of baptism for the remission of sins* down to 1858, when the change was made, and that a doctrine now regarded as a monstrous heresy was believed and taught up to that time. Indeed, it seems hard for the creed-makers to avoid teaching this doctrine even when seeking to avoid it. The Westminster and Cumberland Presbyterian Confessions have both taught it, despite of their efforts to the contrary. They say: "Although it be a great sin to condemn or neglect this ordinance, yet grace and salvation are not so inseparably annexed unto it as that no person can be regenerated or saved without it." Here note the fact that *it is a great sin to condemn or neglect baptism.* Of repentance they say: "As there is no sin so small but it deserves damnation, so there is no sin so great that it can bring damnation upon those who truly repent." Here note the fact that *there is no sin so small but deserves damnation;* hence, if the smallest sin deserves damnation, the great sin of neglecting baptism deserves it none the less. On the attributes of God they say: He "hates all sin, and will by no means clear the guilty." Then they who neglect baptism deserve, and will receive, damnation, if these books be true.

But the last resort is an appeal to the prejudice of the people: "If baptism is for the remission of sins, all our pious fathers and mothers who died unbaptized are lost." As to what God will do with those *who sought to know the truth,* and made an honest mistake with regard to baptism or any thing else, He has not seen fit to reveal, and therefore we will not attempt to decide; but if, like many do now, they allowed prejudice to stop their ears and close their eyes against the truth, then we hesitate not to say that their ignorance of the law will be no excuse. But suppose they were deprived of opportunities which you have, and they honestly believed *non-essential* that which you know to be a solemn requisition of the Lord, will you be excused because they were? But suppose we concede that they were lost, will it benefit them for you to persist in rebellion and be lost also? Would it not be more wise for you to seek a knowledge of your duty, and perform it to your own salvation, than to cling to known error because your parents believed it true? Though you were to weep tears of blood on account of their mistake, you could not correct it. They are in the hands of a God whose infinite love and mercy will secure a just decision as to them: and this is all you can know on the subject. You have an immortal spirit of your own, which must live in endless bliss with God and His Son in heaven, or writhe in eternal misery with the devil and the damned. Oh, then, as you have a heaven to gain and a hell to shun, why not accept salvation upon the terms which God has proposed?

CHAPTER XV.

THE HOLY SPIRIT

It is not our purpose to write a dissertation upon the *nature, origin,* or *relationships* of the Holy Spirit. Paul said, "Foolish and unlearned questions avoid, knowing that they do gender strifes." 2 Tim. ii:23. We are persuaded that there can be but little known of these subjects because there is but little revealed concerning them. "Secret things belong unto the Lord our God: but those things which are revealed belong unto us and to our children forever." Deut. xxiv:29. Why, then, should we worry ourselves over questions which our Father never revealed to us, and therefore never intended us to know?

There are more practical questions connected with the Holy Spirit of which we may know something, because God has spoken to us more definitely concerning them, and it is of them we propose to write. We are aware, too, that even these are not to be comprehended without effort; nor are we vain enough to suppose that we are able to write an unexceptionable essay concerning them. Strong minds and devoted hearts have prayerfully perused the sacred pages of Holy Writ until their eyes have grown dim in age; and, after all their toil, have closed their labors confessedly ignorant of the *modus operandi* of the Holy Spirit. Indeed the incomprehensibility of the subject is the *theory* advocated by many very able pens. By such, those who claim to understand the subject, are at once suspected of denying the influence of the Spirit in conversion entirely. If you deny an incomprehensible influence of the Spirit, they know of no other, and hence conclude that you deny all spiritual influence. They are ever ready to quote John iii:8; "The wind bloweth where it listeth, and thou hearest the sound thereof, but canst not tell whence it cometh, and whither it goeth: so is every one that is born of the Spirit." In vain may you call their attention to the fact that the passage does not say "so is the Spirit," or "so is the operation of the Spirit." They have learned to so interpret it, and this is quite sufficient to end the investigation of the subject. They will regard it presumptuous in us to even attempt an examination of it. They will quote the old adage, "Fools rush on where angels fear to tread." But we beg them to remember that if we are ignorant of the subject, we will not be more likely to remain so, than those who do not examine it at all. If they and we close our Bibles and cease to investigate, we will all remain ignorant together. The divine volume contains many lessons on the subject, and surely our Father would not have said so much to us on a subject of which he intended us to remain entirely ignorant. We are, therefore, encouraged to pursue our study of the sacred pages with all the assistance we can get, in the hope that we may, at least, acquire a sufficient knowledge of what is taught concerning the Holy Spirit, to enable us to enjoy its comforting influences in God's appointed way.

Our Bible teaches us that there is not only one God and Father, and one Lord Jesus Christ the Son of this Father, but also that there is one Holy Spirit which proceeded from God, divine as is God from whom it proceeded. As the sun is the great center of the solar system from which emanate light and heat to the natural world, so God is not only Spirit, but the great center of the spiritual world from whom emanated the Holy Spirit, giving light and comfort to the denizens of earth through the inspired word and the institutions and service appointed therein.

John the Baptist said to those who came to be baptized of him in the Jordan: "I indeed baptize you with water unto repentance; but he that cometh after me is mightier than I, whose shoes I am not worthy to bear; he shall baptize you with the Holy Ghost and with fire." Matt. iii:11.

Paul says, "Now concerning spiritual gifts, brethren, I would not have you ignorant." And again: "Now there are diversities of gifts but the same Spirit." 1 Cor. xii:1, 4.

After Jesus had told His disciples that it was needful for them that He should go away, in order that the Holy Spirit might come to and remain with them as an abiding Comforter. He said to them: "When He is come He will reprove the world of sin, and of righteousness, and of judgment." John xvi:8.

Paul, in his epistle to his brethren at Rome, said: "Ye have received the Spirit of adoption, whereby we cry, Abba, Father." Rom. vii:15. And again: "The Spirit itself beareth witness with our spirit, that we are children of God." Rom. viii:16.

Thus we find the Scripture speaking of the *baptism of the*

Holy Spirit; secondly, of the *gifts of the Spirit;* thirdly, the *operation* or *work* of the Spirit in *reproving* the world of sin, righteousness, and judgment, the *reception* of the Spirit by the children of the Father, and the *witness* of the Spirit. Paul charged Timothy, saying: "Study to show thyself approved unto God, a workman that needeth not to be ashamed, rightly dividing the word of truth." 2 Tim. ii:15. We know of no subject to the study of which this admonition is of more importance than that of the Holy Spirit. If we can rightly divide and apply the word of truth to the subject in hand, we will be aided much in attaining to a knowledge of it. If we fail to do this, we may correctly learn something concerning it, but understand the subject as a system we never will.

We have seen five separate departments of our subject spoken of in the passages quoted. Let us draw the line deep and wide between them, that we may keep them well apart until we examine them in the light of the Scriptures. Should we indiscriminately apply what was written with reference to any one of them, teaching of the Spirit and make an incomprehensible logomachy of the whole subject. Let us rightly divide our subject, and apply the Scriptures accordingly. First in order we examine

THE BAPTISM OF THE HOLY SPIRIT.

That God promised the baptism of the Holy Spirit to certain persons, through John the Baptist and also through Jesus His Son, is not disputed by any one; and that this promise was verified on the day of Pentecost, and at the house of Cornelius, is believed by all. The matter in controversy is as to whether or not the baptism thus promised was to be special or general, temporary or perpetual. In other words, was it confined to the day of miracles? or was it designed for, and promised to, the Christians of our day, yea, of all time?

First, then we will examine the Scriptures relied on, to prove that persons are *now* baptized with the Holy Spirit. The first passage we will examine may be found in the prophecy of Joel ii:28-30. "And it shall come to pass afterward, that I will pour out my Spirit upon all flesh; and your sons and your daughters shall prophesy, your old men shall dream dreams, your young men shall see visions; and also upon the servants, and upon the handmaids in those days will I pour out my Spirit; and I will show wonders in the heavens and in the earth, blood and fire, and pillars of smoke." That this prophecy had reference to the baptism of the Holy Spirit, to take place on the day of Pentecost is certain, from the fact that Peter quotes it as fulfilled in the events of that day. Acts ii:16-19. As it is here said that the Spirit was to be poured out upon *all flesh*, it is insisted that those living now are a part of all flesh as well as those who lived then, and hence it must require all time to fulfill the prophecy, because if its fulfillment was restricted to the events of that day, it was not poured out upon all flesh. But if there are to be no restrictions placed upon the phrase "all flesh" then the passage will prove entirely too much. Paul tells us that "All flesh is not the same flesh: but there is one kind of flesh of men, another flesh of beasts, another of fishes, and another of birds." 1 Cor. xv:39. Therefore, if the phrase "*all flesh*" is not to be limited, we not only have *all men* baptized with the Spirit, but also all beasts, birds, and fish. "Well, but it means *all human flesh.*" This proves too much yet; for this would include the most wicked man of earth, as well as the best Christian. "But it means *all Christians.*" Stop; you set out with the position that there are no restrictions to be put on the phrase all flesh; now you cut off not only all beasts, birds, and fish, but also the larger portion of human flesh, for few go the narrow path, while the many go the broad road; and these you will not allow to be baptized with the Spirit at all. This is doing pretty well. These restrictions are right; may there not be others? The sons and daughters who were the subjects of this baptism were to prophesy, the old men were to dream dreams, and the young men were to see visions. Are these phenomena exhibited by all Christians now? If not, the phrase *all flesh* must be pruned down until it embraces such, and only such, as can do the things spoken of. When Peter said, "This is that which was spoken by the prophet Joel," (Acts ii:16) the disciples were prophesying, speaking with tongues, and doing the things spoken of by Joel; hence we feel authorized to restrict the phrase "*all flesh*" to such as exhibited the signs predicted in the prophecy. Again: We have the fulfillment of this prophecy to take place at a specified time. "It shall come to pass in the *last days*, saith God, that I will pour out of my Spirit upon all flesh." Acts ii:17. Certainly the last days here spoken of can not be the last days of time, for more than eighteen hundred years have gone by since Peter said, "This is that which was spoken by the prophet Joel." And it would require great boldness to affirm that the phrase *last days* was intended to include *all the days* from the day of Pentecost to the end of time; yet such must be the interpretation given to it, to make the fulfillment of Joel's prophecy include the Christians of all time, and therefore those of this day. The *last days* here spoken of by Joel must have been the last days of the Jewish dispensation, for it was in them that Peter tells us, "This is that which was spoken." The argument drawn from this prophecy to support the notion that persons are *now* baptized with the Holy Spirit is, therefore, evidently defective.

The language of John the Baptist next claims our attention. He said to those demanding baptism of him in the Jordan: "I indeed baptize you with water unto repentance; but he that cometh after me is mightier that I, whose shoes I am not worthy to bear: he shall baptize you with the Holy Ghost and with fire: whose fan is in his hand, and he will thoroughly purge his floor, and gather his wheat into the garner; but he will burn up the chaff with unquenchable fire." Matt. iii:11, 12. This address is recorded by Luke (iii:16, 17) in very nearly the same words. Mark records an abridgment of it, thus "There cometh one mightier than I after me, the latchet of whose shoes I am not worthy to stoop down and unloose. I indeed have baptized you with water; but he shall baptize you with the Holy Ghost." Mark i:7, 8. It is not important to our investigation that we stop to inquire who were to be the subjects of the baptism of fire spoken of in the records by Matthew and Luke, as it is the baptism of the Holy Spirit which concerns us at present; nor will we stop to inquire whether this was to be a *figurative* or a literal baptism in the Holy Spirit. That it was *literal* is all that can be claimed, and this we are not only willing to grant, but firmly believe. But do these quotations prove that persons are now baptized with the Holy Spirit? If they prove it at all, they must do it in one of two ways. First, *the language employed must be sufficiently comprehensive to include us, or the principle taught must be applicable to us.* First, then, who were the persons represented by the pronoun *you* in the sentence "He shall baptize *you* with the Holy Ghost"? That this word could not have included even *all John's audience* is clear from the fact that some of them were wicked—comparable to chaff and to be burned with unquenchable fire. But even had it embraced every one to whom he spake, both wicked and good, it would still require very elastic rules of interpretation to make it embrace the Christians of all time. "I indeed baptize *you* with water * * * he shall baptize *you* with the Holy Ghost and with fire." Can any fair rules of interpretation make the last *you* include more than the first *you?* Surely not. Then it follows that those who were here promised the baptism of the Holy Ghost were among those *baptized by John in water.*

Again: We have a rule of grammar saying: *"Pronouns must agree with the nouns for which they stand, in gender, number, and person."* If we respect this rule at all, how can we make these pronouns include more, or other, persons than their antecedents in the preceding part of the chapter?

Once more: *In oral discourse, the persons indicated by pronouns of the second person are always present with the speaker.* This rule knows no exception. In written communications, persons represented by pronouns of the second person may be absent from the writer, but to a speaker they must be present. Let us apply this rule to the speech made by John the Baptist to the multitude on the banks of the Jordan. "I indeed baptize *you* with water* * * he shall baptize *you* with the Holy Ghost." How can these pronouns of the second person embrace any persons not present before John when he used them? If we apply this promise to other persons, we must derive authority for doing so from other sources than the language employed, for evidently it is not there. Then is there a principle taught applicable to us? If so, we can not see it. The passage was a prophetic promise made to certain persons, to be fulfilled to them, and when so fulfilled, there was no general principle remaining applicable to any persons *only such as are shown to be subjects of the baptism in question.* That Christians are now such subjects is the matter to be *proved—to assume it* is to assume the whole controversy. We have seen that the language of John is incapable of proving it, either expressly or by implication. We would not be understood, however, to deny that any were baptized with the Holy Ghost who were not of those baptized by John the Baptist in water. We know that others were so baptized, but this is not quite sufficient to prove that the language employed by John included them. We have been seeking to test the power of this passage to prove the doctrine in question. We know that it is confidently relied on to sustain the theory; hence we have sought for the extent of its application and the time of its fulfillment. When Jesus was assembled with the apostles on one occasion, He "commanded them not to depart from Jerusalem, but wait for the promise of the Father, which, saith he, ye have heard of me; for John ruly baptized with water, but ye shall be baptized with the Holy Ghost not many days hence." Acts i:4, 5. As Jesus here associates this promise of the Father with John's baptism, it is next to certain that He here refers to the *same promise* which the Father made by John. This being so, we can scarcely fail to recognize its fulfillment on the day of Pentecost at Jerusalem, where they were commanded to wait for it. And though, in the three recorded accounts of John's discourse, we have no specific allusion to the *time* of its fulfillment, yet when Jesus quotes it, He says it shall be *not many days hence*, and commanded them not to depart from Jerusalem until it was fulfilled. When, therefore, we connect these passages together, we see not how it is possible to look beyond the day of Pentecost for the complete fulfillment of the promise of the Father made through John concerning the baptism of the Holy Spirit.

But we may be told that Peter quoted this language at the house of Cornelius as applicable to the Gentiles, saying: "As I began to speak, the Holy Ghost fell on them as on us at the beginning. Then remembered I the word of the Lord, how that he said, John indeed baptized with water, but ye shall be baptized with the Holy Ghost." Acts xi:15, 16. This is sufficiently near the language quoted from Acts i:4, 5, to make it probable that both passages refer to the same conversation. As God baptized the disciples with the Holy Spirit when the gospel was first proclaimed to the Jews, it was proper, for reasons which we will see in due time, that He should attend its introduction to the Gentiles by the like gift. But if the baptism of the Holy Spirit was *then bestowed upon all converts, as we are told it now is*, why did Peter associate it with the *beginning?* Why not have said: "As I began to speak the Holy Spirit fell on them as on all others converted?" Surely, some such style would have been appropriate. Many thousands had been converted from the day of Pentecost to that time, yet the language employed is calculated to make the impression that such an event had not come under their notice from the beginning until that time.

We will notice one more passage only. "For by one Spirit are we all baptized into one body, whether we be Jews or Gentiles, whether we be bond or free; and have been all made to drink into one Spirit." 1 Cor. xii:13. Although this passage was written in close proximity to Paul's explanation of the miraculous gifts of the Spirit, yet we are willing to admit the principle taught in it to be applicable to Christians generally, but it falls very far short of proving that they, or any of them, are baptized with the Holy Spirit. So far from it that it says not one word about it. *By one Spirit* are we all baptized into one body. There is one body (Eph. iv:4); This is the church (Col. i:18 and 24). There is one baptism (Eph. iv:5), by which we enter this one body. Are we now prepared to see the import of the passage? By (the teaching of) one Spirit (the Holy Spirit) we are all baptized (in water) into one body (the church). This seems to be the obvious import of the passage, and it is in harmony with the whole tenor of the Spirit's teaching on the subject. But if we insist that it means "*in* one Spirit we are all baptized into one body," then we make Paul contradict himself, saying there is "one baptism." When he says: "There is one Lord, one faith, one baptism, one God and Father of all," he as clearly teaches that there is *but* one baptism, as he does that there is *but* one Lord or *but* one God and Father of all. The denominations themselves agree that *by water baptism we enter the church;* if, therefore, they make this passage mean Holy Spirit baptism, they not only contradict Paul, but they contradict themselves. Surely, they will not do this.

It is admitted by all that God's works, every-where, are a most wonderful exhibition of harmony and order. He has a place for every thing and every thing in its place—an office for every thing to fill, and every thing filling its own office. It is altogether probable, then, that the baptism of the Holy Spirit was designed for some appropriate work, and not given to accomplish any thing, every thing, or nothing, as might chance to happen. It is, then, of the first importance that we seek for the office assigned it in the gospel plan of salvation. What say you, gentle reader, on this subject? What do you want with it? What do you expect it to do for you? The first work usually assigned it in the theories of modern times, is the removal of the depravity or corruption of nature supposed to have been inherited from our illustrious progenitors as a result of their sin, or rather, *our sin in them.* It is assumed that man comes into the world totally depraved, wholly defiled in all the faculties and parts of soul and body, opposed to all good and wholly inclined to all evil, in consequence of which he can not will or desire any thing good accompanying salvation until this depravity is removed or modified by the baptism of the Holy Spirit. For an examination of this assumption the reader is referred to the chapter on Hereditary Depravity.

Suppose, however, that this is really a true picture of man's nature, and he can do nothing until God enables him to do it by baptizing him with the Holy Spirit. What then? If God has to administer it, and man can do nothing until it is done, and it is never done at all, who is to blame for it? Will God sentence the sinner to hell and there punish him forever for not obeying the gospel, when it was no fault of his that he did not do it? The baptism of the Holy Spirit was a *miracle, emphatically a miracle, performed by Jesus Himself.* If, therefore, all converts of our day are baptized with it, it follows that there is a miracle performed every time a conversion takes place, and miracles will continue as long as there is a subject converted to God; and the conversion of every man is suspended upon the performance of a miracle of which he has not the slightest control, for until it is performed he can not even desire it, or will any good thing accompanying it.

But was the removal of depravity the object to be accomplished by the baptism of the Spirit anciently? The first case, of which we have a record, took place on the day of Pentecost, and the disciples were the subjects of it on that occasion. Had the apostles been more than three years with the Lord, and been sent by Him to preach the approach of the kingdom "to the lost sheep of the house of Israel" (Matt. x:5-7), with power to perform miracles in His name, and, finally, to preach the gospel to every creature, with power to bind and loose on earth, with the assurance that their acts should be ratified in heaven, and yet their hearts totally depraved, wholly disposed to evil and opposed to all good until they were baptized with the Holy Spirit on the day of Pentecost? Are we prepared for this?

But we are told that the three thousand converts of that day were also baptized with it. Is there any proof of this? The record says: "Peter stood up in the midst of the *disciples,* the number of names together were about a hundred and twenty." Acts i:5. "And when the day of Pentecost was fully come, *they* were all with one accord in one place * * * and *they* were all filled with the Holy Ghost, and began to speak with other tongues as the Spirit gave them utterance." Who were with one accord in one place? The disciples. Who were all filled with the Holy Ghost? The disciples. Who began to speak with other tongues as moved by the Holy Ghost? The disciples. Not a word about any one else being with them. But "when this was noised abroad, the multitude came together." Ver. 6. Then it was not until after the baptism of the disciples with the Holy Spirit that the multitude came together, from among whom the three thousand were converted. Not a word in the narrative about their having been baptized with the Holy Ghost. They were promised the *gift* of the Holy Spirit if they would "repent, and be baptized in the name of Jesus Christ for the remission of sins;" but even this was not until they had heard and believed Peter's preaching, and were cut to the heart by it, which modern teachers insist they could not have been until they were baptized with it.

We will next examine the case of Cornelius. Please notice his character before he was baptized with the Holy Spirit. He was "a devout man, and one that feared God with all his house, which gave much alms to the people, and prayed to God always." Acts x:2. And was his heart totally depraved, wholly corrupt, the opposite of all good? Really, it seems he had good thoughts and did good deeds before he was baptized, either with Spirit or water. Then it follows, that the baptism of the Holy Spirit was not intended to remove his depravity and make him devoted, charitable, or prayerful, for he was all these before. We insist that if you purify the heart by the baptism of the Holy Spirit, you thereby annul the office of *faith*. With reference to the Gentiles, Peter says: "God, which knoweth the hearts, bare them witness, giving them the Holy Ghost even as he did unto us; and put no difference between us and them, purifying their hearts by faith." Acts xv:8, 9. Here we find, that in cases where the Gentiles received the Holy Spirit, it was not to purify the heart, for this was done by faith. Suppose you have a clock, the machinery of which is propelled by weights. You remove the weights from their place, and propel the machinery of the clock by springs, what further use have you for the weights? So, if you purify the heart by the baptism of the Holy Spirit, what further use have you for faith? But we are sometimes told that the baptism of the Holy Spirit is to produce faith. Then when Paul said, "So then *faith cometh by hearing*, and hearing by the word of God" (Rom. x:17), he should have said, "So then faith cometh by the baptism of the Holy Spirit."

Again: It is insisted that the baptism of the Holy Spirit is for, or in order to, the remission of sins, and that this is its office in the gospel plan of salvation. Then it follows, that the apostles were three years the chosen companions of Jesus, sent by Him to preach to the lost sheep of the house of Israel, with power to perform miracles in His name, and still unpardoned until baptized on the day of Pentecost. "John did baptize in the wilderness and preach the baptism of repentance for the remission of sins. And there went out unto him all the land of Judea, and they of Jerusalem, and were all baptized of him in the river of Jordan, confessing their sins." Mark i:4, 5. Thus John made "Ready a people prepared for the Lord." Luke i:17. Jesus selected His apostles from the material thus prepared for him. Does any one believe that, when they were baptized by John for the remission of sins, that they were still unpardoned until baptized with the Holy Spirit on the day of Pentecost? If not, then the baptism of the Holy Spirit was not for the remission of their sins. Paul informs us that there is "one Lord, one Faith and ONE Baptism." Eph. iv:5. That this one baptism is for the remission of sins, we believe, is admitted by all. All agree that the one Body, Spirit, Hope, Lord, Faith, Baptism, God, and Father of all, spoken of in this connection, by the apostle to his Ephesian brethren, are essential to the remission of sins, spiritual growth, and final happiness of intelligent men and women in a land of Bibles. But those who would disparage the worth of baptism in water always insist that this one baptism is "Holy Ghost baptism." If we can dispel this delusion, we will have done much to settle the unfortunate controversy, with regard to the design of baptism in water. First, then, we would inquire of those who advocate this theory, and believe themselves to have received this *one baptism* in the Holy Spirit, why they still submit to baptism with water in any form? Surely, if they have been baptized with the Holy Ghost, that is *one baptism;* yes, verily, if their theory be true, it is *the one baptism;* hence, if they subsequently add to this another, in water, they have not *one,* but *two* baptisms, and Paul should have said: "There is one Lord, one faith, and *two Baptisms.*" But we may be told that "Cornelius was baptized with the Holy Spirit and was subsequently baptized with water, in obedience to the command of God through Peter, which proves that we may have two baptisms." If this proof is conclusive, will the objector be so good as to assist Paul in extricating himself from the difficulty in which he is placed by saying "There is one baptism." If he will say, with us, that the baptism of the Gentiles at the house of Cornelius, with the Holy Spirit, was a miracle, such as has not occurred from that time to the present (of which we have a record), and allow that, when Paul said "There is one baptism," he alluded to the baptism to which the taught of all nations are to submit (Matt. xxviii:19), and that was enjoined upon "every creature" who would believe the gospel and be saved (Mark xvi:16), which was connected with repentance for the remission of sins (Acts ii:30), that now saves the people who rightly submit to it (1 Peter iii:21), and to which all must submit, or fail to enter the kingdom of God (John iii:5), then we can see perfect harmony in the Scriptures, and a fitness in Paul's language saying: "there is one baptism."

Again: When persons were baptized with the Holy Spirit on the day of Pentecost, "they were all *filled with the Holy Ghost,* and began to speak with other tongues as the Spirit gave them utterance." Acts ii:4. There was an absolute impact of the

Holy Spirit with the human Spirit; and hence, being *filled* with the Holy Spirit, their spirits were energized—inspired by the Holy Spirit, which took possession of them—and through them spake forth the wonderful and mighty works of God in languages hitherto unknown to them. The same cause produces the same effect on all occasions, if surrounded by the same circumstances. Baptism with the Holy Spirit, on the day of Pentecost, enabled those who received it to speak with tongues, hence, if we can find another case on record, we may expect the *same results;* for of this law in nature God is as much the author as he is the author of the Bible. Accordingly, when Cornelius and his house were baptized with it, "they *heard them speak with tongues and magnify God.*" Acts x:46. Now, as this law obtained in the cases recorded, we must insist that those who claim to have been baptized with the Holy Spirit, must, under its influence, speak in languages before unknown to them; or give us some good reason why their cases are exceptions to the rule. And, were they even to speak with other tongues, this would not be conclusive, for although this always followed the baptism of the Holy Spirit, and its absence would bar the claim to such baptism, yet there were persons enabled to speak with tongues, and prophesy, who had not been baptized with the Spirit. This we will see more clearly when we come to examine the subject of spiritual gifts. As Paul tells us that there is "one baptism," we have only to show that baptism in *water* is enjoined upon *all nations,* and *every creature* who believes the gospel and would be saved, in order to show that there is now no such thing as Holy Spirit baptism, and hence, that there is not a man, woman, or child, alive to-day who has been the subject of it. In the commission, Jesus says, "Go ye, therefore, and teach all nations, baptizing them into the name of the Father, and of the Son, and of the Holy Ghost." Matt. xxviii:19. Now, here is *a* baptism to which the taught of all nations are to submit; for it would have been anomalous had Jesus commanded the apostles to baptize them without, at least, an implied obligation on their part to submit to it. Hence, if there be *one* baptism, and *only* one, this is THE baptism, besides which there is not another. There is no escape from this position. Then, the only remaining question to be settled is, *did the Saviour here allude to water baptism?*

Does any one doubt it? If so, from whence comes their authority to baptize with or in water, in the names here set forth; that is, in the names of Father, Son, and Holy Ghost? And as Jesus was to baptize with the Holy Ghost, and no human being ever had power to administer this baptism; and as the apostles were commanded to administer *one*, it is certain that it was not Holy Ghost baptism. Once more: This was to be administered in the *name of the Holy Ghost;* and as it is not probable that the baptism of the Holy Ghost would have been administered in its own name, it is not probable that this was that kind of baptism.

We have seen that there was an implied command in the commission to the taught of all nations to submit to this baptism, and in keeping therewith we find the apostles commanding persons to be baptized: "Repent, and be baptized, every one of you." Acts ii:38. "And he commanded them to be baptized in the name of the Lord." Acts x:48. The baptism of the Holy Spirit was not a *command* but a *promise*. "And being assembled together with them, commanded them that they should not depart from Jerusalem, but wait for the *promise* of the Father, which, saith He, ye have heard of me." What promise? "For John truly baptized with water, but ye shall be baptized with the Holy Ghost not many days hence." Acts i:4, 5. As baptism in water is a command, and the baptism of the Holy Spirit is a promise and not a command, it follows, that when the apostles commanded baptism, they meant water baptism. Paul speaks of himself and Roman brethren as having been buried with Christ by baptism, and finally tells them, "ye have *obeyed* from the heart the form of doctrine which was delivered you; being then made free from sin." Rom. vi:17, 18. When were they made free from sin? When they obeyed the form of doctrine. What form of doctrine? He was speaking of a baptism in submission to which they *obeyed*, and were then made free from sin. Was this Holy Ghost baptism? No; there was no obedience in that —it was a *promise*, not a command. Promises may be enjoyed, but can not be obeyed. Commands are to be obeyed in order that the promises connected therewith, if any, may be enjoyed. Water is the only element in which the Romans were commanded to be baptized; and hence baptism in it was the only baptism they could have obeyed in order that they might be made free from sin. This form of doctrine we have already examined.

But it is insisted that we must have the baptism of the Holy Spirit as *evidence* of pardon and acceptance with God. Then we ask, had the apostles, who received it on the day of Pentecost, no evidence of their acceptance during their personal intercourse with the Saviour prior to that day? And did it give evidence to Cornelius of his acceptance before he obeyed the gospel? Now, we propose to show that persons were pardoned under the gospel dispensation, and had reliable evidence of the fact, who *had not* been baptized with the Holy Spirit. Let us see. "Then Philip went down to the city of Samaria and preached Christ unto them." Acts viii:5. "When they believed Philip preaching the things concerning the kingdom of God and the name of Jesus Christ, they were baptized both men and women." Ver. 12. Now are they saved? Does any one doubt it? Do the advocates of modern Holy Ghost baptism command men and women to be baptized, whom they regard as unsaved, when they have been baptized? Nay, verily! So far from it, that they believe them pardoned before baptism. Then, according to their own theory, these persons were saved. If men are saved by faith only, before baptism they believed and were therefore saved; and if it required faith and baptism, they had believed and been baptized and were still saved. So they were saved in any aspect of the case. But they had still further evidence of pardon. Jesus had said "He that believeth and is baptized shall be saved." Mark xvi:16. This language is not ambiguous, we can not fail to understand it. Luke says they *did believe and were baptized*, hence, if Jesus spake truly when He issued the proclamation, and Luke correctly recorded what they did, it follows, unmistakably, that they were pardoned, and had the word of the Lord as evidence of the fact. Were they yet baptized with the Holy Ghost? "Now when the apostles which were at Jerusalem, heard that Samaria had received the word of God, they sent unto them Peter and John, who when they were come down prayed for them, that they might receive the Holy Ghost, for *as yet he was fallen upon none of them:* only they were baptized in the name of the Lord Jesus." Acts viii:14, 16. While it is true that the baptism of the Holy Spirit was not the measure of it which Peter and John designed to confer upon the disciples at Samaria, yet the context clearly shows that it had not fallen upon any of them in any form, they having only received what ordinarily followed adoption into the family of God; still they were pardoned—saved beyond a peradventure. Then if the Samaritans could and did believe the gospel, and be baptized in the name of the Lord Jesus, and have His word as evidence that they were saved *without* the baptism of the Holy Spirit, *why may we not do the same thing?* If any one supposes himself to have been baptized with the Holy Spirit in order to his conversion, then we would like to know whether or not he supposes himself to have been converted as were the Samaritans? Should he claim to have been pardoned in a different way, then we would inquire how many ways of pardon are there for the same class of persons?

But we have not yet found the purposes for which the baptism of the Holy Spirit was administered in the cases of which we have a record. Soon after His baptism, Jesus selected twelve men, to whom it was His purpose to commit the first proclamation of the gospel which was to be the power of God for the salvation of men; these he required to forsake parents, friends, occupations—every thing—and follow Him, that their minds might be free to receive the instruction necessary to a thorough preparation for the work assigned them. For three and a half years He ceased not to instruct them in the things pertaining to His kingdom; and though they had left all to follow one so poor that He had not where to lay His weary head, He comforted them, saying: "I appoint unto you a kingdom, as my Father hath appointed unto me; that ye may eat and drink at my table in my kingdom, and sit on thrones judging the twelve tribes of Israel." Luke xxii:29, 30. Knowing the events that were soon to occur in their presence—that He should be put to death, and go to His Father, leaving them to plead His cause in the midst of persecution and death—He faithfully told them of all that should befall them, but that He would remember them in prayer to His Father: "I will pray the Father, and he shall give you another Comforter, that he may abide with you forever: even the Spirit of truth; whom the world can not receive, because it seeth him not, neither knoweth him: but ye know him; for he dwelleth with you, and shall be in you." John xiv:16, 17. This Comforter was not, like Him, to be taken from them, but to remain with them forever. But said He: "Because I have said these things unto you, sorrow hath filled your heart. Nevertheless I tell you the truth; It is expedient for you that I go away: for if I go not away, the Comforter will not come unto you; but if I depart, I will send him unto you." John xvi:6, 7. Why was it expedient for them that He should go away? "When the Comforter is come, whom I will send unto you from the Father, even the Spirit of truth, which proceedeth from the Father, he shall testify of me." John xv:26. They "trusted that it had been he which should have redeemed Israel." Luke xxiv:41. But when He was crucified their hopes died with Him, and, in despair, they went, each one, to his former occupation. When He gave them proof that He had risen from the dead, they took courage, and determined to await the promised power from on high. But when the Holy Spirit came from heaven, bearing to them the glorious tidings of His coronation as King of kings and Lord of lords, it filled their hearts with joy and gladness; yea, they rejoiced to know that He was at His Father's right hand, as their adorable High Priest and Mediator, and would there remain to make intercession for His children, until His foes should become His footstool. Truly did the Comforter, on that day, bear witness of Him, for then were they bold to declare that he was "by the right hand of God exalted, and having received of the Father the promise of the Holy Ghost, he hath shed forth this, which ye now see and hear." Acts ii:33.

Again: Notwithstanding He had been with them, and had faithfully instructed them in the great scheme of man's salvation, still they were human, and liable to forget the important lessons He had given them; hence He told them that "the Comforter, which is the Holy Ghost, whom the Father will send in my name, he shall teach you all things, and bring all things to your remembrance, whatsoever I have said unto you." John xiv:26. Though He had many things to say to them which, in their weakness, they were not able to bear, and which, for their good, He graciously declined then to reveal, he assured them that "when he, the Spirit of truth, is come, he will guide you into all truth" (John xvi:13); and thus He prepared them to eventually receive what He could not then tell them.

Once more: their commission required them to "preach the gospel to every creature," to "teach all nations." How could these ignorant Galileans preach the gospel among *all nations*, to *every creature* in the numerous languages then spoken? "There were dwelling at Jerusalem Jews, devout men, out of every nation under heaven." Acts ii:5. Truly, here was a difficulty. But they were to "tarry at Jerusalem until endued with power from on high." This power they were to receive after that the Holy Ghost came upon them. This completed the preparations. How could they then err? They could not despair, for the Spirit gave them comfort from heaven. They could not forget any thing, for the Spirit was to strengthen their memory. What Jesus lacked of perfecting their instructions the Spirit supplied by guiding them in all truth. Were there many nations and divers languages? The baptism of the Holy Spirit enabled them to speak to every man in his own tongue wherein he was born; and thus they were enabled to preach to every creature among all nations; and the Comforter through them reproved the world of sin, of righteousness, and of judgment. Only one thing more and the scheme is complete. "Other sheep have I which are not of this fold: them also I must bring, and they shall hear my voice; and there shall be one fold, and one shepherd." John x:16. But how shall this be done? The Jews then, like the Calvinists now regarded themselves as the favored few for whom Jesus died, and thought it not meet to take the children's bread and give it to dogs. Hence, it took a miracle to convince Peter that it was his duty to preach the gospel to the Gentiles. Six of his Jewish brethren accompanied him to the house of Cornelius, where God poured out the Holy Ghost on the Gentiles as on the disciples at Jerusalem on Pentecost. "And they of the circumcision which believed were astonished, as many as came with Peter, because that on the Gentiles also was poured out the gift of the Holy Ghost. For they heard them speak with tongues and magnify God." Acts x:45, 46. This satisfied those of the Jews who were with Peter and witnessed it; and when he rehearsed the whole matter from the beginning to the apostles and brethren who were at Jerusalem, "they held their peace and glorified God, saying, Then hath God also to the Gentiles granted repentance unto life." Acts xi:18. Thus we see a necessity for God to baptize the Gentiles at the house of Cornelius with the Holy Spirit—*not to convert those who received it,* or in any way benefit them—but that the Jews might "perceive that God is no respecter of persons: but in every nation he that feareth him, and worketh righteousness, is accepted with him." Acts x:34, 35.

We wish, in conclusion, to call attention to the striking difference in the forms of speech used with reference to water baptism and Holy Spirit baptism. "Go teach *all nations,* baptizing them." "Preach the gospel to *every creature;* he that believeth and is baptized shall be saved." *Every creature, among all nations,* who is capable of hearing and believing the gospel, may be baptized with the baptism connected with faith as a condition of salvation.

How very different the style when speaking of Holy Spirit baptism! "He shall baptize *you* with the Holy Ghost and with fire." "*Ye* shall be baptized with the Holy Ghost not many days hence." When speaking of that coming down to us and designed to be perpetual, the style is *all nations, every creature;* but when speaking of Holy Spirit baptism it is *you, ye,* and this is the extent of it. Kind reader, is not this significant?

The Gifts of the Holy Spirit.

Speaking of the Son of God, John the Baptist said: "God giveth not the Spirit by measure unto him." John iii:34. This language clearly implies, as stated elsewhere, that God gave the Spirit by measure to others. Indeed, it may be safely said that Jesus was the only person who ever possessed the Spirit without measure—who was always speaking and doing the things suggested by it. The prophets and apostles spake and acted under it occasionally, He always. But we have seen that there was a baptism with the Spirit which was a measure of it sufficient to temporarily possess and inspire those who received it. This measure of the Spirit was the promise of the Father, and was given by Him through His Son to the disciples on the day of Pentecost, and to the Gentiles at the house of Cornelius. See Acts xi:17. But we must be careful that we do not confound the

Spirit with the gifts of the Spirit. The inspiration and energizing influences of the Spirit are not the Spirit. But there was another measure of the Spirit which was capable of imparting extraordinary gifts to the disciples, which we propose to examine for a time. That this measure of the Spirit was different from the baptism of the Holy Spirit, is evident from the fact that *the latter always required a divine administrator,* while the measure under consideration was imparted by *the laying on of apostolic hands.* That this measure of the Spirit was different from the ordinary measure received by all Christians is clear from several considerations. First: "It was imparted by the apostles through the imposition of their hands, as before stated, while the ordinary measure was received by the hearing of faith. See Gal. iii:2. Second: Miraculous power was always imparted by it, and *manifested* by those who received it, while no such manifestations attend the ordinary measure. Third: At Samaria and other places, persons believed the gospel and were baptized, and, therefore, enjoyed the ordinary measure of the Spirit for some time *before this measure* was imparted to them by the apostles. The power to impart this measure of the Spirit was what Simon sought to purchase with money, and was called by Peter "the gift of God" (Acts viii:20), because God gave it to the apostles, who alone possessed it. Though this power of imparting the Spirit by the imposition of apostolic hands was *the gift of God,* it was neither the Spirit nor the gift of the Spirit. And the Spirit itself, though given in different measures, at different times, to different persons, in different ways, for different purposes, was always *the gift of God* and the *same Spirit.* There is one Spirit, and only one; hence, Paul says: "There are diversities of gifts, but the same Spirit." 1 Cor. xii:4. We have seen that baptism with the Holy Spirit required a divine administrator, hence on the day of Pentecost and at the house of Cornelius it came from heaven in its amplitude—"the self-same Spirit dividing to every man severally as he would" the measures and manifestations appropriate to each.

The phrase "the gift of the Holy Ghost" occurs Acts ii:38, and x:45, and in both places must be understood as equivalent to "the Holy Spirit as a gift," yet we are persuaded that the same measure of the Spirit is not alluded to in both places. "While

Peter yet spake these words, the Holy Ghost fell on all them which heard the word. And they of the circumcision which believed were astonished, as many as came with Peter, because that on the Gentiles also was poured out the gift of the Holy Ghost; for they heard them speak with tongues and magnify God." Acts x:44-46. That this was that measure called the baptism of the Holy Spirit is plain from the fact that when Peter rehearsed the matter before his brethren, he said: "As I began to speak the Holy Ghost fell on them as on us at the beginning. Then remembered I the word of the Lord, how that he said, John indeed baptized with water, but ye shall be baptized with the Holy Ghost" (Acts xi:15, 16); thus quoting the language of the Lord concerning baptism with the Holy Ghost as applicable to this event. But it was not until after the Holy Spirit had been poured out on the disciples "at the beginning," on the day of Pentecost, that the multitude came together, to whom Peter promised the Holy Ghost as a gift; hence, it could not have been the baptism of it to which he referred when he said: "Ye shall receive the gift of the Holy Ghost." Acts ii:38. But did Peter here mean the Holy Spirit itself, in some measure of it; or did he mean that they should receive something imparted to them by the Spirit? Paul says: "There are *diversities of gifts,* but the same Spirit." Peter did not say: "Ye shall receive a gift, some gift, or any gift of the Spirit, but *the gift* of the Holy Spirit." He uses the singular number and definite article; hence we conclude he must be understood to mean some measure of the Holy Spirit itself.

But to what measure of the Spirit did the apostle allude? We have seen that he did not allude to the baptism of it; then it only remains for us to inquire whether he alluded to the ordinary measure which always follows as a necessary result of adoption into God's family; or did he mean to promise them an extraordinary endowment of it peculiar to the apostolic times? We can not regard it very important to settle this matter in favor of one question or the other. All agree that there were extraordinary endowments of the Spirit conferred upon those, or at least many of them, who believed and obeyed the gospel in the apostolic times; and all agree that all Christians, from then until now, receive the Spirit of adoption—that all Christians may unite in saying: "The love of God is shed abroad in our hearts by the Holy Ghost which is given unto us." Rom. v:5. While good and true men differ as to *how* the Spirit is received, all agree that it is received and in some sense dwells in every Christian. It is not important, therefore, whether Peter referred to this or that measure of the Spirit; yet it may not be amiss to state that, as the apostles had power to communicate the Spirit in an extraordinary measure to such as believed and obeyed the gospel under their ministry, and as they deemed it so important that the primitive Christians should thus extraordinarily receive it, as to send Peter and John from Jerusalem to Samaria to confer it upon the disciples first made there, we are inclined to think that Peter intended to promise something more than the ordinary measure of the Spirit to those he addressed at the beginning. Surely, it was as important that the first disciples made at Jerusalem should receive the extraordinary endowment as it was that those of Samaria, Ephesus, and other places should receive it. Nay, more; there were dwelling at Jerusalem Jews, devout men, from every nation under heaven, and it is fair to suppose that some of every nation were converted on that occasion; and it is more than probable that it was through these men that the commission was carried out. The apostles preached to all nations on that day; and when the persons there converted returned to their homes, bearing the gospel to every creature, the commission was carried out—"their sound went into all the earth and their words unto the ends of the world." Rom. x:18. Surely, if these gifts of the Spirit were for the confirmation of the Word in Jerusalem, Samaria, and Ephesus at its first proclamation, it was not less important that these converts, who were to go into all the world with the gospel, should be able to confirm its truth when they first preached it in their respective countries. Hence, we conclude that Peter promised the *Spirit to such as would believe and obey the gospel there in as ample measure as he had power to impart it to them.* Why should he not thus amply bestow it upon them, having the power to do so? and why should he not thus amply *promise* it to them? Did he wish to bestow it upon them without apprising them of it, that he might afford them an agreeable surprise? But as a settlement of this matter could have no practical bearing upon our investigation, the subject is not worth debating, and we will not consume further space with it. Our purpose is, more particularly, to show that there were extraordinary manifestations of the Spirit in the apostolic times, what they were, and how they were conferred, that they were to cease, have ceased, how and when they ceased, and consequently need not be expected now.

Jesus said, in the final commission: "Go ye into all the world, and preach the gospel to every creature. He that believeth and is baptized shall be saved; but he that believeth not shall be damned. And these signs shall follow them that believe; In my name shall they cast out devils; they shall speak with new tongues; they shall take up serpents; and if they drink any deadly thing, it shall not hurt them; they shall lay hands on the sick and they shall recover." Mark xvi:15-18. By this we see that signs were not confined to the apostles alone, but were to follow them that believe. This has been a sweet morsel to infidels from the time miracles ceased until now. The Mormon claims to exhibit these signs now; and he sneeringly tells you that you do not believe your own book. It says: "He that believeth and is baptized shall be saved; but he that believeth not shall be damned." You believe that; oh yes! but when it says "these signs shall follow them that believe," you do not believe that. Yes, we believe it all; but we will not allow an infidel to divide and interpret it for us.

We were once asked by an infidel why these signs do not follow them that believe. Jesus said they should follow them that believe. Persons profess to believe, and still we do not see the signs following. What is the reason? Until such persons learn to discriminate between things *ordinary* and *extraordinary*—until they can "rightly divide the word of truth"—it will ever be unintelligible to them. They never will understand it, and therefore never will have any well-grounded faith in it. Nor do we think it at all strange that persons should fail to understand the subject of the Spirit's influence, and therefore teach that it is enveloped in mystery—entirely incomprehensible to finite minds, who mix up the baptism, gifts, reception, and operation of the Holy Spirit. Nor is it strange that they fail to understand us and continue to misrepresent our teaching; for when we deny them the baptism of the Holy Spirit, which they have failed to distinguish from the operaton of the Spirit, and therefore regard them as one and the same thing, it is natural that they should understand us to deny the operation of the Spirit in denying the baptism of it. But Jesus said these signs should follow them that believe. Did they follow? At Samaria "the people with one accord gave heed unto those things which Philip spake, hearing and seeing the miracles which he did. For unclean spirits, crying with loud voice, came out of many that were possessed with them: and many taken with palsies, and that were lame, were healed. And there was great joy in that city." Acts viii:6-8. Here we find that the very things which Jesus said should follow, really did follow.

We next propose to show that these signs which Jesus said should follow them that believe, and which we have seen did follow, were among the gifts of the Spirit. What were the gifts? "To one is given by the Spirit the word of wisdom; to another the word of knowledge by the same Spirit; to another faith by the same Spirit; to another the gifts of healing by the same Spirit; to another the working of miracles; to another prophecy; to another discerning of spirits; to another divers kinds of tongues; to another the interpretation of tongues: but all these worketh that one and the self-same Spirit, dividing to every man severally as he will." 1 Cor. xii:8-11. Thus we see that these gifts of the Spirit were the same things which Jesus said should follow them that believe, and which we have found, at Samaria and other places, did follow. Before leaving this quotation it may be well to remark that no one man possessed all the gifts, but they were given, one to this, and another to that man—"the self-same Spirit dividing to every man severally" the gifts appropriate to each.

How, then, was the Spirit imparted by which these gifts were conferred? As the baptism of the Holy Spirit enabled those who received it to speak with tongues—and speaking with tongues is here said to be one of the gifts of the Spirit—is it true that all these miraculously-endowed persons were baptized with the Spirit? We think not. The baptism of the Spirit was the gift of the Father (Acts ii:4), sent from heaven by the Son. No human being was ever entrusted with the administration of it; but when these spiritual gifts were to be manifested, "then laid they *their hands on them, and they received the Holy Ghost.* And when Simon saw that through laying on of *the apostles' hands* the Holy Ghost was given, he offered them money, saying, Give me also this power, that on whomsoever I lay hands, he may receive the Holy Ghost." Acts viii:17-19. Then it was through the laying on of the apostles' hands that God gave the Holy Ghost to believers, by which these extraordinary gifts of the Spirit were conferred. And it is expressly said that Simon "had neither part nor lot in this matter" (Acts viii:21); and we suppose he had as much part and lot in it as had any one else save the apostles.

That these spiritual gifts were uniformly imparted by the laying on of apostolic hands, is made probable by the fact that the *presence of an apostle* was indispensable to the reception of them. Had it been possible for the apostles to have imparted these gifts by *prayer,* it occurs to us that a useless trip from Jerusalem to Samaria was imposed upon Peter and John. Certainly, their prayers would have been as efficacious in that city as in this: they would have been addressed to God, who could hear in one place and answer in another—and did so in numerous instances (see Matt. viii:5-13). He was God afar off as well as near by. Paul said to his brethren at Rome: "I long to see you, that I may impart unto you some spiritual gift." Rom. i:11. This shows, most clearly, that, however much Paul desired to impart spiritual gifts, he had not the power until he could visit those to whom he would impart them. When he passed through the upper coasts of Asia and came to Ephesus, he found certain disciples, of whom he inquired: "Have ye received the Holy Ghost since ye believed?" By this it seems to have been customary for the apostles to impart this endowment of the Spirit to the disciples wherever they met them, unless they had previously received it. Hence, finding that these disciples were entirely ignorant of it, and that they had been baptized with John's baptism after its validity had ceased, he instructed them in the way of the Lord more perfectly, after which "they were baptized in the name of the Lord Jesus. And when *Paul had laid his hands upon them,* the Holy Ghost came on them; and they spake with tongues, and prophesied." Acts xix:5, 6. Then, whether this endowment was ever imparted otherwise than by the laying on of apostolic hands or not, it is certain that they did impart it in this way; and we have no account of its ever being imparted in any other way—and they could not impart it without being present, where their hands, at least, *could* have been laid on.

From this stand-point it is easy to see when and how these signs, or spiritual gifts, ceased. As none but the apostles, as instruments in the hands of God, had power to impart this endowment of the Spirit to those who believed and obeyed the gospel, it is obvious that when they died, the power to work miracles necessarily ceased to be conferred upon any person; and when all died who had received the power at the hands of the apostles, they, of course, ceased to be performed. That none but the apostles had power to impart that measure of the Holy Ghost by which these gifts were conferred, is plain from the fact that "when the apostles which were at Jerusalem heard that Samaria had received the word of God, they sent unto them Peter and John: who, when they were come down, prayed for them, that they might receive the Holy Ghost." Acts viii:14, 15. Philip, it seems had the power to exercise the gifts of the Spirit, but, not being an apostle, he could not transfer this power to any one else; hence the necessity of sending Peter and John to them for that purpose—the apostles alone possessing such power.

As we have said that this Philip, who preached the gospel to the Samaritans, was not an apostle, and as one of the apostles was named Philip, it may be well for us to turn aside long enough to examine this matter a little.

The New Testament clearly speaks of three persons named Philip:

First, Philip, the brother of Herod, whose wife was Herodias, at the request of whom Herod had John the Baptist's head taken off. This Philip was "tetrarch of Iturea and of the region of Trachonitis." Luke iii:1.

Second. The apostle Philip, of whom we have an account as one of the twelve—Matt. x:3; Mark iii:18; Luke vi:14; and as one of the eleven, after the fall of Judas, and before the election of Matthias—Acts i:13. This Philip "was of Bethsaida of Galilee." John xii:21.

Third. Philip the evangelist, who lived in Cesarea, into whose house Paul and company entered; and who "had four daughters, virgins, which did prophesy." Acts xxi:8, 9. He "was one of the seven." Acts xxi:8. What seven? "Then the *twelve* called the multitude of the disciples unto them, and said, It is not reason that we should leave the word of God, and serve tables. Wherefore, brethren, look ye out among you seven men of honest report, full of the Holy Ghost and wisdom, and whom we may appoint over this business. But we will give ourselves continually to prayer, and to the ministry of the word. And the saying pleased the whole multitude: and they chose Stephen, a man full of faith and of the Holy Ghost, and *Philip*, and Prochorus, and Nicanor, and Timon, and Parmenas, and Nicolas a proselyte of Antioch; whom they set before the apostles." Acts vi:2-6.

Could any thing be more plain? The apostle Philip was one of the *twelve* who declined to leave the ministry of the Word, and commanded the selection of *seven* others from among the disciples, one of whom was Philip; hence the language: "We entered into the house of *Philip the evangelist, which was one of the seven;* and abode with him." Acts xxi:8. Following up the history of these seven from their appointment in the sixth chapter of Acts, we find in the seventh chapter an account of the death of Stephen. The second verse of the eighth chapter speaks of his burial; then, in close connection, the fifth verse declares that "Philip went down to the city of Samaria, and preached Christ unto them." Then can we be mistaken in saying that this was Philip the evangelist, but not the apostle Philip? "Now when the apostles which were at Jerusalem heard that Samaria had received the word of God, they sent unto them Peter and John: who, when they were come down, prayed for them, that they might receive the Holy Ghost (for as yet he was fallen upon none of them; only they were baptized in the name of the Lord Jesus). Then laid they their hands on them, and they received the Holy Ghost." Acts viii:14-17. Had this Philip, who was already at Samaria, been an apostle, why the necessity of sending Peter and John from Jerusalem to Samaria that they might impart the Holy Spirit to the Samaritan disciples? Surely, one apostle could have done this as well as others. Are our readers sufficiently acquainted with the Samaritan preacher? then we will return to the examination of spiritual gifts.

These gifts were not given as toys, to be sported with by those to whom they were given as they might think proper.

Even the apostles themselves possessed them only to a limited extent. When Paul was shipwrecked on the island called Melita, he gathered a bundle of sticks and laid them on the fire, and there came a viper out of the heat and fastened on his hand; yet he shook off the beast into the fire, and felt no harm. Acts xxviii:3, 5. Did Jesus say "they shall take up serpents; and if they drink any deadly thing, it shall not hurt them?" Surely, the ever-faithful Son of God remembered this promise to His humble, persecuted disciple just then. But this was not all—Jesus further said: "They shall lay hands on the sick, and they shall recover." Hence he not only protected Paul's person from harm, but "it came to pass that the father of Publius lay sick of a fever and of a bloody flux: to whom Paul entered in, and prayed, and laid his hands on him, and healed him. So when this was done, others also, which had diseases in the island, came, and were healed." Acts xxviii:8, 9. By this we learn that Paul possessed in an eminent degree the power to heal the sick, which is enumerated among the spiritual gifts; nevertheless he informs us that *he left Trophimus at Miletum sick.* 2 Tim. iv:20. Why would Paul leave his friend and traveling companion sick, having the power to heal him? Surely, if he could have done so, he would have cured him. The reason why he did not, can only be found in the fact that he only possessed such power when the glory of God would be exhibited by its exercise.

But for what were these spiritual gifts bestowed upon the primitive disciples? After Jesus had given to the apostles their commission to preach the gospel to every creature, promising salvation to those who would believe and obey it, and assuring them that these signs (gifts of the Spirit) should follow them that believe, we learn that "they went forth and preached everywhere, the Lord working with them, and *confirming the word* with signs following." Mark xvi:20. Then these signs were for the confirmation of the Word at its first proclamation. Hence Paul said to the Romans: "I long to see you, that I may impart unto you some spiritual gift, *to the end ye may be established,* that is, that I may be comforted together with you by the mutual faith both of you and me." Rom. i:11, 12.

In the infantile state of the church, when it was dependent upon oral instructions for all things pertaining to life and godliness, the Lord graciously attended, and confirmed the Word preached by these extraordinary demonstrations of the Spirit. Hence, says Paul to the Corinthians: "And I, brethren, when I came to you, came not with excellency of speech or of wisdom, declaring unto you the testimony of God; for I determined not to know any thing among you, save Jesus Christ, and Him crucified. And I was with you in weakness, and in fear, and in much trembling. And my speech and my preaching was not with enticing words of man's wisdom, but in demonstration of the Spirit and of power; that your faith should not stand in the wisdom of men, but in the power of God." 1 Cor. ii:1-5. Persons sometimes say of a preacher, "He is so smart that he can make error appear as truth—he would make you believe a crow is white as a swan were he to make the effort." Though this is not very complimentary to the intelligence of the people, the devil sometimes seeks thus to catch away the seed sown, by making the people believe that it is the shrewdness of the preacher, and not the truth, which makes his positions look plausible. The apostle made no effort to fascinate and charm the Corinthians by his eloquence, excellency of speech; nor by his learning, enticing words of man's wisdom. As to these, he was with them in weakness. But that they might be established and their faith unshaken, his preaching was confirmed by signs following, here called demonstration of the Spirit, and of power that their faith should not stand in the wisdom of men, but in the power of God. When Jesus ascended up on high, he led captivity captive and gave gifts unto men. How did he give these gifts, and what were they? By the Spirit he prepared some men to be "apostles; and some, prophets; and some, evangelists; and some, pastors and teachers." And what were these for? "For the perfecting of the saints for the work of the ministry, for the edifying of the body of Christ." And how long were these gifts to remain? "Till we all come in the unity of the faith and of the knowledge of the Son of God, unto a perfect man [perfect Church], unto the measure of the stature of the fullness of Christ; that we henceforth be no more children, tossed to and fro, and carried about with every wind of doctrine." Eph. iv:11-14. Paul tells us "Whether there be prophecies, they shall fail; whether there be tongues, they shall cease; whether there be knowledge, it shall vanish away." 1 Cor. xiii:8. These were among the spiritual gifts, and it is here expressly stated that they should have an end; and we have clearly seen just how and when they did end. Having a perfect record of these signs given by inspiration of the Holy Spirit, there is no necessity for them to be repeated now; and to wish to see them, is but to confess our want of confidence in the Bible—virtually saying, "I know, God therein says they occurred, but I am not sure the record is true: I would prefer to see them myself." "If the word spoken by angels was steadfast, and every transgression and disobedience received a just recompense of reward, how shall we escape, if we neglect so great salvation, which at the first began to be spoken by the Lord, and was confirmed unto us by them that heard Him; God, also, bearing them witness, both with signs and wonders, and divers miracles and gifts of the Holy Ghost, according to his own will?" Heb. ii:2-4. Kind reader, let us ponder well this soul-stirring question. This great salvation first spoken by the Lord, was confirmed by them that heard him; God, also, bearing them witness with signs, and wonders, and divers miracles and gifts of the Holy Spirit according to His will; and they are written, as were the signs of Jesus, that ye might believe that Jesus is the Christ the Son of God, and that believing ye might have life through His name. Oh! then, how shall we escape if we neglect it? As surely as every transgression and disobedience, under the law, received a just recompense of reward, so surely will we be rewarded according to our works.

The Operation of the Holy Spirit.

That it is necessary that man be *converted* in order to the enjoyment of the favor of God is not a matter of controversy with any save Universalists; and we are not quite sure we could do any good by stopping to debate the question with them just now. They say, they believe the Bible to be a revelation from God, and therefore true. It says "These shall go away into everlasting punishment; but the righteous into life eternal." Matt. xxv:46. "The hour is coming, in the which all that are in the graves shall hear His voice, and shall come forth; they that have done good, unto the resurrection of life, and they that have done evil, unto the resurrection of damnation." John v:28, 29. "The rich man also died, and was buried; and in hell he lifted up his eyes, being in torments." Luke xvi:22, 23. And what more? "The fearful, and unbelieving, and the abominable, and murderers, and whoremongers, and sorcerers, and idolaters, and all liars, shall have their part in the lake which burneth with fire and brimstone." Rev. xxi:8. These are enough for us; and if they will not suffice for those *who profess to believe the Bible*, then they would not be persuaded, though one should arise from the dead. That all intelligent men and women, in a land of Bibles, must be converted or lost, we will assume as a settled fact.

That the Spirit does operate in conversion, is admitted by all who are expected to be benefited by our labors; hence, we offer no argument to prove that which no one denies. Though we have sometimes, nay, often, *heard of a people* who deny the operation of the Holy Spirit in conversion, we have never met a single man who so taught; nor have we ever read any thing from the pen of any man who had so written. Lest, therefore, we waste our ammunition in "shelling the woods" we will wait for the appearance of the enemy, before we make war upon him. Nor do we propose any examination of what the Spirit *can or can not do*. The questions which concern us are, *What does it do, and how does it do it?*

We have seen, in another department of our work, that on the day of Pentecost God established upon the earth a system of government, variously styled, the kingdom of God, the kingdom of heaven, the kingdom of God's dear Son, the Church of God, the temple of God, the house of God, the household of faith, the body of Christ, etc. Concerning this organization, we are now prepared to see:

First, That those who established it were directly instructed by the Holy Spirit.

Second, That, from the time of its organization, it became the dwelling-place of the Holy Spirit through all succeeding time; and,

Third, That it is the medium through which the Holy Spirit puts forth its power for the conversion and salvation of man.

To an examination of these propositions, in their order, we solicit the attention of the reader for a time.

First, then, that those who established it were directly instructed by the Holy Spirit. This has been so thoroughly examined already that it need not detain us long. Still it is important to remember that "they were all filled with the Holy Ghost, and began to speak with other tongues, as the Spirit gave them utterance." Acts ii:4. Then their teaching was but the teaching of the Holy Spirit through them. Every announcement made, every condition imposed, every blessing promised, and every punishment threatened, was spoken by the Holy Spirit through men selected for the work, and was made binding on men here and ratified in heaven.

Second, that it became the dwelling-place of the Holy Spirit through all succeeding time is apparent from several considerations:

1. "The body without the Spirit is dead." Jas. ii:26. "The body is the Church." Col. i:18 and 24. Then if there was ever a time when the Spirit was not in the body of Christ or Church it was surely a dead body.

2. When Paul said, "There is one body and one Spirit," it is next to certain that he meant to teach that there is one body, and one Spirit in this body.

3. In speaking of it as a temple or building, and the disciples as living stones in it, the apostle says: "Know ye not that ye are the temple of God, and that the Spirit of God dwelleth in you." 1 Cor. iii:16.

4. Jesus said to the disciples before His death, "I will pray the Father, and He shall give you another Comforter, that He may abide with you forever." John xiv:16. "The Comforter is the Holy Ghost." Ver. 26. From these Scriptures it is apparent that when the Holy Spirit came, and the Church or body was organized by its directions, it took up its abode in it; not for a season only, but as an abiding guest and Comforter forever; and thus it is that the disciples are "Builded together, for an habitation of God through the Spirit." Eph. ii:22.

Third: We come now to an examination of our third proposition, namely, that the Church, thus organized by the Spirit, is not only its dwelling-place, but is the medium through which it puts forth its power for the conversion and salvation of man.

The kingdom or church of God, and the kingdom of Satan,

are the great antagonistic governments or powers of earth. They are engaged in a perpetual war against each other; and each is seeking to capture the subjects of the other. They do not discharge their prisoners on parole; but each one taken is forthwith made a recruit in the ranks of the captors. Paul minutely describes the armor furnished the soldiers of the cross in this great struggle. After describing the character of the enemy, he says: "Wherefore take unto you the whole armor of God, that ye may be able to withstand in the evil day, and having done all, to stand. Stand therefore, having your loins girt about with truth, and having on the breast-plate of righteousness; and your feet shod with the preparation of the gospel of peace; above all, taking the shield of faith wherewith ye shall be able to quench all the fiery darts of the wicked. And take the helmet of salvation, and the sword of the Spirit, which is the word of God." Eph. vi:13-17. There are many valuable thoughts suggested by the different parts of this armor, which we have not time to notice. We wish to call attention to the fact, that the disciples are to don this armor and use it; not lay it on the centre-table as a keepsake, but *use it*. That this spiritual war is both *offensive* and *defensive* is suggested by the fact that there is both a *sword* and a *shield* belonging to the armor. This is for protection against the darts of the enemy, that is for making wounds upon him. He that enters the army taking only the shield, that he may protect himself, while others fight the enemy, makes rather a worthless soldier. Soldiers of the cross are required to take the *whole armor* of God, that they may "fight a good fight," for their own salvation, and the salvation of others. The Word of God is the sword of the Spirit, and the disciples are to use it in order to rescue their fellow-man from the enemy, and enlist him as a soldier against him—that he may be delivered from the power of darkness and translated into the kingdom of God's dear Son. Are we letting the sword of the Spirit rust in its scabbard? "Ye are the salt of the earth; if the salt have lost his savor, wherewith shall it be salted? It is thenceforth good for nothing, but to be cast out, and to be trodden under foot of men." Matt. v:13.

The Holy Spirit, dwelling in the body, operates through its members with its teaching upon such material as comes within the range of its influence. The teaching of the Spirit, put forth through the members of the body, is both *theoretic* and *practical.* The gospel is the power of God unto salvation to every one that believeth; and he has ordained that it shall be preached to all nations—every creature, that he may learn the theory by which God proposes to save him. But this is not all of it. There must be a practical exhibition of the Christian religion in the life of the disciples; hence Jesus said to them: "Let your light so shine before men, that they may see your good works, and glorify your Father which is in heaven." Matt: v:16. That this be spiritual light, the good works must be those "which God hath before ordained that we should walk in them." Eph. ii:10. Every thing necessary to a thorough exhibition of the Christian religion, both theoretically and practically, is comprehended in the Scriptures, "Given by inspiration of God," for they are "profitable for doctrine, for reproof, for instruction in righteousness; that the man of God may be perfect, thoroughly furnished unto all good works." 2 Tim. iii:16, 17. The man of God is designed to be perfect, and the Scriptures given by inspiration were designed to make him so. They not only *furnish him,* but *thoroughly* furnish him, not only to *some good works* but to *all good works.* Does it not follow, then, that there is nothing left discretionary with man? Nay, if there be any work to which the man of God is not thoroughly furnished by the Scriptures, does it not follow that it is not a good work? "As His divine power hath given unto us all things that pertain unto life and godliness, through the knowledge of him that hath called us to glory and virtue." 2 Peter i:3.

But we have seen that the promised Comforter was to reprove the world of sin, righteousness, and judgment. That this Comforter was the Holy Spirit, and that it did come to the disciples, and was received by them, we have already seen. That it did reprove, and is reproving, the world of sin, righteousness, and judgment is a fact so generally admitted that we need not stop to offer proof of it. The controverted question is, *How did it do it?* To this question we will give our attention for a time. Did the Spirit come from heaven to the *world?* What do we understand the Saviour to mean by the term *world* in the passage under consideration? Certainly, it will be conceded that He did not mean the material universe, but that He meant the wicked people who committed sin of which to be reproved, in contrast with the disciples. Then was the Holy Spirit given directly to the wicked, that it might enter their hearts and reprove them? No; it was promised to the disciples. Jesus said to them: "I will pray the Father, and he shall give *you* another Comforter, that he may abide with you forever; even the Spirit of truth, whom *the world can not receive,* because it seeth him not, neither knoweth him; but ye know him, for he dwelleth with you and shall be in you." John xiv:16, 17. Then, the Spirit was not only promised to the disciples to dwell with and be in them, but it is said, in great plainness, that the world, which was to be reproved by it, *could not receive* it. On the day of Pentecost the promised Spirit came, and through Peter used words calculated to convey to those who heard just such ideas as were necessary to be communicated to them to make them sensible of the sin of which they were to be reproved. Believing Jesus to be an impostor, they had crucified and slain Him; but Peter used such arguments as convinced them that in this they were mistaken. At the close of his speech he said: "Therefore, let all the house of Israel know assuredly, that God hath made that same Jesus, whom ye have crucified, both Lord and Christ. Now, when they heard this, they were pricked in their heart." Acts ii:36, 37. This is all plain. The Spirit reproved them through Peter's words, which they understood and believed, and thus operated sensibly upon them—cut them to the heart. When God created man, He gave him an organization capable of receiving just such impressions as He designed should be made upon him. He placed within him a mind capable of appreciating communications from his Creator and his fellowman; and He gave him certain senses through which to receive such impressions as are necessary to the accomplishment of his mission on the earth. Hence, we conclude that, in order for man to receive instructions from any source, they must be embodied in words adapted to his comprehension and directed to the mind through the avenues which God has opened to it. In keeping with this arrangement, we find that in every period of man's existence, when God wished to communicate an idea to him, He embodied it in words adapted to his capacity, and gave it to him either in person or through some agent selected for that purpose. Even so, when the Spirit reproved man of sin, it is said: "Ye men of Israel, *hear these words:* Jesus, of Nazareth, a man approved of God among you, by miracles, and wonders, and signs, which God did by him in the midst of you, as ye yourselves also know: him, being delivered by the determinate counsel and foreknowledge of God, ye have taken, and by wicked hands have crucified and slain." Acts ii:22, 23.

When the angel of the Lord told John, in the Isle of Patmos, what to write to each of the seven Asiatic churches, each message closed by saying: "He that hath an ear, let him hear what the Spirit saith unto the churches." Hence, the words which John wrote by inspiration of the Spirit were the words of the Spirit, and by hearing them we hear what the Spirit said to the churches. Then, it follows that when we hear the words of an inspired man we hear the words of the Spirit, and when we have the thoughts legitimately belonging to such words, we have the thoughts communicated by the Spirit. In this way even "now the Spirit speaketh expressly, that in the latter times some shall depart from the faith, giving heed to seducing spirits and doctrines of devils." 1 Tim. iv:1. The Spirit, then, does not speak in mysterious and incomprehensible ways, but it speaks expressly—in words easy to be understood. "Holy men of God spake as they were moved by the Holy Ghost." 2 Peter i:21. We have a faithful record of what they said; hence, "they being dead, yet speaketh." Heb. xi:4. Paul said: "Eye hath not seen, nor ear heard, neither have entered into the heart of man, the things which God hath prepared for them that love him. But God hath revealed them unto us by his Spirit; for the Spirit searcheth all things, yea, the deep things of God. * * * Which things also we speak, not in the words which man's wisdom teacheth, but which the Holy Ghost teacheth; comparing spiritual things with spiritual." 1 Cor. ii:9-13.

And again: "For this cause I, Paul, the prisoner of Jesus Christ for you Gentiles, if ye have heard of the dispensation of the grace of God which is given me to you-ward: how that by revelation he made known unto me the mystery (as I wrote afore in few words; whereby, when ye read, ye may understand my knowledge in the mystery of Christ), which in other ages was not made known unto the sons of men, as it is now *revealed unto his holy apostles and prophets by the Spirit.*" Eph. iii:1-5. Here we learn that things which in other ages had been a mystery to other people were by the Spirit revealed and made known to Paul and other apostles and prophets, and that Paul had written them to his brethren, so that when they read they could understand his knowledge of what had previously been a profound mystery. "And what shall I say more? for the time would fail me" to quote all the Scriptures which prove that the lessons taught by the prophets and apostles were nothing less than the teaching of the Holy Spirit. David said: "To-day, if ye will hear his voice, harden not your heart, as in the provocation, and as in the day of temptation in the wilderness, when your fathers tempted me, proved me, and saw my work. Forty years long was I grieved with this generation, and said, It is a people that do err in their heart, and they have not known my ways." Ps. xcv:7-10. Paul quotes this language, saying: "Wherefore, as the Holy Ghost saith, To-day if ye will hear his voice," etc. Heb. iii:7-10. Why did the apostle thus quote the language of David as the language of the Holy Ghost? Because "David, the son of Jesse, said, and the man who was raised up on high, the anointed of the God of Jacob, and the sweet psalmist of Israel, said, The Spirit of the Lord spake by me, and his word was in my tongue." 2 Sam. xxiii:1, 2. Hence it was, too, that Peter quotes David, saying: "The Holy Ghost by the mouth of David spake," etc. Acts i:16. Thus we see why Paul and Peter quote the words of David as the words of the Holy Spirit spoken by him; and, therefore, any effect produced upon the heart as properly growing out of such language can be nothing less than an effect produced by the Holy Spirit.

Having found that the Holy Spirit has clothed its ideas in words adapted to the comprehension of man, we can see a beauty and fitness in the parable of the sower and the explanation of it by the Saviour. He says: "The seed is the word of God. Those by the way-side are they that hear; then cometh the devil, and taketh away the word out of their hearts, lest they should believe and be saved." The devil knows well that if he can keep the people away from the Word of God, or get it away from them after they have heard it, all are his. Hence, he makes every effort he can to keep it from them. He will bolt church doors against it; call it all the ugly names he can think of to keep people from hearing it; if, in spite of him, they hear it, he offers every gratification that the flesh can desire to choke it out. "They on the rock are they, which, when they hear, receive the word with joy; and these have no root, which for awhile believe, and in time of temptation fall away. And that which fell among thorns, are they, which, when they have heard, go forth, and are choked with cares, and riches, and pleasures of this life, and bring no fruit to perfection. But that on the good ground are they, which in an honest and good heart, having heard the word, keep it and bring forth fruit with patience." Luke viii:11-15. As the farmer can not reap a crop without seed has been sown, neither can there be a spiritual crop without spiritual seed; and as *the Word of God is the spiritual seed*, it follows that where the Word of God is not preached, or the seed in some way sown, there can no be spiritual crop. This is so very evident that we need not offer arguments to support it. "Faith cometh by hearing, and hearing by the word of God." Rom. x:17. Where the Word of God is not, it can not be heard, and hence there can be no faith, and "he that believeth not shall be damned." Mark xvi:16. Hence, no word of God, no faith—and no faith, no salvation for intelligent men and women in a land of Bibles. Before there was a written Word, "it pleased God, by the foolishness of preaching, to save them that believe." 1 Cor. i:21. The press is *now* a very extensive sower of the Word of God; but *then* men went everywhere preaching the Word. Hence, Paul asks: "How shall they believe in him of whom they have not heard? and how shall they hear without a preacher? and how shall they preach except they be sent?" Rom. x:14, 15. Before the gospel was written so as to afford preachers an opportunity of learning it by study, God miraculously called, qualified, and sent men to preach; but now, if they would know any thing, they had better observe Paul's charge to Timothy: "Give attendance to reading."

That we may, if possible, more clearly see the medium through which the Spirit operates, we will notice another scripture or two. "The Lord said, My Spirit shall not always strive with man." Gen. vi:3. How did the Spirit of the Lord anciently strive with the people? "Yet many years didst thou forbear them, and testifiedst against them by thy Spirit in thy prophets:

yet would they not give ear." Neh. ix:30. Thus we see that the Spirit strove with, bore with, and testified against, the people, but was located in and did its work through the prophets, and by resisting their words the people resisted the teaching of the Holy Spirit. The devoted Stephen said to his persecutors: "Ye stiff-necked and uncircumcised in heart and ears, ye do always resist the Holy Ghost: as your fathers did, so do ye." How did their fathers resist the Holy Ghost? "Which of the prophets have not your fathers persecuted?" Then, by persecuting the prophets they resisted the Holy Ghost. "When they heard these things they were cut to the heart"—reproved of sin—operated on by the Holy Spirit; but did they receive the Spirit? Surely not. "They gnashed on him with their teeth; but he being full of the Holy Ghost looked up steadfastly into heaven and saw the glory of God, and Jesus standing on the right hand of God, and said, Behold I see the heavens opened, and the Son of man standing on the right hand of God. Then they cried out with a loud voice, and stopped their ears, and ran upon him with one accord and cast him out of the city, and stoned him." Acts vii:57, 58. By this narrative we see clearly that the Spirit was located in Stephen, and through his words operated on the people; yet they did not receive the Spirit, but resisted it. The Holy Spirit was in Stephen, but the spirit of the wicked one was in the people. It is one thing, therefore, to be operated on by the Spirit, and quite another thing to receive the Spirit. On the day of Pentecost the Spirit operated in the same way, but the result was very different. It was in Peter, and through his words cut the people to the heart. "Then they that gladly received his word were baptized: and the same day there were added unto them about three thousand souls." Acts ii:41. In place of gladly receiving Stephen's words, they resisted the Holy Spirit and put Stephen to death. Persons operated on by the Spirit may receive or reject its teaching as they may elect.

All bodies, or organizations, have spirits within them, and can not exist without them. Not only so, but every organization or body has its own peculiar spirit. The Free Mason, Odd Fellow, Sons of Temperance, and Good Templar organizations, each has its own peculiar spirit. And it is a working, operative spirit, too, operating through the members with its teaching on such material as comes within the range of its influence. And when it makes any thing it makes material for its own body and nothing else. That is, the spirit of Masonry, if it makes any thing, makes Masons, and never makes an Odd Fellow or Son of Temperance. The spirit of Odd Fellowship makes Odd Fellows, but never makes Masons, or any thing else. Mormons, Baptists, Presbyterians, Methodists, and Christians, all have spirits peculiar to their own respective organizations or bodies. These spirits, too, are working spirits, operating through their members with their teaching on the people. When the spirit of Catholicism operates it always makes a Catholic, and never makes a Mormon, Baptist, Presbyterian, Methodist, or a Christian. When the Mormon spirit operates, it always makes, if any thing at all, a Mormon, and never makes a Catholic, Baptist, Presbyterian, Methodist, or Christian. To this, all but Catholics and Mormons will agree. Shall we take another step? *When the Holy Spirit operates with its teaching, it always makes Christians, and never makes a Catholic, a Mormon, or any thing else.* Will all agree to this? "No," says an objector; "I see what you are at, and you are mistaken. I will give you an instance where the Spirit made Methodists, Baptists and Presbyterians. There was a protracted *union meeting* in our town (or neighborhood, as the case may be) in which these several denominations were engaged. The Spirit was profusely poured out, and the meeting was abundantly blessed to the conversion of scores of persons, some of whom joined each of the denominations mentioned." Very well. It yet remains to be shown that this was the work of the Holy Spirit. Let us see. Perhaps this meeting was gotten up by these parties, not to oppose the powers of darkness, or put to flight the armies of Satan; but to put down what the preachers were pleased to call Campbellism. They told the people not to hear such stuff. They had bolted their doors against all who dared to say as Jesus did, "He that believeth and is baptized shall be saved," or as did the Spirit, by Peter, "Repent, and be baptized, every one of you, in the name of Jesus Christ, for the remission of sins." But still the people would go to hear, and this *union meeting* was gotten up as an effort to create, if possible, a deeper prejudice in the minds of the people to keep them from hearing. "It is but the teaching of the Bible, and as sure as the people continue to hear it they will believe it. Our peculiarities are all in danger, and we must unite to put them out of the way. This done, we can then fight and devour each other, as we did thirty years ago." Now, as the spirit of this meeting was hatred and malice toward those who taught and acted according to the Spirit's directions, and as Paul tells us, "The fruit of the Spirit is love, joy, peace, long-suffering, gentleness, faith, meekness, temperance," etc. (Gal. v:22, 23), fruit so very unlike the fruit of this meeting, it is clear that the very main spring of the whole affair was not the Spirit of Christ, but the spirit of anti-Christ.

But let us examine the teaching at this meeting, and see whether or not it resembles the teaching of the Spirit. The preachers say to sinners, "Ye wicked and uncircumcised in heart, the Lord's arms of mercy are open wide to receive and bless you, but you will not come to Him that He may bless you." The horrors of hell and the joys of heaven are painted in glowing colors before the audience, until some conclude they will secure these, and avoid those; and they at once put themselves under the instructions of the preachers, with hearts subdued to the will of God, as far as they know it. And how do they direct them? Do they say to them, as the Spirit by Peter said to those wishing to know how to be saved on the day of Pentecost, "Repent, and be baptized, every one of you, in the name of Jesus Christ, for the remission of sins?" Nay, verily! Such a declaration would put out all the excitement as effectually as water puts out fire. What then? "Come into the altar or to the mourner's bench." Did the Spirit so teach the Pentecostian inquirers? Nay, did the Spirit ever teach a son of Adam thus, from the beginning of time until now? Not a word like it. But the sinners, willing to do any thing to obtain the blessing, come to the altar as directed by the preacher (not the Holy Spirit). Then what follows? The congregation must all engage in prayer to God for them; and among the first petitions made in their behalf is something like the following: "O God, come now, we beseech thee, and pardon and bless these mourners." First they told the people God was willing, but they were not willing; now they are willing, but God is not. Hence they pray, beg, and beseech God to do that which they had peviously declared Him always ready and willing to do. Is this the teaching of the Holy Spirit? It can not be.

Surely God trifles not with His creatures in this way. But the preacher prays very earnestly to God, to baptize them (us, says he) "with the Holy Ghost and with fire, right now." And perhaps he has prayed for the same thing at every meeting he has attended, perhaps a dozen times at some of them. Did God anciently baptize the same persons with the Holy Ghost and fire day after day repeatedly? When we hear such a petition, we involuntarily think, if we do not say, Lord, forbid! But the excitement in some is now sufficiently high, and they rise, shouting, jumping, falling over benches, or on the floor, until it has become necessary for the friends to interpose, and restrain them by force, to prevent them from being injured or killed. What is the matter now? Will the Holy Spirit kill the people in converting them? Not so. If we believed it, the operation of the Holy Spirit, we would say, hands off, gentlemen, it is God's work. Fear not, he will do right. If He kills them, they ought to die. Others, who are not blessed with a temperament so highly excitable, are not so easily moved by excitement (which by the way, is the very pabulum upon which the whole meeting subsists); hence the preacher says to them, "You have got it. Get up and shout, and tell the people what the Lord has done for you." And it takes all the assurance the preachers and Spirit can all give to get them through. Others, who have a little higher intellectual development, have to get up and go home without "getting through" at all. What is the reason? Did any of the Pentecostian applicants fail? The preachers told them God was willing, and would bless them if they would come. They have come; and they have honestly and faithfully done as they were directed, and yet they have been disappointed. What is the matter? Were they not as honest and as humble as they ever could be? Had they not full confidence in the efficacy of the blood of Jesus? If they had not, they would not have gone into the altar. Did they not, from the great deep of their hearts, desire pardon? Were they any worse than those who get through, that it should cost them a harder struggle? Then we again ask, why were they disappointed? Not to be tedious, we must leave these unfortunate subjects to brood over, and account for their disappointment upon the ground that they are not of the elect, or by supposing that there is no reality in religion, and thus merge into the stygian pool of infidelity, while we attend to those who were fortunate enough to "get through."

They must each tell an "experience of grace," for which there is not a word of authority in the Bible. Persons under the instruction of the Spirit anciently were required to confess their faith in the Son of God, but these tell the workings of their own imaginations; and, not to be tedious in our examination of the many absurdities detailed, they usually contained the following four main points:

1st. They felt like, and therefore believed themselves the worst sinners living.

2d. They felt like, and therefore believed that their day of grace had forever passed.

3d. They felt like, and therefore believed that God could not be just and pardon persons so wicked as themselves.

4th. They felt like, and therefore believed that God for Christ's sake had pardoned them.

As these four points enter into almost every experience we have listened to, we will examine them briefly.

1st. They never had killed any person or stolen any thing; others, having done both, were worse than they; therefore, when they believed themselves worse than all others, they believed a falsehood.

2d. They were then telling an "experience of grace," claiming to have found a day of grace; hence, when they believed their day of grace forever passed, they believed a falsehood.

3d. They all believed God to be infinitely just, and were then saying that they believed He had pardoned them; so, if in this they were not mistaken, when they believed God could not be just and pardon them, they believed a falsehood.

Now, as their feelings had led them to believe three admitted falsehoods out of but four propositions, may we not at least suspect the truth of the fourth? Paul told his brethren that they were chosen to salvation "through sanctification of the Spirit and belief of the truth." 2 Thess. ii:13. Then, if these persons were not mistaken in thinking themselves pardoned, Paul's rule was reversed as to them, for they were not chosen in the belief of the truth, but in the belief of three falsehoods, as they themselves admit; and as the fourth proposition consists in believing that

God had pardoned them without a compliance upon their part with the conditions upon which He had suspended their pardon, we must be permitted to think that there is as much probability in the truth of either of the other propositions as in this one. The vote is taken, however, and they are received.

But we are rather ahead of the proceedings—we must go back a little. Each one asks: "What church shall I join?" The preachers are all present. No one will say: "Join my church"—that would be too selfish; but they say: "Go to the grove, and secretly pray to God to direct you by the Spirit; then come back and join the church to which the Spirit, through your feelings, may incline you." Very well; all go and pray to the same God, and are guided by the same Spirit, yet when they return, one will join the Presbyterians, and he will have water sprinkled on him as baptism; another, guided by the same Spirit, will join the Methodists, and have water poured on him as baptism; another, under the guidance of the same Spirit, will join the Baptists, and nothing will do him for baptism but immersion; and though, when he "got religion" twelve months before, he may, under direction of the Spirit, have been immersed by one of the Methodist preachers in the present meeting, he must now have it administered by a Baptist minister. The Methodist preacher who immersed him a year before, though now fully competent to preach, pray, exhort, sing, and assist in his present conversion, is nevertheless incompetent to administer baptism, though it be "*a mere non-essential,*" and his former baptism is therefore invalid, though it may have been immersion. Paul says: "By one Spirit are we all baptized into one body." 1 Cor. xii:13. Now, as these were not all baptized into one body, but into several bodies, it is quite clear that they were not guided by the Spirit of which he spake.

Now, kind reader, is this picture over-drawn? Have you not seen all this and much more? We most solemnly aver that we have seen all this and many other things at such meetings too absurd to be spoken of in an essay like this without a compromise of our self-respect. Then, in the fear of God, allow me to ask, Did the Holy Spirit originate, preside over, or conduct the meeting?

There are a few thoughts connected with these revival meetings to which we respectfully invite the attention of those who believe that the Spirit operates directly, abstractly, or immediately on persons to effect their conversion. First: Why is it necessary that there be a meeting? Is it because the Spirit can not or will not operate on the people at their respective homes as well as when they are congregated? Or is it not true that they are called together that the *preacher* may have an opportunity of calling their attention to their spiritual interests. If so, it must follow that the Spirit is expected to operate through the preacher by such preaching, praying, singing, and exhortation as he may be able to bring to bear upon them.

Again: *Why is it important that the best revivalists be secured to conduct the more successful meetings?* If the Spirit operates immediately on the people, we can not see any use for a preacher at all; or, if one must be had, it would not matter whether he have ten talents or one. An *immediate* operation of the Spirit can not be a *mediate* operation, and hence the preacher could have nothing to do with it, and one preacher would do as well as another. From our stand-point, we can easily see why one preacher may be more successful in conducting a meeting than another, but we can not reconcile it with the doctrine of *immediate* spiritual influences. The Spirit is in the church and operates through its members with its teaching upon such material as comes within the range of its influence, and it is to bring the people where they may hear its teaching that the meeting is called in the first place. Then, as the Spirit operates not *immediately* but *mediately,* the stronger the medium the more potent the influence. The Word of God is the sword of the Spirit, and as earthly governments wield their swords through their soldiery, so God wields the sword of the Spirit through His solidery; and as an adroit fencer will use the instrument of death more successfully in carnal warfare, even so will skillful workmen more successfully wield the sword of the Spirit in fighting the battles of the Lord. God gives us bread by giving us soil, rain, and other means of producing grain of which to make it, but the richer the soil and better the season the more abundant will be the crop. So of every thing we enjoy through means—the more potent the means the richer the blessing.

But we are told that the devil operates on the people immediately. It is assumed that he has no written law or revealed will, nor does he make any verbal communications to man; hence he must either operate without words, arguments, or other visible means, or not operate at all. And if the Holy Spirit only operates on man *mediately,* and the devil *immediately,* then it follows, that the latter has more power than the former. We would respectfully suggest that the *modus operandi* of the Holy Spirit is not a question of power. We care not to examine whether the Spirit *can* or *can not* operate in this or that way. It is sufficient that we know how it *does operate.* Nor are we prepared to admit that the devil, even now, makes no verbal communications to men; on the contrary, he makes very many, both oral and written. It is true that there are no books bearing *his name* as author; nor did he write immediately any book known to us. But the same may be said of Jesus and the Holy Spirit. Neither of them wrote any part of the New Testament immediately, yet we accept it as the last will and testament of the one, and inspired by the other. We most firmly believe that four-fifths of the books extant, are doing efficient service in behalf of the devil. Does any one doubt it? Then let him look at the Mohammedan and Mormon Bibles, leading multiplied thousands away from Christ, after Mohammed and Jo Smith. Look, too, at the writings of infidels of every grade and hue, whose avowed purpose is to make the people believe that the Word of God is a fable, and His Son an impostor. The time would fail us to mention even the *genera,* to say nothing of the *species* of the devil's literature, and yet we are told that the devil makes no verbal communications to man at all! Surely, even this is an example of such communications from his satanic majesty. We have seen that God has His government, and operates through His subjects, with His teaching, upon such material as comes within the range of its influence; even so, the devil has his government, and operates through his subjects, with his teachings, upon such material as comes within the range of its influence. Jesus said: "He that is not with me is against me; and he that gathereth not with me, scattereth abroad." Matt. xii:30; Luke xi:23. Therefore, all responsible persons who are not the disciples of the Lord are the children of the devil, and engaged in his service. "Ye are of your father the devil, and the lusts of your father ye will do."

John viii:44. When he wished to operate on our progenitors in the garden of Eden, he *talked* to them; and as there was no human being through whom he might address Adam and Eve, he made a medium of the serpent, the most shrewd of all beasts; for which there would have been no necessity, had wicked men and women been numerous then as now. When he wished to torture Job he *talked* to God about him. When he tempted Christ he *talked* to Him, and offered Him inducements to serve him; some of which are not unlike the inducements presented by him now. It is said in the explanation to the parable of the sower, that the devil catches away the word sown in the heart. Do we not see this verified almost every day? Through his subjects, he calls it "Campbellism," and one of his subjects has recently written a book in which he calls if "Bald-faced infidelity," "water salvation," and many other ugly names, for no other purpose than to make it odious to the people, lest they believe it. Should they believe and obey the gospel, then he appeals to their ambition, by offering them places of honor in his government; or to their avarice by offering them wealth; or to their appetites, passions, or fleshly lusts, by offering them any and every gratification which their carnal natures can desire. Surely his resources are ample without resort to immediate communications upon any person, or class of persons. The Word and service of God are our only sure means of defense against him and his subjects. "Know ye not, that to whom ye yield yourselves servants to obey, his servants ye are to whom ye obey." Rom. vi:16.

If God has given us a full and perfect revelation of His mind and will concerning the redemption, conversion, salvation, government, spiritual growth, and final happiness of man in His Word, what need have we for influences of, or communications from, the Spirit without the Word? We can not conceive of an impression necessary to be made upon the heart of man which the Word of the Lord is not capable of making. If we wish to be enlightened, "The commandment of the Lord is pure, enlightening the eyes." Ps. xix:8. If we wish to be made wise unto salvation, "The testimony of the Lord is sure, making wise the simple." Ps. xix:7. Paul told Timothy that "From a child thou hast known the Holy Scriptures, which are able to make thee wise unto salvation, through faith which is in Christ Jesus." 2

Tim. iii:15. If we wish our souls converted to God, "The law of the Lord is perfect, converting the soul." Ps. xix:7. He that is dead in trespasses and in sins may be quickened by the gospel: "Thy word has quickened me." Ps. cxix:50. "I will never forget thy precepts; for with them thou hast quickened me." *Ibid*, 93. If any one wishes to be spiritually begotten, Paul says: "In Christ Jesus I have begotten you through the gospel." 1 Cor. iv:15. Indeed, the Corinthians were saved by the gospel, if they were saved at all, Paul says: "Moreover, brethren, I declare unto you the gospel which I preached unto you, which also ye have received, and wherein ye stand; by which also ye are saved." 1 Cor. xv:1, 2. "O the depth of the riches both of the wisdom and knowledge of God!" What can we desire to perfect the scheme of salvation to which we are not thoroughly furnished in the gospel?

We can see no use of sending the gospel to the heathen if the doctrine of abstract spiritual influences be true. If God converts sinners here where Bibles are plenty, without the Word, He will certainly be as kind to the heathen and convert them without the Word where they have no chance to hear it. If we believed this doctrine, we would not contribute one dollar to send Bibles or missionaries to them, for God will as surely convert them without the Word as He will any one here. If you tell us you do not want influences of the Spirit without the Word, but an accompanying influence with the Word, then is this not an attack upon the sufficiency and truth of the Word? It seems to virtually say: "I will not believe and obey the Lord in full assurance of faith in His Word until there is the accompanying influence of the Spirit through my own feelings confirming its truth." If the Spirit makes impressions through our feelings not conveyed by words, we would like to have the rule of interpretation. How shall we decide whether it confirms or contradicts the Word? If the message be that God has pardoned our sins, how shall we determine that it is not a message of condemnation? We can not see how communications from a dumb spirit can be reliable. It occurs to us that we would about as soon undertake to translate the tappings of table-legs into good English as any other kind of communications not made through words.

Again: Paul said: "Faith cometh by hearing, and hearing by

the word of God." Rom. x:17. Then, faith that comes by an abstract operation of the Spirit can not be the kind of faith of which Paul wrote. If he had been taught in the theological schools of modern times he would have said: "Faith cometh by feelings, and feelings by the Holy Spirit." If God gives man faith and converts him to Christianity by an abstract operation of the Spirit, we can not see why He will not give him all information necessary for his present and eternal happiness in the same way. Certainly, we can as readily conceive of sanctification by the Spirit without the Word as of justification by the Spirit without the Word. Hence, the Bible is a dead book, if not "a dead letter." A judge of the circuit court, whose name is quite familiar in this country, was celebrated for his ignorance of every thing but the law. On one occasion the connection of Scripture containing the "Lord's prayer" was read in his hearing, whereupon "his honor" remarked, in all sober earnestness, "There is some right good reading in that book." So, we suppose, the Bible may be respected for its antiquity and the "good reading" it contains; but as a way-bill from earth to heaven it is worth nothing if the feelings and speculations of men are allowed to supersede it. It was a useless application of the blood of Jesus when the new covenant was dedicated with it. If there are new revelations being constantly made by the Spirit, they become the last will of the Saviour, and as the last will abrogates all former wills, these abstract revelations must supersede the one dedicated by the blood of Jesus; and if these impressions are not new revelations, but simply the same that are in the Word, made known without the Word, then they are worthless, nay, mischievous, for it were much better to have them in the Word where they may be understood.

Finally, this doctrine opens the door to every species of imposition as wide as the speculations of men may desire it. We can not conceive of a doctrine so odious that it may not be confirmed by the same kind of testimony. The feelings of the Roman Catholic tell him that the priest can pardon his sins for money, and sell him indulgences to commit others. Surely, he believes it real pardon or he would not give his money for it. The feelings of the Moslem tell him that Mohammed was a prophet equal to Jesus of Nazareth, and that he conversed with

God and received the Koran from Him in person as Moses did the law at Sinai. The feelings of Brigham Young tell him that Jo Smith was the prophet of God and that the Book of Mormon, and not the Word of the Lord, is the rule of faith and practice; and can we object to what the Spirit tells him through his feelings, and at the same time offer him the same kind of testimony as evidence of our acceptance with God? We know not how any man, who admits the doctrine of abstract spiritual influences, can object to the faith of the Moslem, the Mormon, the Catholic, the spirit-rapper, or any one else who believes that the Holy Spirit, or any other spirit, communicated to him that upon which his faith is predicated, unless they can discredit the spirit which is said to have made the communication to him. Whenever they claim, as generally they do, that the Holy Spirit was the source of the communication, further objection can not be made by those who are committed to that kind of testimony.

Before dismissing the subject, it may be well to call the attention of the reader to a few things which have been improperly blended with the ordinary influence of the Spirit in conversion, at least by some. The cases of conversion recorded in the Acts, all occurred in the days of miracles, and there were miracles connected with most of them. We have taken some pains to disconnect ordinary from extraordinary manifestations of the Spirit; we need only here remind the reader that, however prominent a miracle may appear in the record of any case of conversion as we do not live in the days of miracles, he must not expect the miracle to be reproduced in him.

Again: the influence of *circumstances*, whether *accidental* or *providential*, are not the work of the Spirit in conversion. A merely accidental circumstance may take a man within range of the Spirit's teaching; *e.g.* a young man goes to meeting to see a young lady—to see some friend—simply to be in company, or transact some business; the gospel is preached, he becomes interested, and is finally converted. The *accidental circumstance*, whatever it may have been, which induced him to go to preaching, was not the influence of the Spirit, for this began when he came in contact with the teaching of the Spirit, through the preaching and other services at the meeting. The Scriptures furnish numerous examples illustrative of this fact. Lydia's occupation as a vender of purple, took her from Thyatira to Philippi, where Paul preached the gospel to her, by which God opened her heart, enlightened her mind, and she was converted; but the influence of the Spirit upon her heart, began not until Paul's preaching saluted her ears.

Again: The Jailer's occupation, as keeper of the prison in the city of Philippi, caused him to hear the Word of the Lord preached by Paul and Silas, by which he was converted, but he had not a spiritual idea until they spoke to him. Even after the miracles had ceased, he would have committed suicide, had they not prevented him. Had some one else been keeper of the prison, such one, and not he, might have been the beneficiary of the preaching.

A *providential circumstance* may prepare a man to favorably receive the Spirit's teaching; *e.g.* the death of a friend or near relative, or physical suffering. When death fastens upon the vitals of a lovely child, brother, sister, or parent, with whom our affections are borne away to the realm of spirits; or when our physical powers are exhausted by the blighting influence of disease and trouble, then it is, that we realize the insufficiency of human aid, and the instability of all earthy things. Our dependence upon God is brought home to us, and thus the heart is prepared for a favorable consideration of spiritual instruction; but not a ray of spiritual light can we derive from such afflictions. We are simply prepared to consider what light we previously had, and to receive additional instruction if it is presented to us. We are not prepared to regard the mellowing influence of such afflictions as the work of the Holy Spirit in conversion; nor are they even within the line of *special providences,* for they are the common lot of all men—the result of *general providence* or *natural law.* Nor would we be understood to deny the doctrine of spcial providence. Nay, we not only admit, but believe it; but *it is for God's children, and not to convert sinners.* Paul says: "We trust in the living God, who is the Saviour of all men, but *specially of those that believe.*" 1 Tim. iv:10. God has a general providence, of which all are the recipients, but He *specially* provides for them that put their trust in Him, according to His Word. Hence, "We know that all things *work together for good to them that love God,* to them who are the called, according to his purpose." Rom. viii:28. "The eyes of the Lord are over the righteous, and his ears are open unto their prayers; but the face of the Lord is against them that do evil." 1 Pet. iii:12. But we have no disposition to enter upon a discussion of this subject here. It is important to a proper understanding of the Holy Spirit's work in conversion, that we keep it disentangled from every thing foreign to it. If we can do this, and then quit hunting for difficulties and mysteries, we will not find many. The truths of God often sparkle as gems upon the surface of His Word, and are unobserved by those who are always digging tunnels, but never examine the virgin soil in its native simplicity.

The Reception of the Holy Spirit.

Having seen that the Spirit dwells in the body or Church—that the disciples are builded together for a habitation of God through the Spirit, and that the church is the medium through which the Spirit's power is exerted for the conversion and salvation of man, we come now to consider the relationship it sustains to each member of the body. Before leaving the disciples, Jesus said to them: "I will pray the Father, and he shall give you another Comforter, that he may abide with you forever; even the Spirit of truth, whom the world can not receive, because it seeth him not, neither knoweth him; but ye know him, for he dwelleth with you, and shall be in you." John xiv:16, 17. There are several very important matters in this quotation, for which we will have use as we proceed; but at present, we are here to see that the Holy Spirit was promised as an abiding guest and comforter to the disciples, and as such it was to dwell with, and be in them forever. That this was not a figurative, but a literal in-dwelling of the Holy Spirit in the disciples is plain, from the fact that when the Spirit came, as promised, "they were all filled with the Holy Spirit, and began to speak with other tongues, as the Spirit gave them utterance." Acts ii:4. It will scarcely be said that the disciples were only figuratively filled with the Holy Spirit on the day of Pentecost. Nay, it was *literally in them*, as the Saviour promised them it should be. Then, are we to believe that it was literally in them as an inspiring monitor, but as a comforter only figuratively? If not, and it was literally in the apostles to inspire them, we can see no reason why it should not be as literally in them as a comforter. And if it dwelt literally in them as a comforter, and as such was to abide with them forever, we conclude that it must dwell in the disciples *now as literally as it was in them.*

And here we must not forget that the Spirit was given to man by measure; and we have seen some of these measures fill their mission and pass away. It was to guide the apostles into all truth, and bring to their remembrance every thing said to them by the Saviour. It has done this, and as we have a perfect record of what they said and did when inspired by it, we have no use for it now as an inspiring monitor; but as a comforter it abideth ever. But we may be told, that this promise was made to the apostles only, and was to them fulfilled. And as they were inspired by its presence, the absence of such inspiration proves the absence of the Spirit in all who are not so inspired.

A careful examination of the Scriptures will show that, while there was no promise that the inspiration should remain, as a comforter it was to abide with the disciples forever. As such, it was to dwell with, and be in them. As an inspiring monitor it did not abide forever. Nay, even the apostles, during their lives, were not always under its inspiration. Paul sometimes spake as a man, at other times he *thought he had the Spirit of God* (See 1 Cor. vii:40). How could he so speak if he knew himself to be at all times under the influence of inspiration? When it was necessary for something to be *revealed* or *confirmed* by the Spirit, it took possession of some spiritual man or men, through whom the work was accomplished. Had Peter been all the time under the influence of inspiration, it would not have taken a special miracle to teach him that he might go to the house of Cornelius with the gospel to the Gentiles. This case clearly shows that the gospel was progressively developed to the apostles, and that they did not know all its provisions, when first baptized with the Holy Spirit on the day of Pentecost. "While Peter thought on the vision, the Spirit said unto him, Behold, three men seek thee, arise, therefore, and get thee down, and go with them, doubting nothing, for I have sent them." Acts x:19, 20. Then he knew something he never knew before. And when the messengers told him for what they had come, he knew something more. And when Cornelius rehearsed the things seen and heard by him "Then

Peter opened his mouth, and said, Of a truth I perceive that God is no respecter of persons; but in every nation, he that feareth God and worketh righteousness is accepted with him." Acts x:34, 35. These important lessons, the other apostles, though inspired, did not know yet. But Peter rehearsed the whole matter to them from the beginning, and "when they heard these things, they held their peace, and glorified God, saying: Then hath God also to the Gentiles granted repentance unto life." Acts xi:18.

Here, for the first time, these inspired men knew that the Gentiles were fellow-heirs with the Jews in the privileges of the gospel. But as a comforter, was it designed for the apostles alone? If so, why did Jesus promise that it should abide with them forever. They could not live here forever; nor can we conclude that Jesus intended to promise them the Holy Spirit as a comforter forever, meaning that it should go with them into the future state; for He assures them that *there* they should again be with Him. "I go," said He, "to prepare a place for you; and if I go and prepare a place for you, I will come again and receive you unto myself; that where I am, there ye may be also." John xiv:2, 3. While clothed with humanity, Jesus was not omnipresent, and hence, could only be with and comfort His disciples in a single place at one time.

As to the apostles alone, this would not have made another comforter necessary, for He could have kept them with Him; but when the time came for them to go into all the world and proclaim the gospel to every creature He could not, as son of man, be in Jerusalem, Rome, Corinth, Philippi, Samaria, and other places at the same time; hence it was expedient, in this respect, as well as others, that He should go away and send another Comforter, even the Holy Spirit, who could dwell with, and be in every disciple, any and every where until He should come again. There is a remarkable similarity in the style of the Saviour when He promised the Comforter to the disciples, and that of Paul in his letter in his brethren at Rome. He says: "But ye are not in the flesh, but in the Spirit, if so be that the Spirit of God dwell in you. Now, if any man have not the Spirit of Christ, he is none of his. And if Christ be in you, the body is dead because of sin; but the Spirit is life because of righteousness. But if the Spirit of him that raised up Jesus from the dead dwell in you, he that raised up Christ from the dead shall also quicken your mortal bodies by his Spirit that dwelleth in you." Rom. viii:9-11. That this passage is applicable to Christians now is admitted by all; how strikingly similar the phraseology to that used by the Saviour. He says: "He *dwelleth with you and shall be in you.*" Paul says: "If so be that the Spirit of God *dwell in you.*" "If the Spirit of him that raised up Jesus from the dead *dwell in you.*" "Shall also quicken your mortal bodies by his Spirit that *dwelleth in you.*" What can this language mean? We can not say that God will quicken our mortal bodies by His Spirit that dwelleth *figuratively* in us; and to say that He will quicken our mortal bodies by His Spirit that dwelleth *metonymically* in us would be no better. Nor will it do to say that God will quicken our mortal bodies by His *disposition* that dwelleth in us. To our mind, the passage admits of one interpretation, and only one; namely, that the Spirit of God—the Holy Spirit—dwells *literally and really* in every Christian, and by it God will re-animate his body in the great day. With this agrees the teaching of Paul, when he wrote to the disciples at Corinth. He says: "What! know ye not that your body is the temple of the Holy Ghost which is in you?" 1 Cor. vi:19. He here manifests astonishment that they should not ever keep this thought before them. And again: "Know ye not that ye are the temple of God, and that the Spirit of God dwelleth in you?" 1 Cor. iii:16. Had Paul been seeking to impress the disciples at Rome and Corinth, with the fact that the Spirit did really dwell in each of them, we know not how he could have selected a set of words better calculated to convey the thought than those he employed in the passages quoted.

Thus far we have not approached our position by any process of reasoning, but by positive declarations of Holy Writ. "*The Spirit dwelleth in you*" has met us everywhere. Upon such scriptures there is not much room to reason, and here we could well afford to rest this position. But we think we can arrive at the same thought by a process of reasoning altogether satisfactory, even in the absence of direct testimony. Paul more than once likens the church to the human body, an example of which may be found, 1 Cor. xii:12-27, to which the reader is referred; we can only transcribe a sentence or two. Addressing the disciples, he says: "Now ye are the body of Christ, and members in particular." The blood freighted with the pabulum of life must freely circulate in all the members of the body, great and small; and should such circulation cease in any member, death and disintegration of such member must inevitably follow, and unless it is separated from the body all must perish. Even so, "the body without the spirit is dead." Jas. ii:26. If the Spirit ceases to dwell in and vitalize every member of the church or spiritual body, spiritual death to such a member is inevitable; and if the circulation can not be restored, painful as the operation may be, the amputating knife must be used, for "when one member suffers all the members suffer with it." As it is "better for one member to perish than for the whole body to be cast into hell" (Matt. v:29, 30), sacred as the relationship may have been, a separation must take place. Are we not here taught that the presence of the Spirit in the Christian is indispensable to the maintenance of Spiritual life?

Again: Jesus illustrated the relationship His disciples sustained to Him by a vine and its branches. See John xv:1-7. Said He: 'I am the vine, ye are the branches. He that abideth in me, and I in him, the same bringeth forth much fruit." As every branch must maintain its connection with the vine, so that the sap may circulate from vine to branch and keep it alive, even so must every member of the church or body of Christ maintain his connection with the body, so that the Spirit circulate in and keep him alive, lest "he be cast forth as a branch and is withered; and men gather such, and cast them into the fire, and they are burned." So the Lord taught, and so we believe.

But we are sometimes told that the Spirit dwells in us simply by its teaching received through the inspired Word; hence all that is meant by it is that we are well instructed by the Spirit. When Paul told the Romans that God would quicken their mortal bodies by His Spirit that dwelt in them, did he only mean to teach that God would reanimate their sleeping dust by the instructions they had received from the Spirit? If this be all, then we see not why the *world can not receive it.* An infidel may be as wise in the Scriptures as the most devoted disciple. It took a man mighty in the Scriptures to meet Mr. Owen in debate upon the authenticity of the Bible, and yet it will scarcely be contended that the Holy Spirit dwelt in his infidel heart. Every man who is adopted into the family of God must be taught by the Spirit before he is adopted: but the Spirit is given to him because he *is a son*, and not to prepare him for adoption or make him a son. If the reception of the Word of truth be all that is meant by the reception of the Spirit, then Paul's rule is reversed, and every man receives the Spirit, not because he is a son, but that he may become one. Yea, Jesus was mistaken when He said: "The world can not receive it," because they must receive its instruction *while of the world,* and *before* entering the church, kingdom, or body, as certainly as hearing precedes faith and faith precedes obedience.

Paul said to the Ephesians that they were sealed with the Holy Spirit after they heard and believed the gospel and trusted in Christ. "In whom ye also trusted after that ye heard the word of truth, the gospel of your salvation: in whom also, after that ye believed ye were sealed with the Holy Spirit of promise, which is the earnest of our inheritance until the redemption of the purchased possession." Eph. i:13, 14. Then it follows, most certainly, that if we are now sealed with the Holy Spirit, as these Ephesians were, it takes place *after,* and is *something more than hearing, believing, and receiving the Word.* Their *sealing* was to them an earnest of their inheritance; that is, a *pledge* of God's faithfulness in giving them the promised inheritance; hence, he admonishes them to faithfulness on their part, that they "grieve not the Holy Spirit of God, whereby ye are sealed unto the day of redemption." Eph. iv:30. The same apostle writes to the Corinthians thus: "For all the promises of God in him are yea, and in him amen, unto the glory of God by us. Now, he which establisheth us with you in Christ and hath anointed us, is God; who hath also sealed us, and given the earnest of the Spirit in our hearts." 2 Cor. i:20-22. God established them in Christ by giving them the Holy Spirit as an earnest or pledge of the fact that His promises were yea and amen in Christ, hence they were sealed with the Spirit. "Now, he that hath wrought us for the self-same thing is God, who also hath given unto us the earnest of the Spirit." 2 Cor. v:5. That God gave these Corinthians the Holy Spirit as an earnest of the promised inheritance is clear; and when we associate these quotations with the language quoted from Eph. i:13, it clearly shows that it was given *after they were instructed in and believed the gospel,* and hence was something more than the information thus received by them. From this conclusion we can conceive of but one possible way of escape—namely, that the measure of the Spirit by which the Ephesians and Corinthians were sealed was the extraordinary measure by which spiritual gifts were imparted, and not the ordinary measure following adoption into God's family. But it is the business of him who so affirms to furnish the proof of such affirmation; and he would do well, in the meantime, to see that he does not explain away all the Bible in special applications of it, leaving nothing applicable to us at all.

It may not be amiss to remark here, that the words in which a truth or thought is expressed are not the thought itself; nor is the thought or truth suggested by a person or thing the person or thing which suggested it. Hence, the words in which a spiritual idea is suggested are not the idea; nor is the idea suggested by the Spirit the Spirit itself. A school-boy may have the words of an author committed to memory most perfectly, and yet not have the thought which the author designed to convey by the words, nevertheless the thought was in the words. Even so, he may get the thoughts of an author without drinking in or imbibing the spirit of the author who suggested the thought, nevertheless, the spirit was in the thought. Hence it is possible for us to comprehend a thought or truth suggested by the Holy Spirit, and yet fail to receive the Spirit which inspired the thought. You will say these are nice distinctions; we admit it; but they are distinctions nevertheless, and he who fails to make them, may never fully understand the subject of the Holy Spirit.

But How do Persons Receive the Holy Spirit?

Suppose we acknowledge ourselves incapable of answering the question at all; what then? Does it follow that we must repudiate a plainly taught fact, because we can not comprehend and explain the philosophy of it? For just such a crime Zacharias was made dumb and not able to speak, until the fulfillment of the words which he refused to believe, because he could not see how he and Elizabeth were to be blessed with a child when both were well stricken in years. When God speaks, the man of faith believes, whether he can or can not explain the philosophy of what He says. Hence, we are prepared to believe that the Holy Spirit dwells in God's people, whether we can or can not explain the manner of its reception, because He says, He will quicken our mortal bodies by His *Spirit which dwelleth in us.* But we would not have the reader suppose the Bible a blank, even on this subject. Paul says: "The love of God is shed abroad in our hearts by the Holy Ghost which is given unto us." Rom. v:5. By this we learn that the Holy Spirit is given to the disciples. But *how is it given?* This is the troublesome question. Well, it is either given *mediately* or *immediately*—through means, or without means. Jesus once said: "If ye then, being evil, know how to give good gifts unto your children, how much more shall your heavenly Father give the Holy Spirit to them that ask him?" Luke xi:13. Here we are taught that the Father gives the Spirit to such of His children as ask Him for it; but we are not told how He gives it to them. He gives us bread, and taught His disciples to pray for it, yet He gives it through means and not otherwise; hence we may find that the Father has provided a system of means by which to convey the Holy Spirit to His children. "This only would I learn of you, Received ye the Spirit by the works of the law, or by the hearing of faith?" Gal. iii:2. Two thoughts are here implied:

First, that the Galatians did not receive the Spirit by the works of the law.

Second, That they did receive it by the hearing of faith.

This question, then, is pertinent to our inquiry. We wish to know *how the Spirit is received,* and it is here assumed to have been *received by the hearing of faith.* But this is a queer sentence; what can it mean? Does hearing belong to faith? No; faith comes by hearing; hence hearing must precede faith; indeed, hearing may be where there is no faith. Then the apostles could not have meant by *faith* that confidence only with which we receive testimony. He must mean something more than that. In this chapter, as in many other places, he is evidently contrasting the *Mosaic Law* and its service with the *gospel* and its service; and the word *faith,* in the verse quoted, is the synonym of *gospel,* and comprehends the whole plan of salvation presented in the gospel. If we comprehend the passage, we must notice the word *hearing*, for it must mean something more than the reception of sound. In the New Testament compiled by A. Campbell, from the works of Doctors George Campbell, Macknight and Doddridge, the passage is rendered, "The *obedience* of faith." We might quote many passages from the common version, where the word *hear* implies *obedience*, but a single example must suffice: "And it shall come to pass, that every soul which will not *hear* that Prophet, shall be destroyed from among the people." Acts iii:23. Certainly the word *hear* must be understood to mean obedience to the commands of Jesus. Collating these items, the account stands thus: The Galatians *received the Spirit by obedience to the gospel*, and hence, obedience to the gospel is the Father's appointed means of imparting the Holy Spirit to His children. Thus we see why it is that the world can not receive the Spirit; they do not obey the gospel that they may receive it. We have seen that it is given by the Father to His children; hence Paul said to them: "Because ye are sons, God hath sent forth the Spirit of His Son into your hearts, crying, Abba Father." The children obey the Father; hence as the gospel is the law by which He governs His children, and as obedience to it is the medium through which He gives them the Spirit, by obeying the gospel the children receive the Spirit.

We have seen that there are two great opposing kingdoms, namely: "The kingdom of God," and the "kingdom of darkness." The subjects of that are called the children or "Sons of God." 1 John iii:1. The subjects of this are called, "the world," and Jesus says they can not receive the Spirit. Nor is it at all strange that they can not receive the Holy Spirit while citizens of the kingdom of darkness, laboring for and serving their father, the devil. If we would receive the Spirit of God we must become citizens of His government—members of His family. Then, and not until then, may we receive the Spirit of the family which entitles us to the privilege of calling God *our Father*. The men of the world have not the Spirit of God and have not the right to call Him their Father. Jesus said to such: "Ye are of your father the devil, and the lusts of your father ye will do." John viii:44. The church is God's spiritual family, into which we enter as "babes in Christ." 1 Cor. iii:1. And we are admonished, "as new-born babes, to desire the sincere milk of the word, that we may grow thereby." 1 Pet. ii:2. Reading and feeding upon this spiritual food, the children of God are "filled with the Spirit"—not because the Word is the Spirit, for it is not—but because the Spirit is ever present in the inspired Word, and the service appointed therein is God's ordained means of giving them the Spirit. Hence, says Paul: "Let the word of God dwell in you richly, in all wisdom." Col. iii:16. By so living we may grow up to the stature of men and women, full grown in Christ Jesus, the Lord, "till we all come in the unity of the faith and of the knowledge of the Son of God, unto a perfect man, unto the measure of the stature of the fullness of Christ." Eph. iv:13. If we take a child of Indian parentage and adopt it into a family of civilization and refinement, it ceases to imbibe the spirit of the family from which it is adopted. It henceforth manifests a different disposition and speaks a different language. Its manners, habits, occupation, every thing save its personality undergoes a corresponding change. So, when a person is taken from "the world" and adopted into the family of God, he or she ceases to imbibe the spirit of the world, and hence to "conform to the world," and imbibes, "drinks into" that measure of the Spirit which the Father promised to His children by living in the Father's family, receiving His instruction, and being governed by His laws.

Every time the faithful child obeys a command of the Father, he drinks into or imbibes a measure of the Spirit connected with that service. It matters not whether it were the service of the Lord's day, worship in the family, visiting the sick, relief of the poor, or any other service required by the Father of His children, He has connected Himself through the Spirit with His service, and he who faithfully serves Him receives the Holy Spirit as an earnest of the promised inheritance. Hence, "he that keepeth his commandments dwelleth in him, and he in him. And hereby we know that he abideth in us, by the Spirit which he has given us." 1 John iii:24. And again: "If we love one another, God dwelleth in us and his love is perfected in us. Hereby we know that we dwell in him, and he in us, because he hath given us of his Spirit." *Ibid,* iv:12, 13. The devoted disciple goes to the house of worship on the Lord's day, and there is greeted heartily by his brethren and sisters in the Lord, and he feels the cords of love strengthen as he takes them by the hand.

He joins with them in singing psalms, and hymns, and spiritual songs; and as he makes melody in his heart to the Lord, his thoughts soar away to a place where he hopes to join with the redeemed in singing the "new song before the throne" in sweeter strains than mortal tongues can make. A lesson of instruction is read from the Word of the Lord "whereby are given unto us exceeding great and precious promises; that by these we might be partakers of the divine nature." 2 Pet. i:4. Are we made partakers of the divine nature by the precious promises of the Lord? Then, what has He promised? Nay, what has He not promised us? Eye hath not seen nor ear heard, neither has it entered into the heart of man to conceive the things which God has in reservation for them that love Him; and though God has revealed them by His Spirit, language is beggared when called upon to furnish drapery in which to present them. He has promised that He will never leave nor forsake His children; that He will comfort and support them while crossing the deep, rolling river, that He will quicken their mortal bodies by His Spirit that dwelleth in them, and give them bodies fashioned like unto the glorious body of His Son; that their homes shall be in the city of God, where God and angels shall be their associates; that they shall have right to the tree of life, and drink of the pure river of life that flows from beneath the throne; that they shall bask in the sunny smiles of God's eternal love forever and ever. Oh, great, *exceeding great and precious promises!* Who can contemplate them without partaking of the divine nature; nay, without drinking copious draughts of the Holy Spirit that is ever present with them?

While the disciple eats of the bread and drinks of the wine which symbolize the broken body and shed blood of a crucified Saviour, who died that he might live, his memory fastens by faith upon the scenes of Calvary, and his heart swells with gratitude and is stirred with deepest emotion as he feels the love of God shed abroad in his heart by the Holy Spirit which is given to him through the appointments of the Lord. He prostrates himself at the golden altar and offers thereon the incense of an humble and devoted heart. Feeling his unworthiness, he pleads for mercy through Jesus Christ. Truly grateful for favors received, he humbly yet in faith asks his Father for blessings and protection in time to come. "Likewise the Spirit also helpeth our infirmities: for we know not what we should pray for as we ought: but the Spirit itself maketh intercession for us with groanings which can not be uttered." Rom. viii:26. Thus God's children are "strengthened with might by his Spirit in the inner man" (Eph. iii:16) by the service of the Lord's day at the house of worship. Oh, precious season of refreshing from the presence of the Lord! Surely, it is good for them to be there, that they may sit together in heavenly places in Christ Jesus, and drink of that measure of the Holy Spirit with which God designed to comfort and strengthen His children amid the persecutions and trials incident to their pilgrimage through life. But Jesus called the Holy Spirit a Comforter, and truly it did comfort them. It not only dwelt in them, but it inspired men to write and speak words of cheer for them. It inspired Paul to write a graphic description of their victory over death and subsequent reign with the Lord. He says: "The Lord himself shall descend from heaven with a shout, with the voice of the archangel, and with the trump of God: and the dead in Christ shall rise first: then we which are alive and remain shall be caught up together with them in the clouds, to meet the Lord in the air: and so shall we ever be with the Lord. Wherefore comfort one another with these words." 1 Thess. iv:16-18.

The Witness of the Spirit.

After Paul had given the disciples at Rome positive assurance of the Spirit's presence in them, and that God would quicken their mortal bodies by it, he tells them that the measure of it received by them was the Spirit of adoption, by which they were authorized to call God THEIR Father; and in further confirmation of this, he said: "The Spirit itself beareth witness with our spirit that we are the children of God." Rom. viii:16. The apostle here speaks of *two* witnesses, the *Spirit itself* and *our spirit*, and these bear witness to the fact that certain characters are children of God. By the phrase *Spirit itself* we suppose we are to understand Paul to mean the Holy Spirit, and by *our spirit* we suppose he means the *human spirit*. Then, the Holy Spirit and the human spirit bear testimony *with* each other that the disciples are children of God. The passage is generally interpreted as though it read thus: "The Spirit itself beareth witness TO our spirit that we are children of God." And though this makes the Holy Spirit the *only witness*, when we inquire of those who thus interpret the passage, for the *testimony* of the witness, they give us the testimony of *their own spirit*, as though *it* were the only witness; and thus the testimony of the Holy Spirit is virtually excluded. Is there not a want of consistency in this? We have listened attentively to many persons when detailing the testimony upon which they predicated their acceptance with God, and of that given by those who believe in the doctrine of abstract spiritual influences; we remember not a sentence that was not a statement of what they had *felt*, imagined, or *dreamed*. In vain have we listened for one word of testimony from the Holy Spirit—it is entirely excluded. That this is true may be seen in the fact that such persons are often *in doubt* upon the subject themselves; and surely they would not *doubt the testimony of the Holy Spirit*. One day their hopes are all bright, and they feel perfectly sure that they are children of God—the next day they are in Bunyan's "slough of despond," and singing, with plaintive voice,

> " 'Tis a point I long to know;
> Oft it causes anxious thought;
> Do I love the Lord or no?
> Am I His, or am I not?"

Indeed, doubts are their counterfeit detector, by which the wheat is separated from the chaff and a genuine conversion is recognized. He who has no doubts of his acceptance with God is, with them, an egotistic, self-righteous Pharisee, who is ignorant of "the work of grace in the soul." Those who thus doubt are not like those to whom Paul said: "Let us draw near with a true heart, in full assurance of faith." Heb. x:22. They can only draw near to God in full assurance of faith *occasionally*, if at all. Their faith is not based upon testimony, but upon their feelings; hence, when they draw near to God it must be in full assurance of *feeling*, and only occasionally at that. We do not object to good feelings; they are proper in their place; but when they constitute *all* the foundation of hope in Jesus, dark days will be sure to come. When the excitement of the protracted meeting passes away and the convert begins to grapple with the trials of life, the ardor of his feelings cools down, and we hear him sing:

> "Dear Lord, *if* indeed I am thine,
>   *If* thou art my sun and my song,
> Say, why do I *languish* and pine,
>   And why are my *winters* so long?
> Oh, drive these *dark clouds* from my sky;
>   Thy soul-cheering presence restore;
> Lord, take me to thee up on high,
>   Where *winter* and *clouds* are no more."

Under such a state of mind, unless another protracted meeting should speedily drive the dark clouds away and renew the soul-cheering presence of the Lord, they are apt to imagine themselves deceived, and go back into sin, or seek another *conversion* by which the feelings of the former excitement may be temporarily renewed; and thus they pass through life alternating between hope and despair.

We do not know that we are pardoned because we feel good, but we feel good because we know we are pardoned. He who believes himself pardoned will feel like a pardoned man whether he be pardoned or condemned, for a falsehood believed will produce just the same feelings that would have been produced had it been true. When Jacob believed Joseph to be dead, he grieved and wept in all the anguish of soul that would have wrung his heart had the fact been really that way. He refused to be comforted, and confidently expected his gray hairs to go down to the grave in sorrow for what he believed to be the sad fate of his dear boy; and it was with great difficulty that he was made to believe that Joseph was alive and governor of Egypt, but when he saw the wagons which Joseph had sent to carry him to Egypt, he said: "It is enough: Joseph, my son, is yet alive; I will go and see him before I die." Gen. xlv:28. He felt like Joseph was dead when really he was alive and governor of Egypt. The Roman Catholic pays his money to the priest to absolve him from guilt, and dies rejoicing in the belief of the imposition as though it were really true; and if good feelings are conclusive proof of pardon, then is he pardoned indeed, for doubtless he feels as much like he was pardoned as does any one else.

Feelings may prove us sincere, but they alone can not prove

the pardon of sin. It is a moral proposition and can not be proved by physical testimony. *Our feelings may prove that which is wrought in us or done by us, but they can not prove that which is wrought in or done by another who is not visible to us.* They may bear witness to the sincerity of our faith and repentance, because they are done by us; they may bear witness to our change of heart, because it is wrought in us; but pardon of sin takes place in the mind of God, the party offended, as far from us as heaven is from the earth, and hence we can not attest the fact by our feelings. When we are *hungry, thirsty, sleepy, sick,* or in *pain,* we know the fact by our feelings, and no amount of moral testimony could convince us to the contrary, for this character of testimony is not capable of proving such a fact; but the fact that Jesus died upon Calvary must be proved by moral testimony, and can not be proved by our feelings, any more than Jacob's feelings could prove that Joseph was slain by a wild beast. Sin is a moral evil, and its forgiveness can not be recognized by *feelings,* like the removal of disease from the body, but must be known by testimony coming from the party who forgives it. By way of illustrating the thought here presented, we beg permission to present the substantial features of an actual occurrence of the late war. A soldier of one of the armies, charged with a crime thought worthy of death, was tried by a court-martial and sentenced to be shot on a specified hour of a certain day. He had been a good soldier, and the commanding general determined to pardon him, and, without mentioning the fact to any one, he wrote out his reprieve early on the morning of the day set for his execution. The condemned man was placed in position, in the care of an officer and squad of soldiers charged with the execution of the order, and the whole army was marched out to witness his death. Within a minute or two of the time appointed for the man to die the reprieve was handed to the officer in charge, and was read to the prisoner, announcing his release. Then he had *knowledge* of his pardon, and for the first time *felt like a pardoned man.* Though pardoned early in the morning, his feelings gave him no evidence of the fact until the written communication came from the pardoning power in words adapted to his comprehension. Why did not his feelings assure him of his pardon as soon as it took place in the mind of the general? Because feelings are not capable of bearing such testimony. Had pardon taken place in his own mind, then his feelings would have given him assurance of the fact. So the sinner is pardoned in the mind of God; and though he may rejoice with joy unspeakable and full of glory, he does it in full assurance of faith in the proclamation which contains the conditions of his pardon.

But will this source of testimony relieve the question of pardon from the doubts which hang about it in the minds of such as rely upon their feelings alone as the evidence of their acceptance with God? We may know that our sins are pardoned with as much certainty as we may know that there is a God against whom we have sinned, a heaven awaiting the saints, a hell to be the abode of the damned, or that we have an immortal spirit within us.

How do we know that there is a God? "No man hath seen God at any time; the only-begotten Son, which is in the bosom of the Father, he hath declared him" (John i:18), yet he is denominated a fool who "hath said in his heart, There is no God." Ps. xiv:1, liii:1. Testimony may be such as to produce a conviction in the mind that amounts to knowledge. We feel just as sure that there is such a place as New York or London, neither of which we have seen, as we do that there is such a place as Nashville, which we have seen; then, if we may thus *know* from human testimony that there is such a place as New York, why may we not know from *divine testimony* that there is a heaven where God and angels dwell? John says: "If we receive the witness of man, the witness of God is greater." 1 John v:9. But does this amount to knowledge? Job says: "I *know* that my Redeemer liveth, and that he shall stand at the latter day upon the earth; and though after my skin worms destroy this body, yet in my flesh shall I see God." Job xix:25, 26. How did Job know these things? Peter said: "Let all the house of Isreal know assuredly, that God hath made that same Jesus, whom ye have crucified, both Lord and Christ." How were the Pentecostians to *know* this? They could not see the Lord as did Stephen, but they must know it through the testimony which Peter presented to them. Paul says: "We know that, if our earthly house of this tabernacle were dissolved, we have a building of God, a house not made with hands, eternal in the heavens." 2 Cor. v:1. How could these Corinthians have known this? Only through testimony; yet it amounted to knowledge. John said: "We know that, when he appears, we shall be like him; for we shall see him as he is." 1 John iii:2. How could the disciples to whom John wrote have *known* this? Only through testimony; yet they *knew* it. Then, if the Pentecostians could *know* from testimony that Jesus was crowned Lord in heaven; if the Corinthians could *know* that there was a building of God awaiting them in heaven after death; if the disciples *knew* that they would be like Jesus Christ when He should appear, why may we not *know our sins forgiven by the same kind of testimony?* Luke says: "Forasmuch as many have taken in hand to set forth in order a declaration of those things which are most surely believed among us, even as they delivered them unto us, which from the beginning were eye-witnesses, and ministers of the word; it seemed good to me also, having had perfect understanding of all things from the very first, to write unto thee in order, most excellent Theophilus, that thou mightest know the certainty of those things wherein thou hast been instructed." Luke i:1-4. Then, we may *assuredly know* the *certainty* of things from written testimony, especially when the Spirit of God guided the pen of the writer. Hence, John says: "These things have I written unto you that believe on the name of the Son of God; that ye may know that ye have eternal life." 1 John v:13. Then, we may *know* ourselves heirs of eternal life by the things which inspired men have written. Jesus says: "I have given them the words which thou hast given me, and they have received them, and have known surely that I came out from thee." John xvii:8. Here we not only learn that the *words* of Jesus were sufficient to let the apostles know assuredly that He came from God, but we also learn that the words spoken and written by them came from God through His Son to them; hence, in these words we have the testimony of Jesus Christ and also of God Himself. What, then, is the testimony?

In the new covenant, which was dedicated with the blood of His Son, God said: "I will be merciful to their unrighteousness, and their sins and their iniquities will I remember no more." Heb. viii:12. This covenant was the consummation of the Promise which God gave to Abraham, "wherein God, willing more abundantly to show unto the heirs of promise the immutability of his counsel, confirmed it with an oath; that by two immutable things, in which it was impossible for God to lie, we might have strong consolation, who have fled for refuge to lay hold upon the hope set before us; which hope we have as an anchor to the soul both sure and steadfast." Heb. vi:17-19. Then, we have the promise of God, confirmed by His oath, that the sins of His people should be remembered no more. But on what conditions, if any, He would blot them from His memory is not here stated.

Jesus was the mediator of this covenant—the *surety* of a better testament than the old; hence, to Him we go for the terms of pardon under the testament of which He is Testator. He says: "He that believeth and is baptized shall be saved." Mark xvi:16. Here we find that pardon is conditional, and the conditions are clearly set out. He further says: "The words that I speak unto you, they are spirit and they are life." John vi:63. We suppose this at least implies that the Spirit is ever present in His Word. In this conditional proclamation of pardon we have the presence of the Spirit, the word of Jesus Christ, and the oath of God the Father; and they are all pledged for the pardon of him who believes and is baptized.

But *our* spirit is also a witness that we are children of God; what testimony does it give? The first condition in the proclamation requires us to believe; but we may profess to believe when we do not; and if so, God is not mocked; "it is with the heart man believeth unto righteousness." Our faith must come from the great deep of our heart; and though others may accuse us of hypocrisy, our own spirit bears us witness that we do believe. Hence, says John: "He that believeth on the Son of God hath the witness in himself." John v:10. The witness of what? that he is pardoned? No; that he does believe. Our spirit is competent to bear witness to the sincerity of our faith, for it is an act of our own; and hence, no amount of testimony can convince us that we do not believe what our spirit tells us we do believe.

But we must be baptized, for this is another condition of the proclamation. This, too, may be done from impure motives, and if so, it is worthless, for Paul says: "Ye have obeyed from the heart that form of doctrine which was delivered you; being then made free from sin." Rom. vi:17, 18. Here again our spirit testifies that we were baptized with a heart sincerely desirous of honoring God's authority in humble obedience to His will. Then, *our spirit testifies that we do believe and have been baptized, and the Holy Spirit testifies, in the words of Jesus, that we are saved, and* GOD HAS CONFIRMED IT WITH HIS OATH.

Thus the Spirit itself beareth witness with our spirit that we are children of God; and now "*believing* ye rejoice with joy unspeakable and full of glory, receiving the end of your faith, even the salvation of your souls." 1 Pet. i:8, 9. Yea, "the God of hope fill you with all joy and peace in *believing*, that ye may abound in hope through the power of the Holy Ghost." Rom. xv:13. Now, like the jailer, we "*rejoice,* believing in God." Acts xvi:34. When the believing eunuch was baptized, "he went on his way rejoicing." Acts viii:39. These were wholly unlike the converts of modern times. They rejoiced in their salvation because they knew they had complied with the conditions of the proclamation. Now, ask that rejoicing convert why he feels happy, and he will tell you he is happy because he knows his sins are pardoned; ask him how he knows he is pardoned, and he will tell you he knows he is pardoned because he feels good. Thus he reasons in a circle, proving his pardon by his feelings and his feelings by his pardon.

Now, is there any room to doubt the pardon of a man who has thus complied with the conditions of the proclamation? None whatever. Can we doubt the word of Jesus and the oath of God? Can you say, "Yes, I know I did believe, and I know I was baptized in good faith, and I know the Lord says, 'He that believeth and is baptized shall be saved, but I am not sure He told the truth; and I know, too, that God confirmed His promise by His oath, but I am in doubt still." Our pen trembles when we record even a supposition of such a thought in any human heart. Have we any stronger testimony that God is, and that He is the rewarder of them who diligently seek Him? Have we any stronger evidence that there is a heaven to be the home of the righteous? Is there any stronger proof that the wicked will be turned into hell with the nations that forget God? Have we any stronger assurance that we have a soul to be saved or lost? It occurs to us that he who will not believe it would not be persuaded though Jesus were on earth and should speak to him in person. We have His word, and it confirmed by the oath of His Father. What more could we have were He here to-day? Many refused to believe on Him when He was among them confirming His word by miracles, which they saw with their own eyes; and they would do so again were He here now; but the responsibility is with them—not with Him—not with us. When all material things shall be wrapped in flame—nay, when they shall have passed away—His word will stand secure.

We had many other thoughts which we were anxious to present, but we have already gone more than one hundred pages over our contemplated limits, and must lay down our pen, though we do it reluctantly. We feel that we have performed our work faithfully as far as we have gone, but we did not wish to leave our readers until we had shown them the road through "the gates into the city." Having told them how to become children of God, we were anxious to tell them how to live as Christians, that they might die in the Lord and enjoy the rest that remains for the people of God. We wanted to go with them to the *house of worship* on the *Lord's day,* where we might teach and admonish each other in *psalms,* and *hymns,* and *spiritual songs,* making melody in our hearts to the Lord. We wanted to surround the *table of the Lord,* and with them partake of the emblems of His broken body and shed blood, in commemoration of the great *sin-offering* made for the world. We wanted to go with them to the *family altar,* whence their prayers might ascend, as sweet incense, to the throne of the Most High. We wanted to go with them through the *trials, temptations,* and *persecutions* incident to their pilgrimage on the earth. We wanted to see them grapple with and overcome the last enemy when crossing the deep rolling river. After sleeping in Jesus for a time, we wanted to see them come forth in His glorified image, clad in the habiliments of immortality and basking in the radiant smiles of God's eternal love, for ever and ever. But all this, for want of room, we must leave for the work of another pen.

Friendly sinner, we have labored for your interest in the preparation of this work under much physical pain, but God has spared us to its completion, for which we have earnestly prayed and feel devoutly thankful; for we feel assured that for every one we may be instrumental in turning to righteousness and guiding in the way of life eternal we will have a star placed in the crown of glory which will wreathe our brow in the presence-chamber of our God. You will read these pages when the hand that guides the pen with which they are written will have grown cold, and the heart that beats with anxious solicitude for your salvation will have been stilled in death; then, even then, though dead, may we yet speak through them some kind word that may feel about the tender chords of your heart and cause you to love God who first loved you, and Jesus Christ who died to redeem you, that you may flee from sin and lay hold upon eternal life.

Jesus says, In my Father's house are many mansions; if it were not so, I would have told you. He has gone to prepare a place for you, that where He is there you may be also. Oh! do you not want to be with Jesus? If so, He says, Come unto me, all ye that are weary, and I will give you rest. The Father says, Look unto me, all ye ends of the earth, and be ye saved; for I am God, and besides Me there is none else. Then, God says, Come—Jesus says, Come—the Spirit and the Bride say, Come; and whosoever will, let him come and take of the water of life freely. Oh! then, will you come?

> "Come, all you who see yourselves lost,
> And feel yourselves burdened with sin;
> Draw near, though with terror you're tossed;
> Obey, and your peace shall begin.
> He, riches has ever in store,
> And treasures that never can waste;
> Here's pardon, here's grace—yea, and more,
> Here's glory eternal at last."

And why should you not come? Is it not strange that, while God, Jesus, angels, and all good men are concerned for you, you, the most directly interested, are still unconcerned for yourself? What has the devil with which to reward you for a life of devotion to him? Esau was regarded as a profane person for selling his birthright for a mess of pottage; are you not doing worse, bartering a home in heaven for the momentary gratification of fleshly lusts, pride, and appetite? Surely these are not sufficient to compensate you for an eternity of misery and woe! Were you to acquire the cattle of a thousand hills, yea, and all the gold of California and Peru, these could not purchase one drop of water with which to cool your parching tongue in the rude flames of an angry hell; then what will it profit if you gain the whole world and lose your soul at last? or what will you give in exchange for your soul? If you could possess the world and its treasures, the time may come when you would give them all for an interest in the blood of Jesus—you may now have it without money and without price. How unwise to reject it! Oh, then flee from the wrath to come and lay hold on eternal life!

INDEX

Aaron's death, 16.
Abraham's faith, 436.
Abraham pardoned, when, 436.
Abrahamic covenant, 327.
Action of baptism—see
  What is baptism, 210
Acts viii: 37, genuine, 198.
Acts ii:38, argument on, 401.
Adam's death, 16.
Adam died literally, 102.
Adam and predestination, 12.
Ænan, a place for baptizing, 254.
All flesh, spirit poured upon, 458.
All bodies have spirits, 493.
Allegory—two covenants, 348.
Altar, Elijah's, baptized, 287.
All things ordained of God, 8.
Amad, Syriac for baptism, 243.
Apostles not always under
  inspiration, 482.
Apostasy proven possible, 22.
Apo, the meaning of, 249.
Apocryphal baptisms, 288.
Apostles, when in the kingdom, 125.
Arguments for sprinkling, etc., 284.
Armor of the Christian, 487.
Atonement, general, 27-32.
Atonement and election, 27, 28.

Baptidzo, lexicons on, 212.
  critics on, 220.
  classic meaning of, 226-233.
Baptism of Jesus, 249.
Baptism a burial, 257-270.
Baptism of the jailer, 276.
  of Paul, 279.
  of the Israelites, 279, 380, 422.
  of suffering, 282.
  of Jewish beds, vessels, etc., 289.
  the action—see What is baptism, 210.
  of the eunuch, 273.
Baptism of the altar, 287.
  of the Holy Spirit, 457.
  a work, therefore classed with works, 419.
  in room of circumcision, 341.
  history of the action, 292.

Baptist, name of a church, 147.
Baptized by one spirit, 462.
Begotten and born, the difference, 160.
Believers unpardoned, examples of, 443.
Believeth on the Son, hath life, etc. 441.
Beza on Baptidzo, 221.
Birth of water—the action, 256.
  the design of, 390.
  theories on, 159.
Born of water and Spirit—how, 162.
Body of sins put off, 418.
Body washed in baptism, 270.
Branch churches, 135-138.
  when organized, 135.

Calvinistic proofs examined, 41-73.
Carson on bapto and baptidzo, 237.
Calvin on baptidzo, 223.
  on change of baptism, 310.
Christ died for all men, 28-32.
  for the elect only, 31.
Christ's mission was to the lost, 35.
Church established, when, 117-133.
Church first composed of whom, 132.
  organized by inspired men, 485.
  the dwelling-place of the Holy Spirit, 486.
  the medium of the Spirit's operations, 486.
Change of heart, what is it, and how effected, 177.
Circumcision, examples of, 317.
  baptism in room of, 341.
  and baptism in force at once, 345.
Circumcised Jews baptized, 345.
Circumstances no part of conversion, 504.
Classic use of baptidzo, 226-233.
Clarke on foreknowledge, 85.
  on 1 Pet. iii:21, 421.
Comforter no confined to the apostles, 508.
Commission made void—infant baptism, 368.
  the action of baptism, 245.

528

INDEX 529

the subjects of baptism, 358.
the design of baptism, 395.
Confession, the good, 198-209.
 what is it, 202.
 how made, 203.
 history of, 207.
Confession, questions concerning, 206.
Convertible terms, 254.
Conscience in baptism, 369.
Cornelius pardoned, when, 444.
Covenants with Abraham, 327.
Critics on baptidzo, seventy, 220.

David at Keila, 10.
David's words were words of the Holy Spirit, 491.
Decrees of God broken, 9.
Dead body, washing from, 288.
Depravity, hereditary, 88-116.
 proofs examined, 106.
 the origin of infant baptism, 373.
Desert conversions by objectors, 411.
Design of baptism, 382.
Derivation of baptidzo—see Webster, Worcester, Liddell & Scott, Groves, etc., 211-213.
Ditzler on Simon's case, 395.
 on Acts ii:38, 404.
Discipline on remission, 452.
Diversity of spiritual gifts, 474.
Divine nature, partakers of, how, 516.
Doctrinal Tracts, Wesley's, 377.
Doubts, the test of conversion, 518.
 no room for, 524.
Dual character of mind, 100.
Dumb spirit unreliable, 502.

Ekk'esia does not necessarily imply a religious assembly, 336.
Election and reprobation, 13-87.
 of Isaac injured none others, 49.
 and the atonement, 27.
 and future judgment, 38.
Enan, a place for baptism, 254.
Episcopalian Catechism, 392.
Establishment of the church, 117-133.
Eunuch's baptism, 273.
Everlasting life, when possessed, 441.

Ewing on depravity, 99.
Examples of baptism, no infants, 362.
Experience of grace examined, 497.

Facts and testimony, suigenerus, 520.
Faith, chapter on, 167-186.
 office of, 176.
 what is it, 168.
 how does it come, 170.
 and repentance, order of, 193.
 differs not in kind, 175.
 Pollok on, 176.
 always a noun, 169.
 prayer for, 172.
 can not be demanded after reception without it, 325.
 is a work, 419.
 only, justification by, 434.
 approved examples of, 435.
 perfected by obedience, 435.
 dead without works, 435.
 as a system, 436.
 imputed for righteousness, 438.
Falling from grace, 23.
Feelings not a test of right, 504.
 the office of, 518.
Final perseverance, or apostasy—which, 23.
Figurative meanings of baptidzo, 236.
Foreknew, predestinated, etc., 43.
Foreknowledge of God, chapter on, 74-87.
 Clarke on, 84.
Form of doctrine obeyed, 411.
Full assurance of faith, 518.

Gal. iii:27, argument on, 414.
Gentiles once not God's people, 37.
Gifts of the Holy Spirit, 473.
 how conferred, 478.
 how ceased, and when, 479.
 are not its baptism, 474.
 are not the ordinary measure, 475.
Glorified with Christ, who, 43.
God grieved by man's wickedness, 11.
 willing to save all men, 34.
 no respecter of persons, 38.
Good conscience—may not be pardoned man, 420.
Greek Church baptizes only by immersion, 309.

Hate, love less, 53.
Heart, change of, 177.
  what is it, 178.
  changed by whom, 264.
Heathens have no spiritual light, 502.
Hearing of faith, 513.
Henry on infant baptism, 323.
Hereditary depravity, 88-116.
Hezekiah's days prolonged, 10.
History of baptism, the action, 293.
  of sprinkling, 302-313.
  of infant baptism, 369.
  of baptism for remission, 449.
Holy Spirit, 455.
  baptism of, 457.
  gifts of, 473.
  operation of, 484.
  reception of, 506.
  how received, 512.
  witness of, 517.
  baptism a promise, 468.
  makes Christians, nothing else, 494.
How the gospel was taken to all nations, 476.
Hughey on the classics, 235.

Identity of the church, 134-150.
Infants non-elect, 00.
  damned by reprobation, 38.
  baptism—see Who should be baptized, 314-381.
  baptism, no precept for, nor example of, 314-317.
  mentioned in various connections, 317.
  baptized because in and not in the church, 322.
  born in the church, yet must enter it, 324.
  not allowed the supper, 325.
  baptism carnalizes the church, 325.
  none in the church, 339.
  none baptized by John, 358.
In Christ, new creatures, 413.
Influence of circumstances, 504.
Inspiration was progressive, 507.
Injured, none by election, 38.
Israel, a remnant of, 63.
  rest blinded, 64.
Israel, reprobates saved, 64.
Israelites baptized, how, 279.
  saved, when, 422.
  had infants with them, 379.

Jacob and Esau, 49-53.
Jacob felt like Joseph was dead, 519.
Jailer's baptism, 276.
  conversion, 408.
James and Paul on justification, 435.
Jesus, baptism of, 249.
  entrance into heaven, 128.
  crowned King, 128.
Jerusalem, water supplies in, 300.
Jews, the election and fall of, 17-21.
  objected to the admission of the Gentiles, 47.
  rejected for unbelief, 48.
  had to be born again, 334.
Jewish beds and vessels baptized, 289.
  proselyte baptism, 350.
Jeter on infantile depravity, 93.
John the Baptist never in the kingdom, 124.
  baptized no infants, 358.
John's raiment, 253.
  baptism for remission of sins, 388.
  disciples not rebaptized, 389.
John i:12—His own, who were they, 439.
  iii:5, authors on baptism, 300.
  iii:15, 16, 18, 36—believeth, etc., 440.
Jordan, Lynch on, 251.
  Randall on, 253.
Josephus, education of, 235.
Judgment and election, 38.
Judith's bathing in the fountain, 288.
Justification, things connected with, 434.

Kingdom established, chapter on, 117-133.
  meaning of, 117.
  established of whom, 132, 390.
  of God vs. the kingdom of Satan, 486.
  visible and invisible, 427.
Know that we are pardoned, 427.

Last days—Joel, Isaiah, Mal., 459.
  will and testament, 503.
Laws of pardon, two, 384.
Law and gospel contrasted, 436.
Learn to baptize infants, how, 321.

INDEX 531

Lexicons on baptidzo, 212.
Liddell & Scott's Lexicon, 213.
Line of separation between church and world obliterated, 368.
Literal presence of the Spirit in Christians, 507.
Luther on baptidzo, 223.
  on taufen, German for baptize, 244.
  on putting on Christ, 414.
Lynch on the Jordan, 251.

Maccalla Debate, quotation from, 407.
Man condemned, reprieved, 520.
Mark xvi:16, canonical, 396.
Marriage, figure of, 156.
McGarvey on Acts xiii:48, 43.
Measure applied to Spirit, 473.
Men and women baptized, 317.
  Mercy to whom shown, 55.
  on whom He will have mercy, 54.
Mind, dual nature of, 100.
Miracles examined, 430.
  no part of conversion, 504.
Moral and physical testimony, 520.
Moses, death of, 15.
  and the brazen serpent, 440.
Mortal bodies quickened by the Spirit, 509.

Nadab and Abihu destroyed, 16.
Naaman dipped himself, 271.
Name Baptist, 147.
  church, etc., 335.
Names, unscriptural, 146.
Natural calamities conditional, 11.
Nebuchadnezzar's dream, 121.
Neocæsarean council, 303.
New birth not a change of heart, 193.
  not a change of life, 154.
  chapter on, 151-166.
  a change of state, 156.
Nicodemus understood not, why, 395.
Nineveh's destruction averted, 11.
Noah's salvation a type, 420.
No efficacy in water, 448.
None elect before conversion, 36.
No spiritual qualifications to enter Jewish church, 325.
Novatian baptized on his bed, 302.

Office of faith, 176.
  of Spirit baptism, 462, 470.
  of Spiritual gifts, 482.
  of feelings, 518.
Olive-tree, parable of, 336.
One body only, 134.
  way only, 140.
  baptism only, 466.
Ordained whatsoever comes to pass, 8.
  to eternal life believed, 42.
Order of faith and repentance, 193.
Oriental church always immerse, 309.
Orthodoxy examined, 140-143.
  defined, 141.
Operation of the Spirit, 484.
  none deny it, 485.
Our spirits' testimony, 522.

Parable of new and old wine, 34.
  of the sower, 419.
Pardon may be known, 522.
Paul's election, 41.
  conversion, 406.
Paul, baptism of, 279.
  and James on faith, 435.
  not sent to baptize, 446.
Persons saved not baptized in Spirit, 469.
  commanded to be baptized, 468.
Peter had the keys, 127.
Pharaoh hardened, 55-57.
Philip the evangelist not an apostle, 480.
Pictures of baptism, 250.
Pious fathers all lost—objection, 454.
Potter and the clay, 58-63.
Predestination, chapter on, 7-12.
Precious promises, 516.
Presbyterian Confession of Faith on baptism, 453.
Primitive and derivative words, 238.
Providence, special and general, 505.

Raiment, John's, 253.
Reasoning in a circle, 524.
Reception of the Holy Spirit, 506.
Regeneration, not born again, 162.
Religion of the Jews not Christian, 338.

Repentance, chapter on, 187-197.
the gift of God, 192, 196,
and faith, order of, 194.
Reprobate infants, 38.
Reprieve of a man condemned, 520.
Respect of persons with God, 38.
Restitution to be made, 191.
Revival of modern type, 496.
Romans ix examined, 47.
Rules of exegesis, 239.
Rupos filth, 421.

Sanctified and cleansed with washing, etc., 417.
Saul elected king and fell, 16.
Saved added to the church, 405.
Schleusner on baptidzo, 218.
Seal of the covenants, 346.
Sealed after believing, 511.
Seven units, argument on, 415.
Seventy critics on baptidzo, 220.
Shifting ground on infant baptism, 325, 341.
Signs followed belief, 477.
Sins remembered every year, 330.
Smith's Bible Dictionary on the birth of the church, 132.
Special and general providence, 505.
Speculations vs. the Word of God, 503.
Spirits from God, 103.
Spiritual power, miraculous limited, 482.
Spirit operates, how, 487.
operated through Stephen's words, 493.
operates best through best revivalists, 49.
of Satan operates through words, 500.
Sprinkling and pouring examined, 284.
first law for, 304.
Stokius on baptidzo, 217.
Stowe on Mark xvi:16, 396.
Stuart on dying, 238.
change of baptism, 310, 311.
bapto and baptidzo, 223.
difference in bapto and baptidzo, 238.
Suffering, baptism of, 282.

Tabernacle of David, 338.

Table of versions, 242.
Tauf, tief, taufen—German, 244.
Taval—Hebrew, lexicons on, 241.
examples of, 240.
The commission, 245, 358, 395.
confession, 198, 209.
new birth, chapter on, 151-166.
Things forbidden come to pass, 8.
never entered the mind of God, 12.
Third parties—objection, 411.
The witness of the Spirit, 517.
Thief's case, 433.
Tseva defined, 245.
Two laws of pardon, 384.
Types and shadows, 419.

Universalism, 484.
Union meeting of modern type, 494.

Versions, table of, 242.
Vessels of wrath, 60, 61.
Visible and invisible kingdoms, 427.

Wall on infantile depravity, 93.
Watson on repentance, 196.
on Col. ii:12, 418.
on 1 Pet. iii:21, 421.
Washing of water by the word, 410.
of regeneration, 418.
Water and Spirit, one birth, 160.
supplies in Jerusalem, 300.
Way, but one, 139.
Webster on baptism, 212.
Wesley on 1 Pet. iii:21, 421.
on Acts xxii:16, 407.
on infantile depravity, 94.
What is baptism—the action, 210-392.
for—the design, 382.
Who should be baptized—not infants, 314-381.
Wicked men inspired, 444.
Wills are arranged during life, 394.
Wind bloweth where it listeth, 164.
With water—in water, 251.
Witness of the Spirit, 517.
Word of the Lord at Philippi, 409.
of God enlightens, quickens, saves, etc., 501.
World can not receive the Spirit, 489.
Worcester on baptism, 211.

THE GOSPEL PLAN OF SALVATION

In presenting the THIRD edition of this work to the public, it is deemed proper to present, with it, a few extracts of notices of former editions by the PRESS; and by *distinguished men* deemed competent to decide upon the merits of the work.

The Christian Quarterly, after naming the subjects treated, says: "These subjects are discussed with great plainness and generally with marked ability. Want of space will not permit us to point out special features; but we have no hesitation in saying that the work, as a whole, is worthy to be studied—not simply read, and then laid aside, but carefully and earnestly studied. It will, we think, be specially acceptable to young preachers and Sunday-School teachers, as it condenses a large amount of valuable information from books accessible to on'y a favored few. While not so pretentious as many works upon the subjects of Anthropology and Soteriology, to the general reader it will be found to contain several advantages over all other works of its kind. It is simple in its arrangement, sufficiently comprehensive in treatment, and relies chiefly on the Word of God to settle all disputed questions."

The Gospel Advocate says: "Bro. Brents is a popular writer for the common people. They read his writings gladly, because they understand them readily. The treatment of his subjects is his own. No man has a more marked individuality as a thinker and writer than Bro. Brents. His association of subjects is also his own. Then the book occupies a place of its own in Christian literature. . . . There is a fuller examination of the subject of baptism, and a more copious collection of authorities on this subject than can be found elsewhere. . . . It is opportune that such full authorities should be presented. We then commend heartily the circulation of the book among all classes who can be induced to read it. It will build up and strengthen the faith of the Christian. It will do much to convince the unbeliever and silence the gainsayer."

The Southern Christian Weekly says: "We have not had the work long enough to examine it thoroughly; but we have known Bro. Brents for a number of years, both as a preacher and writer, and have long been familiar with his method of handling most of the subjects treated in his book. He is a fine reasoner and a good writer. This work is written in a clear, forcible, nervous style—is both readable and instructive, and will, no doubt, prove of incalculable value in clearing away erroneous doctrines which now form one of the chief hinderances to many in receiving and obeying the Gospel. We hope the book will meet with a ready reception, and that it may be widely circu'ated, and thus enabled to accomplish the good it is so well calculated to do. The mechanical execution and material are, in every way, good enough."

"We have not time to enter at large upon an examination of the questions of the work before us. Its style is simple, clear, and natural to the author. The author's heart is loyal to the cause of the Bible as the only source of sound religious instruction. The work is admirably adapted to the average understanding and intelligence of men, and is thus fitted to accomplish a grand work aong the masses of men; we heartily commend it to the brotherhood as one of the best books for their own reading, and for distribution among those who may be willing to be informed concerning our religious teaching."—*Christian Examiner.*

The American Christian Review says: "It is a neatly printed and well bound volume of 667 pages, in good style. The work contains the pith of near a lifetime of thought, much reading and extended experience touching the matters treated, with all the doctrinal difficulties, perplexities, and confusion that lie in the way. He has, with a master hand, met, traced out, and explained the greatest difficulties, and, with the utmost patience and in the most laborious manner, cleared away the perplexities and confusion that have kept thousands out of the kingdom of God, and are now keeping thousands, who honestly desire to be Christians, out of Christ. The work is decidely *well written*. It enters into the matter item by item, and clears up difficult questions lying in the path of every man striving to spread the gospel, and deals with them in a most safe and reliable manner, and makes the truth gleam out at every angle. After c'earing away the difficulties it enters its main work, the 'Plan of Salvation,' and the *Gospel plan* at that. He finds no 'Mosaism' nor 'Legalism' in his way, nor *Pauline* gospel. The gospel of Christ is sufficient for him. We are rejoiced that this book has appeared, and hope it will be extensively read. If our young men desire to understand the gospel, and know how to present it to others so that they can understand it, believe it and be saved by it, they can do no better than to obtain this book, and not only *read* it, but study it."

The Apostolic Times, though dissenting from the chapter on the foreknowledge of God, says: "This entire work is well adapted to the minds of the masses of the people, for whom it was especially written, and it will be read with avidity and delight by thousands. We anticipate for it a large and continuous circulation, and we commend it as a work well worthy of the careful study of our brethren, and of extensive circulation among the thoughtful of other churches and of no church."

The Bible Index says: "It is carefully written, and in good English. The author does not rely very much upon his logic to establish the conclusions which he draws, but rather upon the supreme and final authority of the Holy Scriptures, to which he makes constant reference. In the initial chapters he takes in hand, Predestination, Election, and Reprobation, Hereditary Depravity, etc., and before he gets through with these illogical and anti-scriptural dogmas, there is no breath left in them. They are utterly demolished. And we do earnestly recommend those who are troubled with these creations of the sect-thirst, or have friends or acquaintances so afflicted, to buy and read, or cause to be read, Bro. Brents' book. The identity of the Church, faith, repentance, and baptism—as to what it is and the proper subject—the gifts of the Holy Spirit, the operation of the Holy Spirit, and the witness of the Holy Spirit are all dealt with in a critical and thorough manner. Without a more careful reading than we have yet been able to bestow on the latter portions, we are not prepared to say that all Bro. Brents' conclusions are incontrovertible; but we do earnestly admire the respectful style with which he treats the views which it is his duty to refute, and especially the respects, so uncommon, which he displays for the *very words* of the Scriptures. He does not attempt to jump at a meaning, but is careful to deduce it directly from the words used according to the recognized rules of interpretation, without regard to the consequences to which such a course may lead. These are our impressions of this book, and we shall therefore take pleasure in knowing that it has secured the large demand which its intrinsic merits deserve."

"We call the attention of our readers to this work and ask them to examine it. Bro. Brents is a forcible writer, and he deals with vital questions in the work named. The great questions that distinguish us from other religionists are investigated, and there is a compendium of useful information on these points. The publishers have done their work well, as they always do."—*The Christian*, of Louis, Mo.

"This book is admirable for its correctness of views, its plainness of style, and is adapted for a hand book for young ministers and others wishing an easy compend upon these important elementary principles. We heartily commend it, too, for family reading and a work to be placed in the hands of those untaught upon these themes."—*The Evangelist*, Oskaloosa, Iowa.

"As a clear and skillful disposition of disputed and knotty points in theology, the book has decided value. The author's style is perspicuous and forcible, and he shows a large acquaintance with the Scriptures as well as ability to unfold their meaning and rescue them from false interpretations. . . . To all who are embarrassed with Calvinistic teaching this book ought to have special interest and value, as the author has studied that system of doctrines thoroughly and deals with it faithfully. On the question of Baptism, alike as regards action, subjects, and design, the book is a repository of testimonies and arguments sufficient to meet almost any want in that line, and furnishes, we judge, as cheap and satisfactory a collection of evidences as can be found.

"It is not our purpose to review the chapters in which we are treated to original views and interpretations such as John iii:5, and Rom. viii: 29, or do more than express our dissent from interpretations given. . . . We have no doubt that it will have, as it deserves, a large sale."—*Christian Standard.*

"We have examined the work with care, and read some of the chapters attentively, and regard it as a valuable work for all inquirers after truth, and specially for young preachers whose libraries are small and means limited. It embraces a large amount of valuable information, requiring extensive reading to collect, particularly on the subject of Baptism. The chapter on the 'Foreknowledge of God,' as well as some other matters in the work, contains some statements liable to just criticism. Still the work is valuable on many accounts, and, on the whole, does credit to the author and the subjects discussed; and the disciples generally, and young preachers specially, will find it an excellent compendium of religious information."—*The Watch Tower,* New Berne, N.C.

EXTRACTS OF NOTICES BY DISTINGUISHED PREACHING BRETHREN.

IRA J. CHASE, *Peoria, Ill.*: "I think I own the first copy sold north of the Ohio River. I am just delighted with it, especially *Election* and *The Holy Spirit*. I must be permitted to use the arguments almost *verbatim*. Though strangers, personally, I feel quite well acquainted with you through your book. God bless you. May your book have GREAT SALE."

R. B. TRIMBLE, *Mayfield, Ky.*: "Your book is giving perfect satisfaction. I believe it to be THE BOOK of the brotherhood. I am sure it will more than meet the expectations of the brethren."

J. M. KIDWELL, *Smithville, Tenn.*: "Every one is delighted with it. I think the first four chapters are richly worth many times the price of the book; indeed I think the entire range of subjects well chosen, and brought so completely within comprehension of the ordinary reader that great good must result from it. You have also brought such an amount of critical research to bear on some of the leading questions of the day as will make it profitable to the student of the Bible."

W. C. HUFFMAN, *Enon College, Tenn.*: "It is more eagerly read, and its contents more universally approved than any book published among our brethren for many years. May the Lord bless you in your efforts to do good. Surely your investigations and publications must do great good for the cause of our Redeemer, and add bright stars to your crown."

WASHINGTON BACON, *Tecumseh, Ala.*: "I fear I think too highly of it. There is a vacuum in the literature of this reformation that your book most completely fills. There is no such work amongst us—it is just the thing; and you can use my name in any way you wish in its commendation—you can not exaggerate my estimation of it."

G. W. CONE, *Newburg, Ark.*: "I think the work is well done—variety and exhaustion well combined. It would be difficult to select *five* words in the English language more expressive of the book than the five given, 'THE GOSPEL PLAN OF SALVATION.'"

Dr. J. T. Barclay, *Wheeler's Station, Ala.*: "Am really delighted with the work. It most happily supplies a vacuum in our literature long and seriously felt; and should it not have an extensive circulation I shall be much surprised."

"I consider it the most thorough work of the kind I have ever read. The intelligent reader can not fail to be struck with the force and clearness with which it handles every subject, and on the subjects of baptism and the Holy Spirit the work is peculiarly excellent. I most heartily commend the work to all who feel interested in a clear and lucid exposition of the most important subjects connected with the scheme of salvation.

"You will not find in it the speculative conclusions of an ingenious writer—but the clear and natural deductions of an exhaustive accumulation of Scriptural evidences adroitly linked together, so that the unbiased mind will naturally, easily, and almost, if not quite, unavoidably yield to the same conclusions. And to such minds many hitherto perplexed questions will forever be set at rest."

DAVID ADAMS.

Pine Apple, Ala.

"I consider it a prize work. It is simply powerful. It will take a high position among the standard productions of the literature of the Current Reformation, and will live when the present generation has passed away. I am generally parsimonious, very parsimonious, in my recommendations of latest productions, but I can afford to be liberal in what I say of this work, which does its work respectfully and does it with a masterly hand. I arrive at the same conclusions with our talented brother on every topic, especially on what he calls 'Adam's sin,' on which I may hereafter write an essay if I am spared and feel able, as I am now poorly, and have been for several days past. If I did not possess a copy of this work, nor had the money to purchase it, I would labor and earn the money, and place it in my library, for he has *routed* the Pedobaptist forces, horse, foot, and dragoons, from their hiding-places. I will now make some statements relative to the baptismal controversy. But first I hope our brotherhood will consider the time, expense, labor, research, and learning necessary to the production of such a work, and not only feel grateful to Brother Brents but lessen the expense by taking a copy of the work, as well as to compensate him in some measure for his great mental and bodily labor, and be grateful that they have such a champion of truth in the South."

JACOB CREATH.

Palmyra, Mo.

"I would like to see your book in the hands of every man and woman in Tennessee. I would produce a shaking among the dry bones. It combines more of the elements of Christianity, and concentrates more of the facts, with a clearer view of the whole, than any book in the English language."

E. R. OSBORNE.

Union City, Tenn.

"Every young preacher should at once supply himself with a copy of The Gospel Plan of Salvation, and not only read, but study and digest its arguments. It contains an array of arguments, facts, and authorities nowhere else to be found in so small a compass.

"The authorities may be relied on as correct. They are taken from the original, and not at second hand, as is often done.

"I commend the book most heartily to our brotherhood, and to all who desire to understand the great themes of which it so clearly and fully treats."

W. D. CARNES,
President of Burritt College

Spencer, Tenn.

www.ingramcontent.com/pod-product-compliance
Lightning Source LLC
Chambersburg PA
CBHW050157240426
43671CB00013B/2158